The Neural Basis of Free Will

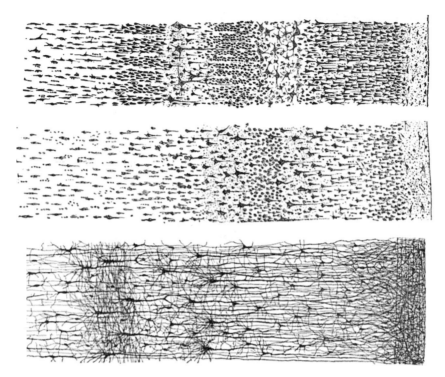

Drawings by Ramón y Cajal of three different cortical cross-sections. The cortical surface is on the right. © Herederos de Santiago Ramón y Cajal.

Y, sin embargo, á despecho de la impotencia del análisis, el problema nos atraía irresistiblemente. Adivinábamos el supremo interés que, para una psicología racional, tenía el formar un concepto claro de la organización del cerebro. Conocer el cerebro—nos decíamos en nuestros entusiasmos idealistas—equivale á averiguar el cauce material del pensamiento y de la voluntad, sorprender la historia íntima de la vida en su perpetuo duelo con las energías exteriores; historia resumida, y en cierto modo esculpida, en esas coordinaciones neuronales defensivas del reflejo, del instinto y de la asociación de las ideas.

[And yet, despite the impotence of our analyses, the problem attracted us irresistibly. We foresaw that forming a clear concept of brain organization was of supreme interest for a rational psychology. To know the brain—we said in our idealistic enthusiasm—is equivalent to discovering the material course of thought and will, to unveiling the intimate history of life in its perpetual duel with external forces, a history summarized, and in a sense sculpted within these defensive neural coordinations of reflex, of instinct and of the association of ideas.]

—Santiago Ramón y Cajal, *Recuerdos de mi Vida*, Moya, Madrid, 1917, courtesy of Javier DeFelipe

The Neural Basis of Free Will

Criterial Causation

Peter Ulric Tse

The MIT Press
Cambridge, Massachusetts
London, England

MIT Press books may be purchased at special quantity discounts for business or sales promotional use. For information, please email special_sales@mitpress.mit.edu or write to Special Sales Department, The MIT Press, 55 Hayward Street, Cambridge, MA 02142.

This book was set in Stone sans and Stone serif by Toppan Best-set Premedia Limited, Hong Kong. Printed and bound in the United States of America.

Library of Congress Cataloging-in-Publication Data

Tse, Peter.
The neural basis of free will : criterial causation / Peter Ulric Tse.
    p. cm.
Includes bibliographical references and index.
ISBN 978-0-262-01910-1 (hardcover : alk. paper)
1. Cognitive neuroscience. 2. Neuropsychology. 3. Science—Philosophy. 4. Free will and determinism. I. Title.
QP360.5.T75   2013
612.8'233—dc23
2012029294

10 9 8 7 6 5 4 3 2 1

For my mother Helga and father Kim Fung

Contents

Preface   xi
Falsifiable Predictions of the Burst Packet Theory of Attention and Consciousness   xv

1 Introduction: The Mind–Body Problem Will Be Solved by Neuroscience   1

2 Overview of the Arguments   11

3 A Criterial Neuronal Code Underlies Downward Mental Causation and Free Will   19
What Is Will?   20
What Is Criterial Causation?   22

4 Neurons Impose Physical and Informational Criteria for Firing on Their Inputs   31
How Can Neurons Realize Informational Criteria?   31
The Bottom-Up Information-Processing Hierarchy for Visual Recognition   36
Decision Making and Action   43
Attention and Top-Down Modulation of Bottom-Up Processing   44
Basic Issues in Neuronal Information Processing: Balancing Excitation and Inhibition   50
Tonic versus Phasic Firing   53
The Sweet Spot of Neural Criticality   57
Synchrony among Inhibitory Interneurons   58
Attentional Binding and Gamma Oscillations   60
Attentional Binding by Neuronal Bursting   64
Neural Epiconnectivity and Rapid Synaptic Resetting   67
Amplifying Microscopic Randomness to Spike Timing Variability   72

5 NMDA Receptors and a Neuronal Code Based on Bursting   79
Spiny and Nonspiny Neurons   79
The NMDA Receptor   81

Long-Term Potentiation Is Not the Mechanism of Rapid Synaptic Plasticity   83
Spike Timing-Dependent Plasticity   87
The Role of Back-Propagating Action Potentials in Rapid Synaptic Plasticity
and Bursting   89
A Neuronal Burst Code   98
Attentional Binding by Bursting: The Role of Cholinergic Feedback   103
Attentional Binding by Bursting: The Role of Noncholinergic Feedback   108
Conclusion   114

6   Mental Causation as an Instance of Criterial Causation   115
Criterial Causation and the Detection of Patterns in Input   115
Criterial Causation: Multiple Realizability Is Not Enough   119
Addressing Kim's Challenge   123
There Is No Backward Causation in Criterial Causation   127
Criterial Causation Is a Causation of Pattern-Released Activity   129

7   Criterial Causation Offers a Neural Basis for Free Will   133
Strong Free Will   133
Criterial Causation Escapes the Basic Argument against Free Will   135
James and Incompatibilist Physicalist Libertarianism   144
Decision Making and Choice   146
Conclusion   148

8   Implications of Criterial Causality for Mental Representation   151
The Neural Code Is Not Algorithmic   151
Criterialism, Descriptivism, and Reference   153
Countering Kripke's Attack   156
Wittgenstein and Criteria   159
Propositions and Vectorial Encodings   162
Mental Operations versus Mental Representations   164
Beyond Functionalism   165

9   Barking Up the Wrong Free: Readiness Potentials and the Role of
Conscious Willing   169
Libet's Experiments Do Not Disprove the Possibility of Free Will   169
Is Conscious Willing Causal?   173
Illusions of Volitional Efficacy   177

10   The Roles of Attention and Consciousness in Criterial Causation   183
Why Are There Qualia?   185
Iconic versus Working Memory   189
Stage 1 Qualia as Precompiled Informational Outputs of Preconscious
Operations   192

Qualia as a Shared Format for Endogenous Attentional Operations   196
Experience Is for Endogenously Attending, Doing, and Planning   198
Volitional Attentional Tracking Requires Consciousness   200
If an Animal Can Attentionally Track, Is It Conscious?   209
Volitional Attention Can Alter Qualia   212
Qualia and Chunking: Types of Qualia   217
Qualia and the Frontoparietal Network   225
The Superpositionality of Qualia   233
Zombies Are Impossible   236
Tying It All Together   237

Appendix 1: Physical Evidence for Ontological Indeterminism   241
Appendix 2: Ontological Indeterminism Undermines Kim's Argument against the
Logical Possibility of Mental Causation   247
Appendix 3: Why There Are No Necessary A posteriori Propositions   257
Notes   261
Glossary   289
References   309
Author Index   411
Subject Index   443

Preface

§0.1 Many neuroscientists, myself included, entered the brain sciences because of a desire to find answers to the deep questions of the neural code, mental causation, free will, and the neural bases of consciousness. Although I am now fortunate to have a passionate group of students in my brain imaging and visual psychophysics lab at Dartmouth, it has sometimes seemed to me that the actual practice of science has driven me away from the deep questions. It has seemed at times as though my life was whizzing by, always focused on the next experiment, paper, or grant application. Some years ago I decided that I needed to counteract this emphasis on the trees by taking a step back to get a bigger picture of the forest. I decided to write a summary of what could be said about the deep, unsolved issues surrounding the mind–body problem from a neuroscientific perspective. The goal would be to listen to what neurons had to tell us, instead of, like most philosophers, using logic to argue from unproven first premises. Since the brain must already embody a solution to the mind–body problem, why not focus on how the brain actually accomplishes mental causation and consciousness, rather than arguing philosophically, typically in the absence of any data, whether mental causation and consciousness are logically possible?

§0.2 Philosophy is regarded with such skepticism by many in science (including, originally, myself) that it may actually hinder scientists from attempting to address the big questions. Young scientists, in particular, seem most inhibited by a fear of being branded "philosophical." The process of professionalization and the pursuit of tenure force young scientists to allocate their efforts to where their payoff is: empirical publications and grants. Once scientists have tenure, they have the freedom to finally speak out on the deep questions from a scientific point of view; but only rare ones do.

§0.3 Two of the rare ones were Francis Crick and Christof Koch. They liberated the field in the 1980s and 1990s by making it legitimate to attempt to give neuroscientific answers to the big questions. A great debt is owed to them for helping neuroscientists get over their behavioristic hang-ups against discussing consciousness, free will, and mental causation. Since then, the field of neuroscientists interested in finding the neural correlates of these processes has grown enormously. A parallel role was played by Patricia and Paul Churchland within philosophy at about the same time. We can only hope that more and more young scientists will take on the deep questions, and that more and more philosophers will embrace empirical data in an attempt to reach the truth via facts as well as argumentation. There is no question that to do so carries some risks. It is safer and easier to focus on the trees within one's own field. When neuroscientists like Crick and Koch begin to venture into philosophy, or philosophers like the Churchlands venture into neuroscience, some on the other side or even on the same side might ridicule or dismiss their efforts as lacking appropriate pedigree or knowledge. So be it. Reality has no arbitrary professional boundaries. Therefore, the pursuit of a complete model of the nature of reality should not be inhibited by professional boundaries. Yes, there is a risk of trying and failing. But the greater risk is always in failing to try.

§0.4   The deepest problems have yet to be solved. We do not understand the neural code. We do not understand how mental events can be causal. We do not understand how consciousness can be realized in physical neuronal activity. We have yet to be liberated by a Darwin who will provide an overarching conceptual framework that unifies all the data in the field. We have yet to find our Watson and Crick who will crack the neural code. It is truly a wonderful time to be in the brain sciences because we know so much, and yet the deepest issues remain wide open. We find ourselves in the midst of one of humankind's greatest ages of exploration and discovery—only it is not exploration of the outer world with ships and sextants. It is exploration of the inner world with scanners and electrodes.

Acknowledgments

First and foremost I thank my family for their love, fun, and support over many years: my children Lilia Grace, Henry Christian, and Eliza Jane, my wife Melinda, my parents Helga and Kim Fung, my brother Michael, and my sister Barbara. Many of the results and ideas discussed here have arisen through experimental collaborations and discussions I have had with my students, including Gideon Caplovitz (now at the University of Nevada at

Reno), Sergey Fogelson, Sebastian Frank, Po-Jang Hsieh (now at Duke-Singapore), Peter Kohler, Katie Porter, Eric Reavis, Mark Samco, and Alex Schlegel, who have done all the hard work. I also wish to thank my colleagues Thalia Wheatley, Adina Roskies, and John Kulvicki of Dartmouth College, Walter Sinnott-Armstrong of Duke University, and Jaegwon Kim of Brown University, for generously commenting on various parts and versions of this manuscript between 2005 and 2010, and for encouraging me to publish my argument. I owe a lot to Mark Greenlee for supporting my sabbatical at the University of Regensburg in 2005–2007, where I started writing this book, and to Alfonso Caramazza, Jens Schwarzbach, Angelika Lingnau, Giorgio Vallortigara, Massimo Turatto, and David Melcher for supporting my sabbatical year at CIMeC and the University of Trento in 2011–2012, affording me the freedom and time to finish this book and its companion *The Cultivation of Will*. My mentors in science, Patrick Cavanagh and Ken Nakayama, have had a lasting impact on my understanding of the mind that is reflected throughout this book. I thank Nikos Logothetis for three years of intense postdoctoral training in monkey fMRI and neurophysiology. Other colleagues and friends who have influenced my thinking include Moshe Bar, Sheng He, Ryota Kanai, Christof Koch, David Leopold, David Sheinberg, Nao Tsuchiya, Steve Macknik, and Susana Martinez-Conde. I would not have been able to fund the research that is the empirical side of some of the ideas described here without the financial support of American taxpayers via the NSF and NIH. The same is true of the generosity of my deans, my past and present colleagues at Dartmouth including Michael Gazzaniga, Scott Grafton, David Bucci, Hany Farid, Howard Hughes, Todd Heatherton, Jim Haxby, and others at the Brain Imaging Center at Dartmouth College, as well as private individuals and foundations, especially the Templeton Foundation, the Alexander von Humboldt Stiftung, and the Big Questions in Free Will project led by Al Mele at Florida State University.

Falsifiable Predictions of the Burst Packet Theory of Attention and Consciousness

• Endogenous attentional binding/tracking is realized in cholinergic/non-cholinergic bursts sent from the basal forebrain and other areas that trigger a transition from tonic to phasic processing in pyramidal circuits from retinotopic areas up to anterior inferotemporal cortex and hippocampus, facilitating recognition. §§4.53, 5.45–5.51

• Gamma synchrony increases with attention because of an inhibitory interneuron "clock." Like decorrelation it is a "shadow" of attentional binding, not its direct cause. §§4.45–4.50

• Bursting is more prevalent inside than outside the attentional window in V4, etc. §5.50

• Ignoring is realized in part via burst suppression; e.g., less LFP high-gamma power. §5.41

• Using NMDA receptor antagonists (e.g., ketamine, PCP or nitrous oxide) or optogenetics to "turn off" postsynaptic NMDA receptors locally in V4 should eliminate attentional binding-by-bursting in the ventral pathway at corresponding retinotopic coordinates. A subject might not notice that he lacked consciousness at a retinotopic location until he tried to attend there. Behaviorally, recognition performance and attentional tracking capacity should decline to the degree that burst packet transmission is blocked.

• Optogenetically triggering localized bursting in V4 should lead to evidence of attentional allocation to the retinotopic location activated. For example, performance on a detection or discrimination task should increase by facilitating bursting at the stimulated retinotopic location, relative to performance at an adjacent "unattended" location. This should artificially bind type 1 into type 3 qualia at that location, and be so experienced.

• Eliminating just the onset transient bursting portion of a spike train may be sufficient to interfere with burst packet transmission. §§4.48, 5.32

• Interfering with burst transmission at any stage of an information-processing hierarchy should interfere with burst transmission in subsequent bottom-up or top-down stages.

• The length of apical dendrites from the pyramidal soma should be given by the speed of a backward-propagating action potential times the optimal time for its arrival at NMDA receptors that are kept open by its arrival, facilitating burst transmission. See ch. 5, n. 8.

• Interfering with back-propagating action potentials should interfere with coupling between post- and presynaptic neurons, and with burst packet transmission across a circuit. §5.20

• What we are conscious of we can endogenously attentionally track and vice versa. §10.28

• To the degree that the stage 1 buffer remains intact, even Balints and neglect patients are predicted to be able to report some aspects of type 1 qualia in unattended regions, such as the mean brightness of, say, the neglected hemifield. §§10.35, 10.77

• In cases where the event-related potential component N2 is present, but the P3b is not, observers will be able to report aspects of "qualia soup" or type 1 features of stimuli, such as location, motion, or brightness, without being able to identify stimuli. §§10.16, 10.75

• Knocking out the frontoparietal circuit, e.g., dorsolateral prefrontal cortex, with transcranial magnetic stimulation should preserve type 1 qualia realized in the stage 1 buffer that do not require attention for their binding into identifiable objects (such as pain, color, brightness, thirst, or hunger), while eliminating type 3 qualia, voluntary tracking, binding into global configurations, or manipulation of contents in working memory. §10.77

• As receptor and spine expression changes at synapses of an attentionally maintained epicircuit, it can consolidate into a learned "burst packet track" that permits bottom-up burst packet transmission up to a level of feature conjunction recognition, subserving the transformation of attentionally bound type 3 into more automatic type 2 qualia. §10.88

1 Introduction: The Mind–Body Problem Will Be Solved by Neuroscience

Given that there are many more synapses than neurons in a typical circuit, the state of a neural network might better be described by specifying the state of its synapses than the firing pattern of its neurons. We might even extend this viewpoint by stating that *the role of synapses is to control neuronal firing within a neural circuit, but the role of neural firing is to set the states of the synapses.*
—Abbott and Regehr (2004, p. 802, italics added)

§1.1   Some actions, whether motoric or internal, are subject to voluntary control. I can choose to stop breathing—for a while—by merely wanting to do so or deciding that I will do so, but I cannot choose to stop my heart with mere thoughts or desires. I can choose to covertly shift my attention to someone sitting at another table, but I cannot choose not to be distracted by sudden movements or loud noises. Willing is whatever it is that triggers actions in the domains of voluntary or endogenous motoric or internal actions. No one doubts that some actions can be voluntarily controlled. But if will is itself entirely determined by preceding facts that are not themselves willed, then it is these facts that ultimately trigger our endogenously chosen acts. The core question, then, is whether willing per se is in any sense causal of our voluntary actions. If yes, then we can be said to have "free will." If not, then voluntariness and the causal efficacy of will are mere illusions. Since the causal efficacy of willing is a subset of the more general question of whether mental events can be in any sense causal, the core issue here is mental causation.

§1.2   This book explores the neural bases of free will and mental causation from the perspectives of neuroscience and psychology. I offer a series of arguments that a particular kind of strong free will and "downward" mental causation is realized in neuronal, dendritic, and synaptic processing. I also address certain views in philosophy of mind about the relationship of brain to mind (e.g., "mental causation is logically impossible," "there is no free will," "consciousness is epiphenomenal," "mind and brain cannot be identical") that are clarified by data about what neurons actually do. My main goal is to look at what nature in fact came up with as a solution to the problem of informational causation realized in the physical causal system of the nervous system. What natural selection came up with is both simple and elegant: Neurons function as criterial assessors of their inputs and are capable of changing the criteria that will make other neurons fire in the future. Informational causation cannot change the physical basis of information realized in the present. But it can change the physical basis of information that may be realized in the immediate future. I explore the ways in which free will might be realized in a particular kind of neuronal and associated information-processing architecture. I then explore the psychological and philosophical implications of having such an architecture realized in our brains.

§1.3   When reading an article or book in science, it is good to first understand the questions that the author hopes to answer. I address several interlinked questions here: If physical causation is sufficient to account for the succession of events in nature, how can mental events be in any sense really causal if they are themselves realized in physical events? How can we have any measure of freedom in a world in which physical events mindlessly obey physical laws? Many philosophers and some psychologists have come to the conclusion that mental events cannot be causal; they have concluded that consciousness and mental causation are "epiphenomenal" (e.g., Dennett, 1990, 2001; Kinsbourne, 1996, 2000; Pinker, 1997). This conclusion flies in the face of common experience; it seems to most people that their thoughts, plans, and percepts lead their bodies to behave differently than they otherwise would have behaved in the absence of such experiences. Is the commonsense point of view, that, for example, we go to the dentist because a tooth hurts, an illusion or delusion as reductionistic materialists typically imply when they dismiss this view as mere "folk psychology?" What exactly do we mean by "information" when we say that neurons process information? Are neurons indeed the fundamental units of information-processing in the nervous system? Is mental activity identical to information-processing? Or do mental events such as qualia afford information processing, without being identical to information? More fundamentally, how can mind arise from matter at all? What is the neural basis of consciousness? What is (are) the neural code(s)? These are some of the deepest issues that humans have yet to solve. Twenty-five centuries of philosophical thought and argumentation since Plato have yet to yield a satisfactory solution to these deep problems of mental causation, free will, and the material realization of mind.

§1.4 Both neuroscience and philosophy find themselves at an impasse in understanding the relationship of the mental to the physical, but for different reasons. Let me start with philosophy.

§1.5 Some leading living philosophers grant that their field is at an impasse. Galen Strawson, a senior philosopher in the free will debate, takes a pessimistic view of his field: "The principal positions in the traditional metaphysical debate [over free will] are clear. No radically new option is likely to emerge after millennia of debate" (Strawson, 1998, 3:749). Another leading philosopher, Jaegwon Kim (1999, p. 127), had this to say about the impasse in philosophy concerning mental causation: "The attempt to 'analyze' causation seems to have reached an impasse; the proposals on hand seem so widely divergent that one wonders whether they are all analyses of one and the same concept." He concedes that the entire program of eliminative physicalist reductionism, of which he is perhaps the leading proponent, fails to fully account for reality: "physicalism will not be able to survive intact and in its entirety" because "phenomenal mental properties are not functionally definable and hence functionally irreducible"; and "if functional reduction doesn't work for qualia, nothing will" (Kim, 2005, pp. 29, 31). On the other hand, anti-epiphenomenalists in philosophy assert that the mental is causal without having the means to propose a brain mechanism whereby this is the case. For example, Tyler Burge (1993, p. 114), an antireductionist and opponent of epiphenomenalism, wrote, "I have no satisfying response to the problem of explaining a mechanism. [. . .] What is unclear is whether the question is an appropriate one in the first place. Demanding that there be an account of mechanism in mind–body causation is tantamount to demanding a physical model for understanding such causation. It is far from obvious that such a model is appropriate. It is not even obvious why any model is needed." I suspect that no neuroscientist would ever say such a thing. Almost all scientists, including myself, assume that there is only energy changing in space and time. Assuming physicalism, it is obvious that to understand the relationship of mind to body will require a physicalist model of mental causation.

§1.6 Why has philosophy been unable to make substantial progress in solving the mind–body problem? The root of philosophy's impasse is that its main tools—logical argumentation, "thought experiments," "intuition pumps," and persuasion—are inadequate to the task.[1] By themselves, these tools are incapable of settling basic debates between scholars with conflicting views rooted in incompatible starting assumptions. Logic can derive conclusions from axioms, but it cannot derive axioms, or, for that matter, the assumptions, biases, hunches, or intuitions that seem to underlie so much philosophical argumentation. With no objective way to settle a conflict, it is rare to find any philosopher who has written, "I was wrong and my rivals were right." Without an objective arbiter of truth such as that imposed by falsifiability, why would a philosopher ever concede, especially when to do so might diminish career standing? A field cannot move forward to the next stage of a problem, and acknowledge that what was once a problem has now been solved, unless those on the wrong side of a debate are forced to concede that they were wrong. Science, in contrast, has nature to falsify theories and models, and the scientific method of experimentation and model-correction/abandonment that forces scientists to stand on the shoulders of giants. Whether or not scientists concede that they were wrong does not matter in the long run. Nature forces their concessions. Scientists who dogmatically maintain a position despite concrete evidence to the contrary are left behind. Whereas philosophers receive acclaim for occupying a position and defending it persuasively, scientists receive acclaim for making new discoveries that push the field to modify existing models of reality. Science makes astonishing progress year after year, whereas philosophy makes slow progress over centuries—at least concerning mental causation, free will, and the mind–body problem—because debates can be objectively settled in science but cannot be objectively settled in philosophy. Given that philosophy seems chronically locked in opposing viewpoints argued from incompatible starting assumptions, progress on the mind–body problem will have to come from neuroscientists themselves and philosophers versed in neuroscience, if there is to be progress at all. Those who do not know much about the brain cannot be expected to make much progress in solving the relationship of the mind to the brain. Neuroscientists can shed useful new light on the various aspects of the mind–body problem, including the problem of how nature instantiated a physical system where voluntary action is executed. Neuroscientists can examine how voluntary actions are carried out by neurons, and learn from what hundreds of millions of years of natural selection have fashioned. It might look nothing like what logicians would come up with on the basis of first principles.

§1.7 Some philosophers reject that qualia can cause subsequent actions. They would say that it is naïve to claim that a person goes to the dentist because a tooth hurts. To most postbehaviorist neuroscientists, what seems naïve is how epiphenomenalists can deny the facts. The fact is that the toothache causes a person to try to find ways to stop the pain. If the pain were not present, no person would try to stop it by going to the dentist. Such philosophers impose their first principles (e.g., reductionism, determinism) on reality and argue that pain must be epiphenomenal and acausal (or worse, they explain consciousness away by claiming that it does not exist) because this conclusion follows necessarily and logically from their "correct" assumptions. Rather than change their first principles, they deny the facts and charge the rest of us with delusion. If our present models of reality based on reductionism lead to the conclusion that pain cannot be causal or does not even exist, and the facts say otherwise, then it is our models and assumptions that need to change, not our recognition that pain exists or affects behavior. Explaining the causal efficacy of pain away with logic based on assumptions that, by definition, rule out the possibility of such causal efficacy does not explain anything; it just sidesteps the problem. We must simply accept that there are subjective experiences, such as pain, because we have immediate, undeniable access to them. Scientists prefer to start with facts rather than with logical assumptions. Facts always trump first principles. With the facts as a starting point, rather than assumptions, we can try to figure out a model of reality that helps us understand the causal efficacy of pain and other experiences.

§1.8   If philosophy is at an impasse because logical argumentation, intuitions, thought experiments, and reason are inadequate to the task of unraveling how the mind–body problem was solved by nature, neuroscience is at an impasse because it has trouble observing information-processing at the level at which it actually occurs, namely, neural circuits. Neural circuits involve thousands if not millions of neurons operating in precise temporal relationships. They carry out operations on their informational inputs. But lacking the ability to measure thousands of neurons that belong to a common circuit simultaneously, each with the precision of an intracellular single-unit electrode, we cannot determine with precision what the information-processing steps within a neural circuit are. Instead, as a field, we are like the person who has lost his or her keys in the dark, but is looking for them under a nearby lamppost, because at least there the light is good. That is, neuroscientists use the methods that are available even though they are inadequate to the task of deciphering information-processing in complex neural circuits that span the brain.

§1.9   In the absence of methods that would let us measure information-processing at the level of circuits, we settle for second best. Many neuroscientists, myself included, use blunt measures of brain activity. We measure electro- or magneto-encephalograms at the scalp and try to infer the sequence of information-processing steps from these signals. The timing of these signals is good, but the spatial resolution is poor. The signal is, after all, the summation of potential changes from millions of cells, most likely not localized to a single source. Alternatively, using functional magnetic resonance imaging (fMRI), we look at where blood flows in response to neural activity. In this case, the spatial resolution is not that bad—on the order of millimeters—but the timing is poor, given that it takes several seconds for oxygenated blood to peak once neural activity has triggered increased blood supply to replenish glucose and oxygen. At the other end of the spectrum, the gold standard in neuroscience remains single-unit recording. Here both the temporal and the spatial resolution of the measured signals are excellent. Yet, understanding information-processing architecture will require an analysis of the sequence and interplay of excitation, inhibition, and neuromodulation at the level of interneuronal (network) and intraneuronal (dendritic) circuits. Just as observing a single brick would not tell you whether it was part of a Georgian, colonial, or baroque building, determining a single neuron's receptive field or tuning properties will offer scant insight into circuit-level information-processing architecture.

§1.10   In visual neuroscience, our most advanced subfield, neuroscientists measure the tuning properties and receptive fields of neurons that detect certain kinds of stimulus energy, such as orientation or "motion energy." But the concept of the receptive field has both helped us and held us back. Once sufficient information has been detected, operations must be carried out that transform detected information and even generate information where there was none in the image. For example, if a woman is half occluded by shrubbery, the visual system must construct the three-dimensional shape of the woman on the basis of input that is highly fragmented at the level of the two-dimensional image. Nothing in the image establishes that the fragments arise from a common object or dictates how the woman should be constructed on the basis of this impoverished information. But this "amodal completion" is child's play for the visual system. The stage of detection of stimulus energies is followed by numerous neuronal and information-processing steps that construct what we experience. Because we cannot easily measure sequential computations in dendrites or networks, we cannot deeply model the neuronal operations that construct informational outputs on the basis of ambiguous, noisy, and often impoverished input. Instead, we settle for vague notions like "Gestalt grouping principles," or "Bayesian priors," regarding the mapping between the image and the constructed experience. But these are more or less just crude descriptions of what must be happening, rather like "explaining" the efficacy of some medical intervention as due to the placebo effect.

What is lacking is a precise analysis of the neuronal and informational operations that take place after the stage of detection. The problem is partly technological: We need more methods that allow us to measure thousands of neurons simultaneously that are known to be part of a common circuit. We need to eventually be able to apply such methods in awake and behaving humans who can tell us, for example, what they experience when certain parts of a known circuit are microstimulated in a particular way. But the problem is not only technological. It is also conceptual.

§1.11 A reductionistic inclination leads many neuroscientists to focus on the properties of single neurons. But circuits, considered as spatiotemporal wholes, exhibit emergent properties that are not possessed by any single neuron. Take, for example, that rare case where neuroscience has had success in understanding at a circuit level of processing: the undulation of a swimming lamprey. Observing only a single neuron might tell you that a muscle contraction is commanded at regular intervals. But it is the temporal or "phase" relationships among many individual such commands that lead to the emergent capacity of locomotion via undulation. The emergent capacity to swim is not a property of any single neuron. It is a property of the whole lamprey, in particular the spatiotemporal pattern of firing in a circuit of neurons, interacting with muscles that can contract and an environment that offers the right kind of resistance. Scramble the timing or locations of those multiple commands, and a lamprey would not swim but instead would thrash about "epileptically." But these phase relationships are not encoded in any single neuron. They are encoded in the circuit, in the precise timing and interplay among excitation and inhibition in a cascade of activity that traverses a network. True, undulation might be released by a "command neuron" (Carew, 2000; Edwards et al., 1999; Korn & Faber, 2005) that triggers a "central pattern generator" that releases the "fixed action pattern" of undulatory motion (Harris-Warrick & Cohen, 1985), but the temporal phase relations among a population of neurons are not encoded in a single command neuron. A command neuron at best releases a complex behavior such as undulation. A full understanding of the human brain and mind will require understanding all our neural circuitry at the level at which we understand the precisely timed sequence of activity in central pattern generators in lampreys that permit them to swim. It is cascades of well-timed excitation and inhibition that allow us to swim as well, or talk, think, attend, and perceive.

§1.12 Neuroscience is unusual among the sciences in that it seeks to understand facts that are not publicly observable. Mental contents, information, consciousness, and attention cannot be directly observed as physical phenomena. We can only observe the physical events that realize mental unobservables, particularly neuronal activity; and we can observe the consequences of mental operations, especially behavior. In addition to being able to measure neuronal activity and psychophysical behavior, we have a third source of information about the brain: our own experience. To date, experience has not been as explored as systematically as the other two handles on information-processing provided by neural activity and behavior. But as neuroscience matures, and outgrows the insecurities that led to behaviorism's rejection of experience as a valid domain of scientific inquiry, I suspect we will see the emergence of a "Gestalt Neuroscience" that will embrace not only the analysis of neuronal activity and behavior, but also the systematic manipulation and analysis of experience via, for example, microstimulation of human brains that can tell us what they are experiencing as a consequence. Experience is, after all, the output of many of the neural circuits we want to understand. Those outputs can inform us about the information-processing steps that led to those outputs.

§1.13 Philosophy and neuroscience find themselves, for different reasons, at an impasse in their attempts to understand mental causation. Facts alone, model-testing alone, or logical argumentation alone are weaker than their combination. Philosophers can benefit by learning neuroscience and collaborating with neuroscientists in developing experiments that can make falsifiable predictions that settle their disputes, and neuroscientists can benefit by collaborating with philosophers in clarifying terms and concepts, in developing experiments that ask the deep questions, and in learning the philosophical literature themselves.

§1.14 Both philosophy and neuroscience are dominated by a form of reductionism that inhibits people from exploring how spatiotemporal patterns in input can be causal. The fear might be that letting go of a strong reductionism might result in a "fluffy dualism" or rejection of physicalism. But that fear is unfounded. One can be a physicalist and still be open to the possibility that spatiotemporal patterns in input can play a role in the causation of subsequent events in a physical system.

§1.15 The difficult question has been how patterns of energy rather than mere amounts of energy might be causal. Van Gulick (1995, p. 252; see also Campbell, 1974, and Deacon, 2007) suggests that patterns can be causal in this sense: "higher-order patterns can have a degree of independence from their underlying physical realizations and can exert what might be called downward causal influences without requiring any objectionable form of emergentism by which higher-order properties would alter the underlying laws of physics. Higher-order properties act by the *selective acti-*

vation of physical powers and not by their *alteration.*" He gives a hurricane as an example. It is a pattern that is realized in constituent particles, but whose constituent particles come and go. A hurricane in the morning may have no constituent particles in common with the "same" hurricane in the afternoon; "there is a very real sense in which the constituents of the pattern are organized as they are because of the pattern. It is because of the existence and persistence of the pattern that the particular constituents of its instances were recruited and organized as they are" (Van Gulick 1995, p. 252). The "downward causation" that Van Gulick argues a hurricane "exerts" on particles, however, can be reduced to the localistic transfer of energy among particles (see appendix 1). Thus, this kind of attack against strong reductionism and epiphenomenalism fails; the hurricane is arguably epiphenomenal because it is not doing causal work when all the causal work is being done by energy transfer among its constituent particles. This is the reductionist's fundamental criticism (see appendix 2). It is one that those who believe in mental causation have so far been unable to refute.

§1.16   A central message of this book is that *patterns in input can be genuinely causal only if there are physical detectors, such as neurons, that respond to patterns in input and then change the physical system in which they reside if the criteria for the presence of a pattern in inputs have been met.* Neurons that respond to patterns in input, such as temporal coincidences, that carry information about spatial and other patterns in the world, such as, say, the spatial pattern of the constellation Orion, can be thought to realize a downwardly causal physical process. The causal efficacy of pattern detection among neurons is fundamentally different from the "downward causation" of a hurricane because pattern detection among neurons cannot be reduced to the localistic transfer of energy among colliding particles. A neuron does not absorb or transfer energy like a billiard ball. It assesses its inputs for satisfaction of physical/informational criteria, which, if met, lead to output. These criteria do not assess the amount of energy in inputs. They assess patterns in input. One of the most important assessments is of the coincidence of input (i.e., arrival within the temporal integration window of neurons). By responding to patterns in energy rather than just amounts of energy, neurons permit spatiotemporal patterns of input to be causal. Without such a mechanism of pattern detection and the triggered physical response of firing, patterns in energy, like hurricanes, would only be epiphenomenally causal. But with a physical mechanism in place that responds to patterns in energy by generating a physical response in a cascade of such pattern detectors, patterns in energetic inputs become genuinely causal.

§1.17 In sum, given that the nervous system realizes mental events such as pain that can cause subsequent actions, our job is to try to understand how this can happen, not to deny that it happens because we cannot explain it given our present assumptions. The physical realizations of consciousness and mental causation have already been "solved" by evolution. If a learned man asserts that you cannot sail westward from Portugal to reach China because the world is flat, and an explorer accomplishes this nonetheless, which one needs to change his view? The solution to the mind–body problem will not come from logical derivations that yield conclusions that follow from unproven assumptions. What if an assumption of reductionism is wrong? What if an assumption of determinism is wrong? The solution to the ancient mind–body problem will eventually emerge as scientists unravel the way that mind is in fact realized in neuronal activity at the level of interneuronal and intraneuronal circuits. New options concerning free will, mental causation, and the mind–body problem can and will emerge in light of neuroscientific data.

2   Overview of Arguments

§2.1   Most readers interested in the neural basis of free will should begin with the next chapter, where the main arguments concerning "criterial causation" in the brain begin. However, for completeness, I have included some material of primarily philosophical interest in the appendixes. Philosophers have confronted the problems of mental causation and free will for much longer than neuroscience has even existed, and their findings and debates need to be addressed, especially since some of their conclusions have been quite radical (e.g., consciousness does not exist, or mental events are not causal, or cannot be identical to brain events). For readers who want to begin at the most fundamental physical level, in appendix 1 I review evidence from physics for the reality of an ontologically indeterministic universe. In light of this, ontological indeterminism is assumed for all other arguments made in this book, although a nonindeterministic form of local randomness alone would suffice for my main argument concerning what neurons do. Neuronal criterial causation is compatible with either determinism or indeterminism. But an assumption of ontological indeterminism is required for the logical arguments in appendix 2 to work. In this second appendix I challenge the central philosophical argument against the logical possibility of mental causation. I argue that the core argument of physical reductionists against the possibility of mental causation (§A2.3) rests on the impossibility of self-causation; if determinism were the case, then these arguments would indeed be correct, and mental causation and a "strong free will" (defined in §7.1) would be logically ruled out. However, the central argument of eliminative reductionism does not follow if ontological indeterminism is the case. I argue that ontological indeterminism undermines the central reductionistic physicalist argument against the possibility of mental causation (§§A2.2–A2.5). If determinism is the case, neuronal criterial causation could be a mechanism underlying a form of free will compatibilism. However, if indeterminism is the case, then a strong free will (§7.1) can exist, because in that case, things really could have turned out otherwise.

§2.2   Readers who do not need convincing that reductionistic materialism does not undermine the possibility of free will can start with chapter 3. Neuroscientists and others interested in how neurons encode information will want to focus on chapters 4, 5, 9 and 10. In chapters 6 through 8, I take a step back from neuroscience to address related problems in psychology and the philosophy of mind, before returning to neuroscience in chapter 9. In chapter 6 I go into further depth concerning what we mean by "mental causation" from a criterialist perspective. Readers who are mainly interested in the argument in favor of the existence of a strong free will can skip to chapter 7. Issues concerning the nature of mental representation from a criterialist perspective are the focus of chapter 8. Those interested mainly in the neural basis of consciousness can go directly to chapter 10.

§2.3   In chapters 3 through 6, a physicalist mechanism of mental causation and volition is described that is consistent with what we currently know about the physical processes that allow neurons to process information. A central argument against the logical possibility of either mental causation or free will has been the impossibility of self-causation: Because mental events, including acts of willing, are realized in (or supervene[1] on) physical events, they cannot alter the physical events in which they are now realized (or on which they now supervene). Higher-level facts in the present are realized in physical facts in the present. In this regard, any information that is realized in neurons that are active now cannot change the physical basis of that information itself. That would be impossible circular causation. However, neurons do not only make other neurons fire; they also recode the informational criteria realized in the physical criteria that will make other neurons fire at some unknown time in the future when the right inputs come along. The central thesis argued here is that physically realized mental events can change the physical basis not of present but rather of *future* mental events by triggering changes in the physical and informational criteria that must be met by future presynaptic inputs before future postsynaptic neuronal firing occurs. The information in the future that will occur when these recoded criteria are met by future incoming neuronal inputs is not information that is realized in the present. The recoding of physical/informational criteria takes place in the present, but the information that occurs when those criteria are met occurs in the future. Such criterial causation does not involve self-causation; arguments that mental causation (§A2.3) and free will (§7.4) are logically impossible because of the impossibility of self-causation therefore do not apply. None of this violates physicalism or requires additional natural or supernatural forces to permit mental-on-physical causation. Information is not reified as something realizable outside matter. But it does allow information now realized in physical neuronal activity to be causal of future information realized in future neuronal activity.

§2.4   It is commonly assumed that information processing and thus informational causation among neurons is primarily a matter of presynaptic action potentials (i.e., neuronal firings) triggering postsynaptic action potentials. Postsynaptic neurons in turn serve as presynaptic neurons to the next level, allowing neuronal causation to be thought of as a sequence of action potentials traversing a neuronal circuit. While this is indeed a central process realizing neuronal and informational causation in the brain, neurons can also rapidly and dynamically change the weights and temporal integration properties of synapses of other neurons without necessarily instantly triggering an action potential in those neurons (§§4.54–4.60). That is, physical criteria for firing are changed by changing synaptic properties. This and other physical mechanisms accomplish a recoding of the inputs that will make a neuron fire. Such recoding changes both the physical and the informational criteria that a neuron places on its inputs. A given physical criterion for firing, such as passing a threshold potential at the axon hillock, can remain constant and yet realize many different informational criteria, depending on the dynamically resettable inputs that drive a neuron above threshold. Evidence suggests that the neural information-processing code is first and foremost a dynamic synaptic code, and is not solely a code in terms of action potentials (§4.56).

§2.5   A central concern of this book is to understand how exactly synapses could be reset fast enough to serve as a mechanism for mental causation and therefore for willing. An important part of the answer lies in the increase in the probability of the opening of NMDA[2] receptors[3] with neuronal bursting. The opening of NMDA receptors both transiently resets the weights, gains, and temporal dynamics of synapses, and also plays a key role in shifting a network into a "phasic" or bursty mode of spiking. It is argued that attentional binding in particular is realized when circuitry enters a "phasic" or bursty mode of firing. In this "binding by bursting" mode (§4.53), bursts function as units of information processing (Lisman, 1997) that are propagated through the perceptual processing hierarchy. Because the bursts are subject to computational operations as they "pass through" the neurons of the information-processing hierarchy, the information realized in a burst changes as it propagates through the hierarchy.

In the absence of attention, it is argued that the network stays in "tonic" or nonbursty firing mode, and the likelihood of complete information processing is diminished.

§2.6 Although neuronal criterial causation could operate deterministically (§7.18), data suggest that random microscopic fluctuations are amplified into randomness in spike timing, which allows any given set of criteria to be met in a nonpredetermined manner. Assuming amplification of microscopic fluctuations, criterial causation permits downward mental causation and a strong free will because neurons can set up criteria for future action potential release that, once satisfied, lead to nondetermined yet self-selected future actions that harness inherent variability in neuronal responses to generate novel solutions that meet the particular criteria that were set. Multiple physical causal chains are possible at any moment, assuming indeterminism. Only a minute subset of these will also be informational causal chains. Criterial causation is powerful because it allows only that subset of possible physical causal chains that are also informational causal chains to occur. In systems that exhibit criterial causation, informational causal chains just are physical causal chains and vice versa. For neuronally and criterially realized informational causal chains, there is no need to talk of mind causing matter or neurons taking information as input rather than material structures such as neurotransmitters: For this unusual subset of possible causal chains among particles, mental causation just is criterial informational causation, which just is criterial physical causation.

§2.7 I propose a three-stage neuronal model of mental causation and free will according to which (1) new physical/informational criteria are set in a neuronal circuit on the basis of preceding physical/mental processing at time t_1, in part via a mechanism of rapid synaptic resetting that effectively changes the inputs to a postsynaptic neuron. These changes can be driven either volitionally or nonvolitionally, depending on the neural circuitry involved. (2) At time t_2, inherently variable inputs arrive at the postsynaptic neuron, and (3) at time t_3 physical/informational criteria are met or not met, leading to postsynaptic neural firing or not. Randomness can play a role in the first two stages, but not substantially in the third, because intracellular potential either passes the threshold for firing or it does not. Such criterial causation is important because it allows neurons to alter the physical realization of *future* mental events in a way that escapes the problem of self-causation of the mental upon the physical. The impossibility of self-causation has been at the root of basic criticisms of the possibility of mental causation (§§A2.2–A2.5) or free will (§§7.1–7.5).

Criterial causation gets around this core problem. In essence, free will is all about setting the physical grounds for unpredictable future mental events and decisions that meet the informational criteria set. Free will is fundamentally about the future, especially the next cycle in iterative information-processing loops.

§2.8 A recurring theme in this book concerns the issue of multiple physical realizability. Although multiple realizability is necessary for criterial causation, it is not sufficient. Criterial causation involves mapping many types and sets of input, each of which meets the criteria that were preset to one output, such as an action potential, that then acts as input to the next stage in a network of criterial decoders (§6.8). As such, criterial decoders exhibit a variant of multiple realizability in that the same mental state can be realized on the basis of numerous inputs, and therefore numerous antecedent physical states. But in addition, criterial causation involves a succession, sequence, or chain of criterial assessments of informational input that transform, complete, and manipulate that information. Because the criteria at each stage can differ, information can be transformed in an informational cascade. Because one informational realization can trigger another, information can be causal, as it is in the brain. On this account, we really do go to the dentist because the pain is unbearable. This is not to deny that we are entirely physical systems subject to the laws of physical causation; we are. It is just that for brains, physical neuronal causal chains are informational causal chains, and vice versa.

§2.9 In chapter 8, I explore various implications of the view that neural information-processing is an instance of criterial causation for psychology, philosophy, and neuroscience. For one, criterial neural information processing need not be algorithmic. Indeed, criterial encoding is not even representational, in the sense that it at best places constraints on inputs rather than specifying exactly what future inputs must be. This implies that there is no necessary causal connection between a proposition or name and things or events in the world. Criterialism hearkens back to the descriptivist account of reference of Russell, Wittgenstein, and Frege, except that most of the criteria imposed by neurons cannot be understood at the level of descriptions, naming, semantics, or words. That said, criterialism rejects Kripke's criticisms of descriptivism. Kripke's main argument against descriptivism is rooted in a category error that confuses statements about the world with statements about models of the world. Although a criterial account of neural information processing is alone insufficient to account fully for certain mental operations, such as mental rotation or syntax, it accounts well for other aspects of cognition, including prototyping, caricaturing, other race effects, generalization, categorization, and semantic priming.

§2.10   When thinking these ideas through, I wanted to see how far I could get in understanding neuronal criterial informational causation without addressing possible causal roles of consciousness. By chapter 9 I can no longer avoid consciousness. In chapter 9 I argue that readiness potentials, believed by some to be a neural signature of conscious willing, in fact are not this signature, and are not relevant to debates about conscious willing or its causal efficacy. In chapter 10 I address the various roles that conscious experience plays in the causal framework of the three-stage process of criterial causation and outcome selection proposed as a neural basis for mental and volitional causation. Given only what was presented up to chapter 10, one could fairly argue that neuronal criterial causation and randomness are at best necessary but cannot alone be sufficient for the physical realization of mental causation and a strong free will, because without a conscious agent with intentional states that could exploit the three-stage process to fulfill its ends, we might be no more than mindless, unpredictable "zombies" (§10.83). In chapter 10, I argue that consciousness plays a key role in mental causation by providing a common format for endogenous attentional and other executive operations that permit the assessment of possible behaviors and thoughts against the highest-level criteria held in working memory for successful attainment of goals and fulfillment of desires. Qualia, I argue, are those representations that can be operated on by endogenous attention, giving rise to the possibility of volitional attentional tracking, which, I argue, cannot happen in the absence of consciousness. Because certain operations can only take place over conscious operands, and motor acts can follow and enact the conclusions of such operations, such mental operations play a necessary causal role in their mental and motoric consequences, and are not mere illusions of volition. How a propositional conclusion, such as "I need to go to the store to buy cranberry sauce," is translated into motor plans and actions is not well understood, but it is likely to occur via the same rapid and dynamic reconfiguration of the physical/informational criteria for neuronal firing via synaptic resetting that underlies the three-stage process. If so, current operations in working memory over endogenously attendable operands do not cause present thoughts, experiences or actions, but instead play a causal role in future thoughts, experiences, and actions, given the arrival of inputs that satisfy the criteria that have been preset.

§2.11   I suggest that there are innate (type 1) qualia, like salty, blue or pain, that form the "basis dimensions" of experience within which both learning and endogenous attention can operate. A type 1 quale, such as red, can "pop out" in a search array among, say, green distractors that lack that quale. Type 2 qualia are chunked combinations of type 1 qualia that are learned with repeated attentional binding; over time they become automatized to serve as a neo-primitive dimension of experience. With practice a type 2 quale can approach "pop out" performance, requiring minimal or no attentional binding in order to be experienced. A type 3 quale is a temporary attentional binding of qualia of types 1 and 2. The neural correlates of types 1 and 2 are to be found in early iconic and mid-level buffers, after a stage of automatic preconscious grouping procedures and other operations. In contrast, the neural correlates of type 3 qualia are to be found in various working memory buffers. Our normal waking experience is comprised of all three types in "superposition." But it is possible to experience only the contents of iconic buffers, as we do in parts of the visual field that we are not attending, and it is possible to experience only the contents of working memory, as we do while dreaming. During

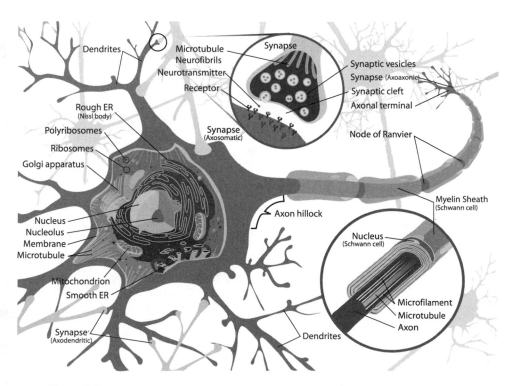

Figure 2.1
A diagram of a neuron. Courtesy of Wikimedia commons.

daydreaming or mental imagery while awake, the contents of both iconic and working memory buffers are experienced in parallel. For example, this would be the superpositional experience we have while driving and day-dreaming. We see and act on the basis of iconic information, while simultaneously experiencing mental imagery and thoughts associated with working memory processing. This places my view in opposition to the now-dominant view that the frontoparietal network is necessary for consciousness or the having of experience (e.g. Dehaene & Changeaux, 2011). I argue that this is correct for type 3 qualia, but not for types 1 or 2. Thus, I argue that a person who lacks working memory and attentional processes, perhaps because they have been thoroughly lobotomized, can still experience pain, hunger, or brightness in the context of "attentionally unbound qualia soup," whereas those who believe that the frontoparietal network is necessary for consciousness do not (§10.65).

3 A Criterial Neuronal Code Underlies Downward Mental Causation and Free Will

Abstract for Chapters 3–6

In the following chapters, I describe a physicalist mechanism of mental causation and volition that is consistent with what is currently known about the physical processes that allow neurons to process information. A central argument against the logical possibility of either mental causation or free will has been the impossibility of self-causation: Because mental events, including acts of willing, are realized in or supervene on physical events, they cannot alter the physical events in which they are presently realized or on which they supervene. Although this claim is true, the central thesis I argue here is that physically realized mental events can change the physical basis of *future* mental events by triggering changes in the physical/informational criteria that must be met by future presynaptic inputs before future neuronal firing occurs. Such criterial causation does not involve self-causation; arguments that mental causation and free will are logically impossible because of the impossibility of self-causation therefore do not apply. Physical criteria for firing are changed via various physical mechanisms, including the dynamic resetting of synaptic properties. Changes in physical criteria for firing can realize changes in informational criteria for firing. A given physical criterion for firing, such as passing a threshold potential at the axon hillock, can remain constant and yet realize many different informational criteria, depending on the dynamically resettable inputs that drive a neuron above its threshold. While neuronal criterial causation could operate deterministically, data suggest that random microscopic fluctuations are amplified into randomness in spike timing, which allows given criteria to be met in a nondeterministic manner. Criterial causation permits downward mental causation and free will because neurons can set up criteria for future action potential release, which, once satisfied, lead to nondetermined yet self-selected future actions that harness inherent variability in neuronal responses to generate novel solutions that meet the criteria that were preset.

What Is Will?

§3.1   An agent's act of will can be defined as the agent's choice or decision to perform or not perform an action, either later (via formation of distal intentions) or right now (via proximal intentions; cf. Haggard et al., 2010). Will is the capacity to so choose or decide to act. But there are actions that are implemented in the world, and actions that are implemented internally. External actions are limited to muscular actions. If it wants to do anything in the world, whether to locomote or move objects, a brain can only contract muscles. Internal actions, however, are more varied and require no muscular contraction. Shifting your attention volitionally from this page to the sensation of the chair against your thighs is an example of an internally willed action. Exerting effort to carry out the computation "42 × 19" or trying to recall all the capitals of Scandinavian countries provide examples of internal actions in the domains of reasoning and recall. Whenever effort is volitionally applied in order to implement a decision or plan, whether muscularly or in terms of subsequent mental operations, we can say that the effort is a willed effort.

§3.2   But the idea of will, whether free or not, is not monolithic. Will appears not to be a thing or event but a durationally extended process. A process, such as driving a car, involves numerous procedures and nested subprocedures. For example, certain areas of the brain might specify a problem or a need that requires possible solutions; other areas of the brain might generate multiple possible solutions; others might evaluate possible solutions on the basis of various criteria while playing out the consequences of a given possible choice internally; others might select the optimal option; others might evoke the motivation and appropriate emotional and physiological states needed to implement the chosen plan; and still other areas might then implement a motoric plan to enact the propositional plan. For example, lesioning the dorsolateral prefrontal cortex (DLPFC) or area 10 might limit the ability to generate multiple possible plans or play them out internally; lesioning the dopaminergic circuitry (e.g., Montague et al., 2004) associated with the ventral striatum might limit the ability to evaluate possibilities for their positive reward value; lesioning frontoparietal attentional areas might limit the ability to select optimal options; lesioning the anterior cingulate cortex might limit the ability to evoke motivation or appropriate emotional and physiological responses for a given plan and inhibit suboptimal or inappropriate plans; lesioning motor planning areas such as the presupplementary and supplementary motor areas might damage the ability to plan motor acts appropriately; and damaging the motor strip might eliminate the ability to carry out muscular actions at all. Because the cascade of steps from an abstract plan to a concrete action occurs in such rapid succession in a normal brain, it may seem that willing is a single process, but it is in fact a concatenation of subprocesses (§10.61). Some might want to associate willing primarily with the ability to freely choose a plan; others might want to associate it primarily with the feeling of effort associated with trying to implement a plan. Confusion arises when people talk about the operations of different neural circuits using the single word "will."[1]

§3.3 Willing concerns at least five separable issues. Most neuroscientists and philosophers who are interested in free will focus on the question of whether our wills and actions are free (in the sense defined in §7.1); incompatibilists believe we are free only if determinism is false, whereas compatibilists think that we may will or act freely even if our wills are determined. A second, separate question is whether our wills are efficacious. This issue is not about what, if anything, causes or constrains our wills, but rather is about what, if anything, our wills cause. A will might be free, but if it is not causally connected to a motor system for generating action, the will would remain ineffective and impotent; for example, patients with "locked-in syndrome" who have lost all voluntary muscle control might have a free but inefficacious will.[2] A third issue is whether conscious contents in general, or consciousness of will or feelings of agency in particular, play any role in causing actions.[3] A fourth issue concerns the magnitude of free will, in the sense that a pianist has more degrees of freedom in that particular domain than someone who cannot play the piano. A fifth issue concerns will in the sense of willpower: the capacity to see our choices through. We may be able to choose freely, have an efficacious motor system and efficacious conscious willing, but if we lack motivation, determination, or the attention, planning, and working memory capacities to see our decisions through, we may be quickly blocked or diverted from enacting our choices, whether because of external impediments or internal ones, such as forgetting or being distracted. Without willpower to enact our choices, it does not matter how free our capacity to choose is.

§3.4 In this book I address only the first and third questions, namely, whether our wills can be free and whether consciousness plays any role in mental causation. In chapters 9 and 10, I ask whether consciousness in general and our conscious feelings of willing in particular are causal of our actions. While questions of causal efficacy are crucial for determining when, if ever, we have free will in the sense of the ability to act freely, it is useful to focus first on freedom of the will in the first sense, setting aside the complex issue of consciousness until the last chapters. In my next book *The Cultivation of Will*, also to be published with MIT Press, I focus on the fourth and fifth issues. The issue of willpower, generally neglected by neuroscientists, needs its own in-depth analysis, and including that topic here would have made this book far too long. So for now, I will put issues of willpower aside and focus on issues of how criterial causation offers a path toward a strong free will that passes between the unfree "Scylla" of determinism and the equally unfree "Charybdis" of randomness.

What Is Criterial Causation?

§3.5   Neuroscientists commonly assume that information-processing and thus information-level causation among neurons is primarily a matter of presynaptic action potentials triggering postsynaptic action potentials. Postsynaptic neurons in turn serve as presynaptic neurons to the next level, allowing neuronal causation to be thought of as a sequence of action potentials through a neuronal circuit. Although this is indeed a central process realizing neuronal and informational causation, neurons can also rapidly and dynamically change the weights, gains, and temporal integration properties of synapses of other neurons without necessarily triggering an action potential in those neurons (§4.54–4.60). This and other physical mechanisms accomplish a recoding of the inputs that will make a neuron fire in the future. Such recoding changes both the physical and the informational criteria that a neuron places on its inputs, even when the threshold for firing at the axon hillock remains constant. Indeed, this physical process of synaptic filter modification can change the "epiconnectivity" of a neuron and effectively sculpt a temporary circuit from the set of all circuits that are possible given a particular network of neurons. A given neuron can belong to many different epicircuits depending on its moment-by-moment epiconnectivity.

§3.6   What are criteria? They are a set of conditions on input that can be met in multiple ways and to differing degrees. A criterion is an aspect or dimension along which something is assessed, typically relative to some benchmark or point of reference (e.g., the resting potential). Criterial assessments are typically accompanied by standards that set a level for acceptance that the criterion or criteria have been met (e.g., the threshold at the axon hillock for the generation of an action potential). When multiple criteria are used for the assessment of input at the same time, many different combinations or degrees of satisfaction are tolerated, when the standard that must be met concerns net satisfaction across all criteria. Each criterial dimension of assessment might be weighted differently in a dynamic manner that changes with the recent history of the assessing system. Any given criterion need not be satisfied at all in order to meet a multi-criterial assessment of input. A threshold need not be imposed on the satisfaction of conditions, but if one is imposed, then beyond a certain threshold of collective satisfaction, the criteria will count as having been met. In the case of a neuron, criteria are assessed over intracellular potential, which, if met, will make the neuron fire once the physical threshold placed on the level of potential has been passed.

§3.7 Criteria are not the same as rules. Rules are directives concerning allowed actions that must be obeyed by an actor or system in order for those actions to be correct. Rules specify the allowability or correctness of outputs whereas criteria assess the degree to which inputs possess specific attributes that typically have nothing to do with allowability or normativity. Rules are typically a proposition of the form "x is allowed" or "y is not allowed." Unlike criteria, rules can easily be reformulated into commands such as "do x" or "do not do y." Unlike criteria, rules can also be reformulated into injunctions such as "you should do x" or "you ought not do y." An example of a rule phrased as an injunction is "when at a stop sign or a red light, (you must/should) stop your car." Such a rule can be rephrased into a format that mimics criteria plus a standard, such as "if the conditions that define a stop sign or red light are met, then stop." Even such a criterial phrasing, however, leaves the rule abstract, operating over propositional representations. Criteria, in contrast, need not be propositional in their assessments, although they can be. For example, in working memory we can apply propositional criteria: a car should look good, accelerate quickly, be cheap, be safe, and get good mileage before we decide to buy one. We must weigh the different criterial fulfillments against each other and assess aggregate criterial fulfillment. But this might not be so simple as crossing some threshold upon the summation of all criterial evaluations. Perhaps a cheap car requires a trade-off in terms of safety or speed, or a car that gets good mileage is more expensive than we might wish. Because there are different ways of weighing evaluations and trade-offs between conflicting criteria, decision making is not ballistic but deliberative, at least among propositional criteria assessed in working memory.[4] But at a neuronal level, there is just excitation and inhibition, assessment of potential level relative to the resting potential, firing and the reweighting of synapses. It is a physical process that can realize information, but it is in no way an inherently propositional process. Neurons criterially assess incoming information in a manner realized in the physical criterial assessment of changes in intracellular potential. Neurons cannot break rules because neurons do not obey rules. Neurons do not evaluate the correctness of outputs, and they certainly do not do this at a propositional level. Neurons assess the degree to which inputs possess informational attributes because they assess the degree to which corresponding physical facts are met. This is realized in the common currency of changes in intracellular potential and the physical threshold for firing. The passage of a potential threshold triggers neurons to do certain things, like fire, or generate dendritic action potentials when certain physical conditions are met.

§3.8   Nonetheless, humans are capable of obeying propositional rules and assessing cars propositionally. We do talk of causation at a propositional level, as when we say "he stopped because the light was red" or "she bought the car because it gets good mileage." But this higher-level propositional causation has to be realized in criterial causation at the neuronal level. Since there are only cells in our brains, propositions and rules must be generated from concatenations of simpler neuronal criterial satisfactions. A central aspect of the human mind appears to be the capacity to set up arbitrary linkages between input and behavior or thought. For example, if the criteria for coming to a red light are met, and one has recognized (i.e., matched input to a memory of) a red light, the arbitrary link to the behavior of braking can be made. In humans, a rule such as "stop at red lights" can be learned in a single shot, just by hearing someone command it. Other animals can come to associate arbitrary classes of input and output, but not in this one-shot way. Animals learn associatively, but they typically require many trials to learn an association. Humans also have associative learning, but in addition we have the capacity to make rapid, flexible mappings between arbitrary inputs and outputs. More generally, we have a capacity to seemingly bind any representation with virtually any other. It is this capacity to make arbitrary linkages or bindings between, for example, input and behavioral output that in part makes the human mind both abstract and flexible (Tse, 2006b). This process has to be realized in criterial neuronal assessments of potential. It will entail a capacity to link the outputs of high-level recognition neurons, such as those that fire upon the presence of a red light, with neurons that trigger stepping on the brakes. Although rules and causation at the level of propositions are central to that which makes human minds remarkable, in this book I will focus on processes that our brains have in common with those of other complex animals, particularly neuronal criterial causation.

§3.9   I will describe a three-stage model of mental causation, according to which (1) new physical/informational criteria are set in a neuronal circuit on the basis of preceding physical/mental processing at time t_1, in part via a mechanism of rapid synaptic resetting that changes the effective inputs to a postsynaptic neuron; these changes can either be driven volitionally or nonvolitionally, depending on the neural circuitry involved. (2) At time t_2, inherently variable inputs arrive at the postsynaptic neuron; and (3) at time t_3 physical/informational criteria are met or not met, leading to postsynaptic neural firing or not. Randomness can play a role in the first two stages, but not substantially in the third, because intracellular potential either passes the threshold for firing or it does not. Such "criterial causation" (see §6.8) is important because it allows neurons to alter the physical realization of future mental events in a way that escapes the problem of self-causation of the mental upon the physical. The impossibility of self-causation has been at the root of the strongest criticisms of the possibility of mental causation (§§A2.2–A2.5) or free will (§§7.1–7.5); criterial causation gets around this problem.

§3.10   The notion of criterial causation sheds light on how mental events cause physical events. A schematic representation of the temporal dynamics of criterial causation is shown in figure 3.1. The criteria for what makes a neuron fire can change. For example, a given physically realized mental event can set up new criterial triggers for future input by changing the code for future neuronal firing, either in the neuron(s) realizing that mental event, or other neurons, presumably using the physical mechanisms summarized in §§4.54–4.60. Any future input that satisfies these new criteria will lead to a response that will in turn either lead to a physical action or a change in how information even further in the future will occur by again changing criteria for neuronal firing. Thus, even though mental events are realized in physical events, they (i.e., their physical realization) can cause subsequent physical and mental events by preparing new decoders, or changing the criteria for firing on already existing decoders. This kind of online and continual resetting of the criteria, or code, whereby decoders decode input, and thereby realize information, is crucial to all aspects of mental life, including volition and mental-on-physical causation. Thus, mental events are not epiphenomenal. They are informational states[5] realized in neural decoders that play a role in determining how future information will be decoded by future neural activity and therefore in determining how the physical/informational system will behave in the immediate and more distant future. Of course, the information realized in

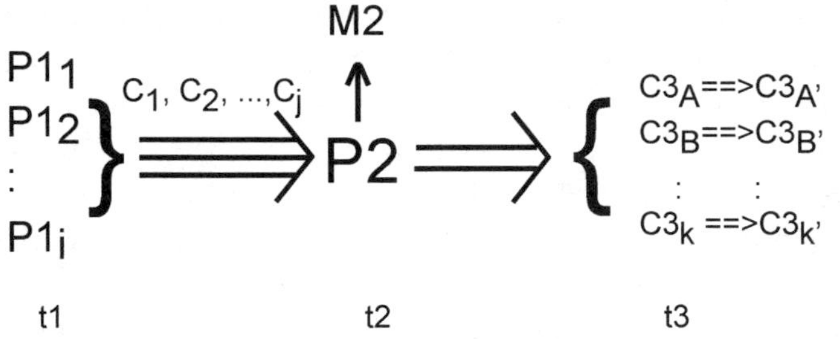

$$M2$$

$$\begin{matrix} P1_1 \\ P1_2 \\ \vdots \\ P1_i \end{matrix} \Bigg\} \xRightarrow{\;C_1, C_2, \ldots, C_j\;} \overset{\uparrow}{P2} \Longrightarrow \left\{ \begin{matrix} C3_A ==> C3_{A'} \\ C3_B ==> C3_{B'} \\ \vdots \quad \vdots \\ C3_k ==> C3_{k'} \end{matrix} \right.$$

t1   t2   t3

Figure 3.1
The prototypical sequence of criterial causation among neurons is represented in terms of the setting and resetting of physical criteria for neuronal firing. The triple arrow here represents physical criterial causation, where some proportion of the criteria $C_1, C_2, \ldots C_j$, must be met before P2 is released. In this case $P1_1, P1_2, \ldots$ $P1_i$ at t_1 are the dynamic neuronal inputs from multiple neurons to a second neuron that fires at t_2 only if these criteria $C_1, C_2, \ldots C_j$, which that neuron imposes on $P1_1, P1_2, \ldots P1_i$, are met beyond a certain threshold. The firing of this second neuron is P2, and information M2 is realized in this firing. The firing of this neuron at t_2 can in turn change the criteria for the firing of multiple neurons at and after t_3. For example, a neuron k that takes input from the neuron that fires at t_2 might have criteria $C3_k$ for firing at t_2, but will have criteria $C3_{k'}$ after t_3. The double arrows represent noncriterial physical causation. The single arrow represents the supervenience relationship of the mental on the physical.

a decoder cannot change the present physical system in which it itself is realized (there can be no *causa sui*). But it can lead to subsequent physical changes, such as the resetting of criteria for neuronal firing, in which future information will be realized upon the satisfaction of those neuronally realized criteria. Thus, we can talk about causation that operates at the level of information processing in the brain, rather than simply of causation at the level of energy transfer among elementary particles (see appendix 1).

§3.11   The multiple physical realizability of the mental, while still a contentious issue (Bechtel & Mundale, 1999; Couch, 2004; Gillett, 2003; Polger, 2004; Shapiro, 2000; Sober, 1999; Witmer, 2003), was used by Putnam (1967; cf. Putnam, 1988) and Fodor (1975; cf. Fodor, 1998) as a central argument against reductionistic accounts of the relationship of mental to physical kinds, principally type-identity theory and eliminative materialism (but see Kim, 1989, 1992, or Bickle, 1998, 2003, 2006a,b, for spirited defenses of reductionism). Multiple realizability, whether across structural types or within a given structure, such as the brain, implies that any microphysical account of mental events would fail to capture psychological kinds. This led these theorists and others, initially, to variants of functionalism, according to which mental events are explained and equated at the level of functional causal relationships rather than particular physical instantiations of those relationships. In the philosophy of mind, multiple realizability is usually considered at an abstract level, according to which mental states are realizable in multiple brain states. But, ultimately, such abstractions have to be understood in terms of neurons embedded in specific neuronal circuits. We must consider what multiple realizability might look like at a neuronal level, given what we presently know in neuroscience about how neurons process information.

§3.12   Although criterial causation is not a functionalist account of causation (§§8.24, 8.25), it does essentially involve multiple realizability. Multiple realizability is necessary for criterial causation, but it is not sufficient. For example, physical systems like locks and keys that are multiply realizable (a key can be made of many kinds of substances and still function as a lock opener; cf. Shapiro, 2000) need not realize criterial causation. Criterial causation involves mapping many types of input to one output, such as an action potential, that then acts as input to the next stage in a network of criterial decoders (§6.8). As such, criterial decoders exhibit a variant of multiple realizability in that the same mental state can be realized on the basis of numerous inputs, and therefore on the basis of numerous antecedent physical states. But more than this, criterial causation involves a succession, sequence, or chain of criterial assessments of informational input realized in physical input. Because the criteria at each stage can differ, information can be transformed, and therefore be causal, as it is in the brain. This is something that a lock and key, or even a succession of locks that in turn open other locks, could not do. Although multiple realizability is not uncommon in nature (§6.8), criterial causation appears to be unique to biological systems.

§3.13   Higher-level facts in the present are realized in physical facts in the present. In this regard, any information that is realized in neurons that are active now cannot change its own physical basis. That would be circular causation. However, neurons do not only make other neurons fire. They also recode the physical criteria that will make other neurons fire in the future when the right inputs come along. This is most likely realized via very rapid mechanisms that reset synaptic weighting, gain, and temporal integration properties (§§4.54–4.60). I will call such mechanisms collectively "synaptic resetting." Concerning temporal integration, synapses can be "facilitating" or "depressive" (Abbott & Regehr, 2004). Facilitating synapses become transiently stronger after a spike, whereas depressive synapses become transiently weaker. This means that facilitating synapses effectively integrate input, and depressive synapses effectively differentiate it. The result of these different temporal response characteristics is that facilitating synapses foster bursting and the enhancement of informational transmission via bursting (Lisman, 1997), whereas depressing synapses foster more regular or "tonic" firing patterns. It is possible that rapid synaptic resetting may involve not just changes in weight and gain, but also changes in the manner in which a synapse integrates input. *If synaptic resetting can be fast enough, the initial spikes of a spike train or burst can reset synapses and later spikes can meet those reset criteria for firing (§5.43). The information in the future that will occur when these recoded criteria are met by future incoming neuronal input is not information that is realized in the present. The recoding of physical/informational criteria takes place in the present, but the information that occurs when those criteria are met occurs in the future, even if only milliseconds after synaptic resetting. This gets around self-causation in the present, because informational transfer and synaptic resetting take place over durations; information is typically transmitted not in isolated spikes, but in spike trains.* None of this violates physicalism or requires additional forces to permit mental-on-physical causation. But it does allow information now realized in physical neuronal activity to play a causal role in future information realized in future neuronal activity. Multiple physical causal chains are possible at any moment, assuming indeterminism. Only a minute subset of these will also be informational causal chains. Criterial causation is powerful because it allows only that subset of possible physical causal chains that are also informational causal chains to occur. In cases exhibiting criterial causation, informational causal chains just are physical causal chains, and vice versa. For physical systems that realize criterial causation, to say "such-and-such physical events caused such-and-such physical events to happen" becomes a different way of saying "such-and-such information caused such and such information to happen."

§3.14   An overview of the main arguments is as follows: (1) Kim's central arguments against the possibility of mental causation (§A2.3) rest on the impossibility of self-causation. (2) Likewise, the central argument against the possibility of free will (§7.4) rests on the impossibility of self-causation. (3) If determinism were the case, then these arguments would be correct, and mental causation and a strong free will would be logically ruled out. However, Kim's argument does not follow if ontological indeterminism is the case (§§A2.2–A2.5). And the basic argument against free will also does not follow, given a degree of randomness in neural spike timing and given neural criterial causation (§§7.5, 7.10). (4) Assuming indeterminism provides a way out of the arguments of (1) and (2) as follows: Physically realized mental events can change the physical basis not of themselves in the present, but of future mental events. They accomplish this by triggering changes in the physically realized informational/physical criteria for firing that must be met by future neuronal inputs before future neuronal firing occurs that realizes future mental events. (5) Such criterial causation does not involve self-causation. It also does not require any strange quantum domain effects to be exploited by consciousness (§A1.8). Even though the amplification of microscopic randomness to randomness at the level of neural spike timing (§§4.66–4.68) is essential to support a strong free will (§7.1), criterial causation could operate in a purely deterministic manner (§7.18). But assuming ontological indeterminism, criterial causation offers a physicalist mechanism that realizes a strong free will and mental causation. Arguments such as Kim's concerning the impossibility of mental causation (§A2.3) or Strawson's concerning the impossibility of free will (§7.4), which are built on the impossibility of self-causation, thus do not apply to criterial causation as realized in neurons.

§3.15   In chapters 4 and 5, I review neuroscientific evidence that suggests that neurons set physical criteria for firing on their physical inputs, which realize informational criteria on informational inputs by virtue of a hierarchy of connectivity and dynamic resetting of synapses. In chapter 6 I argue that if physically realized criteria place conditions on the informational content carried by input, then informational causal chains can be realized in physical causal chains. In chapter 7 I argue that criterial causation provides the key neural mechanism for mental causation and free will.

4   Neurons Impose Physical and Informational Criteria for Firing on Their Inputs

How Can Neurons Realize Informational Criteria?

§4.1   Neurons can be thought to physically realize informational criteria placed on characteristics of their input, which, if met, trigger neuronal firing.[1] But how do they do this? To answer this we must first consider a fundamental puzzle in neuroscience: Why do neural networks "bother" with relatively slow chemical transmission between neurons at the synapse, when electrical communication would be much faster? One answer could be that evolution cannot easily come up with an unbroken reticulum because such a reticulum would have to be constructed of cells, and cells are by their very nature discrete entities. However, there are instances of networks of discrete cells (e.g., in the retina prior to the ganglion cell output stage) that communicate using gap junctions. Such networks are tantamount to a continuous reticulum, since gap junctions allow potential to flow directly from cell to cell. So cellularity alone cannot explain why the nervous system relies on chemical transmission at most synapses. An alternative answer to this puzzle arises from the present view of neurons as criterial decoders. Neurons keep their intracellular potential discrete because they each impose their own discrete set of criteria for firing on their inputs. If they were continual (e.g., if linked by gap junctions) they could not easily enact discrete criteria for firing based upon summation of intracellular potential, since depolarization of one cell would too easily lead to depolarization of its target cell. To enact discrete criteria for firing, it is necessary to keep the summation of potential in one cell separate from that in another cell. In fact, discrete criterial assessments require discrete compartmentalizations of the summation of potential, not only at the level of individual neurons, but also within neurons. As we shall discuss in §§5.15 and 5.16, this may account for the compartmentalization of potential within dendritic arms and spines as well. Finally, criteria are physically

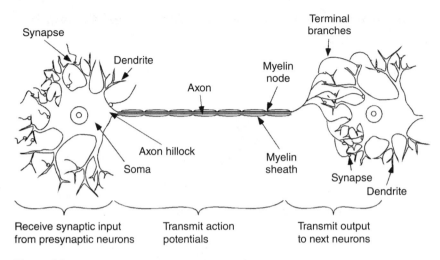

Figure 4.1

A schematization of a basic neuron that takes input from presynaptic neurons and carries out computations over intracellular potential in the dendrites and soma. If the threshold for an action potential is passed at the axon hillock, an action potential is transmitted down the axon and out to the terminals, which in turn synapse on the next neuron or neurons. The traditional model of neuron function is solely feedforward in the sense that dendrites receive no feedback from the soma about whether an action potential has been generated. Recent evidence requires the incorporation of such feedback, revolutionizing our understanding of neural computations.

realized, in part, at the level of receptors in the postsynaptic cell, and receptors are by their nature chemical in the criteria they set, owing to the binding of the neurotransmitter with the receptor (§4.61). Thus, all complex nervous systems that we know of have evolved an alternation between electrical communication (which is not criterial once a ballistic action potential has been set in motion) and chemical communication, allowing discrete summation of potential within each neuron. Physical compartmentalization of potential summation, when combined with a physical assessment of potential level relative to a threshold for the release of some subsequent physical process, realizes the specification of discrete informational criteria placed on informational inputs.

§4.2   All informational criteria are realized in physical processes that place physical criteria on aspects of energy. In the case of neurons, the primary physical mechanism that places physical criteria on aspects of energetic inputs is that which determines whether summed potential at the axon hillock surpasses the critical threshold above which an action potential is generated.[2] One might say that summation of excitatory and inhibitory postsynaptic potentials (EPSPs and IPSPs), whether in a dendrite or later, in the soma, cannot in itself be an assessment of information because this summation is purely mechanistic; potential just goes up or down, and either passes the action potential threshold or not. When a neuron is considered in isolation of all the neurons that give it input, this is correct. A neuron firing in a Petri dish realizes and conveys no information. One could depolarize the neuron and it would fire once the threshold was passed. In a localistic sense, summation of potential at the axon hillock cannot be regarded as placing any criterial conditions on the informational content of the input into a neuron. Similarly, a neuron cannot be thought to assess information criterially when considered in isolation. It just takes chemicals, such as glucose, oxygen, neurotransmitters, and ions, as inputs. But if the threshold for firing is met *if and only if* certain kinds of informational facts are true about the inputs, then the mechanism underlying neuronal firing not only assesses net potential at the axonal hillock, it also assesses these informational facts. In this way, physical criteria placed on physical inputs can realize informational criteria placed on informational inputs.

§4.3   A simple cell in primary visual cortex provides a straightforward example of how this might be done more generally in other neurons whose activity realizes information about more complex representations than just information about the presence of edges or bars at a given location in the visual field. A simple cell could be constructed that fired if, say, at least three out of five on-center off-surround neurons triggered EPSPs in the simple cell within that cell's very brief temporal integration window τ.[3] If these center-surround cells respond to inputs from adjacent regions of the visual field that fall along a line, as shown in figure 4.2, the simple cell fires when a band of light of a particular spatial frequency (visual extent) and orientation appears at a particular location in the visual field. The axon hillock in this simple cell places physical criteria on net potential within a cell before physical firing is triggered, and simultaneously places informational criteria on informational inputs for the realization of certain information (the presence of a bar of light) that occurs when the simple cell fires.

§4.4   The simple cell functions as a coincidence detector in that several lower-level facts (e.g., inputs from lateral geniculate neurons) must hold at the same time. Coincidence is not made of energy in addition to the energy it is realized in. That is, coincidence per se does not have mass or momentum or other attributes of an amount of energy. For example, several temporally coincident action potential inputs are not made of more energy than a staggered sequence of the same number of action potentials. But coincidence detection affords the possibility of detecting spatial patterns that exist at a given time. And these spatial patterns, or spatial relationships among inputs, are likewise not made of energy in addition to the energy in which the pattern is realized. Just as a coincidence has no mass, orientation has no mass. Coincidence detection therefore allows neurons to respond to relationships among material inputs. By coming to encode arbitrary relationships among light, sound, heat, or vibration energy detected locally at the sensory sheet, neurons make explicit information about such relationships that are only implicit in the sensory input.

§4.5   A reductionist would want to say that the assessment of informational criteria is epiphenomenal upon the assessment of physical criteria for neuronal firing. But physical neurons are arranged such that physical criteria for firing are satisfied only when certain information is the case, so that an animal can gain information about its environment and body in order to be able to respond to things and events appropriately. Since evolution operated on perceptual, motor, and cognitive systems to optimize information-processing, one could equally well argue that the particular implementation of information realization that we find in brains in the form of action potentials within neural networks is epiphenomenal upon the information that needs to be realized so that an animal can eat, flee, and mate successfully (§6.22). A given physical criterion for firing, given by summation of potential at the axon hillock, can realize different informational criteria, depending on the connectivity modulated by synaptic weights and other synaptic properties at a given time. For example, given one set of inputs, a neuron in the somatosensory cortex might fire if the face is touched, but given a different set of inputs, it might fire only if the hand is touched. The physical criteria for firing at the axon hillock do not change, but the informational criteria for firing (hand vs. face touch information) change as a function of epiconnectivity; such epiconnectivity can change via extremely rapid dynamic changes in synaptic weights due to the opening or closing of ionotropic receptor[4] pores, and slower changes in synaptic weights that depend on protein synthesis via, for example, long-term potentiation.

§4.6   It seems trivial to say that neurons process information, but how do they carry information at all? Neurons carry, communicate, compute, and transform information by transforming action potential spike inputs into spike trains sent to other neurons. If I say "Please pick up your coffee

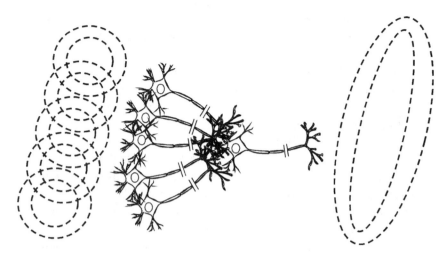

Figure 4.2

How to construct orientation-tuning in a simple cell. Each early visual neuron has a receptive field that responds to stimuli falling within a well-defined local region of retinotopic space. The neurons on the left have circular center-surround opponent receptive fields, shown on the far left. The inner and outer dashed circles indicate that the center is excitatory and the surround is inhibitory, or vice versa. Several such neurons, perhaps residing in the LGN of the thalamus can feed into a single simple cell shown on the right, residing in striate cortex. If the simple cell fires only when some proportion of its presynaptic input cells simultaneously depolarize it, the simple cell will exhibit a receptive field such as shown on the far right. It will also realize information that a bar of light is present at that location when it fires.

cup," and you do, then a pattern of air vibrations has been transduced into neural firing in nerves that receive input from inner hair cells; this is in turn transformed multiple times across neuronal subpopulations until the meaning has been decoded at the level of words and a proposition, allowing you to issue a motor command to carry out my request, perhaps after having considered various other possible courses of action. This can all happen in less than a second after hearing the word "cup." To try to cut information and meaning out of the causal picture here, as radical reductionists and epiphenomenalists do, by arguing that there are only particles interacting with particles, makes a fundamental error. Of course there are only particles interacting with particles. But assuming ontological indeterminism on the basis of evidence in appendix 1, countless sets of particle paths could physically follow my command given your initial physical state and the physical state of the world at the moment of the word "cup."

Why did a subset of possible particle paths occur that was consistent with an information-processing view of the brain, and not other physically allowed sets of particle paths that would have been consistent with the indeterministic laws of particle physics but not consistent with an information-processing account? Because neurons place physical criteria for firing on inputs that are also informational criteria on inputs, such that only those subsets of possible particle paths that meet those criteria can occur, as only those subsets trigger neuronal firing. On this account, mental events can cause future mental and physical events by altering physically realized informational criteria for firing that can be met by future neuronal inputs. This mechanism of physically realized downward mental causation will be more fully examined in chapter 6. The next sections review the basics of neuronal information processing, with a focus on visual processing, in preparation for subsequent sections on the neural code, binding, and the realization of criterial causation at the synaptic and receptor levels.

The Bottom-Up Information-Processing Hierarchy for Visual Recognition

§4.7   Visual information processing begins in the retina (Bear et al., 2007; Gazzaniga, 1995; Kandel et al., 2000). After a stage of light detection by cones and rods and intermediate processing by various classes of retinal cells, information about light reaches a class of neurons in the retina called "ganglion cells," which then transduce this information into action potentials that are primarily, though not solely, transmitted to the lateral geniculate nucleus (LGN) of the thalamus and from there to occipital cortex for further processing. Although there are many classes of retinal neurons, the most fundamental division lies between magnocellular and parvocellular ganglion cells. The former are particularly driven by fast changes in luminance contrast, but are relatively insensitive to color information. They tend to have large receptive fields, making them sensitive to large regions of the visual field and relatively insensitive to fine detail. Parvocellular ganglion cells have the opposite properties: They have relatively small receptive fields, and so are sensitive to fine spatial detail. They are not very sensitive to sudden changes in luminance, but are sensitive to color.

§4.8   This retinal division of labor is the basis of an information-processing division of labor that culminates in two very different ways of processing the visual scene, one for determining where objects are and where they are going, and the other for determining what objects are and what they mean (Ungerleider & Bell, 2011). This functional division of labor corresponds to the anatomical distinction between the dorsal and ventral streams (Mishkin & Ungerleider, 1982; Ettlinger, 1990; Goodale & Milner, 1992). The dorsal or "where is it?" stream extends from the occipital lobe's visual cortical input area "V1" to the parietal lobe and is involved in the processing of where things are and where they are going in space for the purpose of computing bodily actions in body-centric coordinates. This includes grasping in arm-, looking in eye-, orienting in head-, and feeding in mouth-centric coordinates. In contrast, the parallel ventral or "what/who is it?" stream extends from V1 along the lower portion of the temporal lobes, is involved fundamentally in form and object representations, and is tightly linked with processing in the medial temporal lobe involved in memory storage and retrieval. The ventral but not the dorsal stream appears to underlie our conscious visual experience of the world. The dorsal stream takes primary input from the magnocellular processing stream and the ventral system takes primary input from the parvocellular processing stream, although both processing streams receive both types of input. In fact, dorsal "where is it?" and ventral "what/who is it?" processing cannot be functionally segregated either from each other (Farivar, 2009; Van Essen & DeYoe, 1995) or from other semi-modular visual processing streams, including both the tectopulvinar pathway (retina → superior colliculus → pulvinar → amygdala) that leads into the emotional processing of the limbic system (Hannula, 2005) and the medial "where am I?" pathway (V1/V2 → retrosplenial cortex → parahippocampal cortex → entorhinal/subicular cortex → hippocampus) that appears to be crucial for navigation and situating the body and objects in allocentric or world coordinates (§§5.36, 8.22; Doeller et al., 2010; Epstein et al., 2007; Fyhn et al., 2008; Hafting et al., 2005; Moser et al., 2008; Solstad et al., 2008).

§4.9   The advantage of having chains of successive, discrete criterial coincidence detectors is that different criteria can be set at each stage, allowing for ever more complex criteria to be set as one progresses up a hierarchy of such detectors. For example, the famous neurophysiological work of Hubel and Wiesel (1959, 1968) made clear that the visual system is set up to initially detect light at points (via photodetectors), then detect small regions of light, particularly near borders (center-surround opponent receptive fields of ganglion cells and the LGN of the thalamus), then oriented edges and bars at a location (simple cells), then moving edges and bars within a region (complex cells), then moving edges and bars of certain lengths (hypercomplex cells), allowing for curvature detectors, closed region detectors, perhaps then eye and mouth detectors, hand and face detectors (Perrett et al., 1982; Rolls, 1984; Yamane et al., 1988) in the fusiform gyrus and anterior inferior temporal lobe (AIT), and ultimately detectors for many other kinds of complex forms in AIT (Gross, 2000; Logothetis & Sheinberg, 1996; Tanaka, 1996).

§4.10   As ventral stream information passes from V1 to V2 and V4v, each of which has a complete "retinotopic" map[5] of the contralateral visual hemifield, receptive fields increase in size. Beyond V4v retinotopy begins to break down, and activity begins to show evidence of viewpoint and size invariance, as is the case in the occipitotemporal junction area just anterior to V4v called the "lateral occipital complex" (Grill-Spector et al., 1999). This area is thought to be where localistic processing of visual features transitions into more global or configural processing of shape (Grill-Spector et al., 1998; Kanwisher et al., 1996; Lerner et al., 2001; Malach et al., 1995). As information proceeds further along the ventral stream to posterior, central, and anterior inferotemporal cortex, information about retinotopic location is increasingly disregarded in that receptive fields increase ever more in size. In more anterior portions of the ventral temporal lobe, neurons can have receptive fields that span both visual hemifields (Gross et al., 1969, 1972) and that are tuned to complex objects (Bruce et al., 1981; Desimone et al., 1984; Kobatake & Tanaka, 1994; Perrett et al., 1982; Rolls et al., 1977; Tanaka et al., 1991) in a way that is invariant to changes of position or size (Desimone et al., 1984) within the receptive field.

§4.11   Initially it was thought that such a hierarchy would culminate in a stage of "grandmother cells" (Barlow, 1972; Gross, 2002). Very high-level criterial decoders do indeed exist in the hippocampus and AIT (Connor, 2005; Gross, 2000; Kreiman et al., 2000, 2002; Quiroga et al., 2005, 2008). However, because they remain criterial, a wide range of inputs will satisfy them, including things that are potentially not your grandmother. For example, anything that satisfies the holistic criteria of what counts as a face (e.g., two dark eyelike blobs and a mouthlike blob within a round closed region) might trigger some face detectors (Freiwald et al., 2009; Jagadeesh, 2009). This is perhaps why we can will ourselves to see, and sometimes find that we unwillingly see, a face in a house's facade or in the front end of a car.

§4.12   Face processing appears to take place in part in a region on the underside of the temporal lobes called the "fusiform gyrus" (Sergent et al., 1992; Puce et al., 1995, 1996; Kanwisher et al., 1997; for reviews see Tsao & Livingstone, 2008, or Rolls, 2007) as well as in the superior temporal sulcus (Haxby et al., 1999), anterior occipital lobe (Ishai et al., 1999) and anterior temporal lobe (Kriegeskorte et al., 2007; Rajimehr et al., 2009; Tsao et al., 2006) of humans, and in corresponding cortical areas in monkeys (Tsao et al., 2003, 2006; Bell et al., 2009; Pinsk et al., 2005, 2009). It has been shown that face-tuned inferotemporal neurons respond biphasically (Sugase et al., 1999); their initial response, approximately 100–150ms after face image onset, carries information about global face information useful for discriminating faces as members of a face category versus other categories. Immediately subsequent responses carry information about fine spatial detail that would permit recognition of particular facial expressions (§4.38). Facial recognition involves anterior inferotemporal neurons. Eifuku et al. (2004) trained monkeys to match an image of a face to one of many possibilities taken from different viewpoints. They found that the neural latency of anterior inferotemporal face-tuned neurons was correlated with the monkey's behavioral latency, suggesting that these neurons play a role in the decision process. Indeed, microstimulation of such face-tuned cells can lead a monkey to report that it has seen a face given ambiguous input more often than is the case in the absence of microstimulation (Afraz et al., 2006).

§4.13   An instance of a hierarchical architecture of fungible neurons responding criterially to ever more complex features is the Pandemonium model (Selfridge, 1959) depicted in figure 4.3, proposed before Hubel and Wiesel had even discovered neurons in V1 that behaved much like the criterial feature-detectors predicted by this theory. A more recent model of criterial detectors that pool over inputs from progressively more complex lower-level detectors is described in the HMAX model (Riesenhuber & Poggio, 1999, 2000, 2002). Whereas Pandemonium involves linear pooling of responses from one stage in the hierarchy of feature detection to the next, HMAX involves nonlinear pooling, but the general strategy is similar. Both these models are feedforward descriptions of ventral processing between V1 and inferotemporal cortex. Models like the HMAX model accomplish successively more complex neuronal tunings by having neurons take input from lower-level feature detectors in such a way that eventually an inferotemporal neuron fires most to that spatiotemporal arrangement of features that defines, say, a giraffe or helicopter. Hierarchical feature-detection models are some of the best models we have to date concerning stimulus-driven aspects of visual object recognition, and they are built on the hierarchical satisfaction of criteria placed on feature attributes by neurons.

§4.14   Nevertheless, such "stack models" are inadequate. They ignore feedback operations and other complexities such as attention (e.g., Intraub, 1997; Graboi & Lisman, 2003) and corresponding frontoparietal feedback that can modulate functioning of early visual circuitry (e.g., Lauritzen et al., 2009), eye movements (e.g., Henderson & Hollingworth, 1999), top-down

A

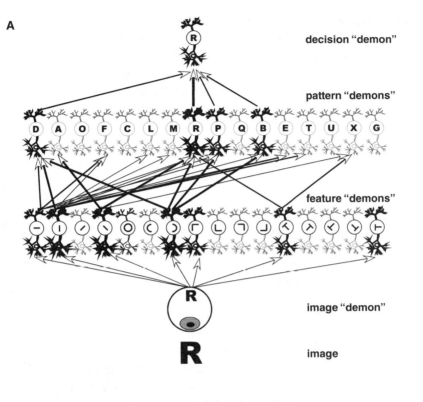

decision "demon"

pattern "demons"

feature "demons"

image "demon"

image

B

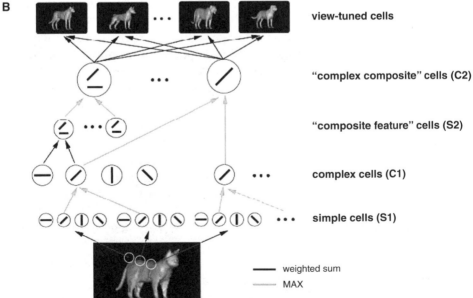

view-tuned cells

"complex composite" cells (C2)

"composite feature" cells (S2)

complex cells (C1)

simple cells (S1)

weighted sum

MAX

knowledge of object properties (e.g., Bar et al., 2006) including biological motion (e.g., Jastorff and Orban, 2009), context (e.g., Chun, 2000; Bar, 2004), or the influence of the amygdala's processing of objects (e.g., Carretié et al., 2005). Moreover, stack models fail to account for the remarkable speed with which we can recognize the general gist of an image as, say, a beach or city scene (e.g., Joubert et al., 2007; Oppermann et al., 2012). They are also unlikely to account for how we set up criteria or solve problems in working memory (§4.26). They offer, in effect, a feedforward and bottom-up cascade of criterial detectors feeding into criterial detectors. Viewing visual object recognition as a cascade of detection ignores operations that construct information on the basis of what has been detected, such as filling-in operations (e.g., Hsieh & Tse, 2009), global motion-from-form operations (e.g., Tse, 2006a), and operations that generate three-dimensional form from contours (e.g., Tse, 1999, 2002). Nonetheless, such models adequately account for affine transformation invariant object recognition (e.g., Hung et al., 2005) in certain cases. More recent models incorporate a role for attention in object recognition (e.g., Cohen et al., 2011), feedback from orbitofrontal cortex (Bar, 2003; Bar et al., 2006), and input from the amygdala (Carretié et al., 2005). Another recent model supported by neurophysiological data suggests that object shape is coded criterially by neurons that respond to equivalence classes of shapes that share certain defining shape attributes (Yamane et al., 2008). In sum, then, criterial encoding and tuning appear to be properties of feature-detection cascades, although this information-processing architecture is not sufficient to capture all aspects of object recognition.

§4.15   When and where does recognition occur? At some point in the ventral information-processing stream, object representations must be compared with representations stored in memory. A decision must then

Figure 4.3
Stack models. According to Selfridge's (1959) Pandemonium model (A), a neuron, thought of as a "demon," that responds to a complex configuration of simple local features in the image, such as the configuration of the letter "R," can be constructed on the basis of a hierarchy of inputs of increasingly complex criterial feature detectors, arranged here from bottom to top. The degree of pyramidal cell firing is indicated by its degree of thickness. Whereas the Pandemonium model involves linear pooling of responses from one stage in the hierarchy of feature detection to the next, the HMAX model (B) of Riesenhuber and Poggio (1999, 2000, 2002) involves nonlinear pooling from stage to stage (here arranged from bottom to top), but the general strategy is similar. Both "stack" models are feedforward descriptions of ventral processing between V1 and inferotemporal cortex.

be made concerning the best match between seen and stored representations. But recognition of what an object is does not occur in isolation within the ventral processing stream. Object recognition is contextualized by information about reward value, meaning, emotional content, and space. In a lovely example of form following the function of neural circuitry, multiple semi-modular visual processing streams converge on the hippocampal formation. Besides the ventral stream, both the medial "where am I?" pathway and the limbic system project to entorhinal cortex and the hippocampus. Concerning limbic inputs, entorhinal cortex receives input from anterior cingulate cortex via the cingulum bundle and projects directly (via the perforant pathway) and indirectly (via the alvear parthway) to the subiculum. This forms a key component of the well-known Papez circuit (Bear et al., 2007) that serves emotional processing and control. Thus, recognition and decision processes may happen at several stages in parallel that converge on a common process of spatially and emotionally contextualized matching to memory in the hippocampal formation.

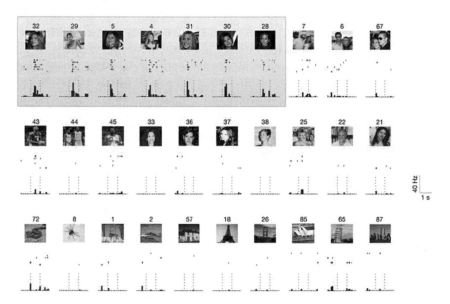

Figure 4.4
Hippocampal face detectors. A hierarchy of criterial feature detectors could account for the rather "grandmother cell"–like nature of neurons in the hippocampus that appear to fire in response to very different images of a single individual, but not to fire much for other people or things (reproduced in grayscale from Quiroga et al., 2005, with permission). This neuron responds well to the actress Jennifer Aniston (shown in the box) and not so well to other people, places, and things.

Decision Making and Action

§4.16   Vision is not only for recognition. It is for planning and acting on objects, fulfilling desires, engaging with other minds and moving about the world as well. Actions can be exogenous, rapid, automatic, and stimulus driven, as when we duck to avoid being hit by a branch. Or actions can be endogenous, considered, and driven by internal planning or assessments of the value of various options. Actions can also be external and muscular, such as reaching or making an eye movement. Or actions can be internal and amuscular, such as shifting attention or willing the recall of someone's name.

§4.17   An ongoing debate among neuroscientists concerns the format of information in which visual decisions for action are made. At one end of the spectrum, decisions could be made in the same informational format as the actions that will execute those decisions. This would mean that the format of decision making is action based, and that a decision is realized in the area of the brain where the programming of the motor act to enact the decision takes place. At the other end of the spectrum, decisions could be made in a more abstract informational format that is not tied to any particular motoric effector. For example, a decision might be made to indicate a particular person in a crowd, but whether this will be done by pointing, nodding the head, or describing the person might not be known at the moment of the decision.

§4.18   The strongest evidence for the view that decisions occur in a motoric format comes from neurons in the lateral intraparietal area (LIP) with spatially specific receptive fields that respond not only to visual stimuli in the receptive field, but also when a saccade is made to the corresponding location or even just planned to this location. This could be because LIP neurons are tuned to salience at a particular location (Goldberg et al., 2006) or because of the plan or intention to move to that location (Snyder et al., 2000). A model (Gold & Shadlen, 2003, 2007; Shadlen et al., 2008) of decisions made in an action format describes LIP neurons as integrators of noisy evidence. As sensory evidence accumulates that a signal is, say, moving to the left, LIP neurons tuned to this direction increase their firing rate relative to neurons accumulating evidence for motion to, say, the right. Once a threshold is passed, a saccade to the left is generated (Huk & Shadlen, 2005; Roitman & Shadlen, 2002; Shadlen & Newsome, 2001) automatically, without the need for propositional thought.

§4.19   One criticism of the view that decisions occur in a motoric format is that almost all evidence for this comes from experiments where the mapping between perceived, say, motion direction, and effector response was known to the responder in advance (Freedman & Assad, 2011). The decision in such experiments is effectively given as soon as the correct direction of motion is perceived. In delayed match-to-sample experiments, in contrast, a sample is shown followed by a delay followed by another stimulus. If the second and first stimuli match, say, by belonging to some common category, one motoric response is called for, and if not, a different response is required. In many experiments with this design, where the correct effector response could not be known during the first stimulus presentation or during the delay period, it has been found that LIP neurons encode information about categories defined on the basis of abstract "rules" (Stoet & Snyder, 2004; Gottlieb, 2007) of any number of different stimulus attributes, such as shape (Freedman & Assad, 2011), color (Toth & Assad, 2002), and motion (Freedman & Assad, 2006). These experiments suggest that LIP and lateral prefrontal (Freedman et al., 2001, 2003) and frontal eye field neurons (Ferrera et al., 2009) do not make decisions in a motoric format in all cases, but can also, or may even exclusively, make decisions based on a more abstract informational format, such as category, which must then be translated into a format executable by a particular effector, such as the arms or eyes.

§4.20   These views are not mutually exclusive. Some plans and decisions might be made in the format of effectors, and other plans might be made in a format that is more abstract. Willing an outcome to occur, such as drinking water, can involve a high-level proposition such as "I should drink more water," a desire for water, a high-level motor plan to get up and walk to the water fountain, and then lower-level motor plans concerned with contracting particular muscles. These plans or decisions are not mutually exclusive. Intentions, plans, decisions, and actions are probably encoded at many levels simultaneously (§§3.2, 10.61).

Attention and Top-Down Modulation of Bottom-Up Processing

§4.21   Apart from motoric commands, volitional control of attention with its consequent mental operations is the primary expression of the endogenous control of action that most people mean when they talk about "will." Attention enhances information processing for a selected subset of inputs and may also suppress information-processing for unselected or ignored inputs. Attention has low-level aspects that can be described as changes in sensitivity to inputs or changes in response or gain control (Desimone & Duncan, 1995; Hillyard et al., 1998; Liu et al., 2009; Reynolds

& Heeger, 2009). Attention also has higher-level aspects, such as binding of features (Allen et al., 2006; Ashby et al., 1996; Engel et al., 1999; Oakes et al., 2006; Reynolds & Desimone, 1999; Shipp et al., 2009; Treisman, 1996), binding of operations and operands in working memory (Tse, 2006b), and tracking (Kahneman et al., 1992; Pylyshyn & Storm, 1988) a figure over time.

§4.22   Attention is commonly believed to have at least two components, one "transient" or "exogenous," and one "sustained" or "endogenous" (Nakayama & Mackeben, 1989), mediated by overlapping but different circuitry and even neurotransmitter systems. The transient or exogenous component of attention is allocated automatically to the abrupt onset of a new stimulus (§10.16; Irwin et al., 2000; Jonides & Yantis, 1988; Remington et al., 1992; Theeuwes, 1994; Yantis & Hillstrom, 1994; Yantis & Jonides, 1984, 1990). This is the process that makes one orient to someone in a crowd who waves his or her hands, for example, or that makes flashing advertisements on the Internet distracting. The processes that specify what is worth shifting attention toward must, by definition, precede attentional allocation, so are best thought of as "preconscious," unconscious, rapid, and automatic (§10.28). A transient event that "grabs" exogenous attention, such as the appearance of something improbable or unexpected, typically leads to marked changes in event-related potentials that are believed to be related to attentional mechanisms (e.g., Garcia-Larrea et al., 1992; Muller-Gass et al., 2007; Polich, 1986; Potts et al., 1996; Salisbury et al., 1992; van Alderen-Smeets et al., 2007). Endogenous attention, in contrast, is allocated relatively slowly but can be sustained through volition, whereas exogenous attention on its own quickly fades away (Nakayama & Mackeben, 1989). In addition, endogenous attention can only be allocated over information that has been processed by grouping procedures, shape formation, and other automatic processes that operate preconsciously (e.g., Baylis & Driver, 1995; Enns & Rensink, 1990, 1991; He & Nakayama, 1992, 1994a,b, 1995; Rensink & Enns, 1995, 1998). Endogenous attention, unlike exogenous attention, appears to be enhanced by increased availability of acetylcholine (§5.38) in the circuitry realizing attended information processing (Rokem & Silver, 2010; Rokem et al., 2010). Yu and Dayan (2005; see also Avery et al., 2012) suggest that acetylcholine projected to cortex from the nucleus basalis of the basal forebrain modulates "expected uncertainty" within a given context, as might occur under conditions of endogenous attentional shifting during visual search, whereas norepinephrine projected from the locus coeruleus mediates sudden changes in context triggered by "unexpected uncertainty," as might occur under conditions of exogenous attentional shifting to a sudden flash of light or a loud noise. In fact, norepinephrine release plays a central role in large-scale shifts in cortical state associated with changes in arousal, awareness, or wakefulness (Constantinople & Bruno, 2011), whereas acetylcholine release is most closely tied to endogenous attentional allocation.

§4.23 Exogenous attention is thought to involve circuitry in the superior colliculus (Valsecchi & Turatto, 2007), and endogenous attention is thought to involve circuitry in the frontal lobe (Mesulam, 1981; Posner & Petersen, 1990) associated with making voluntary eye movements. Thus, the computations involved in shifting attention appear to overlap those involved in computing eye movements. This may be because both involve shifting a center of processing from one location in a representational space to another. The "internal fovea" of attention usually shifts to the same location as shifts of the eyes, although in humans, "covert" shifts of attention can move attention to a nonfoveated location. Like exogenous and endogenous attention, saccade generation involves two parallel subsystems. A subcortical pathway involving the superior colliculus generates reflexive, orienting "exogenous" saccades, and a cortical pathway involving the frontal eye fields generates voluntary, "endogenous" saccades via top-down input into the superior colliculus (e.g., Everling & Munoz, 2000; Hanes et al., 1998; Schall, 1995). Both the "exogenous" eye movement system and exogenous attentional shift system appear to recruit some of the same circuitry in the superior colliculus, one to move the direction of gaze and the other to move the focus of processing without necessarily moving the eyes (Corbetta et al., 1998; Kustov & Robinson, 1996; Rizzolatti et al., 1994; Robinson & Kertzman, 1995). This is probably why shifts of attention lower the probability of simultaneous microsaccades (Engbert & Kliegl, 2003; Hafed & Clark, 2002; Horwitz & Albright, 2003; Rolfs et al., 2004; Tse et al., 2002, 2004b, 2010; Turatto et al., 2007; Valsecchi & Turatto, 2009), as the shared shifting circuitry is utilized for one purpose or the other. Endogenous attentional shifting is likely commanded from the frontal eye fields to the superior colliculus in parallel with "endogenous" saccade circuitry. Thus the attentional command centers lie in a frontoparietal network that includes areas that also process eye movements. The frontoparietal network directly and/or indirectly feeds back to occipitotemporal visual circuitry, altering its dynamics and functionality. Indeed, when attending, the frontoparietal network increases in beta-frequency synchronization (Buschman & Miller, 2007; Donner et al., 2007; Gross et al., 2004; Hipp et al., 2011; Kopell et al., 2000; Pesaran et al., 2008;

Roelfsema et al., 1997), while the occipito-temporal visual processing network increases in gamma and high-gamma frequency synchronization (e.g., Fries et al., 2008; Hipp et al., 2011).[6] The frontoparietal network that subserves endogenous attention appears to overlap with or even perhaps be the same network that subserves free choice (Pesaran et al., 2008) and endogenous decision making (Siegel et al., 2011).

§4.24 Endogenous attention can be flexibly and volitionally allocated to features (Haenny et al., 1988; Hayden & Gallant, 2009; Khayat et al., 2010; Martinez-Trujillo & Treue, 2004; McAdams & Maunsell, 2000; Motter, 1994; Treue & Martinez Trujillo, 1999), a location or object at a location in space (Blaser et al., 2000; Houtkamp et al., 2003; Serences et al., 2004), and durations (Coull & Nobre, 1998; Doherty et al., 2005; Ghose & Maunsell, 2002; Tse et al., 2004a). It has been debated whether feature- and space- or object-selective attention are realized in different types of neural activity, or whether the same mechanism affects different circuits differently (Duncan, 1980; Maunsell & Treue, 2006). If attention involves operations over information from neighboring regions of the visual field, such as perhaps are realized in lateral inhibition among corresponding neurons, the retinotopic organization of visual cortex would afford a natural means of indexing locations and carrying out such operations. Neurophysiology indeed suggests that there is top-down attentional feedback to early visual areas from frontal and parietal areas involved in computing eye movements (Astafiev et al., 2003; Bisley & Goldberg, 2010; Buschman & Miller, 2007; Craighero et al., 1999; Gitelman et al., 1999; Gregoriou et al., 2009a,b; Moore et al., 2003; Moore & Armstrong, 2003; Roelfsema et al., 1998; Saalmann et al., 2007), and microstimulation of eye movement planning areas triggers neuronal effects that resemble those of attention (Armstrong et al., 2006; Cavanaugh et al., 2006; Cavanaugh & Wurtz, 2004; Cutrell & Marrocco, 2002; Herrington & Assad, 2009; Herrington et al., 2009; Moore & Armstrong, 2003; Moore et al., 2003; Moore & Fallah, 2001; Muller et al., 2005).

§4.25 Some have used psychophysical results to argue that spatial and nonspatial attention are mediated by different mechanisms (Kwak & Egeth,1992; Nissen & Corkin, 1985), while others have argued that they are mediated by similar mechanisms (Bundesen, 1990; Duncan, 1980; Keren, 1976; Rossi & Paradiso,1995; von Wright, 1970). Neurophysiological data generally support the latter view that attention of all types share key mechanisms (Assad, 2003; Hayden & Gallant, 2009; Martinez-Trujillo & Treue, 2004; Maunsell & Treue, 2006; McAdams & Maunsell, 2000; Motter, 1994; Reynolds & Chelazzi, 2004; Treue & Martinez Trujillo, 1999; Yantis &

Serences, 2003). Whereas feature-based attention appears to operate globally by altering neural responsiveness to input features across both visual
hemifields, spatial attention appears to operate only on local circuitry
(Cohen & Maunsell, 2011) by increasing the firing rate, decorrelation, and
burstiness of presumed pyramidal cells tuned to the location where attention is allocated (Anderson et al., 2011). Presumably, attention to features
is realized in the same transition to burstiness in the network dynamics of
pyramidal neurons, but in a manner less tied to specific locations.

§4.26   One role of attention appears to be the temporary binding of
various task-relevant representations. This could happen in early areas
where features are themselves processed, or it could happen higher in the
processing hierarchy, in working memory circuitry, such as found in prefrontal and parietal cortex (e.g., Curtis, 2006; Fuster, 2008; Jonides et al.,
2005; 2008; Kravitz et al., 2011; Linden, 2007; Rao et al., 1997; Todd &
Marois, 2004, 2005; Ungerleider et al., 1998; Wager & Smith 2003; Xu &
Chun, 2006) and in the anterior inferior insula (Corbetta & Shulman,
2002). Attention could operate at both early and late levels, as needed
(§10.23). For example, when looking for red fruit anywhere in the visual
field, feature-based attention could operate "early" by changing gains on
color outputs as early as the LGN; When attending to a particular monkey
in a troupe, object-based attention could operate at a "late" level in V4,
LOC, or DLPFC by changing the gain on object-level representations.
Operating on "late" representations in a flexible and dynamic manner
(Freedman et al., 2001) within a working memory area such as the DLPFC
would permit the integration of high-level outputs from modular circuits.
In particular, semantic object representations from the ventral stream
could be integrated with the outputs of dorsal spatial processing areas (Levy
& Goldman-Rakic, 2000). Such an architecture would not only allow the
binding of outputs from "what/ventral" and "where/dorsal" circuits, it would
permit the online monitoring of maintained representations (Owen et al.,
1996; D'Esposito et al., 1999; Linden, 2007).

§4.27   Further evidence that attentional selection can occur at the late
level of working memory occurs in the Stroop task. The Stroop task is to
say the color of written words. If the words are not conflicting color names,
the task is easy. If, say, "penguin" is written in red ink, it is easy to say
"red." But if "blue" is written in red ink, people are slower to say "red" and
might actually say "blue" by mistake. The task is attentionally demanding.
Even with full concentration people typically start reading the color words
despite their intention to name the ink color of the word. This suggests
that a process of inhibition fatigues, allowing the previously suppressed

information to dominate. Because it seems effortless to suppress noncolor words in the Stroop task like "penguin" while naming the color in which the word is written, the problem does not appear to be one of suppressing reading circuitry per se. Rather, the problem appears to occur at the level of selecting the correct output and inhibiting a similar but inappropriate output. There are many variants of the Stroop task, but all involve conflict at the level of identical output type, such as a color name, of which only one token is correct. The attentional load or effort associated with blocking reading output and selecting the ink color name appears to occur within a shared working memory buffer that receives the output of visual color processing circuitry and reading circuitry. The outputs must be in the same format, namely "color name," in order for there to be a conflict. This suggests that attentional selection and ignoring occur at a late stage within a common working memory buffer where multiple completed outputs of different processes or neural circuits are deposited in an amodal format (§10.14) prior to selection for further processing by motor areas that result in saying "blue" or "red."

§4.28   How binding is accomplished at the level of integrating, selecting, and deselecting the outputs of whole circuits is not clear, though such binding would seem to require a solution to an addressing or routing problem whereby outputs of neurons in disparate areas of the brain can be temporarily and precisely addressed as inputs to working memory neurons. It is possible that certain nuclei of the thalamus play such a routing role (e.g., LaBerge, 1995; Crabtree & Isaac, 2002; Sherman & Guillery, 2002). In particular, cortical attentional circuits may excite inhibitory neurons in the thalamic reticular nucleus, which is thought to modulate outputs to and inputs from cortex and other thalamic nuclei, modifying the activity of corticothalamocortical loops. For the case of visual processing, it has been shown that attention modulates LGN signals to V1 via topographically organized collaterals from both cortex and the LGN to and from the thalamic reticular nucleus (McAlonan et al., 2006, 2008), vindicating Crick's (1984) idea that "if the thalamus is the gateway to the cortex, the reticular complex might be described as the guardian of the gateway." How such circuitry could facilitate the outputs of attended circuits and inhibit the outputs of unattended circuits has been developed in depth elsewhere (Ferrarelli & Tononi, 2011; Guillery et al., 1998, 2003; Krause et al., 2003; Mayo, 2009; McAlonan et al., 2000; Zikopoulos & Barbas, 2006, 2007). This suggests that gain on information permitted access to working memory might be realized in a gain control mechanism that operates at the level of entire neural circuits or modules and their outputs, rather than just at the level of individual neurons, as implied by standard gain control models of attention (Reynolds & Heeger, 2009).

Basic Issues in Neuronal Information Processing: Balancing Excitation and Inhibition

§4.29 Certain problems must be solved by any neural circuit capable of processing information. Activity in the circuit must be dynamically changed by sensory or internal input such that changes in neuronal activity carry information about these inputs. If a neural circuit's activity is not perturbable, it cannot carry information in the changes of its activity. Moreover, only perturbations of neural activity that carry information should be allowed to propagate within the neural circuit. All functioning nervous systems that succeed in processing information must therefore tread a fine line between excess excitation and excess inhibition. In neural networks, excitation or inhibition are expressed as an increase or decrease, respectively, of potential across a postsynaptic neural membrane, and ultimately in an increase or decrease of action potential output. Because neuronal excitation and inhibition are inherently dynamic processes, a network that balances excitation with inhibition can only accomplish this dynamically. A set point or baseline level of activation must be realized through some process that interplays excitation and inhibition. This is why baseline levels of neural activity typically express a degree of oscillation, as a dynamic equilibrium is struck between the two opposing processes. Too much excitation (or too little inhibition) at the wrong time can lead to action potentials that carry no information, as in epilepsy. Too much inhibition (or too little excitation) at the wrong time, and there might be no action potentials at all, so again no information processing, as in coma or deep anesthesia. Information processing cannot occur without the interplay of both excitation and inhibition at the level of every neural circuit. There must be excitation such that an action potential can excite read-out neurons in a cascade of such events that realize information processing. But there must be inhibition of any excitation whose information is already transferred to the next stage, and there must be inhibition of any excitation that carries no information.

§4.30 How is this balance between excitation and inhibition neuronally realized? There must be some baseline level of excitation for information processing to be rapid and dynamic in a neural network because if the baseline were zero excitation, the circuit would essentially be offline. If information is encoded not in individual spikes, but in perturbations of spike rate, timing, and phase relationships away from baseline behavior (which itself might carry no information), then there must be baseline activity. By analogy, a car must at least be idling if the engine is to be able to respond rapidly to the excitation of the gas pedal or the inhibition of the brakes.

§4.31   If excitation exceeded inhibition by even a small percentage above this baseline level of activity, on average, during an information-processing cycle, excitation could compound over multiple information-processing cycles, leading to runaway excitation. This might express itself as action potentials that do not carry information, as in epilepsy. Likewise, if inhibition exceeded excitation by even a small percentage on average, inhibition could similarly compound, and all information transmission and all action potentials would cease after some number of cycles. Information processing should therefore occur optimally in that narrow regime where inhibition on balance cancels out excitation. Indeed, cortical circuitry is thought to exist in a configuration that balances excitation and inhibition, which can account for the large variability in cortical spiking (Shadlen & Newsome, 1994; Troyer & Miller, 1997). In such a regime, net excitation beyond the baseline level of excitation across a population would not undergo exponential growth on successive processing cycles, and would not undergo decay to the point that the circuit effectively stops and no information or action potentials are processed at all. For similar reasons, at a synaptic level, long-term potentiation (LTP) of synaptic weights should balance out long-term depression (LTD) across the population of synapses, perhaps through one or more homeostatic processes of weight renormalization. But if net excitation and inhibition, or LTP and LTD, do not change substantially over time, how can information be realized by changes in brain state? What changes is not the amount of net activity, but the pattern of neuronal activity and synaptic reweighting. In general, information in the brain is realized in patterns of activation rather than mere amounts of activation.

§4.32   It has been something of a puzzle that early visual neuronal tuning properties appear to be driven primarily by bottom-up thalamic input (Bruno & Sakmann, 2006; Ferster & Miller, 2000; Priebe & Ferster, 2008; Wilent & Contreras, 2005) when the majority of inputs to such neurons appear to be due to local excitatory and inhibitory recurrent connections (Binzegger et al., 2004; Stepanyants et al., 2008). If recurrent excitation and inhibition are balanced, then the net input to a postsynaptic neuron will be a small fraction of the total excitation or inhibition received by the cell (van Vreeswijk & Sompolinsky, 1998). For uncorrelated inputs, the mean potential induced by balanced excitation and inhibition must be subthreshold so that the postsynaptic neuron fires optimally in response to deviations from this mean (Amit & Brunel, 1997; Ozeki et al., 2009; Troyer & Miller, 1997). If the subthreshold balance point is too low the neuron will not be sensitive to input, increasing the likelihood of "incorrect rejections" in the sense that the neuron will not fire even when there is a signal to which it is tuned and should respond. If the subthreshold balance point is too close to threshold, there will be "false alarms" in that the neuron will fire because of noise in its inputs. Balanced excitation and inhibition are required to keep the mean potential in the optimal subthreshold domain. Empirical evidence suggests that the amounts of excitation and inhibition received by a postsynaptic cell increase and decrease together with the magnitude of signal corresponding to sensory input (Anderson et al., 2000; Ferster, 1986), perhaps via a mechanism of synaptic gain modulation (Abbott et al., 1997; Abbott & Regehr, 2004). Excitation and inhibition even scale together in the absence of sensory input (Haider et al., 2006; Higley & Contreras, 2006; but see Waters & Helmchen, 2006). This rescaling allows neurons to respond to changes in stimulus magnitude in terms of percentage changes from baseline, consistent with Weber's psychophysical "law" that psychological intensity scales logarithmically with stimulus intensity. Normalizing the baseline activity with recurrent local excitation and inhibition allows a neuron to stay in a narrow dynamic range that rarely involves firing rates above 100Hz. It also makes some sensory neurons function essentially as change detectors, where a change in postsynaptic firing rate is driven by a change in presynaptic firing rate. A network of such change detectors will effectively carry information in perturbations from continually renormalized baseline firing rates. (However, not all sensory neurons will function as change detectors; see §5.37.)

§4.33 At a neural level, a balance of excitation and inhibition would mean that neural activity is propagated across a population without growing or decaying on average. In other words, the average number of spikes per unit time will remain roughly constant within a population no matter what duration is averaged across. This also means that the proportion of excitatory and inhibitory inputs into a pyramidal cell remains on average constant over long enough durations (Shu et al., 2003b). That said, the average rate can remain constant, while phase relationships can change. For example, instead of having eight more-or-less randomly spaced spikes occur in one second, as occurs during tonic firing, the dynamics can switch to four pairs spaced at 0ms, 5ms, 300ms, 305ms, 600ms, 605ms, 900ms, 905ms, as occurs during bursty or phasic firing ("tonic" and "phasic" are explained in detail in §4.35). In general, the phase relationships or relative timing of excitation and inhibition are essential, so that information is transferred in an information-processing cascade before inhibition turns no-longer-needed excitation off. Excitation must be subject to immediate inhibition following information transmission. The timing of inhibition is especially important for optimal information-processing (Gupta et al., 2000; Martina et al., 2000). Faulty inhibition in cortical microcircuitry has been linked to various mental disorders (Casanova et al., 2002, 2003; Childs & Blair, 1997; Gustafsson, 1997; Jambaque et al., 2000), including epilepsy (DeFelipe, 1999; Hirsch et al., 1999; Marco et al., 1996; Marco & DeFelipe, 1997).

§4.34 In sum, neural networks must oscillate around some baseline level of alternating excitation and inhibition in order to be dynamically perturbable and therefore capable of carrying information about the source of the perturbation (e.g., sensory input). Thus, to be able to carry information about sensory inputs via perturbation (i.e., deviation from baseline), cortical neurons must spike spontaneously even in the absence of sensory inputs. Spontaneous firing rates are in the 10–15Hz range in motor and association cortex of awake monkeys and cats (Steriade, 2001) and about 15Hz in inferior temporal cortex of awake monkeys (Baddeley et al., 1997).[7] Information can be carried in upward or downward deviations from the baseline firing rate, or changes in phase or spike timing (Dan & Poo, 2004).

Tonic versus Phasic Firing

§4.35 Neurons tend to fire in one of two basic modes. In tonic firing, such as typically occurs at the baseline firing rate, neurons fire irregularly in a way that matches "Poisson" statistics (defined in §4.52), at a more or less constant rate. The average rate of firing per unit time can increase or decrease in an analog manner, even though action potentials are themselves digital in the sense that they occur in an all-or-nothing manner. In phasic firing, action potentials cluster in time in brief but rapid bursts of spikes. Bursts are preceded and followed by periods of relative quiescence. A burst occurs when two or more action potentials are generated within rapid succession, typically at >100Hz with a preceding and subsequent silent period. Three to five spikes separated by ~5ms (200Hz) is common. This suggests that an increase in bursts should be primarily associated with an increase in high-gamma frequency power (80–200Hz and higher) rather than gamma frequency power (30–80Hz; Ray & Maunsell, 2011). Broadband increase in high-gamma power has been observed throughout the

brain (Crone et al., 2006), including in the rat hippocampus during particular behaviors such as exploration (Buzsáki et al., 1992; Ylinen et al.,
1995) and in rat barrel cortex (Jones et al., 2000; Jones & Barth, 1999,
2002). Ray and Maunsell (2011) find that increases in high-gamma power
are most likely tied to transient increases in spiking rather than ongoing
oscillations, consistent with the view that high-gamma power indicates
bursting (but see ch. 5, n. 12, for a caveat). Unlike tonic firing, phasic firing
behavior is thought to involve the interplay of the fast process of spiking
with a slow process modulated by slow voltage-gated (Huguenard &
McCormick, 1992; Wang, 1999) or calcium-gated currents (Kloppenburg
et al., 2000) that "deplete" the capacity for further bursting, and which
must be "replenished" before bursting can recommence. With these two
modes of firing, the nervous system can use the same neurons for at least
two modes of information transmission or functional control, although
there are likely to be even more modes of information processing than just
these two[8] (e.g., Kass & Mintz, 2006).

§4.36 Different receptor classes dominate the two modes of neuronal
behavior. In the case of ionotropic glutamate receptors, tonic firing is primarily subserved by AMPA[9] receptors that, in the aggregate, allow ions to
pass through their pore to the degree that glutamate binds to them. Depolarization therefore will also be graded. NMDA receptors, in contrast, subserve phasic firing or bursting, and such bursts are thought to propagate
across an information-processing network as units of information (Lisman,
1997; Polsky et al., 2009); NMDA antagonists reduce bursting and increase
single spiking. From the perspective that bursts are key units of information during phasic firing, single spikes not occurring in the context of a
burst might be considered "noise" (Jackson et al., 2004; Lisman, 1997).
These issues will be the focus of chapter 5.

§4.37 Let us consider three examples of the same neurons exhibiting
tonic or phasic firing. First (Lin et al., 2006), noncholinergic basal forebrain
neurons that project to prefrontal cortex tend to fire tonically 2–8 times a
second except when rats are awake or in rapid-eye-movement sleep, during
which time spiking becomes more variable without changing the spike
rate, and bursts (typically >100Hz) become more common (Lin et al.,
2006). Ensembles of these neurons burst in synchrony over an average
duration of 160ms.They appear to increase prefrontal cortical activity and
increase gamma oscillations in the prefrontal cortex, suggesting that their
bursting transiently enhances prefrontal processing associated with the
gamma power domain, presumably increasing the probability of cortical
pyramidal cell bursting. It is probable that switching to a bursting mode

in the basal forebrain plays a role in shifting cortical processing to a mode that permits increased alertness or attentiveness, or otherwise modulates consciousness. We will consider the effects of noncholinergic basal forebrain neural outputs again in §5.45 when we consider the mechanisms whereby endogenous attention alters neural properties in visual cortex.

§4.38   As a second example, thalamic dorsal LGN relay neurons fire either tonically or phasically (Grubb & Thompson, 2005; Guido et al., 1992). Although thalamic bursting happens during sleep and in vitro in the absence of stimulation (Sherman & Guillery, 2002), bursting occurs more often in response to visual input, particularly onsets within a receptive field (Guido & Weyand 1995; Weyand et al., 2001). Attention may shift the LGN into phasic firing via excitation of the adjacent, inhibitory thalamic reticular nucleus (McAlonan et al., 2006). Microsaccades trigger bursting in LGN and V1 neurons as new stimulus information is brought into the receptive field (Martinez-Conde et al., 2002), suggesting that bursts carry information about changes in the stimulus or new input into a receptive field. The two modes do not differ in their spatial tuning characteristics, but do differ in their temporal sensitivities (Grubb & Thompson, 2005). Bursts occur more for high-contrast stimuli (Reinagel et al., 1999), where inhibitory input is replaced by excitatory input (Lesica & Stanley, 2004). However, detection of dim stimuli is higher during phasic than tonic firing mode in the LGN (Guido et al., 1995; Lisman, 1997; Mukherjee & Kaplan, 1995). Bursts are phase-advanced relative to tonic firing, making them the first spikes to reach cortex carrying information about the stimulus. Tonic firing tends to vary more linearly with stimulus contrast and is more finely tuned to high temporal frequencies than bursts, so in general carries more detailed information about stimulus attributes. This has led some authors to suggest that bursts "wake" cortical neurons up to the fact that a new visual stimulus has been detected in order to prepare cortical neurons for subsequent finer informational input carried by tonic firing (Guido et al., 1992; Mukherjee & Kaplan, 1995; Sherman, 2001; Sherman & Guillery, 1996, 2002; Swadlow & Gusev, 2001; Swadlow et al., 2002). If a burst precedes the onset of a stimulus, the probability of a stimulus-induced response increases (Fanselow et al., 2001), suggesting that thalamic sensory relay neuron bursting might not necessarily be used by cortical neurons to decode information about stimulus attributes, although bursts do carry this information; rather, bursts might prime cortical neurons for decoding stimulus attributes on the basis of subsequent tonic firing. Nevertheless, burst duration correlates with the degree to which particular stimulus attributes are present (Kepecs & Lisman, 2003), suggesting that bursts do not just "prime the pump" for information transmission, but in fact do transmit information. For example, burst duration encodes information about the degree of stimulus orientation match to the optimal orientation that drives cells in V1 (DeBusk et al., 1997; Martinez-Conde et al., 2002), and burst spike number encodes information about sound amplitude in grasshopper auditory neurons (Eyherabide et al., 2009).

§4.39   The manner in which bursts are generated in the LGN and visual cortex is instructive in that it reveals the fine temporal interplay between excitation and inhibition that is a universal property of neural networks. The spike train that follows the onset or offset of a stimulus arises from adaptation and the balance between excitation and inhibition carried by opponent channels. On-channel neurons are excited by onsets and inhibited by offsets, whereas off-channel neurons are excited by offsets and inhibited by onsets. Upon stimulus onset the on-channel is excited, whereas the off-channel is inhibited. Since these channels are mutually suppressing, probably via GABAergic[10] inhibition, a burst occurs upon stimulus onset because inhibition of the off-channel takes a brief time to dissipate, before it can again suppress the on-channel. The opposite scenario occurs as well, leading to the "after-discharge" burst that occurs upon visual stimulus offset. Bursting in the LGN also appears to be influenced by topographically organized collateral outputs to and inhibitory feedback from the adjacent thalamic reticular nucleus, which can, moreover, modulate LGN activity via cortical input to the thalamic reticular nucleus that mediates attentional control of bottom-up input (Crick, 1984; McAlonan et al., 2006, 2008).[11] Suppression of the onset-associated or offset-associated bursts has perceptual consequences. Suppression of the onset-associated burst leads to a loss of visibility known as "forward masking" whereas suppression of the after-discharge leads to "backward masking." For example, if an abutting masking stimulus appears at the moment of the offset of a target stimulus, its on-response (itself partially suppressed) can suppress the after-discharge in cells that respond to the target, rendering the target perceptually invisible (Judge et al., 1980; Macknik & Livingstone, 1998; Macknik et al., 2000; Macknik & Martinez-Conde, 2004; Richmond & Wurtz, 1980; Schiller, 1968; Tse et al., 2005; Wurtz et al., 1980). If after-discharge bursts did not carry visual information, it is unlikely that suppressing them would lead to perceptual invisibility.

§4.40   As a third example, ventral striatal dopamine neurons can fire either tonically or phasically, permitting two ways of controlling cortico-striatal plasticity (Chergui et al., 1994; Frank, 2005; Goto & Grace, 2005; Shen et al., 2008; Morikawa et al., 2003; Overton & Clark, 1997; Tong et al., 1996; Wang et al., 2004; Zweifel et al., 2009). Tonic activity may trigger the activation of high-affinity dopamine (D2) receptors that underlie LTD of corticostriatal synapses and inhibit medium spiny neurons of the basal ganglia indirect pathway (Goto & Grace, 2005; Grace et al., 2007; Zweifel et al., 2009). Phasic dopamine neuron firing, in contrast, plays a role in enhancing excitatory activity in basal ganglia direct pathway circuitry that is involved in selecting the appropriate action to fulfill a goal. It may trigger the activation of a class of low-affinity dopamine (D1) receptors that bring about LTP among corticostriatal synapses involved in making an association between a stimulus and a reward. To determine what kinds of information-processing the two functional neuronal modes in this circuitry might realize, Zweifel et al. (2009) created knockout mice with genetically inactivated NMDA receptors in dopamine neurons. Tonic firing was unaffected, but bursting was highly attenuated. While these mice showed no deficits in other functions modulated by dopamine release, they had severe deficits in learning reward and punishment-based contingencies, and so could not be conditioned like normal mice. This could be taken to imply that midbrain dopamine neuron bursts carry information about such contingencies, or, more probably, that midbrain dopamine neuron bursts trigger dopamine release in distal synaptic clefts, which in turn affords the learning of the contingency through a Hebbian process. On the latter view, midbrain dopamine bursts carry information about cue reward value, which is lost in these mice. Reinforcement learning is thought to depend on the coincident arrival of dopamine and glutamate at dendritic spines of basal ganglia medium spiny neurons, which facilitates LTP at these excitatory synapses (Goto & Grace, 2005; Grace et al., 2007; Lisman & Grace, 2005).

§4.41   These are only three circuits. How dual transmission modes are taken advantage of may vary from circuit to circuit, and some circuits may only engage in one mode. A key focus of this book is the claim that attention transitions selected circuitry into phasic mode, which facilitates attentional binding, the transfer of attended contents into working memory for endogenous manipulation, and the rapid synaptic resetting that permits top-down mental causation. In order to develop these ideas fully, it is necessary to review the key mechanisms that underlie neural bursting.

The Sweet Spot of Neural Criticality

§4.42   Recent computational and empirical work suggests that the "sweet spot" that balances dynamic excitation with inhibition occurs in a narrow range of moderate excitability. Theoretical work suggests that dynamic systems are maximally perturbable, even for small inputs, when the system operates in a narrow zone known as "criticality" (Buzsáki, 2006; Legenstein & Maass, 2007), which in turn requires a baseline spontaneous firing rate. Early theorists (e.g., Abeles, 1991) found it difficult to model stable low baseline firing rates on the basis of excitation and inhibition alone, because such solutions were not stable. However, adding homeostatic short-term synaptic plasticity (Sussillo et al., 2007) allows neurons to stably return to a low-level tonic firing rate despite perturbations. This criticality domain (Hinrichsen, 2006; Bak et al., 1987) has other interesting properties (Shew et al., 2009, 2011; Yang et al., 2012). It expresses a moderate mean level of synchrony with maximal variability of synchrony. This domain lies at the boundary between excessively low synchrony and excessively high neuronal synchrony in the population.[12] This "criticality" domain also displays neuronal bursts whose probability decreases with duration in a fractal manner (i.e., with a power law whose exponent is ~–1.5; Beggs & Plenz, 2003; Shew et al., 2009; Klaus et al., 2011). The healthy brain therefore appears to operate where unpredictability of network response to a given input is maximal (i.e., entropy is maximal). This high-variability, borderline chaotic behavior of healthy neural networks may account for empirical evidence showing variability in neuronal responses to identical external inputs (Arieli et al., 1996; Cafaro & Rieke, 2010; Poulet & Petersen, 2008) and may arise because of the nonlinear and burst-triggering responses of NMDA receptors (Durstewitz, 2009). If information is carried in perturbations from baseline, this domain is maximally sensitive to perturbations, and thus is maximally capable of carrying information.

Synchrony among Inhibitory Interneurons

§4.43 Without well-timed inhibition, indiscriminate excitation would cease to carry information. In the extreme case, it would lead to epilepsy. For example, the same excitatory input that excites a pyramidal cell will commonly also excite a neighboring interneuron, which will inhibit the same pyramidal cell after a short delay, "sharpening" the timing of its responses (Pouille & Scanziani, 2001; Wehr & Zador, 2003; this can occur via pyramidal cell collaterals, as between the LGN and thalamic reticular nucleus: see McAlonan et al., 2006, 2008). Depending on the delay, the pyramidal cell will have been able to transmit spikes or bursts of spikes to the next level of processing before being inhibited. Information cannot be carried solely by the firing rate of pyramidal cells. Because of the very short temporal integration window of pyramidal cells, timing is essential if post-synaptic neurons are to depolarize efficiently. Information can be transmitted successfully only given the precise timing of inputs needed to drive a postsynaptic neuron. Thus, information must also be carried in the phase relationships or relative timing of action potentials within highly specific neural networks (Foffani et al., 2004; Hasenstaub et al., 2005; Lu et al., 2001; Shadlen & Newsome, 1998; Singer & Gray, 1995; Singer, 1999a,b).

§4.44 GABAergic inhibitory interneurons play a key role in gamma frequency network oscillations that arise from the rapid and precisely timed interplay of excitation and inhibition (in cortex: Bartos et al., 2007; Hasenstaub et al., 2005; in the hippocampus: Buzsáki & Chrobak, 1995; Cobb et al., 1995; Csicsvari et al., 2003; Jefferys et al., 1996; Jonas et al., 2004; Mann et al., 2005b; Miles et al., 1996; Penttonen et al., 1998; Pouille & Scanziani, 2001; Traub et al., 2004; Whittington et al., 1995). Inhibitory interneurons can fire in synchrony, and may themselves be driven by excitatory pyramidal cell input (Csicsvari et al., 2003; Mann et al., 2005a; Traub et al., 2004), in particular from "chattering" pyramidal cells (Cunningham et al., 2004; Gray & McCormick, 1996), or by input via gap junctions made with other interneurons (Deans et al., 2001; Galarreta & Hestrin, 1999, 2002; Gibson et al., 1999, 2005; Hormuzdi et al., 2001). Gap junction coupling increases gamma frequency power but is not necessary for the occurrence of gamma oscillations, since they occur even when gap junctions are blocked (Bartos et al., 2007; Buhl et al., 2003; Hormuzdi et al., 2001; Traub et al., 2000, 2001; see Bibbig et al., 2002, for a model of induced gamma oscillations that is not driven by interneuron synchrony). If interneuron synchrony is accomplished via gap junctions, the network of interneurons will function as a synchronized reticulum, which in turn could synchronize pyramidal cell firing probability and timing, especially in the gamma frequency domain (Bartos et al., 2007; Hasenstaub et al., 2005). Indeed, synchronous inhibition is a more powerful determinant of synchrony among action potentials of excitatory neurons than synchrony of excitatory inputs (Hasenstaub et al., 2005; see also Buzsáki & Chrobak, 1995; Csicsvari et al., 2003; Jonas et al., 2004; Jones et al., 2000). Gamma oscillations generated by fast-spiking inhibitory interneuron input into postsynaptic neurons appear to be a primary source of gamma oscillations in cortex (Bartos et al., 2007), with most evidence implicating parvalbumin-binding basket cells (Kawaguchi et al., 1987). Indeed, these basket cells form a reticulum (Gulyás et al., 1999; Kisvárday et al., 1993; Sik et al., 1995) that can phase lock via gap junctions, and their collective gamma oscillation can be transferred to pyramidal cells via their inhibitory synapses onto pyramidal cell bodies. Rhythmic synaptic inputs modulate postsynaptic membrane potentials rhythmically, generating fluctuations in the local field potential (Buzsáki et al., 1983). Gamma oscillations are a hallmark of actively processing cortex (Gray & Singer, 1989; Ribary et al., 1991) and may serve as a reference signal for phase-locking in a temporal spike code (Buzsáki & Chrobak, 1995; Hopfield, 1995). Gamma oscillations play a role in memory encoding and recall, as well (Lisman & Idiart, 1995; Lisman, 1999). For example, gamma oscillations at different frequencies in CA1 neurons of the hippocampus may arise from different sources of input to those neurons, and may serve to segregate and route those inputs as a part of distinct information-processing operations (Colgin et al., 2009). For our purposes, however, the most important thing about gamma oscillations is that they have been proposed to be the mechanism that realizes informational binding (Gray & Singer, 1989).

Attentional Binding and Gamma Oscillations

§4.45   Timing or phase relationships among spikes of different neurons are likely to be important because the combined effects of many synchronous presynaptic neuronal inputs on a shared postsynaptic dendritic region is greater than for noncoincident or asynchronous inputs (Kelso, 1995; Kopell et al., 2010; Varela et al., 2001; von der Malsburg et al., 2010). Von der Marlsburg and others have argued on theoretical grounds that phase-locking could bind information across a population of neurons and tag a neuron as belonging to a particular assembly (Grossberg & Somers, 1991; Neven & Aertsen, 1992; Reitboeck et al., 1987; Sporns et al., 1991; Tononi et al., 1992; von der Malsburg, 1981, 1985, 1995; von der Malsburg & Schneider, 1986; Wang et al., 1990). Singer and colleagues have argued that such binding occurs in the range of gamma oscillations (Fries et al., 1997, 2001a,b, 2002, 2007, 2008; Gray, 1999; Singer, 1999a,b, 2004; Uhlhaas et al., 2009). Initial studies inferred enhanced gamma frequency spike coherence on the basis of local field potential power (Taylor et al., 2005) or coherence between spiking of single neurons and the LFP (Fries et al., 2001b; Bichot et al., 2005; Womelsdorf et al., 2006). This was not fully convincing evidence of synchronous spiking among individual neuron pairs; and, of course, LFPs are not transmitted to downstream neurons, spikes are. But spike-spike coherence was then shown to occur to bottom-up stimulus changes and top-down attention allocated inside or outside of a receptive field, particularly in the 30–70Hz range (Fries et al., 2008; see their figure 7C). This coherence among spike trains in the gamma frequency domain could arise from tonic gamma oscillations or synchronous bursting behavior.

§4.46   Numerous problems arise with the idea that information is bound by virtue of phase-locking across a neuronal assembly (Shadlen & Movshon, 1999). Synchrony per se does not have to carry information about sensory input or serve as an assembly tag. Certainly, synchrony among neurons oscillating together at baseline, in the absence of sensory input, is not likely to carry much information if information is carried in perturbations away from just such activity. Synchrony generally occurs because neurons are driven by common input. For cortical neurons oscillating with zero phase difference, this will generally mean that they are driven by shared subcortical, particularly thalamic, or local cortical or long-range cortical input. If synchrony arises via long-range connectivity from other subcortical or cortical pyramidal cells, a problem arises because a phase lag will be introduced as a function of the distance that that excitatory input must traverse. Moreover, a long-range driver of synchrony would likely mean that synchrony is driven by some factor other than the information realized in the synchronized ensemble itself. Gamma oscillation synchrony is only likely to be a mechanism of informational binding in an ensemble if the synchrony arises from local connectivity within that synchronized ensemble. As discussed in the previous section, gamma oscillations are likely imposed by the intrinsic network dynamics of an inhibitory interneuron "reticulum" that may get around the phase-lag problem via gap junctions that afford phase-locking over large distances.

§4.47   While the transition to this phase-locked state may be enhanced by attention, gamma oscillations increase with attention *prior* to the arrival of sensory input; as Fries et al. (2008) write: "Selective visual attention modulated synchronization before stimulus onset and during sustained visual stimulation. Attention reduced [alpha] frequency synchronization and enhanced gamma-band synchronization already during the prestimulus period." This was true for both the local field potential power in the gamma frequency domain and the firing rate (see their figure 9). Gamma oscillations may therefore not be the mechanism of attentional binding of sensory information per se, since it can happen in the absence of any sensory input. That is, gamma oscillations occur in the absence of sensory information that needs to be bound, and so is unlikely to be the signature of binding of sensory information. Also, because correlations among neural spikes appear to be driven primarily by local cortical circuitry among similarly tuned neurons (Smith & Kohn, 2008), synchrony would appear to be incapable of binding features belonging to a common object across large expanses of the visual field, unless some mechanism that generates synchrony across widely spaced neurons within, say, V4, is discovered. Finally, Ray and Maunsell (2010) find that gamma oscillations vary in frequency as a function of local stimulus contrast, suggesting that they are a consequence of local excitatory-inhibitory interactions that likely have nothing to do with binding per se. Instead, gamma oscillations may be a correlate of a cortical network that is prepared to process sensory inputs in a particular kind of way, namely, via bursting and firing rate increases to sensory inputs. Attentional binding, I argue, occurs because of a transition to a phasic mode of information processing, rather than via synchrony per se.

§4.48   Importantly, visual inputs substantially *decrease* neuronal spike correlations relative to the no-input case, particularly upon stimulus onset and offset (Smith & Kohn, 2008). Moreover, attention *decorrelates* neuronal activity (Cohen & Maunsell, 2009, 2011; Mitchell et al., 2009) while increasing firing rate (Knudsen, 2007; Reynolds & Chelazzi, 2004; Treue, 2003) and burst activity in those neurons, presumably pyramidal cells (Mitchell et al., 2007), that are modulated when attention is paid to a stimulus in their V4 receptive fields (Anderson et al., 2011). Decorrelation per se is also not likely to be the mechanism of binding, but is instead a correlate of that mechanism, namely, a shift into phasic processing. Cohen and Maunsell (2009, 2011) see neither decorrelation among spike times of neuron pairs, nor an increase in firing rates in individual neurons, until after the onset transient. Thus, decorrelation and firing rate increases begin ~70ms after the neuronal response in V4 begins, and ~130ms after stimulus onset. This long latency of decorrelation and firing rate modulation with attention would seem to imply that attentional binding is not likely to be realized in decorrelation or increased firing rate per se, because this would make attentional binding, and indeed attention, too slow a process to account for psychophysical data showing that effects of attending are apparent in less than 130ms from stimulus onset (e.g., Hilkenmeier & Scharlau, 2010; Nakayama & Mackeben, 1989; Tse et al., 2003). But in the previous paragraph, I argued that attentional binding of stimulus information is also not likely to be realized in increased gamma oscillations, because these precede the onset of the stimulus (Fries et al., 2008). If gamma oscillations appear too soon and decorrelations and firing rate changes appear too late to be the mechanism we are looking for, what might actually realize binding and not be a mere "shadow" of the binding mechanism? If the binding mechanism requires the transition into phasic mode within an information-processing circuit, binding of stimulus information would be realized in the initial bursts to stimulus onset as well as the spikes that occur thereafter while in phasic mode. The first neural correlate of visual feature binding by attention would include the onset burst because it will traverse the entire visual hierarchy as a "burst packet" (§§4.53, 5.36, 5.53) if the circuit is already in phasic mode. If the circuit is in tonic mode (i.e., no attention), there may be an onset response, but it may be less likely to traverse the entire visual hierarchy. Attention may transition visual circuitry into a phasic mode as early as the LGN (see n. 11; McAlonan et al., 2006).

§4.49 The finding that attention decorrelates neural activity (Cohen & Maunsell, 2009, 2011; Mitchell et al., 2007, 2009) can perhaps be reconciled with the claim that synchrony increases with attention in visual cortex by noting that attention and visual stimulation decrease spike coherence and local field potential oscillations at low frequencies, while increasing them transiently at gamma and high-gamma frequencies (Fries et al., 2001b, 2008; see also Donner et al., 2007; Gray & Singer, 1989; Gregoriou et al., 2009a,b; Gruber et al., 1999; Hall et al., 2005; Henrie & Shapley, 2005; Hipp et al., 2011; Jensen et al., 2007; Siegel et al., 2007, 2008; Siegel & König, 2003; Tallon-Baudry et al., 1996; Womelsdorf et al., 2007; Womelsdorf & Fries, 2007; Wyart & Tallon-Baudry, 2008). Gamma-frequency (40–60Hz) coherence is confined to superficial layers of cortex, while deep layers show maximal coherence among low frequencies (6–16Hz); attention increases the former in the ventral stream, while decreasing the latter (Buffalo et al., 2011). Layer five pyramidal cells typically project to the superior colliculus and basal ganglia, and layer six pyramidal cells project to the thalamus as well as making feedback connections to other cortical areas. Meanwhile, layer 2/3 pyramidal cells make feedforward connections to other cortical areas (Barone et al., 2000; Felleman & Van Essen, 1991; Kennedy & Bullier, 1985; Rockland & Van Hoesen, 1994; Salin & Bullier, 1995). This suggests that gamma-frequency coherence operates primarily among networks that feed information forward in cortex, and that attentional boosting of this coherence enhances feedforward processing (Buffalo et al., 2010).

§4.50 While ongoing tonic gamma oscillations are no doubt important, the fact that gamma power in the LFP and gamma-frequency coherence among spike trains increases with attention in superficial cortical layers merely means that gamma frequencies and attention are correlated. No evidence to date has conclusively gone beyond this correlation to prove that gamma-frequency oscillations are the primary causal mechanism underlying binding. Attention does increase power in the gamma-frequency domain, but that does not mean that gamma oscillations serve as a frequency tag for an ensemble or serve as the means of binding. Data suggest that gamma oscillations are a primary indicator of a synchronizing "clock" imposed on pyramidal neuron outputs by inhibitory interneurons (Buzsáki & Chrobak, 1995), while the primary process that realizes attentional binding is neuronal bursting. Indeed, recent evidence (Ray & Maunsell, 2011) implies that gamma- and high-gamma-frequency power arises from different neuronal processes. In particular, high-gamma, but not normal gamma oscillations, may arise from bursts of spikes.

Attentional Binding by Neuronal Bursting

§4.51   The intuition that led to the hypothesis that synchrony could serve as a mechanism for binding comes from the fact that multiple spikes arising from different neurons will be able to drive a single common postsynaptic neuron more efficiently if they arrive simultaneously. But another mechanism, distinct from ensemble-wide synchronous tonic gamma-frequency firing, could exploit postsynaptic coincidence detection (realized in NMDA receptor function, as discussed in chapter 5). If attention increased the probability of bursting such that successive spikes arrived within the temporal integration window of the postsynaptic cell, the cell would also be efficiently driven. The increase in gamma-frequency spike coherence could arise via synchronous bursting in an ensemble, particularly if triggered by stimulus onset and offset (Smith & Kohn, 2008). Moreover, synchronous bursting among a few pyramidal cells itself tends to synchronize large numbers of pyramidal cells within a cortical column because inhibitory interneurons called "Martinotti cells" inhibit in a manner that is frequency dependent; This leads to phase-locking of membrane potentials and synchronous subsequent pyramidal cell spiking, including, presumably, synchronous bursting (Berger et al., 2010). If a typical episode of bursting, particularly synchronous bursting in an ensemble, lasts on the order of 160ms (Lin et al., 2006), it would look similar in power and coherence to a brief period of tonic gamma oscillation, except that more high-gamma power should be present. But bursting behavior is phasic and non-Poisson, whereas ongoing gamma-frequency spiking across an ensemble is tonic and Poisson in its statistics (§4.52). Instead of collective tonic circuit gamma frequency oscillators, neurons would burst in volleys of two to a few spikes that would arrive within the temporal integration window of postsynaptic cells. Bursting depolarizes a postsynaptic neuron more effectively than the same number of spikes transmitted in a tonic manner sequentially because bursts can arrive within the temporal integration window of a downstream pyramidal cell. The most effective driver of postsynaptic activity would likely be a synchronous arrival of bursts from multiple cells. Synchrony without bursting does not appear to carry information to the extent of bursts or burst synchrony. Indeed, some synapses do not respond well to single spikes. They may be thought to filter out single spikes but pass information carried in bursts (Lisman, 1997). At least in terms of encoding information about external events, the neuronal code may not just be a firing rate code, it may also be a neural burst code (§5.29).

§4.52 Until the 1990s, it was widely believed that neural spiking was Poisson in its statistics, meaning (1) that spike probabilities at any given time are largely independent of spike history—beyond the limitations on firing rate imposed by the neuronal refractory period—and (2) that spike count variance is proportional to the mean firing rate (Shadlen & Newsome, 1998; Softky & Koch, 1993; Tolhurst et al., 1983). It is now clear that spiking statistics are not Poisson for all neurons (Bair et al., 1994; Compte et al., 2003; Friedman-Hill et al., 2000; Katai et al., 2010; Joelving et al., 2007; Maimon & Assad, 2009). Spiking statistics of "narrow spiking neurons," presumed to be interneurons, tend to be Poisson in V4 (Anderson et al., 2011), prefrontal, and parietal cortex (Compte et al., 2003; Constantinidis & Goldman-Rakic, 2002). These neurons display a clear refractory period. At least in V4, these neurons are not significantly modulated by attention (Anderson et al., 2011). However, some "broad spiking neurons," presumably pyramidal neurons (Mitchell et al., 2007), have non-Poisson statistics (McCormick et al., 1985; Nowak et al., 2003). These are the neurons most likely to display bursts and firing rate increases in response to attentional allocation to a stimulus falling within their receptive field. In contrast, putative pyramidal cells that display decreases in firing rate with attention are not bursty (Anderson et al., 2011). If the neurons most prone to bursting are pyramidal cells, this suggests that bursting is an excitatory mode of information transmission accomplished via presynaptic pyramidal cell glutamate release onto, especially, postsynaptic pyramidal cells.

§4.53 We will analyze the nature of information transmission via bursting in greater depth in chapter 5. There I will suggest that attentional binding does not consist in transitioning ensembles from a mode tagged by ongoing tonic gamma oscillations, as Singer and colleagues have long argued. Rather, attentional binding, I will suggest, consists in transitioning a neural circuit into a phasic mode of firing, characterized by an increased probability of burst transmission up and down the circuit. The notion that attentional binding occurs via gamma oscillatory "tagging" of an ensemble places emphasis on synchrony at a given layer or ensemble of an information-processing hierarchy. If information processing is thought of as a vertical hierarchy, with simpler representations on the bottom and more complex representations on top, as shown in figure 4.3b, the gamma oscillation synchrony view emphasizes what is going on within one horizontal layer, as neurons in an ensemble synchronize to indicate to read out neurons elsewhere in the hierarchy that they represent something in common. In contrast, the present view, that attentional binding occurs by transitioning an information-processing *circuit* into phasic mode, emphasizes decorrelation in firing (Cohen & Maunsell, 2009, 2011) and an increase in bursting (Anderson et al., 2011) over synchronous firing. On this view, increased power of gamma oscillations with attention (Fries et al., 1997, 2001a,b, 2002, 2007, 2008; Gray, 1999; Singer, 1999a,b, 2004; Uhlhaas et al., 2009) arises not primarily from synchronous firing, although synchronous bursting is important; it arises from the synchronous subthreshold inputs to postsynaptic neurons imposed by the inhibitory interneuron "clock" discussed above (Buzsáki & Chrobak, 1995; Bartos et al., 2007; Kawaguchi et al., 1987). The hallmarks of attention-induced phasic firing include increased burstiness (Anderson et al., 2011), increased decorrelation in spikes after the initial stimulus-triggered onset transient (Cohen & Maunsell, 2009, 2011), and increased gamma range power (Fries et al., 1997, 2001a,b, 2002, 2007, 2008; Gray, 1999; Singer, 1999a,b, 2004; Uhlhaas et al., 2009) due primarily to the oscillation of inhibitory inputs to pyramidal cells. The "binding by bursting" view (§§5.48–5.50) emphasizes the transmission of "burst packets" vertically up and down an attended circuit, which, in the case of figure 4.3b, would be the entire stack. It is a "vertical" view of attentional binding, rather than the standard "horizontal" view of binding by gamma oscillations. What "binding by bursting" provides is not the gluing of features together at a location, but rather the complete information-processing treatment of the entire hierarchical circuit within the attended domain. Processing outside of the attended domain does not receive a circuit's complete information-processing treatment because it remains in tonic firing mode. If single spikes are "filtered out" (Lisman, 1997), then downstream neurons will not respond well to tonic input, unless it arrives synchronously. Each level will process its inputs even in tonic mode. But signals are less likely to reach late stages of a hierarchy in tonic mode. I will argue that entering phasic mode enhances information processing, especially in later stages of a hierarchy, because burst packets corresponding to a given bottom-level input will propagate the entire hierarchy in a coherent sequence. Thus, detected information will be processed from beginning to end, or bottom to top of a stack. In contrast, tonic mode spikes corresponding to a given bottom-level input are less likely to propagate the full extent of the information-processing hierarchy.

Neural Epiconnectivity and Rapid Synaptic Resetting

§4.54   It will doubtless prove easier to discover how "hard-wired criteria" for firing are realized in neural networks, such as are present, at least to a first approximation, in the creation of the tuning properties of a simple cell (figure 4.2) or retinal ganglion cell. But it is likely that certain physical mechanisms are shared between "hard-wired criteria" and temporary "soft-wired criteria" realized in working memory and higher-order cognitive functions, such as thought, planning, and language, where criteria can specify outcomes that are both novel and not specified by sensory input (e.g., if I tell you to imagine an animal that is half goat, half anaconda, and has wings, there cannot have been a neuron whose preexisting criteria for firing were such, since I could have told you to imagine any of an infinity of things). Certainly "hard-wired criteria" are realized in existing axonal inputs, but "soft-wired criteria" for the firing of a neuron must also depend on existing axonal inputs because the axons that synapse on a given neuron cannot rapidly change. It is therefore likely that temporary criteria for firing will be realized in dynamically changing synaptic weights, gain, facilitative versus depressive dynamics, and changes in the temporal window over which EPSPs and IPSPs are integrated. To understand how new criteria for firing are set up in a given neuron, it is not enough to specify how input neurons are physically connected to that neuron, as has been described in traditional neural network theories (e.g., Abeles, 1991; Braitenberg & Schuz, 1991; Hebb, 1949; Hopfield & Tank, 1986; Palm, 1982, 1987; Wennekers et al., 2003; Wickelgren, 1999). It is necessary to model how synaptic weights on inputs to that cell change dynamically (von der Malsburg, 1994; Marder & Buonomano, 2003), effectively changing its neural "epiconnectivity."[13]

§4.55   Synapses express a wide range of both potentiating and depressing weights in the brain (Gloveli et al., 1997; Holmgren et al., 2003; Markram et al., 1998; Reyes et al., 1998; Tsodyks & Markram, 1997; Wang et al., 2006), which can change dynamically using presynaptic and post-synaptic mechanisms (Chung et al., 2002; Deisz & Prince, 1989; Gupta et al., 2000; Markram et al., 1998; Thomson et al., 2002), including rapid changes in spine conformation (Bonhoeffer & Yuste, 2002; Fischer et al.,

2000; Korkotian & Segal, 2001; Majewska et al., 2000; Segal & Andersen, 2000; Verkuyl & Matus, 2006). A common assumption in neuroscience is that information processing in the brain is realized in action potentials and that mental causation must be realized in a succession of action potentials triggering action potentials. This is no doubt part of the story, but recent evidence suggests that dynamic, short-term changes in synaptic plasticity can also play the role of a neural basis for information processing (Abbott & Regehr, 2004; Abbott et al., 1997; Maass & Markram, 2002; Mongillo et al., 2008; Sussillo et al., 2007; von der Malsburg, 1994; Zucker & Regehr, 2002). The rules of the dynamic changes on the weights of inputs are not well understood, but sequences of such dynamic read-out events can be conceptualized as a generative syntax of thought that may even have chunks analogous to words and sentences (Buzsáki, 2010; Pulvermüller, 2010).

§4.56   Many neuroscientists have thought that deciphering the neural code would mean deciphering the information carried by action potentials per se, as if something about a train of action potentials, whether rate, pattern, phase relationships, or something else, were a code that could be deciphered like, say, Morse code or the Enigma code. But which inputs will make a neuron fire is dependent on the synaptic weights that are imposed on incoming presynaptic action potentials at a given moment. If information is physically realized when it is made explicit, and it is made explicit when a neuron fires and passes that information on to other neurons, then the information that a neuron will realize if it fires is implicit in its synaptic weights even before the arrival of any presynaptic action potentials. Facts about action potentials in isolation of the inputs that trigger them will not carry information about anything; a given neuron might fire identically given one set of inputs at t_1 and a different set of inputs at t_2. Since different information would be realized, the information cannot be localized in action potentials per se. If you know that a neuron has fired but you do not know what input has made it fire, then you do not know what information has made it fire. But if you know that a neuron has fired given particular physical inputs, which will only occur when certain informational facts are the case, then you can know what information made it fire.

§4.57   Conversely, if an action potential arriving at a synapse is "multiplied" by a synaptic weight of zero, it contributes nothing to the firing of the postsynaptic neuron and therefore nothing to its information processing. Therefore, observing an action potential without knowing about how it is "filtered" by synaptic weighting cannot tell you what information it conveys, if any. The "voice analogy" of Abbott and Regehr (2004) can be extended to encompass this view of neural information processing: How the mouth is formed determines whether the same vibrating air passing through the mouth will lead to the enunciation of, say, an "ah" or an "oh" sound. The mouth can be formed into an "ah" or an "oh" shape before any air is forced through it, just as neurons can be criterially reset before being driven to fire by input. The bit of information "ah" versus "oh" does not exist in the vibrating air in isolation of the shape of the mouth through which it is filtered. Rather, this information comes into being as the vibrating air passes through either the "oh" or "ah" mouth filters. On this account, action potentials are analogous to the vibrating air, and momentary synaptic weights are like filters that determine the information expressed by action potential input. The search for the neuronal code is likely to be more fruitful if the focus is on neuronal criterial resetting rather than on action potentials in isolation of synaptic recoding. Cracking this kind of criterial neural code poses a major challenge to neuroscience because, given present single- and multi-unit methods, action potentials are easy to observe, whereas dynamic synaptic resetting over thousands of synapses is not. However, if this view is correct, even if neurophysiologists were to measure only action potentials forever, neuroscience would not crack the neuronal code. Doing so would be like trying to decipher what someone is saying by observing air vibrations as they come off the vocal cords without observing how the mouth is formed or how it filters vibrations in highly specific ways. The analogy can be taken further, in the sense that the mouth has to be formed (criteria for firing have to be set) before the air is passed through the mouth (before the arrival of presynaptic action potentials). Indeed, the mouth must be shaped dynamically on a continual basis in order for the mouth to be able to speak. Action potentials are therefore a necessary but not sufficient basis for neural information processing whereby neurons convey information or "talk" to each other. This metaphor is not to be taken too seriously and should be discarded once its weaknesses become apparent.

§4.58   A more useful way to think of the situation, perhaps, is to return to the example of a simple cell. When I learned about simple cells, the situation was portrayed inaccurately, as in figure 4.2, as if only those LGN cells that are activated by inputs along the simple cell's axis of orientation tuning fed input into the simple cell. If that were the case, a simple cell could not change its tuning properties to orientation, size, or position. Imagine instead that the simple cell receives input from many more LGN center-surround cells than portrayed in figure 4.2, most of whose weights are set to zero. Then, by changing the weights, the vertically tuned simple cell's receptive field could change position tuning in retinotopic coordinates without changing orientation tuning, as in (b) or even change orientation tuning, as in (c). Here "0" means the presynaptic cell's input cannot drive the postsynaptic cell, and "1" means that it can. In this example, the cell will be driven by input at the location of a "1, 1, 1" pattern. If synapses are conceived of as switches that can be turned on or off, then perhaps the majority of synapses might be off at any given time. But when needed, switches could be turned on. This permits the possibility of "sculpting" neuronal "epicircuits" on the fly, to construct neural circuits that are needed at a given time, rather like switching the railroad switches on train tracks to create different track connections as needed. The metaphor breaks down because weights need not be limited to the black-and-white case of on or off. They can be modulated up and down, like dimmer switches.

§4.59   In this regard, the rapid synaptic resetting discussed here might have elements in common with the rapid gain control mechanism proposed to underlie attentional modulation (e.g., Reynolds & Heeger, 2009; Salinas & Thier, 2000). But gain control is a rather blunt tool. It can change the number of output spikes per a fixed number of input spikes, or it can change the probability of bursting in relay neurons, for example, in the thalamus (Godwin et al., 1996; Uhlrich et al., 2002). But gain control alone should not change, say, the orientation tuning function of a neuron. To do that, synaptic resetting would have to be much more precise than simply multiplying or dividing all weights by a scalar, or changing the threshold for firing at the axon hillock. One must be able to alter synaptic reweighting in a more tailored fashion to account for cases where attention modulates tuning functions as above.

§4.60   A neuron's firing can even change the criteria that must be realized to make that very neuron fire again, in the future, without in any sense being "self-causal." This occurs, most commonly, when a neuron becomes less likely to fire again immediately after having fired. But it can also happen when a neuron changes its own (future) inputs; in discussing a hierarchy of criterial decoders, it is important to emphasize the role of dynamic feedback from a decoder back on the neurons that provide its inputs. Such feedback may play a role in both learning (e.g., Ahissar et al., 2009) and optimizing the timing (e.g., Sirota et al., 2003, 2008; Buzsáki, 2010), synchrony (Fries, 2005; Womelsdorf et al., 2007), and signal-to-noise ratio (Ahissar & Arieli, 2001; Bremmer et al., 2009; Gutierrez et al., 2010) of information transfer. Such neuronal feedback also plays an important role in top-down processing, including the influence of knowledge,

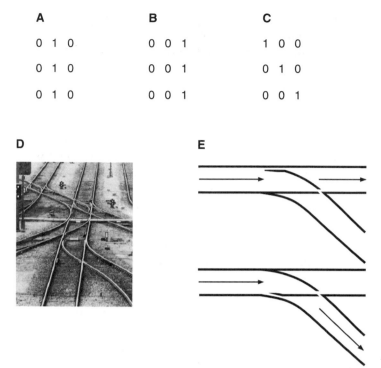

A

0 1 0

0 1 0

0 1 0

B

0 0 1

0 0 1

0 0 1

C

1 0 0

0 1 0

0 0 1

D

E

Figure 4.5
Dynamic synaptic resetting changes informational tuning. By changing the synaptic weights on inputs from zero to one or vice versa, a hypothetical simple cell can be tuned to the different bars of light indicated by (1, 1, 1) in a, b, and c. This mechanism permits the formation of "epicircuits" just as railroad switches (d and e; from Wikimedia Commons) permit the formation of various track connectivities. Rather than a train traversing tracks, in the brain, bursts of information can be thought to traverse neuronal circuits from a given starting point to various destinations, as needed.

expectation, and attention on processing (e.g., Graboi & Lisman, 2003; Reynolds & Heeger, 2009). Corticocortical and corticothalamocortical looping is thus likely to play an important role in the dynamic setting of the physical—and thereby also informational—criteria for the firing of any given neuron at any given moment. Given that criterial resetting of synaptic weights is a distinct functional step from the steps of feedback or feedforward information-processing via criterial satisfaction, making the next neuron in a sequence of neurons fire, it is likely that these functional steps are temporally discretized in a potentiation-action cycle. Some hints that this might be the case can be discerned in the temporal patterns found in cortical microcircuitry (Ikegaya et al., 2004; Luczak et al., 2009; Mao et al., 2001), though the functional role of such information-processing cycles is not yet well understood. A great deal remains to be discovered.[14]

Amplifying Microscopic Randomness to Spike Timing Variability

§4.61   Because receptor binding is a stochastic process, it plays an important role in introducing randomness from the microscopic domain to the macroscopic domain of neural networks. A receptor for some neurotransmitter can be thought of as analogous to a lock. Even though the criteria are not listed anywhere, or represented in software, a lock physically realizes a set of criteria for opening that specify thresholds on the shape and rigidity of a key. The criteria do not assess whether the key is hollow, transparent, warm, red, or platinum versus steel. When it comes to opening the lock, the key's temperature, color, or other nonshape properties simply do not matter (cf. Shapiro, 2000). For the purpose of opening the lock, it is as if these irrelevant properties did not exist, because they play no necessary causal role in opening the lock; but while the key need not be made of steel in order to be able to open the lock, it is necessary that it have a certain shape and rigidity. Of course, the criteria realized in a lock are purely mechanistic, and occur at such a coarse and large scale, that microscopic randomness plays no role in criterial satisfaction. That is, everyday locks can effectively be understood within the framework of deterministic, Newtonian physics. Note that this is not the case with the "lock and key" relationship of a neurotransmitter channel, say, the $5HT_{2A}$ receptor, to a neurotransmitter that binds to it, in this case serotonin. The physical criteria for molecular reconformation realized in the binding properties of this receptor only concern the shape of a small binding portion of a potentially binding molecule. Although the $5HT_{2A}$ receptor evolved to take serotonin as its "key," its criteria for reconformation can also be met by mescaline, LSD, psylocybin, and many other molecules. The physically realized criteria in the receptor are indifferent to the vast majority of facts about the molecule, including which token atoms or even type atoms make up the molecule outside the binding region. Note in figure 4.6 how different the molecules are outside the "key" regions they have in common. Mass, size, momentum, spin, and many other energetic properties play only an incidental role in fulfilling the criteria placed on shape and, therefore, in causing the action that this physical criterial satisfaction releases. The only criterion that must be met for such a membrane receptor is that some portion of some abutting molecule have some approximate shape.

So we can talk about a chain of criterial causality that can be understood only once the "shape code" realized physically in the membrane receptor is understood.

§4.62 This is a type-level criterial causality (§§6.8, 6.10) because there is a many-to-one type mapping where numerous types of molecules (e.g., LSD, mescaline, or serotonin) can bind to a receptor and cause it to trigger the same intracellular cascades. Unlike an everyday lock, a receptor's operation is stochastic because the diffusion of neurotransmitter across the synapse is itself a random walk (§§4.66, 4.67). Even though the physical opening and closing of receptors is entirely mechanistic, involving no criteria placed on information, the fact that their behavior is stochastic is very important in introducing unpredictability to the processing outcomes of neural networks. For random fluctuations in postsynaptic potential (which arise from randomness at the level of individual receptors, neurotransmitters, and ions) to lead to random spike timing differences at the level of neurons and ultimately neural networks, postsynaptic potential must be homeostatically returned to just below the firing threshold after each perturbation. This is likely the reason that in vivo spike timing is not a regular consequence of identical input (Shadlen & Newsome, 1994; Softky & Koch, 1993). The introduction of randomness from the microscopic domain to neural networks, and therefore to the domain of mental causation, is central to having a free will in the strong sense described in §7.1. The special role of NMDA receptors in introducing bursting and erratic spike timing to neural behavior is so fundamental to neural coding,

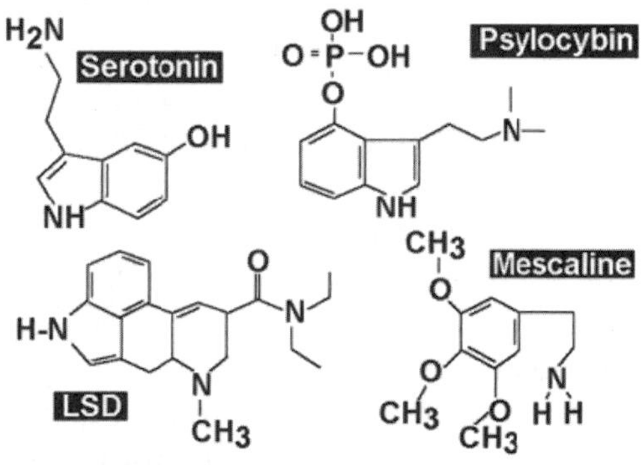

Figure 4.6
Several molecules meet the shape criteria physically realized in the $5HT_{2A}$ serotonin receptor because they share the "key" binding region that releases the receptor's state change and ultimately the postsynaptic neuron's action potential.

and ultimately to the issue of free will, that it will be addressed in its own chapter, chapter 5.

§4.63   Although physical criteria for firing are built into a single neuron, informational criteria for firing need not be physically realized in an individual neuron, but can be realized in the neuronal circuit it finds itself in. A given neuron, for example, may only exhibit visual versus auditory tuning properties by virtue of getting visual versus auditory inputs (cf. Newton et al., 2006). Similarly, the information that there is a bar of light at a particular orientation and spatial frequency at a particular location in the visual field is not available to an observer who observes a single neuron in isolation, who knows nothing about the whole cascade of successive neuronal inputs that led to the firing of, say, our simple cell. The information is not in intracellular potential changes or the axon hillock, or even in the firing of the simple cell in isolation. It occurs when the simple cell fires in the context of a cascade of neurons changing state. The information is thus global in origin, at the level of neural circuitry that causally links a particular kind of input, such as an oriented bar, to the firing of particular cells. Information is as little localized to a single neuron in isolation as gothic or baroque architectural style is isolated to a single brick in a building.

§4.64   One advantage of the architecture of a hierarchy of criterial coincidence-detecting decoders is that individual neurons are as fungible as bricks. If connections change, or if the weights on existing connections change, then criteria or tuning properties change. The physical criteria for neuronal firing change through operations like excitation, inhibition, hyperpolarization, subthreshold depolarization, long-term potentiation, the post-action potential refractory period, the dynamic changing of synaptic weights on existing inputs (§4.56), growing of new dendrites or synapses, expression of proteins in the membrane, changing of thresholds, apoptosis, and changes in the resting potential. A change in physical criteria for firing can change the informational criteria for firing, which, in turn, implies that the information realized in neuronal firing is fungible. Again, a single neuron in somatosensory cortex could realize information about a touch to the face or arm if its inputs were to change.[15]

§4.65   Criteria are generally not so specific that they cannot be met by a range of inputs. Indeed, criteria can generally be satisfied in multiple ways (§6.8). For example, a simple cell might fire equally to an optimally oriented bar of low luminance contrast and to a suboptimally oriented bar of higher luminance contrast. This poses a problem because the firing of a neuron is informationally ambiguous. Its firing can be driven by potentially countless types of inputs; given neural firing, which one in fact is the case is not clear. For example, another neuron taking input from our simple cell cannot decipher the orientation or luminance contrast of the bar of light in the world. One way around this ambiguity problem has been to argue that information must lie in the population of neuronal activity at a given representational level, because although the information realized in each individual neuron's firing is ambiguous, when multiple neurons fire in response to a given input, ambiguity is markedly reduced by virtue of the intersection of criteria for firing that exist across the population. An interesting question is whether one or more read-out neurons are required, which take input from a population, in order for that population to realize information that an animal can use to get around the world, or whether it is enough for the population to enter one state over other possible states in the absence of a read-out neuron (§§8.6, 8.7).[16]

§4.66   Independent informational criterial assessments require compartmentalization of potential (i.e., within neurons and dendrites, §4.1) for those informational criteria that are assessed in the physical realization of threshold assessments of potential. This necessitates a means of communication between neurons that is not reliant on gap junctions, because gap junctions would decompartmentalize physical potential and therefore make informational criterial assessments nonindependent. But chemical transmission between neurons, although slow, introduces additional advantages. A central reason why chemical transmission at the synapse may be beneficial is that neurotransmitter diffusion across the synapse introduces another source of variability in postsynaptic neuronal responses. Variability or noise in neural activity can be harnessed by a neuronal system that realizes discrete criterial detectors to generate novel solutions that meet any given set of neuronally realized criteria. How is this variability realized within a single postsynaptic neuron? Variability exists in the arrival time and magnitude of single postsynaptic potentials or currents because of neurotransmitter binding to postsynaptic receptors and their consequent reconformation. This translates, ultimately, into variability in the timing and rate of firing of postsynaptic neurons. This variability has multiple potential independent sources. According to a realistic model (Franks, Stevens, & Sejnowski, 2003) stochasticity of postsynaptic receptor responses plays a relatively minor role (Faber et al., 1992; Franks et al., 2002). More important are (1) the variability in the amount of neurotransmitter in the synaptic cleft due to variability in the amount contained in vesicles, and therefore in the amount released presynaptically; and (2) variability in the distance of the release site across the synapse on the presynaptic neuron to the site of receptors on the postsynaptic neuron. Modeling the diffusion of neurotransmitter across the synapse using a three-dimensional random walk (i.e., a Monte Carlo algorithm mimicking Brownian motion; Bartol et al., 1991; Stiles & Bartol 2001; Stiles et al., 1996), they find that distances greater than 300nm lead to essentially no postsynaptic response.

§4.67   It is therefore most likely not a coincidence that the synaptic cleft is typically on the order of 20–40nm. There would be little variability in arrival times of neurotransmitter as it diffuses across the synaptic cleft if the synaptic cleft were just 1nm wide, because the random walk of diffusion would not have much distance over which to introduce variability in arrival times of neurotransmitters. Conversely, if the cleft were too big, say, 300nm wide, the neurotransmitter would not even arrive, and even if it did arrive, it would take too long to get there. A reasonable hypothesis, then, is that the cleft has evolved to be the size that it is because this permits the introduction of an optimal level of variability in postsynaptic potential onset time given neurotransmitter diffusion rates, and given the need to arrive quickly. The optimal size of the cleft may also be analogous to the signal detection problem faced in determining the optimal level of subthreshold oscillations (§4.32); if the cleft is too big, there will be "incorrect rejections" in the sense that the postsynaptic cell will not fire when it should because the signal failed to get across the cleft, and if the cleft is too small, there will be "false alarms" in the sense that the postsynaptic cell will fire when it should not, because of an oversusceptibility to being triggered by noise in neurotransmitter release. In sum, neurotransmitter diffusion across the synaptic cleft carries both signal and noise. It is an important cause of variability in the rate and timing of neural activity, and of the neural basis of nonpredetermined but nonetheless self-selected choices, as we shall see in chapter 7 on the neural basis of free will. In effect, diffusion across the synapse is one of several physical mechanisms that permit the amplification of microscopic fluctuations into macroscopic variability in spike timing. Another important physical cause of the introduction of random fluctuations at the level of atoms to randomness in spike timing is the timing of magnesium ion release from NMDA receptors (§§5.6, 5.23, 5.25).

§4.68   Amplification of microscopic fluctuations is not limited to this mechanism, however. Another known mechanism can be found in the retina where a cascading avalanche of signals can follow the detection of even a single photon (Baylor et al., 1979; Barlow et al., 1972). Another mechanism may be found in nonsynaptic electrochemical communication among neurons (e.g., Anastassiou et al., 2011; Jefferys, 1995). In addition, there is good evidence that certain brain processes are inherently chaotic and therefore prone to amplification of microscopic random variability into global state changes (e.g., Faure & Korn, 2001; Grafstein, 2011; Korn & Faure, 2003; Jirsa, 2004; Sarbadhikari & Chakrabarty, 2001; Tsuda, 2001; Vogels et al., 2005). Indeed, particular receptors, such as the NMDA receptor, may introduce chaotic patterns of bursting into neurons and therefore neural network behavior (Durstewitz, 2009), as shall be discussed in depth in the next chapter. Thus, the randomness expressed in the microscopic domain may be amplified into randomness in the behavior of neural circuits via multiple physical mechanisms.

§4.69   It would be misleading to place sole emphasis on the amplification of microscopic to macroscopic randomness, because macroscopic to microscopic causation can also occur in complex systems that operate far from thermodynamic equilibrium. Such "dissipative structures" exchange energy with their environment, increasing entropy globally, while potentially increasing organization locally. When several such structures interact, as occurs within nested hierarchies of cooperating and competing neural circuits in the brain, nonlinear interactions can impose organization at the level of local neuronal activity that could not have been predicted on the basis of full knowledge of any subset of neural circuit activity in isolation. One common nonlinear mechanism occurs when winner-take-all operations lead to the capturing of the entire information-processing system by a random fluctuation at the level of an entire circuit. For example, should a burst from one neuronal subcircuit happen to arrive by chance at neurons that realize a winner-take-all decision before a burst from another subcircuit, the "winning" information could come to dominate subsequent information processing at all levels for a period of time because it flushes new order into the system. Something analogous happens in winner-take-all social systems, where, for example, one candidate wins by chance (e.g. Bush Jr. receiving more votes in Florida in 2000 because of faulty ballots in Palm Beach County) and then imposes a new social order that effectively shuts down potential competitors and dictates the terms of future decisions carried out by the system. Nonlinear dynamic systems are chaotic and unpredictable in principle because global outcomes are dependent on initial or boundary conditions to such a degree that immeasurably small differences in those conditions can lead to radically different outcomes or trajectories of system development (Freeman, 1992, 1999; Prigogine & Stengers, 1984; Prigogine, 1997). Some authors (Bressler & Kelso, 2001; Haken, 1984; Kelso, 1995) emphasize the "circular" nature of causation in chaotic systems like the brain, as winner-take-all and other nonlinear "attractor" mechanisms impose global → local causation that constrains subsequent local neuronal behavior, which in turn realizes local

→ global causation by changing the dynamics of the circuits to which they belong. Neuronal criterial causation harnesses such "circular" causation by presetting criteria at t_1 that must be met, which, when met nondeterministically via bottom-up variability at t_2, bias future behavior in a "downwardly" causal manner.

§4.70   Recent evidence (reviewed in Brembs, 2011) suggests that some neural response variability is not due to amplified microscopic noise, but is instead "injected" by neural responses whose variability can be changed to suit learning or task demands. For example, researchers have found that variability in fly head movements cannot be explained by the level of variability introduced by noise in visual processing (Rosner et al., 2009, 2010), suggesting that behavioral variability has endogenous sources outside the sensory system (Brembs, 2008). Similarly, fly turning behavior is more unpredicatable than can be accounted for by system noise amplification (Maye et al., 2007; Reynolds et al., 2007). This can make behavior vary between completely predictable and random. Fly behavior seems to follow from neural activity that operates in the "sweet spot" of criticality (§4.42), allowing maximum perturbation and unpredictability to input. Flies can be conditioned to reduce the range of behaviors over which variability is expressed (Wolf & Heisenberg, 1991) and specific fly brain circuits are involved in changing the degree of endogenous variability generated (mushroom bodies: Brembs, 2009; Colomb & Brembs, 2010; ellipsoid body: Martin et al., 2001). Similarly, mammals tend to increase behavioral variability when confronting novelty (Bunzeck & Duzel, 2006; Liu et al., 2007; Roberts & Gharib, 2006; Shahan & Chase, 2002), and specific neural sources of endogenous variability have been found (London et al., 2010). Although irregular input is central to neural computation (Destexhe & Contreras, 2006), information-processing circuitry that requires a consistent and stable input–output mapping would presumably amplify local fluctuations or receive endogenous sources of variability to a lesser degree than neural circuitry designed to generate multiple novel courses of action or thought. For example, we would expect to find less neuronally realized "annealing" in cerebellar or basal ganglia circuitry (Balleine & O'Doherty, 2009; Yin & Knowlton, 2006), with their stereotyped input–output transformations, than in the working memory circuitry used in creative problem solving. High variability affords creativity and exploration, but comes at the cost of efficiency and speed (Brembs, 2011). Control of the degree of endogenously generated variability would afford an animal the ability to flexibly optimize its neural processing to meet its needs.

5 NMDA Receptors and a Neuronal Code Based on Bursting

Spiny and Nonspiny Neurons

§5.1   We know that there are many structurally different neuronal types, and it is not likely that neurons of different types are interchangeable (cf. Newton et al., 2006). This suggests that criterial decoding and feature detection are not likely to emerge solely as a result of linear or nonlinear pooling of inputs, as suggested by the pandemonium or HMAX models (see fig. 4.3), respectively. Rather, they are also likely to emerge as a function of structural differences in various types of neurons, which, by virtue of their physical differences, impose different types of criteria for firing on neuronal input. They likely integrate information and fire in inherently different ways that give them particular information-processing properties within a network.

§5.2   Broadly speaking, there are only two basic types of neurons: those that have spines on their dendritic branches and those that have none or almost none (DeFelipe & Fariñas, 1992). Dendritic spines are about 2μm long and are found only at glutamatergic synapses, so are an indicator of excitatory synaptic input (Crick, 1982; Gray, 1959; Matus, 2000). Spiny cells include stellate cells and the only projection neurons of the brain, the glutamatergic pyramidal cells, which make up perhaps three-quarters of all cortical neurons (Jones, 1984). Since this class is thought to generally have excitatory outputs, and this class also has spines, which indicate excitatory inputs, it follows that most stellate and pyramidal cells excite other stellate and pyramidal cells. To prevent runaway excitation or excitation that carries no information, excitation must also trigger inhibition.

§5.3   Inhibition is the job of nonspiny cells. These are generally non-projecting local, GABAergic inhibitory interneurons (Fitzpatrick et al., 1987; Hendry et al., 1987, 1991; Houser et al., 1983). There is a large diversity of inhibitory interneurons (Miles, 2000) in both the hippocampus

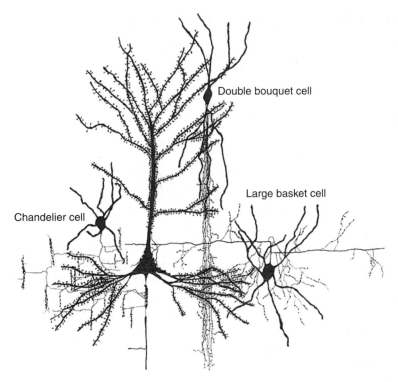

Figure 5.1
Pyramidal cell and inhibitory interneurons. This drawing depicts the synaptic relationships between the three main classes of inhibitory interneurons and pyramidal
cells. From DeFelipe and Fariñas (1992), reprinted with permission.

(Buhl et al., 1994; Freund & Buzsáki, 1996; Pawelzik et al., 2002; Somogyi
& Klausberger, 2005) and cortex (Gupta et al., 2000; Kawaguchi & Kubota,
1997; Soltesz, 2006), but interneurons can be classified as either fast-spiking
or non-fast-spiking, and they tend to inhibit the vicinity of either the soma
or the distal dendrites. They can also be classified by their expression of
neuropeptides and calcium-binding proteins such as parvalbumin (De-
Felipe, 1997; Freund & Buzsáki, 1996). The three most common inhibitory
interneurons are chandelier cells, basket cells, and double bouquet cells.
Their names describe the patterns of their arborizations. Fast-spiking basket
cells tend to wrap around and synapse onto a pyramidal cell's soma and
proximal dendrites, while chandelier cells tend to wrap around and synapse onto the axon hillock or the initial segment of the axon just beyond
the axon hillock (Cobb et al., 1995; DeFelipe et al., 1986, 1990; Hasenstaub
et al., 2005; Kawaguchi & Kubota, 1998; Miles et al., 1996; Pouille & Scan-

ziani, 2001; Somogyi et al., 1998; Tamas et al., 1997). This anatomy implies that these types of interneurons inhibit action potential generation late in the game of potential summation, perhaps even after a pyramidal cell's computations might have otherwise led it to fire. Indeed, pyramidal cells typically have multiple inhibitory chandelier cell inputs at the axon hillock and no excitatory inputs there (DeFelipe et al., 1990; DeFelipe & Fariñas, 1992; DeFelipe & Jones, 1985). The lack of late excitation makes sense, because excitation of the axon hillock would lead to an action potential that carried no information based on the pyramidal cell's own computations. The presence of late inhibition also makes sense, because some outputs are to be vetoed or blocked lest they interfere with other information-processing. Alternatively, fast-spiking basket cells and chandelier cells may play a key role in enforcing strict timing onto pyramidal cell outputs, rather than vetoing them, such that spikes or bursts of spikes will leave an ensemble at the same time to maximize their capacity to depolarize downstream neurons (Hasenstaub et al., 2005). In order to control the timing of pyramidal cells, the temporal integration window of fast-spiking inhibitory interneurons would have to be at least as fast as that of pyramidal cells. In fact, such cells show little adaptation and have shorter membrane time constants than pyramidal cells (McCormick et al., 1985; Nowak et al., 2003). Fast-spiking inhibitory interneurons therefore likely play a key role in setting up gamma oscillations in cortex (Buzsáki & Chrobak, 1995; Cobb et al., 1995; Csicsvari et al., 2003; Jefferys et al., 1996; Jonas et al., 2004; Mann et al., 2005a; Miles et al., 1996; Penttonen et al., 1998; Pouille & Scanziani, 2001; Traub et al., 2004; Whittington et al., 1995), although non-fast-spiking neurons also play a role (Deans et al., 2001; Mann et al., 2005b; Somogyi & Klausberger, 2005). Double bouquet cells, in contrast, tend to synapse on dendritic branches, suggesting that they inhibit dendritic computations or cancel out excitatory dendritic inputs.

The NMDA Receptor

§5.4 The NMDA receptor is an ionotropic channel consisting of four subunits (Laube et al., 1998; Banke & Traynelis, 2003) that together comprise in essence a coincidence detector. Their defining characteristic is that they permit rapid influx of calcium ions. To open, the tetramer requires (1) the simultaneous binding of glutamate to NR2 subunits released by a presynaptic neuron and (2) co-agonist glycine (Kleckner & Dingledine, 1988) or D-serine (Johnson & Ascher, 1987; Schell, 2004) to NR1 or NR3 subunits, as well as (3) the depolarization of the postsynaptic cell in the

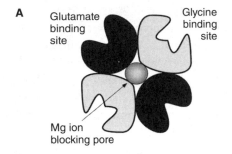

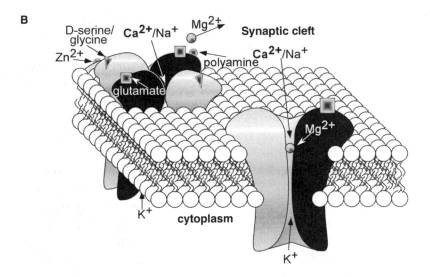

Figure 5.2
The NMDA receptor. (A) A schematic drawing of an NMDA receptor "from above" viewed from inside the synaptic cleft when the postsynaptic neuron is at resting potential. An NMDA receptor is made up of two obligatory NR1 and two NR2A-D or two NR3A-B subunits coded by different genes. Two molecules, each of two different amino acids, glycine and L-glutamate, bind, respectively, to an NR1 and NR2 subunit. A magnesium ion is drawn into the pore by the negative charge of the resting potential, and is released if the postsynaptic neuron depolarizes sufficiently, but only when glutamate and glycine or their agonists are appropriately bound as well. As such, NMDA receptors function as coincidence detectors of these three simultaneously true facts. (B) Another schematic drawing showing how a magnesium ion blocks the pore in the foreground, because glycine has not bound to the appropriate site. In the background NMDA receptor, the magnesium ion has been set free, opening the pore to calcium and sodium ion influx and potassium ion efflux.

immediate vicinity of the NMDA receptor. Unless all three conditions are met, the receptor remains closed.[1] Thus, at resting potential, NMDA receptors are closed.

§5.5   Why would it be important to keep a "door" closed with so many "locks"? Besides the importance of coincidence detection, glutamate-triggered calcium ion influx is potentially highly excitotoxic (Rothman & Olney, 1995). Since D-serine (De Koning et al., 2003) is an endogenous glycine site agonist,[2] and D-serine is produced and released by astrocytes, adding glycine or D-serine binding as a necessary condition for pore opening affords both an added insurance against toxicity and affords glial control over NMDA receptor pore opening. Just as a fuse plays an essential functional role in electrical circuitry, glia are inseparable components of neural circuitry, since they can effectively shut down any part of a neuronal circuit by regulating the expression of a crucial factor for NMDA receptor function and thus information transfer.[3] Should feedback arrive from a dendritic spine that too much calcium has entered the postsynaptic cell, local glial cells could presumably shut the synapse down regardless of how much presynaptic excitatory input were to arrive. Another "safety lock" feature of NMDA receptors might arise from the fact that NMDA receptors are found most typically in dendritic spines, although they are also found extrasynaptically (Hardingham & Bading, 2010) and in axon terminals and astrocyte processes (Conti et al., 1999). Because open NMDA receptors allow potentially excitotoxic Ca^{2+} to enter the dendrite, some researchers have suggested that dendritic spines evolved to compartmentalize calcium ions (Müller & Connor, 1991; Yuste & Denk, 1995; Svoboda et al., 1996; Takechi et al., 1998; Finch & Augustine, 1998). The growth of a new spine can take place within half an hour after excitatory stimulation (Maletic-Savatic et al., 1999; Engert & Bonhoeffer, 1999) and appears to depend on NMDA receptor activity.

Long-Term Potentiation Is Not the Mechanism of Rapid Synaptic Plasticity

§5.6   The traditional understanding of long-term potentiation (LTP) can be understood in terms of a feedback loop. Briefly, the other main ionotropic glutamate binding receptors, namely, the AMPA receptors, permit the local depolarization of the postsynaptic neuron, which clears magnesium ions from blocking nearby NMDA receptors, allowing calcium ion influx, which then triggers secondary cascades within the postsynaptic neuron, enhancing, in turn, AMPA receptor expression (Koester & Sakmann,

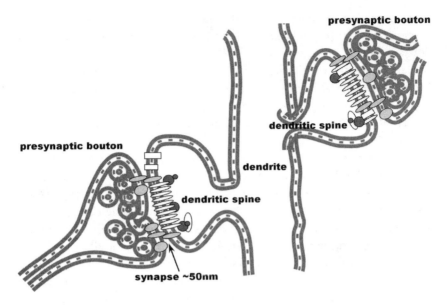

Figure 5.3

A schematic drawing of dendritic spines. Various receptors lie in the pre- and post-synaptic membranes, including NMDA receptors, symbolized here by the white thin ovals. Only glutamatergic synapses occur on ~2μm long dendritic spines. Spines are therefore an indicator of an excitatory synapse.

1998; Malenka & Bear, 2004; Schiller et al., 1998; Yuste & Denk, 1995). Synaptic plasticity via changes in receptor number cannot happen on the scale of a few milliseconds, because it requires signaling from synapses to the nucleus, followed by transcription in the nucleus (Martin et al. 1997a; Miller & Sweatt, 2007; Vecsey et al., 2007). It therefore cannot be the mechanism underlying rapid synaptic resetting that we need to account for mental causation on the millisecond timescale of thoughts. Nonetheless, AMPA and NMDA glutamate receptors and their up-regulation are central to learning. AMPA-expression-mediated LTP can be stimulated artificially with high-frequency stimulation, in the range of 100Hz. This is what one might find in the high-gamma range of inputs of long-range projecting pyramidal cell inputs to other pyramidal cells upon the arrival of bursts. Indeed, in at least some classes of pyramidal cells, LTP at a postsynaptic dendritic spine that has undergone NMDA receptor opening only occurs given that the postsynaptic cell has burst within a specific time window[4] after NMDA receptor opening (Harnett et al., 2009). Other evidence shows that a single presynaptic burst can trigger LTP of a postsynaptic dendritic spine, but only if the burst leads to a dendritically initiated spike that reaches the soma (Remy & Spruston, 2007). In short, postsynaptic bursting enhances LTP (Pike et al., 1999; Wittenberg & Wang, 2006). In contrast, down-regulation of synaptic strength, realized through the mechanisms of long-term depression (LTD), including, especially, down-regulation of AMPA receptor expression, happens optimally when gluta-matergic synapses are given low-frequency input (Bliss & Lomo, 1973; Dudek & Bear, 1992).

§5.7   A positive feedback loop may occur where up-regulation (or down-regulation) of receptor expression increases the likelihood of the conditions that would lead to ever more (or less) receptor expression. If the danger of runaway LTP (or LTD) were not scaled back homeostatically (Davis, 2006; Marder & Goaillard, 2006; Turrigiano, 2008), synapses might suffer from a ceiling (or floor) effect, where postsynaptic neurons could fit no more (or lose all) NMDA or AMPA receptors on a given dendritic spine. Functionally, this could result in the silencing of synapses and whole neurons and the loss of plasticity, learning, or the capacity to process information. Also, glutamate is highly toxic, and too many NMDA receptors would lead to too much calcium ion influx, which could result in cell death. Thus, a constant or periodic process of homeostatic reweighting is required to bring the system back to a baseline far from ceiling or floor, so that long-term plasticity through receptor up- and down-regulation remains possible. Researchers have suggested multiple mechanisms of synaptic weight renormalization (Maffei & Fontanini, 2009; Rich & Wenner, 2007), including changes in connectivity (Nakayama et al., 2005), intrinsic excitability or membrane conductances of pyramidal cells (Desai et al., 1999), presynaptic neurotrans-mitter release, and synaptic depression and potentiation (Royer & Paré, 2003). But the dominant mechanism is likely to be changes in synaptic gain control (Burrone & Murthy, 2003; Pozo & Goda, 2010; Rabinowitch & Segev, 2008; Turrigiano, 2008). If renormalization were a global process, involving down-regulation across all synapses in the brain or even of a single neuron, some synapses might be weighted down to zero even when they had undergone no changes in activity. Even though there is evidence of homeostatic renormalization of weights at the level of whole neurons (Burrone & Murthy, 2003; Goold & Nicoll, 2010; Ibata et al., 2008) and dendrites (Yu & Goda, 2009), synaptic weight renormalization most likely also occurs in each synapse via a local homeostatic process. Indeed, prolonged excitation of a single synapse leads to a reduced number of AMPA receptors in the postsyn-aptic membrane (Hou et al., 2011) in a synapse-specific manner, and pro-longed inhibition of a synapse leads to an increase in AMPA receptor expression and placement in the specific postsynaptic membrane (Béïque et al., 2011; Hou et al., 2008; Lee et al., 2010). How renormalization is orchestrated across levels from single synapses, to dendrites, neurons, and networks of neurons is an open question.

§5.8   In the brain a process of synaptic weight renormalization may occur during slow wave sleep (Tononi & Cirelli, 2003, 2006; cf. Perlmutter & Houghton, 2009); Note that artificially induced AMPA receptor down-regulation (LTD) occurs when input is in the slow-wave domain. Slow-wave sleep renormalization may therefore in part be self-induced LTD, and rapid-eye-movement sleep in part a form of periodic "annealing" to minimize getting stuck in local minima of reweighting as memories are laid down in cortex. On this view, without sleep, the brain could not learn via the synaptic reweighting underlying LTP on a sustained basis (Edelman, 1987). In support of this possibility, researchers have shown that inducing slow wave activity during non-REM sleep enhances memory consolidation (Marshall et al., 2006), and affords ocular dominance plasticity (Frank et al., 2001).

§5.9   While the mechanisms at the molecular level are thought to be homologous in mammals, the majority of molecular work on learning to date has been on animals with much simpler nervous systems, such as *Aplysia*. These sea snails have varieties of short-term (Castellucci et al., 1980) and long-term memory that are realized in different molecular mechanisms, including synaptogenesis and protein synthesis (Bailey et al., 1992; Frey & Morris, 1997; Martin et al., 1997b; Montarolo et al., 1986). Mammals also have short- and long-term memory. Short-term learning on the order of minutes appears to depend on NMDA receptor activity, whereas memories that can last a lifetime appear to be dependent, as in *Aplysia*, on changes in gene expression (Nguyen et al., 1994), protein synthesis (Krug et al., 1984), and synaptogenesis (Maletic-Savatic et al., 1999; Engert & Bonhoeffer, 1999; Moser et al., 1994; Holtmaat & Svoboda, 2009). On the timescale of an hour or so, early-LTD and early-LTP are induced via NMDA receptor-mediated calcium ion influx (Malenka & Bear, 2004). Indeed, Ca^{2+} influx appears to be the key signal that triggers the cascade of postsynaptic intracellular events that lead to both LTP and LTD (Linden, 1999; Sjöström & Nelson, 2002). Brief, massive influx of Ca^{2+} into a dendritic spine under-lies LTP, whereas lower, more sustained amounts of Ca^{2+} influx underlie LTD (Sjöström et al., 2008).[5] Calmodulin responds to LTP- or LTD-inducing calcium signals by triggering the action of certain enzymes (DeMaria et al., 2001; Sjöström & Nelson, 2002; Sjöström et al., 2008; but see also Luu & Malenka, 2008). Low levels of influx associated with LTD activate protein phosphatases (Mulkey et al., 1993), and high levels associated with LTP activate protein kinases (Malinow & Tsien, 1990). These events may lead to the addition or subtraction of AMPA receptors from the postsynaptic membrane via reversible protein phosphorylation (Boehm et al., 2006). Alternatively or additionally, enzyme action may be able to change the number of active NMDA subunits; this may provide a way to rapidly change a synaptic weight without having to change the number of expressed receptors (Lisman, 1985; 1989, 2003; Lisman & Zhabotinsky 2001; Lisman et al., 2002). Beyond about two hours, protein synthesis in the dendrites can occur (Steward & Schuman, 2003), and beyond three hours, protein synthesis in the nucleus strengthens the synapse even more (late-LTP; Frey et al., 1996). Because expression of proteins by the nucleus could affect the entire cell, it has been hypothesized that postsynaptic locations may get tagged (so-called synaptic tagging) so the proteins produced by the nucleus can be delivered where needed (Frey et al., 1996; Frey & Morris, 1997). How synapses communicate the need for protein synthesis to the nucleus rapidly is a matter of debate (Saha & Dudek, 2008). Although feedback mechanisms that change synaptic weights through new protein synthesis or dendritic spine formation are likely to play a central role in learning (Malinow, 1991), and although these mechanisms do depend critically on the timing of presynaptic input (Govindarajan et al., 2011), they are simply too slow to realize the rapid synaptic resetting hypothesized to underlie mental causation. Thoughts do not unfold in minutes or hours; they unfold and trigger one another on a timescale of milliseconds. The physical basis of thoughts must change states at least as fast as thoughts, if they are to realize them.

§5.10   In contrast to long-term synaptic reweighting via protein synthesis and changes in ionotropic glutamate receptor abundance, rapid synaptic resetting might not require renormalization if it is a transient change in gain between presynaptic neurotransmitter input and postsynaptic changes in potential. If rapid synaptic resetting were maintained on a sustained basis, then a process of renormalization would be required for the same reason it is required in the case of Hebbian learning and LTP. However, if rapid synaptic reweighting occurs primarily through NMDA receptor opening, and NMDA receptors close again after the transmission of information via a burst, the synapse returns to baseline automatically as magnesium ions once again block NMDA pores.

Spike Timing-Dependent Plasticity

§5.11   A large body of research and modeling (Abbott & Nelson, 2000; Allen et al., 2003; Bi & Poo, 1998, 2001; Caporale & Dan, 2008; Dan & Poo, 2004, 2006; Jacob et al., 2007; Markram et al., 1997; Meliza & Dan,

2006; Rao & Sejnowski, 2001; Sjöström & Nelson, 2002; Sjöström et al., 2001, 2008; Song et al., 2000; Zhang et al., 1998) has shown that a fast form of long-term potentiation or Hebbian learning (Hebb, 1949) is possible when a single presynaptic spike precedes a single postsynaptic spike by one to a few milliseconds, depending on the type of dendrite and synapse (Abbott & Nelson, 2000; Bi & Poo, 2001). When the opposite is true—when a presynaptic spike follows a postsynaptic spike—LTD ensues (e.g., Bi & Poo, 1998). Such timing-dependent LTP and LTD require NMDA receptor activation (Bi & Poo, 1998; Ganguly et al., 2000). Over time, such spike timing-dependent weight changes could result in the "sculpting" of neural circuits, in which spikes, and the information realized in them, are causal of later spikes and information, from level to level in an information-processing series of stages. Such circuitry allows the encoding and learning of information about external causation in terms of changes in synaptic weights and the ordering of neuronal firing in a network.[6] In a typical experiment (e.g., Bi & Poo, 1998; Markram et al., 1997), a spike is induced presynaptically and postsynaptically in vitro at a fixed temporal offset on a millisecond timescale by injecting a rapid pulse of current. This temporally defined pairing of spikes is repeated a large number of times. After, typically, at least several hundred milliseconds of such "training," the strength of the synapse is inferred by the magnitude of the depolarization in the dendrite following a presynaptic action potential.

§5.12   As important as spike timing-dependent plasticity is, it will not quite be what we are looking for, if many pre- and postsynaptic spike pairings are required to change synaptic weights. The mechanism needed to account for mental causation must not only be rapid, on a millisecond timescale; it must be capable of changing synaptic weights without undue repetition of inputs. The artificial regularity of pre- and postsynaptic depolarization timing accomplished in vitro rarely occurs among neurons *in vivo*, which tend to be highly variable in their timing (Shadlen & Newsome, 1994). Also, the pairing of single pre- and postsynaptic spikes that was the centerpiece of spike timing-dependent plasticity tends to operate less well when neurons burst (Froemke & Dan, 2002; Sjöström et al., 2001; Wang et al., 2005).

§5.13   Ideally, we want to find a mechanism that allows a single spike, coincidence of spikes, burst of spikes, or coincidence of bursts to change synaptic weights without recourse to multiple repetitions or "slow processes" such as enzyme action, transcription, protein synthesis, or receptor addition to the postsynaptic membrane. There is no doubt that there are multiple mechanisms of synaptic plasticity, including these. But what we

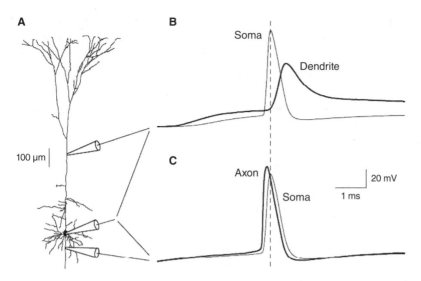

Figure 5.4
Recording of a back-propagating action potential as it passes a recording location going up the apical dendrite column from the axon and soma. Recordings are from (A) a layer-5 pyramidal rat neuron showing (B) somatic and dendritic and (C) somatic and axonal action potential traces triggered by threshold synaptic stimulation. The dashed line indicates the time of the peak of the somatic action potential. Time runs left to right. The axon has been cut off because it could be orders of magnitude longer than the portion of the cell shown here. Reproduced from Stuart et al. (1997) with permission.

are looking for must be even faster than any of these forms of rapid synaptic plasticity. The neuronal criterial causation and rapid synaptic resetting that permits the mental causation of a thought must be at least as fast as the fastest thought that can cause an external or internal action.

The Role of Back-Propagating Action Potentials in Rapid Synaptic Plasticity and Bursting

§5.14   It is now becoming clear that the dominant view of neuronal computation from at least the time of McCulloch and Pitts (1943)[7] until the present day is incomplete. According to the traditional model of neuronal processing, the neuron is the fundamental unit of information processing in the brain and is a feedforward linear classifier. Indeed, neurophysiologists still call neurons "single units." On this view, a neuron "decides" to fire or not on the basis of just one nonlinear operation imposed by the threshold for release of an action potential assessed at the axon hillock; all prior operations up until this nonlinearity arise from analog and linear summation and decay of intracellular potential. In retrospect, this view had to be inadequate to account for certain facts about neurons. For example, the apical dendrites of some pyramidal cells are so far away from the soma that passive summation and propagation of potential would have been insufficient on their own to substantially drive the potential being assessed at the axon hillock above threshold. The traditional view of analog computation followed by a digital output is inadequate because it is now clear that neural computations within dendrites involve numerous linear and nonlinear operations on potential.

§5.15   Depending on the relative locations of excitatory and inhibitory synaptic inputs, dendritic branches can realize Boolean logical operations such as the AND-NOT operation realized in modern computers on the basis of purely passive dendritic mechanisms (Jack et al. 1975; Koch et al., 1983; London & Häusser, 2005; Rall, 1964). If this "Boolean" view of passive dendritic computation is correct, then it is reasonable to view branchpoints on dendrites, where potential from two different branches sums, as the physical realization of a summation over logical gates, allowing a dendritic tree to carry out complex logical operations by summing over simpler ones. Such information processing is entirely dependent on the correct localiza- tion of synaptic inputs and dendritic branchpoints. This gives rise to a seemingly astronomical synaptic addressing problem (Chklovskii et al., 2004; Mehta, 2004; Poirazi & Mel, 2001) that is likely to be solved in part through the "sculpting" of plastic neuronal connectivity by experience such that synchronous inputs are summed within the same dendritic compartments (Takahashi et al., 2012). It is also likely in part solved through genetic programming of connectivity, and in part via the usage of entire genetically preprogrammed modules of many neurons for mul- tiple computational purposes, such as the minicolumn.

§5.16   There are likely to be different units of computation at different levels. A dendritic compartment is a unit at one level, the neuron a unit at a higher level, and microcircuits a unit at an even higher level. A strong case can be made that a fundamental unit of computation in the brain is the 80 to 100 neurons in a minicolumn (Buxhoeveden & Casanova, 2002). There are also hints that modularity is not only spatial, in the sense of having repeated microcircuits, but also temporal, in the sense that certain repeating sequences of neuronal firing within cortical microcircuitry have been observed (Ikegaya et al., 2004; Luczak et al., 2009; Mao et al., 2001). What might be computed by such spatially and temporally defined computational units is not fully understood. Certainly, at a lower level, the temporal integration window of a neuron (imposed by the fact that postsynaptic neurons function as leaky integrators, where EPSPs and IPSPs "leak" back down to baseline) functions as a compartmentalization or quantization of information-processing time. Because all information processing must be realized physically in the brain, it is likely that information-processing modularization in space or time will typically be realized in physical compartmentalization. Conversely, when one finds physical compartmentalizations or encapsulations of processes, such as occur in dendritic spines or branches, or single neurons, or minicolumns, it is useful to wonder what computational modularizations might reasonably be realized in such structures. Likewise, when one finds a temporal quantization in a neuronal process, whether the time constant of the opening of an NMDA channel, the temporal integration window of a pyramidal cell, the duration of a single gamma oscillation cycle or the duration of a single corticothalamocortical loop, one can ask what unit of information processing has been realized. Often information-processing modularizations, though modular, will interact just as modules, such as the heart and lungs, generally interact in complex biological systems. For example, if the temporal quantization introduced by the temporal integration window of pyramidal cells is comparable to the temporal cycling of subthreshold inhibition, as appears to be the case with gamma oscillations introduced by basket cell input, the former can time lock to troughs in the latter, with synchronous ensemble bursting as a potential consequence.

§5.17   On the traditional view of neurons as feedforward linear classifiers, a neuron is an open-loop system that lacks feedback to the dendrites. This traditional feedforward view of neuronal information processing was dominant from the time of the groundbreaking work of Hodgkin and Huxley (1952) until the end of the twentieth century. It became clear that the postsynaptic neuron could influence the presynaptic neuron by feeding retrograde messengers back across the synapse (Abbott & Regehr, 2004; Chavkin, 2000; Fitzsimonds & Poo, 1998; Freund et al., 2003; Kombian et al., 1997; Tao & Poo, 2001; Wilson & Nicoll, 2002). For example, endocannabinoid release triggered by increased levels of calcium or by second messenger systems in the postsynaptic neuron can inhibit presynaptic neurotransmitter release (Kreitzer & Regehr, 2001; Ohno-Shosaku et al., 2001; Wilson & Nicoll, 2001). This gives the postsynaptic neuron the capacity to regulate its neurotransmitter input from presynaptic neurons.

§5.18   Another form of feedback occurs because there are backwardly propagating action potentials (Häusser et al., 1995; Rapp et al., 1996;

Spruston et al., 1995; Stuart & Sakmann, 1995) that proceed from the axon into the soma and dendrites (Stuart et al., 1997),[8] providing feedback to the dendrites that the cell has fired (Häusser et al., 2000), which in turn alter dendritic responses to subsequent synaptic inputs (Euler & Denk 2001, Häusser et al. 2000; Koch & Segev 2000; Linden, 1999; London & Häusser, 2005; Ma & Lowe, 2004; Magee 2000; Magee & Johnston, 1997; Segev & London, 2000; Williams, 2004; Williams & Stuart, 2002, 2003). Dendritic processing can no longer be thought of as passive electrical signaling, and neurons can no longer be thought of as simple feedforward units. Computation also happens inside of neurons, not just within neural networks on the basis of connectivity. Dendritic computation is an exciting area of modeling and research that suggests several mechanisms whereby synaptic weights can be dynamically modified.

§5.19   How could a synaptic weight change dynamically on the order of milliseconds? Ignoring, for now, slower effects of metabotropic receptors, if all ionotropic channels on the postsynaptic membrane were permanently "closed" (or if there were no postsynaptic AMPA receptors), the weight of a synapse would effectively be zero, because no amount of input from a presynaptic neuron would lead to changes in potential within the postsynaptic neuron. However, if presynaptic input or, especially, coincidences of such input could trigger the opening of fast ionotropic channels, the synaptic weight would no longer be zero, since presynaptic inputs would now be able to change the potential within the postsynaptic neuron. Changing the number of such channels or changing the degree to which they, as a group, are open would change the synaptic weight at a given synapse to the degree that they were now open. What possible mechanism could realize such a rapid and dynamic process at the level of a single synapse? Changes in NMDA receptors in the postsynaptic membrane could underlie both dynamic synaptic weight resetting and also the long-term potentiation and depression that is thought to underlie Hebbian learning and memory.

§5.20   Like axonal action potentials, back-propagating action potentials are actively propagated, via voltage-dependent Na^+ channels in the dendrites. Back-propagating action potentials can alter slow dendritic voltage-gated channels, in particular NMDA receptors, which then allow greater depolarization than just prior to the arrival of the back-propagating action potential. The possibility of a feedback loop between depolarization, forward–backward action potential generation, and depolarization is exciting. If the timing of these events is just right, it can function as a "handshake," "resonance," or "coupling" between a neuron and presynaptic neurons whose inputs arrive in synchrony with the arrival of the back-propagating action potential. Such a process would enhance the likelihood of neuronal bursting (Carruth & Magee, 1999; Williams & Stuart, 1999) and presumably the rapid transmission of bursts across a neuronal network. The cessation of a burst would shut the "burst transmission" down in that NMDA receptors would become blocked by magnesium ions, by which point a burst would have passed on to the next level of the information-processing hierarchy.

§5.21   Whether such coupling between the soma and dendritic inputs takes place depends on the timing and spatial localization of dendritic inputs, the time it takes voltage-gated receptors to close (e.g., the time it takes for NMDA receptors to be blocked by magnesium ions upon post-synaptic intracellular hyperpolarization as potential descends to baseline), and the velocity and timing of the arrival of the back-propagating action potential. This in turn depends on dendritic distances, widths, architecture, the distribution of voltage-gated sodium, potassium and calcium channels (Doiron et al., 2002; Mainen, 1999; Mainen & Sejnowski, 1995; Pinsky & Rinzel, 1994; Schaefer et al., 2003; Vetter et al., 2001), dendritic resistances, and the shunting effects of background synaptic activity (Rapp et al., 1996). Because of presumed attenuation of a backwardly propagating action potential, the magnitude of timing-dependent LTP in apical dendrites of pyramidal cells is lower than in proximal dendrites, and the temporal window over which timing-dependent LTD takes place is longer in apical than proximal dendrites (Froemke et al., 2005). This might be influenced by the differential distribution of NMDA and AMPA receptors as well; NMDA receptors are distributed more prevalently on the soma and in proximal dendrites, whereas AMPA receptors are more common in apical dendrites (Dodt et al., 1998). Depending on the timing of the arrival of a backwardly propagating action potential relative to the arrival of presynaptic spikes, apical dendrites might exhibit timing-dependent LTD whereas proximal dendrites might exhibit timing-dependent LTP (Letzkus et al., 2006). Setting up neural processing for the transmission of bursts may in part account for the striking differences in morphology among neurons and among dendrites in particular (cf. Chklovskii, 2004).

§5.22   Dendritic spiking can also operate from the dendrites toward the soma, effectively boosting signals that might otherwise be too weak to affect the generation of action potentials because of distance from the soma. Forward propagating dendritic spikes can be driven by strong, synchronous arrival of presynaptic action potentials (Golding & Spruston, 1998), particularly when there is clustering of voltage-gated channels in the neighborhood of a synapse. A dendritic spike alone may only be able to trigger an action potential if other conditions are also met, amounting to coincidence detection of inputs across different dendrites (Jarsky et al., 2005). Dendritic architecture determines how potential is pooled in segregated sections, whether within spines (Sabatini et al., 2001) or within branches (Polsky et al., 2004), which is the physical basis of a compartmentalized integration of information (Vetter et al., 2001). Dendritic structure, circuitry, and compartmentalizations are plastic: NMDA receptor-mediated circuit remodeling results in dendritic compartmentalization of correlated inputs. This is a dynamic spatial segregation according to the synchrony of local synaptic inputs (Takahashi et al., 2012). Highly branched dendrites, such as those of pyramidal cells, permit the possibility of thresholds for dendritic spikes being assessed at logical and physical branch points that may realize "active" Boolean operations such as AND-OR decisions in an all-or-none fashion before the passage of information up the dendritic decision tree, analogous to the passive Boolean operations suggested by Koch et al. (1983). Forward and backward propagating dendritic spiking gives rise to the possibility of stages of criterial satisfaction entirely within dendrites. The treelike structure of pyramidal cell basal dendrites, for example, could realize a series of criteria placed on potential summed within dendritic arms or compartments, which, if met, would permit information processing to be carried up a hierarchy of decision steps analogous to Boolean logical operations entirely within a single neuron. Ultimately, such a hierarchy of information-processing steps realized in thresholds placed on local potential could result in a "conclusion" that will drive the neuron above its threshold for firing, so that informational conclusions can be passed on to other neurons that take such information as "inputs." In general, all points about criterial causation (and the information processing that is realized in threshold assessments of summed potential) can apply equally well to the intraneuronal level, within dendritic decision trees, as to the interneuronal level of neural networks. Dendritic spiking presumably also occurs because of the assessment of informational criteria that are realized in physical potential being assessed against a physical threshold for spike release.

§5.23   If a backwardly propagating action potential arrives at the same time as glutamate binds with an NMDA receptor, a magnesium ion that normally blocks the channel is "knocked" free,[9] allowing the NMDA channel to open with a greater probability (Kampa et al., 2007). This allows calcium ion influx and an increased likelihood of an action potential in the postsynaptic neuron. An NMDA receptor remains open on the order of one to about five milliseconds (e.g., Howe et al., 1991; Kleckner & Pallotta, 1995). In order to keep it open, a back-propagating action potential would have to arrive within this narrow temporal window of opportunity. Modeling and empirical data suggest that a back-propagating action potential begins reaching the dendrites by one millisecond and peaks within several milliseconds after that, depending on distance from the soma and other factors (Rapp et al., 1996). Since the NMDA receptor only temporarily remains "potentiated" by the arrival of the wave of depolarization from a back-propagating action potential, the synaptic weight resetting will itself be temporary (Stuart et al., 1997). In fact, once depolarization dissipates and potential descends downward toward baseline, a magnesium ion will once again be drawn into the NMDA pore, closing it. This will happen when one of the conditions for NMDA receptor opening is not met, whether the arrival of glutamate, glycine (or D-serine), or postsynaptic depolarization. The NMDA receptor is thus a truly remarkable molecular device for the transmission of information between neurons and the blocking of noninformational input. Because of its functional properties, it suggests that the neuronal code is not only one realized through rapid synaptic resetting or spike rate, but is also one where information is principally carried by bursts and coincident spikes or coincident bursts. In the absence of either bursting or coincidence (synchronous inputs) NMDA receptors will not open with a high probability, and information might not get transferred as readily through an information-processing circuit.

§5.24   On this view, information in the brain, that is, a "signal," is fundamentally carried by neuronal excitation, particularly bursting and spike-rate changes in single neurons, as well as synchronous spiking and bursting among ensembles of neurons. Inhibition is essential for signal enhancement, elimination of excitation that has served its information-processing purposes, and noise and interference reduction. Neuromodulators could dramatically influence how information is processed by changing the balance between excitation and inhibition, or by changing the degree of burst behavior in a neural network. Because the primary cells that trigger excitation of a target cell via NMDA receptor opening are the pyramidal cells that release glutamate at their synapses, their bursting can be seen as a core engine of information realization in the brain, with inhibitory interneurons, neurons that release neuromodulators, glial cells, and other cells playing necessary but supporting or modulatory roles to glutamatergic pyramidal informational operations, transformations, and transfer. The neural correlates of complex informational operations, structures, and states, such as attention, thinking, and consciousness, are therefore likely to be rooted in glutamatergic pyramidal neuronal bursting. At an ensemble level, the signature of these processes will be decorrelation and power in the gamma and especially high-gamma frequency domains rather than slower-frequency domains. Conversely, dysfunction of NMDA receptor mediated bursting should lead to dysfunction of attention, thinking and consciousness. Indeed, there is growing evidence supporting Friston and Frith's (1995) hypothesis that faulty NMDA receptor-mediated neuronal transmission results in functional disconnection of prefrontal executive circuitry (Niswender & Conn, 2010; Roopun et al., 2008; Stephan et al., 2009). This may cause or be caused by faulty "sculpting" of neural circuitry via synaptic pruning (Bullmore et al., 1997; Changeaux & Danchin, 1976; McGlashan & Hofmman, 2000), resulting in the faulty network connectivity found in schizophrenics (Holland & Gallagher, 2004; Lynall et al., 2010; Oh et al., 2009). The psychosis associated with schizophrenia and psychomimetic NMDA receptor antagonists (e.g., phencyclidine or PCP and ketamine; Sharp et al., 2001) in normals may in part be due to faulty NMDA-mediated inhibition of thalamic nuclei by the thalamic reticular nucleus (Ferrarelli & Tononi, 2011).

§5.25 The interplay between back-propagating action potentials and probabilistic atomic events such as magnesium ion displacement from the NMDA channel or magnesium ion reblockage of an NMDA pore may play some role in the possibility that NMDA channels introduce chaotic patterns of bursting into neurons and therefore into neural network behavior (Durstewitz, 2009). Indeed, the duration of an NMDA channel opening and shutting is best modeled as a random process (e.g., Colquhoun & Hawkes, 1981, 1987; Hawkes et al., 1992; Howe et al., 1991; Shelley & Magleby, 2008; but see Liebovitch & Todorov, 1996a,b) taking into account that NMDA receptors can undergo desensitization (Colquhoun & Hawkes, 1995; Lin & Stevens, 1994) and "bursts" of openings (Colquhoun & Hawkes, 1982). NMDA receptors therefore likely play a role in the magnification of microscopic randomness operative at the level of the behavior of a single magnesium ion to the level of spike timing discussed previously (§§4.66, 4.67). It is remarkable that this molecular device can play a role in physically realizing so many of the most fundamental properties of information processing in neuronal circuits: rapid synaptic plasticity, amplification of microscopic randomness to randomness at the level of spike timing in neural circuits, bursting, LTP, and LTD, as well as information-processing via bursting and synchronous bursting. Although a physical mechanism with the properties of NMDA receptors is a necessary condition for the possibility of neuronally realized free will (or of mental causation more generally) in that it permits rapid criterial causation and amplification of randomness at the level of synapses and neurons, NMDA receptors alone are not sufficient.

§5.26   Synaptic resetting could also occur via modulation of the *path* of a back-propagating action potential up the dendritic arbor. The Na$^+$ channels that support back-propagation are low in density. This makes the dendritic action potential susceptible to the influence of synaptic shunting and the particular morphology of the dendritic tree. Inputs onto different dendritic branches could in principle keep the back-propagating action potential from going down certain dendritic arbors while enhancing the likelihood that it will go down others. Dendritic computations could be altered by network inputs that sculpt which branches are "active." This would not necessarily be an all-or-none process, but could be a graded or gain-modulated process that effectively added or decreased resistance to the passage of an action potential up particular dendritic branches. Thus, by exploiting synaptic shunting of potential, the weight of a synapse could be transiently changed by modulating the degree to which it would receive depolarization upon the arrival of an action potential. This would in turn affect the degree to which NMDA receptors can stay open (Kim, Breirlein, & Conors et al., 1995; Rapp et al., 1996).

§5.27   In addition, the danger of failed back-propagation could be countered by strategic placement of dendritic depolarization that could boost the signal (Sjöström & Häusser, 2006). Indeed, dendritic spikes alone could play the role of back-propagating action potentials (Golding et al., 2002) in keeping NMDA receptors open. This mechanism, if it exists, is likely much faster than back-propagating action potentials, so it may not offer optimal timing parameters for keeping NMDA receptors open during bursting. But such a mechanism could change synaptic weights extremely rapidly by opening NMDA receptors in the absence of a postsynaptic spike or subsequent back-propagating action potential. If this initial ultra-rapid synaptic resetting were followed by a barrage of coincident inputs or bursts, the slightly slower resetting afforded by back-propagating action potentials might take over. In this sense, dendritic spiking could serve as an "ignition" that would trigger the "transmission" of presynaptic bursting to postsynaptic bursting. A dendritic spike could trigger the initial NMDA receptor opening that would then evoke a series of bursts in the postsynaptic neuron with accompanying back-propagating action potentials that would keep NMDA receptors open until the burst was fully transmitted from the pre- to postsynaptic cell. Bursts may underlie neuronal information-processing and transfer to a previously unappreciated degree. Indeed, a single burst and dendritic spike can lead to LTP in hippocampal neurons, even without the generation of a postsynaptic somatic action potential (Remy & Spruston, 2007). Burst-based LTP could underlie both single-shot learning and episodic memory.

§5.28   NMDA receptors are not expressed solely in dendritic spines, but also in both excitatory and inhibitory axon terminals and even in distal astrocyte processes (Conti et al., 1999). Presynaptic NMDA channels can acutely enhance the release of glutamate (Bender et al., 2006; Berretta & Jones, 1996; Brasier & Feldman, 2008; Corlew et al., 2007, 2008; Rodríguez-Moreno et al., 2010; Sjöström et al., 2003), and may play a special role in the sculpting of neuronal circuitry via experience during developmental critical periods. During a critical period of early development, special NMDA receptors containing the NR3a subunit are expressed, most likely in the presynaptic axonal bouton, that are not closed by a magnesium ion (Buonanno, 2011; Larsen et al., 2011). This property is not shared by post-synaptic NMDA receptors, which are gated by a magnesium ion, making them coincidence detectors that open and shut acutely as soon as releasing conditions are met or not met, respectively. The presynaptic NR3a subunit NMDA receptors can respond tonically to relatively low levels of presynaptic depolarization, resulting in spontaneous glutamate release. These presynaptic NMDA receptors also afford a kind of spike timing-dependent long-term depression known to occur presynaptically. Once the developmental critical period is over, the tonic variety of NMDA receptor becomes less common and magnesium-gated NMDA receptors are predominantly expressed (Larsen et al., 2011). This mechanism, along with other mechanisms such as apoptosis (cell death) and neural growth factor release, almost surely realizes the sculpting of optimal neuronal circuitry on the basis of experience via Hebbian (LTP) and anti-Hebbian learning (LTD). In the mature brain, presynaptic magnesium-gated NMDA receptors will be coincidence detectors of axonal bouton depolarization and glutamate/glycine binding. This likely makes presynaptic glutamate release in the mature brain not nearly as tonic as in the juvenile brain, but instead primarily acute. This means that glutamate release is not a linear function of axonal bouton depolarization, but is instead highly nonlinear; beyond a certain threshold of depolarization in the axonal bouton, glutamate release will be ballistic and acute. This will generally occur under conditions of the arrival of a burst of presynaptic action potentials.

A Neuronal Burst Code

§5.29   In the adult brain, we see that *the coincidence criteria imposed by pre- and postsynaptic NMDA receptors afford the physical conditions required to have a neuronal code based on transmission of information via bursts of action potentials as informational packets that traverse a neural circuit.* Glutamate will tend to be inordinately released presynaptically with the arrival of a burst; postsynaptically, a burst of action potentials will be released only with the arrival of a burst or large-scale synchronous arrival of input, because only bursts or synchronous inputs are generally capable of triggering the opening of postsynaptic NMDA receptors.

§5.30   Bursts can propagate through a network as units (Lisman, 1997), where burst inputs beget burst outputs that are passed from cell to cell. They drive postsynaptic cells more effectively than an equivalent number of single spikes arriving outside the temporal integration window of a postsynaptic cell (e.g., Rancz et al., 2007), and are thought to carry more information than single spikes (Kepecs & Lisman, 2003). Note, however, that burst propagation may not depend solely on voltage-gated calcium channels in the apical dendrites, or on backwardly projecting action potentials. Basal dendrite computations alone may be sufficient to trigger neuronal bursting. NMDA receptors in the basal dendrites of pyramidal cells play a central role in detecting bursts and then triggering bursts of output to the next stage in an information-processing network (Polsky et al., 2009).

§5.31   The initial spike(s) of a presynaptically arriving burst train or multiple coincident inputs may be sufficient to trigger the opening of postsynaptic NMDA channels via AMPA channel action and subsequent release of blocking Mg^{2+} ions (see fig. 5.5). If this triggers a dendritic spike or somatic action potential and backward action potential that arrives in synchrony with the arrival of presynaptic input (glutamate), NMDA receptors will open or remain open, and back-propagating action potentials might occur until the burst is over. Timing of back-propagating action potential arrival would be important, because a single NMDA channel will only remain open on the order of one to a few milliseconds (e.g., Howe et al., 1991; Kleckner & Pallotta, 1995). After a burst has passed, and a handful of milliseconds has passed without the arrival of a new wave of depolarization from a backwardly traveling action potential, the cell will hyperpolarize back toward its resting potential. NMDA pores will close again as Mg^{2+} ions are drawn back into NMDA channels by the "pull" of the hyperpolarizing postsynaptic intracellular potential. *Thus bursting will trigger information transfer followed by closure of the burst communication channel until the next burst or barrage of coincident inputs arrives.*

§5.32   To open NMDA receptors, it is most advantageous that a spike train start with a burst. Once open, a high but tonic spike rate might suffice to keep the "resonance" of forward and backward waves of depolarization and action potentials going. Therefore, it may not be necessary to have a continual succession of bursts to keep information transfer going, but it appears that initial bursting is essential for getting the nonlinear NMDA-mediated process of burst-mediated information transmission started. An initial burst, as seen upon stimulus onset (and offset) in V1 (Smith & Kohn, 2008), may be followed by a nonbursty tonic series of spikes. A burst code might therefore be inseparable from a more traditional rate code, if increases or decreases in rate are read out more readily when initial bursting triggers the opening of NMDA receptors.

§5.33   It is possible to argue that bursting can occur without changing spike rate. Eight spikes can occur within one second that are evenly spaced or arranged in four bursts of spike pairs (§4.33). But over a short enough time window, an increase in bursting probability will be equivalent to a change in firing rate. For example, over the typical temporal integration window of a pyramidal cell τ, the arrival of a burst of spikes will be tantamount to a substantial increase in rate relative to tonic mode, where subsequent spikes arrive outside τ. Because the postsynaptic neuron functions as a leaky integrator, spikes from a single presynaptic neuron that arrive outside τ will not summate. Thus information carried by bursts may be a special subcategory of information carried by rate, with the advantage that bursts arrive within τ. In real neurons, an increase in burstiness may generally be accompanied by an increase in rate over longer periods, as occurs for purported pyramidal neurons in V4 when attention is allocated to an object in the location of their receptive field (Anderson et al., 2011). Conversely, a postsynaptic pyramidal cell might be "blind" to changes in tonic firing rate of a single presynaptic cell if τ is too brief, because intracellular potential will tend to have descended back to baseline before the arrival of the next spike. However, the probability of postsynaptic spiking would increase with the spike rate of multiple presynaptic neurons all synapsing on the postsynaptic cell, because then the probability of simultaneous EPSPs occurring within τ would increase, especially with synchronous arrival of spikes. Given the brevity of τ, tonic mode firing would seem to require inputs from an ensemble of presynaptic neurons, whereas phasic mode firing could allow, in principle, a small number of presynaptic neurons to drive a single postsynaptic neuron above threshold. Tonic mode may realize a "large ensemble mode" of information processing, whereas phasic mode may realize a "small ensemble mode" of information processing. These may end up being two ends of a spectrum, rather than mutually exclusive circuit states.

§5.34   A burst code affords the possibility of building complex representations like the pattern of Orion (§6.3) on the basis of coincidence detection, at least within τ. A physical mechanism, like NMDA receptors, that functions as a coincidence detector, allows information to be carried by coincidence. This suggests that information transfer among neurons might happen in the form of "burst packets." But the informational content of a burst packet can be thought to change as it passes through a sequence of neurons, unlike, say, TCP/IP packets sent by computers over networks, whose informational content is bound in the structure of the packet itself. Burst packets carry information only to the extent that a decoder existing within a hierarchy of decoding neurons undergoes a bursting episode. Examining a burst in isolation of knowledge of the hierarchy it traverses will tell a neuroscientist nothing about its informational content, because the content cannot be read from the burst, quite unlike a computer information packet. In a physical sense, "a burst is a burst is a burst," regardless of which neuron is bursting. However, different informational conditions are met depending on whether one neuron in an information-processing hierarchy fires or a different neuron fires. For example, returning to a stack model like HMAX (see fig. 4.3), a simple cell will burst if and only if an oriented edge is present at a given location, whereas a "cat detector" will only burst if sufficient cat-defining criteria are met by the stimulus. Even if both cells burst in an identical manner and would be physically indistinguishable otherwise, their burst-releasing conditions differ. The information that an edge or cat is present cannot be thought to reside in the burst itself, or even in an isolated neuron itself, but rather within the physical realization of certain informational criteria being met within a hierarchy of neurons. This physical realization can be seen as the transmission of bursts through the network.[10] For example, let us say that a neuron that fires in response to "cat" is at layer ten of some "stack." Changing the inputs or gain or weights on inputs at any level below this will change the information encoded at every level above it. If feedback is incorporated into the model, changing the inputs (e.g., by changing synaptic weights) at any level will change information encoded at every level. Information therefore is not encoded in single units, neuronal firing rates, or bursts in isolation. Information is encoded in circuits, particularly bursts that traverse a circuit. As noted in §4.63, to think otherwise is like believing that a building's architecture can be decoded from a single brick.[11]

§5.35   What are some advantages of coding information in bursts? Bursts can carry information about input in terms of their timing, number, or duration. For one, bursts can be generated even in the absence of strongly correlated synaptic input (Staff et al., 2000). Although synchronous inputs, and synchrony in general, are potent drivers of postsynaptic depolarization (Tiesinga & Sejnowski, 2004), bursting in a postsynaptic neuron can be generated without them. The key factor that generates bursts is Ca^{2+} influx when NMDA receptors are open. Since this is potently driven by presynaptic bursts, presynaptic bursts can cause postsynaptic bursts. Bursts are therefore a sufficient causal mechanism whereby bursts can propagate through a neural network, potentially realizing at each step a transformation of information. This is not to say that bursting is necessary for information processing in the brain. There are clear examples of tonic firing carrying information, probably in terms of neuronal firing rate, in many if not most neural networks. But phasic neural network behavior may instantiate a certain kind of information processing.

§5.36   Bursts can increase signal-to-noise ratio in information transmission and the probability of signal transmission, particularly for spikes that follow the initial spike of a burst, as long as subsequent spikes arrive within a very narrow time window of under 20ms (Lisman, 1997; see his fig. 3). The first spike of a burst in effect alters the criteria for the depolarization and hence firing of the postsynaptic neuron very rapidly, on the order of the interspike interval in a burst (fig. 5.5). Moreover, bursts in visual cortex carry more information about a visual stimulus than single spikes (Cattaneo et al., 1981; Livingstone et al., 1996). The bursting rate and single-spike rate both increase for a visual neuron in V1, but bursting rate varies with stimulus attributes like orientation (Cattaneo et al., 1981) and spatial frequency (Bonds, 1993), whereas the single-spike rate does not (Lisman, 1997; see his fig. 5B). If bursts encode a particular stimulus attribute, the degree to which that information is present correlates with burst duration (Kepecs & Lisman, 2003) and number (Eyherabide et al., 2009). This suggests that single spikes are noise that needs to be filtered out, presumably by synapses that do not trigger postsynaptic potential changes upon the arrival of a single spike. Similarly, the place-field of hippocampal place cells is more precisely defined on the basis of just bursts than it is on the basis of all spikes (Lisman, 1997; Otto et al., 1991), suggesting that downstream neurons would be able to gain more accurate information about the location of the animal if they only "listened" to bursts. Bursts can also increase the reliability of information transmission at the synaptic level, because their number is robust to noise and burst timing is more precise than that of single spikes (Kepecs & Lisman, 2003). Bursts greatly increase the probability that neurotransmitters will be released into the synaptic cleft from the presynaptic neuron, relative to an equivalent number of spikes occurring at the same average rate but longer interspike intervals (Abbott & Regehr, 2004; Cooper, 2002; O'Donnell & Grace, 1995; Lisman et al., 1998;

Miller & Cohen, 2001; Stevens & Wang, 1995). This will increase the probability that informational signals will propagate through a neural network. Lisman (1997) argues that for some networks in certain states, bursts are the fundamental unit of neuronal information processing. In this case, single spikes can be filtered out because synapses will not trigger postsynaptic changes in potential as a result of isolated presynaptic spikes. This view suggests that single spikes can produce noise that impairs filtering of irrelevant information or that even generates misinformation.

§5.37　Note that information about the stimulus cannot only be carried in a "change-detection code," however, because we are not only sensitive to deviations relative to some baseline, but also absolute levels of stimulus attributes. For example, shifting the baseline relative to which neural activity counts as a change allows a person to see outside in broad daylight, and then, after adjusting the baseline, once that person walks inside (§4.32). But if information were only carried in terms of deviations from a baseline, we could not look at a "ganzfeld" like the sky and know what time of day it was based on the constant level of luminance. In addition to "change detectors," sensory systems need "absolute level detectors." In the visual system, "luxotonic neurons" or "surface neurons" appear to encode absolute levels of luminance in macaques (e.g., Kayama et al., 1979), squirrel monkeys (Bartlett & Doty, 1974) and cats (DeYoe & Bartlett, 1980). Similarly, surface neurons responding to diffuse sustained color have been observed in macaques (von der Heydt et al., 1996, 2003; Zhou et al., 2000). Information encoded in terms of levels and rates of change detection is likely to involve a burst encoding, whereas information encoded in terms of constant levels is less likely to involve burst encoding. Bursting may in effect carry sensory information corresponding to the slope or first derivative of some stimulus attribute (Kepecs & Lisman, 2003). In this sense, bursting may encode information about spatial and temporal discontinuities, at least in the domain of bottom-up sensory processing.

Attentional Binding by Bursting: The Role of Cholinergic Feedback

§5.38　Neuromodulators and neurotransmitters can alter neural excitability and synaptic properties. This can alter the information-processing properties of neurons and neural networks (Berridge & Waterhouse, 2003; Jones, 2008; Robbins, 1997; Steriade & McCarley, 1990). This kind of plasticity need not even occur through rapid or slow synaptic plasticity. There are mechanisms of nonsynaptic plasticity as well (Daoudal & Debanne, 2003; Moore et al., 2009b; Zhang & Linden, 2003). In particular, there are receptors that lie away from the synapse that allow for the regulation of intracellular potential via changes in ligand- and voltage-gated conductances. Extrasynaptic muscarinic acetylcholine receptors are of this class and appear to play an important role in network changes that occur with changes in arousal and attentional allocation (Everitt & Robbins, 1997; Hasselmo, 1995; Sarter et al., 2005). Cholinergic neurons originating in the nucleus basalis of the basal forebrain project widely across cortex (Lehmann et al., 1980). The nonsynaptic "burst plasticity" afforded by the arrival of acetylcholine via these basal forebrain projection neurons is not mediated by AMPA or NMDA receptors, postsynaptic depolarization, dendritic spikes, or backward or forward propagating action potentials. Activation of extrasynaptic muscarinic acetylcholine receptors appears to play a central role in the increased decorrelation (Cohen & Maunsell, 2011; Goard & Dan, 2009) and burstiness that is associated with increases in attention (Anderson et al., 2011; Moore et al., 2009b). In addition, acetylcholine-driven burst enhancement may also play an important role in memory formation, retrieval, and consolidation (Disterhoft et al., 1999; Gold, 2003; Power et al., 2003; §10.88), as well as cortical map reorganization (Kilgard & Merzenich, 1998).

§5.39   Although the effects of acetylcholine are complex and diverse (Hasselmo & Giocomo, 2006), attention may have its effects on local neural circuitry in part via the release of acetylcholine (Furey et al., 2008; Sarter et al., 2005) from cholinergic neurons originating in the basal forebrain nucleus (Everitt & Robbins, 1997) that binds with muscarinic (Herrero et al., 2008) and nicotinic (Disney et al., 2007; Gil et al., 1997) acetylcholine receptors. When such binding occurs, neurons become more excitable (Deco & Thiele, 2009; McCormick & Prince, 1986). Since the majority of muscarinic acetylcholine receptors, at least in V1, lie on inhibitory interneurons (Disney et al., 2006), acetylcholine appears to increase the drive of the inhibitory network that surrounds, synchronizes, and regulates pyramidal cells. This enhancement of the inhibitory network increases gamma oscillations. Via nicotinic receptor activation, acetylcholine also enhances the efficacy of thalamocortical input (Avery et al., 2012; Deco & Thiele, 2011; Disney et al., 2007; Gil et al., 1997). In particular, it improves the reliability of V1 neurons to bottom-up input received from the thalamus (Goard & Dan, 2009). This might account for the decrease in low-frequency power in the deeper layers reported by Fries et al. (2008) as well as the increase in spike-timing decorrelation with attention (Cohen & Maunsell, 2011). Muscarinic acetylcholine receptor activation also reduces glutamate release from excitatory cortical neurons onto other excitatory cortical neurons (Hasselmo & Bower, 1992). Decreasing recurrent excitation may decorrelate pyramidal cell responses, as recently reported (Cohen & Maunsell, 2011; Goard & Dan, 2009), but it would also lower the level of firing within an ensemble, which is difficult to reconcile with the consistent observation that attention leads to increases in firing rates (but see the discussion section of Deco & Thiele, 2011). Muscarinic acetylcholine receptor activation also reduces spike adaptation to a constant input (Hasselmo & Giocomo, 2006), making responses to input more sustained. The probability of burst firing also increases greatly when acetylcholine binds to extrasynaptic muscarinic acetylcholine receptors and glutamate binds to group 1, subtype 1 metabotropic glutamate receptors (mGluR1; see Moore et al., 2009b). Note that this coincidence-detection mechanism appears to be independent of the coincidence-detection mechanism underlying NMDA receptor opening. Given these multiple acetylcholine-mediated effects, attention would enhance the likelihood of signal detection and transmission. It would accomplish this by increasing temporal precision and synchrony of ensemble outputs by enhancing the gamma oscillations of the inhibitory network "clock" (Buzsáki & Chrobak, 1995) and by enhancing bursting in the corresponding pyramidal network. Attention would also increase signal strength by increasing the magnitude of thalamic/sensory input, sustained responses to such input, and the independence of responses to that input, effectively decorrelating output. Assuming that withdrawing attention involves withdrawing acetylcholine release, inattention would exhibit decreased activity of the gamma oscillation "clock," decreased signal throughput from the thalamus, and decreased bursting, but increased correlation among pyramidal cell output.

§5.40   Note that gamma oscillations can be evoked in in vitro hippocampal slices by applying agonists of metabotropic glutamate receptors (Whittington et al., 1995), muscarinic acetylcholine receptors (Fellous & Sejnowski, 2000; Fisahn et al., 1998), and kainate receptors (Fisahn et al., 2004; Hájos et al., 2000). Gamma oscillations arising from all three types of receptor activation are blocked by GABA type A receptor antagonists, revealing that fast inhibition, presumably by basket cells, is necessary for gamma oscillations to occur. Gamma oscillations arising from muscarinic acetylcholine receptor activation require the simultaneous activation of AMPA receptors. This proves that gamma oscillations arising from metabotropic glutamate (Whittington et al., 1995) or kainate receptor (Fisahn et al., 2004) activation depend entirely on fast inhibition, presumably by basket cells. In contrast, gamma oscillations that arise from muscarinic acetylcholine receptors require both this fast inhibition and the rapid excitation afforded by AMPA receptors (Fisahn et al., 1998; Mann et al., 2005a). Bartos et al. (2007) hypothesize that this difference arises because metabotropic glutamate and kainate receptors are activated directly on inhibitory interneurons that generate gamma oscillations, whereas muscarinic acetylcholine receptors are found primarily on pyramidal neurons, which must spike in order to activate the interneurons that generate gamma oscillations. Similar mechanisms of gamma oscillation generation appear to operate in the cortex (Buhl et al., 1998; Cunningham et al., 2004).

§5.41   Interestingly, glutamate release, in the absence of acetylcholine release, decreases the probability of bursting via the action of group 1, subtype 5 metabotropic glutamate receptors (mGluR5). When acetylcholine is released, the up-regulation in bursting dominates, but in its absence, the down-regulation dominates. This suggests not only a mechanism for attentional enhancement of active information-processing via acetylcholine and glutamate coincidence detection in the corresponding neuronal circuits, but also a mechanism for attentional ignoring via burst down-regulation in other active circuits whose information processing is not attended.

§5.42   Increases in cortical alertness are associated with so-called cortical UP states where bursting is more prevalent. During the UP state the postsynaptic neuron receives barrages of input; some barrages are dominated by inhibitory input and others by excitatory input that depolarizes the cell (Hasenstaub et al., 2005). Inhibitory inputs during such barrages are more correlated across neighboring neurons than excitatory inputs, suggesting that the inhibitory inputs operate across a local network (Hasenstaub et al., 2005). Cortical (Battaglia et al., 2004) and subcortical (nucleus accumbens: Lape & Dani, 2004) UP states can be triggered by hippocampal "sharp wave" bursts that provide synaptic inputs that "turn on" the UP state. Artificially inducing a cortical neuron to burst at high-frequency can also cause a switch in global brain state (Li et al., 2009). Cortical UP states might continue via recurrent excitation within local neuronal circuitry, if excitation were not inhibited. Because bursting might lose its information-processing function, as in epilepsy, if not inhibited after that function has been performed, inhibition and not just excitation must enter an UP state as well. GABAergic interneurons are therefore essential for controlling the extent and timing of excitation traversing the network (Sanchez-Vives & McCormick, 2000; Shu et al., 2003b). For example, acetylcholine release associated with changes in alertness may increase the burstiness not only of excitatory neurons, but also of inhibitory interneurons. In particular, acetylcholine bound to muscarinic receptors appears to increase the bursting behavior of inhibitory interneurons that generate inhibitory perisomatic postsynaptic currents (Nagode et al., 2011). Different GABA receptor types appear to inhibit bursting and transition a circuit from an UP into a DOWN (quiescent) state where there is much less synaptic input and the membrane potential is relatively hyperpolarized (Cowan & Wilson, 1994; Mann et al., 2009; Shu et al., 2003a,b; Steriade et al., 1993b, 2001). Power in the gamma frequency domain requires NMDA receptor activation in parvalbumin-expressing (presumably fast-spiking, soma-inhibiting) interneurons just as it does in pyramidal cells; Knockout mice that lack NMDA receptors only in these interneurons display enhanced gamma frequency power in cortex, perhaps because of reduced inhibition of pyramidal cell bursting; Such mice display deficits in habituation, working memory tasks, and associative learning (Carlén et al., 2012).

§5.43   The increase in gamma oscillations with attention rooted in the activity of parvalbumin-binding, fast-spiking basket cells must be related to the tendency of pyramidal cells to burst because of attention. The exact causal relationships between pyramidal bursting and the gamma oscillation "clock" (Buzsáki & Chrobak, 1995) set up by the background inhibitory network acting on pyramidal cells is not fully understood. Fast-spiking interneurons generate an average of 1.2 action potentials per gamma cycle and are phase-locked to the gamma oscillations (Gloveli et al., 2005; see also Hájos et al., 2004; Penttonen et al., 1998). Pyramidal cells, in contrast, fire less frequently. If gamma oscillations arise from inhibitory inputs to pyramidal cells, the probability of bursting would be higher in troughs than peaks, and vice versa, if gamma oscillations arose from excitatory input. In fact, Ray and Maunsell (2011) find that high-gamma-frequency power and firing rates increase in the troughs of the gamma rhythm (see their figs. 5 and 8D,E). This is consistent with the view that gamma oscillations reflect ongoing inhibitory inputs into pyramidal cells from the inhibitory interneurons around them, whereas high-gamma-frequency power may reflect bursting.[12] Future data and modeling will hopefully explain why bursts should be comprised of two to five spikes in succession followed by a burst-free period. One possibility is that attention modulates the temporal integration properties of synapses from a dominantly depressive to a dominantly facilitatory mode (cf. Abbott & Regehr, 2004). Another possibility is that bursts themselves alter synaptic properties, such that they are momentarily depressive following successful neurotransmitter release. Lisman (1997) presented data (see fig. 5.5a,b) that the probability of neurotransmitter release is very high for a second spike of a burst when the initial spike of the burst did not lead to neurotransmitter release, but when it did, there was a ~20ms refractory period during which neurotransmitter release was low. This, combined with gamma-oscillations imposed by inhibitory interneurons, would serve to stagger bursts. Note that the "burst refractory period" appears to be approximately the same duration as one gamma cycle. Future research and modeling will hopefully clarify how exactly attentional input to a circuit increases gamma oscillations, presumably by modifying the properties of the background inhibitory interneuron network, while increasing the probability of bursting in pyramidal cells.

§5.44 Attention-induced increases in burstiness and decorrelation among spikes may be accomplished through the physical mechanism of coincident glutamate and acetylcholine release discussed above. If so, one possibility is that cholinergic projection fibers from the basal forebrain deliver acetylcholine to local circuitry as far away as retinotopic cortex. Another possibility is that cholinergic inputs trigger phasic neural activity at locations on a "master map of locations" (Treisman & Gelade, 1980; Treisman, 1996) perhaps realized in a posterior parietal saliency map (Treue, 2003), which then triggers phasic activity in target neurons in, say, V4, and other target regions. In support of the latter possibility, attentional processing of discrete stimuli, including learning that depends on attention, such as trace conditioning (McAlonan et al., 1995), is damaged by removing cholinergic inputs to posterior parietal cortex (Baxter et al., 1999; Bucci et al., 1998; Voytko et al., 1994) while sparing spatial learning (Baxter et al., 1995) and spatial working memory (Chappell et al., 1998). Cholinergic projections from the nucleus basalis to the frontal lobes appear to play a role in vigilance and divided attention (Everitt & Robbins, 1997; Voytko, 1996; McGaughy et al., 1999; Muir et al., 1994). In general, loss of cortical cholinergic inputs from the basal forebrain results in a decreased ability to detect signals in tasks that require attention, so the "hit rate" goes down (Burk & Sarter, 2001; Pang et al., 1993).

Attentional Binding by Bursting: The Role of Noncholinergic Feedback

§5.45 The basal forebrain also contains noncholinergic neurons (Lau & Salzman, 2008; Lin & Nicolelis, 2008). Even though the role of the basal forebrain in attention and memory is traditionally regarded as arising from the activity of cholinergic neurons that project to cortex (Everitt & Robbins, 1997; Wenk, 1997), the majority of basal forebrain neurons that project to cortex are noncholinergic. Most of these are GABAergic, although a minority of them are glutamatergic (Gritti et al., 1997; Sarter & Bruno, 2002).

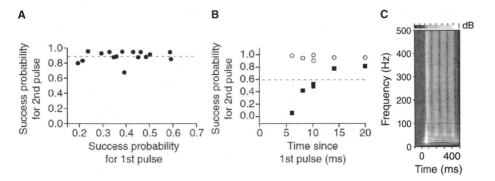

Figure 5.5
Bursts reset synapses within milliseconds and greatly increase the fidelity of information transmission. A, B: reproduced from Lisman (1997; figure 3A,B; adapted by Lisman from Stevens & Wang, 1995) with permission; data from single hippocampal CA1 synapses. (A) The initial spike of a burst had varying neurotransmitter release probabilities, as shown on the x-axis. If the second spike of a burst occurred within 20ms of the first, its release probability was uniformly very high for cases where the first spike had not released neurotransmitter (black disks). (B) However, if the first spike led to release, then the second spike initially had a near-zero probability of release, which had recovered by ~20ms (solid squares). White disks refer to the probability of neurotransmitter release following the second spike of a burst if there was no neurotransmitter released following the first spike of the same burst. (C) Correlation between firing rate and LFP power across frequency bands in a single monkey at 19 locations in V1 when a sinusoidal grating was presented with a counterphasing temporal frequency of 5 Hz. For this and several other temporal frequencies of the stimulus, the firing rate followed the contrast profile of the stimulus, resulting in firing increases at twice the temporal frequency of the counterphasing grating, noticeable as vertical bands every 100ms in this case. Notice that high-gamma LFP power (above 100 Hz) tracked the stimulus-driven changes in firing rate. Ray and Maunsell (2011) find that "high-gamma activity is tightly correlated with the firing rates of neurons near the microelectrode." The authors do not conclude that this is due to an increase in the probability of bursting at peaks in firing rate that follow the contrast modulation of the stimulus, but their data are consistent with this possibility (see n. 12). Reproduced in grayscale from Ray and Maunsell (2011, their figure 5B), with permission.

The GABAergic type innervates GABAergic cortical interneurons, offering the possibility of activating cortex rapidly via disinhibition (Freund & Meskenaite, 1992). This disinhibition is accomplished by inhibiting local inhibitory interneurons (Lin et al., 2006). Inhibition of local inhibition is also consistent with the rate increases and correlation decreases seen in putative pyramidal cells with attentional allocation (Cohen & Maunsell, 2011). Such disinhibition could also change the level or balance of "background" synaptic input to neurons; this has been proposed as a gain control mechanism that modulates neuronal responsiveness to excitatory driving inputs (Chance et al., 2002; Abbott & Chance, 2005). The sources of background synaptic input could be local or long-range (Bastian, 1986; Koch & Ullman, 1985; Hupé et al., 1998; Przybyszewski et al., 2000), but the local balanced excitatory and inhibitory circuitry that presumably exists in cortex (Shadlen & Newsome, 1994; Troyer & Miller, 1997) could serve as a source of the divisive response normalization thought to play a role in attention (Carandini & Heeger, 2012; Chance et al., 2002; Heeger, 1992; Reynolds & Heeger, 2009). In any case, a great deal remains to be clarified concerning the relationship of cholinergic to noncholinergic feedback in realizing attentional modulation of local circuit function. It appears that noncholinergic feedback inhibits local inhibition, whereas cholinergic feedback increases the gamma oscillatory input into postsynaptic pyramidal cells. Could these two processes function in opposition, one as the brakes and the other as the accelerator on local inhibitory circuitry? Do they feed into different cortical layers? Future research will have to answer these questions.

§5.46 Damaging GABAergic basal forebrain cells selectively leads to an increase in false alarms ("detecting" a signal when there was none), perhaps because of a decreased ability to switch rules required for signal-present and signal-absent trials. This may be because these neurons play a role in modulating executive attentional functions (Burk & Sarter, 2001). In particular, certain noncholinergic basal forebrain neurons appear to enhance prefrontal processing by engaging in ensemble bursting, mainly during the awake state, which triggers brief (~200ms) increases in gamma frequency power in the prefrontal cortex, perhaps because prefrontal neurons in turn burst (Lin et al., 2006). This is consistent with other findings that gamma oscillations transiently increase in frontal cortex with attentional allocation (Engel et al., 2001; Ward, 2003).

§5.47 This ensemble bursting among basal forebrain noncholinergic cells is indicative of the motivational salience of a stimulus in a valence-independent manner. Bursting in these cells also improves signal detection, and is a reasonable candidate for a neuronal realization of top-down attention (Lin & Nicolelis, 2008) that disinhibits target cortical pyramidal cells and changes their gain. It is possible that the bursting behavior of noncholinergic basal forebrain neurons not only triggers a transition to bursting in the prefrontal cortex, but in cortical target areas in general. It must still be determined what input drives noncholinergic basal forebrain neurons to burst, and how they acquire the information needed to address burst outputs to appropriate cortex. Presumably, higher-level frontal-parietal executive or eye movement programming areas are driving the basal forebrain.

§5.48   In sum, there is evidence that basal forebrain noncholinergic neuronal bursting may realize top-down attentional modulation of pyramidal cells' behavior. In particular, it may switch pyramidal cell networks from tonic to phasic mode via basal forebrain neurons' inhibition of local inhibitory interneurons. Another possibility is that top-down attention alters the dynamics of the local inhibitory network so that it becomes synchronized, which would increase gamma oscillations in that circuit even prior to bottom-up input and presumably play some role in placing the entire network of inhibitory and excitatory cells in an UP state. A network in an UP state may in turn respond more burstily to bottom-up input. In either case, whether bursty firing is triggered directly by top-down attention or only increases the likelihood of bursts to bottom-up input, a shift to bursting mode would provide a common mechanism underlying the attentional aspects of gain control, normalization, decorrelation, and, of course, bursting. If this view is correct, then attention in its various positive capacities (attentional binding, tracking, selection, increased sensitivity) may be realized in the transitioning of the target cortical circuit from a tonic into a bursting mode mediated by NMDA receptor opening with concomitant increases in firing rate. Meanwhile, attention's negative aspect, ignoring, could be realized in the suppression of bursting and decreases in firing rate.

§5.49   *Attentional binding, then, may be realized in the transitioning of information processing into a phasic mode of information transmission across an information-processing hierarchy* (§4.53). Attentional binding would not be the "gluing" of features together at a location (cf. Treisman & Gelade, 1980); it would instead be the execution of the entire hierarchy of visual processing within the attended figure or location. Within an attended figure, binding by bursting among the entire hierarchy of neurons that make up a circuit would lead to more extensive information processing than carried out by the same circuit in tonic mode. Presumably, neurons processing input from outside the attended figure would remain in tonic mode. Note that for binding by bursting to work, it would not be necessary for attention to be allocated to every level of an information-processing hierarchy. It would suffice for attention to shift the attended portion of one level of the hierarchy, say, V4, from tonic into phasic mode. This could in turn trigger phasic firing in earlier and later levels of the hierarchy through feedback and feedforward connections to retinotopically corresponding regions of lower and higher levels. Indeed, there is evidence that attention-induced increases of firing rates in V4 are stronger than in V2 or V1, and have a shorter latency (Buffalo et al., 2010), suggesting that attention operates via just such feedback connections.

§5.50 Bursting could accomplish selection if triggered only in the circuitry corresponding to that which is selected (cf. Desimone & Duncan, 1995; Börgers & Kopell, 2008). It would enhance the signal-to-noise ratio and more effectively drive downstream neurons than tonic firing (Salinas & Sejnowski, 2001). It would increase firing rates (Hayden & Gallant, 2005; Maunsell & McAdams, 2001; Moran & Desimone, 1985; Reynolds et al., 2000; Treue, 2001), decrease variance and noise correlation (Cohen & Maunsell, 2009, 2011; Mitchell et al., 2007, 2009), enhance gamma-frequency power via the synchronous synaptic inputs of basket cells to pyramidal cells, and increase synchrony of firing if bursts are synchronous. In particular, the firing rate of a given neuron in, say, V4 or MT should be modulated more if the stimulus in the cell's receptive field matches its tuning properties than if it does not. This multiplicative or "tuned normalization" view of attention follows because making a neuron respond more to stimuli to which it already responds should not make it respond more to stimuli to which it does not respond (multiplying 0 by a higher scalar still results in 0). Attentional enhancement of responses to stimuli that drive a neuron also explains why, if a preferred and nonpreferred stimulus both lie in a neuron's receptive field, the cell responds more when attention is directed to the preferred than to the nonpreferred stimulus (Ni et al., 2012). It will also account for changes in the shape of receptive fields; even if an inferotemporal neuron with a large receptive field only receives input that can drive it from V4 neurons that have switched from tonic to phasic firing, attention to a location would effectively reduce the size of the inferotemporal receptive field to the size of the attended location. This would account for findings that inferotemporal neurons respond as if only the attended object were in its receptive field (Moran & Desimone, 1985; see also Chelazzi et al., 1993; Desimone & Duncan, 1995; Reynolds et al., 1999; Sheinberg & Logothetis, 2001). This is depicted schematically in figure 5.6. This effect would be enhanced if unattended regions experience burst suppression or an increase in the ratio of tonic to phasic behavior, perhaps via the mechanism discussed in §5.41. Note that Goard and Dan

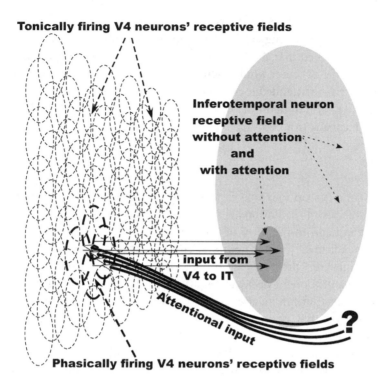

Figure 5.6

Attentional alteration of downstream receptive fields. A schematic drawing of how attention could effectively "shrink" the full hemifield size of the receptive field of an inferotemporal temporal (IT) neuron (i.e. its size in the absence of attention to a particular location, represented by the large, light gray circle on the right) to the size of the attended region (small, dark gray circle on the right), by shifting only a small subset of neurons in V4 with receptive fields in the hemifield (all disks on the left) into bursting mode (the darkened disks) via input from basal forebrain neurons or elsewhere. Because an inferotemporal neuron only responds to its inputs, and its inputs are determined in part by the subset of V4 neurons that fire phasically, the inferotemporal neuron effectively has a smaller receptive field.

(2009) noticed increased decorrelation in V1 when they stimulated presumed cholinergic projecting cells in the nucleus basalis of the basal forebrain, but also noticed that the burstiness of LGN cells decreased. On the present view, tonic behavior would increase outside the retinotopic region corresponding to the attended location (or the region receiving acetylcholine from basal forebrain neurons) in V1, and presumably also in the LGN, perhaps via feedback from cortex.

Conclusion

§5.51   NMDA receptors may play at least four important roles in the neuronal basis of mental causation: (1) they introduce randomness to the macroscopic domain in the form of spike-timing uncertainty, which may then meet or not meet present neuronal criteria; (2) they may play some role in an "annealing" process that minimizes the chances of getting stuck in local minima of thought or behavior, affording the generation of many possible solutions that can meet a set of criteria; (3) they may realize rapid synaptic resetting that permits neurons to escape the impossibility of self-causation by changing the criteria for firing of neurons on the next information-processing cycle; and (4) they transition neural network behavior into a bursting mode that allows for the transfer of bursts as informational packets across a network, which, I argue, is the neural basis of attentional binding. Criterial causation occurs in that the first part of a burst train (or a burst followed by an increased tonic firing rate) can rapidly recode the gain or weight of a synapse. Rapid synaptic resetting occurs via the coincidence detection built into NMDA receptors. Bursts trigger the opening of NMDA receptors. Presynaptically, bursts increase the amount of glutamate released by the presynaptic axonal bouton. Postsynaptically, bursts trigger massive depolarization in postsynaptic dendritic spines. Spikes and bursts of spikes that arrive after this rapid criterial recoding can then meet the rapidly reset criteria. Criterial causation may therefore operate on the millisecond timescale of thoughts by rapid synaptic resetting and transmission of information via "burst packets." Volition is closely tied to endogenous attention, which is in part realized in an enhancement of bursting in corresponding neural circuitry via neuromodulators that shift the circuit into bursting mode. This attentional mode allows the circuit to process information coherently; as bursts traverse an attended circuit, the information realized in that circuit is realized across the entire hierarchy.

6 Mental Causation as an Instance of Criterial Causation

§6.1   In chapters 6 and 7 I address some philosophical points concerning criterial causation. Chapter 6 looks more deeply into the nature of causation realized in neurons. Chapter 7 looks specifically at the question of free will. Chapter 8 examines psychological issues of representation raised by criterial encoding. Those primarily interested in the neuroscience of free will could skip to chapter 9 at this point. Those interested in the present chapter's deeper discussion of causation would benefit from reading appendix 1 at this point, and then returning here. In appendix 1, I provide an overview of different conceptions of causation, arguing that causation was initially conceived to be a transfer of energy. Later notions of causation emphasized how energy is transformed. Criterial causation emphasizes not how energy is transferred or transformed into a different state, but how *patterns* of energy, such as coincidence, are transmitted and transformed. As we saw in chapter 5, this is made possible by highly specialized coincidence detectors operating at the molecular level. Because patterns can be created and destroyed, unlike the physical substrate in which they are realized, patterns are not subject to the same physical laws that constrain amounts of energy. This permits the emergence of higher-level types of causation that exist over a succession of patterns.

Criterial Causation and the Detection of Patterns in Input

§6.2   The claim I develop here is that mental processing accomplishes a downward and nonepiphenomenal causation, where mental events (realized in some neurons' criteria for firing having been met) occur only if elementary particles realize a particular subset of the possible paths open to them. This subset is the subset that embodies not only a physical causal chain of events, but also an informational causal chain of events. Other possible paths that are open to elementary particles which do not also realize an informational causal chain are in essence "deselected" by neurons by virtue of the failure of those paths to meet physical/informational criteria for the release of an action potential. All informational causal chains are also physical causal chains. But the vast majority of physical causal chains in nature are not informational causal chains. What makes some physical causal chains also informational causal chains is that the physically realized criteria for some physical event happening, such as the firing of a neuron, are met only when certain informational criteria are also met. For example, a neuron, thought of solely as a physical device, integrates potential within a temporal integration window. If summed excitatory postsynaptic potentials pass the threshold for firing, the neuron fires. But if inputs to this neuron are such that action potentials sufficient to make it fire only arrive from presynaptic neurons when some informational conditions are met, then this neuron realizes informational criteria by virtue of imposing physical criteria for firing upon its physical inputs. This information is used by a physical organism to do useful things such as find food and mates and avoid dangers.

§6.3   Criterial decoders allow for the emergence of physically realized informational causal chains that are not just physical causal chains (although they are that), but also, in the case of the brain, mental causal chains. What makes one outcome occur rather than others is that certain informational criteria were met in decoders that then triggered consequences that would have differed had these informational criteria not been met. Individual elementary particles are of course "oblivious" to anything about information. They are just mindless, informationless units of energy. Information can lie in a global spatiotemporal configuration or pattern of particles, and, importantly, such a pattern is not itself a particle or collection of particles with material attributes like mass. A pattern is not itself made of energy in addition to the particles in which it is realized. For example, a postsynaptic neuron may only fire if its presynaptic inputs arrive simultaneously. That simultaneity is a temporal relationship among particles, but that temporal pattern is not itself made up of particles in addition to the constituent particles that arrive simultaneously. Similarly, if there are multiple particles they will have a spatial configuration, but that configuration is not itself made up of particles in addition to the constituent particles. Both spatial and temporal patterns of particles are not themselves made of particles beyond their constituting particles (§6.12). A pattern may not even objectively exist in the world, much as a constellation that we see in the sky does not really exist in the universe, although, of course, the individual stars do. The pattern of the constellation Orion, for example, exists only contingently because of the placement of the Earth, and has no objective existence as a real physical object in the world made of energy in addition to that emitted by its constituent suns. Because a pattern of particles, or a pattern of neuronal inputs, lacks mass as such, a pattern of energetic inputs can only have causal efficacy above and beyond the traditional causal modes of energy transfer and transformation (see appendix 1) if there is a criterial detector that responds to that pattern. However, the fact that we can recognize Orion means that we must have a decoder that responds (i.e., some population of neurons presumably fires) if and only if a set of criteria concerning Orion-like spatial relationships among component inputs is satisfied.

§6.4   How might such a decoder be wired up neuronally? Presumably, there are neuronal Orion-pattern detectors that take input from lower-level neurons that fire when there are objects in particular locations at the same time. An Orion-pattern coincidence detector would take input from such lower-level neurons and would only fire when certain relationships among inputs are met. The criteria realized in such a neuronal Orion-decoder would be realized in the particular inputs it gets from lower level neuronal decoders. The neuron itself need not "know" anything about Orion, and the criteria need not be stated anywhere as a rule or if-then statement (§8.1). The criteria might emerge from the particular pattern of neuronal inputs to this Orion-pattern-detecting neuron. Given the particular neurons that send axonal inputs to it, and given its threshold for firing and temporal integration window, it will only fire when the pattern of Orion is present. In this way, a neuron that carries no information when isolated in a Petri dish realizes information when connected to a particular set of input neurons and output neurons. When this neuron fires, the criteria for the pattern of Orion being present have been met, and the information that this Orion-like pattern is present is realized. Note that the criteria for the firing of such an Orion-pattern-decoder might not require much more than a certain set of spatial and temporal relationships in input. If a collection of dots of light, or lemons or inkspots of various sizes, shares these spatial proportions and ratios, this neuron will fire, and the information that there is an Orion pattern present will be realized. That is, such a criterial pattern detector will respond equivalently to countless inputs, and thus will be invariant to differences in those inputs, as depicted in figure 6.1.

§6.5   Vastly different physical patterns or inputs may realize the same information in that they all satisfy the same informational criteria. Indeed, they may have nothing else in common other than that they satisfy the same criteria. To physically realize certain information in the brain just

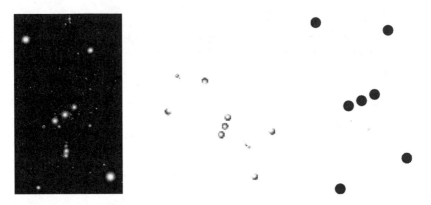

Figure 6.1
Various patterns that meet the same criteria. Many types of input would be sufficient
to meet the configurational criteria imposed by an Orion-pattern detector.

means to meet or be capable of meeting certain physically realized criteria
for the release of neuronal activity. For example, a simple Orion-pattern
detector could be wired up much like a simple cell (see fig. 4.2), on the
basis of coincident inputs from lower-level cells that indicate that something is present at locations consistent with the spatial layout of Orion.
Making it size and orientation invariant would require the encoding of
relationships among such inputs. As far as the Orion-detecting cell is concerned, the different examples of inputs that have the Orion-like spatial
relationships shown in figure 6.1 are all exemplars of "that which activates
this cell in an equivalent manner." The equivalence class of all inputs to
which that neuron responds is the set of inputs that meet the neuron's
criteria for firing. It is the set of all inputs that carry the information "the
Orion pattern is present." The informational criteria are that certain coincident spatial relationships must be present before the neuron will fire.
This will be the class of things that has a spatial set of relationships that
are Orion-like.

§6.6   Such spatial pattern detection would have a temporal component
in the minimal sense that all relevant inputs would have to arrive within
the temporal integration window of the Orion-pattern detector. But more
explicit temporal criteria on inputs could be set by a neuron. For example,
the criteria might be that a certain temporal pattern of input must arrive
over some duration, or else the neuron does not fire. (In fact, there is little
evidence that neurons obey a temporal pattern code; rather, rate, coincidence, and burst coding seem paramount. But to emphasize just how
flexible and general criterial causation can be, one could imagine that some

neurons do exhibit pattern coding.) This hypothetical criterial decoder might respond to the temporal pattern of input "dun—dun-dun-dun-dun––dun-dun," and do so whether that pattern arrives over 200ms or 2,000ms. Of course, even if no such decoder exists, one could be designed that physically realized these criteria for responding. A physically realized criterial decoder could be designed that responds to a temporal pattern of a certain ratio. It would respond in the same manner to many patterns of input so long as they have these ratios, just as we can recognize a melody played at many tempos or in different keys. This pattern, though physically realized, is not itself material. In fact, a pattern that plays out over time does not even exist at a given moment, and so is not itself realized in a particular configuration of energy that exists at any given moment. Such a pattern could even play out over very long durations and would require only that a detector of such a temporal pattern have a physically realized memory store, since, obviously, a pattern that does not exist at an instant cannot be recognized or matched until after some duration has passed. This temporal pattern of physical input would be information for the temporal-pattern-detecting neuron, and this neuron would realize the information that this temporal pattern has occurred, once it fires.

§6.7   Regardless of the informational decoding scheme used to realize information, whether based on temporal pattern, firing rate, coincidence detection, burst encoding, population pattern, pattern of neuronal connectivity as in a simple cell, or some other yet-to-be-discovered neuronal code, a neuron's criteria must be met before triggering activity in the next level up the hierarchy of the network. A neuron's output can trigger a cascade of neuronal activity, magnifying in an instant the amount of information realized in the physical system of the brain. Again, this rapid increase or decrease of information can occur without violating the first or second laws of thermodynamics,[1] which apply to energy, not the information realized in that energy.[2] Moreover, the criteria set by each stage within such a hierarchy of decoders can become more complex, leading to higher and higher levels of informational criteria satisfaction.

Criterial Causation: Multiple Realizability Is Not Enough

§6.8   The essence of criterial causality is a many-to-one mapping[3] between input and output: All criterial decoders effectively lump together many kinds of physical input as indistinguishable insofar as they trigger a common output. All criterial causal chains have this aspect of multiple realizability of input that can trigger a released output, such as an action potential. Note that while criterial causation instantiates multiple realizability, not all instances of multiple realizability in physical systems exhibit criterial causation. This is because criterial causation requires that some output be released upon criterial satisfaction, typically to subsequent stages in a net of criterial decoders. Certainly, some physical systems do exhibit multiple realizability and an indifference to microphysical differences in their evolution, such as exhibited in the evolution of dynamical systems toward the attractor states of condensed matter, chaos, or quantum field theories. But these systems lack output upon criterial satisfaction, and are certainly not processing information or recoding criteria for future output of other physical systems. They therefore do not exhibit criterial causation. Another difference between criterial causation and nonbiological physical systems that exhibit multiple realizability and an indifference to microphysical differences is the fact that neurons place dynamic thresholds for criterial satisfaction on their input before output is released. Moreover, criterial decoders do not function as attractor states toward which input–output mappings inevitably proceed. Indeed, in principle, decades might go by without some neuronal criteria for firing being met, as might occur in certain "recognition neurons" when one meets and recognizes a long-lost childhood friend in middle age.

§6.9 Criterial causality comes in both uninteresting token-level and interesting type-level versions. An example of token-level criterial causation is any basic chemical reaction where two or more reactants (e.g., $2H_2$ and O_2) interact and undergo a chemical change, leading to a product chemical (e.g., $2H_2O$) that typically has different properties than the reactants.[4] Such reactions are criterial in the very limited sense that token molecules or atoms or particles of a given type are fungible or interchangeable. This is uninteresting because such reactions generally involve a one-to-one mapping between types of inputs and types of outputs, even if there is fungibility at the token level of particular molecules or atoms. For example, combining $2H_2$ and X_2 will only result in water if X is oxygen. There is no fungibility at the level of type of element in the equation $2H_2 + X_2 \rightarrow 2H_2O$, even if there is fungibility at the level of token atoms.[5] Of sole interest here are cases of criterial causality where numerous different *types* of input lead to one *type* of output. For example, there is a many-to-one type mapping when numerous types of inputs, such as shown in figure 6.1, can make the Orion-pattern-detecting neuron(s) fire equivalently. Type-level criterial causality is central to biological systems in general, and to brain processing in particular. Indeed, biological systems have evolved to take advantage of this special subclass of physical causal chains that are rare and perhaps nonexistent outside of biological systems.[6] Criterial causality is expressed at almost every level of biological systems, from molecular criterial satisfaction, as occurs in a membrane receptor, to selection of a mate on the basis of visible evidence of genetic health. Criterial causality is realized in the material causality underlying physicalist monism (e.g., Kim, 2005) that is described by the laws of physics, but is not the standard Newtonian or classical mechanical "billiard ball" causality rooted in energy transfer or transformation (§§A1.2, A1.3).[7] This is accomplished by physically realizing a set of criteria for the release of some physical action, where the criteria that are met are about some aspect of energy that is not itself subject to the physical laws obeyed by energy (e.g., spatial or temporal patterns, or information, can be created and destroyed, and are not described by the first law of thermodynamics). The phrase "criterial causality" entails the concept of fungibility of and multiple realizability of *types* of input in triggering a released action.

§6.10   Type-level criterial causality is interesting because it is not reducible to the transfer of energy (noncriterial causality; e.g., classical mechanics, see appendix 1). It is also not reducible to the transformation of energy familiar from chemical reactions (token-level criterial causality). Because the mechanism of causality is indifferent to the physical particulars of the input, so long as the key criteria are met, there can be, and indeed are, higher-level emergent causalities than fundamental particle-level physical causality, even while these higher-level causalities must always be realized in and therefore consistent with lowest-level physical causality. A given low-level (noncriterial) causality, such as operates among strings or whatever is at the lowest level of physical causation, can give rise to countless higher-level (criterial) causalities, assuming ontological indeterminism, some of which can even be mutually inconsistent, such as, for example, the rules of the card games poker and bridge. When, say, poker is being played, only an instance from the subset of all the physical causal chains open to elementary particles that count as a causal chain in the game of poker is realized. The possibility of physically constructing criterial detectors of input that do something or not, depending on how well criteria are met, affords the emergence of causalities that are realized in particle-level causality, but that obey emergent laws. Of course, elementary particles just obey the indeterministic laws of physics. But a succession of criterial satisfactions can be constructed that will obey input–output relations unlike anything obeyed by elementary particles. If determinism were the case, Kim's reductionistic argument (§§A2.3–A2.5) would prove such higher-order causalities to be epiphenomenal. But if ontological indeterminism is the case, then emergent causalities can exist that permit downward causation (§6.14).

§6.11   A criterial causality operates at the level of whatever criteria have been physically realized in some decoder. If physically realized criteria assess, for example, the shape, spatiotemporal pattern, or information of inputs, then the criterial causality that operates among a series of such criterial decoders operates at that level, and the correct level of description for such causal chains is at that level. For example, if the criteria for winning points from a home run are that a pitched baseball has been hit by a batter out of the park, then the level of causal analysis that is useful in understanding the causal effects of a homerun is one at the level of balls, pitchers, scored points, hitters, and parks, not some lower level of particle causation, or higher level of history or economics. The event of a home run is both downwardly multiply realizable, in that infinitely many sets of particle events would be equivalent at the level of the criteria that must be met for something to count as a home run, and upwardly multiply realizable, in that infinitely many societies or universes could have been the context in which this event occurred. This multiple realizability arises because the vast majority of facts about particles, societies, or the universe are irrelevant to the satisfaction of the criteria of what counts as a home run here and now.

§6.12   The rules obeyed by criterial causal chains (i.e., of successions of criterial satisfactions), including informational and mental causal chains, are not bound to obey the laws of physics, even though they are realized in physical causal chains that do obey the laws of physics. For example, a causality based on the meeting of informational criteria need not obey any "law of the conservation of information," because information can be created and destroyed, even when the energy that that information is realized in cannot be created or destroyed. This is because information is realized not in the substance of energy per se, but in its spatiotemporal organization. And relevant organizations or patterns of the fundamental substance can be created and destroyed, whereas the underlying substance itself cannot be. Whereas energy or mass cannot be created or destroyed, information is itself not energy and has no mass. It can easily be created or destroyed because organization of energy can be destroyed. If, for example, I put a music compact disc (CD) into my microwave oven and turn it on for a minute, the CD will crackle and spark. After this, the information that lay *in potential* on the CD will no longer be readable by a CD player, and the potential for informational decoding relative to a CD player will be irretrievably lost, even though energy must be conserved throughout this process of CD destruction. Is this a process of destruction of information? No. It is a process of the destruction of the organization of matter on the CD that gave rise to the potential for information had the intact CD been placed in the correct decoder, namely a CD player. Similarly, information does not obey the conservation of momentum or spin. Indeed, these notions from physics do not even apply to information, because information as such has neither momentum, nor mass, nor spin, nor even a spatial extent. Information does not have to obey the second law of thermodynamics either, in that information can increase within the physical system that realizes it even as net thermodynamic entropy increases. A subset of energy in a system can become more organized even when the total energy in which information is realized does obey the first and second laws of thermodynamics as well as other physical laws. Information is not unique in its seeming disregard for the first and second laws of thermodynamics. I can create and destroy forms in clay, and I can create and destroy social relationships, because form and social relationships do not obey the laws of physics obeyed by energy. They can increase in complexity, even while the physical substrate in which they are realized suffers from increasing net thermodynamic entropy. While information, form, configuration, spatial and temporal patterns, value, and social relationships are realized in physical events, they are themselves not substantial, and do not obey the laws of physics obeyed by fundamental substance.

Addressing Kim's Challenge

§6.13   Let us address Kim's skepticism concerning the possibility of a physicalist account of nonepiphenomenal mental causation (see appendix 2) head on: If the fundamental particle-level of causation is complete and closed, is not any higher-level causation merely epiphenomenal and devoid of any genuine causal efficacy? It follows from ontological indeterminism that many physical causal chains can follow a single physical event and that each of these would be consistent with the laws of physics. For example, whether a particle sent through a double slit ends up at position x or y on a photographic emulsion, energy, momentum, spin, and other physical properties are conserved. By responding to spatial and temporal patterns or relationships among inputs, such as the spatial pattern of Orion or the simultaneity of lower-level inputs, criteria permit the emergence of causalities among successions of patterns that are realized in physical causality. Such emergent causalities cannot violate physical causality, of course, because physical things like receptors and neurons must obey physical laws. Ontological indeterminism (see appendix 1), however, allows the possibility of decoders that might occupy various different physical states at the next moment, because they can amplify fluctuations available in the microscopic domain to the macroscopic domain of neural spike timing (see §§4.66, 4.67). Indeterminism permits the real, as opposed to just illusory, collapse of possibilities that permits information to be a real property of certain physical systems that operate according to a physically realized and informational criterial causality. While all causal chains are necessarily physical causal chains that obey the laws of physics obeyed by energy, some possible physical causal chains following any given neuronal event are also informational causal chains. On this account, only relatively few physical causal chains open to the aggregate of particles comprising a network of neurons are also informational causal chains. What makes this subset of possible causal chains become realized over others is that the neural system is "designed" to operate criterially, where the criteria met are informational in the sense that they are placed upon spatial and temporal relationships among input. But how does criterial causation accomplish downward causation?

§6.14   In figure 6.2 the dashed lines and solid line indicate the possible paths open to a particle, each of which, although different, allows the particle to obey all the physical laws of elementary particles. Some subset of possible paths, if realized, allows the particle to be part of an informational causal chain. This is represented here as the path drawn as a solid line. This path also obeys all the laws of physics because it is a possible path open to elementary particles according to the laws of quantum mechanics, but it is a special path in that it also realizes a link in an informational causal chain, whereas those represented by the dashed lines do not. Setting up physically realized informational criteria in advance of the arrival of input allows the solid path to be realized over the dashed paths at the level of particles. There is downward causation by criterially released detectors of information, such as neurons, because they assure that only those possible paths open to particles that also comprise links in informational causal chains are realized. Only aggregate sets of particle paths that could make a postsynaptic neuron fire will make it fire and thereby play a role in successions of such neuronal firing. None of the laws of physics is violated by this form of downward causation, because the solid path, like dashed paths, obeys all the laws of physics. This type of causation requires that physically realized criteria for the release of an action potential are in place *before* the arrival of inputs that could possibly meet those criteria. This is obviously the case in neural networks. Criterial causation

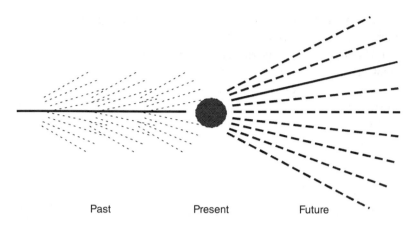

Past   Present   Future

Figure 6.2

An actual and several possible paths. Assuming ontological indeterminism, a particle in the present, represented by the disk, has—and, in the past, had—many paths open to it. The ones that were not realized are symbolized by thin dashed lines. The path that was realized is symbolized by the horizontal solid line. In the present moment the particle again has many possible paths open to it in the next moment, indicated by the thick dashed lines. The one that will be realized is represented by the slanted solid line. Each of these paths, whether dashed or solid, fully obeys the laws of physics, assuming indeterminism. In the case of causation among neurons, this same drawing can be interpreted as follows: Setting up physically realized criteria on neuronal input in advance of the arrival of that input realizes those possible paths at the particle level that are also links in informational causal chains, indicated by the solid line. The dashed lines indicate possible paths open to a particle that would not be part of an informational causal chain. There is downward causation by criterially released detectors of spatiotemporal patterns in input, such as neurons, because they assure that only those possible paths open to particles that also comprise links in informational causal chains are realized. None of the laws of physics is violated by this form of downward causation, because the solid path, like the dashed paths, obeys all the laws of physics.

as realized in neurons offers one solution to Kim's challenge. It is a purely physicalist mode of causation that does not require new physical laws and does not violate existing physical laws. In the absence of criteria placed upon spatiotemporal patterns in input, criterialess physical causation is bottom-up and localistic. But by changing the criteria that future inputs must meet to make a postsynaptic neuron fire, a type of downward causation is physically implemented that biases which possible particle paths will be realized.

§6.15   Although physical causation is indeed closed, in the sense that only possible paths allowed by quantum physics can possibly become real (§A2.5), nonetheless, many possible paths could become real at each moment. Which one becomes real in a functioning brain will be a possible path that contributes to meeting the physical conditions for firing by neurons when a neuron in fact fires. Other possible paths open to particles that do not lead to this criterial satisfaction of a neuron's conditions for firing are not realized. Moreover, when criteria are met, and the neuron fires, the information that, say, an Orion-like pattern is present is realized. One could argue that this approach does not really meet Kim's challenge because a criterial decoder, such as a neuron tuned to an Orion-like pattern, is itself a physical system that responds to its inputs purely according to the laws of physics. This is certainly true. But the inputs that drive a neuron, assuming that they arrive within its temporal integration window, are in fact those that realize some information, such as the presence of an Orion-like pattern; and the reason the system has such a decoder, driven by such inputs and not others, is that the neural system can learn such patterns and "wire up" detectors for them. In other instances, criterial detectors might be innate, such as simple or complex cells in V1, which detect static and moving oriented bars of light. In addition, the criteria that will make neurons fire in the future can be modified by present information-processing realized in neurons that carry out operations such as planning in working memory, mental calculation, and mental imagery that do not require preset, dedicated, and "hardwired" detectors, like our hypothetical Orion detector. When criteria are met in the future, the information realized by those criteria having been met is mental; that those criteria were met implies that those possible particle paths that realized that criterial satisfaction became real, and those that did not, did not become real. In this way, physically realized information can influence which paths open to particles become real. In a sense, it is the realization of this information that "causes" (§6.17) certain possible particle paths to become real over others. Because the criteria are informational (e.g., that a sufficiently Orion-like pattern is present), information can affect which possible particle paths in the microdomain become real. This is an instance where information can downwardly cause particle events.

§6.16   Kim derided the notion that mental events can influence how fundamental particles behave (§A2.2) when those mental events are realized in the physical events they purport to alter. The way around this is to have present physical/mental events set up the physical/informational criteria that are to be met by *future* inputs to neurons, which, when satisfied, lead to future neuronal firing and associated information as schematized in figure 3.1. This gets around the core problem of self-causation, while preserving the influence of physically realized mental events on the particle paths that will be realized when preset criteria are met and a neuron fires in the future. This influence of the mental on the physical is possible only because physically realized criteria are set up in neurons in advance of potential criterial satisfaction by input. If this presetting of the criteria for neuronal firing were not set up in advance of the arrival of potentially satisfying input, information and mental events could not influence which possible particle paths become real.

There Is No Backward Causation in Criterial Causation

§6.17   This view of causation may sound dangerously like backward causation in time, which is obviously impossible. Causality is traditionally schematized as "event A at time t_1 makes event B at later time t_2 happen"; not only must A precede B, but B must not happen if A does not happen. In folk psychology and classical physics, billiard ball A forces billiard ball B to move by transferring energy to it. In neuroscience, this folk way of thinking about causality would lead one to view presynaptic neuron A as forcing postsynaptic neuron B to fire deterministically or with some probability. In either case, the cause is primarily placed with A, not B, which is thought of more or less as an automatic consequence of A. Thus, traditionally, causal efficacy lies with A, and B either necessarily and predeterministically follows A, as Newton would have it, or probabilistically follows A, as quantum mechanics would have it. In either case, B follows passively from A, in that B sets no criterial conditions on properties of A for B's occurrence.

§6.18   But criterial causalities, once set up in physical systems, place primary causal efficacy with B, even though B follows A in time. The firing of neuron A may or may not make neuron B fire, depending on the criteria that B is using at any given moment. A causes B only if B "says so," by virtue of B's criteria having been met. B can be thought of as a "causal filter" that blocks all causal efficacy of A unless A meets B's physically realized criteria about some properties of A and its other inputs. This sort of pseudo-backward causation in time is not seen in the traditional Newtonian energy-transfer type of causality. Criterial causality realizes pseudo-backward causation because the consequences of an action are not determined by the input ("the cause") so much as by the decoder ("the effect") and whatever action is released by the satisfaction of whatever criteria have been set. Of course, there is no true backward causation in time. B gains its causal efficacy over A because the criteria realized in B were set up in B *before* A ever happened. For example, a postsynaptic neuron, whatever its criteria for firing, has to be in place before input ever arrives from a presynaptic neuron that may release the postsynaptic cell's firing.

§6.19   B's criteria can be placed on some aspect of the spatiotemporal pattern of energy, such as the spatial pattern of Orion occurring in the image, rather than the amount of energy or momentum. B's criteria are informational, and not driven primarily by the amount of energy inherent in A's input. A large change in the energy level of A's input might make no difference to B, in that its criteria are not met, whereas a minuscule change in A's energetic input to B might make a big difference (e.g., a delay in input by 1/50th of a second may make a difference in whether B responds or not), in that B's criteria are now met. Or A's input to B might be the same, but A2's input to B changes, leading to B's criteria being met or not. Regardless of how much A fires, under these criteria, B would not fire if A alone fires. Criterial causality is driven more by B than A. Chains of causation among neuronal events can really only be understood at the level of the informational criteria that postsynaptic neurons place on their inputs. Trying to understand causality at a particle level of analysis is pointless, because the system is set up to process information. It is therefore necessary to solve the informational code inherent in B's decoding scheme, because the cause of B's firing is primarily that certain conditions on informational inputs have been met. That this is realized in a particular physical way among neurons is inevitable, since it had to be realized in some physical way, assuming physicalism. But the same information processing could have been realized in many other physical ways. We would never think to analyze even the deterministic chains of causation of a computer program at the level of electrons flowing in wires. Even in this deterministic case, we could never understand why electrons followed the paths that they did without understanding the information processing realized in the implementation of the computer program. To argue that chains of causation among neurons can be reduced to chains of causation among particles is true but useless, since it is criteria set on information that decide which paths open to particles will become real. Whereas every instance of an informational causal chain is also a particle-level physical causal chain, the vast majority of physical causal chains are not informational causal chains. Informational causal chains are realized in the brain because physical criteria are set on physical inputs that only allow informational causal chains to be realized in these physical events.

§6.20   Criterial causation is not reducible to the kind of physical causation described by classical or even relativistic physics, where time can be reversed in principle. Under criterial causation, time cannot be reversed, because there is a many-to-one mapping between types of inputs and the one criterially released action (§6.8). In the context of a brain, a given neuron will fire identically to many different combinations of inputs. Knowing that a neuron has fired does not allow one to recover the particular set of inputs that made it fire. Criterial causation therefore imposes a directionality on time and physical causation that may not be the case at the level of elementary particles. Unlike classical mechanics or even relativity theory, where t can be replaced by $-t$, criterially causal systems cannot be "played backward." Because many inputs can lead to an identical output, information about the particular set of inputs—and therefore information about causation—is lost when an output occurs. Under indeterminism, multiple possible "branches" or possible paths are open to an event, whereas under determinism only one path is possible. Indeterminism can be thought of as a "tree of possibilities" that gets larger the further into the future you go. Interestingly, indeterminism at the particle level permits the possibility of higher-level trees that get larger as you go into the past. Criterial causation is an instance of such a "reverse tree," where "multiple pasts" (e.g., combinations of presynaptic inputs) can lead to the same present outcome, such as the firing of a neuron in the present.

Criterial Causation Is a Causation of Pattern-Released Activity

§6.21   Skeptics could argue that the idea of criterial causality is trivial because one could argue that all causality is criterial causality. They might argue that even a Newtonian billiard-ball type of physical causality entails the placement of criteria on input, which, if met, trigger very specific actions or consequences. Imagine, for example, a baseball physically realizing infinite sets of criteria such as "If hit by an object of mass m at location

x and at speed y, then follow trajectory t"; one for each possible combination of (m,x,y,t). You can even imagine the baseball being "indifferent" to the material of the bat or to its shape on the nonstriking side, or whether it is hollow or not, seemingly satisfying §6.8, but in fact not. Why is the causal chain realized when a bat hits a baseball not logically equivalent to that realized when a neuron fires? The essential difference is that the baseball and bat realize a causality entirely reducible to energy transfer (and also energy transformation when one considers the generation of heat by the ball when it is struck by the bat, or changes in the chemistry of the bat or the ball due to the impact). A neuron tuned to a particular type of incoming information, however, realizes a causal chain that is not reducible to energy transfer or energy transformation, because the criteria physically realized in the response properties of the neuron are not about mass, momentum, heat, or any other aspect of the magnitude or type of energy. The physical neuronal criteria are conditions set on spatiotemporal relationships among some portion of the neuron's physical inputs, realizing informational criteria that are placed on the informational content realized in neuronal input. Relationships among portions of matter that release an action by meeting some decoder's criteria are not themselves material and may only exist by virtue of the fact that the decoder responds to them. The Orion pattern is not necessarily causal in the way the matter is in which it is realized; only because some population of neurons is tuned to an Orion-like spatial pattern does the information "Orion-like pattern has been detected" come into existence. Only by virtue of having a detector that can "read" this pattern in input is this pattern potentially causal, as, for example, when that detector then changes the criteria for firing on other pattern-tuned detectors. A baseball bat does not meet the multiple realizability conditions of §6.8 because a baseball bat specifies no criteria that can be met by multiple types of input. In contrast, neurons place criteria on the spatiotemporal patterns that input must have in order for a response to be triggered, and these criteria can be met by multiple inputs, meeting the multiple realizability conditions of §6.8. Similarly, when water falls down a waterfall, it just happens, passively. The water sets no criteria to be met by the rock, and the rock sets no criteria to be met by the water, before some action is released. Causality here can be reduced to energy transfer among local particles. Global relationships among particles play no role in causal outcomes. In a baseball bat hitting a ball or water falling down a rock face, there is no decoder that waits for the arrival of a specific pattern of physical inputs about nonlocal events before the ball is allowed to fly or the water is allowed to fall.

§6.22   The whole point of setting up a physical causal system to react criterially to input, as we have in the brain, is to make sure that only the subset of possible physical causal chains that are also informational causal chains are the ones that will be realized. Far from being an incidental fact about this subset of physical causal chains, natural selection has operated to optimize the efficiency of information processing within possible informational causal chains to fit the needs of an organism within its niche. The fact that information processing is realized in physical causal chains is, in a sense, beside the point. An animal does not get weeded out because it followed such and such a physical causal chain as opposed to another; it gets weeded out because it failed to recognize the lion when there was one. It gets weeded out or survives to the extent that it processes information poorly or well. Evolution of course operates not only to weed out suboptimal bodies, but also suboptimal perceptual, emotional, and cognitive systems realized in neuronal and endocrine system activity.

§6.23   Criterial decoders potentially interact with the uncertainty, noise, indeterminism, and randomness (e.g., Brownian motion, see §§4.66, 4.67) introduced by particle-level causality in at least two interesting ways. First, they clean up this noise by reducing a great variety of potentially noisy inputs into a single output, such as the firing of a neuron. Second they permit the "harnessing" of noise or randomness for the generation of novel information. By setting up criterial decoders in advance that convert many types of input into one type of output (§6.8), systems that instantiate criterial causal chains effectively take control of randomness and use it to generate outcomes that are caused by the system, rather than outcomes that are determined by randomness per se. Yet these nonarbitrary outcomes are not predictable, and could have turned out otherwise. Because solutions are not predetermined and can vary, yet still satisfy a given finite set of criteria, and because outcomes that satisfy lower level criteria can be compared, modified, and rejected in an open-ended fashion at the level of executive consideration of what has been generated by lower-level systems, genuine novelty can result. This novelty is not itself random, because it meets the criteria that were preset. But a particular solution was not predetermined either. Criterial causality therefore offers a middle path between determinism and randomness (§§7.2, 7.3).

7 Criterial Causation Offers a Neural Basis for Free Will

Abstract

According to the three stage neuronal model (§3.9) of mental causation and free will, (1) new physical/informational criteria are set in a neuronal circuit on the basis of preceding physical/mental processing at time t_1, in part via a mechanism of rapid synaptic resetting that effectively changes the inputs to a postsynaptic neuron. These changes can be driven volitionally or nonvolitionally, depending on the neural circuitry involved. (2) At time t_2, inherently variable inputs arrive at the postsynaptic neuron, and (3) at time t_3 physical/informational criteria are met or not met, leading to postsynaptic neural firing or not. Randomness can play a role in the first two stages, but not substantially in the third, because intracellular potential either passes the threshold for firing or it does not. Such criterial causation is important because it allows neurons to alter the physical realization of *future* mental events in a way that escapes the problem of self-causation of the mental upon the physical. The impossibility of self-causation has been at the root of basic criticisms of the possibility of mental causation (§§A2.2–A2.5) or free will (§§7.1–7.8). Criterial causation gets around this core problem. In essence, free will is all about setting the physical grounds and informational parameters for unpredictable future mental events and decisions that will meet the informational criteria that were preset before the arrival of inputs that might meet those criteria. Free will is fundamentally about the future, especially the next cycle in iterative information-processing loops.

Strong Free Will

§7.1   In this chapter, I argue that it is possible to be a physicalist and ontological indeterminist and adhere to a strong conception of free will. A strong free will requires meeting some very high demands. We must have (a) multiple courses of physical or mental behavior open to us; (b) we must really be able to choose among them; (c) we must be or must have been able to have chosen otherwise once we have chosen a course of behavior;

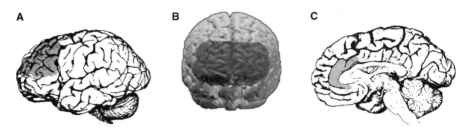

Figure 7.1

Areas of anterior prefrontal cortex thought to be involved in volition. The dorsolateral prefrontal cortex (DLPFC; shown in dark gray in A in the left hemisphere) and Brodmann Area 10 (corresponding to the cortex behind the forehead, shown bilaterally in dark gray in B) appear to be involved in generating possible action plans and sequences. The anterior cingulate cortex (shown in gray in C) appears to be centrally involved in implementing a selected action plan at the level of motivation, emotion, and physiological response. (A and C are modified from Nitschke & Mackiewicz, 2005, and B is modified from Wikimedia Commons.)

and (d) the choice must not be dictated by randomness alone, but by us. This seems like an impossible bill to fill, since it seems to require that acts of free will involve acts of self-causation. The goal of this chapter is to describe a way to meet these demands, assuming ontological indeterminism and criterial causation among neurons, that does not fall into the logical fallacy of self-causation.

§7.2   Neither (pre)determinism nor randomness, whether conceived within a framework of causation via energy transfer (§A1.2) or transformation (§A1.3), offers hope of a truly free will in this strong sense. If determinism is true, we have only one possible course of action at any moment, so we could not have acted otherwise and have no alternatives to choose from. Some, including the Stoics, Hobbes, Hume (1739), or Dennett (1984), have argued that free will is compatible with determinism. Compatibilists typically argue that even though the outcome of any of our acts of choice was predetermined since the beginning of the universe, it was nonetheless a choice made by our nervous system, and so is free, at least in the sense that it was our choice and we were not coerced into our choice by anyone or anything else. Freedom from coercion[1] is a weak conception of free will that fails the strong definition of free will described in §7.1, according to which a choice must have had a real possibility of having turned out otherwise. If the universe were deterministic, strong free will would be ruled out, since things could not have turned out otherwise and the weak compatibilist notion of free will would be the best we could hope for. But since physics provides evidence for ontological indeterminism (see appendix 1), a physical basis for a strong free will is in fact possible.

§7.3   With the randomness offered us by traditional (noncriterial) indeterminism, however, outcomes are as unfree, in the strong sense of §7.1, as under determinism, because any choice that occurs randomly is not chosen by us (Koch, 2009; Pinker, 1997). It just happens randomly, not because we made it happen. Many philosophers have seen no middle path between the equally unfree extremes of determinism and randomness. Hume (1739), for example wrote "'tis impossible to admit of any medium betwixt chance and an absolute necessity." Such philosophers have either concluded that free will does not exist, or tried to argue, I believe in vain, that free will is compatible with predetermined or random choices. A strong conception of free will (i.e., one that meets the conditions described in §7.1) is not compatible with either predetermined or random choices, because in neither case do *we* decide which alternative to actualize from among many that might have been selected. If there are no other physicalist alternatives available besides predetermined or arbitrary random action, there is little hope for strong free will. Criterial causation, however, offers an alternative between the two extremes of predetermined and random effects that Hume was not in a position to see.

Criterial Causation Escapes the Basic Argument against Free Will

§7.4   Strawson (1998/2004) has summarized the impossibility of any kind of *causa sui* free will in what he describes as the traditional or basic argument, which we can paraphrase as follows: (1) One acts or reacts to input in a particular manner because of one's physical/mental organization. (2) If one is to be ultimately responsible for what one does, one must be ultimately responsible for one's physical/mental organization. (3) But one cannot be ultimately responsible for one's physical/mental organization at the time of making a choice, because, simply put, one is what one is when one makes a choice. To choose the physical/mental organization that leads to that same choice, permitting a different choice to be made, would be a case of *causa sui* (self-causation), which is logically impossible. (4) So one cannot help but choose as one does at each instant because one cannot choose what one is at each instant, and one therefore is not ultimately responsible for what one does. The impossibility of self-causation is a valid argument against the possibility of an ability to choose the *present* grounds for making a *present* choice. Note that Kim's argument (§A2.2) against the possibility of downward mental causation also rests on the impossibility of self-causation. Criterial causation gets around the *causa sui* argument against both mental causation and free will by having neurons alter the physical grounds, not of present mental events, but of future mental events, as shown schematically in figure 3.1.

§7.5   Given the conceptual framework of criterial causality, we can reframe this basic argument against free will as follows. The criteria we use to make a present decision exist just before the inputs arrive that led to those criteria being met or not; these criteria are set and are not themselves changeable at the moment the criteria are satisfied. They are what they are, and so we must choose as we choose, making us unfree to have chosen otherwise. We now have, however, a way out of this argument, because this argument rests on the impossibility of self-causation. Self-causation applies only to changing the physical basis of making a *present* decision that is realized in or supervenes on that very same physical basis. *Self-causation does not apply to changing the physical basis of making a future decision.* There can obviously never be a self-caused event, but criteria can be set up in advance, such that when they are met, an action automatically follows; this is an action that we will have willed to take place by virtue of having set up those particular criteria in advance. At the moment those criteria are satisfied at some unknown point in the future, leading to some action or choice, those criteria cannot be changed, but because criteria can be changed in advance, we are free to determine how we will behave within certain limits in the near future. Criterial causation therefore offers a path toward free will where the brain can determine how it will behave given particular types of future input. This input can be milliseconds in the future or, in some cases, even years away.

§7.6   Because any given set of criteria can be met by many types of input (§6.8), and because noise (i.e., physical variability; §§4.66, 4.67) in the system gives rise to input, the timing and particulars of an outcome of a criterial decision are neither predetermined nor random. For a simple noninformational criterial mechanism, such as an ion channel, the outcome will be rather monotonous, even if the timing of its opening or closing is random. But one can build increasingly higher-level criterial decoders in a hierarchy of decoders that take lower-level decoders' outputs as inputs (see fig. 4.3), such that high-level informational criteria such as "is a person who has white hair" can be physically realized in neuronal preconditions for firing (§§3.10, 4.9). A criterial outcome is an outcome that meets certain preset criteria, but what that outcome will be is not foreseeable; had we run the sequence of events over from the same initial conditions, with the same criteria, we may have ended up with a different outcome, because of noise in the system (§§4.66, 4.67). For example, a different person with white hair might have come to mind. In short, free will may be rooted in part in the multiple possible outcomes permitted by the variability caused by neurotransmitter diffusion across the synapse, the randomness of magnesium ion behavior amplified by NMDA receptor opening, and other ultimately microscopic sources of randomness that cause randomness in spike-time intervals. This bottom-up amplification of randomness, in combination with top-down imposition of random outcomes due to winner-take-all and other nonlinear dynamics (§4.69), permits criteria that were satisfied randomly to change all future possibilities open to the system. Free will in the stringent sense of §7.1 would not be possible in a system that lacked inherent variability or noise that could be harnessed to meet prespecified criteria in nonprespecified ways.[2]

§7.7   Any criterial outcome will meet the criteria preset by a given brain, and so will be an outcome that is satisfactory to that brain and caused by that brain, but it will also not be a unique solution predetermined by that brain or coerced upon that brain by external forces. Imagine, for example, Mozart trying to generate a musical sequence that sounds happy. Some part of his brain, perhaps a working-memory area like the dorsal lateral prefrontal cortex, defines criteria that a melody would have to meet in order to sound happy. Various cascades of criterial satisfaction are met that result in possible sequences that might meet the happiness criteria. These are "presented" to Mozart's executive system, and it either accepts them or rejects them, whereupon lower level systems continue to generate possible solutions to the problem.[3] Of course, whatever eventually gets accepted by him as adequate will sound to us like Mozart, because it satisfied the criterial decoding schemes that were unique to his brain. However, if we had "rewound the clock," a different solution to the problem might have been reached than the one that was reached, because of noise in the system. None of his pieces of music was predestined to sound as it did, and each piece could have turned out otherwise, although any piece that met his criteria would have sounded like a piece by Mozart. He could not help but have his style because he could not help but instantiate criteria that would satisfy Mozart, because he was Mozart, with his nervous system. Criterial causal systems, like Mozart's brain, can thus harness randomness to generate novel and creative solutions. His lower-level, nonexecutive systems generated various sequences that met the criteria for happiness that his executive decision to generate a happy melody had set in place. When solutions were presented for executive consideration, his executive system could then further edit these solutions, or reject them, invoking the further generation of possible solutions that might meet the criteria set for a happy melody. Indeed, this editing of, selection among, and invoking of solutions to problems appears to be a central function of the executive subsystems of the frontal lobes.

§7.8   Criterial causality therefore leaves room for nonillusory choice that is a middle path between the extremes of (a) determinism, where there is no ability to choose freely in the strong sense because there is no possibility of an alternative action (§7.1), and (b) criterion-free randomness (§A2.6), where arbitrary choices follow randomly rather than from criteria one sets up oneself. Many people have seen no alternative between predetermined and random choices, neither of which offers a path to a strong free will. But there is a physical mechanism that offers a way of realizing a strong free will, and that is the setting up of physically realized criteria in advance for behaving a certain way given certain types of future input. Again, because criteria can be set up for responding to future input, the problem of self-causation does not arise. Instead, the nervous system can now change the physical grounds for making a future choice by setting up criterial decoders that then wait for relevant input that will meet those criteria. This is accomplished by changing weights on synapses, either rapidly and dynamically (§§4.54–4.60), or more slowly, using mechanisms such as long-term potentiation.

§7.9   Although I disagree with defenders of the basic argument (§7.4) that there is no free will, I do agree that we are not utterly free in making our choices. Defenders of the basic argument would argue against the possibility of free will by arguing that initial criteria must be given by our genetic inheritance and its interaction with our environment or upbringing. They typically (e.g., Strawson, 1998/2004) see nothing that can affect who we are besides our genetic potential as realized by the environments in which we have lived. At some point criteria, and that which satisfies those criteria, must be given by our physical/mental organization. It is correct to say that we cannot choose some of the initial bases of our choices. For example, we cannot choose what smells good or disgusting; what smells good to us is just given by the organization and functioning of our nervous system, which is genetically encoded, expressing itself soon after birth. We are not free to determine our initial conditions, since we have to start with some innate criteria at birth. It is also true that what is genetically given is a potential to realize certain outcomes, and not one that will realize certain outcomes.[4] However, although we cannot choose what smells good, we can choose what we eat. Although Mozart's brain was not free to set up criteria that were criteria set up by Bach's brain, since he did not have Bach's brain, Mozart's executive system was free to reject or modify possible solutions generated by his lower-level systems that met his criteria for a musical sequence that sounds happy. This is an open-ended process that can go through countless iterations. Because of noise in the system, the outcome of this process is not predetermined. It is also not random. Any outcome will have met Mozart's criteria, so will inevitably end up sounding like Mozart and no one else. Thus, although Mozart was not free to preset criteria that belonged to Bach, what his nervous system would create was not foreseeable, in principle, to him or anyone else. Yet, what he ended up composing was shaped by his nervous system alone to meet criteria preset by his nervous system.

§7.10   Criterial causation permits a degree of self-determination that meets the high standards demanded of a strong free will described in §7.1, without permitting, of course, a *causa sui* free will, which is impossible. To reiterate, for us to have a strong free will, multiple courses of physical or mental behavior must be open to us, we must really be able to choose from among them, we must have been able to have chosen otherwise once we have chosen, and the choice must be dictated not by randomness but by us. Returning to our example, Mozart's brain can generate numerous musical sequences that meet his preset criteria for a happy melody, and his executive circuitry can choose from among these on the basis of the degree to which these criteria are met, or on the basis of other criteria realized in his nervous system. Because of noise in the system, there is no guarantee that he would choose the same sequence as the best one if we could "rewind" him in time and play the sequence over. The same musical sequences might not even be generated for executive consideration by the lower-level systems because they in turn generate possible solutions by setting criteria on their own lower-level inputs, and so on. Such hierarchies of criterial selection can, even at the lowest level, harness noise for the generation of novel solutions to problems posed by higher levels in the system. However, the choice is not dictated solely by randomness, but, in the present example, by criteria that Mozart's nervous system set up to solve the problem of finding a happy melody. This meets all the stringent conditions required of a free will described in §7.1, without falling into the trap of a *causa sui* free will (§7.4).

§7.11   Nervous systems can set up different types of criteria in order to be able to assess future inputs for their degree of criterial satisfaction. Criteria can be set up in "hardware," presumably by creating new neural connections or changing weights on existing synapses that then realize new criteria, or wiring up a neuron to have new tuning properties (e.g.,

Logothetis, Pauls, & Poggio, 1995). Or criteria can be set up in "software," as conditions that are met by inputs within a working memory (§§4.54–4.60), as when my executive system commands my lower-level systems to retrieve examples of people who have white hair, or to create a mental image of, say, a tree with wings. Much research implicates prefrontal working-memory areas in the flexible application of decision criteria for action planning and selection (Barcelo, 2003; Boettiger & D'Esposito, 2005; Freedman et al., 2001; O'Reilly et al., 2002; Ragozzino et al., 1999; Rougier et al., 2005; Wallis et al., 2001). The specification in working memory of arbitrary criteria for response selection and the arbitrary specification of mappings between input and output allows for some surprising possibilities. For example, one can set up criteria in working memory that are modeled to be unlike those that one models to be like one's own criteria. For example, Mozart can say to himself, I want to create a musical composition that sounds like Bach. He might be able to do this so well that the result is a composition that experts regard as indistinguishable from one that Bach himself might actually have written. Of course, these criteria would not really have been Bach's, but Mozart's imitation of Bach's criteria. But because there are few necessary limits on what can be imagined in working memory (Tse, 2006b), there is a great deal more flexibility in the kinds of choices one can make than would be the case if criteria could only be realized at a "hardware level," in the tuning properties of neurons dedicated to the detection of a certain feature or configuration. Indeed, what may offer humans a greater range of choice than other animals, and thereby a "freer" free will, is the degree to which we rely on choosing on the basis of arbitrarily defined criteria in open-loop imaginary scenarios realized in working memory, as opposed to closed-loop fixed actions patterns of behavior criterially released by perceptual inputs.[5] Our freedom and flexibility appear to be cortical in origin. In the basal ganglia, option selection appears to be primarily executed on the basis of nonabstract stimulus attributes (Cools et al., 2006), whereas arbitrary, abstract choice criteria can be held in working memory. Criterial resetting in working memory, rather than being hardwired like the criteria for the firing of a simple cell, are most likely realized in the physical mechanisms underlying rapid and dynamic synaptic plasticity discussed in chapters 4 and 5.

§7.12 Some free-will skeptics (e.g., Strawson, 1998/2004, 2002; cf. Cashmore, 2010; Greene & Cohen, 2004) argue as follows that our genetically given potential, realized in a particular environment, entirely determines our character: Since we cannot freely choose our genetics, nor the environment we are born into, we cannot choose the character we develop through the interaction of genetics and environment; thus, we are not responsible for our characters, and therefore cannot be ultimately responsible for actions that arise from our characters. But this argument against both free will and moral responsibility fails to acknowledge that we can now prepare the physical basis of future decisions and that we are, ourselves, part of the environment that shapes how our genetically given potentials are realized. Concerning this second point, when a baby looks at its environment, it sees not only its surroundings but also its own body in those surroundings. Through much potentially frustrating trial and error, it learns that it can control through acts of volition that subset of its environment that is its body, and it learns that it cannot control that portion of its surroundings that is not its body. Of course it is not limitlessly free to will to do with its body whatever it will. It cannot will itself to fly, because it cannot fly, but it can will itself to move its arm. The child also learns that it can, in addition to its body, control the contents of its experience to some degree by willing to have or not have certain kinds of thoughts, by shifting attention at will, and ignoring what it chooses to ignore. Thus, how genetic potential is realized (and, indeed, how genes are regulated up or down through feedback mechanisms such as methylation) is influenced not only by factors in the external environment, but also by choices we make concerning what our bodies and minds will do or become in the future. Our character is not just a passive consequence of genetics and external environment, but is also, in part, the active consequence of choices we make concerning what we think, attend to, and do. We can choose to learn a new language, start exercising, or move to a new location, and these decisions will alter how our bodies and brains will function in the future. For example, in my lab we have shown that studying Chinese leads to increased myelination of underlying language-processing circuitry (Draganski et al., 2004; Schlegel et al., 2012b).

§7.13   The free-will skeptic might then respond by saying that these choices are themselves not free. But they were free when they were made, because they were choices made by virtue of satisfying criteria that our nervous systems had set in place before those choices themselves were made. If we "rewound the clock" and could make the same decision over, we might have decided to learn Hutu this time instead of Tutsi, but in either case the choice was free, because it was a satisfaction of criteria that were set by our nervous system and no one else's. For example, the executive system might have considered various options and then decided that it was best for us to learn a local language to prepare for our posting as ambassador to Rwanda. Such a command can be regarded as a set of criteria that must be met, such as "is a local language in Rwanda," "is easiest to master," "is spoken by the most people," "will make the best impression on my hosts," and the like. The choice of Tutsi over Hutu, say, was neither predetermined nor solely dictated by randomness. That said, while our preset criteria permitted us free will to choose a Rwandan language rather than a non-Rwandan language, they did not permit us the freedom to choose between Rwandan languages; that would have required stipulating more specific criteria than we did, such as "A language spoken by the Tutsi tribe." If criteria are so specific that the class of things that satisfy them contains only one member (e.g., the Tutsi language), then we have free will to choose a specific outcome, such as choosing Tutsi over any other language. The setting up of criteria allows our brains to harness randomness, so to speak, to come up with novel, unforeseeable solutions and choices that have met the criteria of our nervous systems, making them our choices. These can be further rejected, modified, and edited in an open-ended process in working memory. We are therefore responsible, in part, for the characters we have, and we are therefore responsible, in part, for the choices we make, as well as the consequences of our choices and actions.

§7.14   Traditional free-will skeptics might argue that once criteria are met, an action, such as an action potential or a cascade of action potentials leading to, say, pulling a trigger, automatically follows. They might then argue that as a result one is not ultimately responsible for one's actions. Certainly, the moment that criteria are met, the action that follows must follow as surely as an action potential, sneeze, or toilet flush must commence once the critical threshold has been passed. However, a person can be responsible both for setting up the kind of criterial detectors that would lead to certain kinds of actions and also for failing to inhibit criterial satisfaction (i.e., block the passing of the critical threshold) on the basis of higher-order criteria about what counts as right and wrong, through, for example, inhibition from executive centers in the frontal lobe. On this account, one would not be responsible for pulling the trigger at the moment criteria are passed, leading to a motor command to pull the trigger; instead one is responsible for (a) having certain criteria in place, and (b) for failing to inhibit criterial satisfaction on the basis of knowledge of what is right and wrong, in the moments before the criteria are satisfied that lead to the pulling of the trigger. In a moral sense, the crime is not committed at the instant the trigger is pulled, but moments (or even longer spans of time) before that, by one's having made decisions to put criteria in place or having failed to make decisions to train one's nervous system to inhibit criterial satisfaction, which then led one to have the kind of nervous system that would cause one to pull the trigger under circumstances like those where one did pull the trigger.

§7.15 Free-will skeptics might counter that the setting up of any set of criteria to be met by future inputs is itself determined by preexisting sets of criteria that have been met. This is in fact correct. There is no "ghost in the machine." In the end, there are only cells providing criterially assessed input to other cells. This is not to say that all neurons are the same. There can be a hierarchy of neural circuitry with modules and sub-modules just as there is a hierarchy in most information-processing systems, as occurs, for example, in a military, a computer network, or a corporation. Indeed, recent evidence suggests that many neural circuits are comprised of functional subcircuits (Bassett et al., 2008; Ferrarini et al., 2009; He et al., 2009; Meunier et al., 2009). An executive system can demand the generation of multiple possible courses of action. Various cortical or subcortical selection processes can select from among those options based on what optimally satisfies their different criteria for selection. For example, the basal ganglia might select and implement the optimal action sequence to get a task done (Chakravarthy et al., 2010; Stocco et al., 2010) on the basis of concrete stimulus attributes (Cools et al., 2006). The basal ganglia might switch motoric or cognitive action programs automatically, like an "automatic transmission" in a car, or it might be commanded to switch action programs from prefrontal cortex, rather like a stick shift, on the basis of more abstract criteria. But if one pushes choices back far enough in the history of the system, those choices will have to be rooted in criteria that were not themselves selected by the system. We have to be born with a minimal set of criteria to get the whole process of criterial causation going. All later criteriality that is contingent upon a particular history and set of later decisions needs a starting point of criteria that were innately dictated by a genetic plan. This does not mean that there is no free will. It means that free will is constrained (§7.9). We are not utterly free to choose the physical grounds of making a present choice. But our brains can make choices that are neither predetermined nor purely random, which are in part determined by previous decisions of our nervous system. The key point is that criteria will be met in unpredictable ways if there is inherent variability or noise in inputs, such as can be introduced by the randomness inherent in neurotransmitter molecules crossing the synapse (see §§4.66, 4.67) or NMDA receptor behavior that can introduce chaotic behavior into the timing of neural spike trains (Durstewitz, 2009). Just because new criteria are set up by a nervous system in a manner dictated by the satisfaction of preexisting criteria does not mean that either the future or present criteria will be met in a predetermined manner. Moreover, because neurons that realize a decision can reset criteria for the firing of other neurons that can respond to future input in light of that decision, the future acts or thoughts realized in the satisfaction of those reset criteria are neither random nor predetermined; they are self-selected consequences of our own choices, which are choices to set certain criteria for future neuronal response. Ontological indeterminism by itself is not enough for free will, because an indeterministic subatomic outcome is random and not controlled by or selected by our brain. However, ontological indeterminism harnessed by neuronal criterial causation permits a physical causal basis for a strong free will (§7.1), because outcomes are selected by our brain by virtue of having met criteria preset by our brain.

§7.16   This process is dynamic. Once some inputs have satisfied a given set of criteria, the fact that this one has been selected now feeds back on the neurons as input, which can then trigger further criterial causation based on this new fact. Using the example above, if the criteria that were set were "a Rwandan language" and the satisfaction of those criteria resulted in Tutsi being selected rather than Hutu, then the fact that Tutsi is the language that has been chosen can trigger future criterial specification, such as "is a book on the Tutsi language that has a high customer ranking." Then, after some title has been found that meets those criteria, subsequent criteria can be set such as "is a used copy that is in good shape and cheaper than ten dollars." Once we find a copy that is cheap and good, we can purchase it. And so on.

James and Incompatibilist Physicalist Libertarianism

§7.17   The present view is a type of incompatibilist physicalist libertarianism. Its closest relatives are found in two-stage models of free will, first proposed by William James (1884) and elaborated and modified by many others (e.g., Compton, 1931; Dennett, 1978; Doyle, 2011; Heisenberg, 2009; Kane, 1985, 1996, 2005, 2011; LeShan & Margenau, 1982; Mele, 1995, 2006, 2010; Popper, 1972; Popper & Eccles, 1977). In the first Jamesian stage, multiple alternative possibilities[6] for action or thought are generated, in part randomly, and in the second, subsequent stage, an adequately determined volitional mechanism (but see Kane, 1985) or rational faculty, where chance is no longer a factor, evaluates and selects the optimal option. James, Popper, and others viewed the process as akin to a Darwinian two-stage process[7] (Mayr, 1988), where randomness in the microscopic domain at the level of genetic reshuffling and mutation is amplified into variability at the level of animal phenotypic traits, which is then selected among via natural and sexual selection.[8] The present view differs from the traditional Jamesian view in that multiple ideas are not generated, and the selecting faculty is not rational and is not the will, but is instead a postsynaptic neuron. That is, instead of modeling possibility generation and selection at the level of ideas, here the focus is on what happens at the neuronal level. The present view might more profitably be thought of as a three-stage neuronal model, where (1) in the first stage at t_1 new physical/informational criteria are set in a neuron or neuronal circuit on the basis of preceding physical/mental processing, including volitional processing, in part via a mechanism of rapid synaptic resetting that effectively changes the future inputs to a postsynaptic neuron; and (2) in the second stage at later time t_2, inherently variable presynaptic inputs arrive at the postsynaptic neuron; and (3) in the third, later stage at t_3 physical/informational criteria are met or not met, leading to postsynaptic neural firing or not. Randomness can play a role in the first two stages, but not substantially in the third, because potential either passes the threshold for firing or does not.

§7.18   A determinist could correctly argue that neuronal criterial causation could proceed just as depicted in figure 3.1, but that the variability exploited in stage (2) above (§7.17) need not be rooted ultimately in microscopic ontological indeterminacy; it instead could be rooted in, if not quite classical sources, ultimately microscopically determined sources of randomness. For example, even if the universe were deterministic as a whole, with regard to any subset of it such as, say, the human brain, there would be causal influences coming in from the outside that could not be accounted for by causal interactions within the brain alone. This would in effect lead to a kind of "as if" indeterminism from within any framework that regarded brain processing as a closed system. The variability exploited in stage (2) could arise from such external factors, whether cosmic rays or some unknown but deterministic factors that somehow accounted for nonlocal correlations. Although the evidence discussed in appendix 1 supports the case for ontological indeterminism, it might not even be possible to formally settle whether ontological indeterminism or this kind of "as if" indeterminism is the case without access to the entire set of events in the universe (cf. Butterfield, 1998). Given the Gödelian problem associated with our being a subset of the universe, it would seem that the matter cannot be settled in principle. If an issue cannot be settled in principle, such as, for example, whether there are multiple universes or just one, or whether ontological indeterminism or determinism is the case at the level of the whole universe, one need not worry about settling it; one can just decide to ignore the issue or decide to believe in the most appealing option.[9] Regardless, the physical process realizing informational criterial causation is independent of this issue. If ontological indeterminism is the case, then the three-stage process offers a mechanism for a strong free will, and if determinism is the case, then this mechanism can realize a type of compatibilism. If the question of ontological determinism versus indeterminism cannot be settled empirically in principle, then most scientists would abandon the debate as quickly as they would a debate about the existence of other universes. What science can answer is whether causation only works in a bottom-up and reductionistic manner, or whether physical causation can also work in a top-down manner. By setting up physically realized informational criteria to be met by future neuronal activity, present neuronal activity can realize a form of downward causation.

§7.19   Under determinism, a strong free will (§7.1) is ruled out by definition, and Kim's argument (§§A2.2–A2.5) succeeds in eliminating the mental as causal. In contrast, assuming ontological indeterminism, Kim's argument fails to exclude the possibility of mental causation. Given this, the main goal of this book has been to examine a physicalist mode of causation that is also an informational mode of causation that avoids the trap of impossible mental-on-physical self-causation. Neural criterial causation provides this physicalist mechanism. For a determinist to say that this mechanism *could* operate deterministically and therefore that indeterminism is not necessary for my argument concerning criterial causation per se, though correct, would be missing my main point: Assuming ontological indeterminism on the basis of the evidence in §A1, and given empirical evidence that neurons are capable of amplifying microscopic randomness into randomness in the timing of neural spikes (§§4.66, 4.67), mental causation and a strong free will are possible and are in fact implemented in the human brain as three-stage criterial causation at the neuronal level.

Decision Making and Choice

§7.20   So much discussion about free will concerns our ability to influence the body's immediate movements. But it is our propositional choices that can bring about even decades of successive motor acts that are more relevant to free will. Decisions at a propositional level, just like the neuronal processes in which they are realized, are criterial, oriented toward future input, subject to the creativity inherent in harnessing randomness, and ultimately made by passing a threshold for the adequacy of criterial satisfaction.

§7.21 For example, once there was a couple who did not like their stressful lives, so they thought about how to escape the rat-race.[10] To put this in neuronal terms: As a result of the displeasure each felt in their situation, his or her executive system could issue a command like "find me a place to escape from this suffering." The executive system could specify what criteria a solution should meet; for example, the new place should be "peaceful," "far from civilization," "beautiful," "in the United States," "cheaper than twenty thousand dollars," and so on. Once these propositional criteria are set in working memory, the possibility-generation process could search for possible solutions that meet them. That is, the unconscious systems, exploiting randomness and given enough time, could come up with infinite possible solutions that meet those criteria. Options that meet the set criteria would then become conscious, for further consideration and planning using the capacity to play things out internally, using the capacities of working memory and mental imagery. By thus creating pseudo-sensory input internally, those systems that require such input to operate could judge whether they like this (virtual) experience, and vote up or down based on that experience. Unconsciously generated options could be selected, rejected, internally played out or edited, and criteria could be changed in light of possible solutions in an open-ended manner. The unconscious systems could then specify new possible solutions that meet the now modified criteria. The largely unconscious process of criteria-satisfying option-generation can end when the executive system terminates the search or when the best option is selected and the problem is solved. The largely conscious process of option comparison, weighing, consideration, and playing out must also end. Any search for a solution might always lead to a better satisfaction of any set of criteria, so the search for a solution could in principle last forever. Why are we not all paralyzed, like Buridan's ass, by indecision or an infinite loop of weighing our options? A threshold must be set on what counts as sufficiently satisfying of the criteria that were set. This is true at the level of neurons or at the level of personal choice. Because it is not determined which solution will pass this adequacy threshold first, the decision itself is both adequate and random. Among the set of all possible solutions that meet the criteria set, which one is selected is not predetermined by the brain, genetics, society, or anything in the universe, assuming the ontological indeterminism of events at the level of the synaptic cleft and neuronal criterial satisfaction. The couple in the above example ended up buying a small island off the coast of Maine and spent the rest of their lives there. But had some other event influenced random fluctuations at the right moment at the neuronal level—say, a phone had rung at just the right moment to perturb the process that generated possible solutions that met the criteria—they might have spent the rest of their lives in a different place that also met all the criteria they had set for their escape from civilization. Maybe they would have spent their lives on an island in Puget Sound instead (§4.67).

§7.22   The same goes for many of the key decisions we make in life. Why do we marry Bob and not Joe, when both would have met all the criteria one would want to set on a high-quality mate and life partner, and both would have in fact turned out to be perfect husbands? Bob was chosen because Bob passed the threshold for adequacy first (§4.69). This does not mean that Bob and Joe need to be identical. Bob might be more handsome, for example, and Joe a better provider. Whatever the weightings one puts on various criteria, a threshold assessing multiple criterial inputs can equate very different events or inputs.[11] Thus, much in decision making and therefore in life has a random, contingent feel to it. So much comes down to a matter of happenstance and being at the right place at the right time. There is no "fate" in the sense of a predetermined future. What there is, however, are sets of criteria that must be met, some of which are imposed on us by our innate biological organization. We cannot choose what smells delicious. We cannot choose not to feel hungry. What we can influence is the availability of things that might meet innately set criteria that are pressing to be met via ideational and behavioral interrupts and prioritization (what we interpret as desire). For example, we could choose to go to a vegetarian restaurant to fulfill the need to eat. Similarly, a parent may not be able to stop a teenage daughter from going "boy-crazy." But a parent can put his or her daughter in a situation, say, a boarding school, where the kinds of boys who might meet her criteria for a desirable romantic partner would likely also be the kinds of boys who would meet parental criteria for a respectable young man. In the end, quality decision making may in part come from playing the role of such a "parent" with regard to one's own "child."

Conclusion

§7.23   I have proposed a three-stage model of a neuronal mechanism that underlies mental causation and free will, according to which (1) new physical/informational criteria are set in a neuronal circuit on the basis of preceding physical/mental processing at t_1, in part via a mechanism of rapid synaptic resetting that effectively changes the inputs to a postsynaptic neuron. These changes can be driven volitionally or nonvolitionally, depending on the neural circuitry involved. (2) At t_2, inherently variable inputs arrive at the postsynaptic neuron, and (3) at t_3 physical/informational criteria are met or not met, leading to postsynaptic neural firing or not. Such "criterial causation" (§6.8) is important because it allows neurons to alter the physical realization of future mental events in a way that escapes the problem of mental-on-physical self-causation, a problem that has been at the root of basic criticisms of the possibility of mental causation (§§A2.2–A2.5) and free will (§§7.1–7.5). Substantial theoretical work, however, is still required to provide a more complete account of free will and mental causation. One could argue that neuronal criterial causation and ontological indeterminism are at best necessary but cannot alone be sufficient for the physical realization of mental causation and a strong free will, because without a conscious agent with intentional states that could exploit the three-stage process to fulfill its ends, we might be no more than mindless, unpredictable "zombies" (§10.83). We consider the roles of mental operations in exploiting the three-stage process in the next three chapters.

8   Implications of Criterial Causality for Mental Representation

Abstract

Neural information-processing is an instance of criterial causation. Criterial neural information-processing need not be algorithmic. Indeed, criterial encoding is not even representational, since it places constraints on inputs rather than specifying what exactly inputs must be. This implies that no necessary causal connection holds between a proposition or name and things or events in the world. Criterialism hearkens back to the descriptivist account of reference of Russell, Wittgenstein, and Frege, except that the criteria imposed by neurons cannot be understood at the level of descriptions, naming, semantics, or words. That being said, criterialism rejects Kripke's criticisms of descriptivism. Kripke's main argument against descriptivism is rooted in a category error that confuses statements about the world with statements about models of the world. Although a criterial account of neural information processing has some difficulty accounting for mental operations, such as mental rotation or syntax, it accounts well for other aspects of cognition, including prototyping, caricaturing, other race effects, generalization, categorization, and semantic priming.

The Neural Code Is Not Algorithmic

§8.1   It might be tempting to think of a neuronal criterion as a physically realized "if-then" statement, namely, if such-and-such conditions are met by input, then fire. But the criterial if-then relationship realized in a neuron is fundamentally different from an if-then statement coded in software that is implemented on any present-day computer.[1] To understand why neurons and computers are fundamentally different, we must bear in mind that modern computers are algorithmic, whereas the brain and neurons are not. An algorithm is a series of decisions, operations, or instructions that are carried out sequentially, one at a time; when one instruction is finished, the next step in the algorithm is executed, and its output goes to the next step, and so on. In a computer, this series is carried out in a sequential processor known as a central processing unit (CPU) or a core. A "thread" on a computer is one such linear sequence of decisions. Even multithread processing on multiple cores in a single computer, or on a computing grid of many computers, is algorithmic, because each thread is still a linear sequence of instructions executed one at a time. Multithread or grid processing might be parallel in the sense that subroutines run concurrently (Blaise, 2011; Savain, 2010), but in fact each processor carries out sequential algorithmic operations. Despite the speed of CPUs, this algorithmic parallelism can at best mimic the nonalgorithmic parallelism found in the brain, where each neuron is essentially an independent but slow processor. Several attributes distinguish algorithmic processing, as done by single- or even multithread CPUs (or their abstraction, the algorithmic universal Turing machine) from nonalgorithmic processing, as done by neurons: (1) An algorithm handles one input at a time, whereas a neuron or other nonalgorithmic, parallel processors can handle multiple inputs at a time; (2) an algorithm sends output to a single subsequent step in the algorithm, whereas a neuron can send output to many other neuronal processors simultaneously; and (3) because an algorithmic step operates only on a single input, it is by definition not an instance of criterial causal processing, which, according to §6.8, must be able to react to and equate multiple *types* of input. Whereas an if-then statement in a computer program is one step in a sequential algorithm that is not an instance of criterial causation, biological neural networks are not algorithmic and enact an instance of criterial causation. Whereas a step in an algorithm converts a single input to a single output, a parallel processor, such as a neuron, can be thought to transform a vector of inputs (weighted by synaptic strength) into a vector of outputs (action potentials to other neurons; cf. Georgopoulos et al., 1989).

§8.2 Individual neurons do not carry out algorithmic operations sequentially, on one input at a time. Criterial causation realized among neurons involves the operation of criterial satisfaction and a threshold that determines to what extent the criteria have been met. The essence of neuronal processing may involve chained sequences of criterial pattern-matching on the perceptual side, and pattern execution on the motoric side—nothing like numerical or algorithmic computation. If a spatiotemporal pattern of input matches the criteria, the neuron will be driven above threshold and tell other very specific neurons that its criteria—namely, the pattern to which it responds—have been satisfied by sending them an action-potential-modulated signal. At no stage need anything be computed using an algorithm; there is nothing like software or a computer program, and nothing has been represented explicitly as a number. The brain may be as far from an algorithmic computational device as, say, the digestive system; just because a system processes input does not mean it is carrying out algorithmic computations.

§8.3   Of course, any physical process can be redescribed in computational terms. This does not mean that anything is actually being computed. For example, a process such as peristalsis can be described using differential equations, but this does not mean that the esophagus is computing anything using differential equations. The properties of a model of a physical process can be very different from the process itself, even if the model makes perfect predictions. Differential equations help us to predict the direction of the wind tomorrow, but air does not solve differential equations, and models lack wind. We would not want to reduce peristalsis or wind to a Turing machine, yet many want to do this to the brain. But if the brain is not fundamentally a computational or algorithmic device, then it is not subject to problems inherent in computational or algorithmic systems, such as Gödel's incompleteness theorem or Amdahl's (1967) law specifying bottlenecks inherent to any multithreaded parallelization of an algorithm's subroutines.

Criterialism, Descriptivism, and Reference

§8.4   Criteria do not necessarily specify mental content as specific propositions, ideas, or representations. For example, if I want to eat something sweet, I might not know what it is exactly that I want to eat, beyond that it must be sweet. Any number of possible desserts—candy, ice cream, cake—might suffice to satisfy my desire. A criterial account of mental content is not specifically representational, in the sense that criteria themselves offer no specific mental content that is represented to satisfy them; they only offer constraints on what *would* satisfy them. Thus, when I desire something sweet, nothing very specific might be represented. Even if I subsequently narrow my criteria and say that I now desire to eat a piece of chocolate cake in my fridge that has three layers and a cherry on top, these narrowed criteria can still be met by countless possible chocolate cake pieces, any of which will be good enough to meet my new criteria.

§8.5   The nineteenth-century philosopher Franz Brentano (1874) thought that we could not desire something sweet unless something sweet was represented in our minds, presumably as an image of or proposition about chocolate cake or some other specific thing. But criteria are not themselves representations of anything in the world. They are not even themselves information about anything particular in the world, because an infinite number of things in the world can satisfy them. At best, criteria specify the class of all things in the world and/or "possible worlds"[2] that could satisfy them, which is to say that they represent no specific actual thing. They are conditions that must be met by input, whether externally generated, as when we perceive a piece of cake at the other end of the room, or internally generated, as when we survey our memory for possible sweet things that may be in our house. Thus a criterial account of mental content does not require that mental content be about specific things that are referred to, or directed to specific things in the world, or even in our own minds. Specifically, a criterial account of mental content does not require that mental content refer to anything that really exists in the world. I might desire to find an escape from death, when there is in fact no solution (or set of inputs) that can meet the criteria that are pressing to be met. I might desire to see a living *Homo floresiensis*, when this is in fact not possible, since they are extinct. I might even hallucinate one, and believe it to be real, because certain criteria for the detection of such have been met that were triggered not by input from the world, but rather by input due to neural activity generated by a drug that I ingested. As Chisholm (1957) pointed out, the aboutness or intentionality of mental content that Brentano regarded as central cannot be a physical relationship between a mental content and what it refers to in the world, because mental contents can be about nonexistent things.

§8.6   Scientists and many philosophers (e.g., Dretske, 1981; but cf., e.g., Millikan, 1989) tend to adhere to the traditional view of Shannon (1948) that information is effectively epistemological in the sense that it arises as a function of possibilities collapsing in the state of some reader, decoder, or receiver of information sent over some channel by a sender sharing a common informational encoding scheme. But Tononi (2008), in contrast, has recently advocated an ontological conception of information, whereby information simply is the occupying of some possible state in a system that can occupy many possible states. Tononi's view, that a decoder is not needed to generate information, is problematic because information changes depending on how input is decoded. Indeed, one could reasonably argue that there is no information at all in, say, a free-floating strand of DNA or mRNA. Rather, DNA and mRNA contain the *potential* for information, relative to a given decoder that decodes it. But the potential for realizing information relative to a given decoder is not the same as actually realizing information via physical state changes of that decoder. For example, a ribosome that "reads" mRNA will build proteins. But relative to a different decoder, the same mRNA strand might be used to build cities or write sonnets. A central problem for any theory of information is that given any physical configuration, a physically realized decoder can be designed that does whatever you would like in response to that configuration. Fashion the right decoder, and even cracks on a burned tortoise shell can be thought to carry information about the future, the temperature on the sun, or anything else.

§8.7   This seems to run counter to common sense, however, because it seems that for something to be informative about some event in the world, it must derive from that event in the right way. The "right way" is thought by externalist philosophers of mind to be in part a causal chain between the event and our experience of or knowledge of the event that makes our experience or knowledge of the event true (i.e., makes it correspond to facts). On this account, cracks in tortoise shells do not really carry information about the future, even though generations of ancient Chinese thought that they did, because this kind of causal chain is generally regarded as impossible within the modern scientific worldview. Even though we may now think that they were deluded and wrong, for the ancient Chinese who cracked tortoise shells in fire to divine the future, the cracks were very much informative about the future because they believed that they were. If information is only realized within a physical state change of a decoder, the decoder itself has no way to determine whether that which it decodes corresponds to some event in the world. Indeed, we may undergo a scientific revolution someday and come to see that the ancient Chinese were right about tortoise shell cracks after all, and that we were wrong. But then again, in the even more distant future, we might find that in fact we were right after all, and so forth. Does the informativeness of the cracks change with our transient scientific theories? No, the cracks were informative for the ancient Chinese, but are not for us, because they were decoding them according to a different decoding scheme than we use. If someone believes in astrology, horoscopes are informative to them, relative to their decoding scheme, even if objectively, astrology is complete bunk. Thus, *information has no necessary link to truth*, or correspondence with events in the world. Information arises only in the context of some decoding read-out mechanism (cf. Buzsáki, 2010). Information does not even require that a message be sent by a sender; even a random pile of rocks left by a melted glacier can be decoded as informative by a decoder prepared to interpret such input as a pattern that matches its criteria. For example, a religious person might see a meaningful pattern in such a pile and take this to confirm the existence of a caring God who is sending him or her a message.

§8.8   Criterialism rejects the notion that a name (or word or symbol) can only refer to a thing if it has a causal link to that thing in the world. Instead, information and reference arise in the context of the physical reconformation of a decoder or read-out mechanism when its physical/ informational criteria are met, regardless of whether the thing exists in the world or even could exist. According to traditional "descriptivist" theories of reference, like those of Frege, Russell, Wittgenstein, and Searle, a proper name refers to a thing by virtue of its being—or being associated with—a set of descriptions that that thing uniquely satisfies. A criterialist view of reference is related to a descriptivist account in that reference arises from the satisfaction of criteria, which, although they can be satisfied in many and even partial ways, can be thought of as descriptions.[3] Note, however, that the physical/informational criteria that neurons place on their inputs need not be, and typically cannot be, understood in terms of words, semantics, descriptions, or names. Nevertheless, descriptivism can be seen as an example of a criterialist approach to reference at the level of words.[4] Therefore, a criterialist would want to defend descriptivism as an instance of criterialism.

Countering Kripke's Attack

§8.9   The most serious attack on a descriptivist account of reference was Kripke's (1980) argument that reference arises only via a causal link between a proper name and the thing it refers to. He starts with an intuition showing, he argues, that descriptivism is incorrect: If a famous person had died as a baby, all the descriptions that defined his or her fame as an adult would not apply to the baby; but we would nonetheless want to consider him or her the same person regardless of our descriptions. Kripke argues that a proper name (e.g., "Alexander the Great") is therefore a "rigid designator," which means that it refers to the named person or thing in every possible (i.e., conceivable, but not necessarily actually existing) world in which it "exists." In contrast, most descriptions (e.g., "the leader who defeated Darius III and conquered Persia") are not rigid in that they can refer to different referents in different possible worlds. For example, in another possible world, Alexander's father is the one to have defeated Darius III and conquered Persia. A criterialist would say that the criterion "defeated Darius III" would be satisfied only by the mental representation of the adult Alexander, and not by the representation of the baby, and that criterial satisfaction need not depend in any necessary way on Alexander the Great's ever having even existed. That criterion could be satisfied in the context of a comic book by the story's hero. In the real world, it is satisfied by Alexander the Great.

§8.10   Let us define some needed philosophical terms. A necessarily true proposition is conventionally defined as a proposition that could not have been false. A contingently true proposition is defined as one that is true but might have been false. *A priori* knowledge is true by definition and does not require experience to prove it, whereas *a posteriori* knowledge can only be gained via experience or empirical evidence. Kripke's argument against a descriptivist account of reference and his claim that there are necessary *a posteriori* truths results from a category error that arises because of an ambiguity within the symbolism of modal logic that carries over from the ambiguity of ordinary languages from which that symbolism derives. The nature of the category error was first pointed out by Quine (1943, 1960, 1961, 1966). He noted that the central expressions in modal logic are "necessarily" and "possibly," and that modal logic uses these expressions in a referentially opaque manner, undermining their ability to derive true statements. As an example he gives: (1) The number of planets = 9; (2) necessarily (9 > 7); substituting from (1) into (2) yields (3) necessarily (the number of the planets > 7). This false conclusion occurs because substitution is allowed only in cases where reference is direct (Frege's term was *gerade*), as when different names refer to the same thing in the world. Substitution is not allowed when reference is opaque (*ungerade*), as occurs, for example, when terms refer to others' mental states, including what they may believe or know.

§8.11   Stalnaker (1976, 2004) and Chalmers (1996, ch. 2, section 4; 2002, 2005, 2006; but see Soames, 2007, for a defense of Kripke) have recently argued against Kripke in the spirit of Quine's "argument from propositional ambiguity," and pushed for a revival of descriptivism. According to their "two-dimensional semantic analysis," a sentence like "water is H_2O" expresses two propositions: The primary intension of "water" might be a set of descriptions that water meets (e.g., clear, drinkable, freezes at zero degrees); the secondary intension of water is whatever it is in this world that satisfies these descriptions. Since H_2O satisfies these descriptions in our world, "water" in this second sense must refer to H_2O in all possible worlds, because H_2O is H_2O in all worlds. The primary intension is *a posteriori* (and not necessary, since it is only contingently the case that "water" picks out H_2O in our world), and the second intension is necessary (and not *a posteriori*, because a thing, like H_2O, is necessarily identical to itself in all possible worlds). Kripke only concluded that there are necessary *a posteriori* propositions because a single sentence can frame two propositions at the same time.

§8.12   I will continue Quine's, Stalnaker's, and Chalmers's line of attack using the "argument from propositional ambiguity." While related, my argument is that a single sentence can frame a proposition about a thing-in-itself and also frame a proposition about a mental construct of that thing. To make this clear, two things can be mentally identical or not, or noumenally (actually) identical or not. This gives rise to a 2×2 with four cells. An example of "mentally identical and actually identical" would be the morning star and evening star after it was discovered and mentally modeled that both are in fact Venus. An example of "mentally different but actually identical" would be the same, but before this discovery, where the two stars were thought to be different stars, but were in fact both Venus. An example of "mentally the same and actually different" would be two species that we mistakenly think are one species, such as bonobos and chimpanzees were initially thought to be, but which in fact are different species. An example of "mentally different and actually different" would be how we think about these two separate species today.

§8.13   On a criterialist account, necessary *a posteriori* truths are not allowed. Like ordinary English, the symbolism of modal logic makes no distinction between propositions about (1) reality-in-itself (i.e., the "noumenal"[5] world, independent of any perceptions of it) and (2) a perceiver's perceptual and cognitive maps or models of reality-in-itself derived from "phenomenal" experience and the preconditions of that experience. (It is understandable that these two types of propositions are conflated, because we cannot in fact formulate verifiably true propositions about reality-in-itself, because arguably we have no direct access to it (Kant, 1998 [1781]); we only have (2), our perceptual and cognitive maps of it. Nonetheless, we commonly form propositions about things that we cannot access or experience, whether other people's experiences or the noumenal world, by inferring what must be the case given our experience). In ordinary human languages, no distinction is made between propositions of type (1) and (2). If I say "I see a child" or "A child is standing right over there" I mean both (1) that there is a child out there in the world independent of my perception of it, and (2) I have a mental/perceptual model that there is a child out there. Kripke's usage of modal logic similarly conflates propositions of types (1) and (2). Kripke's favorite examples of necessary *a posteriori* truths are "water is H_2O" and "Hesperus (the morning star) is identical with Phosphorus (the evening star)." Using this second example, at some point it was empirically discovered that both stars were in fact the planet Venus. Although they were once thought to be two stars, they were discovered to be in fact one and the same thing. It is essential to realize that "Hesperus is identical with Phosphorus" can frame two distinct propositions, one of type (1) and one of type (2). These are: (1) the noumenal thing-in-itself labeled "Hesperus" is identical in reality-in-itself with the thing-in-itself labeled by "Phosphorus" and (2) the mental model of the thing-in-itself labeled "Hesperus" and the mental model of the thing-in-itself labeled "Phosphorus" are identical mental models. However, that my mental models should be such that the morning and evening star are both modeled as Venus followed the empirical discovery that they were both Venus. The type (2) proposition here must be contingent. However, the above type (1) proposition is necessary if it is true, because a thing-in-itself is necessarily identical with itself, even if it is given two different names. It is only because of the ambiguity introduced by the fact that a single sentence can frame two different propositions, one necessary (1) and the other *a posteriori* (2), that one reaches the mistaken conclusion that there can be necessary *a posteriori* truths. However, we must consider the two different propositions (1) and (2) separately. A given proposition is either necessary and *a priori* or contingent and *a posteriori*. It cannot be both. The end result of Stalnaker's, Chalmers's, or my argument ends the same way, however: against Kripke and in support of descriptivism. Those interested in reading a formal version of the "argument from propositional ambiguity" in terms of modal logic can go to appendix 3.

Wittgenstein and Criteria

§8.14   More than any other philosopher, Wittgenstein (1953) focused on the importance of criteria. He used the term "criteria" in two contexts, one having to do with countering skepticism concerning the existence of other minds,[6] and the other concerning how concepts, categories, and actions are identified and defined. It is this latter usage that is relevant to the notion of criteria as realized in neural systems. He spoke of "family resemblances" (see also Wittgenstein, 1958) among objects or actions, focusing particularly on the plurality of uses of language. His main example concerned games. He noted that many things count as a game, but there is no single feature that is common to all games. There might be a set of features common among games, but there is no single feature or subset of features that is shared by all games. In other words, one or a number of features might be sufficient for something to count as a game if present to a satisfactory degree, but no feature is a necessary component of all games. Because there are no necessary features, there are no strict boundaries on what counts as a game; games share nothing more than a fuzzy similarity structure along numerous potentially orthogonal dimensions, much like relatives in a family can share various features, such as nose shape or skin color, and yet not all share a unique defining feature. This notion of family resemblances is well captured by the idea of criteria. Criteria can be set for what counts as a game in the sense that some subset of features must be present from among a set of features that define "gamehood." The subcriteria can be met in degrees, and no single subcriterion need be met before the threshold for what counts as gamehood is passed, leading to criterial satisfaction. Wittgenstein was taking particular aim against the idea that there is an essence to actions or concepts abstracted away from some unique defining feature or features.

§8.15   Wittgenstein's idea has been developed in psychology (Rosch & Mervis, 1975; Rosch, 1987) in the form of prototype theory, according to which people do not represent objects according to abstract definitions of what counts as membership in a category, using Aristotelian necessary and sufficient logical conditions, but rather represent objects and experiences in terms of psychological distance from one or more prototype objects or experiences that are the most characteristic instances of a category. Distance from or similarity to a prototype can be thought of as one form of a criterial representation of objects and experiences, where the criteria for inclusion in a category are met to the degree that an object or experience is close to a prototype in the relevant representational space. Initially, prototypes were considered the most typical stimulus or the stimulus first associated with a category (Rosch, 1973), and later Rosch regarded prototypes as the most central member of a category. Typically, prototypes are thought to exist at a semantic level that can be specified by a word; for example, "sparrow" is more prototypical of the category "bird" than "emu." This high-level semantic conception of prototypes has proven useful in capturing the graded nature of the representation of semantic categories in human cognition (e.g., Lakoff, 1987; Langacker, 1987).

§8.16   A criterialist would want to bring the idea of prototypes back closer to Wittgenstein's original conception of family resemblances. On this account, a prototype is whatever best fulfills the criteria that define an object or category. Objects are not encoded relative to a unique prototype, but are encoded in terms of the degree to which they fulfill certain criteria. This is why there is no unique prototype for most categories. For example, which is a more prototypical bird, a pigeon or a sparrow? Both meet all the criteria for bird equally well, so both count as a bird prototype.[7] Emphasizing prototypes over criteria confuses the conditions set on category membership with the things that fulfill those conditions. When one thinks about what may be happening at a neuronal level, one can dispense with the idea of prototypes altogether. There can be neuronal criterial satisfaction in the absence of any high-level semantic or imagistic prototypes per se. Neurons may place criteria on their inputs that have nothing to do with semantic categories or prototypes that could be described with a word. The optimal conditions that satisfy low-level criteria that make a neuron fire might look nothing like high-level semantic categories, and they may not even be describable in words. Indeed, the number of dimensions of a representational space, such as "face space," may be given by the number of criteria that are placed on inputs to determine whether something counts as a face. On this account, each individual criterion for some aspect of faceness defines a dimension of face space. Since criteria may look nothing like our concepts of what counts as a face, it is an empirical question what the dimensions of face space are. For example, there may exist neurons that are tuned to the ratio of the distance between the eyes and lips versus the distance between the eyes. If so, that relationship would constitute a dimension of face space. Thus, while prototype theory is a high-level example of criterial encoding, many examples of criterial encoding can be found that are not semantic and that do not involve anything that looks like a prototype.

§8.17   A neural code based on criterial satisfaction expresses several fundamental traits of human cognition. Similarity and categorization fall out of such an architecture, as, for example, countless fonts and sizes of "A" will all meet the criteria that define "A-ness" in terms of the configuration of lower-level features such as T-junctions, L-junctions, lines, and terminators. Two things will be similar to the extent that they meet the same criteria, and will lie in different categories when there is not a spectrum of criterial satisfaction but a clear boundary. Thus criteria underlie both the formation of categories, and a distance metric among categories of things that meet criteria. In short, criteria permit the emergence of representational spaces based on a multidimensional similarity/difference metric. And criteria afford the possibility of generalization, such that all things that obey certain criteria are tokens of a general class, even if they are very different at the level of defining sensory features. Prototyping also emerges via criterial definition of a class, as that which best meets particular criteria. Criteria can also be assessed in parallel at multiple levels within a criterial hierarchy, permitting constraint satisfaction across the hierarchy and a path to recognition exploiting many parallel avenues of matching input to memory (e.g., simultaneously on the basis of various featural, configural, and contextual cues). In particular, partial inputs can nonetheless lead to criterial satisfaction, giving rise to the brain's ability to complete degraded, partial, or occluded patterns. Prototyping can also account for how people make judgments about categories and probabilities. Tversky and Kahneman (1974, 1981; see also Gigerenzer & Gaissmaier, 2011) noticed that, given only information that a person was orderly, shy, helpful and asocial, people assigned a much higher probability that he or she was a librarian than a farmer, even though there are many more farmers in the world than librarians. When given information about type, human judgments tend not to be Bayesian in that they ignore objective prior and even posterior probabilities.[8] Tversky and Kahneman argued such seemingly irrational assessments were rooted in heuristics or rules of thumb. But there may in fact be no explicit rules represented anywhere in the brain or abstract heuristics involved in making such judgments. Instead, judgments concerning category membership are based on criterial satisfaction regarding, say, the traits exhibited by people in different professions. It appears that the default mode of human cognition is closer to criterial pattern matching than it is to deductive logic. Priming also falls out of rapid neuronal criterial resetting. For example, imagine a neuron that fires if and only if the word "soldier" is spoken or read. The firing of this neuron is a physical event that realizes a mental event, namely, the information that there is a soldier, along with that term's associated meanings. Depending on how this neuron is connected to other neurons in a semantic associative network of neurons, the tendency of neurons to fire that were tuned to "tank," "gun," "platoon," "peace," and so forth can change, accounting for positive and negative semantic priming. Semantic priming could be realized in the changing of the "epiconnectivity" of neurons (§§4.54–4.60).

Propositions and Vectorial Encodings

§8.18   Criterial encoding entails that at least some representational spaces have a quasi-vectorial organization, where multidimensional vectors are specified by the degree to which various criteria are met, triggering the firing of neurons that assess their inputs on the basis of those criteria (cf. Hsieh & Tse, 2009; Leopold et al. 2001, 2006; Rhodes et al., 2010, 2011). Norm-based and vector-based models offer a good but rough first approximation of certain types of mental representation. Nevertheless, criterially defined mental representational spaces would not be true vector spaces in the mathematical sense for several reasons: Such a space would have to be bounded rather than infinite, because criteria cannot be satisfied beyond some maximum value, realized presumably in the maximum response of neurons that impose these criteria on their inputs; neurons operate on one another in ways that vectors do not (e.g., vectors do not laterally inhibit one another, do not adapt, and do not express opponency); and at least certain classes of representations, such as trajectories and motor sequences, are inherently dynamic, whereas vectors need not be (but see Churchland & Churchland, 1997). Of course, these biological properties can be added to the vector encoding and transformation idea, but this would no longer be a vector space in the traditional mathematical sense.

§8.19   Neuroscientists do not yet understand how a propositional conclusion in working memory, such as "I need to buy cranberry sauce," can be translated into a motor plan to carry it out (§9.16). But the transformation across types of encoding, from high-level propositional representations in working memory areas to motoric plans and then commands in premotor and motor areas, happens so quickly in a characteristic thought-to-action cascade, that the respective encodings of these various representations must be readily transformable, one into the other. If a criterial encoding of representations could, to a first approximation, be regarded as a vectorial encoding at both the informational level (i.e., the degrees to which a set of informational criteria are met) and at the physical neuronal level (i.e., the degrees to which neurons in a population fire across the dimensions to which they are tuned), a rapid way to transform vectors across different representational spaces would involve linear transformations describable by matrix multiplication. Transformations could be concatenated, "composed," or chunked easily by multiplying their respective matrices, and a transformation could be undone by inverting the transformation matrix. Future neuroscientific research will hopefully determine whether evolution came up with some instantiation of this elegant solution to the representation and transformation problems inherent in neuronal and mental encoding. Most likely, informational transformation in the brain is not likely to be so simple; nonlinear responses likely abound. At present, however, too little is known about the encoding of various types of representation at a neuronal level to solve the problem of transformations between representations of different types (but see Georgopoulos et al., 1989).

§8.20   If we can model certain types of mental representation as vectors deviating from some origin, norm, or population average, information is likely to be encoded in a population of neural responses rather than in the responses of lone neurons, because information is likely carried in the relative responses of neurons, not just in their absolute responses. Adaptation at the level of individual neurons would alter the population response and would account for well-known aftereffects, such as the face aftereffect (Leopold et al. 2001, 2006; Rhodes et al., 2010, 2011), in terms of changes in the population response. Any population of neurons that encoded a representational space should then exhibit both aftereffects and the possibility of caricaturing and anticaricaturing, as any vector can be reflected through or made longer or shorter relative to the origin. That so many things can be caricatured—faces, bodies, gestures, manners of walking or talking, attitudes, personalities, sizes, brightnesses, degrees of motion, and so on—suggests that these things are represented in a norm-based or examplar-based encoding in some population of neurons. Moreover, any given vector can be placed relative to a different origin, allowing us to carry out operations like imagining what a man might look like if his constellation of features were on a woman. Norm-based representational spaces, like human perception, should be prone to "other race" effects, which occur when certain inputs all "look the same." For example, relative to an African male face norm, all Asian male faces might "look the same" because their vectors relative to that norm are all similar. In order to gain expertise in the domain of Asian faces, one would have to judge them relative to the norm of Asian male faces. But if one lacked such a norm, say, because one grew up in rural Benin, then all Asian faces would be confusable.

Mental Operations versus Mental Representations

§8.21   Norm-based encoding might be useful for understanding representations in representational spaces, but it may be less useful for understanding operations carried out in those spaces. Even though mental operations are at least as important as the representations they transform, recall, store, select, and ignore, operations have received only a fraction of the attention that representations have. This is mainly, I think, because they are harder to study. Whereas a single neuron can be thought to represent a bar or a direction of motion in firing behavior that is relatively easily measured, it is likely that an operation such as willing to recall your mother's maiden name involves thousands of neurons that span the brain. Since we cannot measure operations at a neuronal level, we focus on looking where the light is good (§§1.9, 1.10).

§8.22   If representations are rather like the "nouns" of the mind, operations are like the "verbs" of the mind. Mental rotation, for example, is an operation carried out over mental imagery that can possibly be understood in terms of linear transformations of vectors, but what about more complex operations such as combining arbitrary representations in working memory to imagine, for example, an egg with wings? It is doubtful that an operation involving the spatial manipulation and recombination of representations like imagining an egg with wings can be reduced to a description in terms of vectors. It is equally doubtful that an operation like the placing of a spatial coordinate system within the boundaries of a room, as appears to accomplished by grid cells (Hafting et al., 2005; Fyhn et al., 2008; Doeller et al., 2010; Moser et al., 2008) and border cells (Solstad et al., 2008), can be understood in terms of vector-based encoding. This is also true of syntactic operations. Operations, because they involve a sequence of steps over time, are not likely to be easily explained by a model in which information can be thought to exist in a population response at a given time. Operations will require an understanding of criterial neural processing at the level of sequential procedures within a neural circuit rather than at the level of individual neuronal responses. Recent important work tries to root abstract operations—including symbolic and algorithmic processing—in specific types of neuronal operations such as might be carried out in working memory buffers in the frontal lobes (e.g., O'Reilly, 2006; Prince & Smolensky, 2004). Clearly we can carry out syntactic and mathematical operations using only neurons, but the neuronal operations that permit this may be quite different from those that lead to the recognition of an object.

§8.23   Our ability to understand neural processing at the level of neural circuits is hindered by both technological issues, such as an inability to measure all neurons simultaneously known to be part of a common circuit, and conceptual issues, such as the idea of the receptive field of an individual neuron. A receptive field captures the idea that sensory neurons are tuned to or detect particular types of stimulus energy in input. But the visual system does not merely detect information; it also constructs it on the basis of what was detected. Grouping operators, for example, transform sparse visual inputs into full-blown representations of surfaces and volumes when what is detected may be not much more than explicit information about the locations of edges and luminance blobs.

Beyond Functionalism

§8.24   Understanding that neurons and brains need not fundamentally be algorithmic frees us from the confusions that sometimes emerge when we apply the dominant metaphor of our age, namely, that the brain is a kind of computer. The questionable usefulness of this metaphor is apparent once we realize that there is no hardware–software distinction in the brain and computers do not rewire themselves continually as neurons do. Computers also do not enter teleological states, such as lust or hunger, and they lack consciousness. Metaphors are useful in that they help us understand something that we do not understand in terms of something that we do understand. The danger is that two things can be alike in some ways and totally dissimilar in other ways, and unless we pay attention to these differences we are likely to extend the metaphor too far and make conceptual mistakes as a consequence. For example, while a neuron's threshold imposes a point of no return beyond which an action potential will occur, and a toilet's handle does something similar for flushing, it would be absurd to extend the metaphor to the point that one believes that a neuron really functions like a toilet. But precisely such metaphorical overreach has occurred with the computer metaphor in modern neuroscience. While the initial users of this metaphor, particularly the founders of the cognitive revolution, had good reason to do so—they wanted to put something "scientific" in the black box in their efforts to overturn behaviorism— many neuroscientists and cognitive scientists today speak as if the brain really were a kind of computer. If neural information processing is an instance of nonalgorithmic criterial causation, we should search for the answer to the neural code not in computational algorithms, but in a deeper understanding of how criteria are set up and satisfied in dendrites, individual neurons and circuits of neurons. There is much that is yet to be understood in the brain sciences, and the neural code has yet to be deciphered. But we can free ourselves from the misconceptions of at least one brand of functionalism that is presently dominant in neuroscience, namely, machine-state functionalism (Putnam, 1960, 1967, 1975), according to which the brain is a fundamentally algorithmic and computational device equatable with a Turing machine.

§8.25   Functionalists typically argue that the material implementation of a set of functions is irrelevant to its functions. Certainly in the case of, say, a pipe, this is largely true. Whether a pipe is made of copper or steel is irrelevant for most plumbing applications. But in the case of neurons, the particular physical implementation of criteria is likely to be very difficult, if not impossible, to mimic in another physical substrate. For example, a functionalist might say that mental input–output relations and causal chains could be implemented in a series of tin cans connected with strings that is as big as the world, and that implements a millisecond timescale brain operation over weeks of tin can operations. For a functionalist, as long as the functional causal chains were equivalent, then functional relationships would be the same, and the mental state realized in such a collection of tin cans would be the same as that realized in the analogous brain process. The problem here is that neurons take advantage of properties of physical causation in realizing mental events that are not available to tin cans connected by strings. For example, it is only because synapses are the size that they are, and diffusion constants are what they are at the temperatures that real brains are, that neurons can harness the noise of Brownian motion in the synapse to introduce variability and novelty into neural information processing (§§4.66, 4.67). If the functional properties of NMDA receptors can only arise in something the size and shape of NMDA receptors, the function cannot be split off and transferred to a new "platform." If the main idea of functionalism is that mental states are constituted solely by their functional causal role (i.e., causal input–output relations in a way analogous to software), and such functions cannot be divorced from the properties of physical causality in a particular physical implementation, then mental states are not solely constituted by their functional causal roles, but also by the set of causal relationships present in the particular physical implementation. That is, the central claim of "multiple realizability" of functionalism,[9] namely, that mental states can in principle be moved like software across physical platforms without affecting those mental states, would be wrong. It would follow that our kinds of minds require our kinds of brains, or something close enough. The functionalist viewpoint may have given the past two generations of philosophers of mind a "false sense of security" in that they have thought that they could analyze function without having to learn about the details of neuronal processing. I think that view is wrong and that we will only make progress on philosophical questions of mind and brain with a deeper understanding of the brain. My prediction and hope is that the best future graduate programs in the philosophy of mind will require the equivalent of a Ph.D. in neuroscience and psychology.

§8.26   In arguing that neurons are not algorithmic, I am not arguing that the brain cannot realize computations or that brainlike operations cannot be realized in nonbrains. Indeed, certain procedures are algorithmic and are realized in neuronal operations or routines (e.g., Ullman, 1984). Language provides the paradigmatic example of syntactic, and probably algorithmic, computation. Beyond language, we can work out mathematical problems in our working memory. We can even report the algorithm we used to do so. If I ask you what 29×6 is, you may say 174, and report that you solved this by converting "30×6" to "$3 \times 10 \times 6$" to "$3 \times 6 \times 10$"

to "18 × 10," then subtracting 6 from the resultant 180. But that we can carry out algorithmic computations does not prove that all neural processing is algorithmic. It is unlikely that a dog, say, can carry out anything mathematical or syntactic in its brain, but it can recognize a mate, food, or a predator, it can attend, and it is presumably conscious. It can do these things on the basis of criterial satisfaction among the tuning properties of neurons, without necessarily computing anything symbolically or algorithmically. For most animals, and even for most of what we humans do, it may just be criterial satisfaction by patterns of input—and the innate drive to seek out such satisfaction—all the way up the hierarchy of neurons from sensory input to behavior. Nonetheless, what makes us apparently unique among animals is precisely our capacity to process information symbolically and syntactically. How these capacities could have evolved in us via modifications of the attentional network of the more typical mammalian mind–brain of our ancestors will be a focus of my next book, *The Cultivation of Will* (forthcoming; see also Tse, 2006b).

9 Barking Up the Wrong Free: Readiness Potentials and the Role of Conscious Willing

Abstract

Here I argue that conscious feelings of willing or agency are not central to understanding the neural basis of free will. Simple actions, such as repeatedly lifting a finger, or even complex actions, such as driving a car while daydreaming, may not generate conscious feelings of willing at all. Consciousness of willing appears to primarily arise in cases that require endogenous selection and inhibition of options held and assessed in working memory. As such, Libet's paradigm may not particularly evoke conscious feelings of willing. And even if it did, neither the readiness potential nor the lateralized readiness potential appears to be a signature of a neural process involved in conscious willing.

Libet's Experiments Do Not Disprove the Possibility of Free Will

§9.1 The feeling of volitionally causing a motor act may, in some cases, follow the unconscious planning of that motor act, even if it must precede the execution of that motor act to feel causal of it (Wegner & Wheatley, 1999; Wegner, 2002). Although our wills seem to cause our actions, Benjamin Libet's experiments raised doubts about this (Libet et al., 1982, 1983a,b; Libet, 1985). Libet and colleagues had subjects make a motor movement, such as pressing a button or lifting a finger at will. They estimated the earliest conscious awareness of a will or urge to move (W) by asking subjects to recall where on a clock a fast-moving clockhand had been at the moment when they first felt an urge to move.[1] Elaborating the event-related potential method of Kornhuber and Deecke (1965), Libet et al. (1982, 1983a,b) found that a particular EEG marker of brain activity time-locked to the motor act, dubbed the "readiness potential" (having two components, the RP and the LRP or "lateralized readiness potential"[2]), occurred 200–400 ms before the average reported time of W. This has been replicated many times (e.g., Haggard & Eimer, 1999; Lau et al., 2004; Sirigu et al., 2004). Libet concluded that conscious will could not be what initiates the causal process that leads to action, since the early part of the RP precedes W.[3] What has surprised people most is just how late W is in the process that leads from motor planning to action.

§9.2 It would indeed be surprising and troubling if our proximal conscious intentions or wills did not initiate our actions and if, instead, all of our actions were initiated in a wholly unconscious or automatic manner. Libet's results raise a crucial question: Is the RP part of a causal chain that is sufficient to produce action without any essential intervening causal role for will or for consciousness? If so, moral responsibility and the efficacy of will and consciousness are in doubt. In the end, Libet did not deny free will but instead located it in a veto power that could stop the execution of unconsciously computed actions shortly before the command to execute. However, many scientists and philosophers have used Libet's and similar results to argue against the existence of free will and responsibility (cf. Sinnott-Armstrong & Nadel, 2010). Despite three decades of philosophizing about Libet's results, the precise roles of components of the readiness potential have not been empirically established. It is still unclear whether the readiness potential is a neural correlate of the motor act, the planning of the motor act, expectation of a motor act, or the act of consciously willing.[4]

§9.3 Haggard and Eimer (1999) found that (1) early and late RPs were not correlated with early and late reported consciousness of willing (W), but (2) early and late LRPs were correlated with early and late W. These and other data support the view that the neural processes that give rise to the RP do not cause W. They are also consistent with the possibility that the LRP might be a neural signature of a process that causes W. But correlation is not evidence of causation. Just because some event precedes some other event does not mean it causes it; for example, no educated person would conclude that the arrival of dawn causes the sun to rise just because it always precedes it. There might be some other process or "lurking third variable" (e.g., analogous to the rotation of the Earth) that leads both to the LRP and to W. Just as dust in the nose might trigger a conscious feeling of having a nasal itch and also trigger a sneeze—without the itch itself causing the sneeze—some third variable might trigger both W and the LRP, as well as the actions we mistakenly assume W to cause. Whether this hidden causal process is conscious or unconscious, if it exists, is not known.

§9.4 Other data cast doubt on the possibility that the LRP is a signature of neural activity that prospectively causes a conscious will to move. In particular, an intention to move may unfold over time and arise at multiple levels of processing. It is possible that the awareness of wanting to move,

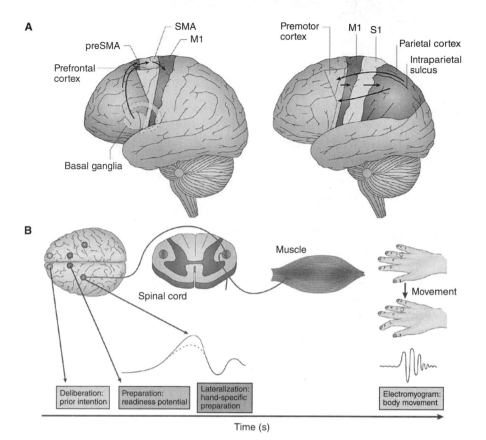

Figure 9.1

Neural circuits involved in volitional movement. (A) M1 or the motor strip on the precentral gyrus is the last cortical stage before motor commands are sent down the spinal cord leading to muscle contraction. M1 receives two broad classes of input (Passingham, 1987), corresponding to voluntary/deliberated (A, left) and stimulus-driven/immediate action commands (A, right). The voluntary input to M1 comes via the supplementary motor area (SMA) from the presupplementary motor area (preSMA), which itself received input from both the "drive" system of the basal ganglia (Akkal et al., 2007; Jahanshahi et al., 1995; Loukas & Brown, 2004; itself modulated by input from the "reward" system of the striatum and substantia nigra) and the planning areas of the anterior prefrontal cortex (Haggard, 2008). The early part of the readiness potential has been localized to the preSMA (Shibasaki & Hallett, 2006; Lang et al., 1991; Yazawa et al., 2000). In contrast, environmentally driven actions, such as catching, involve action plan selection in the parietal lobes, which then send a signal to premotor cortex, which in turn triggers M1 neurons. (B) Before the right finger is voluntarily moved, an action plan from anterior prefrontal is prepared in preSMA and SMA, generating the early part of the readiness potential measured at the midline (position Cz). Before M1 sends its command to the muscles, there is a difference in the readiness potentials measured ipsilaterally (dashed curve) and contralaterally (solid curve) to the moved finger. This difference, the lateralized readiness potential, measured at C3 and C4, likely corresponds to activity in M1 in the region of the finger motor neurons. Reproduced from Haggard (2008) with permission.

reported as the time of W, is a final stage of a process that begins much earlier, perhaps even before the beginning of the LRP. In an attempt to address this, and to counteract the problematic need to rely on self-report and memory to estimate the time of W, Matsuhashi and Hallett (2008; following the method of Smallwood & Schooler, 2006) used a tone probe to ask subjects whether they had any intention to move at the time of the tone. They reported that "the time when subjects have access to movement genesis as intention" could be accessed via an external probe more than one second before W. This cued awareness of a nascent intention to move occurred on average 1420 ms before movement. This is well before the onset of the LRP. If this probed type of awareness is equivalent to W, then W occurs after the RP, but *before* the LRP, implying that the LRP is not the cause of a conscious intention to move. Even if it is not equivalent to W, it would appear to be an early stage of an intention or urge to move that is not accessible to or reportable by observers without cuing. The authors suggest that an awareness of an intention to move indeed does develop over time, and may only reach a full metacognitive level of awareness (i.e., where one is aware that one is aware of an intention to move; see Smallwood & Schooler, 2006) at the relatively late timepoint associated with W. Probing allows one to become aware of a developing intention to move at an earlier stage. Even if not W, some information that subjects can use to infer the genesis of a motor intention is available to probed subjects after the RP but before the LRP (Schlegel et al., 2012a), suggesting that the LRP is not the signature of a neural process that is the sole cause of an intention to move.

§9.5   My colleagues[5] and I are collaborating on a project aimed at finding out what the readiness potential is in fact a signature of. We want to determine which mental states correspond to components of the RP or its preconscious segment, whether anticipation independent of movement, anticipation of movement, or preparation to move. We are experimentally asking whether the RP arises in cases of willing without movement and of movement without willing (or without consciousness of willing). If, for example, we find that the RP reflects only anticipation or preparation that does not ensure action without a later choice or will that is necessary for the action, and if we find that the LRP reflects the command to move, then the efficacy of the will is not undermined by the main arguments of Libet and his followers. However, if either component of the RP instead reflects processes that lead to action regardless of what the agent wills or is conscious of willing, then the will and consciousness of will are inefficacious. Given that such basic issues concerning the significance of the RP are not settled, there is no basis for arguing that Libet's results

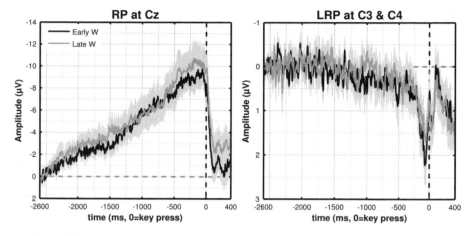

Figure 9.2

No differences exist between early and late time of willing (W) RPs or LRPs. Subjects (n=20; Schlegel et al., 2012a) took part in a Libet-like experiment where they had to report the time of onset of the will to move W. No significant differences exist between early and late awareness RPs at Cz, as shown on the left, or LRPs at C3 and C4, as shown on the right. We have therefore failed to replicate the main finding of Haggard and Eimer (1999) that the onset of the LRP is correlated with the timing of W.

undermine free will. To my knowledge, no data involving RPs or LRPs provide conclusive evidence that undermines the efficacy of the will. It may in fact turn out that the RP and LRP alone cannot prove much about the causal efficacy of W, in which case the field may have taken a wrong turn in focusing on these markers as directly relevant to the free will debate, when they are not. Given our data, shown in figures 9.2 and 9.3, we fail to replicate Haggard and Eimer's (1999) main finding that LRP onset is correlated with the time of W. We conclude that the RP, but not the LRP, appears to be closely tied to anticipation of a motor act or preparation of a motoric plan (Haggard, 2008; Roskies, 2010), whereas the LRP, but not the RP, appears to be closely tied to motor execution. If this is true, then neither the RP nor the LRP have much to teach us about the neural correlates of consciously willing an action to take place.

Is Conscious Willing Causal?

§9.6   In addition, it is not at all clear what is being described when the time of W is estimated by subjects. Is W the conscious feeling of being

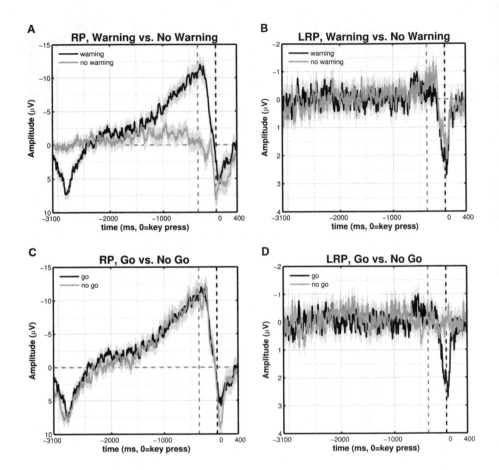

Figure 9.3

Comparison of readiness potential before movement with and without a warning 3 seconds before the imperative stimulus that commanded subjects to press a button. The gray vertical dashed line is the mean imperative stimulus time. The black vertical dashed line is the time of key press. (A) The RP occurred only when the participant was forewarned of imperative stimulus time. (B) The LRP occurred whether or not the participant was forewarned. (C) Comparison of RP when a warning stimulus precedes a prompt to either move ("go") or not move ("no-go"). For the "no-go" condition, data are time-locked to the imperative stimulus and shifted to the right by the mean reaction time in "go" trials. The RP occurred whether or not movement occurred. (D) The LRP only occurred if movement occurred. (Figures 9.2 and 9.3 by Alex Schlegel [Schlegel et al., 2012a].)

about to move? Of intending to move? Of having an urge or desire to move? A feeling that an imminent motion is agentically authored by oneself? Is W a conscious content that is prospectively causal of the subsequent motion? Or is it only retrospectively causal of motion? Perhaps W is a conscious correlate of a form of "efference copy"[6] that marks motion execution as self-caused as opposed to caused by some external factor. Even if W—whatever W is—turns out not to be causal of our actions, that does not allow one to jump to the conclusion that no conscious contents can be causal of our actions. There might be other conscious contents that are not W, and that long precede W, that are causal of our actions. For example, holding a plan in working memory to "move the right index finger every so often during this experiment" might or might not be capable of triggering processing that then leads to unconscious action preparation and execution, and then later, a causally inefficacious W or feeling of authorship of an action.

§9.7 The search for a conscious feeling of willing that is causal of our actions may be misguided in the sense that, for many cases where conscious operands may play a causal role in the occurrence of our actions, we may never experience any feeling of willing at all. In general, most processes that can be dealt with automatically seem to be placed on the unconscious side of the conscious–unconscious divide. Some processes, like monitoring blood pressure, cannot be moved to the conscious side of that divide. Other processes that are normally unconscious, such as breathing, can be moved to the conscious side of the divide when they need to be brought under voluntary control. In general, only processes that require open-ended and endogenously controlled—as opposed to closed-ended or ballistic, exogenously controlled—computations of what to do next are made conscious. If there is only one possible sensible course of action, there is no need to make that process conscious. To do so would waste time and energy in a system designed to minimize both. It would be like having a window pop up in an operating system that needlessly states "the optimal course of action is x, which will now be implemented"; it only makes sense to invoke such an interrupt when a choice between two or more genuinely possible processes or courses of action needs to be made via endogenous consideration of options in working memory.

§9.8 The consciousness associated with full endogenous attentional engagement may not even be needed when multiple courses of action are possible but the optimal path can be selected on the basis of information available in the input. For example, there are multiple ways of driving down the highway, but the process may unfold largely automatically as long as nothing too unexpected happens—that is, as long as we can act according to script. There may be processes that generate possible courses of action automatically, and there may be processes that select the optimal option automatically when we are in auto-pilot mode driving down the highway. For example, the basal ganglia may select and switch to the optimal motoric (e.g., Chakravarthy et al., 2010), cognitive (Cools et al., 2003, 2004; Ragozzino et al., 2002; Ravizza & Ciranni, 2002; Ravizza & Ivry, 2001; Stocco et al., 2010), or emotional (Saint-Cyr et al., 1995; the amygdala also plays a role in emotional switching: Herry et al., 2008) action program at each moment as needed. This can happen automatically, analogous to how an automatic transmission selects the optimal gear when driving.

§9.9   But when something happens that is unexpected because it has not been learned or genetically preprogrammed in an action script, the "automatic transmission mode" of action and thought selection may shift into "stick shift mode," as actions and thoughts are now selected endogenously or voluntarily on the basis of information beyond what can be handled by any action script. That is, concrete and stimulus-driven basal ganglia action program selection (Cools et al., 2006) can be handed over to and influenced by executive cortical circuitry that incorporates information beyond that present in the stimulus, including abstract relations such as rules for behaving (Cameron et al., 2010). Say a clown skips across the highway. This event lies outside information available within the driving script, so control is handed over to endogenous attentional, planning, and selection circuitry that can decide what to do in a context-sensitive and flexible manner.

§9.10   As such, the only time most of our actions require a conscious feeling of willing will be cases where the action involves a decision point that cannot be preprogrammed or a conflict that must be resolved, but cannot be resolved by faster, automatic processing. For a simple action such as repeatedly lifting a finger, or even a complex one such as driving a car down an open highway, there might be no associated conscious feeling of willing even though brain circuits are generating possible courses of action and choosing among them. However, should a clown leap across the road, a feeling of willing may arise as one of multiple possible courses of action are considered (e.g., braking, honking, waving, swerving to the left or right), one action plan is endogenously selected, others are inhibited, and the selected one is implemented. The feeling of willing generally arises in situations where there is either some conflict that must be resolved with endogenous attentional control, as in the Stroop task (§4.27),[7] or some process that must be endogenously considered, selected, or inhibited, as in the clown example just given.

§9.11   More common than feelings of willing may be the sense of authorship over an action, which could arise as a form of efference copy. In short, we may feel authorship but no effortful willing when we are in automatic transmission mode of action selection and implementation, but feel both authorship and effortful willing when in stick shift mode, facing a complex situation or one that requires endogenous attentional selection and inhibition of prepotent responses. Given that W may not typically arise for the kinds of nondeliberative actions that Libet and his followers have studied, the entire research program may be in need of revision. Libet's standard paradigm, in asking subjects to report the timing of W, may be asking them to report the timing of something which they do not particularly experience. Estimated times of W may then be cognitive inferences of the sort "Given that I moved at time x, I must have felt an urge to move at x minus y milliseconds," instead of being reports of the time when an urge to move was actually experienced.

§9.12   What role, then, might any conscious contents play in causing action if not feelings of willing or feelings of authorship? In the next section, I will consider cases of deliberative processing, in particular the open-ended modification and selection of action plans after conscious deliberation. Such deliberative processing precedes the execution of those plans and may in part play a causal role in their selection and implementation.

Illusions of Volitional Efficacy

§9.13   A feeling W that one is the agent that causes a motor act M could be an "illusion of agency" (Wegner & Wheatley, 1999; Wegner, 2002), as shown in figure 9.4a,b, rather than being directly causal of M, as in figure 9.4c, or indirectly causal of M, as in figure 9.4d, where a solid arrow means causal and a dashed arrow means only illusorily causal. In figure 9.4a or 9.4b, W might be an experiential report to executive and planning centers that an action has now been prepared, initiated, or even executed up to some stage, rather like the cocking of a gun. As such, some feelings of volition W may be a form of efference copy (see n. 6) that indicates to planning centers that commands have been prepared as planned. Whatever mechanism "pulls the trigger" on an action, whether unconscious or conscious, planning centers may need to know which actions have been potentiated before any one of them can be triggered. Feelings of agency

(Spengler et al., 2009), then, could arise to indicate to planning processes that planned actions have been prepared, though not necessarily because those feelings of agency themselves cause the actions. A more extreme version of the view that W is not causal of action would assign feelings of agency only to actions where the return of reafferent kinesthetic feedback (generated *after* the command to execute a movement) matched the efference copy of planned movements. A sensed action congruent with the predicted result would be marked as self-generated and felt to have been freely willed (Feinberg, 1978; Frith, 1992; Frith et al., 2000; Frith, 2004, 2005; but see Synofzik et al., 2008). Assignment of agency would follow rather than precede action, making it a type of postdiction, depicted in figure 9.4e.

§9.14   On the other hand, just as the existence of visual illusions does not prove that all vision is illusory, the existence of illusions of conscious agency does not prove that conscious operations cannot be causal of action in certain cases. Wegner and Wheatley's (1999) and Wegner's (2002) examples of illusory conscious agency all involve the execution of a simple action, such as moving or stopping one's hand. Such actions could be caused by unconscious processes that lack access to the flexible manipulation of representations of competing options and the selection of optimal considered possibilities that is afforded by working memory. Indeed, building on the finger movement task of Libet et al. (1983a,b), neuroscientists have written numerous articles since Wegner (2002), arguing on the basis

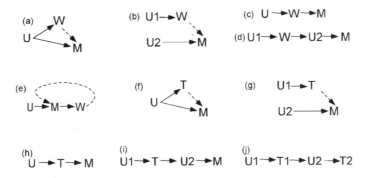

Figure 9.4
Possible causal relationships between unconscious processing, willing, and motor acts. Solid arrows represent causal paths and dotted arrows represent apparently but only illusorily causal paths. Time runs left to right in each case. U=unconscious processing, M=motor act, T=thought, W=conscious willing. See text for a description of the various scenarios.

of simple (i.e., nondeliberative) actions that free will is an illusion because neural activity precedes the consciousness of willing to act, and can even imperfectly predict how one will act (e.g., Bode et al., 2011; Fried et al., 2011; Soon et al., 2008). What is puzzling to me is the apparent enthusiasm that some of my neuroscientist colleagues have exhibited in seeming to claim to provide evidence that the brain lacks a causally efficacious will when the evidence is equally consistent with alternative explanations (cf. Cashmore, 2010; Green & Cohen, 2004; Murphy et al., 2009). Imperfect predictability in no way proves that our decisions are set in stone before we become conscious of those decisions; it proves only that some neuronally realized preconscious patterns of activity play some role in how we will make subsequent simple actions. That it is possible to predict with 70 percent accuracy how a person will respond in advance of his or her awareness of having made a choice to respond does not mean or prove that he or she lacks an efficacious will. It is merely evidence of preconscious biasing factors (Roskies, 2010). That something, say, income, is in part biased or influenced by some preceding factor, say, gender, does not prove in any way that it is solely caused by it. One does get the feeling, however, that some neuroscientists and psychologists, who have been addressing issues of volition since Libet, are jumping to the conclusion that free will is an illusion on the basis of sparse and ambiguous neuronal or behavioral evidence obtained using simple, repetitive, nondeliberative acts.

§9.15   Even if feelings of agency genuinely do precede motor acts, they must themselves be caused. Some neural activity—possibly including the RP or the portion of it that precedes consciousness of willing—that is ultimately neither volitional nor conscious itself must precede and play a role in causing conscious willing. Assuming physicalism, mental events, including feelings of agency, are realized in present brain events that they themselves could not have caused. If this were not the case, an act of conscious willing would be an uncaused cause, which is impossible, assuming physicalism. Since all physical events have physical/informational causal antecedents, feelings of agency must be preceded and caused by brain events that were not themselves consciously agentic. Conscious events are realized in neuronal events that are triggered by preceding events; thus, it has to be the case that conscious events are preceded by preconscious neuronal events that cause them. Far from being astounding, something like Libet's results simply had to be the case. How could it have been otherwise? It does not follow that we are agentic automata or zombies (§10.83) whose experience is epiphenomenal and noncausal of our behavior, however, because experience, possibly even including experience of agency, can play other causal roles than being the causal process necessary for "pulling the trigger" in the initiation of planned actions.

§9.16   In contrast to simple actions, there are action commands that can only follow from the conclusion of deliberative working memory operations that may in part be experienced. For example, I can walk through a decision tree of what to make for dinner given the constraints imposed by my guests' needs and tastes, the ingredients I have on hand, and the fact that it will be Thanksgiving dinner. Only after numerous operations in working memory, some of which may be experienced as propositions or as motoric, visual, or other mental imagery, might I reach the conclusion T that I am out of cranberry sauce and need to go buy some. The motor planning that leads to my getting into my car to drive to the supermarket, even if itself unconscious, follows the conscious propositional conclusion T that I need to go get cranberry sauce and is in part caused by having reached that conclusion even if there is no accompanying feeling of agency W. The command to carry out this motor sequence cannot have been generated before the conscious operations needed to come to this conclusion, because the conclusion came into existence only through conscious operations, namely, the playing out, selection, and deselection of possible scenarios in working memory.

§9.17   The fact that the decision to buy cranberry sauce necessarily preceded the motor planning needed to execute this decision does not prove, however, that it was the conscious decision per se that triggered the subsequent motor planning. A Wegner and Wheatley (1999) type of argument, depicted in figure 9.4a or 9.4b, could still be made; namely, both the conscious decision to buy cranberry sauce and the motor planning to do so were generated by a common (fig. 9.4f) or two separate (fig. 9.4g) preceding unconscious operations, which were the actual causes of motor planning. In this case, consciousness or a consciously derived decision would yet again fail to be causal of motor planning or acts. Indeed, there may be cases where conscious operations resulting in T are only illusorily causal of M, as in figure 9.4f,g and other cases where T is directly or indirectly causal of M, as in figure 9.4h,i. One can imagine that a quadriplegic whose EEG pattern once associated with the intention to move a functioning arm is now instead used to control the motions of a robotic arm. If the latencies are correct, this person would presumably feel that the robot arm is part of his body even if it is located in Tibet and he is watching it in real time over a video link. He might feel that T directly causes M, but T would only indirectly cause M via EEG traces on the scalp, a satellite, and computer. Imagine now that such EEG patterns were used to do more radical things, such as move objects or change the color of the sky. The patient might now feel that his thoughts could change reality when it was really all a kind of magic show.

§9.18   In order to establish that a decision to act, such as to go buy cranberry sauce, could only be reached via conscious operations, it would have to be shown that operations that result in the decision can operate over only conscious (experienced) operands; they cannot operate unconsciously. I believe we and others have shown that this is true for certain endogenous attentional operations, but to understand why, I must first make several points about the nature of conscious operands (qualia) and the nature of the operations that operate over them, particularly endogenous attention. This will be the focus of the next and final chapter.

10 The Roles of Attention and Consciousness in Criterial Causation

Abstract

The goal of this chapter is to understand the various roles that conscious experience plays in the causal framework of the three-stage process of criterial causation and outcome selection proposed as a neural basis for mental and volitional causation. Given only what was presented up to this point, one could argue that neuronal criterial causation and ontological indeterminism are at best necessary but cannot alone be sufficient for the physical realization of mental causation and a strong free will, because without a conscious agent with intentional states that could exploit the three-stage process to fulfill its ends, we might be no more than mindless, unpredictable "zombies." Here I argue that consciousness plays a key role in mental causation in providing a common format for endogenous attentional and other executive operations, which permit the assessment of possible behaviors and thoughts against highest-level criteria for successful attainment of goals and fulfillment of desires. Qualia are those representations that can be (or now are) operated on by endogenous attention, giving rise to the possibility of volitional attentional tracking, which, I argue, cannot happen in the absence of consciousness. Because certain operations can take place only over conscious operands, and motor acts can follow and enact the conclusions of such operations, such mental operations can play a necessary causal role in subsequent thoughts and motor acts. Such mental operations cause their mental and motoric consequences, and are not mere illusions of volition. How propositional conclusions are translated into motor plans and actions is not well understood, but it is hypothesized to occur via the same rapid and dynamic reconfiguration of the physical/informational criteria for neuronal firing that underlies the three-stage process. If so, current operations in working memory over endogenously attendable operands do not cause present thoughts, experiences or actions, but instead cause future thoughts, experiences and actions, given the arrival of inputs that satisfy the criteria that are preset as a consequence of those operations. Finally, I argue that there are qualia of at least three different types, only one of which is likely realized in frontoparietal cortical function. The neural correlates of qualia that do not require attentional binding can be found elsewhere in cortex or even perhaps subcortically.

§10.1   Before tackling the deep issue of the causal role of consciousness in volition, it is useful to summarize the arguments so far. The previous chapters can be summarized as follows. Assuming ontological indeterminism, Kim's argument does not rule out the logical possibility of mental causation (§§A2.2–A2.5). Both Kim's argument against downward mental causation (§A2.3) and the basic argument against free will (§7.4) rest on the impossibility of self-causation. The central thesis argued here is that the problem of self-causation can be avoided if physically realized mental events can change the physical basis of potential *future* mental events by changing the physical/informational criteria for future neuronal firing. This can happen as fast as an initial neuronal burst triggering the opening of NMDA receptors, which in turn transiently changes responsiveness to subsequent spikes on the millisecond timescale needed to account for the rapidity of mental causation. Only an instance from the subset of all possible paths open to all particles in the brain that comprises physical as well as informational causal chains can occur, because only those paths play a role in criterial satisfaction and the successive firings of neurons. This realizes a form of downward mental causation that is consistent with the known laws of physics (§§6.14–6.20). Assuming that neurons can amplify microscopic randomness into randomness in the timing of neural spikes (§§4.66, 4.67), a strong free will (§7.1) can proceed by changing synaptic weights dynamically (§§4.54–4.60), which can then act as criterial triggers for other, later mental and physical events, if and when specified criteria are satisfied by inputs. Neuronal criterial causation is fundamentally nonalgorithmic (§§8.1, 8.2) and accounts for many of the remarkable traits of our cognition (§8.20), including pattern recognition and creativity.

§10.2   The goal of this chapter is to understand the various roles that conscious experience[1] plays in the causal framework of the three-stage process (§7.17) of criterial causation and outcome selection proposed as a neural basis for mental and volitional causation. One could argue that neuronal criterial causation and ontological indeterminism are at best necessary but cannot alone be sufficient for the physical realization of mental causation and a strong free will, because without a conscious agent with intentional states that could exploit the three-stage process to fulfill its ends, we might be no more than mindless, unpredictable "zombies" (§10.83). To talk of mental causation in the absence of intentionally causal minds would seem contradictory. But to regard "experienceless" brains as mindless might be a prejudiced view; perhaps some mental and even volitional causal chains can operate independently of experience.

§10.3   Indeed, there may be neural systems that instantiate a three-stage process (§7.17) of criterial causation and outcome selection where experience plays no role in biasing neuronal outcomes or behaviors. For example, while it is not possible to know whether insects experience anything, cockroaches do exhibit behaviors that appear to be randomly or at least unpredictably selected from among a finite set of possible discrete behaviors (Domenici et al., 2008; Brembs, 2011). This occurs so rapidly that experience, which at least in humans takes relatively long to generate, is unlikely to play a determining role in the stage of outcome selection at a neuronal level in a cockroach. Instead, outcome selection appears to be a rapid and unconscious reflex in these insects, even if selection is criterial and probabilistic.

§10.4   Humans can also behave in response to external events and objects in the absence of experiencing them, as occurs with blindsight (Koch, 2004, ch. 13). Such reflexive "zombie" behaviors tend to be rapid and ballistic, be entirely stimulus driven, be associated more with dorsal than ventral processing, and lack access to working-memory processes that afford nonreflexive, flexible, and voluntary manipulation and comparison of potential options. Because such unconscious processes are instantiated by fulfillment of neurons' criteria for firing, experience is not a necessary component of at least some neuronal criterial causal chains.

Why Are There Qualia?

§10.5   The eliminative materialist stance toward qualia (Churchland, 1985, 2007; Dennett, 1990; Jackson, 1982; Rey, 1983) maintains the internal consistency of a solely physical-on-physical conception of causation at the cost of having to dismiss experience as epiphenomenal. The problem is that it is undeniable that we do experience ("sentio ergo sum") and that without experience we would act differently than we do, which, if granted, implies that experience plays some role in the causation of our actions. For example, if tissue damage did not hurt, we probably would not try to stop it; individuals with a rare congenital disorder of pain fibers (CIPA/HSAN-1V; Axelrod & Gold-von Simson, 2007) experience no pain, so often injure themselves because they do not bother to avoid tissue damage. One could argue that it is not the lack of pain per se that is causal of their unusual behavior, but instead their unusual physical organization. However, there are numerous syndromes where the experience of pain arises psychogenically and centrally in the absence of sensory input or abnormal neuronal organization. One example is Couvade syndrome, where a man experiences nausea or labor pains when he *believes* that his wife is pregnant. This is accompanied by measurable changes in hormone levels in such men (Storey et al., 2000). People can even die if they believe a death spell has been cast upon them (Cannon, 1942). Conversely, the experience of pain can also be terminated centrally, regardless of pain fiber input. A dramatic example occurs in patients who feel that their phantom hand is painfully clenched; when provided with visual feedback that the nonexistent hand has opened, the pain stops (Ramachandran & Altschuler, 2009; Weeks et al., 2010). Pain can therefore be triggered because of informational input (e.g., a belief) as in Couvade syndrome, and eliminated because of informational input, as in phantom limbs (i.e., recognition of one's open hand; consider also the placebo effect), so pain is itself an informational state that is part of an informational causal chain that is realized in physical causal chains. If physically realized pain, or experience more generally, can in turn alter the physically realized informational criteria for future neuronal firing, as argued in this book, then experience can be causal.

§10.6   Why do we experience anything at all? Why not just have a vast array of reflexive zombie agents for every possible input–output contingency? For a complex animal, there would be countless such contingencies. A brain could not store infinitely many reflexive input–output mappings, even if it could know them all in advance. In addition, reflexes, while fast, are not flexible in their mapping of input to output, are locally and slavishly driven by the input stimulus, and do not permit dynamic, open-loop selection among alternative options. In contrast, experience is closely linked to both working memory and attentional processes that do permit dynamic, open-loop selection among alternative options (Moss et al., 2005). Koch (2004, p. 233) suggested that experience provides an "executive summary" to planning areas that can initiate voluntary motor outputs.

§10.7   Working-memory systems presumably evolved in part because the playing out of virtual scenarios and possible courses of action had clear survival value, in that doing so "permits our hypotheses to die in our stead" (Popper, 1979, p. 244). For example, a fish that could represent a predator even after it disappeared behind a coral reef and that could play out its likely possible behaviors within working memory, probabilistically predicting the places where the threat might reappear, would have a survival advantage over another fish that could reflexively flee from the predator only when it was visible. By permitting the consideration of possible courses of action in light of information not present in the stimulus, and by permitting the playing out of possible consequences of actions internally and virtually, working memory allows for global, as opposed to just local, optimization of action. Stimulus-driven behavior permits the selection of the locally best option, but this approach can lead to "garden paths" where successive choices of what is locally optimal results in a globally bad outcome, such as getting eaten. Experience presumably evolved because it enhanced the range and types of possibilities that could be considered, assessed, and selected over. Experience linked sensory input with evaluative desires, emotions and executive processes that could plan on the basis of possibilities held within working memory. This permitted the possibility of "desert paths" where choosing what is locally suboptimal might result in a globally optimal outcome, such as finding a mate or food after some period of enduring lack or want.

§10.8   As long as the necessary and sufficient releasing conditions for a reflexive response are in the sensory input, desires and drives are not needed to release the behavior. Desire can play a role in the shaping of behavior only when sensory releasing conditions are no longer necessary and sufficient for behavioral release—which is to say that behavior is no longer reflexive—or when behavior can be triggered in the absence of any particular releasing conditions in the input. Once working memory freed behavior from being driven solely by the stimulus, desires, emotions, and cognitive consideration of options could evolve so that animals would become driven to do things that benefitted them and the species even when information about the desired or avoided object was unavailable in the sensory input.

§10.9   Animals with a desire to end the causes of tissue damage fared better than those without such a desire. Animals with a desire to have even more tissue damage, for example, who felt pleasure when injured, would have been weeded out. Desire can be thought of as a criterion that demands or seeks criterial satisfaction as opposed to passively waiting for fulfillment. How might such a demand be realized? In the sculpting of the architecture of experience by natural selection, desires have evolved as interrupts that automatically grab attention and drive ideation and behavior toward goals that require gratification. The anterior cingulate cortex appears to be central in this process. If it fails to reset after gratification, this circuitry can lead to obsessive thoughts or behavior. But in the normal range, such interrupting guarantees an enforced prioritization of behavior. If tissue damage were associated only with uninterruptive, demand-free information that there is tissue damage, it could have been ignored. But when associated with an overriding "obsession" to make it stop, realized through interrupts and high prioritization, pain cannot be ignored. Pain is organized to capture attention and trigger output of solutions to the problem of stopping the pain. If no pain were experienced, there would be nothing to seek cessation of. Satisfaction is criterial insofar as any means that stops the tissue damage is adequate. Similarly, if thirst demands finding something to drink and lust demands finding a mate, many inputs can quench these respective desires, but only if they satisfy certain criteria. We can drink lemonade, for example, but not gasoline; we can mate with a conspecific, but not with a cloud. In the absence of, say, desire for a mate, and in the absence of any sensory information that a potential mate is present, it is unlikely that an animal would seek a mate in a flexible and globally contextualized manner.

§10.10   Add to the various desires the evolution of an emotional system that invokes further prioritization via endogenous reward/punishment, attachment, evaluation, or attraction/repulsion, and certain desirables— whether sex, territory, rank, food, offspring, or the termination of tissue damage—can become overwhelming and irresistible for the animal driven by corresponding emotions and desires. Yes, reflexive and experienceless mate-search behaviors could have evolved, but these would at best be locally optimized, because reflexes are inflexible responses to immediate input. The evolution of desire and emotions made animals less driven by present inputs, and more driven to seek out particular future inputs. Knowledge and executive control allowed animals to plan to fulfill desires in a manner contextualized by yet other information not in the input, such as a cognitive map of local terrain or of one's social network. Behaviors that do not require contextualized flexibility of response and that can be driven sufficiently by the stimulus can be relegated to innate or learned stimulus-driven reflexes that can operate automatically, in the absence of the consideration of options in working memory.

§10.11   Why should desires and emotions be experienced as opposed to being mere unconscious information-prioritization procedures? If desires and emotions are criteria that seek certain types of input as fulfillment, they are criteria that must operate at the level of representation of the inputs that can gratify them. If those representations are experienced, then desires and emotions must operate at a level where particular experiences can be sought out. In evaluating and assigning value to experiences that might fulfill them, they change experience and thus are experienced as such, as positive and negative values or valence. Desires and emotions create teleological attractors within the dynamics of the representational space that is our experience.

Iconic versus Working Memory

§10.12   In a groundbreaking psychophysical study (Sperling, 1960) subjects were briefly presented (~50ms followed by a mask) with a three-by-four array of 12 letters. Subjects could only report an average of 4.4 letters correctly. In a partial-report condition, subjects were cued which row to report with a tone that occurred when the letters disappeared. In this case subjects could report an average of 3.3 of the four letters in the attended row. But if the auditory cue was delayed until one second after the visual presentation, subjects could only report 1.5 letters within the cued row, which is about how many they would have been able to report on average for any given row had they not been cued at all. Because the tone occurs only after the visual array disappears, it follows that subjects have momentary access to the whole array but can only report the identity of letters that they have attended. Unless queried within 200ms of display offset, observers cannot report the identity of items not yet visited by attention (Shih and Sperling, 2002; Sperling, 1960). This implies that there is a brief, high-capacity, parallel iconic buffer that stores the preprocessed visual array for about 200 ms (Neisser, 1967), and that attentional selection permits iconic information to be stored in a more durable format that survives stimulus offset and masking, and that also permits object identification. This format is thought to be the format of visual working memory.

§10.13   Thus, according to the "standard model," visual perception appears to proceed in at least two stages. The first stage involves rapid and automatic operations whose outputs are briefly held in a high-capacity, parallel, short-duration iconic buffer. Here preprocessed outputs are made available to attention for selection for more in-depth processing. The second stage involves transfer of attentionally selected iconic contents to the low-capacity visual working memory buffer (Chun & Potter, 1995; Makovski et al., 2008; Sperling, 1960). The working memory buffer permits temporally extended access to what was presented even after it has disappeared (Makovski & Jiang, 2007; Miller et al., 1996; Phillips, 1974; Vogel et al., 2001) as well as online manipulation of those contents (Courtney et al., 1998); Attention is not only necessary for transferring attentionally selected iconic contents to working memory (Griffin & Nobre, 2003; Lepsien et al., 2005; Neisser, 1967; Rensink et al., 1997; Schmidt et al., 2002; Shih & Sperling, 2003; Sperling, 1960), attention is required to maintain representations in working memory (Fougnie & Marois, 2006; Makovski et al., 2006, 2008). Without attentional selection, contents of the iconic buffer are written over by the next set of outputs into the iconic buffer and are simply lost.

§10.14 Multiple intermediate or subsidiary working memory systems likely feed attended content into a highest-level working memory realized in the processing of the dorsolateral prefrontal cortex (DLPFC; §4.27). Miller and colleagues (Miller & Desimone, 1994; Miller et al., 1996) have shown that neurons in this prefrontal area can maintain their selectivity for a task-relevant feature over extended durations in the absence of stimulus input, whereas the neurons they measured in inferotemporal cortex could not. The DLPFC appears to be a key hub in a frontoparietal network that maintains representations in "executive working memory" via attention. Human imaging studies have shown that both prefrontal and posterior parietal cortex are activated regardless of the type of information that is held in working memory (Song & Jiang, 2006; Todd & Marois, 2004; Xu & Chun, 2006), revealing the executive system to be amodal, as opposed to subsidiary working memory systems, which are capable only of maintaining a particular class of information, such as faces or spatial layout. For example, inferior temporal areas are only activated when specific types of information are held in working memory (e.g. activity is seen in the fusiform face area only when faces are maintained in working memory during a retention interval; Druzgal & D'Esposito, 2003). This supports the idea that executive working memory may utilize or be gated by "subsidiary systems" as posited in the models of working memory of Baddeley (1986) and Logie (1995).

§10.15 Recent authors (Griffin & Nobre, 2003; Landman et al., 2003, 2004; Makovski et al., 2008; Makovski & Jiang, 2007; Matsukura et al., 2007; Sligte et al., 2008, 2009, 2011) have argued that there may actually be three stages of visual processing: (1) a high-capacity, retinotopic iconic buffer realized in V1–V3 processing that encodes features that remain unbound, (2) a high-capacity spatiotopic "fragile visual short-term memory" realized in V4 and perhaps posterior inferotemporal processing, that encodes bound object information that lasts a few seconds, and (3) a low-capacity, potentially viewpoint-invariant visual working memory that can sustain information as long as attention is engaged, realized in part in the frontoparietal attentional network (Sligte et al., 2011). Since the first two stages on this view can apparently proceed without attention or involvement of frontoparietal feedback, for present purposes, I will group (1) and (2) together as "stage 1," and call iconic and fragile visual short-term memory, together, the "stage 1 buffer." This buffer holds the results of automatic "stage 1 processing" made available for attentional selection and possible transferral to working memory. I do not mean to suggest that iconic and fragile visual short-term memory are the same thing, but if, in normal vision, information processing in (1) and (2) is usually completed automatically in a rapid sequence, they may be thought of as two substages of automatic bottom-up visual processing that runs from V1 through V4 into posterior inferotemporal cortex.

§10.16   The automatic first stage is associated with event-related potentials N1 and P1. Indeed, approximately the first 200ms of visual event related potentials do not discriminate whether observers can report what they have seen or not (Dehaene et al., 2001; Dehaene & Changeux, 2011; Del Cul et al., 2007; Fahrenfort et al., 2007; Koivisto et al., 2006, 2009; Lamy et al., 2009; Melloni et al., 2007; Railo & Koivisto, 2009; Schiller & Chorover, 1966; Sergent et al., 2005; van Aalderen-Smeets et al., 2006; Vogel et al., 1998). These early components are generated in occipital and posterior inferotemporal cortical areas that presumably process visual input in a bottom-up fashion independent of attention. The influence of attentional selection is first evident in the N2 waveform, which is generated in these areas beginning at about 200ms. Even though the N2 varies in magnitude with the degree to which observers can identify what was presented, it is also evident for stimuli that could not be identified. Beginning at about 270ms (Sergent et al., 2005; Dehaene & Changeux, 2011) after stimulus onset, the P3 waveform is evident in both these areas and in frontal cortex as well. The P3 can be subdivided into a P3a subtype associated with exogenous attentional orienting (Muller-Gass et al., 2007; Salisbury et al., 1992; van Alderen-Smeets et al., 2006), and a P3b subtype associated with endogenous attentional processing (§4.22). The P3b is associated with activation of attentional and working memory circuitry including the hippocampus and association areas of temporal, frontal and parietal cortex (Halgren et al., 1998; Mantini et al., 2009). The P3b appears to be closely tied to the ability to subjectively report the identity of what one has seen (Babiloni et al., 2006; Del Cul et al., 2007; Fernandez-Duque et al., 2003; Gaillard et al., 2009; Koivisto et al., 2008; Lamy et al., 2009; Niedeggen et al., 2001; Pins and Ffytche, 2003; Sergent et al., 2005). Unlike the N2, which is even evident for stimuli that cannot be subsequently identified, the P3b is only evident when observers can identify what they had seen. Dehaene and colleagues (Dehaene et al., 2006; Dehaene & Changeux, 2011; Sergent et al., 2005) take the capacity to identify what was seen as the best evidence that it was consciously experienced, and assume that an inability to identify is evidence of a lack of consciousness of a visual stimulus. They have therefore argued that the outputs of the first stage are not experienced, even though the N2 varies with stimulus identifiability, whereas the outputs of the second stage are. But there are reasons to believe that contents of both the stage 1 buffer and visual working memory are experienced, as visual ground and visual figure, respectively.

§10.17 In the Sperling (1960) experiment it is not the case that subjects can report only the contents of the row that they have attended; they can only report the *identities* of the attended letters. But even for those letters that were not attended, subjects can often report that something was there, roughly how big the array and items were, roughly how many items there were, and any number of other features that are processed automatically, even without attention. This implies that while objects and their identities may require attentional binding, low-level features are both experienced in unattended locations and reportable there, at least to some degree. This would suggest that the contents of the iconic and "fragile visual short-term buffer" (together the "stage 1 buffer") are experienced as the visual background. If the neural correlates of the stage 1 buffer lies in V1-V3 (iconic) or V4 and adjacent posterior, inferotemporal regions ("fragile visual short-term memory; Sligte et al., 2011), then this would suggest that the neural correlates of at least some conscious contents do not require frontoparietal processing (see Dehaene et al., 2006, Dehaene & Changeux, 2011, and Cohen et al., 2012, for the opposing view). I will return to the relationship of the frontoparietal network to experience and qualia in §10.62, but before returning to this central issue, it is important to get our terms straight, so that we know what we are talking about when we talk about qualia.

Stage 1 Qualia as Precompiled Informational Outputs of Preconscious Operations

§10.18 Consideration of apparent motion makes clear the kinds of operations carried out in stage 1 processing. When two nonoverlapping static images of a luminance-defined spot are alternated in succession within a certain range of spatiotemporal offsets (Korte, 1915), they appear to comprise a single object jumping smoothly back and forth in apparent motion. Because no object actually moves, the appearance of continual motion must be a construction of the visual system. Since the position of the second spot cannot be known in advance, it must be the case that perceived motion is constructed only after the onset of the second image. Thus the apparent motion from position 1 to position 2 must be experienced after the visual system constructs the motion that it "infers" must have happened prior to the appearance of the spot at position 2 (Beck et al., 1977; Choi & Scholl, 2006; Eagleman & Sejnowski, 2000; Tse & Logothetis, 2002). This implies that our experience is not of events as they are happening now, but of events as they happened in the recent past constructed on the basis of present *and past* input. This implies, moreover, that there must be a short-term preconscious perceptual buffer within which past and present inputs are integrated and operated upon, before a "commitment" is made to how past events gave rise to present inputs, which is how they will be experienced. This preconscious buffer permits the influence of stages of form analysis (Tse & Caplovitz, 2006; Tse, 2006a) and expectations (Tse & Cavanagh, 2000) on the construction of motion paths. Tse and Logothetis (2002) estimated that this buffer compares form and motion inputs over the past 100ms, and Eagleman and Sejnowski (2000) estimated a comparable 80ms of comparison between past and present inputs, during which perceptual events are constructed into a "cover story," "postdiction," or "unconscious inference" of what must be happening now given recent inputs.

§10.19   Two types of inference can be distinguished, deriving, respectively, from the psychological and philosophical traditions. Perceptual psychologists often talk of "Bayesian inferences" whose conclusions are integrated into our conscious experience as it is delivered to us by unconscious operations that implicitly manifest prior assumptions about the correct image to world mapping. These unconscious operations are also "preconscious" because they are completed prior to the experience of their results (see n. 1). Philosophers, in contrast, prefer to talk of inferences that are based on the facts as we apprehend them, namely, that present themselves in our experience, and which therefore follow consciousness in time. We thus distinguish between "unconscious, perceptual, or preconscious inferences" (Helmholtz, 1910 [1867]) that go into the construction of experience and "cognitive inferences" that are based on what is experienced. Unconscious inferences are largely generated by perceptual modules or modular subsystems, such as the visual motion, face, color, or form-processing subsystems.[2] They are typically automatic, dedicated, rapid, and "cognitively impenetrable" (Fodor, 1983). Cognitive inferences, in contrast, are not perceptual, but are instead cognitive operations over information derived from what we learn from the contents of experience. Cognitive inferences follow experience both temporally and logically.

§10.20   For example, if I go outside and see that the ground is wet, I do not have to cognitively infer that the ground is wet based on low-level cues. My visual system has made a preconscious and automatic unconscious inference that the ground is wet and constructed an experience to that effect, even though there is no explicit information about wetness at the level of the retinal image. In this sense, "seeing is seeing as"; although many possible worlds could have given rise to any given retinal image, a commitment is made preconsciously to a particular interpretation and image-to-world mapping. Consciousness comes "precompiled" in the sense that I cannot choose not to see the ground as wet. For example, I cannot choose to see the world as a collection of colors that have not been automatically preinterpreted by my visual system into materials, surfaces, spatial layout, reflectances, shadow, lighting, and so forth. The world is presented to attentional and planning operators as such by the visual module in a manner that is rapid but inflexible. When I infer that it must have rained given that the ground looks wet, however, I am making a cognitive inference that is open ended, slow, and flexible. I could make countless cognitive inferences from the fact that the ground looks wet. I might notice that the sky is blue, and instead infer, cognitively, that the gardener must have hosed the ground down with water.

§10.21 Ignoring for now the important ways in which attention, expectation, and other top-down processes can alter experience, the output of automatic, stimulus-driven, early modular processing comprises a precompiled, preinterpreted, and preevaluated account of events and objects in the world—as well as of the states and needs of the body. These outputs are made available to brain areas that can make cognitive inferences and plan to do something given these facts, whether motorically or internally by, for example, volitionally shifting attention or exerting effort to recall a name. What is remarkable is that unconscious inferences can come to some surprisingly complex conclusions. For example, there is no information about causation as such in the succession of images, as Hume pointed out long ago. Causation is, as it were, invisible. But we nonetheless experience one event as causing another, given particular spatial or temporal juxtapositions of events. This can lead to illusions of causation. For example, if an accomplice secretly turns the light on or off a split second after I bang the table at a party, everyone present will have the experience that my banging the table itself caused the light to turn on or off. Another example is that we experience the contents of others' minds when these, obviously, are invisible. Faces, in particular, are rich in social meaning and allow us to largely automatically infer the thoughts, intentions, and desires of other minds, unless we are autistic or have some other problem with the "theory-of-mind inference module," forcing us to rely on slow and open-ended cognitive inferences about other minds. The fact that neurons can be tuned to head orientation (Desimone et al., 1984; Perrett et al., 1985), gaze direction (Perrett et al., 1985), and facial expressions (Hasselmo et al., 1989) as confirmed by brain imaging of cortex (Hadj-Bouziane et al.,

2008) and the amygdala (Hoffman et al., 2007), suggests that the face-processing system is inextricably linked with not only the recognition of faces as visual objects, but the rapid and automatic inference of social meaning and decipherment of other minds. This is likely to be true for other classes of objects as well, particularly animate ones. Thus, unconscious inferences can automatically draw conclusions about not only physical, visible properties of objects such as wetness, but also about nonphysical, invisible properties of objects and events such as causation and mental contents. The temporal and logical boundary between unconscious stage 1 inferences and cognitive inferences is experience itself.

§10.22   On this account, experience is an internal, "virtual reality" of objects, events, and internal imaginings, complete with an awareness of causation, the contents of other minds, and social and other meanings. This construction, derived from but very different from the visual image and other sensory and physiological inputs, is normally in such good correspondence with what is actually happening in the world-in-itself and in the body that for the experiencer it is as if the world-in-itself and the body were experienced directly and without delay. However, visual illusions, dreams, hypnosis, and hallucinations can reveal that experience is not of the world-in-itself per se.[3] Feeling that an object is part of your body when it is not, as in the rubber hand illusion, shows that experience is not of the body in some direct, uninterpreted way. Rather, experience is constructed on the basis of ambiguous, sparse, and noisy sensory inputs mediated by numerous preconscious operations, such as shape, color- and size-constancy operations, heuristics (e.g., Gigerenzer & Gaissmaier, 2011; Tversky & Kahneman, 1974), and implicit assumptions about the likely mapping between patterns of sensory activation and the objects and events in the world from which they presumably arise (e.g., Kersten et al., 2004).[4] For example, we experience objects made of materials that are laid out in or move about in three dimensions, when there is no explicit information about objects, three-dimensionality, materials, or motion present at the level of retinal activation. All of this must be, in Helmholtz's sense, inferred from the input.

§10.23   Experience can also be generated by multiple systems in parallel. Obviously, we can see red and feel joy at the same time, but even our experience of redness can be simultaneously one thing and something seemingly incompatible. For example, say I hold up a white piece of paper with a red sunset behind my back. Because of color constancy operations, I will see the paper as having white pigment. But if I now decide to attend to the color being reflected off the paper, I can now experience the paper as pink. Experience can thus be a "superposition" of information that becomes explicit at different stages of an information-processing hierarchy. When attending to the paper and seeing it as white, I am specifying information (such as perhaps realized in V4 or beyond) that has been subject to color constancy operations. And when attending to the paper and seeing it as pink, I am specifying information (presumably in iconic memory, such as perhaps realized in V1–V3), that has not been subject to color constancy operations (§4.26). Another example occurs with practice with mirrors. When a novice driver looks in the rearview mirror, he might see a car, but not really know where it is relative to his own car. With practice, the experience of seeing a car in the mirror becomes precompiled into an experience of a car at a particular position behind oneself. The car can be experienced to be at its location in the mirror if that is attended, or at its inferred world location, if that now automatized output is attended. One role of attention then appears to be to tune in to the right conscious outputs for a given task. It ignores irrelevant conscious outputs and selects relevant ones.

Qualia as a Shared Format for Endogenous Attentional Operations

§10.24   The word "quale" is so poorly defined that many neuroscientists and philosophers cannot easily answer a question as simple as "is the experience of a familiar face or the taste of pineapple a quale?" The initial motivation to use this word was to capture the notion of some irreducible units of experience. But what are these irreducible units, from a neuroscientific perspective? Perhaps the analogy "qualia are to subjective qualities as quanta are to objective quantities" is faulty in the sense that experience is not quantized.[5] Are irreducible experiences the experiences present in neonates? Are they the simplest dimensions of a given type of experience, just as, say, saltiness, bitterness, sweetness, and sourness might be for taste? Why have experiences at all? We have essentially been discussing an information-processing architecture up until this point. Why could such an architecture not lack experience?[6] A partial answer is that a common, endogenously attendable format is required so that the outputs of different subsystems can be evaluated along a common metric, by a common set of criteria assessing input, which, if satisfied, releases a decision to act.[7] Qualitative, subjective experience is the common output format of numerous relatively modular subsystems that process fundamentally different types of input. For example, one subsystem outputs the experience of hunger. Another outputs an experience of seeing food on your neighbor's plate.

Another then evokes awareness of the thought that one should not just take food from someone without asking. If outputs were not in a common format, they could not be assessed as "apples to apples" against a common criterion assessing optimality of potential behavior. Having a highest level of assessment of multiple lower-system outputs in a common format permits the overall system to find a solution that maximizes global benefit to the animal, as opposed to locally, within the representational space of any submodule. A common format is required so that all submodules' outputs can contextualize one another, can be "time-stamped" as occurring in the same moment, and can be stored in the quasi-experiential, spatiotemporal format of episodic memory. If lower-level outputs were not in a common format, there might not be a single endogenous attentional tracking operator, say, that operated on all types of input, whether visual, auditory, motoric, or emotional. Having experience in a common qualia format allows executive, planning, attentional, and working memory processes to have all relevant information about goings-on in the world and body at one time. In the absence of a common format, the relevance or salience of an output from one module, say, redness, might not be comparable to the output of another, say, hunger. Their relative salience, importance, or priority would not be rapidly decidable. If there were multiple endogenous attentional operators, it would be as if multiple minds "lived" in the same brain, as may occur in split-brain patients. Executive processing and experience would be splintered. What was salient for one executive might have nothing to do with the priorities for another executive, even if they both operated over identical qualia. Executive decisions and therefore motor acts would likely conflict if there were more than one master endogenous attentional operator in control of suboperations. Finally, if outputs of different subsystems were not in a common format, it might not be possible to bind them into a common unit for attentional tracking (§10.30). By analogy, computer code can only be run or compiled together if it is written in a common programming language.

§10.25 This shared format allows executive processes to consider, compare, track, and select from among possible courses of action in a unified way. In the absence of a common format for planning and executive operations such as endogenous attention to work on, there could be no hierarchical chain of command in volitional control of behavior. Indeed, the brain instantiates many types of plans in such a chain of command, from planning at the level of propositions such as "I should drink more water" to planning at the level of strategy such as "I will go to that water fountain rather than that one" to commands at the level of motor sequences such as "get up and follow this optimal path to the goal" to commands at the level of contracting particular muscles in specific sequences. All such commands might be thought of as plans that involve executive selection at the appropriate level. But the highest-level executive centers that make plans propositionally, at the level of ideas, need not worry about the details of muscle sequencing and contraction, just as a president, general, or CEO ideally need not worry about the local decisions of lower-level managers or foot soldiers. Propositional commanders just need to say "get *x* done" and the hierarchical chain of "subcommanders" can find the best way to get it done, flexibly working around local difficulties as needed. In the absence of a chain of command in a common format with flexibility at each level of subcommand, commands could fail to be executed. However, if the chain of command from propositional to, ultimately, muscular encoding is to be flexibly contextualized at each stage, this requires a common or at least readily translatable format that commanders and subcommanders can operate on and communicate in. Just as in a military chain of command, each level has to communicate with at least the level above and below it, to flexibly adapt to changing local circumstances, needs, facts, and commands, as well as to provide feedback that commands have been received and tasks have been completed.[8] But the command structure would be inefficient if the commander who said "invade country *x*" had to worry about how each bullet was fired. Flexibility within a chain of command requires a common informational code if there is to be communication between levels of a command-processing hierarchy. This code appears to be the spatialized representation of events and objects in the world, and of the body moving in that world, contextualized in working memory by desires, emotions, and knowledge. Without such a format, behavior would be locally but not globally optimized, driven inflexibly by the stimulus, rather than by goals and information not available in the stimulus.

Experience Is for Endogenously Attending, Doing, and Planning

§10.26   The feeling of agency associated with being the general or CEO might be very high, if things just seem to happen "automatically" after a command to make them happen has been issued, even though the details of lower-level subcommands and execution might be cognitively impenetrable.[9] Endogenous attention operating on experienced representations in working memory is rather like a general or CEO who is ignorant of and indeed indifferent to the lower-level premotoric and motoric commands needed to enact a high-level propositional command at the muscular level. When subcommands that are normally enacted automatically and unconsciously fail to get carried out at all or fail to be carried out within a short enough timespan after a command, or when endogenous attention must try to execute commands at lower levels, the feeling of executive agency likely diminishes. If a subcommander is no longer under the control of a higher-level commander, as may occur in "alien hand syndrome"[10] (Assal et al., 2007), it would seem that the actions generated are not under volitional control. The same would be true if feelings of agency arise as a result of correspondence between planned and executed actions and the process of efference copy matching were damaged (Frith et al., 2000; Frith, 2004, 2005). The corporate and martial metaphor of executive control is, of course, imperfect, particularly because there appear to be several executive centers in the brain, each specialized for a different decision-making domain. Perhaps a more appropriate metaphor would be a family of interacting agents who are each the boss in different domains, and who sometimes collaborate and other times conflict and inhibit one another. Whichever metaphor is most useful, high-level goals are typically represented propositionally and semantically at a level of representation such as "food," "mate," or "territory," at the same time as being driven by associated desires for food, mates, and territory. As such, highest-level criteria that assess path optimization to the fulfillment of such goals will themselves be ideational rather than motoric. Conflicts need to be resolved at a premotoric level in order to prevent conflicts at the motoric level, because one must in the end act or inhibit action, and muscles are slave systems. They are not themselves informational structures capable of placing informational criteria on inputs. If one chose to act but then tried to execute several motor plans simultaneously, muscles, which can only contract or not contract, might cause the arm, say, to seize up as commands to move in opposing directions conflicted. Such cases of "bodily stuttering" would likely lead to failure to execute any plan at all. Because the body cannot carry out all possible behaviors at once, the best option must be selected and implemented while other options are inhibited at a stage prior to the stage of motor commands. If one has highest-level criteria for optimal behavior, the various potentially conflicting options can be assessed relative to these criteria, and the optimal one selected before one behaves. The selection of the optimal option and suppression of other options must happen centrally, most likely not in a "muscle command" format, but rather at the level of evaluated propositions or abstract motor plans.

§10.27   How does experience play a role in mental causation and volitional acts at a neuronal level? By allowing the consideration of multiple
internally generated courses of action or thought in working memory, and
the endogenous attentional manipulation (i.e., selection, deselection,
binding, unbinding, and tracking) of those contents, an animal can recode
the criteria that will make neurons fire given particular future inputs.
Sequences of such criterial recodings can realize the future enactment of a
currently considered propositional plan. How a propositional plan processed in working memory is translated into a potentiated motor plan that
can then be released by a future executive command or future sensory
input is not yet understood, though one possibility is discussed in §8.19.
But we know that a propositional code does get translated into a motor
code, because I can go from thinking "I should buy cranberry sauce" to
reaching for my car keys a second later. This view does not allow experience or consciousness to play any role in influencing the outcomes of the
actions currently experienced. It does not allow experience to alter its own
present neural basis. Experience allows planning and executive centers to
alter the physical/informational criteria that will allow neurons to fire differently in the future than they would have, had there been no experience
or if experience had been different. For example, consciously coming to
the conclusion that I need to buy cranberry sauce leads rather automatically to the formulation of possible abstract and concrete motor plans that
might realize this intention.

Volitional Attentional Tracking Requires Consciousness

§10.28   It is important to understand that even seemingly high-level,
executive processes, such as those involved in shifting attention, must
involve unconscious and preconscious processes. Indeed, recently, some
authors have argued that there is attentional salience specification or selection without consciousness (Jiang et al., 2006; Koch & Tsuchiya, 2007; see
also Bressan & Pizzighello, 2008; McCormick, 1997; Robitaille & Jolicoeur,
2006; Woodman & Luck, 2003). For the system to make a decision about
where to allocate attention (or shift the eyes) in the next moment, a
saliency map must be in place to compute the highest-value location to
shift toward. The computations underlying the formation of this saliency
map must logically and temporally precede an attentional shift to the
maximum peak on this saliency map. Thus, by definition, some saliency-
defining operations must precede attentional shifting and allocation to
that location. This might sound circular, but it is not circular at all once

one realizes that there is a hierarchy of types of attention. From the most primitive to the most complex these are: (i) retinotopically location-based salience specification, (ii) object-based salience specification (also at this level would be feature-based attention), (iii) exogenous or automatic and stimulus-driven object tracking, and (iv) endogenous or volitional object tracking.

§10.29 Even if it is the case that certain low-level aspects, such as orienting to peaks in preconsciously computed salience or changes in gain control, can happen in the absence of qualia (i.e., unconsciously), this does not mean that high-level aspects of attention such as endogenous attentional tracking can operate unconsciously. When there is only a single thing in a display, attentional selection does not appear to be necessary to gain conscious access to the identity of that thing (Wyart & Tallon-Baudry, 2008, 2009); however, when there are multiple things in a cluttered display, attentional selection is required to be able to gain conscious access to the identity of any particular item (Dehaene & Naccache, 2001; Mack & Rock, 1998, 2009). Qualia may be the representational format that can be bound into attentionally selectable and trackable objects.

§10.30 Another way of putting this is that qualia are potential contents of "object files." An object file (Kahneman et al., 1992; Tse, 2006b) is a metaphor for attentional processes that combine multiple features existing over various modalities into a common bound representation of an object. An object file is an attentionally tracked "figure" (Lamy & Tsal, 2000) integrated as a temporary episodic representation in a working memory buffer (Kahneman et al., 1992; Schneider, 1999) that maintains a coherent identity even as the particular contents defining that identity change over time. For example, if we say, "it's a bird, it's a plane, it's Superman!" the features change and the identification changes; what does not change is that this single object is tracked through space over time. Indeed, working memory appears to be a buffer that permits the processing and maintenance of object representations per se, rather than feature representations. For example, working memory operations appear to be limited by a capacity of three to four objects (Fukuda et al., 2010; Magnussen, 2000; Pasternak & Greenlee, 2005; Todd & Marois, 2004). This capacity can be increased by chunking subunits into higher-level units that can be treated as an object (Cowan, 2001). Features can be added to an object without changing an EEG signature of working memory load, the "contralateral delay amplitude." But increasing the number of objects does increase this signal (Luria & Vogel, 2011). Researchers disagree about how object tracking works (Pylyshyn & Storm, 1988; Carey & Xu, 2001; Feigenson et al.,

2002; Scholl et al., 2001), but all conceptions have in common a psychological entity that keeps track of an object over time, within some space. For example, one can listen to a symphony and track the oboe. One can then listen to the same symphony again and this time track the lead violin. In both cases the sensory input is the same. What differs is the nature of the object file one constructs. The contents of an object file are thought to be mid- to high-level contents. That is, there is widely thought to be a "preattentive" stage of representation that cannot be attended and whose contents cannot be added to an object file (Wolfe, 2003; Treisman & Gelade, 1980). This would correspond to information prior to the stage where preprocessing is completed and made available for attentional selection in the stage 1 buffer. Possible object file contents can be perceptual features, such as color and texture, that may exist on feature maps (Treisman, 1992; Quinlan, 2003), midlevel structures such as surfaces (He & Nakayama, 1992), abstract identity tags (Gordon & Irwin, 1996), or higher-level conceptual information (Gordon & Irwin, 2000).

§10.31 Jiang et al. (2006) have provided evidence that (i) computations of salience occur at locations unconsciously, and that these in turn influence the conscious placement of attention. In addition, others have recently shown (Chou & Yeh, 2012) that attention in the sense of (ii) appears to be allocated to objects even in the absence of any awareness of the objects that have been attended. Data collected in my lab suggest that (iii) unconscious attentional allocation to an object does not trigger automatic, unconscious tracking of that object. Finally, (iv) endogenous attentional selection, tracking, and inhibition of nontracked items over seconds is quintessentially a conscious set of operations that cannot take place unconsciously, probably because unconscious operators lack full access to working memory. Volitional attentional allocation entails the specification of voluntary criteria to be met by what will be attended. These criteria are maintained in working memory. An executive system can set the criterion that the color of a stimulus will be attended, rather than the form, and then switch criteria and attend to the form. This process is not driven by the stimulus, because the stimulus can remain constant while first its color and then its form is attended. This flexible remapping of criteria for subsequent endogenous attentional allocation appears to be a conscious process, because only conscious processes have access to the contents of working memory. In short, unconscious processing, including unconscious attentional processing, appears to be limited to automatic and rather ballistic processes that are driven by the stimulus, whereas conscious processing affords the possibility of flexible remapping of the criteria that will determine immediately future responses, such as where endogenous attention will next be allocated.

§10.32 It might seem obvious that there can be no volitional, top-down attentional tracking of unconscious targets among distractors that are equally salient in a bottom-up sense. Even without doing experiments to test for the possibility of volitional multiple object tracking (Pylyshyn & Storm, 1988; Scholl et al., 2001), it seems prima facie impossible that spatial attention could be volitionally allocated to the coordinates of information that cannot be accessed, when no bottom-up cue drives differences in salience that could specify the target (as in e.g., Jiang et al., 2006) in the presence of multiple equally salient, unconscious distractors. If attention were to deviate from tracking a moving, unconscious target, there would be no error or difference signal between the target and the location of attentional focus, because the former would be unconscious and the latter conscious with no ability to compare their respective location signals. If there were such an error signal, it would provide accessible information about location of the target; but since we have agreed that such information is not accessible, no such error signal can exist. This situation would be like aiming and shooting at a subset of birds in a flock that one can neither see nor hear. This may be why location-based endogenous attention can be allocated only to conscious contents, whereas feature-based endogenous attention can be allocated to unconscious contents (Kanai et al., 2006). Presumably, feature-based attention might be allocatable to the entire visual field, possibly as changes in gains of low-level feature detectors, realized, perhaps, as early as the LGN (Desimone & Duncan, 1995; Hillyard et al., 1998; Liu et al., 2009; Reynolds & Heeger, 2009). There would be no need for an error signal to "stay on track" in the case of feature-based attention, as long as feature detectors were reasonably broadly tuned and attention changed gains across the whole visual field. This is not the case with space-based or object-based attention, however, because this kind of attention cannot be allocated across the whole visual field equally and still be specific to a location or particular object. Recent evidence shows that attention to a feature such as orientation or spatial frequency increases the firing rate and decreases correlatedness of neurons tuned to that feature, and decreases the firing rate and increases the correlation among neurons not tuned to that feature across both visual hemifields; in contrast, spatial attention operates on local populations of neurons within a hemifield, decorrelating them and increasing their firing rates (Cohen & Maunsell, 2011; §4.25). This establishes that volitional attentional tracking can occur only in the domain of conscious information.

§10.33   The contents of consciousness certainly include that which one is volitionally attending now. But other contents of consciousness might include that which one could attend in the next moment, if one chose to do so. Access consciousness is sometimes delimited as comprising those contents that one can report voluntarily or access voluntarily, whereas phenomenal consciousness is what is experienced (Block, 1997). The two types of consciousness might be united by the fact that whatever can be reported can be endogenously attended, and whatever is endogenously attended is reportable, at least by humans. Unconscious contents, in contrast, would be those that one cannot access or report voluntarily and that cannot be endogenously attended. To the degree that these definitions of consciousness are valid, volitional or endogenous object tracking in the absence of consciousness would be impossible by definition.[11] If endogenous object tracking in the absence of consciousness were logically possible, it would imply that we could voluntarily operate on or manipulate representations that we cannot access and for which there are no error signals allowing correction. This notion is bizarre, and it would seem to rule out volitional object tracking in the absence of consciousness as impossible in principle, not simply as has been shown empirically (Kanai et al., 2006). On this view, consciousness or experience is that domain of representations that permits volitional or endogenous attentional tracking and manipulation over sustained durations. We are given proto-objects unconsciously, through Gestalt-like stage 1 operations that specify surfaces and coherent sets of features that belong together by virtue of having probably arisen from a common object in the world. But we are given an experienced object by virtue of attentional tracking that binds local features over time. This applies to any representational space that can be thought of as having a spatial or distance metric, for which an error signal would be necessary in order to carry the tracking operation out. This would include endogenously attentionally tracking an oboe in a symphony, one bird in a flock of similar birds, or a thought among distracting thoughts. None of this is possible without consciousness.

§10.34   It may be that lower-level outputs are placed into a common quale format so that they can all be, but need not be, attentionally tracked in the next moment, should the need arise. If this view of qualia is correct, no evidence will be found of unconscious, volitional feature binding into trackable objects, because these require the qualia format to carry out the operations of endogenous attentional tracking. In short, the link between qualia and endogenous attention is very close: Qualia are those features that can potentially be endogenously attentionally bound and tracked over time, and everything that can be so tracked if need be includes all current qualia (i.e., all that is now experienced). On this account, all that is presently experienced includes that which is attended now and that which could be endogenously attended if we shifted our attention to it in the next moment. Note that this does not mean that only attended contents are conscious. Consciousness or experience includes the "qualia soup" of the background of iconic contents that are not attended or only minimally attended, but could be endogenously attended if need be.

§10.35   Just because qualia evolved to be the operands of the attentional tracking operator does not mean that they cannot exist in the absence of being attentionally tracked. A normal brain is typically endogenously binding some small percentage of available qualia into tracked objects, and the rest, I argue, may be unbound in a state of "qualia soup." In the extreme case, where a person's left- and right-hemispheric attentional tracking systems have been damaged, all qualia might remain unbound outside the single object attended by virtue of the exogenous attentional system, as occurs in Balint's patients (Jackson & Swainson, 2009). Note that a kind of attentionless binding of features to each other, or to locations, might still occur automatically in Balint's patients because of spatiotemporal grouping procedures that would continue to operate preconsciously during stage 1 processing (Conci et al., 2009; Kim & Robertson, 2001; Mattingley et al., 1997). Despite this, the experience of someone with severe bilateral frontoparietal damage, as occurs in Balint's patients, might be one of ongoing "qualia soup," except for the one object that was attended at any given moment. They would nonetheless continue to have a kind of impoverished experience, at the level of "qualia soup." But a surprising amount might be "prebound" and precompiled by preconscious operations, including layout, shape, surfaces, and even occluded shapes and surfaces (Enns & Rensink, 1990, 1991; He & Nakayama, 1992, 1994a,b, 1995; Rensink & Enns, 1995, 1998). It is possible that such preconscious and automatically constructed complex representations are experienced even by Balint's patients. Thus, Balint's or neglect patients should not be blind or experience-free in the endogenously unattendable regions of space, since they would be experiencing "qualia soup" there. Presumably they could report certain attributes even where they could not bind features into objects, such as the overall luminance level of the background.

§10.36   If only conscious contents can be volitionally attentionally tracked, then consciousness or experience may conversely be the domain of representations that permit the possibility of endogenous attentional tracking.[12] On this account, unconscious operations may be driven by input rather transiently, on the timescale of the rapid allocation and rapid decay of exogenous attention. In contrast, conscious operations may be driven by input in a sustained fashion, on the timescale of the slow allocation, but slow decay of endogenous attention. Unconscious processing may be driven by the stimulus in a bottom-up fashion independently, "stationarily," or "nonhistorically" from moment to moment (i.e., what is most salient now is largely independent of what was most salient in the past). Indeed, no effects of unconscious processing are detected beyond 500ms (Dupoux et al., 2008; Greenwald et al., 1996; Mattler, 2005). Processing of unconscious inputs tends to involve the automatic analyses of dedicated modules, but tends to be weak or nonexistent for tasks requiring flexible cognition or decision-making tasks (Dehaene, 2008; van Gaal et al., 2008). Consistent with the automaticity of unconscious processing, errors or conflicts appear not to influence performance in unconsciously processed inputs to nearly the extent that occurs during conscious processing, if at all (Kunde, 2003; Nieuwenhuis et al., 2001; but see Logan & Crump, 2010; Van Gaal et al., 2010). In particular, neither executive control nor volitional, endogenous attentional allocation, tracking or shifting are invoked by unconsciously processed stimuli (Dehaene and Changeux, 2011; Heinemann et al., 2009; Kinoshita et al., 2008; Merikle & Joordens, 1997; Van den Bussche et al., 2008; Posner & Snyder, 1975). Finally, effective top-down inhibition of a prepared or automatic action requires consciousness (even though acts fail to be inhibited unconsciously, there may be evidence of some initial, automatic components of inhibition; Van Gaal et al., 2011). In contrast, conscious processing appears to be required for all those above-mentioned processes that cannot be carried out unconsciously.

§10.37 *Consciousness is thus required for endogenous attentional allocation, shifting and tracking, volitional executive control, flexible cognitive processing and manipulation of representations in executive working memory, complex concatenations of simpler mental operations, contextually appropriate management of detected errors, and effective top-down inhibition of imminent acts.* Acts that follow these types of endogenous attentional, executive operations over conscious operands are potentially causal of the motor acts that follow from the conclusion of those operations. To the extent that such operations are volitional, will can be causal of subsequent acts, such as going to the store to buy cranberry sauce.

§10.38 Conscious operations may be driven "historically" or "nonstationarily." Indeed, attentional tracking, unlike salience specification, requires a durational analysis by definition, because to track something, one needs to hold onto (1) where that thing is in the input at the present time 2, and (2) where that thing was in the previous input at time 1, in order to match it to itself across times 1 and 2. Because endogenous attentional tracking requires the durational maintenance of information (and flexible specification of criteria for tracking) held in working memory, and only conscious processes have access to the contents of working memory, endogenous attention is a conscious process. It follows that conclusions of endogenous attentional manipulations in working memory cause subsequent thoughts and motor acts that follow from those conclusions. For such operations the relationships shown in figure 9.4h, i, or j hold. For example, a train of operations carried out by endogenous attention in working memory may reach the conclusion that it is time to recall your mother's maiden name. Within a fraction of a second of this thought T1, your mother's maiden name T2 presents itself in working memory and is experienced as information that you can report and operate on further. The causal relationship in this case would best be represented by figure 9.4j, because the operations that go from the conclusion that certain information is needed to the appearance of that information in working memory are entirely unconscious. Note that no feeling of agency or conscious willing W need intervene between a thought such as "What is my mother's maiden name?" and the appearance of her maiden name in working memory. Such recall might happen quite automatically. This is different from cases where a feeling of willing occurs in the flow of thoughts, such as occurs when trying to recall information when experiencing the tip-of-the-tongue phenomenon. The "flow of consciousness" may involve very little in the way of feelings of effort or even feelings of willing. But it would nonetheless count as volitional in the sense that a thought that was only reachable via operations over attendable, reportable contents causes further thoughts, such as recalling a maiden name, or causes motor planning and actions, such as going to the supermarket to buy cranberry sauce.

§10.39 But if endogenous attention can operate only over conscious operands, does this mean that consciousness per se is causal of motor acts or thoughts? No, it does not. It is generally the case that certain operations can take place only within a particular space. To use a metaphor,[13] I can only turn (an operation) a screw (an operand) with an electric drill (the operator) in three-dimensional space. While this space affords me the possibility of carrying out this action, it is not itself a sufficient cause of any particular action. Similarly, consciousness need not itself be sufficiently causal. It can be thought of as a space or domain of a particular type of representation. Certain operations, particularly those associated with endogenous attentional manipulation and the tracking of representations accessible to this operator, may be possible only within the conscious domain. Primary causation lies with the "operation of the operator on the operand" in the conscious domain, not with consciousness per se. An alternative metaphor is that the electricity needs to be on in order to afford the use of an electric drill to screw in a screw, but that the electricity is on does not guarantee that any operations requiring electricity will be carried out. Consciousness, in the sense of everything experienced now, would, according to this metaphor, play a necessary but not sufficient role in certain kinds of operations.[14] Consciousness is necessary but not sufficient for endogenous attentional operations, while endogenous attentional operations are sufficient for consciousness (for an opposing view, see Cohen et al., 2012).

§10.40   In certain disorders, particularly associated with damage to the medial and orbital prefrontal cortex (Fuster, 2008), a person seems to have experience, yet neither plans nor does anything on the basis of that experience. It is as if the electricity were on, but no operations using the tools that one has on hand were deemed worthy of execution. That one can have qualia, and yet do nothing on the basis of them, suggests that it is not the qualia themselves that trigger or directly cause action. Rather, it is operations that may act on the basis of and act over such representations that cause action. And such operations appear to require the evaluation, motivational drive, and planning afforded by areas such as orbital prefrontal cortex, the anterior cingulate cortex (ACC) and dorsolateral prefrontal cortex (Fuster, 2008).

§10.41   If it is correct that endogenous attentional operations require conscious representations, we might ask: Why is this so? Is there some deep link between endogenous attention, working memory, and experience? I believe that the answer is yes, there is a deep link: If multiple possible courses of action or thought are internally generated, there must be a level where potentially competing solutions to the problem of what to do next can be assessed against criteria that effectively optimize, modify, execute, and sequence behaviors to best satisfy the overarching needs and goals of the organism. On the basis of experience, executive planning centers can assess events, weigh possible plans and meanings against one another, and decide on the best course of action from moment to moment. This is particularly required in cases where responses must be flexibly selected and contextually modified in light of novel or unpredictable circumstances that can be met with multiple possible courses of action. But as soon as multiple possible courses of action can be generated and evaluated against domain-general criteria for optimality, there must be processes that select on the basis of those criteria as well as processes that inhibit deselected possibilities, because a body can only carry out one possible course of action at a time; otherwise, unwanted possibilities could interfere with the execution of the optimal choice. The evolution of attentional processes that select and inhibit representations in working memory therefore goes hand in hand with the evolution of working memory representations that can be endogenously manipulated. Internal comparison, selection, sequencing, and inhibition of possible actions freed behavior from being driven reflexively by sensory input. Having dynamically changing highest-level criteria for optimal behavior that can invoke further processing from lower-level systems allows the generation of solutions to problems that are neither predetermined, nor ballistic, nor insensitive to context. This process is open ended, because solutions can be rejected again and again, or can be modified and optimized before they are carried out.

If an Animal Can Attentionally Track, Is It Conscious?

§10.42   If the above view is correct, it would follow that any animal that demonstrated evidence of endogenous attention, in particular, of volitional attentional tracking, could be inferred to be conscious. For example, if a bird or octopus could show that it is capable of nonmotorically tracking even a single object among distractors in the multiple object tracking task (Pylyshyn & Storm, 1988; Scholl et al., 2001), then this would count as evidence that it is conscious, because attentional tracking is an operation that requires consciousness. On the other hand, if a subsystem's response can be ballistic, because it does not require modification in light of either context or the outputs of other subsystems, its outputs need not be made conscious, because such online and contextually sensitive modification, optimization, and selection of invoked possible solutions appear to be the point of having a conscious subsystem.

§10.43   Koch (2004) has made a related point concerning trace conditioning (see also Bekinschtein et al., 2011). Trace conditioning occurs when there is a temporal gap between the offset of the conditioned stimulus and the onset of the unconditioned stimulus. These authors argue that unlike delay conditioning, an animal has to be conscious of the contingency between the conditioned and unconditioned stimulus in order for trace conditioning to occur. But an animal might exhibit trace conditioning and not have any experience or qualia. It would just need a sensory buffer that held a representation of the unconditioned stimulus for long enough that associations could be made with the conditioned stimulus, once it appears. For example, the sea slug aplysia (Glanzman, 1995; Grol et al., 2006) exhibits trace conditioning, as do fruit flies (Galili et al., 2011; Shuai et al., 2011). This proves only that these invertebrates have such a buffer. It does not prove that they have experience. Even if trace conditioning happens in us only when we are conscious of a contingent relationship across time, it does not follow that a sea slug is conscious of a contingent relationship across time. It might entirely lack experience and still be able to associate events over time if it has an appropriate memory buffer where associations can be made across temporal intervals that are free of input.

§10.44   Note that the converse, namely that any animal that is conscious will exhibit trace conditioning, is patently false. There is a clear counterexample to this. People who lack hippocampi (Bangasser et al., 2006; Corkin, 2002; Feinstein et al., 2010; cf. Solomon et al., 1986) are unable to exhibit trace conditioning,[15] but they are clearly conscious. They in fact appear to be normal in all regards except that they lack consciousness of relationships of events over time because of their complete anterograde amnesia. It follows that a lack of trace conditioning cannot prove that someone is not conscious. It can only prove that he or she lacks an awareness of how events are related to one another over time. Like patient H. M. (Corkin, 2002), a person who exhibited no trace conditioning might have awareness only of the here and now. For example, he or she might be experiencing ongoing pain while in a vegetative state, yet exhibit no trace conditioning.

§10.45   On the other hand, if an animal could carry out attentional tracking, as in the multiple object tracking task, I would accept this as the best available evidence that it is conscious in the sense that it has experience. Granted, this would not be absolute proof that the animal has experience, since it might be organized differently than we are, and possess the capacity to track without experience. But since there is no way to absolutely prove that even another human has experience, this level of evidence might be the best we can hope for. For example, an octopus, cuttlefish, chick, fish or even honeybee could be trained to respond to a sphere that had been momentarily lit to get a food reward, when presented with two or more unlit spheres (e.g., they might be identical translucent white plastic balls lit by internal LEDs). It could then be shown, say, twelve such spheres behind a glass divider, one or more of which would be lit up for a moment. The twelve identical spheres would then move about in the tank for some variable number of seconds. The divider would then be removed. If the, say, octopus tended to pounce on the object(s) that had been lit at a rate higher than chance, it would have to at least be granted that it exhibited endogenous attentional tracking. Since this capacity in humans operates over experienced representations, it would not be a big leap to conclude that this invertebrate also had experience. Promising recent work suggests that even fruit flies can shift a locus of attention to specific locations in the visual field, depending on task demands (Heisenberg et al., 2001; Zhang et al., 2007) and may even be able to do so endogenously (Greenspan & van Swinderen, 2004; van Swinderen, 2005, 2007; van Swinderen & Brembs, 2010; van Swinderen & Greenspan, 2003), which would be an indication of volition or even free will in drosophila (Heisenberg, 1983, 2009), and perhaps consciousness (van Swinderen, 2005).

§10.46   A skeptic could deny this, and say it was only evidence of attentional tracking; but a skeptic can deny that other people have minds as well, and even be a solipsist. Such skepticism can never be disproven, but a reasonable person will grant other people consciousness and the world an external reality. Or a skeptic could say, "if you argue that trace conditioning could happen without experience, why can't attentional tracking happen without experience in other species, even if it cannot happen in us without experience?" The answer is that the contingent association that is conditioned in trace conditioning can be passively learned. If information about the conditioned stimulus is held in a buffer long enough that information about the unconditioned stimulus is simultaneously present with it in the buffer, the association can be made by simple juxtaposition in the buffer. No internal volitional or endogenous operations are necessary for the animal to make or learn this link. The entire process can unfold automatically, without the animal having to make any choices about what to do with the information it has. In contrast, endogenous attentional tracking requires the animal to make choices about which stimuli to maintain or mark as an enduring object over time, and which stimuli to ignore. This is an active, endogenous, volitional process in us, and would have to be an active, endogenous, volitional process of marking, tracking, and ignoring in any species because sensory input itself does not specify the target.

§10.47   But the skeptic could return and ask: Why couldn't this tracking process operate in the absence of experience in, say, an octopus? The first answer is that in the absence of access to the representations that it has to track, its tracking system could not track anything. The second answer is that the criteria upon which it tracks one object over all the other competing objects would have to be held in an online buffer that maintained tracking on the basis of the fulfillment of those critieria. The skeptic could return and say that this would only prove that the analogue of an attentional system in an octopus can access objects and other high-level representations on the basis of information held in a buffer, but it does not prove that the tracked informational structures are experienced. At this point I would say that experienced representations are those that endogenous attentional allocation and tracking operators are now operating on or could operate on in the next moment, if needed. This might not satisfy a skeptic, but by this definition of experienced representations, an octopus that showed evidence of endogenous attentional tracking would show evidence of having experience (see the discussion of zombies in §10.83).[16]

Volitional Attention Can Alter Qualia

§10.48   So far I have talked about stage 1 processing as if it were entirely bottom-up. But attention can alter experience, so it cannot be the case that attention cannot influence the outputs of stage 1 processing. That is, the contents of an object are not simply dictated by the flux of bottom-up sensory input. They can be changed through the manipulations of numerous cognitive operations, such as mental rotation or volitional shifts of attention. An interesting example of this is shown in figure 10.1 (Tse, 2005; see also Carrasco et al., 2004; Tse et al., 2011). Here, if one fixates on one of the spots and attends to one of the three disks, that disk will seem to change its brightness. Tse et al. (2012) theorize that attention can influence preconscious operations either by specifying the domain over which they operate, without changing how those preconscious "operations operate on their operands," or, alternatively, by changing the relative gain on such operations or their outputs. In the particular case shown in figure 10.1, it is theorized that the filling-in of features occurs within figural boundaries, so that features spread freely within a closed figural boundary. This process of filling-in features within a boundary appears to operate in tandem with the placement of layers at relative depths, the specification of transparency or opaqueness, and color constancy operations that recover intrinsic reflectance. Attention may bias the unconscious and automatic filling-in process to operate within the attended figure's boundary and depth by biasing which figural boundaries are dominant. When a distinct object at a distinct depth can be specified by the attended boundaries, the filling-in process results in a weighted average of the features present within the attended figure's boundary (Hsieh & Tse, 2006, 2009).

   §10.49   A related example occurs in the endogenous attentional modulation of afterimages (Reavis et al., 2012a).[17] Early research (Hering, 1878;

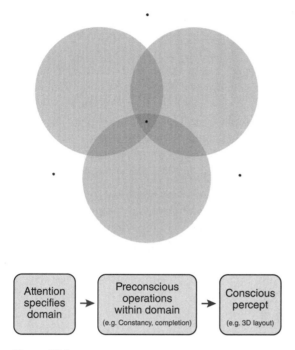

Figure 10.1

Attentional modulation of qualia. Fixate on any of the black fixation spots, such as the one in the very middle of the three disks above. Whichever disk is volitionally attended appears to change in brightness (Tse, 2005; Tse et al., 2012). Here it appears to darken, but in other arrangements the attended disk can appear to brighten or change color (e.g., see back cover). Below this is a schematic of a class of theories that can account for this phenomenon and the one shown in figure 10.2. Attention specifies the domain of preconscious operations such as filling in, motion matching, constancy operations, surface completion, and segmentation, resulting in the conscious experience of these outputs, typically as a 3-D object/scene.

Craik, 1940) suggested that afterimages involve retinal adaptation mechanisms. More recent work, however, has found evidence of extraretinal contributions to afterimage formation as well (Brescamp et al., 2010; Daw, 1962; Gilroy & Blake, 2005; Shevell et al., 2008; Shimojo et al., 2001; Suzuki & Grabowecky, 2003; van Lier et al., 2009). Suzuki and Grabowecky (2003), for example, found that attending to one of two overlapping figures diminishes the strength of the afterimage arising from the previously attended figure. They, however, did not carry out the converse case, where one attends instead to different portions of the blank field corresponding to different portions of the adapted region. Doing so demonstrates that attention can dramatically modulate the content of the perceived afterimage, at least in the present case of perceived overlapping transparent surfaces in the afterimage. To experience this firsthand, fixate on and attend equally to all portions of the image (a) in figure 10.2. After adapting for approximately one minute, fixate on the fixation point in the empty outline image shown in (b). Assuming a purely retinal origin for afterimages, the expected afterimage should be the negative composite shown in (c). However, attention can influence which pattern is seen in the afterimage. When observers attend to the horizontal outline rectangle, they tend to report seeing an after-image of horizontal negative bars with an increased probability, as depicted in (d). In contrast, an after-image of vertical negative bars, as in (e), is more frequently reported when observers attend to the vertical outline rectangle. Note that switching attention from one rectangle to the other while continually fixating on (b) leads to a corresponding switch in the perceived afterimage.

§10.50   What might cause this surprising influence of attention on afterimage perception? Visual afterimages were initially thought to be solely caused by bleaching of photochemical pigments or neural adaptation in the retina (Hering, 1878; Craik, 1940). A number of results, however, suggest a contribution of cortical processing (Brescamp et al., 2010; Daw, 1962; Gilroy & Blake, 2005; Shevell et al., 2008; Shimojo et al., 2001; Suzuki & Grabowecky, 2003; van Lier et al., 2009). The first study to report a central process in the determination of afterimage color was by Fuchs (1923). He used a 3×3 array of colored dots to create nine dot afterimages. He reported that whether one "sees" the afterimage of the central dot as belonging to its row versus its column can alter its perceived color. He did not, however, manipulate afterimages of overlapping surfaces or attention to their boundaries, as here. The present results are not consistent with an account based solely on retinal cone or ganglion cell adaptation, but instead require a cortical contribution (Shimojo et al., 2001). Because the afterimages have been segmented into horizontal versus vertical bars, it appears that the adaptation underlying the afterimages occurs at a level of surface representation where the two transparent layers overlapping in figure 10.2a have been segmented from one another. This effect can be thought of as an endogenous attentional version of the stimulus-driven effect of van Lier et al. (2009), who, like Suzuki and Grabowecky (2003), had observers adapt to two overlapping colored figures. When they briefly flashed a black outline of only one of these figures, the negative afterimage for the corresponding figure was seen, whereas that of the other figure was not seen. Other research (Breitmeyer et al., 2006; De Weerd et al., 1998;

Grossberg & Mingolla, 1985a,b; Macknik, 2006; Macknik, et al., 2000) has established that boundaries play an important role in the filling-in of visual features such as color, and that boundary strength plays a role in whether features are consciously perceived or not. In addition, attention has been shown to strengthen boundary signals (De Weerd et al., 2006; Lou, 1999; Qiu et al., 2007) and this in turn influences the filling-in of features within boundaries (Wede & Francis, 2007). The present example is consistent with past results and theories that suggest that afterimages, like other features, are filled in within visible boundaries at a cortical stage of processing (Wede & Francis, 2007). Here, however, the boundary that is filled in is determined by top-down attentional selection rather than a single bottom-up outline in the image presented by the experimenters, as was the case in van Lier et al. (2009).

§10.51　Although outlines in the afterimage enhance both the probability and duration of perceiving the rivalrous component of the afterimage consistent with voluntary attentional allocation, explicit outlines during this phase are not necessary, probably because the afterimage itself has borders that can be attended. For example, one could stare at figure 10.2a and then attentionally modulate the afterimage while looking at a large blank wall. Because attention is cortical in origin, this finding lends additional support to the growing body of evidence that afterimages derive in part from cortical processes of surface formation, feature filling-in within boundaries, and adaptation over segmented surface-level representations.

§10.52　Attentional modulation of experienced features, whether for the case of visible overlapping transparent surfaces (Tse, 2005; fig. 10.1), or overlapping transparent surfaces in afterimages (fig. 10.2), can be explained with a simple series of processing steps: First, voluntarily attending to a given figure leads to strengthening of that figural boundary; second, assuming the attended boundary can be individuated into a unique object with a uniform reflectance, filling-in of features occurs within those boundaries and is effectively averaged within those attentionally defined figural boundaries (Hsieh & Tse, 2006, 2009, 2010). The effect happens only in those cases where transparency can be perceived, because only in the transparency case can multiple overlapping boundaries undergo segmentation into multiple, simultaneously existing colored surfaces, even if the backmost object is typically perceived as opaque. In the absence of transparency, segmentation into multiple overlapping colored objects fails, and filling-in cannot operate within a single object to the exclusion of other objects that could have been attended.

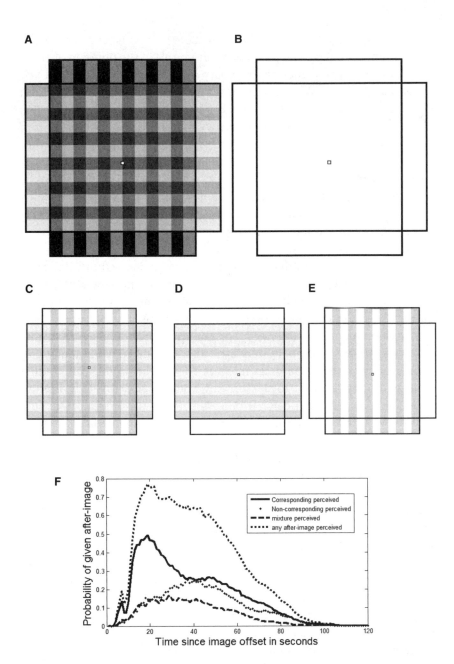

Qualia and Chunking: Types of Qualia

§10.53   Experience is not only essential for planning processes or the selection, inhibition, and tracking of high-level representations in working memory by endogenous attention; experience also plays a central role in chunking of simpler representations and operations, which can in turn facilitate future volitional processes by allowing them to operate on these more complex operands. One possibility is that attention plays a role in converting criteria expressed at the level of working memory to a format expressed at the level of criterial decoders realized in dedicated neurons or groups of neurons. For example, it may take some attentional effort to convert a novel sight-read piano chord to a hand position, but with practice this becomes chunked and automatized, such that one "hardwires" both the recognition of this novel pattern of notes and the motoric commands that realize a hand position, without the need for attention. Consciousness, therefore, may exist not only so that relatively high-level representations, in the form of qualia, can be endogenously attended and otherwise operated upon; it may exist so that attention can chunk, automatize, and hardwire recognition of feature patterns and execute action patterns, automatizing these in order to make processing faster and potentially unconscious. Like a good teacher, attention might have the "goal" of making itself superfluous.

§10.54   Chunking may happen even at the level of qualia themselves.[18] We may be born with a basic basis-set of qualia primitives or "simple qualia," such as sweet, sour, bitter, salty, and so forth. But we are not born with a quale for the taste of a pineapple. If chunking happens at the level of qualia as well, we might expect the hardwiring of neurons or groups of

Figure 10.2
Attentional modulation of experienced after-images. Fixate on the fixation spot in the center of image (a) for sixty seconds, then fixate on the fixation spot in (b). Half of observers were told to attend to the horizontal outline rectangle, and the other half were told to attend to the vertical outline rectangle. Observers then described the afterimage that they perceived. Rather than perceive an afterimage such as shown in (c), which would be the complement of the adapted image in (a), observers who attended to the horizontal empty rectangle in (b) reported seeing horizontal bars as in (d), whereas observers who attended to the vertical empty rectangle in (b) reported seeing vertical bars as in (e). (f) Data averaged across six subjects shows the probability that a given type of afterimage was perceived. The solid curve shows the probability that the afterimage corresponding to the attended box and stripe orientation was perceived after the offset of the image shown in (a).

neurons to be tuned to pineapple per se. As such, the relatively complex flavor pineapple becomes a "neoprimitive" quale. To the extent that we can "wire up" dedicated detectors for complex scenes, such as a beach or city, we can talk of these as comprising high-level qualia too. Similarly, we are not born with 5 and 2 detectors, but humans can learn these to the point that they pop out in visual search arrays (Wang et al., 1994; that is, they demonstrate approximately flat search times as a function of the number of distractors; when rotated 90 degrees, however, they no longer pop out). My colleague Mark Greenlee and our students (Frank et al., 2012) have recently found a similar result for the red and green disks shown in figure 10.3. Initially, when presented with an array of 32 items, the one red–green oddball does not pop out among the 31 green–red distractors. Finding it

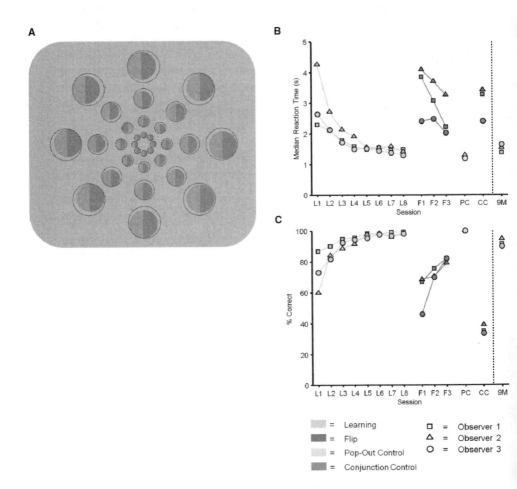

requires effortful, serial attentional search over each item. However, after a week of daily training, reaction times and accuracies are almost as good as for a pop-out task defined by simple feature pop-out. Indeed, having been one of the subjects, I can say that before training, I saw just a mishmash of red and green, but with training, the target seemed to "announce itself" almost as much as if the target had been a red disk among green disks. We ran this training regimen in an fMRI scanner and found clear evidence of increased processing in the attentional network initially. But over the week of training, this subsides, as shown in figure 10.4. As this occurs, we found increased processing in early visual areas in the occipital lobe. This is remarkable, and it suggests that attention is no longer needed to the same degree to locate the target and that processing in the occipital lobes changes with learning. If the account given here is correct, then the red–green target becomes a neoprimitive at the level of not only neuronal detection, but also qualia. This is consistent with the possibility, raised by Tse et al. (2005), that certain visual qualia that do not require (or that no longer require)

Figure 10.3
From parallel to serial search in a week. Behavioral results from a visual search task that progressed from a serial to a nearly parallel "pop-out" search task after eight days of daily training. (A) Depiction of example search stimuli. The correct response for this trial would be "Target in ring 2." To counteract perceptual fading, stimuli were spatially jittered every 100 ms within the stationary dark gray bounding rings. Each search display contained 32 stimuli in this arrangement and was presented for 4 sec. in an MRI scanner (corresponding to the duration to collect a single brain volume). The fixation spot changed color at the end of each to indicate a correct or incorrect response. (B) Reaction times as a function of experimental session, in the original sequence of data collection. Note the initial eight training sessions on the left, and a single retest at nine months on the right with no intervening training, showing that pop-out behavior persisted. Second data series from left: After eight days of training red and green were reversed for three days so that what was the target was now the distractor and vice versa; Behavior returned to a serial search state. The datapoint labeled "PC" for "pop-out control" was a control condition of search for red–green among green–red bull's-eye patterns, which displayed pop-out without training. The datapoint labeled "CC" for "conjunction control" indicates untrained search for a difficult conjunction search (color/aspect ratio conjunction, containing the same amount of red and green stimulus area as the other three stimulus sets). (C) Accuracy rates. Conventions as above. See Frank et al. (2012) for details and corresponding brain data. Key: L1 = learning day 1; F1 = flipped arrangement day 1; PC = pop-out search control; CC = conjunction search control; 9M = retest in the same subjects after nine months of no intervening training. (Figure by Eric Reavis [Frank et al., 2012].)

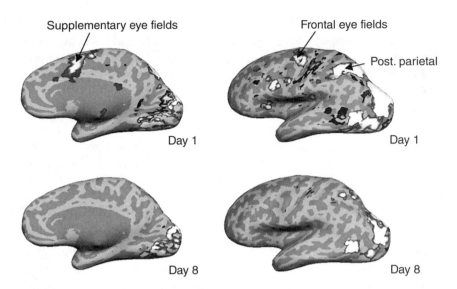

Figure 10.4
The brain changes with chunking. After extensive practice in the conjunction search task described in figure 10.3, there was less activity in the attentional network defined by the frontal and supplementary eye fields, and the posterior parietal cortex and precuneus, perhaps because the target was found more rapidly, but stronger activation in retinotopic visual areas. Left-hand images are of the medial surface of the right hemisphere, and right-hand images are of the lateral view of the left hemisphere. See Frank et al. (2012) for details. (Figure by Eric Reavis and Sebastian Frank.)

endogenous attentional binding are physically realized in the occipital lobe whether attended or not (but see Dehaene et al., 2006, and Dehaene & Changeux, 2011, for an opposing view).

§10.55 Qualia may come in different types (Koch, 2004): (1) simple qualia for which we have innate neuronal systems, presumably like brightness or pain; (2) "configural" or chunked qualia, for which we have learned, through experience or practice, neoprimitive detectors as discussed above; and (3) attentionally bound combinations or conjunctions of simple or configural qualia. Type 1 or "simple" qualia can be surprisingly complex. Emotions such as anger, jealousy, or grief appear to be innate and richly experienced. Desires, such as thirst, hunger, lust, pleasure, or pain, can become all-consuming experiences that appear to be primitive yet complex. For example, lust drives a mind to a specific class of things, namely potential mates, and evokes complex behaviors. Type 1 qualia may actually involve hardwired binding in the sense that two orthogonal features are detected as a unit, as when a simple cell simultaneously detects orientation, spatial frequency, position, luminance, and potentially color. That is, primitive stimulus energy detectors appear to be tuned to multiple dimensions. There is no evidence that simple cells are a neural correlate of experience, but for pure brightness or redness or orientation to count as an independent quale, it would have to be unbound from other features. Low-level feature binding is not attentional binding.

§10.56   Attentional binding defines type 3 experiences, where numerous primitive (type 1, simple) and neoprimitive (type 2, configural) features are bound into a tracked object in an object file. Attentional binding and its associated bound qualia give us a "gorilla" in the wonderful movie[19] by Simons and Chabris (1999; see also Levin et al., 2002; Simons & Levin, 1998; Simons & Ambinder, 2005) based on a film by Neisser (1967). In this film, a team wearing white passes a ball among themselves, intermixed with a team wearing black passing a different ball among themselves. When naïve viewers are told to count the number of the white team's ball passes, they often miss seeing a black gorilla that walks right across the screen and even pounds its chest, because they are attending to the white team and ignoring the black team. This "inattentional blindness" (i.e. not being able to report objects that one is not attending to) leads to only the white team being bound into coherent objects. The black features of the gorilla are not bound into an object, and so are not experienced as a gorilla. This does not mean that no features were experienced at the location of the gorilla. Presumably the motion and blackness of the gorilla were still experienced as "qualia soup" of type 1 and 2 features, say, moving local black shapes in the background. Only if bound together, however, are features experienced as objects and high-level events. Type 3 bound features can, with practice or extensive experience, move from type 3 to type 2 qualia. If this is correct, then the totality of experience comes down to experiencing configurations of qualia of these three types.

§10.57   Type 3 qualia are limited to the figure that we are attending or tracking, although an attentionally tracked figure can include all three types. The background of experience would include qualia of only types 1 and 2, and would comprise the "qualia soup" of what we experience. It would include all experience that the attentional system is not binding into object representations. If it were the case that we only experience that which we are currently attending, then we would only experience a figure and no ground. But we do experience a background against which a figure is defined. Qualia of types 1 and 2 may be the contents of various stage 1 buffers, as well as the outputs of emotional and desire systems, such as pain or hunger, that do not require attentional binding. Qualia of type 3, however, likely reside in short term or working memory buffers that can maintain information even in the absence of bottom-up input. I say "buffers" here and not "buffer" because although there is a highest-level multimodal working memory buffer, probably realized in the frontoparietal network in general, and the dorsolateral prefrontal cortex in particular, there are also intermediate working memory buffers associated with different processing streams, such as visual or auditory working memory, and these are likely to be realized outside of frontoparietal executive circuitry. This would be an instance of the "subsidiary systems" discussed in §10.14. Because qualia of type 3 are posited to be the contents of working memory, and these contents are processed in the frontoparietal network and subsidiary systems, it follows that the neural correlates of type 3 qualia both require the fronto-parietal working-memory/attention network, and are to be found in the DLPFC-parietal network or extra-frontoparietal subsidiary systems.

§10.58   A type 3 quale, because it is by definition an attended figure rather than ground, "pops out" against its background of unbound type 1 and 2 features. Because to pop out means to be immediately attendable upon presentation, that which is presently attended pops out simply by virtue of being attended, even if the type 1 and 2 qualia that are attention-ally bound would not pop out if they were not presently attended. But even type 1 and 2 features might best be thought of in terms of pop-out. On this account, at least in the sensory domain, *a quale is a simple or chunked experienced feature that can pop out in a search array in which distrac-tors lack the feature in question.* On this account of sensory qualia of types 1 and 2, as those features that can pop out during search, we are born with a set of primitive qualia, but can effectively "wire up" new dedicated crite-rial decoders or feature detectors, that permit the formation of neoprimi-tives, or higher-order qualia that we are not born with, such as the taste of pineapple, or even a particular person's face. This chunking, storing, and detection of chunked or bound simple qualia frees attention from having to bind simple and configural qualia anew each moment. Attention then operates over relatively high-level precompiled features, which can then themselves be bound in working memory when attended (but not otherwise; Horowitz & Wolfe, 1998), and potentially then themselves be chunked and stored as even higher level neoprimitive features that can be stored and criterially detected without the need for attention later on. This allows a neoprimitive such as the taste of pineapple to be detected as a chunk, as when we taste pineapple in a complex gustatory ground, such as the flavor of curry. Pineapple effectively becomes a new dimension in taste space, where the taste of the curry becomes a vector in that space that can be projected onto this neoprimitive axis.

§10.59   If endogenous attention is thought of as the binding of representations in working memory, or, as Anne Treisman put it, a "feature glue," it is a "glue that can harden," making future binding unnecessary. (See §10.88 for a neuronal mechanism.) To the extent that consciousness is the domain of present actual and potential future endogenous attentional bindings, one might say that one reason that we have consciousness is to make as much processing automatic as possible so as not to have to waste expensive endogenous attentional resources. Endogenous attentional manipulation, while flexible because any representation can be "glued" with any other, is slow and inefficient. "Preglued" or precompiled representations and motor sequences, while inflexible, are processed efficiently and rapidly. The structure of experience or consciousness will therefore change as we create more and more neoprimitive features or dimensions. This is also why learning will be optimal in a "sweet spot" where representations are not too simple for us, and not too complex, as argued by developmental psychologists Piaget, Vygotsky and others.

§10.60   It might be useful to construct a taxonomy of other types of qualia than types 1–3. One could distinguish between nonvirtual experiences that are generally driven by external sensory inputs, such as occur in normal vision, and virtual experiences (those driven by virtual scenarios played out in working memory buffers and other brain areas), such as those found in mental imagery, daydreaming or dreaming. One could also distinguish teleological versus nonteleological qualia. The latter are not associated with any desire. Redness is an example of a quale that typically lacks an associated desire to do or have something. The teleological type, in contrast, is associated with a desire. Among these, some come associated with a bodily sensation, such as pain, itchiness, hunger, or thirst, and others seem to involve pure desire, in the absence of associated bodily sensations, such as wanderlust, the desire to learn something new, or the desire to laugh. Many teleological qualia involve a desire to put an end to the associated sensation (e.g., itchiness, thirst, lust, hunger, pain; Denton, 2006); others, like the various pleasures, we would usually like to have more of. It would be bizarre to separate the sensation of pain from the associated desire of pain. If one could eliminate the desire that pain stop but still feel the sensation, one could say, "I am in agony, but it does not hurt." It would be equally bizarre to have the desire that the pain stop in the absence of a sensation of tissue damage at any particular location. One possibility is that nonteleological qualia exist in order to permit the experience of a world that we can then operate within and on, in order to try to satisfy the criteria pressing for fulfillment in the form of teleological qualia that are driving us to certain ends. In the absence of nonteleological qualia, we would be left feeling thirst, for example, with no way to find something to drink that is open ended, sensitive to context, and capable of virtual enactment, selection, and deselection.

§10.61   What qualia or experiences are associated with volition? Willing is generally thought of as a single kind of psychological operation, but there are in fact several different types of volition (§3.2). Causation may work differently for different types of volition, and various components of volitional operations might be themselves conscious or not conscious. There could be different volitional operations (perhaps with different types of experience) associated with the preparation of an action before its release, the triggering of a prepared action, the inhibition of a prepared action, the suppression of a thought, the suppression of an emotion, the inhibition of a desire to do something such as scratch an itch, or the inhibition of the outputs of automatic processing, as in the Stroop task. Volitional operations that require endogenous attentional selection, tracking, and inhibition are those likely to be associated with feelings of agency. Similarly, the brain may have different types of executive centers, all of which may mutually interact in determining behavior. For example, area 10 (Shallice & Burgess, 1991; Fuster, 2008) may be involved in operations that maintain a "stack" of plans to be addressed or generate decision or intention trees at an abstract level, and come to executive decisions of the form "I want to get married before turning 30." The dorsal anterior cingulate may regulate, evaluate, motivate, and monitor potentially competing cognitive processes, while the ventral and subgenual anterior cingulate may potentially regulate conflicting emotional processes. Finally, the anterior insula and ventral striatum may realize processing associated with certain desires and feelings of reward, respectively. Each of these types of operations may have a different associated experience or feeling of agency and/or feeling of planning. Whereas qualia of type 1 or 2 may be realized in disparate areas (e.g. hunger or lust in part in the insula, or pleasure partially in the nucleus accumbens), when qualia of types 1 or 2 are attentionally bound into qualia of type 3, these qualia, like all type 3 qualia, are realized in frontoparietal processing or subsidiary systems elsewhere. There may be qualia associated with low-level forms of willing that do not require frontoparietal processing to be experienced, such as pain (with an associated will to make it stop) or thirst (a will to drink something). Thus, pain, itchiness, thirst, or hunger can be thought to include precompiled and automatic volition. Then there may be qualia associated with volition that require frontoparietal processing, such as attentional tracking, as when one concentrates on hearing one voice in a noisy restaurant (with an associated experience of a will to hear that voice).

Qualia and the Frontoparietal Network

§10.62   Experience plays a causal role in subsequent actions by serving as the format upon which endogenous attentional and planning operations can operate in order to generate plans that can be potentiated in advance by reprogramming appropriate neural circuits such that, when the inputs that satisfy those neurons' criteria arrive, the motor act will be executed. Experience may also permit prepotentiated actions to be released by executive processes themselves, because those same executive processes that operate on the experienced format and prepotentiate various possible actions can send outputs that later meet the criteria of the corresponding neurons, triggering one of those actions to happen. That is, neuronal executive and planning operations can recode the criteria for future firing on other neurons, and then later send a command that meets those very same criteria, in effect releasing prepotentiated actions. All of this can occur on the millisecond timescale of concluding that one must do x and then doing it.

§10.63   To be clear, it is not that consciousness or experience is itself necessarily directly causal of present action. Rather, experience and working memory permit operations that model possible future courses of action, select from among them, potentiate the chosen action and then possibly trigger the optimal response not right now, but in the future. Some aspects of these planning, selecting, executing, and tracking operations may themselves be experienced, but presumably large swathes of these operations are themselves carried out in the absence of experience. An experience of, say, planning, willing, tracking, or selecting may have evolved so that subsequent such operations are provided with feedback so that they can be maintained, updated, and corrected flexibly.

§10.64   There is no reason why the outputs of lower-level systems have to be placed in the experienced or endogenously attendable format at a single location in the brain. Consciousness could be distributed across the brain (cf. Zeki, 2001; Tse et al., 2005). Different levels and types of experienced outputs, whether hunger, seeing food, or having thoughts of food, may be made explicit simultaneously in many different locations in the brain.

§10.65   There is currently a schism in the field of researchers looking for the neural correlates of consciousness. The debate has not yet been settled, although it is an empirically decidable issue. Some argue that the frontoparietal network is necessary for consciousness (Dehaene et al., 2006; Dehaene & Changeux, 2011; Del Cul et al., 2009; Laureys, 2004; Sergent & Dehaene, 2004; see also Naghavi & Nyberg, 2005), and others, myself included, argue that it is not (e.g., Lamme, 2004; Tse, 2005; Zeki, 2001). Similarly, some argue that attention is necessary for consciousness (e.g. Cohen et al., 2012), whereas I argue that there can be a type of experience even without attention. Both sides may be partly right (Pins & Ffytche, 2003). The frontoparietal network contains circuitry that realizes attentional and executive operations. The frontoparietal network allows us to attentionally track and manipulate objects in the highest-level multimodal working memory, presumably realized in the dorsolateral prefrontal cortex. In the absence of attention we cannot bind qualia into trackable figural representations, so in effect we would be unable to experience a world of volitionally attendable, trackable, recognizable or identifiable objects and events. In this section I will elaborate on the argument that qualia need not be attended, although they are potentially endogenously attendable in normal individuals.

§10.66   What would we experience in the absence of the frontoparietal network? Those who believe it is necessary for consciousness would assert that eliminating attentional circuitry would eliminate consciousness entirely. On the account developed here, we might experience unbound qualia or "feature soup" of the first two types of qualia, but not the third, since the third type requires attentional binding and this would be missing. The outcome of this debate has moral implications; I argue that someone may lack frontoparietal function yet still experience pain (Boly et al., 2008; but see Laureys, 2004), because pain is evidently an innate, primitive quale that automatically pops out even without attentional binding, chunking, or tracking.[20] If a person cannot think, recognize, track or otherwise volitionally act, because he or she lacks the frontoparietal circuits that realize such processing, but this person could nonetheless experience extreme pain realized in subcortical or insular processing, would we be under a moral obligation to minimize this type 1 experience of pain? If such a patient had no other experience but this pain, would we be under a moral obligation to keep him or her alive? Those who argue that there is no experience without attentional circuits would say that such patients experience nothing. If they wince when we stick a pin in their finger, on their account, it is only because they exhibit unconscious reflexes. On my account, it is possible that they experience pain.

§10.67   Dehaene and Changeux (2011, p. 202) counter my view that there can be varieties of qualia, experience or consciousness even in the absence of frontoparietal processing by saying: "Some authors have found correlations of fMRI activation with visibility of masked versus unmasked [unattended] stimuli exclusively in posterior visual areas (e.g., Tse et al., 2005). However, in their paradigm, even the unmasked stimuli were probably not seen because they were unattended and irrelevant, which can prevent conscious access (Dehaene et al., 2006; Kouider et al., 2007; Mack and Rock, 1998)." This seems to be arguing that unattended stimuli probably cannot be conscious because, according to their theory, unattended stimuli cannot be conscious. Mack and Rock (1998) engage in a similar kind of self-supporting argument about their own data that appears to disconfirm their theory of inattentional blindness (i.e., that unattended information cannot be conscious and therefore cannot be reportable) when they write in their first chapter: "about 75% of the subjects detected the presence, color, and location of the critical shape stimulus in the inattention condition, even though they were unable to identify its shape. . . . Since we found that color, numerosity, motion, flicker, and location were properties of objects that subjects generally reported under conditions of inattention in our original experiments, we had concluded that at least these properties were perceived without attention. However, once one concludes that there is no perception without attention, it of course follows that anything that is perceived must be perceived because attention is engaged. If some critical stimulus is perceived in our inattentive condition, it must be because it has captured or attracted attention."[21] I believe that their own results, namely, that many observers can report aspects of an unattended stimulus, already disconfirms their view that nothing can be experienced without attention.

§10.68   I argue that masked and unmasked unattended stimuli can be conscious as type 1 qualia, extant in the stage 1 buffer. This is why we found only occipital activation in the unmasked-greater-than-masked contrast for the case where the stimuli were unattended (Tse et al., 2005). Dehaene and colleagues argue that such stimuli cannot be conscious, because to be conscious is to be what I would call type 3 qualia, involving, we all agree, frontoparietal processing. The point of contention is whether unattended information is experienced in any sense. This is no doubt a tricky issue. The problem is analogous to the "refrigerator light problem": How do I know if the light is on when the door is closed if I have to open the door to see inside? Perhaps it only turns on when I open the door. Similarly, how do I know if I am conscious of unattended contents at a given location if in order to report anything about them I must attend to that location?

§10.69   When it comes to consciousness, I place primary stock in subjective report and am as skeptical of attempts to define consciousness according to objectively measurable criteria as are Dehaene and Changeux (2011); if some objectively measurable physiological marker x leads to the assertion that a person is (or is not) experiencing qualia y, and the person says that he is not (or is) experiencing y, the person wins, and the objective marker loses. That is, the final arbiter of experience is the experiencer. Therefore, I think that the strongest evidence that there can be unattended conscious contents is that people can report quite a lot about what they were not attending, even when they cannot report the identity of individual elements. This failure to report identity or recognize objects without attention occurs because individuation into individual trackable objects and identifying them requires attentional binding of qualia of type 1 or 2 into qualia of type 3. But *we should not confuse the capacity to identify an attended object with experience of that object*. It is possible to experience, for example, the color, size or location of an object without being able to identify what it was.

§10.70   It is true that in many psychophysical paradigms, people can only report the identity of attended items (Shih & Sperling, 2003; Sperling, 1960). However, an important point that is often overlooked in these arguments, is that, if queried to report whatever they can about what was present at unattended locations, observers typically do not report nothing. In the case of Sperling's famous experiment (Sperling, 1960; §10.12), observers can report layout, contrast, approximate number and size and other basic features of elements whose identities are not reportable. If subjective report is the measure of consciousness that we wish to use in the case of normal humans, and humans can report something about what was present at unattended locations, then they were conscious at those locations, at least at the level of the types of contents that they can report correctly. Even if observers can only say "something was there, but I have no idea what it was" they are reporting an experience of something. This falls far short of identification, but it is nonetheless experience in the absence or near-absence of attention. As the Gestalt psychologists argued, experience does not only encompass the attended "figure" at any given moment, it includes the unattended "ground." On my view, the ground of experience takes the form of type 1 and 2 "qualia soup" which may itself include surprisingly complex outputs of the automatic grouping and other processes that operate within the preconscious buffer.

§10.71   But Sperling's (1960; Shih & Sperling, 2003) or Mack & Rock's (1998) paradigms might not have induced complete inattention. Perhaps the reportability of some aspects of unattended stimuli arises because they are still somewhat attended. One way to try to get around this "residual attention" problem is to present people with so much information for such a brief period of time that they could not possibly have paid attention to every object or location. Even in these situations, observers can report a great deal about entire scenes, including the semantic gist, the approximate number of elements, the spatial layout, whether there were animals or people present, average sizes of objects, average expressions across potentially hundreds of faces, and much else besides (e.g., Joubert et al., 2007; Li et al., 2002; Oppermann et al., 2012).

§10.72   But one could still argue that there had to be at least some minimal residual attention floating about outside the main focus of attention in order for capacities like gist recognition to work. At first, it may seem like there is a certain unfairness in this argument, rather like the witch trials of the past, where they supposedly threw a woman into water; if she floated she was judged to be a witch and was sentenced to death, but if she drowned, she was judged not to be a witch. By analogy, if something is reportable/experienced it must have been attended, but if it is not reportable/experienced, then it must not have been attended. There is an apparent circularity in arguing that stimuli that were experimentally designed not to be attended were nonetheless attended because they were reportable. But I think the witch trial analogy is itself not entirely fair. Although a person is either a witch or not, attention may not be a black and white affair. Perhaps attention can be allocated in degrees like a dimmer switch. Similarly, inattention need not be all or none. A very small amount of residual attention might go a long way toward affording both reportability and experience, though I think no one would want to argue that the entire contents of iconic or visual short-term memory are transferred into visual working memory. By way of analogy, if a dimmer switch is off, one sees nothing, but even if it is on at its minimal setting, an entire room can be dimly seen.

§10.73   Other psychophysics has directly addressed the question of whether attention is necessary for experience. Initially, Braun and colleagues reported that numerous stimulus attributes are reportable even when attention is soaked up in a demanding primary task besides the secondary task of reporting features presented in locations that were, presumably, not attended (Braun & Sagi, 1991; Braun, 1994; Braun & Julesz, 1998). Joseph and colleagues (Joseph et al., 1997) argued that a dual task paradigm does not soak up all attention, and that Braun's results were due to residual attention. To address this, they replaced the dual task paradigm with an attentional blink paradigm (Raymond et al., 1992), where attention was presumed to effectively "turn off" for a moment shortly after a target has been detected; they found that an orientation oddball that would normally pop out during normal attentive vision did not pop out during the attentional blink. Braun (1998) then replicated their results using novice observers, but found that practiced observers could still report pop-out stimulus features during the attentional blink. Joseph and colleagues (Joseph et al., 1998, following Norman & Bobrow, 1975) replied that highly trained observers differ from novice observers because experts can reach a high level of detection with minimal attention—but not without any attention whatsoever—because practice reduces the attentional load associated with the attentional blink. This is the residual attention argument again; trained observers can report features of a pop-out stimulus because they had more residual attention than novice observers during the attentional blink. This might be true, but if so, it either means that the attentional blink does not knock out all attention on each trial, at least for expert observers, or it knocks it out in an all-or-none fashion on some trials but not others, and less often for expert observers.

§10.74 Sergent and Dehaene (2004) argue that they found evidence supporting the all-or-none possibility. Observers were asked to evaluate the visibility of target words on a continuous scale during the attentional blink. Observers moved a cursor on a horizontal bar that was labeled "not seen" on the left and "maximal visibility" on the right. The authors argue that observers responded in an all-or-none fashion; Targets were either identified (i.e., read) as well as targets presented outside the attentional blink or reported as not seen at all. If observers took "not seen" to mean "not identifiable" or "not readable," however, it might be that they experienced something, but could not identify or read what word they had seen. For example, since Mack and Rock (1998) reported that color is often reportable during inattention though shape is not, it might be possible that observers could still report the color of targets that varied in color on each attentional blink trial at an above-chance level, even when they could not identify/read the object. For example, if words were presented in white on a black background or black on a white background at random, it could be that observers would be able to report in which of these formats the word was presented at an above-chance level of performance, even when they could not identify/read the word during the attentional blink. In addition, observers did not actually respond only at the left- and rightmost positions of the scale, but responded at a low rate at other positions on the scale. One possibility is that these intermediate responses are due to noise overlaid on an all-or-none effect. Another possibility is that we should take observers' responses as reflective of their experience, such that when they mark the subjective visibility of a stimulus at 50 percent, they indeed saw something even if they could not identify it.

§10.75   Sergent et al. (2005) followed this up with an event-related potential variant of this experiment, and found that early components N1 and P1, primarily localized to posterior occipital and temporal cortex, were the same regardless of word visibility during the attentional blink. Beyond 270ms, however, brain responses diverged depending on word visibility. In particular, the component P3b, arising with increased neural activity in frontoparietal cortex and other areas, was evident when words could be identified, but not when they could not. They take this as evidence that this brain activity is correlated with experience, and that the activation prior to 270ms outside the frontoparietal network was not a neural correlate of experience. But this appears to equate the ability to identify something with the ability to experience it; again, I argue that it is possible to experience aspects of an object or event without necessarily being able to identify it. Sergent et al. (2005) have trouble explaining why the N2 component, localized to posterior inferotemporal cortex and beginning at about 200ms after word onset during the attentional blink, varies in magnitude with the ability to identify an object, yet remains apparent even in cases when no identification is possible. An alternative view of their results (§10.16) is that (1) pre-200ms components N1 and P1 correspond in part to neural activity that realizes early processing that feeds into the stage 1 buffer, (2) the N2 component starting at about 200ms varies with the degree to which attention has been allocated to the contents of the stage 1 buffer, and (3) the P3b component starting at about 270ms corresponds in part to neural activity that realizes type 3 qualia, attentional individuation and object identification. Under the view of Dehaene and colleagues, the earliest neural correlates of experience begin with (3), whereas I would argue that experience of type 1 and 2 qualia can already begin with the stage 1 buffer in (2). Cases where the N2 is apparent, but the P3b is not, would correspond to cases where identification was not possible, but an object was nonetheless experienced to some degree. My prediction is that observers would be able to report primitive features of words in such cases, such as size or color, even though they could not identify/read them. This remains to be tested.

§10.76   A truly minimal allocation of attentional resources appears to be sufficient to lead to the experience of pop-out features in the background.

At this point some more radical method than the attentional blink or the conditions that induce inattentional blindness would seem to be required to entirely eliminate attention in normals on every trial, although I am sure that the residual attention argument would again be made if anything were reportable under conditions of inattention using this new method for eliminating attention. In one sense, the debate becomes largely academic; if a truly minimal amount of residual attentional is enough to lead to an experience of a perceptual ground where oddball features can pop out, and normal conditions afford such minimal residual attention, then normal experience includes a background of "qualia soup" comprised of features that could undergo pop-out.

§10.77   There is a crucial experiment that can decide between my view and the view of Dehaene and colleagues. They predict that "lesioning or interfering with prefrontal or parietal cortex activity, at sites quite distant from visual areas, should disrupt conscious vision" (Dehaene & Changeux, 2011, p. 216) and in fact eliminate not just visual experience, but all experience. In contrast, I predict that knocking out the frontoparietal circuit, for example, with transcranial magnetic stimulation (TMS), should preserve unattended qualia realized in processes that do not require attention for their binding into identifiable objects (such as pain, color, brightness, thirst or hunger), while eliminating type 3 qualia and concomitant voluntary tracking and manipulation of contents of working memory.[22] If observers can report experiencing anything whatsoever upon application of TMS to, say, the dorsolateral prefrontal cortex, then it is not true that this brain area is necessary for consciousness. On my account, a patient who lacked frontoparietal function might nonetheless scratch a location where he or she experienced an itch, whereas on their account such a patient would not feel an itch or pain or anything else. Balint's patients, who typically have bilateral damage to posterior parietal cortex appear to nonetheless have experience of one object. The posterior parietal cortex is therefore not necessary for consciousness, although it does appear to be necessary for attentional shifting. To my knowledge, no one has tested whether they (or neglect patients in the neglected hemifield; Valler et al., 2001) can nonetheless experience and report aspects of the unattended background, such as, say, its average brightness or color. If so, this would be evidence that they continue to have a "qualia soup" level of experience even at unattendable locations. Similarly, patients with frontal lobe damage severe enough to compromise executive working memory function also appear to have experience, even if impoverished by the lack of executive and attentional function (Pollen, 1999), as Dehaene and Changeux (2011) concede. In addition, dorsolateral prefrontal cortex appears to be deactivated during dreaming relative to wakefulness (Hobson & Pace-Schott, 2002; Nir & Tononi, 2010), yet we would not want to deny that we have experience during dreams.

The Superpositionality of Qualia

§10.78   What would we experience in the absence of type 1 and type 2 qualia? In the case of vision, this would mean loss of experience of the contents of the stage 1 buffer (Neisser, 1967; Sperling, 1960). This is in fact what happens during various internally generated forms of mental imagery in the absence of external inputs, so we know from experience what type 3 qualia may be like in isolation. The experience of dreams may be an instance of this. It is experience realized in attentional manipulation of the contents of various working memory buffers in the absence of sensory processing. These perceptual, emotional and cognitive working memory buffers are presumably realized in frontoparietal processing and subsidiary systems outside the frontoparietal network. In the case of dreams, dorsolateral prefrontal cortex and V1 are actually less active than during waking, suggesting that the mental imagery and visual qualia associated with dreaming are realized in areas that are active during dreaming, such as visual association areas in the medial occipital cortex and temporal subsidiary systems (Hobson & Pace-Schott, 2002; Nir & Tononi, 2010).

§10.79   In wakeful, attentive vision I argue that we experience both the contents of the stage 1 buffer and of visual working memory. When we watched the gorilla movie for the first time and failed to see the gorilla, we nonetheless experienced the blackness and motion at the locations of the gorilla that were represented in the stage 1 buffer. When we watched the movie a second time and saw the gorilla, because we attended to its location, we simultaneously experienced types 1, 2 and 3 qualia there and the neural correlates of this experience were simultaneously in the occipito-temporal stage 1 buffer and working memory areas. The isolated type 3 qualia of dreams seem to be a pale copy of the vividness of the qualia of waking consciousness probably because of the lack of qualia associated with the contents of the stage 1 buffer.

§10.80   An interesting case occurs when we are awake, but daydreaming, such as when we are driving down a familiar stretch of highway on "automatic pilot." In this case, we experience type 1 and type 2 qualia that are realized in our sensory stage 1 buffers, but simultaneously[23] experience unrelated type 3 qualia realized in working memory buffers. Thus consciousness can comprise a superposition of multiple subsystems' outputs, and need not be unified, as in the case where we are fully attending to the contents of a stage 1 buffer. The superpositional character of consciousness affords flexibility in that it allows us to attend to the outputs of one submodule over others, or one level in the hierarchy of processing over others, even while continuing to be conscious of all modular outputs and all levels simultaneously, some as type 3 qualia, others as 'background' qualia of types 1 and 2.

§10.81 This superpositionality of consciousness may even lead to a certain degree of false confidence in the veridicality of our experience, or what might be called "the illusion of precise representation," as when we feel that we see the whole visual scene clearly, when we do not. More specifically, we see the whole visual scene as precise qualia of types 1 and 2 at each location, but only the attended subset of these as type 3 qualia, which is to say, as individuated, identifiable, trackable objects. This means that we do not have precise information about individuated, identified objects at each location. But naïve observers might believe that they do, and certainly, any time they need more information they can just look or shift attention to that location and type 3 qualia suddenly come into existence there. Similarly, neglect patients may believe that they see the whole visual field clearly because they indeed do experience the entire visual field as type 1 and 2 qualia, including in the neglected hemifield, but can only attentionally bind, and therefore experience type 3 qualia, in the nonneglected hemifield. Similarly, we may have the illusory impression that we have precise information about distance or surface orientation, when in fact we do not, perhaps because we do have precise information about features and their locations in the stage 1 buffer. The notion that the visual system does not calculate a precise map of surface orientations is an important one supported by the work of several authors (e.g., Koenderinck et al., 1992, 1994, 1995, 1996; Reichel, Todd, & Yilmaz, 1995; Todd & Norman, 1995; Tse, 1998, 1999, 2002; Tse & Albert, 1998), who have disproved Marr's (1982) central thesis that vision recovers a precise representation of surface orientation and depth. Todd and Norman (1995) conclude that our representation of 3-D structure is not metrical insofar as relative depth and surface orientation are not precisely represented by the visual system. What then can account for our phenomenal impression that the surfaces that we experience have definite surface orientations that vary smoothly over the surface? One possibility raised by Todd and Norman (1995) is that surface smoothness is conveyed by other properties, such as smooth variations of shading, texture, motion, or disparity. Another alternative is that we misattribute the precision of early representations such as orientation to the more complex, derived representations of surface orientation and depth. The illusion of precision occurs because of misattribution of precision from one level of qualia to a different, simultaneously experienced level. This may occur because consciousness, although in fact superpositional, is taken to be a unified, monolithic space of representation, probably because endogenous attention has the freedom to jump to any level of any modular outputs as needed. Another possibility is the notion that "an ambiguous representation is not the same as a representation of ambiguity." We simply may not represent surface geometry metrically, and so do not notice information that is "missing." That is, we may not notice the ambiguity in our representations of depth and surface orientation because surfaces have definite layout in the world. This allows us to gather more precise information about surface layout when we need it without having to explicitly or precisely represent it.

§10.82   This is analogous to the idea of the world as an "outside memory" (O'Regan, 1992), according to which most information about objects can be stored "in the world" such that when we need more information about them, we can simply look.[24] Of course, it cannot be true that nothing is internally represented, as some seem to have argued (O'Regan & Noë, 2001), because enough information must be internally represented so that we at least know where to look to gather more information. Instead, what is represented across the visual field is the contents of the stage 1 buffer, such that anytime we need identifiable objects, we can shift attention to the corresponding features or location of the stage 1 buffer. So it is not that the world is an outside memory. It is that stage 1 buffers hold massively parallel contents about all preprocessed sensory inputs that allow endogenous attention to shift to locations, levels and types of information that will then yield the type 3 experiences of identifiable, trackable objects that are needed for a given task. In this sense, stage 1 qualia play the role of an "outside memory," not the world. The world is not a memory at all. The world outside the brain is just the world, and represents and stores nothing like a memory system would. Stage 1 qualia serve as "pointers" to potential type 3 qualia. Alone, type 1 and 2 qualia may not be sufficient to get the attentional system to attend to the correct subset of features to yield needed information. In addition, there may have to be knowledge about what kinds of stage 1 qualia are likely to yield what kinds of type 3 qualia once attention has shifted to them. For example, if one is looking for a Christmas tree, one must have knowledge that a dark green blur in the visual periphery has a relatively high probability of being experienced as a Christmas tree once attention, or more commonly, both attention and the eyes, have shifted to the location specified by the green blur "pointer." This system is not infallible; we might shift our eyes and find a painting of a fig tree there instead of what we are looking for. But this architecture of information processing, search and indeed of consciousness, affords us an experience of what we need, when we need it, without wasting neural resources binding irrelevant information.

Zombies Are Impossible

§10.83 If experience is that set of neurally realized "precompiled" information that endogenous attentional and planning circuitry can access and operate on (or that they are now operating on), a zombie (cf. Chalmers, 1996) that had no experience would have nothing to operate on with its endogenous attention. It would therefore lack an endogenous attention that could do anything. It would have nothing to manipulate in working memory for purposes of planning or internal visualization. It would therefore not be "just like us in every way" save for qualia. But a defender of zombies could counter that zombies could be wired up to be able to access and voluntarily shift attention around information that was not associated with experience. This unexperienced information could even be assigned weights on some unconscious saliency map that indicated importance, emotional value, or desirability. A zombie would feel no desires or emotions and yet have an information-processing architecture that made it behave as if it did. It could access information and voluntarily operate on it, without experiencing the results of those operations. For example, it could watch the gorilla movie and fail to report a gorilla because it had attended only to the white players, which it did not experience, and then, upon attending to the black players, report a gorilla walking among them. If qualia necessarily co-occurred with endogenous attentional operations, a zombie that had endogenous attention would have qualia—and thus not be a zombie. Therefore, for the zombie argument to work, it must be possible to peel qualia away from their accessibility to the operations of endogenous attention, whether binding or tracking. Let us peel them away. A zombie has everything a conscious person has except whatever it is we just peeled away. Call these peelings endogenously "inaccessible qualia," or "i-qualia." Can i-qualia exist? If they cannot be accessed by endogenous attention, they cannot be voluntarily accessed or reported at all, just like unconscious information. In normal people, there are no known types of information that can be experienced yet cannot be voluntarily attended.[25] Zombies are like us in every way, including having endogenous attention, except that they lack i-qualia. But we ourselves lack i-qualia. So zombies are like us in every way. If experience is the set of all information that is accessible to or pops out for or is trackable by or could be bound by endogenous attention, and zombies have such information, they would have experience. They would have qualia. This is related to the argument given in §10.32 that in order to attentionally track, there must be an error signal between the location of the focus of endogenous attention and the location of an experienced target. If no target were experienced, then no error signal would be possible. Zombies would be unable to attentionally track anything. Zombies would lack the capacity to endogenously attend.

Tying It All Together

§10.84   Until these last two chapters I had avoided dealing with the issue of how consciousness can influence behavior in a downwardly causal manner. In the previous chapter I concluded that presumed neural signatures (readiness potentials) of conscious feelings of willing are in fact not such signatures, and that, in any case, conscious feelings of willing, agency or authorship are not where the action is, so to speak, in mental causation. In this chapter, I argue that consciousness plays a key role in mental causation by providing a common format for endogenous attentional and other executive operations that permit the assessment of possible behaviors and thoughts against highest-level criteria for successful attainment of goals and fulfillment of desires. Qualia are those representations that are now (type 3) or momentarily could be (types 1 and 2) operated on by endogenous attention, giving rise to the possibility of endogenous attentional tracking, which, I argue, cannot happen in the absence of consciousness. Because certain operations can only take place over conscious operands, and thoughts and motor acts can follow and build upon or enact the conclusions of such operations, such operations over conscious operands can be causal of subsequent thoughts and motor acts. Such mental operations within the domain of experience play a necessary (though not necessarily sufficient) causal role in their mental and motoric consequences and are not mere illusions of volition. How a propositional conclusion, such as "I need to go to the store to buy cranberry sauce," is translated into motor plans and actions is not yet known, but it is hypothesized to occur via the same rapid and dynamic reconfiguration of the physical/informational criteria for neuronal firing that underlies the three-stage process. If so, current operations in working memory over endogenously attendable operands do not cause present thoughts, experience, or actions, but instead cause future thoughts, experience and actions, given the arrival of inputs that satisfy the criteria that are preset as their consequence.

§10.85   It was essential to focus on the neural bases of endogenous attention and consciousness in a book about the neural basis of free will, because it is precisely endogenous attentional operations over externally generated qualia (i.e. that which is selectable in the stage 1 buffer) or internally generated qualia (e.g. mental imagery and the internal "playing things out" of dreaming and daydreaming) that allow us to come to conclusions such as "I need to buy cranberry sauce" that can then cause subsequent actions like going to the store. It is the deliberative and volitional manipulation of contents of working memory via endogenous attentional operations that offers the primary causal role of consciousness and the primary domain of free will, regardless of whether or not such operations are associated with conscious feelings of willing or agency. Free will is not limited to the kinds of decisions that are reached by tracking or playing things out endogenously in working memory. Free will also includes the creative ability to imagine, regardless of whether any physical act follows from that which has been imagined.

§10.86   I have focused on endogenous attentional tracking and manipulation of the contents of working memory (type 3 qualia) as the key example where a volitional, experienced process plays a necessary causal role in the subsequent enactment of the conclusions of its operations. However, this is not the only example of a close relationship between qualia and volition. Volition is not only limited to operations over type 3 qualia, which we might call "endogenous volition"—what people traditionally mean when they talk about volition. If to will something is to want it to happen and to try to do what is required to make it happen, desires can be thought of as examples of "exogenous volition" that we do not endogenously will to have. Rather, they are wants and drives that happen to us in the sense that they just "appear" in our experience uncalled for by executive processes. Type 1 qualia, such as pain or thirst, instantiate a primitive form of exogenous volition for that which can bring about their respective cessation. An inherent aspect of teleological qualia like these is that they are associated with some want or desire for that which would fulfill them, such as objects that meet the criteria defining what counts as food or an appropriate mate. Without the experience of these desires, nothing would be done to satisfy these desires. Things that meet the criteria for what counts as food or a mate, say, would not be sought. Thus even type 1 qualia can be causal of thoughts, motor planning and motor acts that proceed as a consequence of their occurrence, even if these proceed automatically without endogenous willing. For example, a toothache can indeed cause subsequent acts, like thinking of going to the dentist and then going to the dentist. The ideas and motor plans that seem to pop into one's head to terminate, say, pain, thirst, lust or hunger can be thought of as "bottom-up mental causation" facilitated by the occurrence of qualia that are not necessarily attended. In contrast, the ideas and motor plans that result from endogenous attentional manipulation of contents in working memory can be thought of as "top-down mental causation" facilitated by the occurrence of qualia that are necessarily attended. Exogenous and bottom-up forms of mental causation would not count as freely willed or endogenous mental causation. But qualia play a central causal role in both exogenous and endogenous forms of mental causation and volition.

§10.87   The central argument of chapters 3 through 6 was that neuronal bursting triggered by the opening of NMDA receptors plays a central role in attentional processing and mental causation on a millisecond timescale by rapidly resetting synapses such that later spikes can potentially meet the physical/informational criteria for postsynaptic neuronal activation that are realized in part in those synapses (§§3.13, 5.51). In particular, endogenous attention, via cholinergic and noncholinergic feedback from the basal forebrain, itself presumably ultimately driven by decisions made in the frontoparietal executive network, can transition "attendable" neural circuits from tonic to phasic mode. This is the neural basis of attentional binding, because attentional binding is complete information processing up until the level of object identification by a circuit such as that underlying the ventral "what/who is it?" processing stream. We can now unify this view of attention with the view of consciousness developed in this chapter. Qualia of types 1 and 2 are the contents of stage 1 buffers. They do not require attentional binding to come into being within various submodules (e.g., vision, audition, pain, touch) with different associated stage 1 buffers. It is not clear whether they are realized in tonic (AMPA-mediated) or phasic (NMDA-mediated) neural activity (§4.36). If they are realized in phasic neural responses, perhaps carried in part by the onset and offset bursts associated with stimulus discontinuities (§4.38), those phasic responses (i.e. burst packets) do not automatically get transferred up the object processing hierarchy from the stage 1 buffer. This is why we are not, for example, conscious of identifiable objects at all locations in the visual field. Transfer from stage 1 to subsidiary working memory buffers, such as visual working memory, and from there into executive working memory, presumably realized in the frontoparietal network, especially the dorsolateral prefrontal cortex, depends crucially on attention. Attention converts selected qualia of type 1 and 2 (potentially endogenously trackable "qualia soup") into qualia of type 3 (endogenously tracked contents of an "object file"). Qualia of type 3 are therefore likely realized in phasic neural responses realized in frontoparietal executive working memory, presumably realized in the dorsolateral prefrontal cortex, or subsidiary working memory systems, such as may be found in the fusiform face area for the specific case of face information. This transition from tonic to phasic mode by attention realized in the frontoparietal network can be thought of as the "ignition" of not only the entire sensory processing hierarchy to the level of object recognition, it is the ignition of object representations in working memory, and it is the ignition of type 3 qualia associated with experiencing objects or figures against a ground of qualia of types 1 and 2.

§10.88   In this chapter (§10.53) I focused on the role of attention in learning, particularly the chunking of qualia. It is possible to link chunking with the view of neural circuitry, learning, and NMDA receptors developed in chapter 5 if attentional allocation alters the expression of NMDA and other receptors as well as dendritic spine formation within a neural hierarchy (see figure 4.3). Indeed, cholinergic release facilitates "muscarinic LTP" at the precise location on a dendrite where there has been Ca^{2+} influx, and locations that do not undergo such influx undergo LTD (Cho et al., 2012). Presumably, before chunking, burst packets only reach a level of "feature recognition," whereas after learning, a burst packet now "automatically" reaches the level of conjunctive pattern-matching neurons given certain low-level featural inputs and only minimal or even no attentional allocation. Attention presumably facilitates the binding of features in part by altering epiconnectivity such as shown in figure 4.5. As receptor and spine expression changes at corresponding synapses of an attentionally maintained epicircuit, the temporary epicircuit "hardens" into a more stable circuit that permits a "burst packet track" to form. This permits bottom-up burst packet transmission up to a level of recognition, subserving the transformation of type 3 into type 2 qualia. Thus learning may proceed not only at the level of synapses, but also at the level of circuits and epicircuits.

§10.89   Future work will have to determine how exactly top-down attention facilitates bottom up information transfer and binding. It would be elegant if not only the bottom-up consequences of endogenous attention, but also the top-down effects of endogenous attention themselves were realized in a neural code based on the transmission of burst packets across entire circuits. If so, the principle neural correlates of consciousness, attentional binding, downward mental causation and free will would be the bursting and associated firing rate changes of pyramidal cells that reset criteria for future neural firing via rapid synaptic resetting.

Appendix 1: Physical Evidence for Ontological Indeterminism

§A1.1 Physicalism is the monistic[1] framework within which causality is understood by most scientists and philosophers of mind, and it is the framework adopted here. Physicalism maintains that there is only one fundamental substance or substrate, namely, energy,[2] changing within space-time in a manner that is best described by the laws of physics. Physicalist stances fall into different camps. One division occurs between deterministic and indeterministic versions of physicalism; determinism essentially asserts that there is only one possible future course of events, whereas indeterminism asserts that there are many possible future courses of events that might occur at any moment, perhaps with different likelihoods, even when only one actually occurs. Another division lies between reductive and nonreductive versions of physicalism.

§A1.2 For centuries following Newton, causality was understood in terms of a "colliding billiard ball" model of particles, based on the idea of "energy transfer" among particles that obey the laws of classical mechanics, including the fundamental laws of conservation of energy and momentum. Fundamental particles were assumed not to transform into different fundamental particles. Particle trajectories were thought to be entirely determined by physical properties such as mass and momentum. This energy transfer conception of causality was deterministic. If a demon (Laplace, 1902 [1814]) could know with absolute precision the locations, masses, momenta, and all other physical properties of all elementary particles everywhere, the whole future and past of the universe could in principle be known to it.[3]

§A1.3 With the advent of modern chemistry, however, greater attention was paid to how energy undergoes transformations and exhibits new properties as fundamental particles combine and recombine in chemical reactions. Even though this "energy transformation" conception of physical causation was no longer a simple Newtonian "energy transfer" conception of particle collisions, it remained in essence deterministic. Physical causality was thought by most scientists to be fully or very nearly fully described by the laws of classical physics and chemistry until approximately the turn of the twentieth century. These laws described how energy was transferred among particles and fields, and how energy was transformed through chemical reactions.

§A1.4   The first hint that the fundamental laws governing particle behavior might be probabilistic rather than deterministic arose with the realization that closed systems tend to approach equilibrium (Eddington, 1932). If water at one end of a bathtub is hot, and at the other end cold, the two will tend to mix with a much higher probability than the probability that they will remain segregated. The second law of thermodynamics[4] implied not only that nature might be probabilistic, but that time might have a directionality that contradicted the temporal reversibility implicit in classical mechanics. However, thermodynamics could still be regarded as an instance of epistemological rather than ontological indeterminism in that underlying particle behavior might still be entirely determined by the physical properties of particles and forces acting on particles such that at each instant a particle has only one possible path open to it. An epistemological indeterminist would maintain that it is only because we cannot obtain complete knowledge of these properties that we must be satisfied with higher-level stochastic laws, such as the laws of thermodynamics (Brush, 1976).

§A1.5   Not until the development of quantum theory were the physical properties of particles regarded as ontologically indeterministic by many if not most physicists. Nonetheless, determinists did not simply concede that nature, as Einstein put it, "plays dice"; he and other physicists argued that the fundamental level of causation must still be deterministic (e.g., Einstein et al., 1935), despite the probabilistic character of quantum theory. According to advocates of such "hidden variables determinism," the probability density functions whose dynamics are given by the equations of quantum physics describe uncertainty in our knowledge of particle locations and movements, not any kind of actual nonspecificity of particle locations, momenta, energies, or durations. The dominant "Copenhagen interpretation" of quantum mechanics (Bohr, 1934, 1958, 1963), however, regarded uncertainty concerning measurement outcomes to be a fundamental fact about reality, rather than simply a problem concerning the limits of our knowledge about particle properties.

§A1.6   Bell argued, against Einstein's deterministic view, that no physicalist theory based on local hidden variables could account for quantum level effects. He proved mathematically (Bell, 1966, 1971, 1981, 1987; see also Fine, 1996; Selleri, 1988), and subsequent experiments have confirmed (Aspect et al., 1981, 1982a,b; Gröblacher et al., 2007; Matsukevich et al., 2008; Rowe et al., 2001), that any local hidden variables version of quantum mechanics can be ruled out, and that allowable versions of quantum mechanics must either allow for nonlocal[5] coordination or correlation of the states of distant physical events, or they must violate "counterfactual definiteness." Counterfactual definiteness refers to the idea that certain properties, such as momentum or position, have a definite state, even when they are not measured and are not known. Since determinists are loath to give up the idea that unmeasured properties nonetheless occupy a definite state at each moment, even if that state cannot be known to us, versions of nonlocal hidden variables determinism have been proposed. Perhaps the best known of these was proposed by Bohm (1952a,b; Bohm & Hiley, 1993). According to this interpretation of quantum mechanics, particles continually "coordinate" with all other particles in the universe instantaneously. Non-Bohmian nonlocal hidden variables quantum theories have also been formulated, but most of these have been ruled out by recent experiments (Gröblacher et al., 2007; Paterek et al., 2007).

§A1.7   Determinists thus appear to be forced into one of two uncomfortable corners. Either determinists must accept that there are causal chains involving nonlocal correlations that are instantaneous (leaving them with the problem of explaining how coordination of particle attributes, such as spin state, can occur at faster than the speed of light with other "entangled" particles over arbitrarily large distances), or they must accept that unmeasured properties do not have a definite ontological state at times when they are not measured. The former notion, that correlatedness can occur apparently instantaneously with events outside the light cone, appears to violate relativity theory, where simultaneity is not absolutely defined. On the other hand, to accept that particle properties are ontologically unspecified when not measured would be tantamount to accepting ontological indeterminism, since nonspecific properties are by definition indeterminate. Thus, to preserve a belief in determinism, it appears that one is driven to accept the reality of instantaneous particle correlatedness outside the light cone, and by implication some as yet unspecified notion of universal instantaneity.[6] Extensive empirical evidence supports the reality of nonlocality (Aspect et al., 1981, 1982a,b; Gröblacher et al., 2007; Matsukevich et al., 2008; Rowe et al., 2001). Although maintaining a belief in determinism may require accepting the reality of nonlocality, that nonlocality is the case is not sufficient to establish whether determinism or indeterminism is the case. That said, nonlocality is a logical consequence of Heisenberg's uncertainty principle (Oppenheim & Wehner, 2010), so accepting determinism may ironically drive one to have to accept the reality of quantum uncertainty or indeterminacy[7] after all. Henceforth, I will accept the weight of empirical evidence from modern physics, and assume ontological indeterminism to be the case. Indeed, the critiques of reductionistic physicalist theories of mind discussed in appendix 2 apply only if reality is in fact indeterministic.

§A1.8   A veritable cottage industry has emerged among physicists who have suggested that mental events somehow follow from quantum domain entanglement and nonlocality (e.g., Hameroff, 2001; Penrose, 1989, 1994) or electron tunneling (Walker, 2001; cf. Macgregor, 2006). Such claims are improbable (Tegmark, 2000; Grush & Churchland, 1995: but see Penrose & Hameroff, 1995, for a rebuttal) and are not needed to account for mental causation. In contrast, criterial detectors, such as receptors or neurons, can operate in the domain of ordinary temperatures where the kind of coherence that would be necessary to realize entanglement would be made incoherent (Koch & Hepp, 2006). There is no need to invoke quantum nonlocality, superposition, entanglement, coherence, tunneling, quantum gravity, or any new forces to understand informational causal chains in the brain. Criteria can be realized in the input–output mechanisms of relatively large scale, high-temperature entities, such as receptors or neurons, in the absence of nonlocality effects. What is needed, however, is some degree of noise in the system that arises from amplified microscopic fluctuations that manifest themselves as randomness concerning the timing of EPSPs and IPSPs and therefore neural dynamics (§§4.64, 4.65). Because of such noise at the synapse and within neurons themselves, there is no guarantee that identical presynaptic input will lead to identical postsynaptic output, even if time could be "rewound" and initial conditions were truly identical. But noise could also be introduced by external factors, such as, say, noise in perceptual inputs, or cellular damage due to free radicals or cosmic rays, or many other possible causes that have nothing to do with nonlocal quantum level effects. While I argue that noise can be harnessed for the purposes of generating novel solutions using criterial causality, this is a far cry from notions that nonlocal quantum-level effects are in some mysterious way responsible for mental events. It is improbable that any of the strange, nonlocal quantum coherence effects can have any influence on how neurons behave, or how consciousness or information is realized in neural events. The brain is, simply put, too "warm" to support this kind of quantum-domain coherence, and synapses are too wide to support electron tunneling. Just because some quantum effects are mysterious and the physical realization of mental phenomena is also mysterious does not mean they are related. In short, I doubt that quantum-domain effects— beyond the variability in neural dynamics introduced by amplification of microscopic fluctuations (§§4.64, 4.65)—are required to account for how information is processed by neurons.

§A1.9   Some physicists and philosophers have argued that quantum indeterminism permits a gap in physical causal chains that can be exploited by consciousness to bias which possibilities become real (cf., e.g., Hodgson, 1993; Penrose, 1989, 1994; Stapp, 2004). The view developed here is unlike such views because consciousness, in the sense of experience, is not seen to play a necessary role in determining which possibility is actualized. Rather, consciousness, and the entertainment of possible scenarios and courses of action in working memory, plays a role in changing the criteria for firing on neurons that might lead to future mental events. In other words, experience and online manipulation of representations in working memory allow the potentiation of future mental events and actions, not present ones. This view is developed further in chapter 10.

§A1.10   I must also express skepticism toward my skepticism, however, because it has been shown that even massive molecules such as C_{60} (Fullerene, molecular weight 720.6468 g/mol; diameter ~0.7nm) exhibit interference effects when passed through a double slit one molecule at a time (Arndt et al., 1999; Nairz et al., 2003). By comparison, neurotransmitters are typically much smaller than this (e.g., glutamate: 147.13g/mol; GABA: 103.12g/mol; serotonin: 176.22g/mol; glycine: 75.01g/mol) and the ions that pass through ionotropic receptors are even smaller (sodium: 22.99g/mol; calcium: 40.08g/mol; potassium: 39.10g/mol). The diameter of an open NMDA receptor pore is only 5.5Å (Villarroel et al., 1995), whereas cation-selective ligand-gated ion channels range between 7Å for acetylcholine receptors in frog muscles (Dwyer et al., 1980; Huang et al., 1978) and 7.6Å for $5HT_3$ receptors in neuroblastoma cells (Yakel et al., 1990; Yang, 1990), and anion selective GABA and glycine receptors in neurons range from 5.2 to 5.4Å (Bormann et al., 1987). By way of comparison, slits that are orders of magnitude larger generate interference effects when electrons are passed through them (50x0.3µ; Jönsson, 1974). Given their small size (Rambhadran et al., 2010; Salussolia et al., 2011), NMDA receptor can be packed together much more closely than this, which, if simultaneously open, as occurs during bursting, would create the conditions for two- or multislit interference. So certainly wave-particle effects could in principle be expressed among neurotransmitters in the synapse. The key question is whether such effects matter in the functioning of a neuron. If so, this would be another mechanism for introducing indeterminacy from the quantum domain to the level of variability in spike and burst timing.

§A1.11   The relevant insight from the double-slit experiment is that a particle must in some sense have wave-like properties in order for it to be able to interfere with itself. This can be thought of as a "probability wave" that passes through space, where the magnitude of the wave indicates the probability of, for example, the detection of a particle. According to Feynman's (1965) path integration account, the wavelike aspects of a particle can be modeled as arising from the integration of all possible particle paths between two points, such as the emitter and the photographic plate in the double-slit experiment. Both of these accounts seem to imply that the path that a particle realizes is in part a function of its (future) possibilities, which can interfere and sum with one another. This seems to imply that what can happen in the future influences what particle paths can be realized now. Even though I did not make reference to possible quantum domain effects in discussing pseudo-backward causation in time (§6.17), a case could be made. Quantum nonlocality is so strange that particles' paths can even be influenced by physical events at locations through which they have no possibility of passing, such as between the two slits (Aharonov & Bohm, 1959; Peshkin & Tonomura, 1989). Thus, although I think it is important to remain skeptical about the role of quantum domain coherency effects in neural processing, it is equally important not to be dismissive of the possibility that certain events involve unusual quantum effects. Likely candidates where microscopic randomness is amplified to the level of neural spike time randomness include the path of a neurotransmitter across the synapse that gives rise to variability in the timing of its arrival at a receptor, or the timing of the release of a magnesium ion from an NMDA receptor. I have made a case for mental causation that does not need strange quantum effects beyond randomness of events at the level of receptors and ions, but time will tell.

Appendix 2: Ontological Indeterminism Undermines Kim's Argument against the Logical Possibility of Mental Causation

Abstract

Kim's argument excluding mental activity from playing a role in physical causation rests on a premise of the causal or dynamical closure of the physical. If determinism is the case, this premise holds, and Kim is correct that mental causation is impossible. However, ontological indeterminism undermines this premise. If ontological indeterminism is correct, then the assumption of the closure of physical causation among *actual* events is incorrect, because any particular present microphysical state e is not necessitated by its antecedent microphysical state c, and the antecedent microphysical state c is not a sufficient cause of e, because some other event than e might have happened. Attempts to base Kim's argument on the closure of physical causation among *possible* events, however, do not work. Therefore, if ontological indeterminism is the case, Kim's argument does not rule out the logical possibility of downward mental causation.

§A2.1   Even though ontological indeterminism has become the dominant framework for understanding reality among quantum physicists, determinism still remains a popular position among some reductionist philosophers of mind. Reductionist physicalist philosophers of mind, exemplified by Kim (e.g., Kim, 2003, 2005, 2006, 2007; see also Churchland, 2007), argue that there is no other causality than fundamental particle-level causality.[1] On this account, all higher-level causalities described by the "special sciences,"[2] such as psychology and neuroscience, are epiphenomenal and reduce, ultimately, to the physical causality operative among elementary particles. To be caused, on Kim's reductionistic physicalist account, is to be caused solely at the level of elementary particles, because causality at the lowest level is "closed." In contrast, the chains of causation modeled by the special sciences are not closed. "Causal closure" means that causality at the level of elementary particles is sufficient to explain all events at the level of elementary particles. Kim (2005, p. 17), applying Occam's razor, advocates the "exclusion of over-determination" when modeling physical causation. In his words: "If event e has a sufficient cause c at t, no event at t distinct from c can be a cause of e." Since particle-level causality, on his account, is sufficient to account for particle behavior, and neurons are made of particles, it follows that mental events, which must supervene on neuronal events, can play no causal role in neuronal behavior and are epiphenomenal. In other words, mental events cannot cause fundamental particles to behave differently than they otherwise would have behaved, had they only moved and interacted according to the laws of particle physics. According to reductive physicalism, the appearance of mental causality "seeps away" (Block, 2003) into the one and only true causality, which is the causality operative among elementary particles. This notion of causality reduces all causation to the transfer and transformation of energy among particles and their aggregates, because the equations of physics describe only how energy moves, is transferred, and transforms, as it changes and combines or otherwise moves through space-time. Physics has no need to refer to mental events to describe how particles move, because particles are mindless bits of energy. As all higher-level events supervene on particle-level events, reductive physicalists maintain that mental events are epiphenomenal and not in any sense causal of brain events or even other mental events, despite our intuitions that our percepts, thoughts, and desires motivate our decisions to act. Their charge of epiphenomenalism is not a criticism of mental causation per se; it applies to causation at *any* level higher than causality at the root-most level of causation operative at the level of fundamental particles, which is where true causation solely lies. Thus, even a physically realized informational mode of causation such as genetic inheritance would be regarded by reductive physicalists as epiphenomenal.[3]

§A2.2   Nonreductive physicalists (e.g., Antony, 2007; Campbell, 1974; Deacon, 2007; Earley, 2008; Hendry, 2006; Humphreys, 1997; Newman, 1996; Sperry, 1986; Van Gulick, 1995) reject the uncompromising reductionism of Kim and other reductive physicalists, while nonetheless accepting physical monism. Nonreductive physicalists attempt to show in various ways that there can indeed be causation of the mental upon the physical. Kim (2005) dismisses nonreductive physicalism as "property dualism" and characterizes the position as one where "The psychological character of a creature may supervene on and yet remain distinct and autonomous from its physical nature" (p. 14). Kim says that all nonreductive physicalists advocate downward causation, which means that they must advocate that mental events can influence how fundamental particles behave. This view

M1 ⊠ M2
↑   ↑
P1 ⇨ P2

Figure A2.1
Mental causation as epiphenomenal. (a) According to Kim's (2005) reductive physicalist account, mental event M1 supervenes (thin arrow) on physical brain state P1 at t_1 and M2 supervenes on P2 at t_2, and P1 causes (white arrow) P2. But M1 does not and cannot cause (arrow with x) M2, on Kim's account, because mental events are epiphenomenal, and can affect physical events as little as shadows can shove other shadows or change the physical objects whose shadows they are; that is, there can be no nonepiphenomenal mental-on-mental or mental-on-physical causation.

is "wishful thinking" (ibid., p. 15) because it is circular in its logic. This circularity can be made explicit by pondering a question: How can mental events realized in or supervening on neuronal and, ultimately, particle-level events change the very physical events that give rise to them or on which they supervene? Self-causation is correctly regarded by reductive physicalists to be as impossible as picking oneself up by one's bootstraps. Kim argues that no convincing account of downward causation has been provided, and he is skeptical that one can ever be provided. The proposition that a believable account of downward causation cannot be given has been called "Kim's challenge" (Earley, 2008). Indeed, reductive physicalists are correct that mental or physical events cannot change the *present* particle-level physical events that give rise to them or on which they supervene. A central theme of this book, however, is that they can trigger changes in the physical basis of *future* mental events, and that this offers a way to meet Kim's challenge.

§A2.3 Kim's view can be summarized in figure A2.1, where the solid white arrow indicates causation, and thin arrows indicate that mental states, where they occur at all, supervene on their respective associated physical states. The causal relationship with an X through it is not possible on Kim's account, where mental events are akin to nothing more than "shadows" that cannot cause each other to do anything, even if it may look like they interact, since they supervene on objects, where the true causation lies. Kim's argument can be succinctly summarized as follows (Kim, 1993, pp. 206–210): If (i) the "realization thesis" is the case, then each mental state is synchronically[4] determined by underlying microphysical states, and if (ii) "the causal or dynamical closure of the physical thesis" is the case, then all microphysical states are completely diachronically necessitated by antecedent microphysical states, then it follows that (iii) there is no causal work left for mental states as such, or conscious states as a subclass of mental states, to do. It follows from Kim's argument that there are no gaps in the chain of physical upon physical causation for mental events or conscious will to fill. It must be conceded that if (i) and (ii) are correct, then Kim and other reductionist philosophers of mind are indeed correct in saying that there is no place for nonepiphenomenal mental causation in nature. If, however, either (i) or (ii) is wrong, then there is potentially room to develop a theory of genuine mental causation. So any theory of mental causation that attempts to meet Kim's challenge must explicitly state which premise, (i) and/or (ii), is incorrect. If nature were deterministic, (i) and (ii) would be correct, and (iii) would logically follow. Thus, if determinism is the case, there can be no mental causation. In §§A2.4 and A2.5 I explain why ontological indeterminism entails that premise (ii) is incorrect, and in §A2.7, although not central to meeting Kim's challenge, I suggest that even (i) might be incorrect.

§A2.4   The sole white arrow in figure A2.1 belies an implicit assumption of determinism, where only one physical event necessarily follows a preceding physical event. However, assuming ontological indeterminism, a physical event can instead be followed by any one of multiple possible physical events. Indeed, any particular $P2_i$ need not have happened at all, given P1, so P1 is not a sufficient cause of $P2_i$. Many other physical brain states could have followed P1 and been consistent with all the laws of physics that are obeyed by energy. Indeterminism introduces a fundamental challenge to premise (ii, §A2.3) above, namely, that all microphysical states are completely necessitated by antecedent microphysical states. If ontological indeterminism is correct, then (ii) is incorrect, because any particular present microphysical state is not necessitated by its antecedent microphysical state or states. The antecedent microphysical state P1 might have occurred, and then caused any of a number of different possible microphysical states than the one that realizes M2 in figure A2.1. Indeterminism does not require that all possibilities occur (although Everett, 1957, did posit this untestable thesis; cf. DeWitt & Graham, 1973). It requires only that at each instant multiple $P2_i$ can really occur, mutually exclusively, perhaps each with a different nonzero probability. An indeterministic version of figure A2.1 is provided in figure A2.2, where some of these $P2_i$ realize the same mental state M2 as shown in figure A2.1, others realize various other mental states, and yet others realize no mental states whatsoever.

§A2.5   One could try to sidestep this challenge to the causal closure thesis ((ii), §A2.3) by arguing that ontological indeterminism does not

M1

↑

P1 ⇨ **P2₁→M2**   or ...

P1 ⇨ **P2₂→M2**   or ...

:

:

P1 ⇨ **P2ⱼ→M2**   The above set of possible P2 states would
                          realize M2.

――――――

P1 ⇨ **P2ₐ→M2ₐ**   or ...

P1 ⇨ **P2ᵦ→M2ᵦ**   or ...

:

:

P1 ⇨ **P2ₖ→M2ₖ**   This middle set of P2 states would realize
                          various different mental states other than M2.

――――――

P1 ⇨ **P2ₐ**   or ...

P1 ⇨ **P2ᵦ**   or ...

:

:

P1 ⇨ **P2ₓ**   This last set of P2 states would realize no
                          mental states if they were to occur.

Figure A2.2

An indeterministic version of figure A2.1 is shown here. As in figure A2.1, mental event M1 supervenes (thin arrow) on physical brain state P1 at t_1. The subsequent brain state can occupy any of a number of different physical states $P2_i$ at t_2, some of which realize the same mental state M2 as in figure A2.1, some of which realize different mental states than shown in figure A2.1, and some of which realize no mental states at all. In all cases, however, P1 causes (white arrow) $P2_i$, and each transition from P_1 to $P2_i$ obeys all the laws of physics (e.g., conservation of energy, momentum, spin, etc.). Thus, each row represents a different possible physical outcome at t_2 following the occurrence of P1 at t_1. The different $P2_i$ may have different nonzero probabilities of occurrence. At t_2 only one of these possibilities will become real.

negate this thesis; it merely makes it a probabilistically causally closed physical process rather than a deterministically closed one. Indeterministic causal closure, on this account, would be as complete as deterministic causal closure, but now, instead of all particle paths being fixed for all future times at the beginning of the universe, as in determinism, it is the entire set of all *possible* particle paths that are fixed at the beginning of the universe. At any given instant t_1, for any given physical system P1, the set of all possible states open to it at time t_2 (and all later times) will be closed. This notion of indeterministic causal closure is internally coherent and seems intuitively obvious: The set of all possibilities open to the universe is fixed at any given timepoint.

§A2.6   Closure, therefore, applies to different types of events under ontological determinism and indeterminism. "Closure" means that the set of outcomes is closed: Any particular outcome will be a member of the set. Determinism is closed at the level of actual outcomes: Any particular outcome of any event will be a member of the set of all actual outcomes or events in the universe across all time. Indeterminism, in contrast, is not closed at the level of actual outcomes or events: A particular outcome that could have happened but did not is not a member of the set of actual outcomes. Rather, indeterminism entails closure at the level of possible event outcomes rather than actual event outcomes: Any particular outcome or event will be a member of the set of all *possible* outcomes or events in the universe across all time. Since the set of all possible outcomes is fixed at the beginning of the universe, this can be rephrased: Under indeterminism, any particular outcome or event will be a member of the set of all *possible* outcomes or events at the beginning of time.

§A2.7   Figure A2.2 might be taken to show the entire closed set of t_2 possibilities open to P1 at t_1. This is again not to say that all P2$_i$ actually occur. All possible P2$_i$ must have some nonzero probability of actually occurring at t_2, assuming indeterminism, but we can safely assume that only one actually will occur at any given time. Thus, any given microphysical state is followed by only one microphysical state, albeit probabilistically or stochastically. But the probabilistic succession of such states is not causally closed because, again, any particular present microphysical state is not necessitated by its antecedent microphysical state or states, negating (ii). If it were necessitated, it would have had to have happened, but since it might not have happened, even if it did happen, it was not necessitated by its antecedent states. Assuming indeterminism, or a probabilistic or stochastic succession of events, the only causal closure—which is to say necessity in event succession—is to be found at the level of the set of all possibilities that can follow any actual microphysical event or preceding set of possible physical states. But this new indeterministic notion of causal closure would require the causal closure thesis to be restated as follows: "(ii*) the set of all possible microphysical states is completely diachronically necessitated by antecedent microphysical states." For Kim's argument against mental causation to work, the realization thesis would also need to be reformulated for the indeterministic case as follows: "(i*) all mental states are synchronically determined by underlying sets of possible microphysical states." That is, (i*) and (ii*) together entail (iii; §A2.3), that there is no causal work left for mental events as such to do, just as (i) and (ii) together entail (iii). But (i) and (ii*) together, or (i*) and (ii) together, do not entail (iii), because an actual microphysical state and the set of all possible microphysical states are not the same thing.

§A2.8   Moreover, (i*) is contrary to the definition of supervenience. Mental events do not supervene on sets of possible physical states, they supervene on specific, actually occurring physical states. To my knowledge, no one has ever maintained that (i*) is the case, probably because it is bizarre. It would entail that there are "metamental" states that supervene on sets of possible physical states, where each possible physical state might realize its own different mental state, as shown in figure A2.2. We should rule out such metamental states that "metasupervene"[5] on multiple possible mental states that in turn supervene on specific possible physical states, because a central tenet of the supervenience thesis is that only one mental state can supervene on a given physical substrate at a given time.

§A2.9   It follows from these arguments that (iii) does not follow from Kim's argument if ontological indeterminism is the case. Unlike determinism, ontological indeterminism therefore does not rule out the logical possibility of mental causation, at least on the basis of Kim's exclusion argument, and does pose a fundamental challenge to claims of mental epiphenomenalism. For that matter, these arguments could also be used to free other modes of physically realized criterial causation, such as genetic inheritance, from the charge of epiphenomenal inefficacy.

§A2.10   One might try to escape this conclusion by claiming that (ii*) follows only if one thinks that indeterminism requires that all possibilities are in some sense actualized or real. But nothing like that is needed, since indeterminism does not require this. Indeterminism requires only that multiple singular outcomes might occur, each with a nonzero probability. Under a stochastic view of causation, microphysical events/states would necessitate the occurrence of some singular/concrete microphysical events/ states, but which single one occurs is not necessitated, because it might not have happened. If one tries to keep causal closure of the physical by resorting to saying something like "the probability of something happening following P1 is 1," one is really talking about necessity at the level of the evolution of a probability density function, as one sees in Schrödinger's famous equation. But this is not necessity at the level of microphysical states necessarily causing particular singular microphysical states with a probability of 1. It is necessity at the level of sets of possible outcomes and their concomitant probabilities of occurring. Thus, even if one argues that stochastic laws stochastically necessitate future microphysical events, and that all future microphysical events are exclusively a function of said laws plus initial/boundary conditions, the only causal closure of the physical that yields necessity at the level of successive events is to be found at the level of all possible outcomes, rather than individual outcomes. The failure to localize causal necessity at the level of sequences of particular event outcomes or particular microphysical states occurs because any particular individual microphysical state might not have happened, and so was not necessitated by preceding events. Thus, even a stochastic conception of natural laws requires the causal closure thesis to be (ii*) rather than (ii). Since it is absurd to maintain that mental events synchronically supervene on sets of possibilia, we can rule out (i*). Thus, even a stochastic conception of causation fails to yield (iii), because (ii*) without (i*) cannot yield (iii). Assuming indeterminism, mental causation is not logically ruled out by Kim's argument.

§A2.11   If the particles that collectively comprise brain state P1 are allowed to each realize their next state randomly, we would expect the brain state $P2_i$ to itself occur randomly, and therefore we would expect the supervening mental state, if any, to occur randomly. A problem with indeterministic accounts of causation in general is that if events occur randomly, there would seem to be no room left for either self-determined actions or coherent, nonrandom, and therefore nonarbitrary chains of causation. The version of this problem of relevance here is that a purely random realization of successive mental states undermines any notion of coherent sequences of mental events, which in turn undermines the notion of mental causation. The question then is how to give a physicalist account that explains how those $P2_i$ that realize either M2 or other mental states that would coherently follow M1 are more likely to occur than other $P2_i$ that realize arbitrary mental events or even no mental states, which are nonetheless permissible at the level of possible paths open to particles. If the system is designed to trigger a $P2_i$ that realizes M2 with a high probability after the occurrence of the P1 that realizes M1, then it follows that the system of successive neuronal events is organized such that mental states trigger other mental states in nonrandom ways. In other words, the system has evolved such that M2 follows M1 with a reasonably high probability. Such mental causation is not epiphenomenal, because physical causation allows for many causal chains that are not mental at all or, if mental, not conducive to the formation of coherent sequences of mental events. It is because certain mental causal chains are coherent and useful for an animal that they are realized. In other words, particular physical causal chains have evolved to occur only because they realize useful mental causal chains. But how can an indeterministic and physicalist account be given that does not fall into the trap of randomly generated sequences of mental events? If $P2_i$ that realize M2 can "influence" P1 such that those $P2_i$ are likely to occur, wouldn't that be like an event at t_2 influencing an event at t_1? Since backward causation in time is not possible, is the situation hopeless?[6]

§A2.12   Another assumption built into Kim's view of supervenience and causation schematized in figure A2.1 is that mental states are synchronically determined by underlying microphysical states (the realization thesis; claim (i), §A2.3). But certain physical attributes are inherently durational, and it is possible that mental events might not be well defined at a given instant. If mental events are processes, they might be realized in physical processes that are extended in time. For example, if information is realized in action potentials, and action potentials are not instantaneous, the realization thesis may need to be modified such that mental states are not synchronically or instantaneously determined by underlying microphysical states. For example, the realization thesis might be wrong if it is the temporally extended *transition* from P1 to $P2_i$ that gives rise to $M2_i$, rather than the occurrence of $P2_i$ in isolation at an instant. On Kim's account, whether a physical state $P1_1$ leads to $P2_i$ or a different physical state $P1_2$ leads to the same $P2_i$, $P2_i$ realizes $M2_i$ identically. On the present account, however, the mental states realized by these two different transitions to $P2_i$ could differ. If that were the case, then two different mental states could supervene on two identical brain states, because of the two different paths taken to that brain state, in violation of the fundamental assumption of supervenience.

Conclusion

Kim's argument (§A2.3) excluding mental activity from playing a role in physical causation rests on a premise of the causal or dynamical closure of the physical. If determinism is the case, this premise holds, and Kim is correct that there cannot be mental causation. However, I argue that ontological indeterminism undermines this premise (§§A2.2–A2.5). One could protest that it is a logical error to say that ontological indeterminism is a sufficient condition for defeating causal closure of the physical, because indeterminism and closure are orthogonal issues. I disagree. Causal closure means that particle-level event c is sufficient to account for the specific outcome e that happens after c. If c is a sufficient cause of e, then the occurrence of c necessarily implies the occurrence of e. But if several outcomes are possible under ontological indeterminism given the occurrence of c, some of which are not e, then c is not a sufficient cause of e because the occurrence of c does not necessarily imply the occurrence of e. Attempts to skirt this by claiming causal closure of the physical at the level of all possible event outcomes following c, however, undermines Kim's argument. What remains to be done is to describe a plausible physicalist account of mental causation, now that one is not logically ruled out; this work is taken up in the main text.

Appendix 3: Why There Are No Necessary *A posteriori* Propositions

This appendix is for those who would like a formal version of the defense of descriptivism discussed in §§8.9–8.13. The modal logical proof forming the backbone of the argument that led Kripke (1980) to claim the existence of necessary *a posteriori* propositions can be rewritten in a way that disambiguates the ambiguity between propositions of type (1) and (2).

The original proof, due to Barcan (1946), has four steps, {A}–{D}:

{A} $(x)(y)[(x=y) \supset (Px \supset Py)]$ (read: For any objects x and y such that x is identical with y, if x has a given property P, y also has this property);

{B} $(x)\square(x=x)$ (read: For any object x, x is necessarily identical with x);

{C} $(x)(y)(x=y) \supset [\square(x=x) \supset \square(x=y)]$ (read: For any objects x and y such that x is identical with y, letting P be the property of being necessarily identical with x, we see, applying {A}, that if x has this property, y has it too; According to {B}, however, x has the property of necessarily being identical to x);

{D} $(x)(y)((x=y) \supset \square(x=y))$ (read: Therefore, for any objects x and y such that x is identical with y, y is necessarily identical with x.

However, if the second equal sign in {D} is taken to stand for an identity between (type 2) mental models of things-in-themselves and the first equal sign in {D} is taken to stand for an identity between (type 1) things-in-themselves in reality-in-itself, we will be violating the rules of logic, because the equal signs stand for different equalities. From such a confusion, we can draw no true conclusions. It is precisely this mistake, due to an ambiguity in the formalism inherited from ordinary language, that led Kripke to the wrong conclusion that there are necessary *a posteriori* truths.

To make this point more explicitly, let the subscript 1 mean that we are talking about things-in-themselves. On this account "x_1" means thing-in-itself x_1 and "$=_1$" means "identical in reality-in-itself" or "noumenally identical." Let subscript 2 mean that we are talking about mental models or percepts of things-in-themselves. Then "x_2" means mental model x_2 or experience x_2, and "$=_2$" means "identical in the mind" or "phenomenally identical." Substituting propositional type (1) into the Barcan proof, we end up with:

{D1} $(x_1)(y_1)((x_1=_1y_1) \supset \square(x_1=_1y_1))$ (read: For any things-in-themselves x_1 and y_1, such that x_1 is noumenally identical with y_1, y_1 is necessarily noumenally identical with x_1; In other words, a thing-in-itself is, not surprisingly, necessarily identical with itself).

Substituting propositional type (2) into the Barcan proof, we end up with:

{D2} $(x_2)(y_2)((x_2=_2y_2) \supset \square(x_2=_2y_2))$ (read: For any mental models or experiences x_2 and y_2, such that x_2 is identical with y_2 in someone's mind, y_2 is necessarily identical with x_2 in that mind; In other words, a mental model or experience is, not surprisingly, necessarily identical with itself.

How then did Kripke reach the astounding result that an identity of two mental models, which everyone grants is an *a posteriori* identification, is also a necessary identity if it is true? He did so by conflating propositions of type (1) and (2). There is, to my knowledge, no logical way to prove:

{D3} $(x_1)(y_1)(x_2)(y_2)$ $((x_1=_1y_1) \supset \square(x_2=_2y_2))$ (read: For any things-in-themselves x_1 and y_1 and mental constructs x_2 and y_2 such that x_1 is noumenally identical in reality-in-itself with y_1, it is necessary that the mental construct x_2 is phenomenally identical with the mental construct y_2).

That people once thought the morning star and evening star were different shows that {D3} is wrong.

And to my knowledge there is also no logical way to prove:

{D4} $(x_1)(y_1)(x_2)(y_2)$ $((x_2=_2y_2) \supset \square(x_1=_1y_1))$ (read: For any things-in-themselves x_1 and y_1 and mental constructs x_2 and y_2 such that x_2 is mentally identical with y_2, it is necessary that the thing-in-itself x_1 is noumenally identical with the thing-in-itself y_1).

{D4} is what Kripke claimed, and it is false, and follows from the Barcan proof only because of a category error between propositions of type (1) and (2).

Kripke claimed, on the basis of this interpretation of the Barcan proof, that if the identification of the thing-in-itself called "a mental state" with the thing-in-itself called "a brain state" is a true identification, it is necessarily true. And since, he argues, mind–brain identity theorists admit that this identity is contingent—which, on his account, it cannot be—the identity is not true at all, but false (cf. similar arguments by Chalmers, 1996, pp. 146–149). Since, however, Kripke's criticism of identity theory rests on a conflation of propositional categories that should be kept distinct, his argument does not in fact rule out mind–brain identity theories.

Notes

1 Introduction: The Mind–Body Problem Will Be Solved by Neuroscience

1. According to "The Philosophy of Neuroscience" in the *Stanford Encyclopedia of Philosophy* (2012; http://plato.stanford.edu/entries/neuroscience/) "actual neuroscientific discoveries have exerted little influence on the details of materialist philosophies of mind" in part because functionalism lulled many philosophers of mind into a belief that the specifics of neural circuitry are not essential; what matters to functionalists is information processing, not plumbing details that happen to realize any given function. The entry continues: "The functionalists' favorite argument was based on multiple realizability: a given mental state or event can be realized in a wide variety of physical types. . . . So a detailed understanding of one type of realizing physical system (e.g., brains) will not shed light on the fundamental nature of mind." Overcoming her field's complacent ignorance of neuroscience was a central goal of Patricia Churchland's (1986) book *Neurophilosophy*. Since then, more and more philosophers have embraced neuroscientific data to guide their arguments. Paul Churchland (1989) has gone so far as to say that it will no longer be possible to do serious work in the philosophy of mind or science without a firm grounding in empirical brain science. I fully agree, and believe both sides need to try to learn the other's field and collaborate in order to make progress. Although still a minority, philosophers who have studied neuroscience are leading the way out of the impasse of relying solely on argumentation from unproven first principles. A few of these philosophers are Kathleen Akins, William Bechtel, John Bickle, Ned Block, David Chalmers, Patricia and Paul Churchland, C. Craver, Dan Dennett, Fred Dretske, Jerry Fodor, Al Mele, Adina Roskies, Michael Tye, and Walter Sinnott-Armstrong. Ironically, some of these philosophers, especially the Churchlands and Bickle, have argued for eliminative materialism on the basis of findings in neuroscience, whereas most neuroscientists I know look for physical mechanisms underlying information processing, but would not dismiss the reality of consciousness. I think this difference emerges because philosophers emphasize axiomatic assumptions such as reductionism and determinism which rule out the possibility of mental causation (see appendix 2), whereas scientists start from empirically known facts.

For the same reason, there are likely to be more determinists among philosophers than quantum physicists (see appendixes 1 and 2).

2 Overview of Arguments

1. The essence of the supervenience relationship is that a higher-level entity is realized in a lower-level entity, such that any change in the former entails a change in the latter. In the context of a physicalist philosophy of mind, the supervenience relationship is as follows: 2P→1M allowed; 1P→2M not allowed; 2P→2M allowed; 1P→1M allowed; where the first relationship can be read "two physical states can realize or give rise to one mental state" or "one mental state can supervene on two physical states," and so on for the other relationships. What is not allowed under any supervenience theory, or for that matter, any identity theory, is that one physical state simultaneously or even sequentially gives rise to two or more mental states. I will use the expressions "supervenes on" and "is realized in" interchangeably.

2. NMDA = N-methyl-D-aspartate. The NMDA receptor is actually a family of ionotropic receptors that bind presynaptically released glutamate. NMDA is a molecule, itself not found in biological tissue, that binds to NMDA receptors but not to other glutamatergic receptors, such as AMPA receptors. Under normal circumstances, NMDA receptors would never bind NMDA, so it is a somewhat misleading name.

3. A receptor is a protein that lies in the plasma membrane or cytoplasm of a cell. One or more mobile molecules or "ligands" must bind to specific sites on this protein for a conformational change to take place. This reconformation initiates a change inside the cell. There are two basic types of neurotransmitter receptors: ionotropic and metabotropic. The former are proteins or "channels" that can open a "pore" that allows ions to cross the membrane. They are associated with rapid neurotransmission because potential in the postsynaptic neuron either increases ("depolarization") in the case of excitation, or decreases ("hyperpolarization") in the case of inhibition, almost immediately after the neurotransmitter released from the presynaptic neuron binds to the receptor. Metabotropic receptors are polypeptides that undergo intracellular changes when a neurotransmitter binds to them, which then activate G-proteins that trigger various intracellular cascades. A single transmitter can trigger different intracellular effects when bound to different receptors. For example, dopamine increases versus decreases cAMP production when it binds to D1 versus D2 receptors (Fuster, 2008); glutamate binds both to ionotropic NMDA and AMPA receptors and to metabotropic G-protein-coupled glutamate receptors. Remarkably, ionotropic glutamate receptor-like genes are even found in plants (Chiu et al., 1999) where the non-NMDA-like coded proteins may play a role in light signal transduction (Lam et al., 1998) or carbon and nitrogen metabolism (Kang & Turano, 2003). This suggests that ionotropic glutamate receptors descend from an ancient eukaryotic signaling mechanism, perhaps a ligand-binding periplasmic bacterial protein (Madden, 2002; Chen et al., 1999). In contrast, Schell (2004) estimates that

the NMDA receptor glycine site evolved after the divergence of arthropods, but before the divergence of amphibians.

3 A Criterial Neuronal Code Underlies Downward Mental Causation and Free Will

1. The history of science has seen several cases where a new field started with an assumption that some semantic construct was monolithic, typically because the concept was borrowed from English, which had a single word for the construct. Over time it was discovered that, in fact, the construct involved the operation of multiple processes realized in multiple neural circuits. For example, attention has turned out to involve several interacting processes (exogenous vs. endogenous allocation, tracking, eye movements, inhibition of return to previously attended locations, etc.) subserved by different neural circuits. Similarly, although initially thought of monolithically, we now talk of several different types of memory, such as episodic, iconic, working, or procedural memories, each subserved by specialized brain processes, mechanisms, and circuits. The same can be said for intelligence, morality, learning, and volition.

2. A choice to perform an action counts as an act of will even if it does not cause or initiate the willed action, so it is an open question whether our wills cause our actions. Both of these issues need to be resolved by any fully satisfying account of free will. Since free will is or underlies the ability to act freely or perform free actions (cf. Haggard et al., 2010), neither an unfree but effective will nor a free but ineffective will is what people desire when they desire free will. Here I will assume that willed actions are connected to a motor system that can carry out those actions, and so avoid complications posed by unusual situations such as locked-in syndrome. That is, I will ignore the second issue.

3. It seems that agents sometimes have a free and effective will without reflexive consciousness or awareness of either the will or the willed action. This occurs when we are on "auto-pilot" as might occur when we drive home while daydreaming, or when we react rapidly without thinking about it, as might occur when playing ping pong or squash. In contrast with such habitual actions or reflexes, perhaps governed by dorsal "zombie agents" (Koch, 2004, §10.83), consciousness of will does seem necessary for control and for free will in some other cases. Many people who act under posthypnotic suggestions or who suffer from alien hand syndrome do not act freely or from free will, arguably because they are not aware of any choice and form no conscious intention to act (cf. Wheatley & Haidt, 2005).

4. A subfield of mathematical decision theory called "multiple criteria decision analysis" studies how to optimize decisions when there are trade-offs imposed by conflicting criteria. The simplest aggregation procedure is the weighted sum of evaluations across all criteria. More complex aggregation procedures are possible that allow for interaction among criteria. Since my focus is criterial assessment and

causation at the level of neurons, I will not emphasize propositional criterial causation. A central problem is how propositional criterial causation is realized in neuronal criterial causation.

5. A criterial account of representation and information-processing suggests that it is useful to distinguish between three meanings of information or representation: (1) that certain inputs are presently occurring, which can be thought of as informational input into a postsynaptic neuron; (2) that certain criteria have been set, which can be thought of as conditions placed on informational input by a postsynaptic neuron; and (3) that these criteria have been met, which is the realization of information in the postsynaptic neuron when the neuron fires.

4   Neurons Impose Physical and Informational Criteria for Firing on Their Inputs

1. Criterial causality does not require that a response be all or none, like an action potential. Criteria can be physically realized such that they can be met to degrees or not, amounting to fuzzy or hard thresholds for criterial satisfaction. For example, there are full and partial agonists for many ion channels, leading to maximal and partial ion flow across the membrane, respectively.

2. The axon must be more excitable than the soma to be able to generate an action potential (Rapp et al., 1996); It can either have many more of the soma's kind of sodium channels (Wollner & Catterall, 1986; Westenbroek et al., 1989), or it can have fewer sodium channels of a different type (Colbert & Johnston, 1996) that are activated at a lower negative potential.

3. This "membrane time constant" is typically on the order of 10–30 ms for pyramidal cells (Koch et al., 1996) and varies depending on several factors, including the presence of neuromodulators (Destexhe et al., 2003), which can change the properties of neural networks, in part, by changing τ. Because τ is so brief, only many nearly simultaneous inputs can lead to the firing of a neuron, generally achievable either through synchrony of inputs from many neurons (e.g., Abeles, 1991; Engel et al., 2001; Fries, 2005; Hansel & Sompolinsky, 1992; Singer, 1999a,b), or neural bursting of one or more neurons, or both. In order for inputs to arrive "synchronously" within the temporal integration window τ, it behooves presynaptic neurons to be synchronized, at a population level, to a "clock" (Buzsáki & Chrobak, 1995) whose oscillatory unit is no longer than $1000\text{ms}/\tau$. Thus, the gamma frequency domain is likely to be a signature of synchronization among neurons that feed into neurons whose membrane time constant $\tau < 30\text{ms}$.

4. Ionotropic receptors are fundamental to neuronally realized information processing because they mediate all fast synaptic transmission. The ionotropic glutamate receptors include several classes: the NMDA (N-methyl-d-aspartate) receptor, the AMPA (α-amino-3-hydroxy-5-methylisoxazole-4-propionic acid) receptor, the kainate receptor, and the δ-opioid receptor. Other ionotropic receptors include nAch

(nicotinic acetylcholine) receptors, P2X receptors, GABA (γ-aminobutyric acid A/C) receptors, serotonin (5-HT3R or 5-hydroxytryptamine) receptors, and Gly (glycine) receptors. (For further details, see Chiu et al., 1999; Dingledine et al., 1999; Frank, 2011). The glutamatergic ionotropic receptors are especially important in nervous system design, because glutamate is the main neurotransmitter associated with postsynaptic excitation. Each of these has receptor subtypes with differential functions that are encoded by different genes (Paoletti, 2011). Indeed, different NMDA and AMPA subtypes are expressed differentially on various synapses of a single cell, suggesting that the postsynaptic cell is excited differently depending on the source of presynaptic glutamatergic input (Nusser, 2000). Although the reasons for such diversity of receptor subtypes across synapses of a single cell is not known, to the extent that different receptor subtypes differ in their delays until postsynaptic depolarization, only simultaneous presynaptic inputs to similar subtypes will result in the coincidence that leads to massive depolarization in a postsynaptic dendritic spine via NMDA receptor opening. This would allow dendrites to segregate different classes of input by a temporal phase encoding (cf. Takahashi et al., 2012).

5. Cortex is said to be retinotopically organized when neighboring locations within a visual quadrant are mapped onto neighboring portions of cortex (Van Essen, 2004; Horton & Hoyt, 1991).

6. Typical domains of brainwave oscillations include delta (0.5–3Hz), theta (3–8Hz), alpha (8–14Hz), beta (14–30Hz), gamma (30–90 Hz), and high-gamma (90–200+Hz). There is some fuzziness in the definition of these ranges. For example, some authors will regard 35Hz as high-beta, and others as low-gamma.

7. Cortical neurons typically have a baseline firing rate whereas cerebellar and basal ganglia neurons do not, suggesting that these systems are not processing information in the same way or for the same purpose as the cortex (Buzsáki, 2006). Perhaps these noncortical areas are not carrying information about external events in terms of perturbations from a baseline firing rate, but rather doing something more akin to transforming one matrix of inputs into another.

8. A third mode of information transfer involves spontaneous glutamate release at synapses in the absence of the arrival of a presynaptic action potential. Spontaneous release involves a single vesicle releasing its contents into the synaptic cleft on the order of once a minute, in contrast to the large number of vesicles that release glutamate into the cleft when evoked by an action potential. Recent work suggests that spontaneous signaling involves a segregated mode of communication that is apparently mediated by different classes of NMDA receptors (Atasoy et al., 2008; Kavalali et al., 2011; Sutton & Schuman, 2009). Although it is not known what type of information or homeostatic regulation is mediated by this communication channel, remarkable evidence suggests that blockade of the spontaneous channel's NMDA receptors with ketamine induces plasticity that has the surprising behavioral consequence of serving as a rapid antidepressant (Autry et al., 2011).

9. AMPA= α-amino-3-hydroxy-5-methyl-4-isoxazolepropionic acid.

10. GABA = γ-aminobutyric acid, the main inhibitory neurotransmitter.

11. McAlonan et al. (2006, p. 4449) describe how this might occur via the thalamic reticular nucleus (TRN) inhibiting the LGN as follows:

If we assume that the TRN affects early visual processing by its inhibitory influence on the LGN, then the predominant attentional effect acting through the TRN [. . .] transiently increases the inhibitory GABAergic drive on the LGN. How could an increase in inhibition on the LGN enhance visual processing? If visual TRN neurons project back to the LGN neurons from which they receive their inputs (to the neurons representing the same part of the visual field), they would form "closed loop" connections, resulting in feedback inhibition. It has been suggested that during wakefulness, feedback inhibition initiates a rhythmic burst firing in LGN relay neurons, which may serve to alert visual cortex of behaviorally relevant sensory input (Crick, 1984; Sherman and Guillery, 1996) and facilitate signal transmission during visual target acquisition and early phases of fixation (Guido and Weyand, 1995; also see Ramcharan et al., 2000). The predominant increase in visual TRN activity that we have shown would be consistent with this view, because this increase in activity would be passed to the LGN as an increase in inhibition, resulting in the hyperpolarization of the LGN membrane and the consequent switching of these visual thalamic relay neurons from tonic to burst mode (Llinas and Jahnsen, 1982; Jahnsen and Llinas, 1984a,b; Sherman and Koch, 1986). This would then facilitate visual detection and discrimination by the generation of a burst of activity rather than by simply modulating the average discharge rate. If this hypothesis turns out to be correct, it would provide exceptional validation of a change in behavioral state being translated into a change in membrane properties and then into a change in the pattern of neuronal discharge. Alternatively, or additionally, visual TRN neurons may project to LGN neurons in adjacent areas of the visual field, forming an open loop connection. In this case, the effect of a focal increase in TRN activity would be lateral or surround inhibition rather than a change in firing mode. Consequently, initial discriminability and detectability would be improved by elevating the signal-to-noise ratio in the LGN and, therefore, the entire ensuing visual processing stream. Such lateral inhibition may preclude the relay of nearby irrelevant information, thus rendering attended information more salient or conspicuous. Anatomical evidence of predominantly open loop connections between TRN and LGN neurons in rodents suggests that TRN mediates its attentional effect primarily through lateral or surround inhibition (Pinault and Deschenes, 1998).

12. Abnormally low synchrony is associated with schizophrenia (Spencer et al., 2003; Uhlhaas & Singer, 2010) and autism (Wilson et al., 2007; Yizhar et al., 2011), while abnormally high synchrony is associated with epileptic seizure (Dichter & Ayala, 1987; Garcia Dominguez et al., 2005; Steriade, 2003) and Parkinson's disease (Boraud et al., 2005; Uhlhaas & Singer, 2006).

13. Epigenetic mechanisms such as methylation or histone deacetylation can change gene expression without changing the underlying sequence of DNA. Analogously, dynamic synaptic reweighting can change functional neuronal circuitry without changing underlying long-term neuronal connectivity.

14. Perhaps neuroscience today is roughly where biology was under Linnaeus. We know a lot at a descriptive level, but we have yet to discover a deep, unifying principle that ties all observations together, such as the theory of evolution by natural selection did for biology. And we have yet to crack the neural code. It is an exciting

time to enter the field. I often tell my students that they might be the future Darwin or Watson and Crick of neuroscience. The greatest problems are wide open: What is the neural code? What is the neural basis of consciousness? How can mental events cause physical events, given that they themselves are physically realized (§0.4)?

15. Indeed, exactly this phenomenon is known to occur in certain cases of the phantom limb syndrome, presumably because, as a result of cortical plasticity and remapping, face touch input expands to feed into cells that previously only took input from touch to the now missing arm (Flor et al., 1995; Ramachandran, et al., 1992; Ramachandran & Hirstein, 1998).

16. If it turns out that the latter is the case, we will have to reconceptualize information as possibility reduction at the level of large-scale brain states, as opposed to possibility reduction at the level of individual neurons, such as simple cells, grandmother cells (Barlow, 1972), or read-out neurons. However, for an argument that read-out or decoding is necessary for the existence or occurrence of information, see §§8.6–8.7.

5   NMDA Receptors and a Neuronal Code Based on Bursting

1. The story may not be as simple as this. "Coincidence detection" may depend on more factors than glutamate, glycine, and Mg^{2+} ion placement on the NMDA receptor. Other synaptic proteins may play a role (Shen & Meyer, 1999), as may the cytoplasmic C-terminal domain (Chen & Huang, 1992; Husi et al., 2000; Kelso et al., 1992; Lieberman & Mody, 1994; Sprengel et al., 1998; Strack & Colbran, 1998; Wang & Salter, 1994) and NMDA-dependent intracellular signaling molecules (Bading & Greenberg, 1991; Greengard et al., 1991; Halpain et al., 1990; Malinow et al., 1989; McGlade-McCulloh et al., 1993).

2. Intriguingly, D-serine is found in cerebral gray matter, especially in the frontal lobes of mammals. It is actively inhibited via enzymatic action in the cerebellum and brainstem of mammals and across the entire adult brains of the carp, frog, or chicken (Nagata et al., 1994; Schell, 2004; cf. Horiike et al., 2001). Although NMDA receptors are widespread both subcortically and cortically in mammals (Petralia et al., 1993), they are expressed at much higher levels in frontal cortex than temporal or parietal cortex (Akbarian et al., 1996). The frontal bias of D-serine suggests that the frontal lobes are the brain region with the greatest capacity for rapid and long-term synaptic plasticity in mammals. Indeed, the loss of D-serine removal in mammalian frontal areas may have accompanied the mammalian adaptation to lifelong synaptic plasticity. Whereas glycine appears to be released by neurons transiently and locally within a synapse, where it is rapidly removed, D-serine appears to linger and spread via diffusion, potentially increasing the excitability of NMDA receptors on other synapses. Such a physical annealing-like process could play some role in

the mammalian capacity to generate novel mental connections (Schell, 2004). In contrast, as a rule, nonmammals likely express relatively limited cortical, behavioral, or neural plasticity once this endogenous glycine agonist is effectively turned off by their genetically set developmental programs. An exception would appear to be the behavioral and cognitive flexibility that has convergently evolved in parrots and crows. It would be interesting to measure areas of parrot or crow brains that continue to express D-serine in contrast to the brain of a behaviorally more stereotyped bird, such as a chicken. This would provide evidence for the neural plasticity that presumably underlies their behavioral and cognitive flexibility. Perhaps the animal phylogenetically most distant from humans that expresses a measure of behavioral and cognitive flexibility is the octopus. Although there are receptors in invertebrates that have NMDA receptor-like properties (see Schell, 2004, for a review), not enough is known about plasticity in invertebrate neural circuitry to hazard a guess about how the octopus brain might have evolved to accomplish its amazing feats.

3. When medullary dorsal horn astrocytes fail to limit D-serine production in pain circuits, NMDA receptors remain open, which can be experienced as allodynia, a condition in which all touch is painful (Miraucourt et al., 2011). This in turn suggests the testable hypothesis that consciousness of pain may be mediated by transition of pain circuitry into phasic mode, and that the gating of pain may be realized by a transition back to tonic mode.

4. The 500ms to 1000ms delay between conditioned stimulus appearance and appearance of the unconditioned stimulus, which Harnett et al. (2009) report to be necessary for this type of LTP to occur, is consistent with the optimal temporal parameters for delay conditioning. Thus this type of burst-dependent LTP in midbrain dopaminergic neurons might be a neural basis for delay conditioning (i.e., when the conditioned stimulus occurs and then the unconditioned stimulus occurs before offset of the conditioned stimulus). Note that this form of LTP is distinct from the spike timing-dependent plasticity described in §5.11 (but see Drew & Abbott, 2006), which has also been observed in midbrain dopaminergic neurons (Liu et al., 2005; Luu & Malenka, 2008).

5. This "calcium hypothesis" is too simple because metabotropic glutamate receptors (Nevian & Sakmann, 2006) and voltage-gated calcium channels (Bi & Poo, 1998; Magee & Johnston, 1997) also contribute to postsynaptic events that result in synaptic reweighting. To complicate matters, presynaptic NMDA receptors (§5.28) also play a role in spike time-dependent synaptic reweighting (Sjöström et al., 2003; Rodriguez-Moreno & Paulsen, 2008).

6. Hume emphasized that causation is not itself in the input. We now know that the brain imposes a causal analysis on a succession of inputs because the tight temporal windows imposed by spike timing-dependent plasticity at the level of synapses shapes neural networks that respond to temporal timing and ordering relations among inputs. Neural networks can therefore also learn temporal orderings

and predict causal consequences on the basis of a given input (Abbott & Blum, 1996; Dan & Poo, 2004; Roberts, 1999). Ultimately, such circuitry allows us to "perceive" causal relations rather than having to cognitively infer them (Fugelsang et al., 2005; Roser et al., 2005).

7. The traditional view may even go as far as back as Ramón y Cajal (1911), who argued on anatomical grounds that information flows only one way in the nervous system, from dendrites toward the soma and out via the axon.

8. Action potentials that propagate along an axon to the soma are "antidromic," whereas those that propagate away from the soma are "orthodromic." Here we are talking about action potentials that are not in the axon at all, but rather in the soma and dendrites. Back-propagating action potentials have been measured to travel at a velocity of 0.15m/sec (Stuart & Sakmann, 1995; Rapp et al., 1996). This propagation is notably slower than the velocity of a typical axonal action potential. This may be "by design" if the timing of the arrival of a back-propagating action potential is key to keeping NMDA receptors open during the arrival of a burst of presynaptic input. If action potentials traveled the same velocity in apical dendrites as they do in axons, apical dendrites might have to be much longer than they actually are to foster synchrony between postsynaptic depolarization, NMDA opening, and presynaptic glutamatergic input.

9. The negative resting membrane potential of neurons leads to blockage of the NMDA channel pore with one Mg^{2+} ion (Evans et al., 1977). When the membrane potential depolarizes beyond a threshold that varies by receptor subtype (Kuner & Schoepfer, 1996), the ion is set free. Therefore, non-NMDA receptors, such as AMPA receptors, must cause the initial depolarization that can in turn cause the subsequent opening of NMDA receptors (Collingridge, 1985; Ben-Ari et al., 2007).

10. Even though bursts traveling through neuronal networks are not things but rather events, it might prove useful for purposes of modeling a neuronal burst code to reify them the way physicists do when they think about solitons or "holes" as particles that obey higher-order lawlike behavior.

11. On the other hand, appropriately microstimulating motion-processing area MT presumably triggers motion phosphenes or other experiences of motion. Does this mean that MT in isolation is the neural correlate of a motion "microconsciousness" as Zeki (2001; see also Tse et al., 2005) has argued? Not necessarily, because microstimulating MT may generate reverberant activity in the neuronal hierarchy in which MT is embedded, some or all of which may be involved in realizing an experience of motion (cf. Pascual-Leone & Walsh, 2001).

12. Ray and Maunsell (2011; Ray, pers. comm.) found a high correlation between high-gamma power and the firing rate profile of the *population* multi-unit activity, not individual neural spikes, which they could not resolve given the low signal to noise ratio of the chronic arrays from which they recorded. Moreover, the population

firing rate varied smoothly with changes in the stimulus contrast in a smooth fashion. In a stimulus that undergoes a sudden onset, there is commonly a barrage of bursts associated with that onset in early visual areas. They did not observe this, possibly because their stimulus varied in contrast smoothly over time. That is, they did not find evidence of an increase in firing rate at any particular phase of the contrast profile which could indicate bursting at that phase. It is, however, possible that different neurons burst at different phases of the contrast profile. If so, the phase of individual neural bursting would have to be uniformly distributed across the population such that the population firing rate would vary smoothly with the stimulus contrast profile, in order to account for their data. Only future data that can resolve individual neuronal spikes will be able to settle whether a burst model of their data is correct or incorrect.

6   Mental Causation as an Instance of Criterial Causation

1. According to the second law of thermodynamics, net thermodynamic entropy must increase globally, within an isolated system not at equilibrium, but that does not rule out the possibility of local decreases. Living systems create a net increase of thermodynamic entropy globally, in accordance with the second law, but can become locally more organized, "disposing of disorder" through, for example, engaging sodium pumps in neurons, emitting heat, or excreting. This gives rise to the possibility of creating order that can carry information for a decoder. From the point of view of that decoder, the amount of information has increased in the system, even though global thermodynamic entropy has increased. In other words, informational entropy can increase or decrease relative to a particular decoder, even as thermodynamic entropy must always increase. For example, I can write a message on paper. This increases thermodynamic entropy at the same time as increasing information for the message's reader. One must be careful not to confuse thermodynamic (or Gibbs') entropy or quantum domain entropy (von Neumann entropy) with Shannon's informational entropy. Even though all are described by a very similar formula, they are merely analogous, but not identical. All types of entropy quantify uncertainty and vary as a function of the number of states that can be occupied, weighted by their probability of being occupied. It was because of this *analogy* that Shannon chose to make a link between the concepts of information and thermodynamic entropy. But thermodynamic entropy is a measure that varies as a function of the number and likelihood of physical states that a physical system can occupy, whereas informational entropy is a measure of the amount of uncertainty associated with a discrete random variable, such as the outcome of a die toss. Shannon's source coding theorem established that the number of bits of information gained upon learning of the outcome of an uncertain event is given by that event's informational entropy. Informational entropy is therefore a measure of the information gained by a decoder upon some event outcome. Information is reduction in uncertainty for a decoder. In contrast, nothing like a decoder concerning thermo-

dynamic entropy is necessary. For example, energy will tend to become less organized (e.g., dissipated as heat) in physical systems not at equilibrium, whether they are being decoded or observed or not.

2. And even to say that the information is realized in the energy or pattern of energy of a physical system, such as an mRNA strand or a presynaptic neuron, is inaccurate because the information is realized not in that energy, but in the decoding of that energy's spatiotemporal pattern by a different physical system, the decoder, such as a ribosome or a postsynaptic neuron. This point is made in more depth in §§8.6–8.7.

3. Many-to-fewer mappings are also possible. An example is a ribosome, which synthesizes proteins by translating different codons (three nucleotides along a strand of mRNA) into specifically mapped amino acids. Such mappings could be thought of as a "state system" where multiple criteria are physically instantiated in a single physical system: e.g., "If criteria x are met, then do y"; "If criteria f are met, then do g" (but see §8.1). A neuron could in principle be designed that fires with pattern y if it receives input x, and with pattern g if it receives pattern f. Here we only focus on the many-to-one type of mapping, because many-to-fewer mappings are reducible, in principle, to a set of several many-to-one mappings.

4. This general notion of an energy transformation describable by a chemical equation applies equally well to transformation of elementary particles or nuclear reactions.

5. There is fungibility at the level of type of atom for X satisfying $2H_2 + X_2 \rightarrow 2H_2X$. For example, substituting sulfur (S) for X allows this reaction to generate hydrogen sulfide. This kind of type-level criterial satisfaction occurs because this kind of chemical reaction is driven by the number of electrons in the outermost shell, where both O and S have six electrons. This is not relevant here, however, because the kind of criterial causality at issue collapses many types of input to a single type of output, such as water or an action potential.

6. If criterial causation and ontological indeterminism allow for mental causation and a strong free will, couldn't mental causation and a strong free will be physically realized in nonbiological systems? I do not see why not. However, I do not know of any nonbiological instances of criterial causation. On the face of it, it would seem that there are nonbiological physical systems that exhibit some of the properties of criterial causation. Many dynamic physical systems exhibit multiple realizability in the sense that multiple microphysical states converge on the same final attractor state. But while criterial causation requires multiple realizability, this alone is not enough; criterial causation requires a many-to-one mapping between input and output in a net of criterial decoders that process information (§6.8). There do not appear to be nonbiological systems with this property, although future, nonalgorithmic computer hardware modeled on neuronal criteriality could possibly accomplish this.

7. There could well be universes in which the only causalities evident involve energy transfer and transformation. Our own universe could have existed for a long

time without any physical system having evolved a type-level criterial trigger for the release of some action. Presumably this was the case for billions of years before the first biological systems evolved.

7   Criterial Causation Offers a Neural Basis for Free Will

1. James's term for compatibilism was "soft determinism," which he called a "quagmire of evasion" in his essay "The Dilemma of Determinism" (1884 [1956]). Similarly, Kant (1997), in his *Critique of Practical Reason*, called Hobbes's and Hume's compatibilism a "wretched subterfuge" and mocked it by saying that on this account a wound-up clock has free will because it turns its hands free of external coercion.

2. One reason present-day computer programs have thus far failed to deeply mimic human cognition or creativity is in part that computer programs are based on algorithms that are intentionally deterministic, rather than being based on a feedforward/feedback hierarchy of criterial pattern detectors that can harness randomness to generate novel solutions to unforeseen problems (§8.1).

3. If my executive system commands the delivery of my mother's maiden name, the answer "Behrens" pops into my mind some time later with no explanation or understanding about how this information was retrieved. It seems that the propositions considered at the executive level can be consciously experienced and reported, whereas the lower-level operations that carry out tasks such as recall or that generate possible solutions to a problem generally are not.

4. A cactus and an oak tree planted under a rock will both fail to grow at all. But given ideal conditions that optimally satisfy the criteria that need to be met for a flourishing life, one will grow to be small and the other large. For a life-form like a plant that cannot choose among possible courses of action, it is indeed correct to assert that genetic potential and environmental conditions account for the life outcome entirely. But for life-forms that can select from among possible courses of action and possible environments, another factor plays a role besides genetic potential and the external environment, described in §7.12.

5. Humans still have fixed action patterns, such as yawning when seeing someone else yawn (Provine, 1986).

6. James equated chance with the existence of multiple possible outcomes, any of which might be chosen: "This notion of alternative possibility, this admission that any one of several things may come to pass is, after all, only a roundabout name for chance." He goes on to say: "What is meant by saying that my choice of which way to walk home after the lecture is ambiguous and matter of chance? . . . It means that both Divinity Avenue and Oxford Street are called but only one, and that one[,] either one, shall be chosen" (James, 1956).

7. One can apply the Darwinian metaphor of a cycle of variability subject to a process of selection to many different adaptive systems that are creative in a bottom-up, decentralized fashion. Examples include immune system generativity and selection of antibodies, selection of patterns of synaptic connectivity in dynamic neural networks (Changeux et al., 1973; Edelman, 1987), or the selection of worthy companies in successive generations of the boom (loose credit) and bust (tight credit) cycle in free markets (e.g., Hayek, 1945). What is often missed by theorists who extend the Darwinian metaphor beyond biology is that natural selection is not only expressed as weeding out of the least fit individuals; in addition, ecological boundary conditions imposed by limits on food and the carrying capacity of the environment prevent runaway takeover by any actor. If a predator is too successful, it will eat most of its prey and undergo a population crash by starvation (e.g., Stenseth et al., 1997); if an animal destroys its environment or a parasite its host, it will destroy itself. The Darwinian metaphor fails for information-processing systems, such as markets, that can have runaway feedback such that one winner comes to dominate the entire system. If unchecked, monopolization occurs because there is no limit to the control or generation of information (§§6.7, 6.12), even when the amount of energy within which information is realized is finite. The Darwinian metaphor fails when applied to information-processing systems because natural selection is premised upon limited energy/food/resources, whereas the amount of information can always grow. Actors that "feed on information" rather than food are not limited by any inherent finiteness of information. Interestingly, Hayek (1994) argued that central planning tends to lead to totalitarianism because the information required to adequately centrally plan is so decentralized that it has to be subject to surveillance and control at every level, including especially universal suppression of information counter to the central planners' goals. But what those against regulation of the market fail to recognize is that unregulated free flow of information leads to monopolies, as power begets more power and corporations capture government (as is now the case). One way to counter monopolization is regular renormalization of the distribution of information to prevent its concentration to a degree that it undermines the creativity of the cyclical Darwinian variation/selection process. In markets, this can take the form of limits on concentration of the means of informational exchange, including especially access to money, political power, markets, and educational opportunity. Similarly, without governmental regulation and redistribution of information and its access, free markets could not maximize creative destruction via the other normalizing process of failure. The information-processing capability of capitalism is undermined by both unchecked entrepreneurship (analogous to neural excitation), and by unchecked regulation and central planning (inhibition). Both monopolization and totalitarianism tend to thwart innovation and competition. While both freedom and restraint are needed to maintain creative information processing in markets as well as in the brain, finding the sweet spot where they are balanced is the key. Maximal potential impact of the individual

occurs when local innovations have maximal potential to affect the whole system, and cannot be easily damped by corporate or governmental monopolies. Just as is the case in the brain (§4.42), this occurs in the domain of criticality in complex information processing systems, such as markets. In my next book, *The Cultivation of Will*, also with MIT Press, I will argue that criterially causal information processing, as realized in the brain, is a more accurate metaphor for understanding economic and social interaction than the standard metaphor of thermodynamics that has dominated economics since the views of Paul Samuelson became dominant in the 1940s.

8. Dennett (1978), although himself a determinist and compatibilist, gives a clear description of the traditional two-stage Jamesian model where multiple possible ideas are generated and a rational will then selects from among these ideas: "The model of decision making I am proposing has the following feature: when we are faced with an important decision, a consideration-generator whose output is to some degree undetermined produces a series of considerations, some of which may of course be immediately rejected as irrelevant by the agent (consciously or unconsciously). Those considerations that are selected by the agent as having a more than negligible bearing on the decision then figure in a reasoning process, and if the agent is in the main reasonable, those considerations ultimately serve as predictors and explicators of the agent's final decision."

9. In April 1870, William James realized this after having suffered from severe depression for years over the potential unreality of free choice, and he concluded that his first act of free will would be to believe in free will. If we take as a fact that certain mental events can cause future mental and physical events, as when a toothache causes us to go to the dentist, we can take the existence of mental causation to be evidence that the universe is indeterministic.

10. See http://www.nytimes.com/2003/02/13/garden/living-to-the-power-of-two.html.

11. According to Leibniz's principle of the identity of indiscernibles, two things are identical if they share all their properties. Conversely, according to the principle of the indiscenibility of identicals, if two things are identical, they will share all of the same properties. These principles do not apply to decisions or information as realized in neurons because neurons equate properties subject to a threshold of adequacy. If the criteria are set, for example, as "a fruit that I can eat" and "available in my kitchen now," both apples and oranges will be equivalent because they both satisfy these criteria. Criterial equivalence is not the same as identity because things with different properties are equated. As far as meeting the conditions imposed by some criteria or desire, apples can be equated with oranges. Information is realized in the brain when criteria for firing are satisfied and neurons fire. Because many sets of physical inputs can lead to firing, information in the brain can be multiply realized. It follows that information is not identical to any particular brain state, although it is always realized in a particular brain state. Rather, information is

equivalent but not necessarily identical in a brain or across brains when identical informational criteria have been met.

8 Implications of Criterial Causality for Mental Representation

1. Present-day computers execute instructions sequentially, one by one, based on von Neumann's architecture that separates the computing processor from memory storage and involves communication between these two halves via a bus.

2. This term, "possible worlds," has become fashionable among philosophers in recent decades. The danger is that one might reify such worlds and think they have some kind of real, even if Platonic, existence. It might be better to use terms like "conceivable worlds" or "imaginable worlds" to avoid this danger.

3. It is doubtful that any finite set of criteria can be set that can only be met uniquely by a single thing among all conceivable things. However, in the real world, there may in fact be only one thing that satisfies a finite set of criteria. For example, "the leader of the richest country in the world" could refer to infinitely many possible beings if the criteria were imposed on all possible or imaginable worlds or times, but may only apply to one person now in our particular world.

4. In general, language itself is criterial. If I say "He took his wallet out of his pocket," my listener might conjure up or imagine countless different men, wallets, or pockets, any of which would meet the criteria imposed by this sentence. But in practice, it is generally not required to conjure up any particular person in order to understand this sentence. This is because *propositions are not particular, referring to specific facts; they are constraints that are met by particular facts.* To understand the meaning of a proposition is to model these constraints. In everyday language use, people resolve the ambiguity introduced by the fact that there are many ways to satisfy constraints by accessing information that may not be provided by the sentence in need of interpretation. We use common sense, body language, tone, context, and our knowledge of others, and, when in doubt, we simply ask "what do you mean by that?" Sometimes two sentences of opposite literal meaning can have the same actual meaning, as when I say "I could care less about his problems" or "I could not care less about his problems." And sometimes a single sentence can carry opposite meanings, as when I say "Have a nice day" to mean that I want people to go away and leave me alone, or when I say this to genuinely wish them a nice day.

5. The idea of the noumenal world is due to Kant: "The concept of a noumenon [is that] of a thing that is not to be thought of as an object of the senses but rather as a thing in itself" (Kant, 1998 [1781], p. 362).

6. According to Malcolm (1962), Wittgenstein (1953) argued that criteria can be used to rebut the skeptic who maintains that we cannot know that there are other

minds, because we possess criteria that, if fulfilled, lead us to the knowledge that another person is feeling something. This is a problematic notion of the idea of criteria, because whatever criteria are set in place for, say, concluding that another person is in pain—say, that he or she has to grimace in a certain way—some conditions can arise that meet those criteria that occur in the absence of the person feeling pain, as when an actor grimaces. This might be done so perfectly that we infer that the actor is in pain when he or she is not. While we no doubt have criteria for inferring the contents of others' minds, such as the tuning functions of neurons tuned to facial expressions, this move fails to eliminate the possibility of skeptical stances concerning other minds, such as solipsism.

7. The focus of work on criteria has generally been on the criteria that specify *inclusion* in some category. For example, birds lay eggs, typically fly, have feathers and beaks, and are warm blooded. But certain facts, if true, would be sufficient to *exclude* a thing from a category. Something that meets all the criteria counting as a bird but appeared in a movie on TV would not count as a real bird. Something made of metal would not count as a real bird, even if it met all other bird-defining criteria, because birds cannot be made of metal. It is generally more informative to say what something is than to say what it is not. Recognition and categorization are therefore more likely to be based on the optimal, smallest set of features or properties that define a thing, rather than on the endless class of features or properties that specify only what a thing is not. That being said, a neuron whose criteria for firing are met, and which would be driven above its threshold, can still be inhibited by other inputs. Commonly, excitatory inputs arrive in the more distal dendrites, whereas inhibitory inputs arrive closer to the cell body and the axon hillock. Such an arrangement gives inhibition the potential for a "veto" before action potential release. Top-down inhibition could realize an executive veto over prepared plans and actions, and more local such inhibition might realize "exclusionary criteria." Similarly, we might not know exactly what we are looking for, though we know what we are not looking for, thus defining "negative criteria" for fulfilling the search. For example, I might be at an airport where everything is written in a script I cannot read, so that I have to find my airline by its logo. I might know many such logos, but not the one of my airline. I can nonetheless search by rejecting what I don't want, rather than accepting what I do want. Positive criteria that allow me to locate what I want will be more efficient than negative criteria that allow me to rule out what I do not want. In fact, both types of processes operate in us. We find things both beautiful and ugly, delicious and repulsive. If positive and negative criteria and associated desire systems operate in parallel, then we can find something simultaneously beautiful and ugly, or attractive and repulsive, to the degree that the respective criteria for triggering associated categorization judgments and desires are fulfilled.

8. A prior probability is the probability distribution that reflects one's assessment of likelihoods of randomly selected outcomes before one ever sees actual data. For example, the chances of it raining in September on a given day are 18 percent. A

posterior probability is the conditional probability that one assigns after seeing the data, for example, the probability that it has rained given that the ground is wet.

9. Contrary to Putnam (1960, 1967, 1975), there are some functionalist accounts that deny multiple realizability (e.g., Armstrong, 1968; Lewis, 1980).

9 Barking Up the Wrong Free: Readiness Potentials and the Role of Conscious Willing

1. Libet's clock method is flawed because it relies on subjective recall that can be biased by retrospective construction (Dennett & Kinsbourne, 1992) and backward referral (Libet, 1985). It also takes time to read and memorize the clockhand location, which might bias estimates of W (Rollman, 1985; Gomes, 2002). Moreover, Keller and Heckhausen (1990) make the valid point that the paradigm may have turned voluntary behavior into a reaction triggered by W. The probe method of Matsuhashi and Hallett (2008) remedies most of these flaws (§9.3).

2. What Libet called an RP—both RPI (for preplanned acts) and RPII (for unplanned acts)—may best be characterized as a GRP (for "generalized readiness potential") to distinguish it from an LRP. The GRP—henceforth just "RP"—and LRP are thought to be two distinct phases of the overall readiness potential. The RP is an early phase that is equally distributed across hemispheres and maximal at medial location Cz (at the top of the scalp; originating in the location of the middle pair of circles shown in fig. 9.1b). The RP has been associated with anticipation of a motor act or preparation of a motoric plan (Haggard, 2008; Herrmann et al., 2008; Roskies, 2010; Haggard et al., 2004; Moore et al., 2009a). The LRP is a later phase, lateralized to the hemisphere contralateral to a unimanual movement, originating in M1 or the motor strip, at the locations of the lateral pair of circles in figure 9.1b. Movement initiation correlates with the occurrence of an LRP, but not a RP (Trevena & Miller, 2010). The LRP, therefore, appears to be closely tied to the command to execute a movement, presumably in the motor strip, whereas the RP occurs regardless of whether a motor command is executed or not. Haggard and Eimer (1999) argue that this later phase may, but only may, constitute a neural correlate of the conscious decision to act. Some researchers do not call an event-related potential (ERP) wave form an RP unless it precedes motion, but it seems reasonable to refer to RPs even when there is a looser connection to action, such as anticipation of or preparation for an action that is never actually performed, provided that the waveform exhibits the characteristics of the RP.

3. Libet's claim that the beginning of the RP precedes consciousness of will or intention does not apply to distal intentions formed long before the action. After all, Libet's subjects formed intentions to follow his instructions, and nothing in Libet's experiments suggests that those distal intentions did not affect what they did. Libet's results also do not show that will or consciousness is impotent in general. Even if the preconscious segment of the RP occurs earlier than will and consciousness, and

even if that RP segment is necessary to cause the action, will and consciousness still might be necessary subsequent elements of the causal chain that produces action. In short, the RP, will, and consciousness might all have causal roles to play (Roskies, 2010). No RP or LRP data published to date rule this out.

4. ERP waveforms that look like the RP have long been known to precede events that are not necessarily movements (e.g., Trevena & Miller, 2010). These are called "contingent negative variations" (CNVs; Walter et al., 1964). While there may be some components of the CNV that are related solely to stimulus anticipation, others may be related to anticipation of movement or preparation for movement (e.g., Schröter & Leuthold, 2008; Van Boxtel & Brunia, 1994). To the extent that the CNV correlates with anticipation rather than motor planning or execution, however, the existence of the CNV causes problems for Libet's basic argument against the efficacy of conscious free will. Given that one typically anticipates making a movement as one prepares to move, some early components of the RP might in fact incorporate the anticipatory component of the CNV. These early components of the RP might then reflect unconscious or conscious expectations that one will move, but they would not have anything to do with initiation of movement or conscious willing to move, as Libet's argument requires. This may not be as dire for Libet's interpretation of the RP as it may seem. Gomes (2010) argues that RPs have higher amplitudes (~10μV vs. ~2μV) and a different timecourse than CNVs; CNVs are small and tend to ramp up slowly over 2500ms whereas the RP is a larger waveform that can be more clearly distinguished from the tracing preceding it. However, as these waveforms are spatially and temporally coincident, a clear understanding of the RP requires separating expectation or anticipation components from movement components of the RP. Comparing the ERP signatures of movement-independent anticipation, movement-related anticipation, and movement preparation should accomplish this.

5 My collaborators include philosophers Walter Sinnott-Armstrong and Adina Roskies, and neuroscientists Alex Schlegel, Scott Alexander, and Thalia Wheatley. The project is supported by the Big Questions in Free Will initiative directed by philosopher Al Mele at Florida State University. Some paragraphs in this chapter are modified from an article co-authored with them (Schlegel et al., 2012a).

6. This term, also known as "corollary discharge," derives from Helmholtz (1910 [1867]), who argued for the existence of a comparator that compares predicted and estimated actual states as a means of sensorimotor control, the detection of errors, and the assignment of causation by self. In the domain of sensorimotor control in humans, this comparator model is amply supported by data (Blakemore et al., 1998; Haarmeier et al., 2001; Lindner et al., 2006; Shergill et al., 2003; Synofzik et al., 2006; Voss et al., 2006).

7. The possibility that the von Economo neuron system may play a role in resolving conflicts between circuits "vying" for control of behavior and thought will be covered in depth in the upcoming sister volume to this book, *The Cultivation of Will.*

10   The Roles of Attention and Consciousness in Criterial Causation

1. I have tried to avoid the word "consciousness" thus far, because it is fraught with ambiguities. If by "consciousness" we mean current subjective experience, then it is better to just use the word "experience" in the sense of "phenomenological experience" to avoid confusion with other meanings of the word "conscious" such as "awake," "alert," "self-aware," or "capable of responding or reporting." I will use the word "consciousness" as a synonym for "experience," and the word "conscious" as a synonym for "experienced." I will use the word "preconscious" to mean "occurring temporally after sensory detection but prior to experience." Note, that I do not mean by "preconscious" what some recent authors have meant by it (Dehaene & Changeux, 2011; Kanai et al., 2010). These authors use the term "preconscious" to mean "not conscious, but potentially conscious if attended." I find this to be a loaded usage of the term because it presumes that to be conscious is to be necessarily attended, which I am arguing against here. These authors use a term "subliminal" to mean "not possibly conscious even if attended," for which I will use "unconscious." In comparing my view with that of Dehaene and colleagues, I would argue that what they call "preconscious" I would call conscious, but experienced as unattended and unbound qualia of types 1 and 2, held in high-capacity but short duration iconic or visual short-term memory buffers, and what they call "conscious" I would also call conscious, but experienced as qualia of type 3, in low-capacity but longer-duration working memory buffers, particularly involving the dorsolateral prefrontal cortex of the frontoparietal attentional or executive circuit, or subsidiary systems elsewhere. The key difference between our views concerns whether qualia realized in non-frontoparietal non-working-memory buffers are experienced. I argue yes, as the "background of experience," and they argue no. I will focus on the debate between those who believe that frontoparietal processing is necessary for experience and those who believe it is not starting in §10.62.

2. Losing these subsystems leads, respectively, to akinetopsia, prosopagnosia, achromatopsia, and apperceptive agnosia. Modularity and the superpositionality of consciousness are evidenced by the fact that one can lose one kind of processing and corresponding experience without losing the others.

3. Illusions can only be understood to be illusions once one realizes that there is a disconnect between what ones sees and what must be the case. Naïve people might feel that what they see is the case, and rather than question the veracity of their experience, assume that reality is as it seems. For example, one might experience a "floating" migraine aura that seems to drift across the visual field and grow/shrink as ones looks at further/nearer surfaces, and leap to the conclusion that it is a really existing ghost or spirit. Possibly many delusional memes have started this way, namely, as one person's mistake.

4. The product of these rapid, preconscious operations can be thought of as a "veridical hallucination." Of course, experience is typically not a hallucination,

because we can assume that experienced content generally corresponds to actual goings-on in the world. But the same constructive and inferential processes that, when untethered from sensory input, can result in hallucinations or dreams, are, broadly speaking, the same as those that result in everyday experience. A riddle that makes this point: "What lies beyond the farthest constellation that you can see?" Answer: "your skull."

5. The notion that experience might be quantized goes back in neuroscience at least as far Wilhelm Wundt, and in philosophy even further, to at least John Locke. Wundt's psychophysics laboratory was driven, perhaps implicitly, by the metaphor of the periodic table; just as complex molecules are made of combinations of simpler elements, complex mental events and experiences, it was assumed, could be decomposed into simpler mental "atoms." The same metaphor underlay a parallel reductionistic movement in philosophy called "logical atomism," evident in works by Russell and the *Tractatus* of Wittgenstein. The atom metaphor is both reductionistic and mentalistic. Introspectionists, such as Titchener, thought the atoms of experience could be apprehended by "observing" one's own experience methodically. This seemed so unscientific to James B. Watson and his followers in the United States that they founded a psychology based solely on the observation of measurable behaviors. Behaviorism was a backlash against the introspectionism of Titchener's brand of Wundt's structuralism. Whereas behaviorism rejected the introspectionistic and mentalistic impulses of Wundt and his students, the Gestalt movement in Germany rejected its reductionism and pushed for holism while maintaining mentalism and a focus on phenomenology. When Gestalt psychologists fled Nazi Germany, upon arriving in the United States most were forced to take jobs at teaching colleges because research universities were dominated by behaviorists who rejected their premises of holism, phenomenology, and mentalism.

6. The same question can be asked of the popular global workspace model of consciousness (Baars, 1988, 1997; Dehaene et al., 1998, 2006; Dehaene & Changeux, 2011). Why should being globally broadcast entail being experienced at all, let alone being experienced in a particular way?

7. On this account, consciousness can emerge only in those systems that instantiate physically realized informational criterial causality, not more general types of physical causation based solely on energy transfer or chemical transformation. Against panpsychism, the vast majority of nonbiological nature would be nonconscious, and those parts of it that are conscious but not biological we have yet to discover. It would also not be enough to just process information, because information can be processed in a manner that does not involve criterial causation, as in computers as currently constructed. Similarly, organizations of individual animals, such as beehives, cities, corporations, or countries, would also lack consciousness.

8. Many hierarchical organizations, such as corporations or the military, involve communication primarily between an operator and other operators at the same level, or the level one up or one down from this level. This organization minimizes

the need for redundant communication. In the brain, such a localistic top-down, bottom-up feedback loop would also minimize axonal length and therefore brain size and energy use. Even if each layer can only speak to adjacent levels, however, communication between levels requires a common code and a mechanism for indicating that information, once transmitted, has been received, in order to terminate repeated sending. This architecture would necessitate as many axons from level 1 to level 2 as level 2 to level 1. To the extent that information is encoded differently in different levels, there must be a transformation or translation step. Certainly this must happen in the brain as propositional plans in say, area 10, are converted into abstract and then concrete motor plans as one moves posteriorly toward the motor strip.

9. We could learn to feel agency over a mechanical arm remotely controlled by patterns of activity measured from our cortex if the timing between mental command and action were not too delayed (cf. Carmena et al., 2003; Lebedev et al., 2005; Lebedev & Nicolelis, 2006; Musallam et al., 2004; Serruya et al., 2002; Taylor et al., 2002; Velliste et al., 2008; Wessberg et al., 2000). Similarly, a muscle need not be our own for us to feel that we govern it if it contracts as soon as we send the command for it to contract, and if it consistently did whatever we wanted it to do. An extreme case of this in nature is the parasite *Cymothoa exigua*, which bites off the tongue of its host fish, attaches itself to the stump, and proceeds to act just as a tongue would act, taking its movement cues from the stump. The fish gets a tongue that functions as well as its own perhaps, and may not notice the difference (although taste would be lost), while the parasite gets a food supply. One can imagine a Borgesian thought experiment where every organ, muscle, and neural circuit gets replaced by a specialized parasite that exactly reproduces the function of the subsystem it replaces. Would a collection of such specialized parasites become functionally identical to a fish or a human? If yes, then functionalism would be correct, but if no, then functionalism has work to do. In the simple case of discrete parasites the answer would be "no," because the sensory, cognitive, and motoric systems of each parasite would be distinct. Sensory information would not get integrated across the whole parasite collection, so there could not be a sensory consciousness that covers the whole collection of parasites. Nor could there be an executive issuing commands based on such global integration of information. If the sensory, cognitive, and motoric systems became integrated across parasite modules, then the collection of parasites might become functionally indistinguishable from the original parasite-free organism. In one sense, we are such integrated systems, and we can view ourselves as vast colonies of specialized cells. But would there be some systems that could not be replaced by a parasite without losing the coherence of a functioning system? One candidate would be the attentional system, which can bind information from many sensory modules at will. For there to be a parasite that could replace the attentional system, its nervous system would have to become integrated with the nervous systems of component parasites, such that their sensory inputs became its sensory inputs and its executive commands were obeyed by their

nervous systems. A simple functionalism based only on local fungible functionality is not tenable. At the very least, what is required is not functional equivalence, but architectural equivalence at the level of global information processing.

10. Some prefer the expression "anarchic hand syndrome" because although the hand is generally viewed as belonging to oneself and sensations of the hand are experienced as happening to one's own body, "the owner of the hand is no longer the *agent* of the movement" (Walter, 2001, p. 281). This syndrome can arise because of hemispheric disconnection in the region of the anterior cingulate cortex (ACC; Ay et al., 1998; Gasquoine, 1993; Scepkowski & Cronin-Golomb, 2003; Tibbetts, 2001). A more extreme variant of this syndrome is called "utilization behavior." Arising from bilateral frontal damage, the hand(s) are no longer inhibited from carrying out action patterns triggered by objects within reach. For example, a comb automatically triggers combing. Such evidence has led some to view the ACC as central to agency or at least feelings of agency. Francis Crick went so far as to say, "Free Will is located in or near the anterior cingulate sulcus" (1994, p. 268). To this claim, Fuster (1999, p. 296) replies, "to assign will to any [particular] region obviously begs the question of prior command on that region from another structure." Not surprisingly, others have attributed will to other areas, particularly those that provide input to the ACC, such as the dorsolateral prefrontal cortex. Liddle et al. (2001) suggest that "the anterior cingulate cortex is principally engaged in making and monitoring of decisions, while dorsolateral and ventral lateral prefrontal sites play a specific role in response inhibition."

11. There are, however, unusual cases such as split-brain patients who seem to have two consciousnesses in a single body and two separate endogenous attentional systems.

12. It is not known how attentional processing in the absence of consciousness occurs. The attentional salience map, residing in part in the inferior posterior parietal lobes, is driven in part by dorsal stream input, which is generally thought not to be conscious, as instances of blindsight reveal (Koch, 2004). Another possibility is that the tectopulvinar pathway provides input to the salience map. This pathway is thought to project information from the retina to the superior colliculus to the pulvinar and other posterior thalamic nuclei, on to the amygdala and cortex; the tectopulvinar projection appears to play a role in the rapid object processing exhibited by the amygdala (Hannula et al., 2005), but does not appear to play an important role in cortical object recognition or visual consciousness. In particular, lesioning the pulvinar and superior colliculus has no measurable effect on visual object discrimination (Chow, 1951; Ungerleider & Pribram, 1977).

13. This metaphor was suggested to me by my colleague at Dartmouth Thalia Wheatley.

14. An alternative version of this metaphor would be that consciousness is analogous to a light that goes on any time the electricity is on. Such a light would play

no causal role in the operation of any operator, which would be to say that consciousness is epiphenomenal; it might always accompany, say, attentional processing, but would play no role in its operations. Other examples of accompanying epiphenomena are the sound of a train moving, which does not cause it to move, or the heat from a lightbulb, which does not cause the bulb to give off light. To prove that something that might be epiphenomenal is in fact not, one would have to show that the operator functions differently in its absence, or that some other process that causes later events takes this as its input. For example, if a detector took the sound of a train of a certain pitch as a signal that the brakes should be applied, then one could argue that the whistling sound causes the train to slow down. Pain, for example, might make us stop doing what we are doing in this sense, making experience causal. Alternatively, in the absence of ongoing experience, it might be impossible to attentionally track some component of experience; this too would show that consciousness is not epiphenomenal.

15. Other areas that, when lesioned, damage an animal's ability to learn via trace conditioning include the mediodorsal nucleus of the thalamus (Powell & Churchwell 2002), entorhinal cortex (Ryou et al. 2001), and medial prefrontal cortex (mPFC; Kronforst-Collins & Disterhoft 1998; Weible et al. 2000, 2003; McLaughlin et al. 2002). Circuitry that relates an event to its consequences over temporal gaps likely spans many brain areas (Weiss & Disterhoft 1996; Green & Woodruff-Pak, 2000), particularly those subserving attentional and working-memory processing. An NMDA receptor-dependent process in the mPFC mediates acquisition and the early stages of consolidation of a trace conditioned response (Takehara-Nishiuchi et al., 2005), whereas the cerebellum (Woodruff-Pak et al., 1985; Takehara et al., 2003) and hippocampus (Kim et al., 1995b; Takehara et al., 2002) mediate trace-conditioned response retention.

16. In collaboration with Giorgio Vallortigara and his students at the University of Trento using chicks, and with Roger Hanlon and his group at Woods Hole Oceanographic Institute using cuttlefish, we hope to learn soon whether some of our distant cousins can attentionally track one or more moving targets among identical moving distractors. It would certainly be wonderful to see a taxonomy of animals capable of endogenous attentional tracking. It would be even more wonderful to see a taxonomy of animals that have experience. Unfortunately we cannot observe experience, consciousness, information or attention directly. We can only observe behavioral and neuronal correlates of operations that we reasonably assume to occur over unobservable experience.

17. Following the flash of a camera, one typically sees a spot in the visual field that persists at the retinal position of the flash. Such visual afterimages can occur after fixating colored images as well. For example, after fixating on a static, solid red disk for half a minute, one will continue to see a green afterimage of the disk when staring at a blank white screen. This afterimage will move over the screen with one's eye movements because the cells that have adapted are either in the retina or in an

area of the brain where information is still represented in retinotopic coordinates. Although afterimages are thought to have rather complex temporal dynamics, the dominant stage is one where a complementary color is seen. What was blue (red, white) in the adapting image appears yellow (green, black) in this "negative afterimage," and vice versa. It was precisely this complementarity of afterimages that led Ewald Hering (1878) to the now widely accepted opponent process theory of color perception, overturning the then-leading color vision theories of Thomas Young and Hermann von Helmholtz, according to which there are three primary colors, red, green, and blue. According to Hering's opponent color theory, in contrast, there are six primary colors arranged in three opponent channels, red–green, blue–yellow, and black–white. Colors are opponent because responses to a given color are antagonistic to those of its paired color. Hering's theory could account for negative afterimages, whereas the Young–Helmholtz theory could not. This is an example where phenomenology—an analysis of the structure of experience—made clear and correct predictions about neural information processing architecture.

18. This idea emerged in discussions with Nao Tsuchiya and Ryota Kanai at Caltech in 2007.

19. See http://www.youtube.com/watch?v=vJG698U2Mvo; even more amazing is http://www.youtube.com/watch?v=ubNF9QNEQLA; http://www.youtube.com/watch?v=3Vz_YTNLn6w.

20. Even premature babies appear to experience pain (Bartocci et al., 2006; Oberlander et al., 2002; Slater et al., 2006).

21. Mack and Rock (1998, ch. 1) continue "In experiments in which a familiar, colored, geometric shape appears in a quadrant of a cross centered at fixation, many instances occur in which the subjects correctly report the color of the [unattended] stimulus and its quadrant location but fail to identify its shape. If retinal input is processed to the level of recognition and perhaps meaning, why this failure of shape perception? There are also other troubling cases in which the critical stimulus is detected—that is, the subjects report they have seen something that was not present on earlier trials—but they are unable to identify it. If it is detected, an occurrence that, according to the theory of late selection, entails the involvement of attention at the late level of processing, why is its identity not perceived?" An alternative interpretation to the view of Dehaene and Changeux (2011) or Mack and Rock (1998) (i.e., that there is no conscious experience without attention) can explain what puzzles them in the above quote. Namely, type 1 qualia can be experienced and potentially reported without attention, but to have reportability of object identity, and perhaps even global shape, attention is needed.

22. A more subtle version of this crucial experiment makes more subtle predictions. Applying transcranial magnetic stimulation (TMS) to the dorsolateral prefrontal cortex (DLPFC) should knock out type 3 qualia, but leave qualia in the stage 1 buffer intact. Dehaene and colleagues would predict that nothing is reportable about the

stimuli without a functioning frontoparietal network. I would predict that observers could report both local and global type 1 and type 2 features, such as color and layout, respectively. But knocking out both the DLPFC and V4/posterior inferotemporal cortex simultaneously, should leave only the iconic buffer intact. I would predict that only local type 1 and type 2 features, such as color and orientation, would be reportable. However, not reportable would be nonlocal bound features realized in what Lamme's group (Sligte et al., 2011) calls "fragile visual short-term memory" realized in V4 and posterior inferotemporal cortex, such as contour closedness and layout.

23. Dreaming and internal visualization engage the "default mode network" (Buckner et al., 2008; Raichle et al, 2007) involving dorsal and ventral anterior medial prefrontal, posterior cingulate, retrosplenial, parahippocampal, entorhinal, lateral temporal and inferior, lateral parietal cortex near the temporal-parietal junction. This "introspective network" appears to operate in an anticorrelated manner with the "extrospective network," which is engaged when the external world and sensory input are processed in depth. The extrospective circuit may have two subcomponents subserving, respectively, endogenous and exogenous attention (Corbetta & Schulman, 2002; Fox et al., 2006). The endogenous or "dorsal attentional network" includes the intraparietal sulcus, DLPFC, the frontal eye fields, anterior insula, and the dorsal anterior cingulate. The introspective and extrospective circuits may comprise two mutually inhibiting components of a more general wakeful, attentional system, where attention is either engaged with sensory input or recalled/internally generated representations. Daydreaming and mental visualization therefore would not engage the DLPFC as an executive working memory buffer, but more likely, instead, the anterior dorsal and/or ventral medial prefrontal cortex.

24. I believe the idea of "summoning what is needed as needed" actually came from industry, although it was foreshadowed in some ways by Stanisław Lem's 1961 novel *Solaris* and the 1920s cartoon character "Felix the Cat" who always produced whatever he needed from his bag of tricks. I first heard this idea in the 1980s when I was working at a Kobe Steel factory in Takasago Japan. Taiichi Ohno of Toyota had initiated a revolution in cost-saving and manufacturing efficiency that exploited the real-time information monitoring afforded by computers. The basic idea was to have all the car parts required for producing the planned number of cars arrive from suppliers on the day that they were needed. The supply chain then acted as its own "warehouse." In contrast, the Detroit model of production required expensive physical warehouses to store car parts for some period of production. The brain instantiates something like the cheap and efficient "just-in-time manufacturing" of the Japanese model in that type 3 qualia of identifiable, trackable objects are "manufactured" from stage 1 qualia on an as-needed basis. The metaphor breaks down because stage 1 buffers are not fixed supply chains. They are far more flexible because they provide vast stores of pre-processed sensory information that an animal itself seeks out to fulfill its needs. It would be as if a company

could switch between entirely different supply chains as needed on a millisecond timescale, depending on what it needed to produce. Working memory buffers also do not only produce one kind of thing, like Toyota produces cars, but instead can realize anything that we can attend to. Because the contents of working memory can even be self-generated, as in dreams, mental imagery and daydreams, there are very few constraints placed on what is manufactured by this information-processing architecture. It would be as if Toyota produced anything imaginable "from the ether," as needed.

25. Even in the "tip-of-the-tongue" phenomenon, where we have an experience of knowing information that we cannot access, we can access and volitionally attend to this experience.

Appendix 1   Physical Evidence for Ontological Indeterminism

1. There can be nonphysicalist monisms. There have been proponents of the idea that everything is mind, or ideas, or information. As dubious as such notions are, they are at least logically consistent, unlike dualism, which posits two mutually irreducible fundamental substances, typically matter and mind (or soul or spirit). The problem for this view is that mental events affect physical events and vice versa, so they must form a causal chain. The two substances must interact in this causal chain if they are to affect each other. The interaction must be realized in these two substances. If they are mutually irreducible, however, we can separate the portion of the interaction that is mental from the portion that is physical. We can then ask how these portions interact. Since they must interact if the two portions can affect one another, we can divide their interaction into two portions, and so on, ad infinitum. Since this is illogical, there must be just one fundamental substrate in which all events are realized.

2. The fundamental substrate or "substance" is best described as having the units of "action," or energy-time or momentum-space. Action can be thought of as spatially and temporally extended energy. Perhaps a better name for the fundamental substrate would therefore have been "change." Planck's constant, which has the units of action, implies that the fundamental substrate is quantized.

3. Several authors have argued that such a demon is impossible, because its acts of gathering information would disturb that which it is gathering information about (cf. Szilard's [1929] arguments concerning the related problem of Maxwell's demon; Landauer, 1961; Bennett, 1982, 2003) or else would trigger a Gödelian incompleteness problem because of the need to gather information about itself (Binder, 2008; Wolpert, 2008). But even if a determinist agreed that complete information about the universe is impossible to attain in practice, making deterministic *prediction* impossible, a determinist could still maintain that the universe nonetheless develops deterministically; we just cannot know how it will develop.

4. The first law of thermodynamics states that energy can be transformed, but it can neither be created nor destroyed. It is an expression of the law of the conservation of energy that is a cornerstone of physics. The second law states that the thermodynamic entropy of an isolated system that is not at equilibrium will tend to increase over time, approaching a maximum value at equilibrium.

5. "Nonlocality" means that when two or more spacelike separated physical systems are measured, outcomes can be correlated. That is, particle behavior can be correlated with that of particles outside the light cone, even if locally this conveys no information about any distant particle's state. Measurement results cannot be correlated to an extent that this would allow information signaling between distant systems. Thus, even under quantum mechanics, information cannot travel faster than the speed of light. It has recently been proven mathematically that the strength of nonlocal correlations is fixed by the uncertainty relation (Oppenheim & Wehner, 2010).

6. The question "why is there a now?" is a deep one that is not raised often in science. The concept of universal simultaneity is not consistent with relativity theory. Because possibilities do not collapse into a real outcome under determinism, a challenge that determinists face but indeterminists do not is to explain why any particular momentary subset of all predetermined events should be privileged as being in the present. Indeterminists can just say that everything that is possible comprises the future, and that the present is the subset of possibilities that are realized. A present might emerge within an ontologically indeterministic interpretation of quantum theory more naturally, as the moment when the wave function collapses. Under indeterminism, even a directionality of time is given by the fact that only that which is possible can possibly happen. Thus both a now and its "directionality" into the future seem to fall out of indeterminism naturally, but cannot be easily accounted for assuming determinism (Prigogine, 1997). While physics may or may not have to accommodate some conception of universal simultaneity, this is an entirely different matter than the now as experienced. The relationship between subjective and objective time is much debated (cf. Tse et al., 2004). However, it can at least be inferred from the fact that experience is not static that the universe in which it is realized is also not static.

7. In the body of his paper, Heisenberg (1927) uses the word *Unbestimmtheit* for his principle. The correct English translation of this is "indeterminacy" rather than "uncertainty" (*Unsicherheit*). Like Bohr, who called it "complementarity," he regarded this indeterminacy to be an ontologically real fact.

Appendix 2   Ontological Indeterminism Undermines Kim's Argument against the Logical Possibility of Mental Causation

1. Kim's reductionism does not claim to account for qualia or consciousness. He states that "physicalism will not be able to survive intact and in its entirety" because

"phenomenal mental properties are not functionally definable and hence functionally irreducible" and "if functional reduction doesn't work for qualia, nothing will"
(2005, pp. 29, 31). A more radical proponent of physical reductionism would reject
this and argue that qualia are epiphenomenal or do not really exist (e.g., Bickle,
2003; Dennett, 1988, 1992; Jackson, 1982; Rey, 1983; see also Churchland, 1985).
The issues of eliminative materialism and qualia are taken up in chapter 10.

2. Special sciences include any science beyond elementary particle physics that
describe how higher-level entities than particles interact and develop.

3. Criterial causation operates in the domain of genetic inheritance as well as many
other domains of life, such as embryogenesis. If radical reductionists argued that
genetics and inheritance, operating via the information realized in DNA and its
cellular decoding, were utterly noncausal because the only true causation operates
among strings (or whatever lies at the bottom-most physical level), it would be easier
to see the poverty of their position. But because they make these arguments about
the information realized in neural activity, and this informational encoding/decod-
ing scheme has not yet been cracked by science, their arguments have caused undue
worry. Criterial causation operates at higher levels as well, including the domains
of sociology and economics. For example, if Japan needs iron ore to build cars, it
might not matter whether this comes from Brazil or Australia, so long as certain
criteria are met by the ore.

4. "Synchronic" means "at a given instant," such as the present moment, whereas
"diachronic" means "happening over time."

5. This problem of metasupervenience has arisen before in a different context. Ned
Block's (1980b) "Chinese nation" argument against the central multiple realizability
thesis of functionalism, involves Chinese individuals playing the exact same functional role as individual neurons. If functionalism is correct, then, Block argues, the
set of all of these interacting Chinese people itself has mental states. Block argues
that this is absurd, since, nations do not have minds, and even if they did, China's
"metamind" would supervene on individual Chinese minds/brains. This metamind
that is purported to metasupervene on minds supervening on matter would violate
the central thesis of supervenience, which states that only one mental state can
supervene on a single physical state. Some have bitten the bullet, so to speak, and
argued that China would in fact experience qualia (Lycan, 1987), but that we cannot
imagine what it might be like to be China in the sense meant by Nagel (1974)
because of limitations within our own theory of mind systems (Baron-Cohen et al.,
1985). Dennett (1990) agrees that functionalism entails that there are qualia in all
physical implementations of brain states; if one finds this absurd, the only alternative, he argues, is to accept the conclusion that qualia do not exist in any physical
implementation.

6. One goal of §§6.17–6.20 is to offer a solution to this seeming problem of backward causation.

Glossary

Cross-referenced terms are italicized. Paragraphs where a concept is discussed are listed at the end of each entry.

Action Potential The firing of a neuron after the level of potential inside the cell has increased (*depolarized*) beyond a threshold. A wave of activity is sent down the axon, typically increasing the probability of release of neurotransmitter into the *synaptic cleft*. §2.4.

Alpha Brainwave 8–14 Hz oscillation evident in the *electroencephalogram* and the *local field potential*. §§4.47, 4n6.

AMPA α-amino-3-hydroxy-5-methyl-4-isoxazolepropionic acid. The AMPA receptor is a primary *ionotropic glutamate receptor*. Unlike the *NMDA* receptor, response varies in a graded manner with the amount of *glutamate* released into the *synaptic cleft* by the *presynaptic neuron*. Its function therefore plays a central role in *tonic* firing. §§2n2, 2n3, 4.36, 4n4, 5.6–5.9, 5.19, 5.21, 5.31, 5.38, 5.40, 5n9.

A Posteriori Knowledge Knowledge that can only be gained via *experience* or empirical evidence. Compare *A priori knowledge*. §§8.10–8.13, A3.

A Priori Knowledge Knowledge that is true by definition and does not require *experience* to establish that it is true. Compare *A posteriori knowledge*. §§8.10–8.13.

Attention Enhances *information*-processing for a selected subset of inputs and may also suppress information-processing for unselected or ignored inputs. Attention may be realized in the transitioning of a neural circuit into a *phasic* from a *tonic* mode of information transmission. See *Endogenous attention, Exogenous attention*. §§2.5, 2.10, 2.11, 4.14, 4.21–4.28, 4.38, 4.39, 4.45–4.53, 4.59, 4.60, 4n11, 5.38–5.51, figure 5.6, §§7.12, 9.8–9.11, 10.6, 10.12, 10.6–10.17, 10.23–10.87, figures 10.1, 10.2, 10.4, §§10n9, 10n11, 10n12, 10n21.

Attentional Tracking See *Endogenous attention*. §§2.10, 10.24, 10.28–10.47.

Back-propagating Action Potentials Potentials that travel from the soma of the neuron to the apical *dendrites*, and serve as a signal to the dendrites that an *action* *potential* has been released. They are thought to play a role in *burst* transmission by keeping *NMDA* receptors open. §§5.14–5.28, 5.31, figure 5.4, §5n8.

Baseline Firing Rate   The rate at which a neuron fires spontaneously. *Information* can be carried in both increases and decreases in rate from this level. §§4.29–4.35, 4.42, 4.46, 4n7, 5.37.

Beta Brainwave   14–30 Hz oscillation evident in the *electroencephalogram* and the *local field potential*. §§4.23, 4n6.

Binding Problem   Certain object features, such as color and motion, appear to be analyzed by distinct processing neural circuits or "modules." The binding problem arises because the brain must somehow represent disparately processed features as belonging to the same object. Attentional binding may be realized in the transitioning of a neural circuit into a *phasic* mode of information transmission. §§2.5, 2.11, 4.21–4.28, 4.45–4.53, 5.38–5.51, 10.17, 10.27, 10.34, 10.35, 10.54, 10.55–10.57, 10.59, 10.66, 10.69, 10.77, 10.83, 10.87.

Bottom-up   When referring to neural information processing, bottom-up processing is driven by virtue of *information* available in the stimulus. §§4.7, 4.14, 4.32, 4.39, 4.45, 4.69, 5.37, 5.39, 5.48, 10.15, 10.16. When referring to physical causation, bottom-up processing is driven solely by particle interactions that are not part of a criterial causal chain §§6.14, 7.6, 7.18. See *Reductionism, Criterial causation*.

Burst   A burst occurs when two or more *action potentials* are generated in rapid succession, typically at >100Hz with a preceding and subsequent silent period. Three to five spikes separated by ~5ms (200Hz) is common. Bursts can reset *synapses* within milliseconds and greatly increase the fidelity of *information* transmission. §§2.5, 3.13, 4.33, 4.35–4.48, 4.51–4.53, 4.59, 4.62, figure 4.5, §§4n11, 5.3, 5.6, 5.10, 5.12–5.51, figures 5.5, 5.6, §§5n8, 5n10, 5n12, 10.1, 10.87, A1.10.

Burst Packet   *Bursts* that traverse an *information*-processing hierarchy as a unit. The coincidence *criteria* imposed by pre- and postsynaptic *NMDA receptors* afford the physical conditions required to have a neuronal code based on transmission of information via bursts of *action potentials* as informational packets that traverse a neural circuit. The arrival of a burst will trigger information transfer followed by closure of the communication channel until the next burst or barrage of coincident inputs arrives. §§4.48, 4.53, 5.34, 5.51.

Causal Closure   When *causality* at the level of elementary particles is sufficient to explain all events at that and all higher levels; all microphysical states are completely *diachronically* necessitated by antecedent microphysical states. §A2.

Causality   An event A plays a role in causing event B to happen or not happen if A precedes B, and B has an altered probability of happening or not happening if A does not happen. §§A1.2, A1.3.

Causa Sui Self-causation. §§2.1, 2.4, 2.7, 3.9, 3.10, 3.13, 3.14, 5.51, 6.16, 7.1, 7.4, 7.5, 7.8, 7.10, 7.19, 7.25, 10.1, A2.2.

Change Blindness Under normal circumstances, an abrupt change draws *exogenous attention* to its location, which then affords the ability to identify the change in the object at that location by triggering spatiotemporal *binding* of features present at the attended location over time. Change blindness typically occurs because one has difficulty identifying changes in objects when the motion (i.e., change localization) processing system is swamped by motion energy (e.g., by changes everywhere or in many locations at once) or is otherwise circumvented (e.g., by very slow changes). §10.56.

Chunking Attention can chunk, automatize, and "hardwire" recognition of feature patterns and execution of action patterns, automatizing these in order to make processing faster and potentially unconscious. §§10.30, 10.53–10.61.

Closure When a set of outcomes is closed: Any particular outcome will be a member of the set. See *Causal closure*. §A2.

CNV Contingent negative variation; an *ERP* waveform that looks like the *readiness potential*. §9n4.

Compatibilism The view that we may will or act freely even if our *wills* and actions are (pre)determined. Compatibilists typically argue that even though the outcome of any of our acts of choice was predetermined since the beginning of the universe, it was nonetheless a choice made by our nervous system, and so is free, at least in the sense that it was our choice and we were not coerced into our choice by anyone or anything else. §§2.1, 3.3, 7.2, 7.18, 7n1.

Consciousness That which is (subjectively and phenomenally) experienced. Consciousness or *experience* is the domain of *information* or representation that permits the possibility of *endogenous* attentional tracking. More generally, consciousness is required for endogenous attentional allocation, shifting and tracking, volitional executive control, flexible cognitive processing and manipulation of representations in executive *working memory*, complex concatenations of simpler mental operations, contextually appropriate management of detected errors, and effective top-down inhibition of imminent acts. See *Qualia, Experience*. §§2.10, 2.11, 4.8, 5.24, chapters 9–10.

Contingent A contingently true proposition is defined as one that is true but might have been false. See *Necessary*. §§8.10–8.13.

Corollary Discharge See *Efference copy*.

Counterfactual Definiteness The idea that certain properties, such as momentum or position, have a definite state, even when they are not measured and are not known. §A1.6.

Criteria A set of conditions on input that can be met in multiple ways and to differing degrees. A criterion is an aspect or dimension along which something is assessed, typically relative to some benchmark or point of reference (e.g., the *resting potential*). Criterial assessments are typically accompanied by standards that set a level for acceptance that the criterion or criteria have been met (e.g., the threshold at the axon hillock for the generation of an *action potential*). §§3.5–3.7.

Criterial Causation Causation that involves a succession of criterial assessments of physically realized informational input that transforms, completes, and manipulates that *information*. Among neurons, informational criterial assessments are realized in physical assessments of intracellular potential that, when satisfied, release a physical change that can carry information for a subsequent stage of decoding. Because intracellular potential decays rapidly, assessment of potential level is tantamount to coincidence detection. Coincidence detection is a key mechanism permitting spatiotemporal patterns to become causal of subsequent activity in a neural net. The essence of criterial causality is a many-to-one mapping between input and output: All criterial *decoders* effectively lump together many kinds of physical input as indistinguishable insofar as they trigger a common output. All criterial causal chains have this aspect of *multiple realizability* of input that can trigger a released output, such as an *action potential*. Note that while criterial causation instantiates multiple realizability, not all instances of multiple realizability in physical systems exhibit criterial causation. This is because criterial causation requires that some output be released upon criterial satisfaction, typically to subsequent stages in a net of criterial decoders. §§2.3, 2.6–2.8, chapter 3, §§4.61, 5.62, 4.69, 4n1, 5.25, 5.51, 6.2, 6.8–6.14, 6.17–6.23, 7.4–7.11, 7.18, 7.19, 7.25, 10.1–10.4, A3n3, figure 3.1.

Criterialism View that maintains that a higher level of organization of aggregates of particles, whether people, neurons or a ribosome, can impose criteria on inputs that, if met, release subsequent behaviors within a dynamic complex system, such that there can be *downward causation*. Criterialism also maintains that *information* and reference arise in the context of the physical reconformation of a *decoder* or read-out mechanism when its physical/informational *criteria* are met, regardless of whether the thing exists in the world or even could exist. *Descriptivism* is an instance of criterialism at the level of words. See *Criteria, Criterial causation*. §§2.3, 2.6–2.8, 3.5–3.15, figure 3.1, §§3n5, 4.61, 4.62, 4.69, 4n1, 5.25, 5.51, chapters 6–8, 10.

Criticality A domain of complex system dynamics expressing high variability and borderline chaotic behavior. Healthy neural networks exhibit this behavior. If *information* is carried in perturbations from *baseline firing rate*, this domain is maximally sensitive to perturbations, and thus is maximally capable of carrying information. Neural behavior in this domain expresses a moderate mean level of synchrony with maximal variability of synchrony. This domain lies at the boundary between excessively low synchrony and excessively high neuronal synchrony in the population.

This domain also displays neuronal *bursts* whose probability decreases with duration in a fractal manner. §4.42.

Decoder   A physical system that imposes a set of physical/informational criteria on inputs, which, when met, release a physical action. A decoder permits the physically realized detection of information or satisfaction of informational criteria to become physically causal. §§2.8, 3.10, 3.12, 4.10. 4.9, 4.11, 4.60, 5.34, 6.3–6.8, 6.11, 6.12, 6.15, 6.18, 6.21, 6.23, 6n1, 6n3, 7.6, 7.8, 8.6–8.8, 10.58.

Delay Conditioning   Conditioning that occurs when there is a temporal overlap between the conditioned stimulus and the subsequent onset of the unconditioned stimulus, which it signals. §§5n4, 10.43.

Delta Brainwave   0.5–3 Hz oscillation evident in the *electroencephalogram* and the *local field potential*. §§4n6, 5.8.

Dendrite   Neuronal processes or "branches" that receive input from other neurons A pyramidal cell has both apical and basal dendrites. Figure 2.1.

Depolarization   An increase in the level of the intracellular potential of a neuron due to an increase in the proportion of positively charged ions in the cell. This is typically a result of *excitation* (see *Glutamate*) that increases the probability of an *action potential*. §§2n3, 4.1, 4.2, 4.36, 4.43, 4.51, 4.64, 4n4, 5.2–5.4, 5.6, 5.11, 5.12, 5.20, 5.23, 5.26–5.36, 5.42, 5.51, figure 5.2, §§5n8, 5n9.

Depressive Synapses   Synapses that become transiently weaker after a *spike*. §3.13.

Descriptivism   A theory of reference according to which a proper name refers to a thing by virtue of its being or being associated with a set of descriptions that that thing satisfies or uniquely satisfies. See *criterialism*. §§2.9, 8.8–8.13, A3.

Determinism   The view that any given fundamental particle, and indeed the set of all particles, has only one path open to it at any time. This implies that there is only one possible future course of events. This view cannot easily explain why there is a now, why there is an apparent arrow of time, or why there are processes that are apparently nonreversible. §A1.

Diachronic   Happening over time. §§A2.3, A2n4.

DLPFC   Dorsolateral prefrontal cortex. §§3.2, 4.26, figure 7.1, §§10.14, 10.57, 10n22.

Dorsal Stream   An *information*-processing circuit that runs from *V1* to the posterior parietal lobes that is concerned with determining where things are and where they are going, typically relative to the body or some part of the body, facilitating internal actions such as shifting attention or motoric actions such as shifting the eyes or grasping. Also known as the "where is it?" stream. Compare *Ventral stream* and *Medial stream*. §§4.8, 4.26, 10n12.

Downward Causation   The thesis that physically realized *mental* events at t_1 can influence in a nonrandom manner the probabilities of possible fundamental particle path outcomes at later time t_2, particularly those involved in realizing mental events at t_2. In the brain, according to *criterial causation*, this occurs because neurons set *criteria* placed on inputs for the release of an *action potential*, which are not only physical criteria placed on the level of intracellular potential, but also realize informational criteria placed on informational inputs realized in presynaptic neural activity. See *Criterial causation, Emergent property, Phase*. §§1.15, 1.16, 6.10, 6.14, figure 6.2, §§7.18, A2.2.

Dualism   The view that there exist two mutually irreducible fundamental substances, typically matter and mind. This view cannot explain how these two substances can causally interact. §§A1n1, A2.2.

EEG   See *Electroencephalogram*.

Efference Copy   The model that there exists a neural circuit that compares predicted (i.e., efferently copied) signals and signals fed back from actually executed motor acts as a means of sensorimotor control, the detection of errors, and the assignment of causation by self. §§9.6, 9.11, 9.13, 9n6, 10.26.

Electroencephalogram   A measurement of changes in potential measured, typically, at the scalp or subdurally. Chapter 9.

Emergent Properties   Properties of a global system that are not possessed by any local component of the system in isolation. For example, no local component of an airplane can fly in isolation, no cell in a vein can function as a tube, and no neuron isolated from its inputs and outputs can realize *information*. Typically, emergent properties emerge because of spatiotemporal or *phase* relationships, including causal relationships among the components. The phase of energy and not just the amplitude or power of energy can be causal given *criterial causation*. In the brain, coincidence detection is a key physical mechanism permitting spatiotemporal patterns in input that realize information for a *decoder* to be causal of subsequent neural activity. See *Burst packet, Criterial causation*, and *NMDA*. §§1.11, 1.15, 1.16, 6.10, 6.13.

Endogenous   Considered and driven by internal planning or assessments of the value of various options.

Endogenous Attention   Attention that is allocated relatively slowly but can be sustained through volition. Endogenous attention can be flexibly and volitionally allocated to a location or object in any representational space to which we have conscious access. If the attended object changes its position in that space, the object is attentionally tracked in that space. For example, we can track an oboe in a symphony volitionally, and then volitionally track the touch of one ant among several crawling over our arm. The endogenous attentional process is commanded by an executive frontoparietal circuit involving the *DLPFC* and posterior parietal cortex, but has consequences, such as a transition to *phasic* neural activity in targeted circuits throughout cortex and subcortical structures. §§2.10, 2.11, 4.22–4.24, 9.8–9.10, chapter 10.

Epiconnectivity Synaptic weight, gain, or filter modification can effectively sculpt a temporary circuit from the set of all circuits that are possible given a particular network of neurons. A given neuron can belong to many different epicircuits depending on its moment-by-moment epiconnectivity. §§3.5, 4.54–4.60, 8.17.

Epiphenomenalism The view that mental events cannot cause fundamental particles to behave differently than they otherwise would have behaved, had they only moved and interacted according to the laws of particle physics. This view follows from the assumption that particle-level *causality* is sufficient to account for all aspects of particle behavior because of *causal closure* at the level of particle interactions. Since neurons are made of particles, it follows that *mental* events, which must *supervene* on neuronal events, can play no causal role in neuronal behavior and are epiphenomenal. Causal closure of particle interactions also entails that genetic inheritance is epiphenomenal, and that genes are in no sense really causal of particle activity. Against epiphenomenalism, *criterialism* maintains that a higher level of organization of aggregates of particles, whether people, neurons, or a ribosome, can impose criteria on inputs that, if met, release subsequent behaviors within a dynamic complex system, such that there can be *downward causation*. See *Causal closure, Determinism, Compatibilism, Strong free will.* §§A2.1, A2.3, 1.3, 1.5, 1.7, 1.15, 1.16, 3.10, 4.5, 4.6, 6.2, 6.10, 6.13, 9.15, 10.5, 10n14.

EPSP Excitatory postsynaptic potential.

Event-related Potential Typically the average *EEG* waveform timelocked to some event, such as the appearance of a cue. Chapter 9.

Excitation An increase in the probability of *action potential* generation due to *depolarization,* typically because of *glutamatergic* input. §§2n3, 4.1, 4.2, 4.36, 4.43, 4.51, 4.64, 4n4, 5.2–5.4, 5.6, 5.11, 5.12, 5.20, 5.23, 5.26–5.36, 5.42, 5.51, figure 5.2, §§5n8, 5n9.

Exogenous Driven automatically by the stimulus in a bottom-up manner.

Exogenous Attention The transient or *exogenous* component of *attention* is allocated automatically and nonvolitionally to, for example, the location of the abrupt onset of a new stimulus. §§4.22, 4.23, 10.16, 10.35, 10.36.

Experience Another word for consciousness; the domain of representations that permit the possibility of endogenous attentional tracking. These subjective, phenomenological representations are associated with *qualia*. In normal individuals experience can be thought of as an internal "virtual reality" of objects, events, and internal imaginings, complete with an awareness of causation, the contents of other minds, and social and other meanings. This construction, derived from but very different from the visual image and other sensory and physiological inputs, is normally in such good correspondence with what is actually happening in the world-in-itself and in the body that for the experiencer it is as if the world-in-itself and the body were experienced directly and without delay. However, illusions, dreams, hypnosis, phantom limbs and hallucinations can reveal that experience is not of the world-in-itself per se. §§1.7, 1.10, 1.12, 4.8, 2.10, 2.11, 5.24, chapters 9–10.

Facilitating Synapses   Synapses that become transiently strengthened after a spike. §3.13.

Family Resemblances   Because there are no necessary features that define membership in some category x, there are no strict boundaries on what counts as an instance of x. Such instances share nothing more than a fuzzy similarity structure along numerous potentially orthogonal dimensions, much like relatives in a family can share various features, such as nose shape or skin color, and yet not all share a unique defining feature. In other words, one or a number of features might be sufficient for something to count as an x if present to a satisfactory degree, but no feature is a necessary component of all instances of category x. §§8.14–8.17.

First Law of Thermodynamics   Energy can be transformed, but it can neither be created nor destroyed. §§A1n4, 6.9, 6.12.

fMRI   Functional magnetic resonance imaging.

Fragile Visual Short-term Memory   A posited high-capacity spatiotopic buffer realized in V4 and perhaps posterior inferotemporal processing, that encodes bound object information that lasts a few seconds. §§10.15, 10.17.

Free Will   That which underlies the ability to act freely or perform free actions. See *Will, Strong free will, Compatibilism, Incompatibilism.* §§1.1, 2.3, 2.6, 2.7, 3.1, 3.3, 3.14, 3n2, 3n3, 4.62, 5.25, chapters 7, 9–10.

Functionalism   The view that mental events are best explained and equated at the level of functional causal relationships rather than particular physical instantiations of those relationships. Functionalists typically argue that the material implementation of a set of functions is irrelevant to its functions. §§1n1, 3.11, 3.12, 8.24, 8.25, 8n9, 10n9, A2n5.

GABA   γ-aminobutyric acid, the primary inhibitory neurotransmitter. §§4.39, 4.44, 4n4, 4n11, 5.3, 5.40, 5.42, 5.45, 5.46, A1.10.

Gain Control   A mechanism that can change the number of output spikes per a fixed number of input spikes, and thereby change the sensitivity to input. A gain control mechanism is thought to play a role in attentional modulation. §§4.21, 4.28, 4.59, 5.7, 5.45 5.48, 10.29.

Gamma Oscillation or Brainwave   30–90 Hz oscillation evident in the *electroencephalogram* and the *local field potential.* §§4n6, 4.37, 4.44–4.53, 5.3, 5.16, 5.39–5.48.

Gap Junctions Junctions that allow potential to flow directly from cell to cell. §§4.1, 4.44, 4.66.

Glutamate The primary excitatory neurotransmitter. §§2n2, 2n3, 4.36, 4.40, 4.52, 4n4, 4n8, 5.2, 5.4–5.7, 5.23, 5.28–5.31, 5.39, 5.41, 5,44, 5.45, 5.51, 5n1, 5n5, A1.10, figures 5.2, 5.3.

Grandmother Cells Cells at the top of a "stack" of lower-level feature detectors that respond to complex objects, such as grandmothers. §§4.11, 4n16, figure 4.4.

Gyrus A convexity in the folded cortical sheet. See *Sulcus*.

High-gamma Oscillation or Brainwave 90–200+ Hz oscillation evident in the *electroencephalogram* and the *local field potential*. §§4n6, 4.23, 4.35, 4.49–4.52, 5.6, 5.24, 5.43, 5n12, figure 5.5.

Hyperpolarization A decrease in the level of the intracellular potential of a neuron. This is a result of *inhibition* (see *GABA*) that decreases the probability of an *action potential*. §§2n3, 4n11, 5.31, 5.42.

Iconic Buffer A high-capacity, parallel, short-duration, rapid, automatic, *retinotopic* buffer probably realized in V1-V3 processing that encodes detected feature primitives. §§2.11, 10.12–10.17, 10n22.

Identity Theory The view that mental states are identical to brain states. §§2n1, 3.11, A3.

Inattentional Blindness A paradigm where objects that are not attended often fail to be identified. §§10.67, 10.71, 10.74, 10n21.

Incompatibilism The view that free will is possible only if determinism is false.

Indeterminism The view that there are many possible future courses of events that might occur at any moment, perhaps with different likelihoods, even when only one actually occurs. Ontological indeterminism views this to be true of real events, whereas epistemological indeterminism accepts uncertainty in our knowledge of event outcomes even when they may be in fact predetermined. §§A1, 2.1, 2.6, 3.13, 3.14, 4.6, 6.10, 6.13, 6.20, 6.23, figure 6.2, 7.1, §§7.15, 7.18–7.22, 7.25.

Information Arises in the context of some criterial decoding or read-out mechanism, such as a neuron, capable of occupying many possible physical states; when physical/informational criteria are met, a decoder undergoes a physical change into a particular state that realizes the information that those criteria have been adequately met. As in the firing of an action potential, this can cause subsequent changes in an information-processing system comprised of communicating decoders that each set distinct criteria for firing. Information is therefore realized in physical changes that can in turn induce physical changes in a criterial causal sequence of decoding (criterial satisfaction) events. If the threshold for neuronal firing is met if and only if certain kinds of informational facts are true about the inputs, then the mechanism underlying neuronal firing not only assesses net potential at the axonal hillock, it also assesses these informational facts. Neurons carry, communicate and transform information by transforming action potential spike inputs into spike trains sent to other neurons. A criterial account of representation and information-processing suggests that it is useful to distinguish between three meanings of information or representation: (1) that certain inputs are presently occurring, which can be thought of as informational input into a postsynaptic neuron; (2) that certain criteria have been set, which can be thought of as conditions for assessing informational input by a postsynaptic neuron; and (3) that these criteria have been met, which is the realization of information in the postsynaptic neuron when the neuron fires. Information is realized not in the substance of energy per se, but in its spatiotemporal organization. See *Downward causation, Criteria, Criterial causation, Phase, Emergent property.* §§1.2, 1.10, 1.16, 2.3, 2.4–2.8, 3.5, 3.7, 3.9–3.14, figure 3.1, 3n5, 4.1–4.15, 4.17, 4.19, 4.29–4.66, 4.69, figures 4.2, 4.5, §§4n11, 4n16, 5.2, 5.3. 5.5, 5.11, 5.14–5.17, 5.22–5.37, 5.49, 5.51, figure 5.5, §§6.2–6.16, 6.19–6.23, figure 6.2, §§6n1, 6n2, 7.6, 7.17, 7n11, 8.5–8.8, 8.19–8.23, 8n4, 10.5, 10.9–10.23, 10.32, 10.81–10.83.

Inhibition   A decrease in the probability of neuronal firing induced by a decrease in intracellular potential (*hyperpolarization*), typically because of *GABA*ergic input. §§2n3, 4.39, 4.44, 4n4, 4n11, 5.3, 5.31, 5.40, 5.42, 5.45, 5.46, A1.10.

Ionotropic Receptors   Proteins or "channels" that can open a "pore" that allows ions to cross the cell membrane. They are associated with rapid neurotransmission because potential in the *postsynaptic* neuron either increases (*depolarization*) in the case of *excitation*, or decreases (*hyperpolarization*) in the case of *inhibition*, almost immediately after the neurotransmitter released from the *presynaptic* neuron binds to the receptor. Ionotropic receptors are fundamental to neuronally realized *information*-processing because they mediate all fast synaptic transmission. §§2n3, 4.5, 4.36, 4n4, 5.4, 5.6, 5.10, 5.19, A1.10. See *Metabotropic.*

IPSP   Inhibitory postsynaptic potential. 4.2, 4.54, 5.16.

Kim's Challenge   The proposition that a believable account of downward causation cannot be given. §§A2.2, 6.13.

LFP   See *Local field potential.*

LGN   Lateral geniculate nucleus of the thalamus. §§4.7, 4.9, 4.26, 4.28, 4.38, 4.39, 4.43, 4.48, 4.58, figure 4.2, §§4n11, 5.50, 10.32.

LIP   Lateral intraparietal area. §4.18.

LOC   Lateral occipital complex.

Local Field Potential   The ambient extraneuronal potential arising from changes in potential of many cells within a relatively large neighborhood around an electrode. §§4.44–4.47.

LRP Lateralized readiness potential. §§9.1, 9.3–9.5, figures 9.2, 9.3.

LTD Long-term depression (of synaptic weights); down-regulation of synaptic weighting or gain, realized in part via down-regulation of AMPA receptor expression. LTD happens optimally when glutamatergic synapses are given low-frequency input. §§4.31, 4.40, 5.6–5.11, 5.21.

LTP Long-term potentiation (of synaptic weights). §§4.31, 4.40, 5.6–5.11, 5.21, 5.25–5.28, 5n4.

M1 The motor strip on the precentral gyrus. The likely locus of the *LRP*. Figure 9.1.

Medial Stream An information-processing circuit that includes V1 → retrosplenial → parahippocampal → entorhinal cortex → hippocampus that analyzes where an animal is in a world-centered reference frame. Also called the "where am I?" pathway. See *Ventral stream, Dorsal stream*. §§4.8, 4.15.

MEG Magnetoencephalogram. Typically measurements at the scalp of changes in magnetic flux due to neuronal activity.

Mental See *Mind and mental events*.

Metabotropic Receptors Polypeptides that undergo intracellular changes when a neurotransmitter binds to them, which then activate G-proteins that trigger various intracellular cascades. Unlike *ionotropic* receptors, they do not permit ions to cross the cell membrane. §§2n3, 5.39–5.41, 5n5.

Microconsciousness The claim that different aspects of consciousness are realized in different neural circuits, without a need to bind their outputs together in a single final circuit. §§5n11, 10.23.

Mind and Mental Events Informational states realized in physical neural *decoders* that play a role in determining how future *information* will be decoded by future neural activity and therefore in determining how the physical/informational system will behave in the immediate and more distant future. See *Information, Experience, Qualia, Consciousness*.

Monism The view that there is only a single fundamental substance or substrate for all that exists. Physicalism maintains that the fundamental substance is material, while variants of idealism maintain that it is mind, spirit, consciousness, or information. See *Physicalism, Dualism*. §§A1n1, A2.2.

MRI Magnetic resonance imaging.

Multiple Realizability The view that supervenient states can be realized in multiple supervened-upon states; for example, the view that mental states can be realizable in multiple brain states. §§1n1, 2.8, 3.11, 3.12, 6.8–6.12, 6.21, 6n6, 8.25, 8n9, A2n5.

Necessary A necessarily true proposition is conventionally defined as a proposition that could not have been false. See *Contingent*. §§8.10–8.13, A3.

Neuromodulator   A neurotransmitter that modulates neural responsiveness to input. While *glutamate* and *GABA* are the dominant neurotransmitters underlying *postsynaptic excitation* and *inhibition*, respectively, other neurotransmitters, such as dopamine, acetylcholine, norepinephrine, and serotonin can alter the way in which a postsynaptic neuron responds to glutamatergic or GABAergic input. For example, a neuron can shift from a *tonic* to a *phasic* mode of firing to a given input via neuromodulatory input. §§4n3, 5.24, 5.38, 5.51.

NMDA   N-methyl-D-aspartate. The NMDA receptor is actually a family of *ionotropic* receptors that bind presynaptically released *glutamate*. The NMDA receptor consists of four subunits that together comprise in essence a coincidence detector. Their defining characteristic is that they permit rapid influx of calcium ions. To open, the tetramer requires (1) the simultaneous binding of *glutamate*, (2) co-agonist glycine or D-serine, and (3) the *depolarization* of the *postsynaptic* cell in the immediate vicinity of the NMDA receptor. Unless all three conditions are met, the receptor remains closed. Thus, at *resting potential*, NMDA receptors are closed. §§2.5, 2n2, 2n3, 4.36, 4.40, 4.42, 4n4, chapter 5, §§7.6, 7.15, 8.25, 10.87, 10.88, 10n15, A1.10, A1.11, figures 5.2, 5.3.

Nonlocality   When two or more spacelike separated physical systems are measured, outcomes can be correlated. That is, particle behavior can be correlated with that of particles outside the light cone, even if locally this conveys no *information* about any distant particle's state. §§A1.7, A1.8, A1.11.

Normalization   The process of dividing all activity by some mean level, in order to bring it back to some baseline. §§4.31, 5.7, 5.8, 5.10, 5.45, 5.48–5.50.

Noumenal   Referring to things and events as they are, independent of any *experience* of them. Kant: "The concept of a noumenon [is that] of a thing that is not to be thought of as an object of the senses but rather as a thing in itself." §§8.12, 8.13, 8n5, A3.

Object file   An attentionally tracked "figure" integrated as a temporary episodic representation in a working memory buffer that maintains a coherent identity even as the particular contents defining that identity change over time. Attentional processes combine multiple features existing over various modalities into this common bound representation of an object. §§10.30, 10.56, 10.87.

Pattern Causation   Another term for *criterial causation*. Patterns or *phase* relationships in input can be genuinely causal only if there are physical detectors, such as neurons, that respond to patterns or phase in input and then change the physical system in which they reside if the criteria for the presence of a pattern in inputs have been met. Among neurons, a central physical mechanism that facilitates this is coincidence detection. See *Emergent property*, NMDA, *Criterial causation*. §§2.3, 2.6–2.8, chapter 3, figure 3.1, §§4.61, 5.62, 4.69, 4n1, 5.25, 5.51, 6.2, 6.8–6.14, 6.17–6.23, 7.4–7.11, 7.18, 7.19, 7.25, 10.1–10.4, A3n3.

Phase A temporal or spatial offset or shift relative to some point of reference. A waveform has an amplitude and wavelength, but also a phase relative to some point of reference, such as an origin. Amplitude varies independently of phase. For example, if the amplitude of spatial frequencies in an image is scrambled while maintaining phase, the image is still recognizable. However, if phase is scrambled, the image is typically no longer recognizable. Thus information can lie in phase for a system that can decode phase relationships. Under Newtonian and other classical conceptions of causation, the magnitude, amplitude, and frequency of energy were thought to be central to causal efficacy. Indeed, the notion of the conservation of energy applies only to amounts of energy and not phase relationships realized in energy, which are not necessarily conserved. Information and patterns realized in the phase relationships of energy can be created and destroyed. Criterial causation, in contrast to classical conceptions of physical causation, places central causal efficacy in the phase relationships among physical inputs to a physical decoder that responds when criteria for decoding have been met by sending outputs to other decoders that can reset or meet subsequent decoders' criteria. Regarding neurons the term "phase" is used to capture the importance of timing and coincidence detection in neural events both within a neuron and between neurons within a neural circuit. Compare *Pattern causation, Criterial causation, NMDA, Emergent property*, and *Downward causation*. §§1.11, 4.30, 4.33–4.34, 4.43–4.47, 4.51, 4n3, 4n4, 5.43, 5n12.

Phasic Bursty. In phasic as opposed to tonic firing, action potentials cluster in time in brief but rapid *bursts* of *spikes*. Bursts are preceded and followed by periods of relative quiescence. §§2.5, 4.33, 4.35–4.41, 4.47, 4.48, 4.51, 4.53, 5.29–5.51, 10.87.

Physicalism A view that maintains that there is only one fundamental substance or substrate, namely, energy, changing within space-time in a manner that is best described by the laws of physics. See *Monism*. §§1.5. A2.1, A2.2.

Poisson Statistics (1) Spike probabilities at any given time are independent of spike history and (2) spike count variance is proportional to the mean firing rate. §§4.35, 4.51, 4.52.

Possible Worlds Imaginable or conceivable worlds under some assumed set of physical laws. These worlds in no sense really exist. §§8.5, 8.9, 8.11, 8n2.

Posterior Probability The conditional probability that one assigns after seeing the data, for example, the probability that it has rained given that the ground is wet. §§8.17, 8n8.

Postsynaptic Referring to the dendritic side of a synapse.

Preconscious Occurring temporally after sensory detection but prior to experience. §§2.11, 4.22, 9.14, 10.18–10.23, 10.28, 10.29, 10.35, 10.48, 10n1, figure 10.1.

Preconscious Perceptual Buffer   A buffer within which past and present inputs are integrated and operated upon, before a "commitment" is made to how past events gave rise to present inputs, which can be how they will be experienced. This preconscious buffer permits the influence of stages of form and motion analysis that result in the forms and motions that we perceive. §§2.11, 4.22, 9.14, 10.18–10.23, 10.28, 10.29, 10.35, 10.48, 10n1, figure 10.1.

preSMA   Presupplementary motor area. Figure 9.1.

Presynaptic   Referring to the axonal bouton side of a synapse, or the neuron providing input to the synapse.

Principle of the Identity of Indiscernibles   Two things are identical if they share all their properties. §7n11.

Principle of the Indiscernibility of Identicals   If two things are identical, they share all of the same properties. §7n11.

Prior Probability   The probability distribution that reflects one's assessment of likelihoods of randomly selected outcomes before one ever sees actual data. §8n8.

Property Dualism   The monistic or pseudomonistic thesis that a single physical substrate can nonetheless have mutually irreducible properties. §A2.2.

Prototype Theory   The view that people do not represent objects according to abstract definitions of what counts as membership in a category, using Aristotelian *necessary* and sufficient logical conditions, but rather represent objects and experiences in terms of psychological distance from one or more objects or experiences that are the most characteristic instances of a category. *Criterialism* views such prototypes as nonunique instances of the class of things that can optimally meet certain criteria. §§8.15–8.17.

Proposition   An abstraction of that which meets certain criteria. Propositions are not particular, referring to specific facts; they are constraints that are met by particular facts. To understand the meaning of a proposition is to model these constraints. For example, the proposition "fish" is an abstraction of that which any particular concrete fish will be an instance or satisfaction of. §§8n4, 2.9, 2.10, 3.2, 3.7, 3.8, 3n4, 4.6, 7.20, 7.21, 8.4, 8.5, 8.10–8.13, 8.19, 9.16, 10.25–10.27, 10.84, 10n8.

Qualia   Those representations that can be (or now are) operated on by endogenous attention, giving rise to the possibility of volitional attentional tracking, which cannot happen in the absence of this format. They are the representational format that can be bound into attentionally selectable and trackable objects. Qualia are potential contents of *object files*. A quale is a simple or chunked experienced feature that can pop out in a search array in which distractors lack the feature in question. See *Type 1 qualia, Qualia soup, Consciousness, Experience, Information, Criterial causation.* Chapter 10.

Qualia Soup The background of *type 1 qualia* and *type 2 qualia* that are not attended or only minimally attended, but could be endogenously attended if need be. Chapter 10.

Readiness Potential A particular event-related potential waveform typically time-locked to a motor act that has been argued by various researchers to reflect neural activity leading up to either an act, expectation of an act, an intention to act or the conscious willing of an act. There are two components, the readiness potential (RP), which is most evident at medial position Cz, and the lateralized readiness potential (LRP) most evident at lateral positions C3 and C4. Chapter 9.

Realization Thesis Each mental state is *synchronically determined* by underlying microphysical states. See *Causal closure*. §A2.3.

Realized in See *Supervene*.

Receptive Field Also known as a "response field." In vision, the region of the visual field where a stimulus can drive a given neuron. §§1.9, 1.10, 4.7–4.10, 4.18, 4.58, figure 4.2, §5.5, figure 5.6.

Receptor A protein that lies in the plasma membrane or cytoplasm of a cell that responds to input. One or more mobile molecules or "ligands" must bind to specific sites on this protein for a conformational change to take place. This reconformation initiates a change inside the cell. See *Ionotropic*, *Metabotropic*. §§2n2, 2n3, 4.36, 4n4.

Recognition A match to a stored representation in long-term memory. §§4.11, 4.12, 4.14, 4.15, 8.17, 8n7, 10.53.

Reductionism The view that there is no other causality than fundamental particle-level causality, that *emergent properties* are *epiphenomenal*, and that there is no *downward causation*. See *Causal closure*. §A2.1.

Refractory Period The duration over which a neuron cannot be induced to fire again after it has fired. §§4.52, 5.43.

Resting Potential The level of intracellular potential in a neuron "at rest" when the cell is neither excited nor inhibited. §§3.6, 5.4, 5.31, figure 5.2.

Retinotopic Cortex is said to be retinotopically organized when neighboring locations within a visual quadrant are mapped onto neighboring portions of cortex. Each early visual neuron has a receptive field that responds to stimuli falling within a well-defined local region of visual space relative to the point of fixation. §§4.7–4.10.

RP See *Readiness potential*.

Saccade A ballistic eye movement from one location to another. §§4.18, 4.23.

Second Law of Thermodynamics   The entropy of an isolated system that is not at equilibrium will tend to increase over time, approaching a maximum value at equilibrium. §6n1.

SMA   Supplementary motor area. Figure 9.1.

Special Sciences   Any science beyond elementary particle physics that describes how higher-level entities than particles interact and develop. §A2.1.

Spike   A single firing or *action potential* of a neuron.

Spike Timing-dependent Plasticity   A fast form of synaptic potentiation that occurs when a single presynaptic spike precedes a single postsynaptic spike by one to a few milliseconds, depending on the type of dendrite and synapse. §§5.11–5.13.

Stage 1 Buffer   In the case of vision, this is the union of (1) a high-capacity, *retinotopic iconic buffer* probably realized in *V1–V3* processing that encodes features that remain unbound, and (2) a high-capacity spatiotopic *"fragile visual short-term memory"* probably realized in *V4, LOC,* and posterior inferotemporal processing, that encodes bound object information that lasts a few seconds. §§10.15–10.17, 10.30.

Strong Free Will   *Free will* that meets the following conditions: There are (a) multiple courses of physical or mental behavior open to us; (b) we are really be able to choose among them; (c) we must be or must have been able to have chosen otherwise once we have chosen a course of behavior; and (d) the choice must not be dictated by randomness alone, but by us. §7.1.

Sulcus   A concavity in the folded cortical sheet. See *Gyrus*.

Supervene   A higher-level entity supervenes on or is realized in a lower-level entity, if any change in the former entails a change in the latter. What is not allowed under any supervenience theory, or for that matter, any identity theory, is that one physical state simultaneously or even sequentially gives rise to two or more mental states. §2n1.

Synaptic Cleft   The gap between an axonal bouton and a dendrite.

Synaptic Resetting   May involve not just changes in synaptic weight and gain, but also changes in the manner in which a synapse integrates input. §§2.7, 3.9, 3.13, 4.54–4.60, figure 4.5.

Synchronic   "At a given instant," such as the present moment. §§A2.3, A2n4.

Synchrony   Occurs when the probability of neural activity varies sinusoidally at a particular frequency in a population of neurons. §§4.37, 4.42, 4.44–4.47, 4.51, 4n3.

Theta Brainwave   3–8 Hz oscillation evident in the *electroencephalogram* and the *local field potential*. §4n6.

Thing-in-itself   See *Noumenal*.

Three-stage Model of Mental Causation   (1) New physical/informational criteria are set in a neuronal circuit on the basis of preceding physical/mental processing at time t_1, in part via a mechanism of rapid *synaptic resetting* that changes the effective inputs to a *postsynaptic* neuron; (2) At time t_2, inherently variable inputs arrive at the postsynaptic neuron; and (3) at time t_3 physical/informational *criteria* are met or not met, leading to postsynaptic neural firing or not. §§3.9, 7.25.

TMS   Transcranial magnetic stimulation. One or more pulses of magnetic flux at the scalp that disturb underlying neuronal activity are used as a probe of information-processing mediated in part by those neurons.

Tonic Firing Mode   Neurons fire irregularly in a way that matches *Poisson statistics*, at a more or less constant rate. *Bursting* is not present. An example occurs at the *baseline firing rate*. This mode of firing is driven especially by the graded *depolarization* afforded by *AMPA* receptors as opposed to the acute depolarization afforded by *NMDA* receptor opening (see *Phasic*). §§2.5, 3.13, 4.33, 4.35–4.41.

Top-down Processing   The processing of input that is not driven solely by the contents of the input, but also by internal factors. Different types of top-down processing exist. Endogenous attentional processing and the influence of knowledge on processing are instances of cognitive effects on bottom-up processing. Top-down also refers to neuronal feedback from "higher" to "lower" levels of an information-processing hierarchy. §§4.14, 4.21–4.28, 4.45, 4.60, 5.47–5.51.

Trace Conditioning   Occurs when there is a temporal gap between the offset of the conditioned stimulus and the onset of the unconditioned stimulus. §§10.43–10.46.

Tracking   See *Endogenous attention*.

TRN   Thalamic reticular nucleus. §§4.27, 4.28, 4.39, 4.43, 4n11, 5.24.

Type 1 Qualia   *Qualia* that comprise the "basis dimensions" of *experience* within which both learning and *endogenous attention* can operate. Examples include salty, blue, or pain. A type 1 quale, such as red, can "pop out" in a search array among, say, green distractors that lack that quale. It is argued that these are *realized* in the *stage 1 buffer*. §§2.11, 10.55, 10.68, 10.86.

Type 2 Qualia   *Qualia* that are chunked combinations of *type 1 qualia* that are learned with repeated attentional binding; over time they become automatized to serve as a neo-primitive dimension of experience. With practice a type 2 quale can approach "pop out" performance, requiring minimal or no attentional binding in order to be experienced. It is argued that these are realized in the *stage 1 buffer*. §§2.11, 10.56, 10.78, 10.80, 10.88, 10n22.

Type 3 Qualia   *Qualia* that are temporary attentional bindings of *type 1* and *type 2 qualia*. It is argued that these are realized in various working memory buffers, including the executive working memory buffer located in part in circuitry found in the *DLPFC*. §§2.11, 10.56–10.59.

Type-level Criterial Causality   Causality that is not reducible to the transfer of energy (noncriterial causality; e.g., classical mechanics, see appendix 1). It is also not reducible to the transformation of energy familiar from chemical reactions (token-level criterial causality). Because the mechanism of causality is indifferent to the physical particulars of the input, so long as the key criteria are met, there can be, and indeed are, higher-level *emergent* causalities than fundamental particle-level physical causality, even while these higher-level causalities must always be realized in and therefore consistent with lowest-level physical causality. See *Criterial causation, Emergent property, Phase, Information*. §§4.62, 6.9, 6.10, 6n5.

V1   Cortical visual input area, also known as striate cortex, Brodmann area 17, and primary visual cortex. §§4.8, 4.10.

V2   Cortical visual area that is a subdivision of extrastriate cortex. Also known as Brodmann area 18. §§4.8, 4.10.

V4   A visual processing area known to be modulated by *top-down* attentional input. §§4.10, 4.26, 4.47, 4.48, 4.52, 5.33, 5.44, 5.49, 5.50, 10.15, figure 5.6.

Ventral Stream   Visual processing running from V1→V2→V4→inferotemporal lobe, involved in processing what or who is in the input. Also called the "what/who is it?" stream. See *Medial stream, Dorsal stream*. §§4.8, 4.10, 4.15, 4.49.

Volition   See *Will*.

W   The earliest conscious awareness of a *will* or urge to move. Chapter 9.

Will   That mental/neural process which triggers actions in the domains of voluntary or *endogenous* motoric or internal actions. An agent's act of will can be defined as the agent's choice or decision to perform or not perform an action, either later (via formation of distal intentions) or right now (via proximal intentions). Will is the capacity to so choose or decide to act. §§1.1, 3.1–3.4.

Working Memory   Memory that permits temporally extended access to what was presented even after it has disappeared, as well as online manipulation of those contents. It is thought to be low-capacity, and capable of sustaining potentially viewpoint-invariant information as long as attention is engaged. Its bottom-up contents are attentionally selected contents of the *stage 1 buffer*. There may be multiple working memory buffers for different types of representations. For example, a "subsidiary" working memory may be realized for faces in the fusiform face area. An amodal executive working memory area appears to be realized in part in the fronto-parietal attentional network, particularly the *DLPFC*. This is at least the case when processing the external environment. When engaged in internal visualization or daydreaming, a "default network" becomes active, including medial prefrontal cortex, posterior cingulate and the temporoparietal junction. Thus, the working memory that subserves internal visualization does not appear to engage the *DLPFC* as much as when sensory input is attended. §§10.13–10.15, 10.30, 10.31, 10.37–10.41.

Zombie A hypothetical being that is like us in every way and that acts like us in every way except that it lacks *experience*. §10.83.

References

Note: Section, chapter, and figure numbers at the end of each entry indicate where in the present volume the work is mentioned.

Abbott, L. F., & Blum, K. I. (1996). Functional significance of longterm potentiation for sequence learning and prediction. *Cerebral Cortex, 6,* 406–416. §5n6.

Abbott, L. F., & Chance, F. S. (2005). Drivers and modulators from push-pull and balanced synaptic input. *Progress in Brain Research, 149,* 147–155. §5.45.

Abbott, L. F., & Nelson, S. B. (2000). Synaptic plasticity: Taming the beast. *Nature Neuroscience, 3,* 1178–1183. §5.11.

Abbott, L. F., & Regehr, W. G. (2004). Synaptic computation. *Nature, 431,* 796–803. §§3.13, 4.32, 4.55, 4.57, 5.17, 5.36, 5.43.

Abbott, L. F., Varela, J. A., Sen, K., & Nelson, S. B. (1997). Synaptic depression and cortical gain control. *Science, 275,* 220–224. §§4.32, 4.55.

Abeles, M. (1991). *Corticonics: Neural circuits of the cerebral cortex.* Cambridge: Cambridge University Press. §§4.42, 4.54, 4n3.

Afraz, S. R., Kiani, R., & Esteky, H. (2006). Microstimulation of inferotemporal cortex influences face categorization. *Nature, 442*(7103), 692–695. §4.12.

Aharonov, Y., & Bohm, D. (1959). Significance of electromagnetic potentials in quantum theory. *Physical Review, 115,* 485–491. §4.12.

Ahissar, E., & Arieli, A. (2001). Figuring space by time. *Neuron, 32,* 185–201. §4.60.

Ahissar, M., Nahum, M., Nelken, I. and Hochstein, S. (2009). Reverse hierarchies and sensory learning. *Philosophical Transactions of the Royal Society of London, Series B: Biological Sciences, 12,* 364(1515), 285–299. §4.60.

Akbarian, S., Sucher, N. J., Bradley, D., Tafazzoli, A., Trinh, D., Hetrick, W. P., et al. (1996). Selective alterations in gene expression for NMDA receptor subunits in prefrontal cortex of schizophrenics. *Journal of Neuroscience, 16*(1), 19–30. §5n2.

Akkal, D., Dum, R. P., & Strick, P. L. (2007). Supplementary motor area and pre-supplementary motor area: Targets of basal ganglia and cerebellar output. *Journal of Neuroscience, 27,* 10659–10673. Figure 9.1.

Allen, C. B., Celikel, T., & Feldman, D. E. (2003). Long-term depression induced by sensory deprivation during cortical map plasticity in vivo. *Nature Neuroscience, 6,* 291–299. §5.11.

Allen, R. J., Baddeley, A. D., & Hitch, G. J. (2006). Is the binding of visual features in working memory resource-demanding? *Journal of Experimental Psychology: General, 135*(2), 298–313. §4.21.

Amdahl, G. (1967). Validity of the single processor approach to achieving large-scale computing capabilities. *AFIPS Conference Proceedings* (30), 483–485. http://www-inst. eecs.berkeley.edu/~n252/paper/Amdahl.pdf. §8.3.

Amit, D., & Brunel, N. (1997). Model of global spontaneous activity and local structured activity during delay periods in the cerebral cortex. *Cerebral Cortex, 7,* 237–252. §4.32.

Anastassiou, C. A., Perin, R., Markram, H., & Koch, C. (2011). Ephaptic coupling of cortical neurons. *Nature Neuroscience, 14*(2), 217–223. §4.68.

Anderson, E. B., Mitchell, J. F., & Reynolds, J. H. (2011). Attentional modulation of firing rate varies with burstiness across putative pyramidal neurons in macaque visual area V4. *Journal of Neuroscience, 31*(30), 10983–10992. §§4.25, 4.48, 4.52, 4.53, 5.33, 5.38.

Anderson, J. S., Carandini, M., & Ferster, D. (2000). Orientation tuning of input conductance, excitation, and inhibition in cat primary visual cortex. *Journal of Neurophysiology, 84,* 909–926. §4.32.

Antony, L. (2007). Everybody has got it: A defense of non-reductive materialism. In B. McLaughlin & J. Cohen (Eds.), *Contemporary debates in the philosophy of mind* (pp. 143–159). Malden, MA: Blackwell. §A2.2.

Arieli, A., Sterkin, A., Grinvald, A., & Aertsen, A. (1996). Dynamics of ongoing activity: Explanation of the large variability in evoked cortical responses. *Science, 273,* 1868–1871. §4.42.

Armstrong, D. M. (1968). *A materialistic theory of the mind.* London: Routledge & Kegan Paul. §8n9.

Armstrong, K. M., Fitzgerald, J. K., & Moore, T. (2006). Changes in visual receptive fields with microstimulation of frontal cortex. *Neuron, 50,* 791–798. §4.24.

Arndt, M., Nairz, O., Vos-Andreae, J., Keller, C., van der Zouw, G., & Zeilinger, A. (1999). Wave–particle duality of C_{60} molecules. *Nature, 401,* 680–682. §A1.10.

Ashby, F. G., Prinzmetal, W., Ivry, R., & Maddox, T. (1996). A formal theory of illusory conjunctions. *Psychological Review, 103,* 165–192. §4.21.

Aspect, A., Grangier, P., & Roger, G. (1981). Experimental tests of realistic local theories via Bell's theorem. *Physical Review Letters*, *47*, 460. §§A1.6, A1.7.

Aspect, A., Grangier, P., & Roger, G. (1982). Experimental realization of Einstein-Podolsky-Rosen-Bohm Gedankenexperiment: A new violation of Bell's inequalities. *Physical Review Letters*, *49*, 91. §§A1.6, A1.7.

Aspect, A., Dalibard, J., & Roger, G. (1982). Experimental test of Bell's inequalities using time-varying analyzers. *Physical Review Letters*, *49*, 1804. §§A1.6, A1.7.

Assad, J. A. (2003). Neural coding of behavioral relevance in parietal cortex. *Current Opinion in Neurobiology*, *13*, 194–197. §4.25.

Assal, F. D. R., Schwartz, S., & Vuilleumier, P. (2007). Moving with or without will: Functional neural correlates of alien hand syndrome. *Annals of Neurology*, *62*(3), 301. §10.26.

Astafiev, S. V., Shulman, G. L., Stanley, C. M., Snyder, A. Z., Van Essen, D. C., & Corbetta, M. (2003). Functional organization of human intraparietal and frontal cortex for attending, looking, and pointing. *Journal of Neuroscience*, *23*, 4689–4699. §4.24.

Atasoy, D., Ertunc, M., Moulder, K. L., Blackwell, J., Chung, C., Su, J., et al. (2008). Spontaneous and evoked glutamate release activates two populations of NMDA receptors with limited overlap. *Journal of Neuroscience*, *28*, 10151–10166. §4n8.

Autry, A. E., Adachi, M., Nosyreva, E., Na, E. S., Los, M. F., Cheng, P., et al. (2011). NMDA receptor blockade at rest triggers rapid behavioural antidepressant responses. *Nature*, *475*, 91–97. §4n8.

Avery, M. C., Nitz, D. A., Chiba, A. A., & Krichmar, J. L. (2012). Simulation of cholinergic and noradrenergic modulation of behavior in uncertain environments. *Frontiers in Computational Neuroscience*. §§4.22, 5.39.

Axelrod, F. B., & Gold-von Simson, G. (2007). Hereditary sensory and autonomic neuropathies: Types II, III, and IV. *Orphanet Journal of Rare Diseases*, *2*, 39. §10.5.

Ay, H., Buonanno, F. S., Price, B. H., Le, D. A., & Koroshetz, W. J. (1998). Sensory alien hand syndrome: Case report and review of the literature. *Journal of Neurology, Neurosurgery, and Psychiatry*, *65*, 366–369. §10n10.

Baars, B. (1988). *A cognitive theory of consciousness*. New York: Cambridge University Press. §10n6.

Baars, B. (1997). *In the theater of consciousness: The workspace of the mind*. New York: Oxford University Press. §10n6.

Baars, B. J. (2002). The conscious access hypothesis: Origins and recent evidence. *Trends in Cognitive Science*, *6*(1), 47–52. §10n6.

Babiloni, C., Vecchio, F., Rossi, S., De Capua, A., Bartalini, S., Ulivelli, M., & Rossini, P. M. (2007). Human ventral parietal cortex plays a functional role on visuospatial attention and primary consciousness: A repetitive transcranial magnetic stimulation study. *Cerebral Cortex, 17*, 1486–1492. §10.16.

Baddeley, A. D. (1986). *Working memory*. Oxford: Oxford University Press. §10.14.

Baddeley, R., Abbott, L. F., Booth, M. C., Sengpiel, F., Freeman, T., Wakeman, E. A., et al. (1997). Responses of neurons in primary and inferior temporal visual cortices to natural scenes. *Proceedings: Biological Sciences, 264*, 1775–1783. §4.34.

Bading, H., & Greenberg, M. E. (1991). Stimulation of protein tyrosine phosphorylation by NMDA receptor activation. *Science, 253*, 912–914. §5n1.

Bailey, C. H., Montarolo, P., Chen, M., Kandel, E. R., & Schacher, S. (1992). Inhibitors of protein and RNA synthesis block structural changes that accompany long-term heterosynaptic plasticity in *Aplysia*. *Neuron, 9*, 749–758. §5.9.

Bair, W., Koch, C., Newsome, W., & Britten, K. (1994). Power spectrum analysis of bursting cells in area MT in the behaving monkey. *Journal of Neuroscience, 14*, 2870–2892. §4.52.

Bak, P., Tang, C., & Wiesenfield, K. (1987). Self-organized criticality: An explanation of 1/f noise. *Physical Review Letters, 59*, 381–384. §4.42.

Balleine, B. W., & O'Doherty, J. P. (2009). Human and rodent homologies in action control: Corticostriatal determinants of goal-directed and habitual action. *Neuropsychopharmacology, 35*, 48–69. §4.70.

Bangasser, D. A., Waxler, E., Santollo, J., & Shors, T. J. (2006). Trace conditioning and the hippocampus: The importance of contiguity. *Journal of Neuroscience, 26*(34), 8702–8706. §10.44.

Banke, T. G., & Traynelis, S. F. (2003). Activation of NR1/NR2B NMDA receptors. *Nature Neuroscience, 6*, 144–152. §5.4.

Bar, M. (2003). A cortical mechanism for triggering top-down facilitation in visual object recognition. *Journal of Cognitive Neuroscience, 15*(4), 600–609. §4.14.

Bar, M. (2004). Visual objects in context. *Nature Reviews: Neuroscience, 5*(8), 617–629. §4.14.

Bar, M., Kassam, K. S., Ghuman, A. S., Boshyan, J., Schmid, A. M., Dale, A. M., et al. (2006). Top-down facilitation of visual recognition. *Proceedings of the National Academy of Sciences of the United States of America, 103*(2), 449–454. §4.14.

Barcan (Marcus), R. C. (1946). A functional calculus of first order based on strict implication. *Journal of Symbolic Logic, 11*, 1–16. §A3.

Barcan (Marcus), R. C. (1947). The identity of individuals in a strict functional calculus of second order. *Journal of Symbolic Logic, 12*, 12–15. §A3.

Barcelo, F. (2003). The Madrid Card Sorting Test (MCST): A task switching paradigm to study executive attention with event-related potentials. *Brain Research Protocols, 11*, 27–37. §7.11.

Barlow, H. B. (1972). Single units and sensation: A neuron doctrine for perceptual Psychology? *Perception, 1*, 371–394. §§4.11, 4.68.

Baron-Cohen, S., Leslie, A., & Frith, U. (1985). Does the autistic child have a "theory of mind"? *Cognition, 21*, 37–46. §A2n5.

Barone, P., Batardiere, A., Knoblauch, K., & Kennedy, H. (2000). Laminar distribution of neurons in extrastriate areas projecting to visual areas V1 and V4 correlates with the hierarchical rank and indicates the operation of a distance rule. *Journal of Neuroscience, 20*, 3263–3281. §4.49.

Bartlett, J. R., & Doty, R. W. (1974). Response of units in striate cortex of squirrel monkeys to visual and electrical stimuli. *Journal of Neurophysiology, 37*, 621–641. §5.37.

Bartocci, M., Bergqvist, L. L., Lagercrantz, H., & Anand, K. J. S. (2006). Pain activates cortical areas in the preterm newborn brain. *Pain, 122*, 109–117. §10n20.

Bartol, T. M., Jr., Land, B. R., Salpeter, E. E., & Salpeter, M. M. (1991). Monte Carlo simulation of miniature endplate current generation in the vertebrate neuromuscular junction. *Journal of Biophysics, 59*, 1290–1307. §4.66.

Bartos, M., Vida, I., & Jonas, P. (2007). Synaptic mechanisms of synchronized gamma oscillations in inhibitory interneuron networks. *Nature Reviews: Neuroscience, 8*, 45–56. §§4.44, 4.53, 5.40.

Bassett, D. S., Bullmore, E., Verchinski, B. A., Mattay, V. S., Weinberger, D. R., & Meyer-Lindenberg, A. (2008). Hierarchical organization of human cortical networks in health and schizophrenia. *Journal of Neuroscience, 28*(37), 9239–9248. §7.15.

Bastian, J. (1986). Gain control in the electrosensory system mediated by descending inputs to the electrosensory lateral line lobe. *Journal of Neuroscience, 6*, 553–562. §5.45.

Battaglia, F. P., Sutherland, G. R., & McNaughton, B. L. (2004). Hippocampal sharp wave bursts coincide with neocortical "up-state" transitions. *Learning & Memory, 11*, 697–704. §5.42.

Baxter, M. G., Bucci, D. J., Gorman, L. K., Wiley, R. G., & Gallagher, M. (1995). Selective immunotoxic lesions of basal forebrain cholinergic cells: Effects on learning and memory in rats. *Behavioral Neuroscience, 109*, 714–722. §5.44.

Baxter, M. G., Bucci, D. J., Holland, P. C., & Gallagher, M. (1999). Impairments in conditioned stimulus processing and conditioned responding after combined selective removal of hippocampal and neocortical cholinergic input. *Behavioral Neuroscience, 113,* 486–495. §5.44.

Baylis, G., & Driver, J. (1995). One-sided edge assignment in vision: 1. Figure–ground segmentation and attention to objects. *Current Directions in Psychological Science, 4,* 140–146. §4.22.

Baylor, D., Lamb, T., & Yau, K.-W. (1979). The membrane current of a single rod outer segment. *Journal of Physiology, 288,* 589–611. §4.68.

Bear, M. F., Connors, B., & Paradiso, M. (2007). *Neuroscience: Exploring the brain.* Hagerstown, MD: Lippincott Williams & Wilkins. §§4.7, 4.15.

Bechtel, W., & Mundale, J. (1999). Multiple realizability revisited: Linking cognitive and neural states. *Philosophy of Science, 66,* 175–207. §3.11.

Beck, J., Elsner, A., & Silverstein, C. (1977). Position uncertainty and the perception of apparent movement. *Perception & Psychophysics, 21*(1), 33–38. §10.18.

Beggs, J. M., & Plenz, D. (2003). Neuronal avalanches in neocortical circuits. *Journal of Neuroscience, 23,* 11167–11177. §4.42.

Béïque, J. C., Na, Y., Kuhl, D., Worley, P. F., & Huganir, R. L. (2011). Arc-dependent synapse-specific homeostatic plasticity. *Proceedings of the National Academy of Sciences of the United States of America, 108,* 816–821. §5.7.

Bekinschtein, T. A., Peeters, M., Shalom, D., & Sigman, M. (2011). Sea slugs, subliminal pictures, and vegetative state patients: Boundaries of consciousness in classical conditioning. *Frontiers in Psychology, 2,* 337. §10.43.

Bell, A. H., Hadj-Bouziane, F., Frihauf, J. B., Tootell, R. B., & Ungerleider, L. G. (2009). Object representations in the temporal cortex of monkeys and humans as revealed by functional magnetic resonance imaging. *Journal of Neurophysiology, 101*(2), 688–700. §4.12.

Bell, J. S. (1966). On the problem of hidden variables in quantum mechanics. *Reviews of Modern Physics, 38,* 447. §A1.6.

Bell, J. S. (1971). Introduction to the hidden variable question. In *Proceedings of the International School of Physics "Enrico Fermi," Course IL, Foundations of Quantum Mechanics,* 171–181. Academic Press. §A1.6.

Bell, J. S. (1981). Bertlmann's socks and the nature of reality. *Journal de Physique,* Colloque C2, no. 3, bk. 42, 41–61. §A1.6.

Bell, J. S. (1987). *Speakable and unspeakable in quantum mechanics.* Cambridge: Cambridge University Press. §A1.6.

Ben-Ari, Y., Gaiarsa, J.-L., Tyzio, R., & Khazipov, R. (2007). GABA: A pioneer transmitter that excites immature neurons and generates primitive oscillations. *Physiological Reviews, 87,* 1215–1284. §5n9.

Bender, V. A., Bender, K. J., Brasier, D. J., & Feldman, D. E. (2006). Two coincidence detectors for spike timing—dependent plasticity in somatosensory cortex. *Journal of Neuroscience, 26*, 4166–4177. §5.28.

Bennett, C. H. (1982). The thermodynamics of computation—A review. *International Journal of Theoretical Physics, 21*, 905–940. §A1n3.

Bennett, C. H. (2003). Notes on Landauer's principle, reversible computation, and Maxwell's demon. *Studies in History and Philosophy of Modern Physics, 34*, 501–510. §A1n3.

Berger, T. K., Silberberg, G., Perin, R., & Markram, H. (2010). Brief bursts self-inhibit and correlate the pyramidal network. *PLoS Biology, 8*(9), e1000473. §4.50.

Berretta, N., & Jones, R. S. (1996). Tonic facilitation of glutamate release by presynaptic N-methyl-D-aspartate autoreceptors in the entorhinal cortex. *Neuroscience, 75*, 339–344. §5.28.

Berridge, C. W., & Waterhouse, B. D. (2003). The locus coeruleus-noradrenergic system: Modulation of behavioral state and state-dependent cognitive processes. *Brain Research Reviews, 42*, 33–84. §5.38.

Bi, G. Q., & Poo, M. M. (1998). Synaptic modifications in cultured hippocampal neurons: Dependence on spike timing, synaptic strength, and postsynaptic cell type. *Journal of Neuroscience, 18*, 10464–10472. §§5.11, 5n5.

Bi, G. Q., & Poo, M. M. (2001). Synaptic modification of correlated activity: Hebb's postulate revisited. *Annual Review of Neuroscience, 24*, 139–166. §5.11.

Bibbig, A., Traub, R. D., & Whittington, M. A. (2002). Synapses: A network model and the plasticity of excitatory and inhibitory long-range synchronization of γ and β oscillations. *Journal of Neurophysiology, 88*, 1634–1654. §4.44.

Bichot, N. P., Rossi, A. F., & Desimone, R. (2005). Parallel and serial neural mechanisms for visual search in macaque area V4. *Science, 308*, 529–534. §4.45.

Bickle, J. (1998). *Psychoneural reduction: The new wave.* Cambridge, MA: MIT Press. §3.11.

Bickle, J. (2003). *Philosophy and neuroscience: A ruthlessly reductive account.* Dordrecht: Kluwer Academic. §§3.11, A2n1.

Bickle, J. (2006a). Reducing mind to molecular pathways: Explicating the reductionism implicit in current cellular and molecular Neuroscience. *Synthese, 151*, 411–434. §3.11.

Bickle, J. (2006b). Ruthless reductionism in recent neuroscience. *IEEE Transactions on Systems, Man and Cybernetics, Part C: Applications and Reviews, 36*, 134–140. §3.11.

Binder, P.-M. (2008). Philosophy of science: Theories of almost everything. *Nature, 455*, 884–885. §A1n3.

Binzegger, T., Douglas, R. J., & Martin, K. A. (2004). A quantitative map of the circuit of cat primary visual cortex. *Journal of Neuroscience, 24*(39), 8441–8453. §4.32.

Bisley, J. W., & Goldberg, M. E. (2010). Attention, intention, and priority in the parietal lobe. *Annual Review of Neuroscience, 33*, 1–21. §4.24.

Blaise, B. (2011). Introduction to parallel computing. https://computing.llnl.gov/tutorials/parallel_comp/. §8.1.

Blakemore, S. J., Wolpert, D. M., & Frith, C. D. (1998). Central cancellation of self-produced tickle sensation. *Nature Neuroscience, 1*(7), 635–640. §9n6.

Blaser, E., Pylyshyn, Z. W., & Holcombe, A. O. (2000). Tracking an object through feature space. *Nature, 408*, 196–199. §4.24.

Bliss, T. V., & Lomo, T. (1973). Long-lasting potentiation of synaptic transmission in the dentate area of the anaesthetized rabbit following stimulation of the perforant path. *Journal of Physiology, 232*, 331–356. §5.6.

Block, N. (Ed.). (1980a). *Readings in Philosophy of Psychology*, 2 vols. Cambridge, MA: Harvard University Press. §A2n5.

Block, N. (1980b). Troubles with functionalism. In N. Block (Ed.), *Readings in Philosophy of Psychology*, 2 vols. Cambridge, MA: Harvard University Press. §A2n5.

Block, N. (1997). On a confusion about a function of consciousness. In N. Block, O. Flanagan, & G. Güzeldere (Eds.), *The Nature of Consciousness*. Cambridge, MA: MIT Press. §10.33.

Block, N. (2003). Do causal powers drain away? *Philosophy and Phenomenological Research, 67*(1), 133–150. §A2.1.

Bode, S., He, A. H., Soon, C. S., Trampel, R., Turner, R., & Haynes, J.-D. (2011). Tracking the unconscious generation of free decisions using ultra-high field fMRI. *PLoS ONE, 6*(6), e21612. §9.14.

Boehm, J., Kang, M. G., Johnson, R. C., Esteban, J., Huganir, R. L., & Malinow, R. (2006). Synaptic incorporation of AMPA receptors during LTP is controlled by a PKC phosphorylation site on GluR1. *Neuron, 51*, 213–225. §5.9.

Boettiger, C. A., & D'Esposito, M. (2005). Frontal networks for learning and executing arbitrary stimulus-response associations. *Journal of Neuroscience, 25*, 2723–2732. §7.11.

Bohm, D. (1952a). A suggested interpretation of the quantum theory in terms of "hidden variables," I. *Physical Review, 85*, 166–179. §A1.6.

Bohm, D. (1952b). A suggested interpretation of the quantum theory in terms of "hidden variables," II. *Physical Review, 85*, 180–193. §A1.6.

Bohm, D., & Hiley, B. J. (1993). *The undivided universe*. London: Routledge. §A1.6.

Bohr, N. [1934] (1987). *Atomic theory and the description of nature*. Reprinted as *The philosophical writings of Niels Bohr* (Vol. I). Woodbridge: Ox Bow Press. §A1.5.

Bohr, N. (1958/1987). *Essays 1932–1957 on atomic physics and human knowledge*. Reprinted as *The philosophical writings of Niels Bohr* (Vol. II). Woodbridge: Ox Bow Press. §A1.5.

Bohr, N. (1963/1987). *Essays 1958–1962 on atomic physics and human knowledge*. Reprinted as *The philosophical writings of Niels Bohr* (Vol. III). Woodbridge: Ox Bow Press. §A1.5.

Boly, M., Faymonville, M. E., Schnakers, C., Peigneux, P., Lambermont, B., Phillips, C., Lancellotti, P., Luxen, A., Lamy, M., Moonen, G., Maquet, P., & Laureys, S. (2008). Perception of pain in the minimally conscious state with PET activation: An observational study. *Lancet Neurology*, *7*(11), 1013–1020. §10.66.

Bonds, A. B. (1993). The encoding of cortical contrast gain control. In R. Shapley & D. M.-K. Lam (Eds.), *Contrast Sensitivity* (pp. 215–230). Cambridge, MA: MIT Press. §5.36.

Bonhoeffer, T., & Yuste, R. (2002). Spine motility: Phenomenology, mechanisms, and function. *Neuron*, *35*(6), 1019–1027. §4.55.

Boraud, T., Brown, P., Goldberg, J. A., Graybiel, A. M., & Magill, P. J. (2005). Oscillations in the basal ganglia: The good, the bad, and the unexpected. In J. P. Bolam, C. A. Ingham, & P. J. Magill (Eds.), *The basal ganglia VIII* (pp. 3–24). New York: Springer. §4n12.

Börgers, C., & Kopell, N. J. (2008). Gamma oscillations and stimulus selection. *Neural Computation*, *20*, 383–414. §5.50.

Bormann, J. O., Hamill, P., & Sakmann, B. (1987). Mechanism of anion permeation through channels gated by glycine and gamma-amino butyric acid in mouse cultured spinal neurons. *Journal of Physiology*, *385*, 243–286. §A1.10.

Braitenberg, V., & Schuz, A. (1991). *Anatomy of the cortex: Statistics and geometry*. Berlin: Springer-Verlag. §4.54.

Brasier, D. J., & Feldman, D. E. (2008). Synapse-specific expression of functional presynaptic NMDA receptors in rat somatosensory cortex. *Journal of Neuroscience*, *28*, 2199–2211. §5.28.

Braun, J. (1994). Visual search among items of different salience: Removal of visual attention mimics a lesion in extrastriate area V4. *Journal of Neuroscience*, *14*(2), 554–567. §10.73.

Braun, J. (1998). Vision and attention: The role of training. *Nature*, *393*, 424–425. §10.73.

Braun, J., & Julesz, B. (1998). Withdrawing attention at little or no cost: Detection and discrimination tasks. *Perception & Psychophysics*, *60*(1), 1–23. §10.73.

Braun, J., & Sagi, D. (1991). Texture-based tasks are little affected by second tasks requiring peripheral or central attentive fixation. *Perception, 20*(4), 483–500. §10.73.

Breitmeyer, B. G., Kafaligönül, H., Öğmen, H., Mardon, L., Todd, S., & Ziegler, R. (2006). Para- and metacontrast masking reveal different effects on brightness and contour visibility. *Vision Research, 46*, 2645–2658. §10.50.

Brembs, B. (2008). The importance of being active. *Journal of Neurogenetics, 23*, 120–126. §4.70.

Brembs, B. (2009). Mushroom bodies regulate habit formation in Drosophila. *Current Biology, 19*, 1351–1355. §4.70.

Brembs, B. (2011). Towards a scientific concept of free will as a biological trait: Spontaneous actions and decision-making in invertebrates. *Proceedings of the Royal Society of London: Biological Sciences, 278*(1707), 930–939. §§4.70, 10.3.

Bremmer, F., Kubischik, M., Hoffmann, K. P., & Krekelberg, B. (2009). Neural dynamics of saccadic suppression. *Journal of Neuroscience, 29*, 12374–12383. §4.60.

Brentano, F. (1874). *Psychologie vom empirischen Standpunkt.* Leipzig: Duncker & Humblot. §8.5.

Brescamp, J. W., van Boxtel, J. J., Knapen, T. H., & Blake, R. (2010). A dissociation of attention and awareness in phase-sensitive but not phase-insensitive visual channels. *Journal of Cognitive Neuroscience, 22*(10), 2326–2344. §§10.49, 10.50.

Bressan, P., & Pizzighello, S. (2008). The attentional cost of inattentional blindness. *Cognition, 106*, 370–383. §10.28.

Bressler, S. L., & Kelso, J. A. S. (2001). Cortical coordination dynamics and cognition. *Trends in Cognitive Neuroscience, 5*, 26–36. §4.69.

Bruce, C., Desimone, R., & Gross, C. G. (1981). Visual properties of neurons in polysensory area in superior temporal sulcus of the macaque. *Journal of Neurophysiology, 46*(2), 369–384. §4.10.

Bruno, R. M., & Sakmann, B. (2006). Cortex is driven by weak but synchronously active thalamocortical synapses. *Science, 312*, 1622–1627. §4.32.

Brush, S. G. (1976). Irreversibility and indeterminism: Fourier to Heisenberg. *Journal of the History of Ideas, 37*(4), 603–630. §A1.4.

Bucci, D. J., Holland, P. C., & Gallagher, M. (1998). Removal of cholinergic input to rat posterior parietal cortex disrupts incremental processing of conditioned stimuli. *Journal of Neuroscience, 18*, 8038–8046. §5.44.

Buckner, R. L., Andrews-Hanna, J. R., & Schacter, D. L. (2008). The brain's default network: Anatomy, function, and relevance to disease. *Annals of the New York Academy of Sciences, 1124*, 1–38.

Buffalo, E. A., Fries, P., Landman, R., Liang, H., & Desimone, R. (2010). A backward progression of attentional effects in the ventral stream. *Proceedings of the National Academy of Sciences of the United States of America, 107*(1), 361–365. §§4.49, 5.49.

Buffalo, E. A., Fries, P., Landman, R., Buschman, T. J., & Desimone, R. (2011). Laminar differences in gamma and alpha coherence in the ventral stream. *Proceedings of the National Academy of Sciences of the United States of America, 108*(27), 11262–11267. §4.49.

Buhl, E. H., Tamás, G., & Fisahn, A. (1998). Cholinergic activation and tonic excitation induce persistent gamma oscillations in mouse somatosensory cortex *in vitro*. *Journal of Physiology, 513*, 117–126. §5.40.

Buhl, E. H., Halasy, K., & Somogyi, P. (1994). Diverse sources of hippocampal unitary inhibitory postsynaptic potentials and the number of synaptic release sites. *Nature, 368*, 823–828. §5.3.

Buhl, D. L., Harris, K. D., Hormuzdi, S. G., Monyer, H., & Buzsáki, G. (2003). Selective impairment of hippocampal gamma oscillations in connexin-36 knock-out mouse in vivo. *Journal of Neuroscience, 23*, 1013–1018. §4.44.

Bullmore, E. T., Frangou, S., & Murray, R. M. (1997). The dysplastic net hypothesis: An integration of developmental and dysconnectivity theories of schizophrenia. *Schizophrenia Research, 28*, 143–156. §5.24.

Bundesen, C. (1990). A theory of visual attention. *Psychological Review, 97*, 523–547. §4.25.

Bunzeck, N., & Duzel, E. (2006). Absolute coding of stimulus novelty in the human substantia nigra/VTA. *Neuron, 51*, 369–379. §4.70.

Buonanno, A. (2011). Presynaptic NMDA receptors also make the switch. *Nature Neuroscience, 14*(3), 274–276. §5.28.

Burge, T. (1993). Mind-body causation and explanatory practice. In J. Heil & A. Mele (Eds.), *Mental causation* (pp. 96–120). Oxford: Clarendon Press. §1.5.

Burk, J. A., & Sarter, M. (2001). Dissociation between the attentional functions mediated via basal forebrain cholinergic and GABAergic neurons. *Neuroscience, 105*, 899–909. §§5.44, 5.46.

Burrone, J., & Murthy, V. N. (2003). Synaptic gain control and homeostasis. *Current Opinion in Neurobiology, 13*, 560–567. §5.7.

Buschman, T. J., & Miller, E. K. (2007). Top-down versus bottom-up control of attention in the prefrontal and posterior parietal cortices. *Science, 315*, 1860–1862. §§4.23, 4.24.

Butterfield, J. (1998). Determinism. In E. Craig (Ed.), *Routledge encyclopedia of philosophy* (Vol. 3, pp. 33–39). London: Routledge. §7.18.

Buxhoeveden, D. P., & Casanova, M. F. (2002). The minicolumn and evolution of the brain. *Brain, Behavior and Evolution, 60*(3), 125–151. §5.16.

Buzsáki, G. (2006). *Rhythms of the brain.* New York: Oxford University Press. §§4.42, 4n7.

Buzsáki, G. (2010). Neural syntax: Cell assemblies, synapsembles, and readers. *Neuron, 68*, 362–385. §§4.55, 4.60, 8.7.

Buzsáki, G., & Chrobak, J. J. (1995). Temporal structure in spatially organized neuronal ensembles: A role for interneuronal networks. *Current Opinion in Neurobiology, 5*, 504–510. §§4.44, 4.50, 4.53, 4n3, 5.3, 5.39, 5.43.

Buzsáki, G., Horvath, Z., Urioste, R., Hetke, J., & Wise, K. (1992). High-frequency network oscillation in the hippocampus. *Science, 256*, 1025–1027. §4.35.

Buzsáki, G., Leung, L. S., & Vanderwolf, C. H. (1983). Cellular bases of hippocampal EEG in the behaving rat. *Brain Research Reviews, 6*, 139–171. §4.44.

Cafaro, J., & Rieke, F. (2010). Noise correlations improve response fidelity and stimulus encoding. *Nature, 468*, 964–967. §4.42.

Cameron, I. G., Watanabe, M., Pari, G., & Munoz, D. P. (2010). Executive impairment in Parkinson's disease: Response automaticity and task switching. *Neuropsychologia, 48*(7), 1948–1957. §9.9.

Campbell, D. T. (1974). "Downward causation" in hierarchically organized biological systems. In F. J. Ayala and T. Dobzhansky (Eds.), *Studies in the philosophy of biology* (pp. 179–186). London: Macmillan. §§1.15, A2.2.

Cannon, W. (1942). Voodoo death. *American Anthropologist, 44*, 169–181. §10.5.

Caporale, N., & Dan, Y. (2008). Spike timing-dependent plasticity: A Hebbian learning rule. *Annual Review of Neuroscience, 31*, 25–46. §5.11.

Carandini, M., & Heeger, D. J. (2012). Normalization as a canonical neural computation. *Nature Reviews: Neuroscience, 13*, 51–62. §5.45.

Carew, T. (2000). *Behavioral neurobiology.* Sunderland, MA: Sinauer. §1.11.

Carey, S., & Xu, F. (2001). Infants' knowledge of objects: Beyond object files and object tracking. *Cognition, 80*, 1–2, 179–213. §10.30.

Carlén, M., Meletis, K., Siegle, J. H., Cardin, J. A., Futai, K., Vierling-Claassen, D., et al. (2012). A critical role for NMDA receptors in parvalbumin interneurons for gamma rhythm induction and behavior. *Molecular Psychiatry, 17*, 537–548. §5.42.

Carmena, J. M., Lebedev, M. A., Crist, R. E., O'Doherty, J. E., Santucci, D. M., Dimitrov, D. F., et al. (2003). Learning to control a brain-machine interface for reaching and grasping by primates. *PLoS Biology, 1*(2), E42. §10n9.

Carrasco, M., Ling, S., & Read, S. (2004). Attention alters appearance. *Nature Neuroscience, 7*(3), 308–313. §10.48.

Carretié, L., Hinojosa, J. A., Mercado, F., & Tapia, M. (2005). Cortical response to subjectively unconscious danger. *NeuroImage, 24*(3), 615–623. §4.14.

Carruth, M., & Magee, J. C. (1999). Dendritic voltage-gated ion channels regulate the action potential firing mode of hippocampal CA1 pyramidal neurons. *Journal of Neurophysiology, 82,* 1895–1901. §5.20.

Casanova, M. F., Buxhoeveden, D., & Gomez, J. (2003). Disruption in the inhibitory architecture of the cell minicolumn: Implications for autism. *Neuroscientist, 9*(6), 496–507. §4.33.

Casanova, M. F., Buxhoeveden, D., Switala, A., & Roy, E. (2002). Minicolumn pathology in autism. *Neurology, 58,* 428–432. §4.33.

Cashmore, A. R. (2010). The Lucretian swerve: The biological basis of human behavior and the criminal justice system. *Proceedings of the National Academy of Sciences of the United States of America, 107,* 4499–4504. §§7.12, 9.14.

Castellucci, V. F., Kandel, E. R., Schwartz, J. H., Wilson, F. D., Nairn, A. C., & Greengard, P. (1980). Intracellular injection of the catalytic subunit of cyclic AMP-dependent protein kinase simulates facilitation of transmitter release underlying behavioral sensitization in *Aplysia. Proceedings of the National Academy of Sciences of the United States of America, 77,* 7492–7496. §5.9.

Cattaneo, A., Maffei, L., & Morrone, C. (1981). Patterns in the discharge of simple and complex visual cortical cells. *Proceedings of the Royal Society of London, Series B: Biological Sciences, 212,* 279–297. §5.36.

Cavanaugh, J., Alvarez, B. D., & Wurtz, R. H. (2006). Enhanced performance with brain stimulation: Attentional shift or visual cue? *Journal of Neuroscience, 26,* 11347–11358. §4.24.

Cavanaugh, J., & Wurtz, R. H. (2004). Subcortical modulation of attention counters change blindness. *Journal of Neuroscience, 24,* 11236–11243. §4.24.

Chakravarthy, V. S., Joseph, D., & Bapi, R. S. (2010). What do the basal ganglia do? A modeling perspective. *Biological Cybernetics, 103*(3), 237–253. §§7.15, 9.8.

Chalmers, D. (1996). *The conscious mind.* Oxford: Oxford University Press. §§8.11, 10.83, §A3.

Chalmers, D. (2002). On sense and intension. *Philosophical Perspectives, 16,* 135–182. §8.11.

Chalmers, D. (2005). Two-dimensional semantics. In E. Lepore & B. Smith (Eds.), *The Oxford handbook of philosophy of language.* Oxford: Oxford University Press. §8.11.

Chalmers, D. (2006). Foundations of two-dimensional semantics. In M. Garcia-Carpintero & J. Macià (Eds.), *Two-dimensional semantics: Foundations and applications* (pp. 55–140) Oxford: Oxford University Press. §8.11.

Chance, F. S., Abbott, L. F., & Reyes, A. D. (2002). Gain modulation from background synaptic input. *Neuron, 35,* 773–782. §5.45.

Changeux, J. P., Courège, P., & Danchin, A. (1973). A theory of the epigenesis of neuronal networks by selective stabilization of synapses. *Proceedings of the National Academy of Sciences of the United States of America, 70*(10), 2974–2978. §7n7.

Changeux, J. P., & Danchin, A. (1976). Selective stabilisation of developing synapses as a mechanism for the specification of neuronal networks. *Nature, 264,* 705–712. §5.24

Chappell, J., McMahan, R., Chiba, A., & Gallagher, M. (1998). A re-examination of the role of basal forebrain cholinergic neurons in spatial working memory. *Neuropharmacology, 37,* 481–487. §5.44.

Chavkin, C. (2000). Dynorphins are endogenous opioid peptides released from granule cells to act neurohumorly and inhibit excitatory neurotransmission in the hippocampus. *Progress in Brain Research, 125,* 363–367. §5.17

Chelazzi, L., Miller, E. K., Duncan, J., & Desimone, R. (1993). A neural basis for visual search in inferior temporal cortex. *Nature, 363,* 345–347. §5.50

Chen, G. Q., Cui, C., Mayer, M. L., & Gouaux, E. (1999). Functional characterization of a potassium-selective prokaryotic glutamate receptor. *Nature, 402,* 817–821. §2n3.

Chen, L., & Huang, L. Y. (1992). Protein kinase C reduces Mg2+ block of NMDA-receptor channels as a mechanism of modulation. *Nature, 356,* 521–523. §5n1.

Chergui, K., Akaoka, H., Charlety, P. J., Saunier, C. F., Buda, M., & Chouvet, G. (1994). Subthalamic nucleus modulates burst firing of nigral dopamine neurones via NMDA receptors. *Neuroreport, 5,* 1185–1188. §4.40.

Childs, J. A., & Blair, J. L. (1997). Valproic acid treatment of epilepsy in autistic twins. *Journal of Neuroscience Nursing, 29,* 244–248. §4.33.

Chisholm, R. (1957). *Perceiving: A philosophical study.* Ithaca: Cornell University Press. §8.5.

Chiu, J., DeSalle, R., Lam, H.-M., Meisel, L., & Coruzzi, G. (1999). Molecular evolution of glutamate receptors: A primitive signaling mechanism that existed before plants and animals diverged. *Molecular Biology and Evolution, 16*(6), 826–838. §§2n3, 4n4.

Chklovskii, D. B. (2004). Synaptic connectivity and neuronal morphology: Two sides of the same coin. *Neuron, 43,* 609–617. §5.21.

Chklovskii, D. B., Mel, B. W., & Svoboda, K. (2004). Cortical rewiring and information storage. *Nature, 431,* 782–788. §5.15.

Cho, K. H., Jang, H. J., Jo, Y., Singer, W., & Rhie, D. J. (2012). Cholinergic induction of input specific late-phase LTP via localized Ca2+ release in the visual cortex. *Journal of Neuroscience, 32*(13), 4520–4530. §10.88.

Choi, H., & Scholl, B. J. (2006). Perceiving causality after the fact: Postdiction in the temporal dynamics of causal perception. *Perception, 35*(3), 385–399. §10.18.

Chou, W.-L., & Yeh, S.-L. (2012). Object-based attention occurs regardless of object awareness. *Psychonomic Bulletin & Review.* doi:10.3758/s13423-011-0207-5. §10.31.

Chow, K. L. (1951). Effect of partial extirpations of the posterior association cortex on visually mediated behavior. *Comparative Psychological Monographs, 20,* 187–217. §10n12.

Chun, M. M. (2000). Contextual cueing of visual attention. *Trends in Cognitive Sciences, 4*(5), 170–178. §4.14.

Chun, M. M., & Potter, M. C. (1995). A two-stage model for multiple-target detection in rapid serial visual presentation. *Journal of Experimental Psychology: Human Perception and Performance, 21*(1), 109–127. §10.13.

Chung, S., Li, X., & Nelson, S. B. (2002). Short-term depression at thalamocortical synapses contributes to rapid adaptation of cortical sensory responses in vivo. *Neuron, 34,* 437–446. §4.55.

Churchland, P. M. (1985). Reduction, qualia and the direct inspection of brain states. *Journal of Philosophy, 82,* 8–28. §§10.5, A2n1.

Churchland, P. S. (1986). *Neurophilosophy.* Cambridge, MA: MIT Press. §1n1.

Churchland, P. M. (1989). *A neurocomputational perspective.* Cambridge, MA: MIT Press. §1n1.

Churchland, P. S. (1986). *Neurophilosophy.* Cambridge, MA: MIT Press. §1n1.

Churchland, P. (2007). The evolving fortunes of eliminative materialism. In B. McLaughlin & J. Cohen (Eds.), *Contemporary debates in the philosophy of mind* (pp. 160–181). Malden, MA: Blackwell. §§10.5, A2.1.

Churchland, P. M., & Churchland, P. S. (1997). Recent work on consciousness: Philosophical, theoretical, and empirical. *Seminars in Neurology, 17*(2), 101–108. §8.18.

Cobb, S. R., Buhl, E. H., Halasy, K., Paulsen, O., & Somogyi, P. (1995). Synchronization of neuronal activity in hippocampus by individual GABAergic interneurons. *Nature, 378,* 75–78. §§4.44, 5.3.

Cohen, M. A., Alvarez, G. A., & Nakayama, K. (2011). Natural-scene perception requires attention. *Psychological Science, 22*(9), 1165–1172. §4.14.

Cohen, M. A., Cavanagh, P., Chun, M. M., & Nakayama, K. (2012). The attentional requirements of consciousness. *Trends in Cognitive Sciences, 16,* 8,411–417. §§10.17, 10.39, 10.65.

Cohen, M. R., & Maunsell, J. H. R. (2009). Attention improves performance primarily by reducing interneuronal correlations. *Nature Neuroscience, 12,* 1594–1600. §§4.48, 4.49, 4.53, 5.50

Cohen, M. R., & Maunsell, J. H. R. (2011). Using neuronal populations to study the mechanisms underlying spatial and feature attention. *Neuron, 70,* 1192–1204. §§4.25, 4.48, 4.49, 4.53, 5.38, 5.39, 5.45, 5.50, 10.32.

Colbert, C. M., & Johnston, D. (1996). Axonal action-potential initiation and Na$^+$ channel densities in the soma and axon initial segment of subicular pyramidal neurons. *Journal of Neuroscience, 16*(21), 6676–6686. §4n2.

Colgin, L. L., Denninger, T., Fyhn, M., Hafting, T., Bonnevie, T., Jensen, O., et al. (2009). Frequency of gamma oscillations routes flow of information in the hippocampus. *Nature, 462,* 353–357. §4.44.

Collingridge, G. L. (1985). Long term potentiation in the hippocampus: Mechanisms of initiation and modulation by neurotransmitters. *Trends in Pharmacological Sciences, 6,* 407–411. §5n9.

Colomb, J., & Brembs, B. (2010). The biology of psychology: "Simple" conditioning? *Communicative & Integrative Biology, 3,* 142–145. §4.70.

Colquhoun, D., & Hawkes, A. G. (1981). On the stochastic properties of single ion channels. *Proceedings of the Royal Society of London, Series B: Biological Sciences, 211*(1183), 205–235. §5.25.

Colquhoun, D., & Hawkes, A. G. (1982). On the stochastic properties of bursts of single ion channel openings and of clusters of bursts. *Philosophical Transactions of the Royal Society of London, Series B: Biological Sciences, 300,* 1–59. §5.25.

Colquhoun, D., & Hawkes, A. G. (1987). A note on correlations in single ion channel records. *Proceedings of the Royal Society of London, Series B: Biological Sciences, 230*(1258), 15–52. §5.25.

Colquhoun, D., & Hawkes, A. G. (1995). Desensitization of N-methyl-D-aspartate receptors: A problem of interpretation. *Proceedings of the National Academy of Sciences of the United States of America, 92,* 10327–10329. §5.25.

Compte, A., Constantinidis, C., Tegner, J., Raghavachari, S., Chafee, M. V., Goldman-Rakic, P. S., et al. (2003). Temporally irregular mnemonic persistent activity in prefrontal neurons of monkeys during a delayed response task. *Journal of Neurophysiology, 90,* 3441–3454. §4.52.

Compton, A. H. (1931). The uncertainty principle and free will. *Science, 74,* 1911. §7.17.

Conci, M., Böbel, E., Matthias, E., Keller, I., Müller, H. J., & Finke, K. (2009). Preattentive surface and contour grouping in Kanizsa figures: Evidence from parietal extinction. *Neuropsychologia, 47*(3), 726–732. §10.35.

Connor, C. (2005). Friends and grandmothers. *Nature, 435*(7045), 1036–1037. §4.11.

Constantinidis, C., & Goldman-Rakic, P. S. (2002). Correlated discharges among putative pyramidal neurons and interneurons in primate prefrontal cortex. *Journal of Neurophysiology, 88*, 3487–3497. §4.52.

Constantinople, C. M., & Bruno, R. M. (2011). Effects and mechanisms of wakefulness on local cortical networks. *Neuron, 69*(6), 1061–1068. §4.22.

Conti, F., Barbaresi, P., Melone, M., & Ducati, A. (1999). Neuronal and glial localization of NR1 and NR2A/B subunits of the NMDA receptor in the human cerebral cortex. *Cerebral Cortex, 9*, 110–120. §§5.5, 5.28.

Cools, R., Barker, R. A., Sahakian, B. J., & Robbins, T. W. (2003). L-Dopa medication remediates cognitive inflexibility, but increases impulsivity in patients with Parkinson's disease. *Neuropsychologia, 41*, 1431–1441. §9.8.

Cools, R., Clark, L., & Robbins, T. W. (2004). Differential responses in human striatum and prefrontal cortex to changes in object and rule relevance. *Journal of Neuroscience, 24*, 1129–1135. §9.8.

Cools, R., Ivry, R. B., & D'Esposito, M. (2006). The human striatum is necessary for responding to changes in stimulus relevance. *Journal of Cognitive Neuroscience, 18*(12), 1973–1983. §§7.11, 7.15, 9.9.

Cooper, D. C. (2002). The significance of action potential bursting in the brain reward circuit. *Neurochemistry International, 41*, 333–340. §5.36.

Corbetta, M., & Shulman, G. L. (2002). Control of goal-directed and stimulus-driven attention in the brain. *Nature Reviews: Neuroscience, 3*(3), 201–215. §4.26.

Corbetta, M., Akbudak, E., Conturo, T. E., Snyder, A. Z., Ollinger, J. M., Drury, H. A., et al. (1998). A common network of functional areas for attention and eye movements. *Neuron, 21*(4), 761–773. §4.23.

Corkin, S. (2002). What's new with the amnesic patient H.M.? *Nature Reviews: Neuroscience, 3*(2), 153–160. §10.44.

Corlew, R., Wang, Y., Ghermazien, H., Erisir, A., & Philpot, B. D. (2007). Developmental switch in the contribution of presynaptic and postsynaptic NMDA receptors to long-term depression. *Journal of Neuroscience, 27*, 9835–9845. §5.28.

Corlew, R., Brasier, D. J., Feldman, D. E., & Philpot, B. D. (2008). Presynaptic NMDA receptors: Newly appreciated roles in cortical synaptic function and plasticity. *Neuroscientist, 14*, 609–625. §5.28.

Couch, M. (2004). Discussion: A defense of Bechtel and Mundale. *Philosophy of Science, 71*, 198–204. §3.11.

Coull, J. T., & Nobre, A. C. (1998). Where and when to pay attention: The neural systems for directing attention to spatial locations and to time intervals as revealed by both PET and fMRI. *Journal of Neuroscience, 18*, 7426–7435. §4.24.

Courtney, S. M., Petit, L., Haxby, J. V., & Ungerleider, L. G. (1998). The role of prefrontal cortex in working memory: Examining the contents of consciousness. *Philosophical Transactions of the Royal Society of London, Series B: Biological Sciences, 353*(1377), 1819–1828. §10.13.

Cowan, N. (2001). The magical number 4 in short-term memory: A reconsideration of mental storage capacity. *Behavioral and Brain Sciences, 24*(1), 87–185. §10.30.

Cowan, R. L., & Wilson, C. J. (1994). Spontaneous firing patterns and axonal projections of single corticostriatal neurons in the rat medial agranular cortex. *Journal of Neurophysiology, 71*, 17–32. §5.42.

Crabtree, J. W., & Isaac, J. T. (2002). New intrathalamic pathways allowing modality-related and cross-modality switching in the dorsal thalamus. *Journal of Neuroscience, 22*(19), 8754–8761. §4.27.

Craighero, L., Fadiga, L., Rizzolatti, G., & Umilta, C. (1999). Action for perception: A motor-visual attentional effect. *Journal of Experimental Psychology: Human Perception and Performance, 25*, 1673–1692. §4.24.

Craik, K. J. W. (1940). Origin of visual after-images. *Nature, 145*, 512. §§10.49, 10.50.

Crick, F. (1982). Do dendritic spines twitch? *Trends in Neurosciences, 5*, 44–46. §5.2.

Crick, F. (1984). Function of the thalamic reticular complex: The searchlight hypothesis. *Proceedings of the National Academy of Sciences of the United States of America, 81*, 4586–4590. §§4.27, 4.39, 4n11.

Crick, F. (1994). *Astonishing hypothesis: The scientific search for the soul.* New York: Scribner's. §10n10.

Crone, N. E., Sinai, A., & Korzeniewska, A. (2006). High-frequency gamma oscillations and human brain mapping with electrocorticography. *Progress in Brain Research, 159*, 275–295. §4.35.

Csicsvari, J., Jamieson, B., Wise, K. D., & Buzsáki, G. (2003). Mechanisms of gamma oscillations in the hippocampus of the behaving rat. *Neuron, 37*, 311–322. §4.44, 5.3.

Cunningham, M. O., Whittington, M. A., Bibbig, A., Roopun, A., LeBeau, F. E., Vogt, A., et al. (2004). A role for fast rhythmic bursting neurons in cortical gamma oscillations in vitro. *Proceedings of the National Academy of Sciences of the United States of America, 101*, 7152–7157. §§4.44, 5.40.

Curtis, C. E. (2006). Prefrontal and parietal contributions to spatial working memory. *Neuroscience, 139*(1), 173–180. §4.26. Cutrell, E. B., & Marrocco, R. T. (2002). Electrical microstimulation of primate posterior parietal cortex initiates orienting and alerting components of covert attention. *Experimental Brain Research, 144,* 103–113. §4.24.

Dan, Y., & Poo, M. M. (2004). Spike timing-dependent plasticity of neural circuits. *Neuron, 44*(1), 23–30. §§4.34, 5.11, 5n6.

Dan, Y., & Poo, M. M. (2006). Spike timing-dependent plasticity: From synapse to perception. *Physiological Reviews, 86*(3), 1033–1048. §5.11.

Daoudal, G., & Debanne, D. (2003). Long-term plasticity of intrinsic excitability: Learning rules and mechanisms. *Learning & Memory, 10,* 456–465. §5.38.

Davis, G. W. (2006). Homeostatic control of neural activity: From phenomenology to molecular design. *Annual Review of Neuroscience, 29,* 307–323. §5.7.

Daw, N. W. (1962). Why after-images are not seen in normal circumstances. *Nature, 196,* 1143–1145. §§10.49, 10.50.

Deacon, T. W. (2007). Three levels of emergent phenomena. In N. C. Murphy & W. R. Stoeger (Eds.), *Evolution and emergence: Systems, organisms, persons* (pp. 88–110). Oxford: Oxford University Press. §§1.15, A2.2.

Deans, M. R., Gibson, J. R., Sellitto, C., Connors, B. W., & Paul, D. L. (2001). Synchronous activity of inhibitory networks in neocortex requires electrical synapses containing connexin36. *Neuron, 31,* 477–485. §§4.44, 5.3.

DeBusk, B. C., DeBruyn, E. J., Snider, R. K., Kabara, J. F., & Bonds, A. B. (1997). Stimulus-dependent modulation of spike burst length in cat striate cortical cells. *Journal of Neurophysiology, 78,* 199–213. §4.38.

Deco, G., & Thiele, A. (2009). Attention: Oscillations and neuropharmacology. *European Journal of Neuroscience, 30,* 347–354. §5.39.

Deco, G., & Thiele, A. (2011). Cholinergic control of cortical network interactions enables feedback-mediated attentional modulation. *European Journal of Neuroscience, 34,* 146–157. §5.39.

DeFelipe, J. (1997). Types of neurons, synaptic connections, and chemical characteristics of cells immunoreactive for calbindin-D28K, parvalbumin, and calretinin in the neocortex. *Journal of Chemical Neuroanatomy, 14*(1), 1–19. §5.3.

DeFelipe, J. (1999). Chandelier cells and epilepsy. *Brain, 122,* 1807–1822. §4.33.

DeFelipe, J., & Fariñas, I. (1992). The pyramidal neuron of the cerebral cortex: Morphological and chemical characteristics of the synaptic inputs. *Progress in Neurobiology, 39,* 563–607. §§5.2, 5.3, figure 5.1.

DeFelipe, J., Hendry, S. H. C., & Jones, E. G. (1986). A correlative electron microscopic study of basket cells and large GABAergic neurons in the monkey sensory-motor cortex. *Neuroscience, 17,* 991–1009. §5.3.

DeFelipe, J., Hendry, S. H. C., Hashikawa, T., Molinari, M., & Jones, E. G. (1990). A microcolumnar structure of monkey cerebral cortex revealed by immunocytochemical studies of double bouquet cell axons. *Neuroscience, 37,* 655–673. §5.3.

DeFelipe, J., & Jones, E. G. (1985). Vertical organization of γ-aminobutyric acid-accumulating intrinsic neuronal systems in monkey cerebral corex. *Journal of Neuroscience, 5,* 3246–3269. §5.3.

Dehaene, S. (2008). Conscious and nonconscious processes: Distinct forms of evidence accumulation? In C. Engel & W. Singer (Eds.), *Better than conscious? Decision making, the human mind and implications for institutions.* Strüngmann Forum Report. Cambridge, MA: MIT Press. §10.36.

Dehaene, S., & Changeux, J. P. (2011). Experimental and theoretical approaches to conscious processing. *Neuron, 70*(2), 200–227. §§2.11, 10.16, 10.17, 10.36, 10.54, 10.65, 10.67, 10n1, 10n6, 10n21.

Dehaene, S., Changeux, J. P., Naccache, L., Sackur, J., & Sergent, C. (2006). Conscious, preconscious, and subliminal processing: A testable taxonomy. *Trends in Cognitive Sciences, 10*(5), 204–211. §§10.16, 10.17, 10.54, 10.65, 10.67, 10.69, 10.77.

Dehaene, S., Kerszberg, M., & Changeux, J. P. (1998). A neural model of a global workspace in effortful cognitive tasks. *Proceedings of the National Academy of Sciences of the United States of America, 95,* 14529–14534. §10n6.

Dehaene, S., & Naccache, L. (2001). Towards a cognitive neuroscience of consciousness: Basic evidence and a workspace framework. *Cognition, 79,* 1–37. §10.29.

Dehaene, S., Naccache, L., Cohen, L., Bihan, D. L., Mangin, J. F., Poline, J. B., & Rivière, D. (2001). Cerebral mechanisms of word masking and unconscious repetition priming. *Nature Neuroscience, 4,* 752–758. §10.16.

Deisz, R. A., & Prince, D. A. (1989). Frequency-dependent depression of inhibition in guinea-pig neocortex in vitro by GABAB receptor feed-back on GABA release. *Journal of Physiology, 412,* 513–541. §4.55.

De Koning, T. J., Snell, K., Duran, M., Berger, R., Poll-The, B. T., & Surtees, R. (2003). l-Serine in disease and development. *Biochemical Journal, 371,* 653–661. §5.5.

Del Cul, A., Baillet, S., & Dehaene, S. (2007). Brain dynamics underlying the nonlinear threshold for access to consciousness. *PLoS Biology, 5,* e260. §10.16.

Del Cul, A., Dehaene, S., Reyes, P., Bravo, E., & Slachevsky, A. (2009). Causal role of prefrontal cortex in the threshold for access to consciousness. *Brain, 132*(9), 2531–2540. §10.65.

DeMaria, C. D., Soong, T. W., Alseikhan, B. A., Alvania, R. S., & Yue, D. T. (2001). Calmodulin bifurcates the local Ca^{2+} signal that modulates P/Q-type Ca^{2+} channels. *Nature, 411,* 484–489. §5.9.

Dennett, D. (1978). On giving libertarians what they say they want. In *Brainstorms: Philosophical essays on mind and psychology* (pp. 295–297). Cambridge, MA: MIT Press. §7.17, 7n8.

Dennett, D. (1984). *Elbow room: The varieties of free will worth wanting.* Cambridge, MA: MIT Press. §7.2.

Dennett, D. (1988). Quining qualia. In A. Marcel & E. Bisiach (Eds.), *Consciousness in contemporary science* (pp. 42–77). New York: Oxford University Press. §A2n1.

Dennett, D. (1990). Quining qualia. In W. Lycan (Ed.), *Mind and Cognition: A Reader.* Oxford: Blackwell. §§1.3, 10.5, A2n5.

Dennett, D. (1992). *Consciousness explained.* Boston: Back Bay Books. §A2n1.

Dennett, D. C. (2001). Are we explaining consciousness yet? *Cognition, 79,* 221–237. §1.3.

Dennett, D. C., & Kinsbourne, M. (1992). Time and the observer—the where and when of consciousness in the brain. *Behavioral and Brain Sciences, 15,* 183–201. §9n1.

Denton, D. (2006). *The primordial emotions: The dawning of consciousness.* Oxford: Oxford University Press. §10.60.

Desai, N. S., Rutherford, L. C., & Torrigiano, G. G. (1999). Plasticity in the intrinsic excitability of cortical pyramidal neurons. *Nature Neuroscience, 2,* 515–520. §5.7.

Desimone, R., Albright, T. D., Gross, C. G., & Bruce, C. (1984). Stimulus-selective properties of inferior temporal neurons in the macaque. *Journal of Neuroscience, 4*(8), 2051–2062. §§4.10, 10.21.

Desimone, R., & Duncan, J. (1995). Neural mechanisms of selective visual attention. *Annual Review of Neuroscience, 18,* 193–222. §§4.21, 5.50, 10.32.

D'Esposito, M., Postle, B., Ballard, D., & Lease, J. (1999). Maintenance versus manipulation of information held in working memory: An event-related fMRI study. *Brain and Cognition, 41*(1), 66–86. §4.26.

Destexhe, A., & Contreras, D. (2006). Neuronal computations with stochastic network states. *Science, 314*(5796), 85–90. §4.70.

Destexhe, A., Rudolph, M., & Paré, D. (2003). The high-conductance state of neocortical neurons in vivo. *Nature Reviews. Neuroscience, 4,* 739–751. §4n3.

De Weerd, P., Desimone, R., & Ungerleider, L. G. (1998). Perceptual filling-in: A parametric study. *Vision Research, 38,* 2721–2734. §10.50.

De Weerd, P., Smith, E., & Greenberg, P. (2006). Effects of selective attention on perceptual filling-in. *Journal of Cognitive Neuroscience, 18,* 335–347. §10.50.

DeWitt, B. S., & Graham, N. (Eds.). (1973). *The many-worlds interpretation of quantum mechanics*. Princeton: Princeton University Press. §A2.4.

DeYoe, E. A., & Bartlett, J. R. (1980). Rarity of luxotonic responses in cortical visual areas of the cat. *Experimental Brain Research, 39*, 125–132. §5.37.

Dichter, M., & Ayala, G. F. (1987). Cellular mechanisms of epilepsy: A status report. *Science, 237*, 157–164. §4n12.

Dingledine, R., Borges, K., Bowie, D., & Traynelis, S. F. (1999). The glutamate receptor ion channels. *Pharmacological Reviews, 51*, 7–61. §4n4.

Disney, A., Domakonda, K., & Aoki, C. (2006). Differential expression of muscarinic acetylcholine receptors across excitatory and inhibitory cells in visual cortical areas v1 and v2 of the macaque monkey. *Journal of Comparative Neurology, 499*, 49–63. §5.39.

Disney, A., Aoki, C., & Hawken, M. (2007). Gain modulation by nicotine in macaque v1. *Neuron, 56*, 701–713. §5.39.

Disterhoft, J. F., Kronforst-Collins, M., Oh, M. M., Power, J. M., Preston, A. R., & Weiss, C. (1999). Cholinergic facilitation of trace eyeblink conditioning in aging rabbits. *Life Sciences, 64*, 541–548. §5.38.

Dodt, H.-U., Frick, A., Kampe, K., & Zieglgaensberger, W. (1998). NMDA and AMPA receptors on neocortical neurons are differentially distributed. *European Journal of Neuroscience, 10*, 3351–3357. §5.21.

Doeller, C. F., Barry, C., & Burgess, N. (2010). Evidence for grid cells in a human memory network. *Nature, 463*(7281), 657. §§4.8, 8.22.

Doherty, J. R., Rao, A., Mesulam, M. M., & Nobre, A. C. (2005). Synergistic effect of combined temporal and spatial expectations on visual attention. *Journal of Neuroscience, 25*, 8259–8266. §4.24.

Doiron, B., Laing, C., Longtin, A., & Maler, L. (2002). Ghostbursting: A novel neuronal burst mechanism. *Journal of Computational Neuroscience, 12*, 5–25. §5.21.

Domenici, P., Booth, D., Blagburn, J. M., & Bacon, J. P. (2008). Cockroaches keep predators guessing by using preferred escape trajectories. *Current Biology, 18*(22), 1792–1796. §10.3.

Donner, T. H., Siegel, M., Oostenveld, R., Fries, P., Bauer, M., & Engel, A. K. (2007). Population activity in the human dorsal pathway predicts the accuracy of visual motion detection. *Journal of Neurophysiology, 98*, 345–359. §§4.23, 4.49.

Doyle, B. (2011). *Free will: The scandal in philosophy*. Cambridge, MA: I-Phi Press. §7.17.

Draganski, B., Gaser, C., Busch, V., Schuirer, G., Bogdahn, U., & May, A. (2004). Changes in grey matter induced by training. *Nature, 427*, 311–312. §7.12.

Dretske, F. (1981). *Knowledge and the flow of information.* Cambridge, MA: MIT Press. §8.6.

Drew, P. J., & Abbott, L. F. (2006). Extending the effects of spike-timing-dependent plasticity to behavioral timescales. *Proceedings of the National Academy of Sciences of the United States of America, 103*(23), 8876–8881. §5n4.

Druzgal, T. J., & D'Esposito, M. (2003). Dissecting contributions of prefrontal cortex and fusiform face area to face working memory. *Journal of Cognitive Neuroscience, 15*(6), 771–784. §10.14.

Dudek, S. M., & Bear, M. F. (1992). Homosynaptic long-term depression in area CA1 of hippocampus and effects of N-methyl-D-aspartate receptor blockade. *Proceedings of the National Academy of Sciences of the United States of America, 89,* 4363–4367. §5.6.

Duncan, J. (1980). The locus of interference in the perception of simultaneous stimuli. *Psychological Review, 87,* 272–300. §§4.24, 4.25.

Dupoux, E., de Gardelle, V., & Kouider, S. (2008). Subliminal speech perception and auditory streaming. *Cognition, 109,* 267–273. §10.36.

Durstewitz, D. (2009). Implications of synaptic biophysics for recurrent network dynamics and active memory. *Neural Networks, 22*(8), 1189–1200. §§4.42, 4.68, 5.25, 7.15.

Dwyer, T. M., Adams, D. J., & Hille, B. (1980). The permeability of the endplate channel to organic cations in frog muscle. *Journal of General Physiology, 75,* 469–492. §A1.10.

Eagleman, D. M., & Sejnowski, T. J. (2000). Motion integration and postdiction in visual awareness. *Science, 287,* 2036–2038. §10.18.

Earley, J. E. (2008). How philosophy of mind needs philosophy of chemistry. *HYLE— International Journal for Philosophy of Chemistry, 14*(1), 1–26. §A2.2.

Eddington, A. S. (1932). The decline of determinism. *Mathematical Gazette, 16,* 66–80. §A1.4.

Edelman, G. (1987). *Neural Darwinism: The theory of neuronal group selection.* New York: Basic Books. §5.8, §7n7.

Edwards, D. H., Heitler, W. J., & Krasne, F. B. (1999). Fifty years of command neurons: The neurobiology of escape behavior in the crayfish. *Trends in Neurosciences, 22,* 153–161. §1.11.

Eifuku, S., De Souza, W. C., Tamura, R., Nishijo, H., & Ono, T. (2004). Neuronal correlates of face identification in the monkey anterior temporal cortical areas. *Journal of Neurophysiology, 91*(1), 358–371. §4.12.

Einstein, A., Podolsky, B., & Rosen, N. (1935). Can quantum-mechanical description of physical reality be considered complete? *Physical Review, 47*, 777–780. §A1.5.

Ellis, W. D. (Ed.) (1938). *A source book of Gestalt psychology*. New York: Harcourt, Brace & World. §10.50.

Engbert, R., & Kliegl, R. (2003). Microsaccades uncover the orientation of covert attention. *Vision Research, 43*, 1035–1045. §4.23.

Engel, A. K., Fries, P., König, P., Brecht, M., & Singer, W. (1999). Temporal binding, binocular rivalry, and consciousness. *Consciousness and Cognition, 8*(2), 128–151. §4.21.

Engel, A. K., Fries, P., & Singer, W. (2001). Dynamic predictions: Oscillations and synchrony in top-down processing. *Nature Reviews: Neuroscience, 2*, 704–716. §§4n3, 5.46.

Engert, F., & Bonhoeffer, T. (1999). Dendritic spine changes associated with hippocampal long-term synaptic plasticity. *Nature, 399*, 66–70. §§5.5, 5.9.

Enns, J. T., & Rensink, R. A. (1990). Influence of scene-based properties on visual search. *Science, 247*(4943), 721–723. §§4.22, 10.35.

Enns, J. T., & Rensink, R. A. (1991). Preattentive recovery of three-dimensional orientation from line drawings. *Psychological Review, 98*(3), 335–351. §§4.22, 10.35.

Epstein, R. A., Parker, W. E., & Feiler, A. M. (2007). Where am I now? Distinct roles for parahippocampal and retrosplenial cortices in place recognition. *Journal of Neuroscience, 27*(23), 6141–6149. §4.8.

Ettlinger, G. (1990). "Object vision" and "spatial vision": The neuropsychological evidence for the distinction. *Cortex, 26*(3), 319–341. §4.8.

Euler, T., & Denk, W. (2001). Dendritic processing. *Current Opinion in Neurobiology, 11*, 415–422. §5.18.

Evans, R. H., Francis, A. A., & Watkins, J. C. (1977). Selective antagonism by Mg^{2+} of amino acid-induced depolarization of spinal neurones. *Experientia, 33*, 489–491. §5n9.

Everett, H. (1957). Relative state formulation of quantum mechanics. *Reviews of Modern Physics, 29*, 454–462. §A2.4.

Everitt, B. J., & Robbins, T. W. (1997). Central cholinergic systems and cognition. *Annual Review of Psychology, 48*, 649–684. §§5.38, 5.39, 5.44, 5.45.

Everling, S., & Munoz, D. P. (2000). Neuronal correlates for preparatory set associated with pro-saccades and antisaccades in the primate frontal eye field. *Journal of Neuroscience, 20*(1), 387–400. §4.23.

Eyherabide, H. G., Rokem, A., Herz, A. V., & Samengo, I. (2009). Bursts generate a non-reducible spike-pattern code. *Frontiers in Neuroscience, 3*(1), 8–14. §§4.38, 5.36.

Faber, D. S., Young, W. S., Legendre, P., & Korn, H. (1992). Intrinsic quantal variability stochastic properties of receptor-transmitter interactions. *Science, 258,* 1494–1498. §4.66.

Fahrenfort, J. J., Scholte, H. S., & Lamme, V. A. (2007). Masking disrupts reentrant processing in human visual cortex. *Journal of Cognitive Neuroscience, 19,* 1488–1497. §10.16.

Fanselow, E. E., Sameshima, K., Baccala, L. A., & Nicolelis, M. A. (2001). Thalamic bursting in rats during different awake behavioral states. *Proceedings of the National Academy of Sciences of the United States of America, 98,* 15330–15335. §4.38.

Farivar, R. (2009). Dorsal–ventral integration in object recognition. *Brain Research: Brain Research Reviews, 61,* 144–153. §4.8.

Faure, P., & Korn, H. (2001). Is there chaos in the brain? I. Concepts of nonlinear dynamics and methods of investigation. *Comptes Rendus de l'Académie des Sciences. Série III, Sciences de la Vie, 324*(9), 773–793. §4.68.

Feigenson, L., Carey, S., & Hauser, M. (2002). The representations underlying infants' choice of more: Object files versus analog magnitudes. *Psychological Science, 13*(2), 150–156. §9.33.

Feinberg, I. (1978). Efference copy and corollary discharge: Implications for thinking and its disorders. *Schizophrenia Bulletin, 4*(4), 636–640. §9.13.

Feinstein, J., Rudrauf, D., Khalsa, S., Cassell, M., Bruss, J., Grabowski, T., et al. (2010). Bilateral limbic system destruction in man. *Journal of Clinical and Experimental Neuropsychology, 32*(1), 88–106. §10.44.

Felleman, D. J., & Van Essen, D. C. (1991). Distributed hierarchical processing in the primate cerebral cortex. *Cerebral Cortex, 1,* 1–47. §4.49.

Fellous, J. M., & Sejnowski, T. J. (2000). Cholinergic induction of oscillations in the hippocampal slice in the slow (0.5–2 Hz), theta (5–12 Hz), and gamma (35–70 Hz) bands. *Hippocampus, 10,* 187–197. §5.40.

Fernandez-Duque, D., Grossi, G., Thornton, I. M., & Neville, H. J. (2003). Representation of change: Separate electrophysiological markers of attention, awareness, and implicit processing. *Journal of Cognitive Neuroscience, 15,* 491–507. §10.16.

Ferrarelli, F., & Tononi, G. (2011). The thalamic reticular nucleus and schizophrenia. *Schizophrenia Bulletin, 37*(2), 306–315. §§4.27, 5.24.

Ferrera, V. P., Yanike, M., & Cassanello, C. (2009). Frontal eye field neurons signal changes in decision criteria. *Nature Neuroscience, 12,* 1458–1462. §4.19.

Ferrarini, L., Veer, I. M., Baerends, E., van Tol, M. J., Renken, R. J., van der Wee, N. J., et al. (2009). Hierarchical functional modularity in the resting-state human brain. *Human Brain Mapping, 30*(7), 2220–2231. §7.15.

Ferster, D. (1986). Orientation selectivity of synaptic potentials in neurons of cat primary visual cortex. *Journal of Neuroscience, 6*, 1284–1301. §4.32.

Ferster, D., & Miller, K. D. (2000). Neural mechanisms of orientation selectivity in the visual cortex. *Annual Review of Neuroscience, 23*, 441–471. §4.32.

Feynman, R. P. (1965). *The Feynman lectures on physics* (Vol. 2 and 3). Boston: Addison-Wesley. §A1.11.

Finch, E. A., & Augustine, G. J. (1998). Local calcium signalling by inositol-1,4,5-trisphosphate in Purkinje cell dendrites. *Nature, 396*, 753–756. §5.5.

Fine, A. (1996). *The shaky game: Einstein, realism and the quantum theory* (2nd ed.). Chicago: University of Chicago Press. §A1.6.

Fisahn, A., Pike, F. G., Buhl, E. H., & Paulsen, O. (1998). Cholinergic induction of network oscillations at 40 Hz in the hippocampus in vitro. *Nature, 394*, 186–189. §5.40.

Fisahn, A., Contractor, A., Traub, R. D., Buhl, E. H., Heinemann, S. F., & McBain, C. J. (2004). Distinct roles for the kainate receptor subunits GluR5 and GluR6 in kainate-induced hippocampal gamma oscillations. *Journal of Neuroscience, 24*, 9658–9668. §5.40.

Fischer, M., Kaech, S., Wagner, U., Brinkhaus, H., & Matus, A. (2000). Glutamate receptors regulate actin-based plasticity in dendritic spines. *Nature Neuroscience, 3*(9), 887–894. §4.55.

Fitzpatrick, D., Lund, J. S., Schmechel, D. E., & Towles, A. C. (1987). Distribution of GABAergic neurons and axon terminals in the macaque striate cortex. *Journal of Comparative Neurology, 264*, 73–91. §5.3.

Fitzsimonds, R. M., & Poo, M. M. (1998). Retrograde signaling in the development and modification of synapses. *Physiological Reviews, 78*, 143–170. §5.17.

Flor, H., Elbert, T., Knecht, S., Wienbruch, C., Pantev, C., Birbaumer, N., et al. (1995). Phantom-limb pain as a perceptual correlate of cortical reorganization following arm amputation. *Nature, 375*, 482–484. §4n15.

Fodor, J. (1975). *The language of thought.* New York: Thomas Crowell. §3.11.

Fodor, J. (1983). *The modularity of mind.* Cambridge, MA: MIT Press. §10.19.

Fodor, J. (1998). Special sciences: Still autonomous after all these years. *Philosophical Perspectives, 11*, 149–163. §3.11.

Foffani, G., Tutunculer, B., & Moxon, K. A. (2004). Role of spike timing in the forelimb somatosensory cortex of the rat. *Journal of Neuroscience, 24*, 7266–7271. §4.43.

Fougnie, D., & Marois, R. (2006). Distinct capacity limits for attention and working memory—evidence from attentive tracking and visual working memory paradigms. *Psychological Science, 17*(6), 526–534. §10.13.

Fox, M. D., Corbetta, M., Snyder, A. Z., Vincent, J. L., & Raichle, M. E. (2006). Spontaneous neuronal activity distinguishes human dorsal and vertral attention systems. *Proceedings of the National Academy of Sciences of the United States of America, 103,* 100046–100051.

Frank, M. G., Issa, N. P., & Stryker, M. P. (2001). Sleep enhances plasticity in the developing visual cortex. *Neuron, 30,* 275–287. §5.8.

Frank, M. J. (2005). Dynamic dopamine modulation in the basal ganglia: A neurocomputational account of cognitive deficits in medicated and nonmedicated Parkinsonism. *Journal of Cognitive Neuroscience, 17,* 51–72. §4.40.

Frank, R. A. W. (2011). Endogenous ion channel complexes: The NMDA receptor. *Biochemical Society Transactions, 39,* 707–718. §4n4.

Frank, S. M., Reavis, E. A., Tse, P. U. and Greenlee, M. W. (2012). From inefficient search to pop-out in one week: Neural mechanisms of feature conjunction learning. Submitted. §10.54, figure 10.3, figure 10.4.

Franks, K. M., Bartol, T. M., Jr., & Sejnowski, T. J. (2002). A Monte Carlo model reveals independent signaling at central glutamatergic synapses. *Biophysical Journal, 83,* 2333–2348. §4.66.

Franks, K. M., Stevens, S. F., & Sejnowski, T. J. (2003). Independent sources of quantal variability at single glutamatergic synapses. *Journal of Neuroscience, 23*(8), 3186. §4.66.

Freedman, D. J., & Assad, J. A. (2006). Experience-dependent representation of visual categories in parietal cortex. *Nature, 443,* 85–88. §4.19.

Freedman, D. J., & Assad, J. A. (2011). A proposed common neural mechanism for categorization and perceptual decisions. *Nature Neuroscience, 14*(2), 143–146. §4.19.

Freedman, D. J., Riesenhuber, M., Poggio, T., & Miller, E. K. (2001). Categorical representation of visual stimuli in the primate prefrontal cortex. *Science, 291*(5502), 312–316. §§4.19, 4.26, 7.11.

Freedman, D. J., Riesenhuber, M., Poggio, T., & Miller, E. K. (2003). A comparison of primate prefrontal and inferior temporal cortices during visual categorization. *Journal of Neuroscience, 23,* 5235–5246. §4.19.

Freeman, W. J. (1992). Tutorial on neurobiology: From single neurons to brain chaos. *International Journal of Bifurcation and Chaos, 2,* 451–482. §4.69.

Freeman, W. J. (1999). Consciousness, intentionality, and causality. *Journal of Consciousness Studies, 6,* 142–192. §4.69.

Freiwald, W. A., Tsao, D. Y., & Livingstone, M. S. (2009). A face feature space in the macaque temporal lobe. *Nature Neuroscience, 12*(9), 1187–1196. §4.11.

Freund, T. F., & Buzsáki, G. (1996). Interneurons of the hippocampus. *Hippocampus*, *6*, 347–470. §5.3.

Freund, T. F., & Meskenaite, V. (1992). Gamma-aminobutyric acid-containing basal forebrain neurons innervate inhibitory interneurons in the neocortex. *Proceedings of the National Academy of Sciences of the United States of America*, *89*, 738–742. §5.45.

Freund, T. F., Katona, I., & Piomelli, D. (2003). Role of endogenous cannabinoids in synaptic signaling. *Physiological Reviews*, *83*, 1017–1066. §5.17.

Frey, U., Frey, S., Schollmeier, F., & Krug, M. (1996). Influence of actinomycin D, a RNA synthesis inhibitor, on long-term potentiation in rat hippocampal neurons in vivo and in vitro. *Journal of Physiology*, *490*, 703–711. §5.9.

Frey, U., & Morris, R. G. (1997). Synaptic tagging and long-term potentiation. *Nature*, *385*, 533–536. §5.9.

Fried, I., Mukamel, R., & Kreiman, G. (2011). Internally generated preactivation of single neurons in human medial frontal cortex predicts volition. *Neuron*, *69*(3), 548–562. §9.14.

Friedman-Hill, S., Maldonado, P. E., & Gray, C. M. (2000). Dynamics of striate cortical activity in the alert macaque. I. Incidence and stimulus-dependence of gamma-band neuronal oscillations. *Cerebral Cortex*, *10*, 1105–1116. §4.52.

Fries, P. (2005). A mechanism for cognitive dynamics: Neuronal communication through neuronal coherence. *Trends in Cognitive Sciences*, *9*, 474–480. §§4.60, 4n3.

Fries, P., Neuenschwander, S., Engel, A. K., Goebel, R., & Singer, W. (2001a). Rapid feature selective neuronal synchronization through correlated latency shifting. *Nature Neuroscience*, *4*(2), 194–200. §§4.45, 4.53.

Fries, P., Reynolds, J. H., Rorie, A. E., & Desimone, R. (2001b). Modulation of oscillatory neuronal synchronization by selective visual attention. *Science*, *291*, 1560–1563. §§4.45, 4.49, 4.53.

Fries, P., Roelfsema, P. R., Engel, A. K., König, P., & Singer, W. (1997). Synchronization of oscillatory responses in visual cortex correlates with perception in interocular rivalry. *Proceedings of the National Academy of Sciences of the United States of America*, *94*, 12699–12704. §§4.45, 4.53.

Fries, P., Schröder, J.-H., Roelfsma, P. R., Singer, W., & Engel, A. K. (2002). Oscillatory neuronal synchronization in primary visual cortex as a correlate of stimulus selection. *Journal of Neuroscience*, *22*(9), 3739–3754. §§4.45, 4.53.

Fries, P., Nikolic, D., & Singer, W. (2007). The gamma cycle. *Trends in Neurosciences*, *30*(7), 309–316. §§4.45, 4.53.

Fries, P., Womelsdorf, T., Oostenveld, R., & Desimone, R. (2008). The effects of visual stimulation and selective visual attention on rhythmic neuronal synchronization in macaque area V4. *Journal of Neuroscience, 28,* 4823–4835. §§4.23, 4.45, 4.47, 4.48, 4.49, 4.53, 5.39.

Friston, K. J., & Frith, C. D. (1995). Schizophrenia: A disconnection syndrome? *Clinical Neuroscience, 3,* 89–97. §5.24.

Frith, C. (1992). *The cognitive neuropsychology of schizophrenia.* Hillsdale, NJ: Lawrence Erlbaum. §9.13.

Frith, C. (2004). Comments on Shaun Gallagher: Neurocognitive models of schizophrenia: A neuro-phenomenological critique. *Psychopathology, 37*(1), 20–22. §§9.13, 10.26.

Frith, C. (2005). The self in action: Lessons from delusions of control. *Consciousness and Cognition, 14*(4), 752–770. §§9.13, 10.26.

Frith, C. D., Blakemore, S., & Wolpert, D. M. (2000). Explaining the symptoms of schizophrenia: Abnormalities in the awareness of action. *Brain Research: Brain Research Reviews, 31*(2–3), 357–363. §§9.13, 10.26.

Froemke, R. C., & Dan, Y. (2002). Spike-timing-dependent synaptic modification induced by natural spike trains. *Nature, 416,* 433–438. §5.12.

Froemke, R. C., Poo, M. M., & Dan, Y. (2005). Spike-timing-dependent synaptic plasticity depends on dendritic location. *Nature, 434*(7030), 221–225. §5.21.

Fuchs, W. (1923). Experimentelle Untersuchungen über die Änderung von Farben unter dem Einfluss von Gestalten. *Zeitschrift für Psychologie, 92,* 249–325. Translated as selection 7 in W. D. Ellis (Ed.) (1938). *A source book of gestalt psychology.* New York: Harcourt, Brace & World. §10.50.

Fugelsang, J. A., Roser, M. E., Corballis, P. M., Gazzaniga, M. S., & Dunbar, K. N. (2005). Brain mechanisms underlying perceptual causality. *Cognitive Brain Research, 24*(1), 41–47. §5n6.

Fukuda, K., Awh, E., & Vogel, E. K. (2010). Discrete capacity limits in visual working memory. *Current Opinion in Neurobiology, 20*(2), 177–182. §10.30.

Furey, M., Pietrini, P., Haxby, J., & Drevets, W. (2008). Selective effects of cholinergic modulation on task performance during selective attention. *Neuropsychopharmacology, 33,* 913–923. §5.39.

Fuster, J. M. (1999). *Memory in the cerebral cortex: An empirical approach to neural networks in the human and nonhuman primate.* Cambridge, MA: MIT Press. §10n10.

Fuster, J. M. (2008). *The prefrontal cortex* (4th Ed.). New York: Academic Press. §§2n3, 4.26, 10.40, 10.61.

Fyhn, M., Hafting, T., Witter, M. P., Moser, E. I., & Moser, M.-B. (2008). Grid cells in mice. *Hippocampus, 18*(12), 1230. §§4.8, 8.22.

Gaillard, R., Dehaene, S., Adam, C., Clémenceau, S., Hasboun, D., Baulac, M., Cohen, L., & Naccache, L. (2009). Converging intracranial markers of conscious access. *PLoS Biology*, *7*, e61. §10.16.

Galarreta, M., & Hestrin, S. (1999). A network of fast-spiking cells in the neocortex connected by electrical synapses. *Nature*, *402*, 72–75. §4.44.

Galarreta, M., & Hestrin, S. (2002). Electrical and chemical synapses among parvalbumin fast-spiking GABAergic interneurons in adult mouse neocortex. *Proceedings of the National Academy of Sciences of the United States of America*, *99*, 12438–12443. §4.44.

Galili, D. S., Lüdke, A., Galizia, C. G., Szyszka, P., & Tanimoto, H. (2011). Olfactory trace conditioning in Drosophila. *Journal of Neuroscience*, *31*(20), 7240–7248. §10.43.

Ganguly, K., Kiss, L., & Poo, M. M. (2000). Enhancement of presynaptic neuronal excitability by correlated presynaptic and postsynaptic spiking. *Nature Neuroscience*, *3*, 1018–1026. §5.11.

Garcia Dominguez, L., Wennberg, R. A., Snead, O. C., III, Gaetz, W., Perez Velazquez, J. L., & Cheyne, D. (2005). Enhanced synchrony in epileptiform activity? Local versus distant phase synchronization in generalized seizures. *Journal of Neuroscience*, *25*, 8077–8084. §4n12.

Garcia-Larrea, L., Lukaszewicz, A.-C., & Mauguiere, F. (1992). Revisiting the oddball paradigm: Non-target vs. neutral stimuli and the evaluation of ERP attentional effects. *Neuropsychologia*, *30*, 723–741. §4.22.

Gasquoine, P. G. (1993). Alien hand sign. *Journal of Clinical and Experimental Neuropsychology*, *15*, 653–667. §10n10.

Gazzaniga, M. S. (Ed.). (1995). *The cognitive neurosciences*. Cambridge, MA: MIT Press. §4.7.

Georgopoulos, A., Lurito, J., Petrides, M., Schwartz, A., & Massey, J. (1989). Mental rotation of the neuronal population vector. *Science*, *243*(4888), 234–236. §§8.1, 8.19.

Ghose, G. M., & Maunsell, J. H. R. (2002). Attentional modulation in visual cortex depends on task timing. *Nature*, *419*, 616–620. §4.24.

Gibson, J. R., Beierlein, M., & Connors, B. W. (1999). Two networks of electrically coupled inhibitory neurons in neocortex. *Nature*, *402*, 75–79. §4.44.

Gibson, J. R., Beierlein, M., & Connors, B. W. (2005). Functional properties of electrical synapses between inhibitory interneurons of neocortical layer 4. *Journal of Neurophysiology*, *93*, 467–480. §4.44.

Gigerenzer, G., & Gaissmaier, W. (2011). Heuristic decision making. *Annual Review of Psychology*, *62*, 451–482. §§8.17, 10.22.

Gil, Z., Connors, B., & Amitai, Y. (1997). Differential modulation of neocortical synapses by neuromodulators and activity. *Neuron, 19,* 679–686. §5.39.

Gillett, C. (2003). The metaphysics of realization, multiple realization, and the special sciences. *Journal of Philosophy, 100,* 591–603. §3.11.

Gilroy, L. A., & Blake, R. (2005). The interaction between binocular rivalry and negative after-images. *Current Biology, 15,* 1740–1744. §§10.49, 10.50.

Gitelman, D. R., Nobre, A. C., Parrish, T. B., LaBar, K. S., Kim, Y. H., Meyer, J. R., et al. (1999). A large-scale distributed network for covert spatial attention: Further anatomical delineation based on stringent behavioural and cognitive controls. *Brain, 122,* 1093–1106. §4.24.

Glanzman, D. L. (1995). The cellular basis of classical conditioning in Aplysia californica—it's less simple than you think. *Trends in Neurosciences, 18,* 30–36. §10.43.

Gloveli, T., Schmitz, D., Empson, R. M., & Heinemann, U. (1997). Frequency dependent information flow from the entorhinal cortex to the hippocampus. *Journal of Neurophysiology, 78,* 3444–3449. §4.55.

Gloveli, T., Dugladze, T., Saha, S., Monyer, H., Heinemann, U., Traub, R. D., et al. (2005). Differential involvement of oriens/pyramidale interneurones in hippocampal network oscillations in vitro. *Journal of Physiology, 562,* 131–147. §5.43.

Goard, M., & Dan, Y. (2009). Basal forebrain activation enhances cortical coding of natural scenes. *Nature Neuroscience, 12*(11), 1440–1447. §§5.38, 5.39, 5.50.

Godwin, D. W., Vaughan, J. W., & Sherman, S. M. (1996). Metabotropic glutamate receptors switch visual response mode of LGN cells from burst to tonic. *Journal of Neurophysiology, 76,* 1800–1816. §4.59.

Gold, J. I., & Shadlen, M. N. (2007). The neural basis of decision making. *Annual Review of Neuroscience, 30,* 535–574. §4.18.

Gold, J. I., & Shadlen, M. N. (2003). The influence of behavioral context on the representation of a perceptual decision in developing oculomotor commands. *Journal of Neuroscience, 23,* 632–651. §4.18.

Gold, P. E. (2003). Acetylcholine modulation of neural systems involved in learning and memory. *Neurobiology of Learning and Memory, 80,* 194–210. §5.38.

Goldberg, M. E., Bisley, J. W., Powell, K. D., & Gottlieb, J. (2006). Saccades, salience, and attention: The role of the lateral intraparietal area in visual behavior. *Progress in Brain Research, 155,* 157–175. §4.18.

Golding, N. L., & Spruston, N. (1998). Dendritic sodium spikes are variable triggers of axonal action potentials in hippocampal CA1 pyramidal neurons. *Neuron, 21,* 1189–1200. §5.22.

Golding, N. L., Staff, N. P., & Spruston, N. (2002). Dendritic spikes as a mechanism for cooperative long-term potentiation. *Nature, 418*, 326–331. §5.27.

Gomes, G. (2002). The interpretation of Libet's results on the timing of conscious events: A commentary. *Consciousness and Cognition, 11*, 221–230; discussion 308–313, 314–325. §9n1.

Gomes, G. (2010). Preparing to move and deciding not to move. *Consciousness and Cognition, 19*, 457–459. §9n4.

Goodale, M. A., & Milner, A. D. (1992). Separate visual pathways for perception and action. *Trends in Neurosciences, 15*(1), 20–25. §4.8.

Goold, C. P., & Nicoll, R. A. (2010). Single-cell optogenetic excitation drives homeostatic synaptic depression. *Neuron, 68*, 512–528. §5.7.

Gordon, R. D., & Irwin, D. E. (1996). What's in an object file? Evidence from priming studies. *Perception & Psychophysics, 58*(8), 1260–1277. §10.30.

Gordon, R. D., & Irwin, D. E. (2000). The role of physical and conceptual properties in preserving object continuity. *Journal of Experimental Psychology: Learning, Memory, and Cognition, 26*(1), 136–150. §10.30.

Goto, Y., & Grace, A. A. (2005). Dopaminergic modulation of limbic and cortical drive of nucleus accumbens in goal-directed behavior. *Nature Neuroscience, 8*, 805–812. §4.40.

Gottlieb, J. (2007). From thought to action: The parietal cortex as a bridge between perception, action, and cognition. *Neuron, 53*, 9–16. §4.19.

Govindarajan, A., Israely, I., Huang, S.-Y., & Tonegawa, S. (2011). The dendritic branch is the preferred integrative unit for protein synthesis-dependent LTP. *Neuron, 69*, 132–146. §5.9.

Graboi, D., & Lisman, J. (2003). Recognition by top-down and bottom-up processing in cortex: The control of selective attention. *Journal of Neurophysiology, 90*, 798–810. §§4.14, 4.60.

Grace, A. A., Floresco, S. B., Goto, Y., & Lodge, D. J. (2007). Regulation of firing of dopaminergic neurons and control of goal-directed behaviors. *Trends in Neurosciences, 30*, 220–227. §4.40.

Grafstein, B. (2011). Subverting the hegemony of the synapse: Complicity of neurons, astrocytes, and vasculature in spreading depression and pathology of the cerebral cortex. *Brain Research Reviews, 66*(1–2), 123–132. §4.68.

Gray, C. M. (1999). The temporal correlation hypothesis of visual feature integration: Still alive and well. *Neuron, 24*, 31–47. §§4.45, 4.53.

Gray, C. M., & McCormick, D. A. (1996). Chattering cells: Superficial pyramidal neurons contributing to the generation of synchronous oscillations in the visual cortex. *Science, 274*, 109–113. §4.44.

Gray, C. M., & Singer, W. (1989). Stimulus-specific neuronal oscillations in orientation columns of cat visual cortex. *Proceedings of the National Academy of Sciences of the United States of America, 86,* 1698–1702. §§4.44, 4.49.

Gray, E. (1959). Electron microscopy of synaptic contacts on dendrite spines of the cerebral cortex. *Nature, 183,* 1592–1593. §5.2.

Green, J. T., & Woodruff-Pak, D. S. (2000). Eyeblink classical conditioning: Hippocampal formation is for neutral stimulus associations as cerebellum is for association-response. *Psychological Bulletin, 126,* 138–158. §10n15.

Greene, J., & Cohen, J. (2004). For the law, neuroscience changes nothing and everything. *Philosophical Transactions of the Royal Society of London, Series B: Biological Sciences, 359*(1451), 1775–1785. §§7.12, 9.14.

Greengard, P., Jen, J., Nairn, A. C., & Stevens, C. F. (1991). Enhancement of the glutamate response by cAMP-dependent protein kinase in hippocampal neurons. *Science, 253,* 1135–1138. §5n1.

Greenspan, R. J., & van Swinderen, B. (2004). Cognitive consonance: Complex brain functions in the fruit fly and its relatives. *Trends in Neuroscience, 27,* 707–711. §10.45.

Greenwald, A. G., Draine, S. C., & Abrams, R. L. (1996). Three cognitive markers of unconscious semantic activation. *Science, 273,* 1699–1702. §10.36.

Gregoriou, G. G., Gotts, S. J., Zhou, H., & Desimone, R. (2009a). Long-range neural coupling through synchronization with attention. *Progress in Brain Research, 176,* 35–45. §§4.24, 4.49.

Gregoriou, G., Gotts, S., Zhou, H., & Desimone, R. (2009b). High-frequency, long-range coupling between prefrontal and visual cortex during attention. *Science, 324,* 1207–1210. §§4.24, 4.49.

Griffin, I. C., & Nobre, A. C. (2003). Orienting attention to locations in internal representations. *Journal of Cognitive Neuroscience, 15*(8), 1176–1194. §§10.13, 10.15.

Grill-Spector, K., Kushnir, T., Edelman, S., Avidan, G., Itzchak, Y., & Malach, R. (1999). Differential processing of objects under various viewing conditions in the human lateral occipital complex. *Neuron, 24*(1), 187–203. §4.10.

Grill-Spector, K., Kushnir, T., Hendler, T., Edelman, S., Itzchak, Y., & Malach, R. (1998). A sequence of object-processing stages revealed by fMRI in the human occipital lobe. *Human Brain Mapping, 6*(4), 316–328. §4.10.

Gritti, I., Mainville, L., Mancia, M., & Jones, B. E. (1997). GABAergic and other noncholinergic basal forebrain neurons, together with cholinergic neurons, project to the mesocortex and isocortex in the rat. *Journal of Comparative Neurology, 383,* 163–177. §5.45.

Gröblacher, S., Paterek, T., Kaltenbaek, R., Brukner, C., Zukowski, M., Aspelmeyer, M., et al. (2007). An experimental test of non-local realism. *Nature, 446,* 871–875. §§A1.6, A1.7.

Grol, M. J., deLange, F. P., Verstraten, F. A., Passingham, R. E., & Toni, I. (2006). Cerebral changes during performance of overlearned arbitrary visuomotor associations. *Journal of Neuroscience, 26,* 117–125. §10.43.

Gross, C. G. (2000). Coding for visual categories in the human brain. *Nature Neuroscience, 3,* 855–856. §§4.9, 4.11.

Gross, C. G. (2002). Genealogy of the "grandmother cell." *Neuroscientist, 8*(5), 512–518. §4.11.

Gross, C. G., Bender, D. B., & Rocha-Miranda, C. E. (1969). Visual receptive fields of neurons in inferotemporal cortex of the monkey. *Science, 166*(910), 1303–1306. §4.10.

Gross, C. G., Rocha-Miranda, C. E., & Bender, D. B. (1972). Visual properties of neurons in inferotemporal cortex of the Macaque. *Journal of Neurophysiology, 35*(1), 96–111. §4.10.

Gross, J., Schmitz, F., Schnitzler, I., Kessler, K., Shapiro, K., Hommel, B., et al. (2004). Modulation of long-range neural synchrony reflects temporal limitations of visual attention in humans. *Proceedings of the National Academy of Sciences of the United States of America, 101,* 13050–13055. §4.23.

Grossberg, S., & Mingolla, E. (1985a). Neural dynamics of form perception: Boundary completion, illusory figures, and neon color spreading. *Psychological Review, 92,* 173–211. §10.50.

Grossberg, S., & Mingolla, E. (1985b). Neural dynamics of perceptual grouping: Textures, boundaries, and emergent segmentations. *Perception & Psychophysics, 38*(2), 141–171. §10.50.

Grossberg, S., & Somers, D. (1991). Synchronized oscillations during cooperative feature linking in a cortical model of visual perception. *Neural Networks, 4,* 453–466. §4.45.

Grubb, M. S., & Thompson, I. D. (2005). Visual response properties of burst and tonic firing in the mouse dorsal LGN. *Journal of Neurophysiology, 93*(6), 3224–3247. §4.38.

Gruber, T., Müller, M. M., Keil, A., & Elbert, T. (1999). Selective visual-spatial attention alters induced gamma band responses in the human EEG. *Clinical Neurophysiology, 110*(12), 2074–2085. §4.49.

Grush, R., & Churchland, P. (1995). Gaps in Penrose's toilings. *Journal of Consciousness Studies, 2*(1), 10–29. §A1.8.

Guido, W., Lu, S. M., Vaughan, J. W., Godwin, D. W., & Sherman, S. M. (1995). Receiver operating characteristic (ROC) analysis of neurons in the cat's lateral geniculate nucleus during tonic and burst response mode. *Visual Neuroscience, 12*, 723–741. §4.38.

Guido, W., & Weyand, T. (1995). Burst responses in thalamic relay cells of the awake behaving cat. *Journal of Neurophysiology, 74*, 1782–1786. §§4.38, 4n11.

Guido, W., Lu, S. M., & Sherman, S. M. (1992). Relative contributions of burst and tonic responses to the receptive field properties of lateral geniculate neurons in the cat. *Journal of Neurophysiology, 68*, 2199–2211. §4.38.

Guillery, R. W., Feig, S. L., & Lozsadi, D. A. (1998). Paying attention to the thalamic reticular nucleus. *Trends in Neuroscience, 21*, 28–32. §4.27.

Guillery, R. W., & Harting, J. K. (2003). Structure and connections of the thalamic reticular nucleus: Advancing views over half a century. *Journal of Comparative Neurology, 463*, 360–371. §4.27.

Gulyás, A. I., Megias, M., Emri, Z., & Freund, T. F. (1999). Total number and ratio of excitatory and inhibitory synapses converging onto single interneurons of different types in the CA1 area of the rat hippocampus. *Journal of Neuroscience, 19*, 10082–10097. §4.44.

Gupta, A., Wang, Y., & Markram, H. (2000). Organizing principles for a diversity of GABAergic interneurons and synapses in the neocortex. *Science, 287*, 273–278. §§4.33, 4.55, 5.3.

Gustafsson, L. (1997). Inadequate cortical feature maps: A neural circuit theory of autism. *Biological Psychiatry, 42*, 1138–1147. §4.33.

Gutierrez, R., Simon, S. A., & Nicolelis, M. A. (2010). Licking-induced synchrony in the taste-reward circuit improves cue discrimination during learning. *Journal of Neuroscience, 30*, 287–303. §4.60.

Haarmeier, T., Bunjes, F., Lindner, A., Berret, E., & Thier, P. (2001). Optimizing visual motion perception during eye movements. *Neuron, 32*(3), 527–535. §9n6.

Hadj-Bouziane, F., Bell, A. H., Knusten, T. A., Ungerleider, L. G., & Tootell, R. B. (2008). Perception of emotional expressions is independent of face selectivity in monkey inferior temporal cortex. *Proceedings of the National Academy of Sciences of the United States of America, 105*(14), 5591–5596. §10.21.

Haenny, P. E., Maunsell, J. H. R., & Schiller, P. H. (1988). State dependent activity in monkey visual cortex. II. Retinal and extraretinal factors in V4. *Experimental Brain Research, 69*, 245–259. §4.24.

Hafed, Z. M., & Clark, J. J. (2002). Microsaccades as an overt measure of covert attention shifts. *Vision Research, 42*, 2533–2545. §4.23.

Hafting, T., Fyhn, M., Molden, S., Moser, M.-B., & Moser, E. I. (2005). Microstructure of a spatial map in the entorhinal cortex. *Nature, 436*(7052), 801–806. §§4.8, 8.22.

Haggard, P. (2008). Human volition: Towards a neuroscience of will. *Nature Reviews: Neuroscience, 9*(12), 934–946. §9.5, figure 9.1, §9n2.

Haggard, P., Cartledge, P., Dafydd, M., & Oakley, D. A. (2004). Anomalous control: When "free-will" is not conscious. *Consciousness and Cognition, 13*(3), 646–654. §9n2.

Haggard, P., & Eimer, M. (1999). On the relation between brain potentials and the awareness of voluntary movements. *Experimental Brain Research, 126*(1), 128–133. §§9.1, 9.3, 9.5, figure 9.2, 9n2.

Haggard, P., Mele, A., O'Connor, T., & Vohs, K. (2010). Lexicon of terms. http://www.freewillandscience.com/wp/?page_id=63. §§3.1, 3n2.

Haider, B., Duque, A., Hasenstaub, A. R., & McCormick, D. A. (2006). Neocortical network activity in vivo is generated through a dynamic balance of excitation and inhibition. *Journal of Neuroscience, 26*, 4535–4545. §4.32.

Hájos, N., Katona, I., Naiem, S. S., MacKie, K., Ledent, C., Mody, I., et al. (2000). Cannabinoids inhibit hippocampal GABAergic transmission and network oscillations. *European Journal of Neuroscience, 12*, 3239–3249. §5.40.

Hájos, N., Pálhalmi, J., Mann, E. O., Németh, B., Paulsen, O., & Freund, T. F. (2004). Spike timing of distinct types of GABAergic interneuron during hippocampal gamma oscillations *in vitro*. *Journal of Neuroscience, 24*, 9127–9137. §5.43.

Haken, H. (1984). *The science of structure: Synergetics*. New York: Van Nostrand Reinhod. §4.69.

Halgren, E., Marinkovic, K., & Chauvel, P. (1998). Generators of the late cognitive potentials in auditory and visual oddball tasks. *Electroencephalography and Clinical Neurophysiology, 106*, 156–164. §10.16.

Hall, S. D., Holliday, I. E., Hillebrand, A., Singh, K. D., Furlong, P. L., Hadjipapas, A., et al. (2005). The missing link: Analogous human and primate cortical gamma oscillations. *NeuroImage, 26*, 13–17. §4.49.

Halpain, S., Girault, J. A., & Greengard, P. (1990). Activation of NMDA receptors induces dephosphorylation of DARPP-32 in rat striatal slices. *Nature, 343*, 369–372. §5n1.

Hameroff, S. (2001). Biological feasibility of quantum approaches to consciousness. In P. van Loocke (Ed.), *The physical nature of consciousness* (pp. 1–62) Amsterdam: John Benjamins. §A1.8.

Hanes, D. P., Patterson, W. F., & Schall, J. D. (1998). Role of frontal eye fields in countermanding saccades: Visual, movement, and fixation activity. *Journal of Neurophysiology, 79*(2), 817–834. §4.23.

Hannula, D. E., Simons, D. J., & Cohen, N. J. (2005). Imaging implicit perception: Promise and pitfalls. *Nature Reviews: Neuroscience, 6*, 247–255. §10n12.

Hansel, D., & Sompolinsky, H. (1992). Synchronization and computation in a chaotic neural network. *Physical Review Letters, 68*, 718–721. §4n3.

Hardingham, G. E., & Bading, H. (2010). Synaptic versus extrasynaptic NMDA receptor signalling: Implications for neurodegenerative disorders. *Nature Reviews: Neuroscience, 11*, 682–696. §5.5.

Harnett, M. T., Bernier, B. E., Ahn, K. C., & Morikawa, H. (2009). Burst-timing-dependent plasticity of NMDA receptor-mediated transmission in midbrain dopamine neurons. *Neuron, 62*(6), 826–838. §§5.6, 5n4.

Harris-Warrick, R. M., & Cohen, A. H. (1985). Serotonin modulates the central pattern generator for locomotion in the isolated lamprey spinal cord. *Journal of Experimental Biology, 116*, 27–46. §1.11.

Hasenstaub, A., Shu, Y., Haider, B., Kraushaar, U., Duque, A., & McCormick, D. A. (2005). Inhibitory postsynaptic potentials carry synchronized frequency information in active cortical networks. *Neuron, 47*, 423–435. §§4.43, 4.44, 5.3, 5.42.

Hasselmo, M. E. (1995). Neuromodulation and cortical function: Modeling the physiological basis of behavior. *Behavioural Brain Research, 67*, 1–27. §5.38.

Hasselmo, M. E., Rolls, E. T., & Baylis, G. C. (1989). The role of expression and identity in the face-selective responses of neurons in the temporal visual cortex of the monkey. *Behavioural Brain Research, 32*(3), 203–218. §10.21.

Hasselmo, M., & Giocomo, L. (2006). Cholinergic modulation of cortical function. *Journal of Molecular Neuroscience, 30*, 133–135. §5.39.

Hasselmo, M., & Bower, J. (1992). Cholinergic suppression specific to intrinsic not afferent fiber synapses in rat piriform (olfactory) cortex. *Journal of Neurophysiology, 67*, 1222–1229. §5.39.

Häusser, M., Stuart, G., Rocca, C., & Sakmann, B. (1995). Axonal initiation and active dendritic propagation of action potentials in substantia nigra neurons. *Neuron, 15*, 637–647. §5.18.

Häusser, M., Spruston, N., & Stuart, G. J. (2000). Diversity and dynamics of dendritic signaling. *Science, 290*, 739–744. §5.18.

Hawkes, A. G., Jalali, A., & Colquhoun, D. (1992). Asymptotic distributions of apparent open times and shut times in a single channel record allowing for the omission of brief events. *Philosophical Transactions of the Royal Society of London, Series B: Biological Sciences, 337*(1282), 383–404. §5.25.

Haxby, J. V., Ungerleider, L. G., Clark, V. P., Schouten, J. L., Hoffman, E. A., & Martin, A. (1999). The effect of face inversion on activity in human neural systems for face and object perception. *Neuron, 22*(1), 189–199. §4.12.

Hayden, B. Y., & Gallant, J. L. (2005). Time course of attention reveals different mechanisms for spatial and feature-based attention in area V4. *Neuron, 47*, 637–643. §§4.25, 5.50.

Hayden, B. Y., & Gallant, J. L. (2009). Combined effects of spatial and feature-based attention on responses of V4 neurons. *Vision Research, 49*, 1182–1187. §4.24.

He, Z. J., & Nakayama, K. (1992). Surfaces versus features in visual search. *Nature, 359*(6392), 231–233. §§4.22, 10.30, 10.35.

He, Z. J., & Nakayama, K. (1994a). Apparent motion determined by surface layout not by disparity or three-dimensional distance. *Nature, 367*(6459), 173–175. §§4.22, 10.35.

He, Z. J., & Nakayama, K. (1994b). Perceived surface shape not features determines correspondence strength in apparent motion. *Vision Research, 34*(16), 2125–2135. §§4.22, 10.35.

He, Z. J., & Nakayama, K. (1995). Visual attention to surfaces in three-dimensional space. *Proceedings of the National Academy of Sciences of the United States of America, 92*(24), 11155–11159. §10.35.

He, Y., Wang, J., Wang, L., Chen, Z. J., Yan, C., Yang, H., et al. (2009). Uncovering intrinsic modular organization of spontaneous brain activity in humans. *PLoS ONE, 4*(4), e5226. §7.15.

Hebb, D. O. (1949). *The organization of behavior: A neuropsychological theory*. New York: Wiley. §§4.54, 5.11.

Heeger, D. J. (1992). Normalization of cell responses in cat striate cortex. *Visual Neuroscience, 9*, 181–198. §5.45.

Heil, J., & Mele, A. (Eds.). (1993). *Mental causation*. Oxford University Press. §1.5, §A2.2, §A2.3.

Heinemann, A., Kunde, W., & Kiesel, A. (2009). Context-specific primecongruency effects: On the role of conscious stimulus representations for cognitive control. *Consciousness & Cognition, 18*, 966–976. §10.36.

Heisenberg, M. (1983). Initiale Aktivität und Willkürverhalten bei Tieren. *Naturwissenschaften, 70*, 70–78. §10.45.

Heisenberg, M. (2009). Is free will an illusion? *Nature, 459*, 164–165. §§7.17, 10.45.

Heisenberg, M., Wolf, R., & Brembs, B. (2001). Flexibility in a single behavioral variable of Drosophila. *Learning & Memory, 8*, 1–10. §10.45.

Heisenberg, W. (1927). Über den anschaulichen Inhalt der quantentheoretischen Kinematik und Mechanik. *Zeitschrift für Physik, 43*(3–4), 172–198. §A1n7.

Helmholtz, H. L. (1910 [1867]). *Handbuch der physiologischen Optik.* Leipzig: L. Voss. Reprinted in A. Gullstrand, J. von Kries, & W. Nagel (Eds.). Handbuch der physiologischen Optik (3rd edn.). Hamburg: L. Voss. §§9n6, 10.19.

Henderson, J. M., & Hollingworth, A. (1999). High-level scene perception. *Annual Review of Psychology, 50,* 243–271. §4.14.

Hendry, R. (2006). Is there downward causation in chemistry? In D. Baird & E. Scerri (Eds.), *Philosophy of chemistry: Synthesis of a new discipline* (pp. 207–220). Dordrecht: Springer. §A2.2.

Hendry, S. H., Schwark, H. D., Jones, E. G., & Yan, J. (1987). Numbers and proportions of GABA-immunoreactive neurons in different areas of monkey cerebral cortex. *Journal of Neuroscience, 7,* 1503–1519. §5.3.

Hendry, S. H., & Jones, E. G. (1991). GABA neuronal subpopulations in cat primary auditory cortex: Co-localization with calcium binding proteins. *Brain Research, 543*(1), 45–55. §5.3.

Henrie, J. A., & Shapley, R. (2005). LFP power spectra in V1 cortex: The graded effect of stimulus contrast. *Journal of Neurophysiology, 94,* 479–490. §4.49.

Hering, E. (1878). *Zur Lehre vom Lichtsinn.* Vienna. §§10.49, 10.50, 10n17.

Herrero, J., Roberts, M., Delicato, L., Gieselmann, M., Dayan, P., & Thiele, A. (2008). Acetylcholine contributes through muscarinic receptors to attentional modulation in v1. *Nature, 454,* 1110–1114. §5.39.

Herrington, T. M., & Assad, J. A. (2009). Neural activity in the middle temporal area and lateral intraparietal area during endogenously cued shifts of attention. *Journal of Neuroscience, 29,* 14160–14176. §4.24.

Herrington, T. M., Masse, N. Y., Hachmeh, K. J., Smith, J. E., Assad, J. A., & Cook, E. P. (2009). The effect of microsaccades on the correlation between neural activity and behavior in middle temporal, ventral intraparietal, and lateral intraparietal areas. *Journal of Neuroscience, 29,* 5793–5805. §4.24.

Herrmann, C. S., & Knight, R. T. (2001). Mechanisms of human attention: Event-related potentials and oscillations. *Neuroscience and Biobehavioral Reviews, 25,* 465–476. §5.46.

Herrmann, C. S., Pauen, M., Min, B.-K., Busch, N. A., & Rieger, J. W. (2008). Analysis of a choice-reaction task yields a new interpretation of Libet's experiments. *International Journal of Psychophysiology, 67*(2), 151–157. §9n2.

Herry, C., Ciocchi, S., Senn, V., Demmou, L., Müller, C., & Lüthi, A. (2008). Switching on and off fear by distinct neuronal circuits. *Nature, 454*(7204), 600–606. §9.8.

Higley, M. J., & Contreras, D. (2006). Balanced excitation and inhibition determine spike timing during frequency adaptation. *Journal of Neuroscience, 26,* 448–457. §4.32.

Hilkenmeier, F., & Scharlau, I. (2010). Rapid allocation of temporal attention in the attentional blink paradigm. *European Journal of Cognitive Psychology, 22*(8), 1222–1234. §4.48.

Hillyard, S. A., Vogel, E. K., & Luck, S. J. (1998). Sensory gain control (amplification) as a mechanism of selective attention: Electrophysiological and neuroimaging evidence. *Philosophical Transactions of the Royal Society of London, Series B: Biological Sciences, 353*(1373), 1257–1270. §§4.21, 10.32.

Hinrichsen, H. (2006). Non-equilibrium phase transitions. *Physica A, 369,* 1–28. §4.42.

Hipp, J. F., Engel, A. K., & Siegel, M. (2011). Oscillatory synchronization in large-scale cortical networks predicts perception. *Neuron, 69,* 387–396. §§4.23, 4.49.

Hirsch, J. C., Agassandian, C., Merchan-Perez, A., Ben-Ari, Y., DeFelipe, J., Esclapez, M., et al. (1999). Deficit of quantal release of GABA in experimental models of temporal lobe epilepsy. *Nature Neuroscience, 2,* 499–500. §4.33.

Hobson, J. A., & Pace-Schott, E. F. (2002). The cognitive neuroscience of sleep: Neuronal systems, consciousness and learning. *Nature Reviews: Neuroscience, 3*(9), 679–693. §§10.77, 10.78.

Hodgkin, A. L., & Huxley, A. F. (1952). Resting and action potentials in single nerve fibres. *Journal of Physiology, 104*(2), 176–195. §5.17.

Hodgson, D. (1993). *The mind matters: Consciousness and choice in a quantum world.* New York: Oxford University Press. §A1.9.

Hoffman, K. L., Gothard, K. M., Schmid, M. C., & Logothetis, N. K. (2007). Facial expression and gaze-selective responses in the monkey amygdala. *Current Biology, 17*(9), 766–772. §10.21.

Holland, P. C., & Gallagher, M. (2004). Amygdala-frontal interactions and reward expectancy. *Current Opinions in Neurobiology, 14,* 148–155. §5.24.

Holmgren, C., Harkany, T., Svennenfors, B., & Zilberter, Y. (2003). Pyramidal cell communication within local networks in layer 2/3 of rat neocortex. *Journal of Physiology, 551,* 139–153. §4.55.

Holtmaat, A., & Svoboda, K. (2009). Experience-dependent structural synaptic plasticity in the mammalian brain. *Nature Reviews: Neuroscience, 10,* 647–658. §5.9.

Hopfield, J. J. (1995). Pattern recognition computation using action potential timing for stimulus representation. *Nature, 376,* 33–36. §4.44.

Hopfield, J. J., & Tank, D. W. (1986). Computing with neural circuits: A model. *Science, 233*, 625–633. §4.54.

Horiike, K., Ishida, T., Tanaka, H., & Arai, R. (2001). Distribution of d-amino acid oxidase and d-serine in vertebrate brains. *Journal of Molecular Catalysis, B: Enzymatic, 12*, 37–41. §5n2.

Hormuzdi, S. G., Pais, I., LeBeau, F. E., Towers, S. K., Rozov, A., Buhl, E. H., et al. (2001). Impaired electrical signaling disrupts gamma frequency oscillations in connexin36 deficient mice. *Neuron, 31*, 487–495. §4.44.

Horowitz, T. S., & Wolfe, J. M. (1998). Visual search has no memory. *Nature, 394*(6693), 575–577. §10.58.

Horton, J. C., & Hoyt, W. F. (1991). The representation of the visual field in human striate cortex: A revision of the classic Holmes map. *Archives of Ophthalmology, 109*(6), 816–824. §4n5.

Horwitz, G. D., & Albright, T. D. (2003). Short-latency fixational saccades induced by luminance increments. *Journal of Neurophysiology, 90*, 1333–1339. §4.23.

Hou, Q., Gilbert, J., & Man, H.-Y. (2011). Homeostatic regulation of AMPA receptor trafficking and degradation by light-controlled single-synaptic activation. *Neuron, 72*, 806–818. §5.7.

Hou, Q., Zhang, D., Jarzylo, L., Huganir, R. L., & Man, H. Y. (2008). Homeostatic regulation of AMPA receptor expression at single hippocampal synapses. *Proceedings of the National Academy of Sciences of the United States of America, 105*, 775–780. §5.7.

Houser, C. R., Hendry, S. H., Jones, E. G., & Vaughn, J. E. (1983). Morphological diversity of immunocytochemically identified GABA neurons in the monkey sensory-motor cortex. *Journal of Neurocytology, 12*, 617–638. §5.3.

Houtkamp, R., Spekreijse, H., & Roelfsema, P. R. (2003). A gradual spread of attention during mental curve tracing. *Perception & Psychophysics, 65*, 1136–1144. §4.24.

Howe, J. R., Cull-Candy, S. G., & Colquhoun, D. (1991). Currents through single glutamate receptor channels in outside-out patches from rat cerebellar granule cells. *Journal of Physiology, 432*, 143–202. §§5.23, 5.25, 5.31.

Hsieh, P.-J., & Tse, P. U. (2006). Illusory color mixing upon perceptual fading and filling-in does not result in "forbidden colors." *Vision Research, 46*(14), 2251–2258. §§10.48, 10.52.

Hsieh, P.-J., & Tse, P. U. (2009). Feature mixing rather than feature replacement during perceptual filling-in. *Vision Research, 49*(4), 439–450. §§4.14, 8.18, 10.48, 10.52.

Hsieh, P.-J., & Tse, P. U. (2010). "Brain-reading" of perceived colors reveals a feature mixing mechanism underlying perceptual filling-in in cortical area V1. *Human Brain Mapping, 31*(9), 1395–1407. §10.52.

Huang, L. Y., Catterall, W. A., & Ehrenstein, G. (1978). Selectivity of cations and nonelectrolytes for acetylcholine-activated channels in cultures muscle cells. *Journal of General Physiology, 71*, 397–410. §A1.10.

Hubel, D. H., & Wiesel, T. N. (1959). Receptive fields of single neurones in the cat's striate cortex. *Journal of Physiology, 148*, 574–591. §4.9.

Hubel, D. H., & Wiesel, T. N. (1968). Receptive fields and functional architecture of monkey striate cortex. *Journal of Physiology, 195*(1), 215–243. §4.9.

Huguenard, J., & McCormick, D. (1992). Simulation of the currents involved in rhythmic oscillations in thalamic relay neurons. *Journal of Neurophysiology, 68*(4), 1373–1383. §4.35.

Huk, A. C., & Shadlen, M. N. (2005). Neural activity in macaque parietal cortex reflects temporal integration of visual motion signals during perceptual decision making. *Journal of Neuroscience, 25*, 10420–10436. §4.18.

Hume, D. (1739). *A treatise on human nature.* London: Clarendon Press. §§5n6, 7.2, 7.3.

Humphreys, P. (1997). How properties emerge. *Philosophy of Science, 64*, 1–17. §A2.2.

Hung, C. P., Kreiman, G., Poggio, T., & DiCarlo, J. J. (2005). Fast readout of object identity from macaque inferior temporal cortex. *Science, 310*(5749), 863–866. §4.14.

Hupé, J. M., James, A. C., Payne, B. R., Lomber, S. G., Girard, P., & Bullier, J. (1998). Cortical feedback improves discrimination between figure and background by V1, V2, and V3 neurons. *Nature, 394*, 784–787. §5.45.

Husi, H., Ward, M. A., Choudhary, J. S., Blackstock, W. P., & Grant, S. G. (2000). Proteomic analysis of NMDA receptor—adhesion protein signaling complexes. *Nature Neuroscience, 3*, 661–669. §5n1.

Ibata, K., Sun, Q., & Turrigiano, G. G. (2008). Rapid synaptic scaling induced by changes in postsynaptic firing. *Neuron, 57*, 819–826. §5.7.

Ikegaya, Y., Aaron, G., Cossart, R., Aronov, D., Lampl, I., Ferster, D., et al. (2004). Synfire chains and cortical songs: Temporal modules of cortical activity. *Science, 304*, 559–564. §§4.60, 5.16.

Intraub, H. (1997). The representation of visual scenes. *Trends in Cognitive Sciences, 1*(6), 217–222. §4.14.

Irwin, D. E., Colcombe, A. M., Kramer, A. F., & Hahn, S. (2000). Attentional and oculomotor capture by onset luminance and color singletons. *Vision Research, 40*, 1443–1458. §4.22.

Ishai, A., Ungerleider, L. G., Martin, A., Schouten, J. L., & Haxby, J. V. (1999). Distributed representation of objects in the human ventral visual pathway. *Proceedings of the National Academy of Sciences of the United States of America, 96*(16), 9379–9384. §4.12.

Jack, J. J. B., Noble, D., & Tsien, R. Y. (1975). *Electric current flow in excitable cells.* Oxford: Oxford University Press. §5.15.

Jackson, F. (1982). Epiphenomenal qualia. *Philosophical Quarterly, 32,* 127–136. §§10.5, A2n1.

Jackson, G. M., & Swainson, R. (2009). Attention, competition, and the parietal lobes: insights from Bálint's syndrome. *Psychological Research, 73*(2), 263–270. §10.35.

Jackson, M. E., Homayoun, H., & Moghaddam, B. (2004). NMDA receptor hypofunction produces concomitant firing rate potentiation and burst activity reduction in the prefrontal cortex. *Proceedings of the National Academy of Sciences of the United States of America, 101*(22), 8467–8472. §4.36.

Jacob, V., Brasier, D. J., Erchova, I., Feldman, D., & Shulz, D. E. (2007). Spike timing-dependent synaptic depression in the in vivo barrel cortex of the rat. *Journal of Neuroscience, 27,* 1271–1284. §5.11.

Jagadeesh, B. (2009). Recognizing grandmother. *Nature Neuroscience, 12*(9), 1083–1085. §4.11.

Jahanshahi, M., Jenkins, I. H., Brown, R. G., Marsden, C. D., Passingham, R. E., & Brooks, D. J. (1995). Self-initiated versus externally triggered movements. I. An investigation using measurement of regional cerebral blood flow with PET and movement-related potentials in normal and Parkinson's disease subjects. *Brain, 118,* 913–933. Figure 9.1.

Jahnsen, H., & Llinas, R. (1984a). Voltage-dependent burst-to-tonic switching of thalamic cell activity: An in vitro study. *Archives Italiennes de Biologie, 122,* 73–82. §4n11.

Jahnsen, H., & Llinas, R. (1984b). Electrophysiological properties of guinea-pig thalamic neurones: An in vitro study. *Journal of Physiology, 349,* 205–226. §4n11.

Jambaque, I., Chiron, C., Dumas, C., Mumford, J., & Dulac, O. (2000). Mental and behavioural outcome of infantile epilepsy treated by vigabatrin in tuberous sclerosis patients. *Epilepsy Research, 38,* 151–160. §4.33.

James, W. (1884). What is emotion? *Mind, 9,* 189. §7.17.

James, W. (1956 [1884]). The dilemma of determinism. In *The will to believe.* New York: Dover. §7.17, §7n1, §7n6.

James, W. (1956). *The will to believe.* Mineola, NY: Dover. §7.17, §7n1, §7n6.

Jarsky, T., Roxin, A., Kath, W. L., & Spruston, N. (2005). Conditional dendritic spike propagation following distal synaptic activation of hippocampal CA1 pyramidal neurons. *Nature Neuroscience, 8,* 1667–1676. §5.22.

Jastorff, J., & Orban, G. A. (2009). Human functional magnetic resonance imaging reveals separation and integration of shape and motion cues in biological motion processing. *Journal of Neuroscience, 29*(22), 7315–7329. §4.14.

Jefferys, J. G. (1995). Nonsynaptic modulation of neuronal activity in the brain: Electric currents and extracellular ions. *Physiological Reviews, 75*(4), 689–723. §4.68.

Jefferys, J. G., Traub, R. D., & Whittington, M. A. (1996). Neuronal networks for induced "40 Hz" rhythms. *Trends in Neurosciences, 19,* 202–208. §4.44, 5.3.

Jensen, O., Kaiser, J., & Lachaux, J. P. (2007). Human gamma-frequency oscillations associated with attention and memory. *Trends in Neurosciences, 30,* 317–324. §4.49.

Jiang, Y., Costello, P., Fang, F., Huang, M., & He, S. (2006). A gender- and sexual orientation-dependent spatial attentional effect of invisible images. *Proceedings of the National Academy of Sciences of the United States of America, 103,* 17048–17052. §§10.28, 10.31, 10.32.

Jirsa, V. K. (2004). Connectivity and dynamics of neural information-processing. *Neuroinformatics, 2*(2), 183–204. §4.68.

Joelving, F. C., Compte, A., & Constantinidis, C. (2007). Temporal properties of posterior parietal neuron discharges during working memory and passive viewing. *Journal of Neurophysiology, 97,* 2254–2266. §4.52.

Johnson, J. W., & Ascher, P. (1987). Glycine potentiates the NMDA response in cultured mouse brain neurons. *Nature, 325,* 529–531. §5.4.

Jonas, P., Bischofberger, J., Fricker, D., & Miles, R. (2004). Interneuron diversity series: Fast in, fast out—temporal and spatial signal processing in hippocampal interneurons. *Trends in Neurosciences, 27,* 30–40. §§4.44, 5.3.

Jones, B. E. (2008). Modulation of cortical activation and behavioral arousal by cholinergic and orexinergic systems. *Annals of the New York Academy of Sciences, 1129,* 26–34. §5.38.

Jones, E. G. (1984). Laminar distribution of cortical efferent cells. In A. Peters & E. G. Jones (Eds.), *Cerebral cortex: Cellular components of the cerebral cortex* (pp. 521–553). New York: Plenum Press. §5.2.

Jones, M. S., & Barth, D. S. (1999). Spatiotemporal organization of fast (>200 Hz) electrical oscillations in rat Vibrissa/Barrel cortex. *Journal of Neurophysiology, 82,* 1599–1609. §4.35.

Jones, M. S., & Barth, D. S. (2002). Effects of bicuculline methiodide on fast (>200 Hz) electrical oscillations in rat somatosensory cortex. *Journal of Neurophysiology, 88*, 1016–1025. §4.35.

Jones, M. S., MacDonald, K. D., Choi, B., Dudek, F. E., & Barth, D. S. (2000). Intracellular correlates of fast (>200 Hz) electrical oscillations in rat somatosensory cortex. *Journal of Neurophysiology, 84*, 1505–1518. §§4.35, 4.44.

Jonides, J., Lacey, S. C., & Nee, D. E. (2005). Processes of working memory in mind and brain. *Current Directions in Psychological Science, 14*(1), 2–5. §4.26.

Jonides, J., Lewis, R. L., Nee, D. E., Lustig, C. A., Berman, M. G., & Moore, K. S. (2008). The mind and brain of short-term memory. *Annual Review of Psychology, 59*, 193–224. §4.26.

Jonides, J., & Yantis, S. (1988). Uniqueness of abrupt visual onset in capturing attention. *Perception & Psychophysics, 43*, 346–354. §4.22.

Jönsson, C. (1974). Electron diffraction at multiple slits. *American Journal of Physics, 4*, 4–11. Translated from Jönsson, C. (1961). Zeitschrift fur Physik, 161, 454–474. §A1.10.

Joseph, J. S., Chun, M. M., & Nakayama, K. (1997). Attentional requirements in a preattentive feature search task. *Nature, 387*(6635), 805–807. §10.73.

Joseph, J. S., Chun, M. M., & Nakayama, K. (1998). Vision and attention: The role of training. *Nature, 393*, 425. §10.73.

Joubert, O. R., Rousselet, G. A., Fize, D., & Fabre-Thorpe, M. (2007). Processing scene context: Fast categorization and object interference. *Vision Research, 47*(26), 3286–3297. §§4.14, 10.71.

Judge, S. J., Wurtz, R. H., & Richmond, B. J. (1980). Vision during saccadic eye movements. I. Visual interactions in striate cortex. *Journal of Neurophysiology, 43*, 1133–1155. §4.39.

Kahneman, D., Treisman, A. M., & Gibbs, B. J. (1992). The reviewing of object files: Object-specific integration of information. *Cognitive Psychology, 24*, 175–219. §§4.21, 10.30.

Kampa, B. M., Letzkus, J. J., & Stuart, G. J. (2007). Dendritic mechanisms controlling spike-timing-dependent synaptic plasticity. *Trends in Neurosciences, 30*, 456–463. §5.23.

Kanai, R., Tsuchiya, N., & Verstraten, F. A. (2006). The scope and limits of top-down attention in unconscious visual processing. *Current Biology, 16*(23), 2332–2336. §§10.32, 10.33.

Kanai, R., Walsh, V., & Tseng, C. H. (2010). Subjective discriminability of invisibility: A framework for distinguishing perceptual and attentional failures of awareness. *Consciousness & Cognition, 19*, 1045–1057. §10n1.

Kandel, E., Schwartz, J. and Jessell, T. (2000). *Principles of neural science* (4th Ed.). New York: McGraw-Hill Medical. §4.7.

Kane, R. (1985). *Free will and values*. Albany: SUNY Press. §7.17.

Kane, R. (1996). *The significance of free will*. New York: Oxford University Press. §7.17.

Kane, R. (2005). *A contemporary introduction to free will*. New York: Oxford University Press. §7.17.

Kane, R. (Ed.). (2011). *The Oxford Handbook of free will* (2nd Ed.). New York: Oxford University Press. §7.17.

Kang, J., & Turano, F. J. (2003). The putative glutamate receptor 1.1 (AtGLR1.1) functions as a regulator of carbon and nitrogen metabolism in Arabidopsis thaliana. *Proceedings of the National Academy of Sciences of the United States of America, 100,* 6872–6877. §2n3.

Kant, I. (1998 [1781]). *Critique of pure reason*. P. Guyer & A. W. Wood (Eds.). Cambridge: Cambridge University Press. §§8.13, 8n5.

Kant, I. (1997). *Critique of practical reason*. Cambridge: Cambridge University Press. §7n1.

Kanwisher, N., Chun, M. M., McDermott, J., & Ledden, P. J. (1996). Functional imaging of human visual recognition. *Brain Research: Cognitive Brain Research, 5*(1–2), 55–67. §4.10.

Kanwisher, N., McDermott, J., & Chun, M. M. (1997). The fusiform face area: A module in human extrastriate cortex specialized for face perception. *Journal of Neuroscience, 17*(11), 4302–4311. §4.12.

Kass, J. I., & Mintz, I. M. (2006). Silent plateau potentials, rhythmic bursts, and pacemaker firing: Three patterns of activity that coexist in quadristable subthalamic neurons. *Proceedings of the National Academy of Sciences of the United States of America, 103*(1), 183–188. §4.35.

Katai, S., Kato, K., Unno, S., Kang, Y., Saruwatari, M., Ishikawa, N., et al. (2010). Classification of extracellularly recorded neurons by their discharge patterns and their correlates with intracellularly identified neuronal types in the frontal cortex of behaving monkeys. *European Journal of Neuroscience, 31,* 1322–1338. §4.52.

Kavalali, E. T., Chung, C., Khvotchev, M., Leitz, J., Nosyreva, E., Raingo, J., et al. (2011). Spontaneous neurotransmission: An independent pathway for neuronal signaling? *Physiology, 26,* 45–53. §4n8.

Kawaguchi, Y., & Kubota, Y. (1997). GABAergic cell subtypes and their synaptic connections in rat frontal cortex. *Cerebral Cortex, 7,* 476–486. §5.3.

Kawaguchi, Y., & Kubota, Y. (1998). Neurochemical features and synaptic connections of large physiologically-identified GABAergic cells in the rat frontal cortex. *Neuroscience, 85,* 677–701. §5.3.

Kawaguchi, Y., Katsumaru, H., Kosaka, T., Heizmann, C. W., & Hama, K. (1987). Fast spiking cells in rat hippocampus (CA1 region) contain the calcium-binding protein parvalbumin. *Brain Research, 416,* 369–374. §§4.44, 4.53.

Kayama, Y., Riso, R. R., Bartlett, J. R., & Doty, R. W. (1979). Luxotonic responses of units in macaque striate cortex. *Journal of Neurophysiology, 42*(6), 1495–1517. §5.37.

Keller, I., & Heckhausen, H. (1990). Readiness potentials preceding spontaneous motor acts: Voluntary vs. involuntary control. *Electroencephalography and Clinical Neurophysiology, 76,* 351–361. §9n1.

Kelso, J. A. S. (1995). *Dynamic patterns: The self-organization of brain and behavior.* Cambridge, MA: MIT Press. §4.69.

Kelso, S. R., Nelson, T. E., & Leonard, J. P. (1992). Protein kinase C-mediated enhancement of NMDA currents by metabotropic glutamate receptors in *Xenopus* oocytes. *Journal of Physiology, 449,* 705–718. §§4.45, 5n1.

Kennedy, H., & Bullier, J. (1985). A double-labeling investigation of the afferent connectivity to cortical areas V1 and V2 of the macaque monkey. *Journal of Neuroscience, 5,* 2815–2830. §4.49.

Kepecs, A., & Lisman, J. (2003). Information encoding and computation with spikes and bursts. *Network, 14*(1), 103–118. §§4.38, 5.30, 5.36, 5.37.

Keren, G. (1976). Some considerations of two alleged kinds of selective attention. *Journal of Experimental Psychology: General, 105,* 349–374. §4.25.

Kersten, D., Mamassian, P., & Yuille, A. (2004). Object perception as Bayesian inference. *Annual Review of Psychology, 55,* 271–304. §10.22.

Khayat, P. S., Niebergall, R., & Martinez-Trujillo, J. C. (2010). Attention differentially modulates similar neuronal responses evoked by varying contrast and direction stimuli in area MT. *Journal of Neuroscience, 30,* 2188–2197. §4.24.

Kilgard, M. P., & Merzenich, M. M. (1998). Cortical map reorganization enabled by nucleus basalis activity. *Science, 279,* 1714–1718. §5.38.

Kim, H. G., Breierlein, M., & Connors, B. W. (1995a). Inhibitory control of excitable dendrites in neocortex. *Journal of Neurophysiology, 4,* 1810–1814. §5.26.

Kim, J. (1989). The myth of nonreductive physicalism. *Proceedings and Addresses of the American Philosophical Association, 63,* 31–47. §3.11.

Kim, J. (1992). Multiple realization and the metaphysics of reduction. *Philosophy and Phenomenological Research, 52,* 1–26. §3.11.

Kim, J. (1993). The non-reductivist's troubles with mental causation. In J. Heil & A. Mele (Eds.), *Mental causation*. Oxford: Oxford University Press. §A2.3.

Kim, J. (1999). Causation. In R. Audi (Ed.), *The Cambridge dictionary of philosophy* (2nd. Ed.) (pp. 125–127). Cambridge: Cambridge University Press. §1.5.

Kim, J. (2003). Blocking causal drainage and other maintenance chores with mental causation. *Philosophy and Phenomenological Research, 67*(1), 151–176. §A2.1.

Kim, J. (2005). *Physicalism, or something near enough*. Princeton: Princeton University Press. §§1.5, 6.9, A2.1, A2.2, figure A2.1, A2n1.

Kim, J. (2006). Emergence: Core ideas and issues. *Synthese, 151*, 547–559. §A2.1.

Kim, J. (2007). Causation and mental causation. In B. McLaughlin & J. Cohen (Eds.), *Contemporary debates in the philosophy of mind* (pp. 227–242). Malden, MA: Blackwell. §A2.1.

Kim, J. J., Clark, R. E., & Thompson, R. F. (1995b). Hippocampectomy impairs the memory of recently, but not remotely, acquired trace eyeblink conditioned responses. *Behavioral Neuroscience, 109*, 195–203. §10n15.

Kim, M. S., & Robertson, L. C. (2001). Implicit representations of space after bilateral parietal lobe damage. *Journal of Cognitive Neuroscience, 13*(8), 1080–1087. §10.35.

Kinoshita, S., Forster, K. I., & Mozer, M. C. (2008). Unconscious cognition isn't that smart: Modulation of masked repetition priming effect in the word naming task. *Cognition, 107*, 623–649. §10.36.

Kinsbourne, M. (1996). What qualifies a representation for a role in consciousness? In J. D. Cohen & J. W. Schooler (Eds.), *Scientific approaches to consciousness* (pp. 335–355). Hillsdale, NJ: Erlbaum. §1.3.

Kinsbourne, M. (2000). How is consciousness expressed in the cerebral activation manifold? *Brain and Mind, 2*, 265–274. §1.3.

Kisvárday, Z. F., Beaulieu, C., & Eysel, U. T. (1993). Network of GABAergic large basket cells in cat visual cortex (area 18): implication for lateral disinhibition. *Journal of Comparative Neurology, 327*, 398–415. §4.44.

Klaus, A., Yu, S., & Plenz, D. (2011). Statistical analyses support power law distributions found in neuronal avalanches. *PLoS ONE, 6*, e19779. §4.42.

Kleckner, N. W., & Dingledine, R. (1988). Requirement for glycine in activation of NMDA-receptors expressed in Xenopus oocytes. *Science, 241*, 835–837. §5.4.

Kleckner, N. W., & Pallotta, B. S. (1995). Burst kinetics of single NMDA receptor currents in cell-attached patches from rat brain cortical neurons in culture. *Journal of Physiology, 486*(2), 411–426. §§5.23, 5.31.

Kloppenburg, P., Zipfel, W., Webb, W., & Harris-Warrick, R. (2000). Highly localized Ca2+ accumulation revealed by multiphoton microscopy in an identified motoneuron and its modulation by dopamine. *Journal of Neuroscience, 20*(7), 2523–2533. §4.35.

Knudsen, E. I. (2007). Fundamental components of attention. *Annual Review of Neuroscience, 30,* 57–78. §4.48.

Kobatake, E., & Tanaka, K. (1994). Neuronal selectivities to complex object features in the ventral visual pathway of the macaque cerebral cortex. *Journal of Neurophysiology, 71*(3), 856–867. §4.10.

Koch, C. (2004). *The quest for consciousness: A neurobiological approach.* Englewood, CO: Roberts. §§3n3, 10.6, 10.43, 10.55, 10n12.

Koch, C., & Hepp, K. (2006). Quantum mechanics in the brain. *Nature, 440*(7084), 611. §A1.8.

Koch, C., Poggio, T., & Torre, V. (1983). Nonlinear interactions in a dendritic tree: Localization, timing, and role in information-processing. *Proceedings of the National Academy of Sciences of the United States of America, 80,* 2799–2802. §§5.15, 5.22.

Koch, C., Rapp, M., & Segev, I. (1996). A brief history of time (constants). *Cerebral Cortex, 6,* 93–101. §4n3.

Koch, C., & Segev, I. (2000). The role of single neurons in information-processing. *Nature Neuroscience, 3*(Suppl.), 1171–1177. §5.18.

Koch, C. (2009). Free will, physics, biology, and the brain. In N. Murphy, G. Ellis, & T. O'Connor (Eds.), *Downward causation and the neurobiology of free will* (pp. 31–52). Berlin: Springer. §7.3.

Koch, C., & Tsuchiya, N. (2007). Attention and consciousness: Two distinct brain processes. *Trends in Cognitive Sciences, 11*(1), 16–22. §10.28.

Koch, C., & Ullman, S. (1985). Shifts in selective visual attention: Towards the underlying neural circuitry. *Human Neurobiology, 4,* 219–227. §5.45.

Koenderink, J. J., van Doorn, A. J., & Kappers, A. L. M. (1992). Surface perception in pictures. *Perception & Psychophysics, 52*(5), 487–496. §10.81.

Koenderink, J. J., van Doorn, A. J., & Kappers, A. L. M. (1994). On so-called paradoxical monocular stereoscopy. *Perception, 23,* 583–594. §10.81.

Koenderink, J. J., van Doorn, A. J., & Kappers, A. L. M. (1995). Depth relief. *Perception, 24,* 115–126. §10.81.

Koenderink, J. J., Kappers, A. M. L., Todd, J. T., & Norman, J. F. (1996). Surface range and attitude probing in stereoscopically presented dynamic scenes. *Journal of Experimental Psychology: Human Perception & Performance, 22*(4), 869–878. §10.81.

Koester, H. J., & Sakmann, B. (1998). Calcium dynamics in single spines during coincident pre- and postsynaptic activity depend on relative timing of back-propagating action potentials and subthreshold excitatory postsynaptic potentials. *Proceedings of the National Academy of Sciences of the United States of America, 95,* 9596–9601. §5.6.

Koivisto, M., Revonsuo, A., & Lehtonen, M. (2006). Independence of visual awareness from the scope of attention: An electrophysiological study. *Cerebral Cortex, 16,* 415–424. §10.16.

Koivisto, M., Lähteenmäki, M., Sørensen, T. A., Vangkilde, S., Overgaard, M., & Revonsuo, A. (2008). The earliest electrophysiological correlate of visual awareness? *Brain and Cognition, 66,* 91–103. §10.16.

Koivisto, M., Kainulainen, P., & Revonsuo, A. (2009). The relationship between awareness and attention: Evidence from ERP responses. *Neuropsychologia, 47,* 2891–2899. §10.16.

Kombian, S. B., Mouginot, D., & Pittman, Q. J. (1997). Dendritically released peptides act as retrograde modulators of afferent excitation in the supraoptic nucleus *in vitro. Neuron, 19,* 903–912. §5.17.

Kopell, N., Ermentrout, G. B., Whittington, M. A., & Traub, R. D. (2000). Gamma rhythms and beta rhythms have different synchronization properties. *Proceedings of the National Academy of Sciences of the United States of America, 97,* 1867–1872. §4.23.

Kopell, N., Kramer, M. A., Malerba, P., & Whittington, M. A. (2010). Are different rhythms good for different functions? *Frontiers in Human Neuroscience, 4,* 187. §4.45.

Korkotian, E., & Segal, M. (2001). Spike-associated fast contraction of dendritic spines in cultured hippocampal neurons. *Neuron, 30*(3), 751–758. §4.55.

Korn, H., & Faber, D. S. (2005). The Mauthner Cell half a century later: A neurobiological model for decision-making? *Neuron, 47,* 13–28. §1.11.

Korn, H., & Faure, P. (2003). Is there chaos in the brain? II. Experimental evidence and related models. *Comptes Rendus Biologies, 326*(9), 787–840. §4.68.

Kornhuber, H. H., & Deecke, L. (1965). Hirnpotentialänderungen bei Willkürbewegungen und passiven Bewegungen des Menschen: Bereitschaftspotential und reafferente Potentiale. *Pflügers Archiv für die Gesamte Physiologie des Menschen und der Tiere, 284,* 1–17. §9.1.

Korte, A. (1915). Kinematoscopische Untersuchungen. *Zeitschrift für Psychologie mit Zeitschrift für Angewandte Psychologie, 72,* 193–206. §10.18.

Kouider, S., Dehaene, S., Jobert, A., & Le Bihan, D. (2007). Cerebral bases of subliminal and supraliminal priming during reading. *Cerebral Cortex, 17,* 2019–2029. §10.67.

Krause, M., Hoffmann, W. E. & Hajos, M. (2003). Auditory sensory gating in hippocampus and reticular thalamic neurons in anesthetized rats. *Biological Psychiatry*, *53*, 244–253. §4.27.

Kravitz, D. J., Saleem, K. S., Baker, C. I., & Mishkin, M. (2011). A new neural framework for visuospatial processing. *Nature Reviews: Neuroscience*, *12*, 217–230. §4.26.

Kreiman, G., Koch, C., & Fried, I. (2000). Category specific visual responses of single neurons in the human medial temporal lobe. *Nature Neuroscience*, *3*, 946–953. §4.11.

Kreiman, G., Fried, I., & Koch, C. (2002). Single-neuron correlates of subjective vision in the human medial temporal lobe. *Proceedings of the National Academy of Sciences of the United States of America*, *99*(12), 8378–8383. §4.11.

Kreitzer, A. C., & Regehr, W. G. (2001). Retrograde inhibition of presynaptic calcium influx by endogenous cannabinoids at excitatory synapses onto Purkinje cells. *Neuron*, *29*, 717–727. §5.17.

Kriegeskorte, N., Formisano, E., Sorger, B., & Goebel, R. (2007). Individual faces elicit distinct response patterns in human anterior temporal cortex. *Proceedings of the National Academy of Sciences of the United States of America*, *104*(51), 20600–20605. §4.12.

Kripke, S. (1980). *Naming and necessity*. Cambridge, MA: Harvard University Press. §8.9, §A3.

Kronforst-Collins, M. A., & Disterhoft, J. F. (1998). Lesions of the caudal area of rabbit medial prefrontal cortex impair trace eyeblink conditioning. *Neurobiology of Learning and Memory*, *69*, 147–162. §10n15.

Krug, M., Lössner, B., & Ott, T. (1984). Anisomycin blocks the late phase of long-term potentiation in the dentate gyrus of freely moving rats. *Brain Research Bulletin*, *13*, 39–42. §5.9.

Kunde, W. (2003). Sequential modulations of stimulus-response correspondence effects depend on awareness of response conflict. *Psychonomic Bulletin & Review*, *10*, 198–205. §10.36.

Kuner, T., & Schoepfer, R. (1996). Multiple structural elements determine subunit specificity of Mg^{2+} block in NMDA receptor channels. *Journal of Neuroscience*, *16*, 3549–3558. §5n9.

Kustov, A. A., & Robinson, D. L. (1996). Shared neural control of attentional shifts and eye movements. *Nature*, *384*(7), 74–77. §4.23.

Kwak, H. W., & Egeth, H. (1992). Consequences of allocating attention to locations and to other attributes. *Perception & Psychophysics*, *51*, 455–464. §4.25.

LaBerge, D. (1995). *Attentional processing: The brain's art of mindfulness.* Cambridge, MA: Harvard University Press. §4.27.

Lakoff, G. (1987), *Women, fire and dangerous things: What categories reveal about the mind.* Chicago: University of Chicago Press. §8.15.

Lam, H. M., Chiu, J., Hsieh, M. H., Meisel, L., Oliveira, I. C., Shin, M., et al. (1998). Glutamate receptor genes in plants. *Nature, 396,* 125–126. §2n3.

Lamme, V. A. (2004). Separate neural definitions of visual consciousness and visual attention: A case for phenomenal awareness. *Neural Networks, 17*(5–6), 861–872. §10.65.

Lamy, D., & Tsal, Y. (2000). Object features, object locations, and object files: Which does selective attention activate and when? *Journal of Experimental Psychology: Human Perception and Performance, 26*(4), 1387–1400. §10.30.

Lamy, D., Salti, M., & Bar-Haim, Y. (2009). Neural correlates of subjective awareness and unconscious processing: An ERP study. *Journal of Cognitive Neuroscience, 21,* 1435–1446. §10.16.

Landauer, R. (1961). Irreversibility and heat generation in the computing process. *IBM Journal of Research and Development, 5,* 183–191. §A1n3.

Landman, R., Spekreijse, H., & Lamme, V. A. F. (2003). Large capacity storage of integrated objects before change blindness. *Vision Research, 43*(2), 149–164. §10.15.

Landman, R., Spekreijse, H., & Lamme, V. A. F. (2004). The role of figure-ground segregation in change blindness. *Psychonomic Bulletin & Review, 11*(2), 254–261. §10.15.

Lang, W., Cheyne, D., Kristeva, R., Beisteiner, R., Lindinger, G., & Deecke, L. (1991). Three-dimensional localization of SMA activity preceding voluntary movement: A study of electric and magnetic fields in a patient with infarction of the right supplementary motor area. *Experimental Brain Research, 87,* 688–695. Figure 9.1.

Langacker, R. W. (1987). *Foundations of cognitive grammar* (Vol. I): *Theoretical prerequisites.* Stanford: Stanford University Press. §8.15.

Lape, R., & Dani, J. A. (2004). Complex response to afferent excitatory bursts by nucleus accumbens medium spiny projection neurons. *Journal of Neurophysiology, 92,* 1276–1284. §5.42.

Laplace, P.-S. (1902 [1814]). *A philosophical essay on probabilities.* New York: John Wiley & Sons. §A1.2.

Larsen, R. S., Corlew, R. J., Henson, M. A., Roberts, A. C., Mishina, M., Watanabe, M., et al. (2011). NR3A-containing NMDARs promote neurotransmitter release and spike timing—dependent plasticity. *Nature Neuroscience, 14*(3), 338–344. §5.28.

Lau, B., & Salzman, C. D. (2008). Noncholinergic neurons in the basal forebrain: Often neglected but motivationally salient. *Neuron, 59,* 6–8. §5.45.

Lau, H. C., Rogers, R. D., Haggard, P., & Passingham, R. E. (2004). Attention to intention. *Science, 303,* 1208–1210. §9.1.

Laube, B., Kuhse, J., & Betz, H. (1998). Evidence for a tetrameric structure of recombinant NMDA receptors. *Journal of Neuroscience, 18,* 2954–2961. §5.4.

Laureys, S. (2004). Functional neuroimaging in the vegetative state. *NeuroRehabilitation, 19*(4), 335–341. §§10.65, 10.66.

Lauritzen, T. Z., D'Esposito, M., Heeger, D. J. and Silver, M. A. (2009). Top-down flow of visual spatial attention signals from parietal to occipital cortex. *Journal of Vision, 9*(13):18, 1–14. §4.14.

Lebedev, M. A., Carmena, J. M., O'Doherty, J. E., Zacksenhouse, M., Henriquez, C. S., Principe, J. C., et al. (2005). Cortical ensemble adaptation to represent velocity of an artificial actuator controlled by a brain-machine interface. *Journal of Neuroscience, 25*(19), 4681–4693. §10n9.

Lebedev, M. A., & Nicolelis, M. A. (2006). Brain-machine interfaces: Past, present, and future. *Trends in Neurosciences, 29*(9), 536–546. §10n9.

Lee, M. C., Yasuda, R., & Ehlers, M. D. (2010). Metaplasticity at single glutamatergic synapses. *Neuron, 66,* 859–870. §5.7.

Legenstein, R., & Maass, W. (2007). Edge of chaos and prediction of computational performance for neural circuit models. *Neural Networks, 20*(3), 323–334. §4.42.

Lehmann, J., Nagy, J. I., Atmadia, S., & Fibiger, H. C. (1980). The nucleus basalis magnocellularis: The origin of a cholinergic projection to the neocortex of the rat. *Neuroscience, 5,* 1161–1174. §5.38.

Leopold, D. A., O'Toole, A. J., Vetter, T., & Blanz, V. (2001). Prototype-referenced shape encoding revealed by high-level aftereffects. *Nature Neuroscience, 4,* 89–94. §§8.18, 8.20.

Leopold, D. A., Bondar, I., & Giese, M. A. (2006). Norm-based face encoding by single neurons in the monkey inferotemporal cortex. *Nature, 442,* 572–575. §§8.18, 8.20.

Lepsien, J., Griffin, I. C., Devlin, J. T., & Nobre, A. C. (2005). Directing spatial attention in mental representations: Interactions between attentional orienting and working-memory load. *NeuroImage, 26*(3), 733–743. §10.13.

Lerner, Y., Hendler, T., Ben-Bashat, D., Harel, M., & Malach, R. (2001). A hierarchical axis of object processing stages in the human visual cortex. *Cerebral Cortex, 11*(4), 287–297. §4.10.

LeShan, L. & Margenau, H. (1982). *Einstein's space and Van Gogh's sky: Physical reality and beyond*. New York: Macmillan. §7.17.

Lesica, N. A., & Stanley, G. B. (2004). Encoding of natural scene movies by tonic and burst spikes in the LGN. *Journal of Neuroscience, 24*, 10731–10740. §4.38.

Letzkus, J. J., Kampa, B. M., & Stuart, G. J. (2006). Learning rules for spike timing-dependent plasticity depend on dendritic synapse location. *Journal of Neuroscience, 26*, 10420–10429. §5.21.

Levin, D. T., Simons, D. J., Angelone, B. L., & Chabris, C. F. (2002). Memory for centrally attended changing objects in an incidental real-world change detection paradigm. *British Journal of Psychology, 93*, 289–302. §10.56.

Levy, R., & Goldman-Rakic, P. S. (2000). Segregation of working memory functions within the dorsolateral prefrontal cortex. *Experimental Brain Research, 133*(1), 23–32. §4.26.

Lewis, D. (1980). Mad pain and martian pain. In N. Block (Ed.), *Readings in philosophy of psychology* (Vol. 1, pp. 216–222). Cambridge, MA: Harvard University Press. §8n9.

Li, C. T., Poo, M., & Dan, Y. (2009). Burst spiking of a single cortical neuron modifies global brain state. *Science, 324*(5927), 643–646. §5.42.

Li, F. F., VanRullen, R., Koch, C., & Perona, P. (2002). Rapid natural scene categorization in the near absence of attention. *Proceedings of the National Academy of Sciences of the United States of America, 99*(14), 9596–9601. §10.71.

Libet, B. (1985). Unconscious cerebral initiative and the role of conscious will in voluntary action. *Behavioral and Brain Sciences, 8*(4), 529–566. §§9.1, 9n1.

Libet, B., Wright, E. W., Jr., & Gleason, C. A. (1982). Readiness-potentials preceding unrestricted "spontaneous" vs. pre-planned voluntary acts. *Electroencephalography and Clinical Neurophysiology, 54*, 322–335. §9.1.

Libet, B., Gleason, C. A., Wright, E. W., & Pearl, D. K. (1983a). Time of conscious intention to act in relation to onset of cerebral activity (readiness-potential): The unconscious initiation of a freely voluntary act. *Brain, 106*(3), 623–642. §§9.1, 9.14.

Libet, B., Wright, E. W., Jr., & Gleason, C. A. (1983b). Preparation- or intention-to-act, in relation to pre-event potentials recorded at the vertex. *Electroencephalography and Clinical Neurophysiology, 56*, 367–372. §§9.1, 9.14.

Liddle, P. F., Kiehl, K. A., & Smith, A. M. (2001). Event-related fMRI study of response inhibition. *Human Brain Mapping, 12*(2), 100–109. §10n10.

Lieberman, D. N., & Mody, I. (1994). Regulation of NMDA channel function by endogenous Ca2+-dependent phosphatase. *Nature, 369*, 235–239. §5n1.

Liebovitch, L. S., & Todorov, A. T. (1996a). What causes ion channel proteins to fluctuate open and closed? *International Journal of Neural Systems, 7*(4), 321–331. §5.25.

Liebovitch, L. S., & Todorov, A. T. (1996b). Using fractals and nonlinear dynamics to determine the physical properties of ion channel proteins. *Critical Reviews in Neurobiology, 10*(2), 169–187. §5.25.

Lin, F., & Stevens, C. F. (1994). Both open and closed NMDA receptor channels desensitize. *Journal of Neuroscience, 14*, 2153–2160. §5.25.

Lin, S. C., Gervasoni, D., & Nicolelis, M. A. (2006). Fast modulation of prefrontal cortex activity by basal forebrain noncholinergic neuronal ensembles. *Journal of Neurophysiology, 96*, 3209–3219. §§4.37, 4.50, 5.45, 5.46.

Lin, S. C., & Nicolelis, M. A. (2008). Neuronal ensemble bursting in the basal forebrain encodes salience irrespective of valence. *Neuron, 59*(1), 138–149. §§5.45, 5.47.

Linden, D. (1999). The return of the spike: Postsynaptic action potentials and the induction of LTP and LTD. *Neuron, 22*, 661–666. §§5.9, 5.18.

Linden, D. E. J. (2007). The working memory networks of the human brain. *Neuroscientist, 13*(3), 257–267. §4.26.

Lindner, A., Haarmeier, T., Erb, M., Grodd, W., & Thier, P. (2006). Cerebrocerebellar circuits for the perceptual cancellation of eyemovement-induced retinal image motion. *Journal of Cognitive Neuroscience, 18*, 1899–1912. §9n6.

Lisman, J. (1985). A mechanism for memory storage insensitive to molecular turnover: A bistable autophosphorylating kinase. *Proceedings of the National Academy of Sciences of the United States of America, 82*, 3055–3057. §5.9.

Lisman, J. (1989). A mechanism for the Hebb and the anti-Hebb processes underlying learning and memory. *Proceedings of the National Academy of Sciences of the United States of America, 86*, 9574–9578. §5.9.

Lisman, J. E. (1997). Bursts as a unit of neural information: Making unreliable synapses reliable. *Trends in Neurosciences, 20*, 38–43. §§2.5, 4.36, 4.38, 4.50, 4.53, 5.30, 5.36, 5.43. figure 5.5.

Lisman, J. E. (1999). Relating hippocampal circuitry to function: Recall of memory sequences by reciprocal dentate-CA3 interactions. *Neuron, 22*, 233–242. §§4.44, 5.9.

Lisman, J. (2003). Long-term potentiation: Outstanding questions and attempted synthesis. *Philosophical Transactions of the Royal Society of London, Series B: Biological Sciences, 358*, 829–842. §5.9.

Lisman, J., Fellous, J., & Wang, X. (1998). A role for NMDA-receptor channels in working memory. *Nature Neuroscience, 1*, 273–275. §5.36.

Lisman, J. E., & Grace, A. A. (2005). The hippocampal-VTA loop: Controlling the entry of information into long-term memory. *Neuron, 46,* 703–713. §4.40.

Lisman, J. E., & Idiart, M. A. (1995). Storage of 7 +/– 2 shortterm memories in oscillatory subcycles. *Science, 267,* 1512–1515. §4.44.

Lisman, J., & Zhabotinsky, A. (2001). A model of synaptic memory: A CaMKII/PP1 switch that potentiates transmission by organizing an AMPA receptor anchoring assembly. *Neuron, 31,* 191–201. §5.9.

Lisman, J., Schulman, H., & Cline, H. (2002). The molecular basis of CamKII function in synaptic and behavioural memory. *Nature Reviews: Neuroscience, 3,* 175–190. §5.9.

Liu, L., Davis, R. L., & Roman, G. (2007). Exploratory activity in Drosophila requires the kurtz nonvisual arrestin. *Genetics, 175,* 1197–1212. §4.70.

Liu, Q. S., Pu, L., & Poo, M. M. (2005). Repeated cocaine exposure in vivo facilitates LTP induction in midbrain dopamine neurons. *Nature, 437,* 1027–1031. §5n4.

Liu, T., Abrams, J., & Carrasco, M. (2009). Voluntary attention enhances contrast appearance. *Psychological Science, 20*(3), 354–362. §§4.21, 10.32.

Livingstone, M. S., Freeman, D. C., & Hubel, D. H. (1996). Visual responses in V1 of freely viewing monkeys. *Cold Spring Harbor Symposia on Quantitative Biology, 61,* 27–37. §5.36.

Llinas, R., & Jahnsen, H. (1982). Electrophysiology of mammalian thalamic neurones in vitro. *Nature, 297,* 406–408. §4n11.

Logan, G. D., & Crump, M. J. (2010). Cognitive illusions of authorship reveal hierarchical error detection in skilled typists. *Science, 330,* 683–686. §10.36.

Logie, R. H. (1995). *Visual-spatial working memory.* New York: Psychology Press. §10.14.

Logothetis, N. K., Pauls, J., & Poggio, T. (1995). Shape representation in the inferior temporal cortex of monkeys. *Current Biology, 5*(5), 552–563. §7.11.

Logothetis, N. K., & Sheinberg, D. L. (1996). Visual object recognition. *Annual Review of Neuroscience, 19,* 577–621. §4.9.

London, M., & Häusser, M. (2005). Dendritic computation. *Annual Review of Neuroscience, 28,* 503–532. §§5.15, 5.18.

London, M., Roth, A., Beeren, L., Hausser, M., & Latham, P. E. (2010). Sensitivity to perturbations in vivo implies high noise and suggests rate coding in cortex. *Nature, 466,* 123–127. §4.70.

Lou, L. (1999). Selective peripheral fading: Evidence for inhibitory sensory effect of attention. *Perception, 28,* 519–526. §10.50.

Loukas, C., & Brown, P. (2004). Online prediction of self-paced hand-movements from subthalamic activity using neural networks in Parkinson's disease. *Journal of Neuroscience Methods, 137*, 193–205. Figure 9.1.

Lu, T., Liang, L., & Wang, X. (2001). Temporal and rate representations of time-varying signals in the auditory cortex of awake primates. *Nature Neuroscience, 4*, 1131–1138. §4.43.

Luczak, A., Barthó, P., & Harris, K. D. (2009). Spontaneous events outline the realm of possible sensory responses in neocortical populations. *Neuron, 62*, 413–425. §§4.60, 5.16.

Luria, R., & Vogel, E. K. (2011). Shape and color conjunction stimuli are represented as bound objects in visual working memory. *Neuropsychologia, 49*(6), 1632–1639. §10.30.

Luu, P., & Malenka, R. C. (2008). Spike timing-dependent long-term potentiation in ventral tegmental area dopamine cells requires PKC. *Journal of Neurophysiology, 100*(1), 533–538. §§5.9, 5n4.

Lycan, W. (1987). *Consciousness*. Cambridge, MA: MIT Press. §A2n5.

Lycan, W. (Ed.). (1990). *Mind and cognition: A reader*. Oxford: Blackwell. §A2n5.

Lynall, M. E., Bassett, D. S., Kerwin, R., McKenna, P. J., Kitzbichler, M., Muller, U., & Bullmore, E. (2010). Functional connectivity and brain networks in schizophrenia. *Journal of Neuroscience, 30*, 9477–9487. §5.24.

Ma, J., & Lowe, G. (2004). Action potential backpropagation and multiglomerular signaling in the rat vomeronasal system. *Journal of Neuroscience, 24*(42), 9341–9352. §5.18.

Maass, W., & Markram, H. (2002). Synapses as dynamic memory buffers. *Neural Networks, 15*, 155–161. §4.55

Macgregor, R. J. (2006). Quantum mechanics and brain uncertainty. *Journal of Integrative Neuroscience, 5*(3), 373–380. §A1.8.

Mack, A., & Rock, I. (1998). *Inattentional blindness*. Cambridge, MA: MIT Press. §§10.29, 10.67, 10.71, 10.74, 10n21.

Macknik, S. L. (2006). Visual masking approaches to visual awareness. *Progress in Brain Research, 155*, 177–215. §10.50.

Macknik, S. L., & Livingstone, M. S. (1998). Neuronal correlates of visibility and invisibility in the primate visual system. *Nature Neuroscience, 1*(2), 144–149. §4.39.

Macknik, S. L., & Martinez-Conde, S. (2004). The spatial and temporal effects of lateral inhibitory networks and their relevance to the visibility of spatiotemporal edges. *Neurocomputing, 58–60*, 775–782. §4.39.

Macknik, S. L., Martinez-Conde, S., & Haglund, M. H. (2000). The role of spatiotemporal edges in visibility and visual masking. *Proceedings of the National Academy of Sciences of the United States of America, 97*(13), 7556–7560. §§4.39, 10.50.

Madden, D. R. (2002). The structure and function of glutamate receptor ion channels. *Nature Reviews: Neuroscience, 3*, 91–101. §2n3.

Maffei, A., & Fontanini, A. (2009). Network homeostasis: A matter of coordination. *Current Opinion in Neurobiology, 19*, 168–173. §5.7.

Magee, J. C. (2000). Dendritic integration of excitatory synaptic inputs. *Nature Reviews: Neuroscience, 1*, 181–190. §5.18.

Magee, J. C., & Johnston, D. (1997). A synaptically controlled, associative signal for Hebbian plasticity in hippocampal neurons. *Science, 275*, 209–213. §§5.18, 5n5.

Magnussen, S. (2000). Low-level memory processes in vision. *Trends in Neurosciences, 23*(6), 247–251. §10.30.

Maimon, G., & Assad, J. A. (2009). Beyond Poisson: Increased spike-time regularity across primate parietal cortex. *Neuron, 62*, 426–440. §4.52.

Mainen, Z. F. (1999). Functional plasticity at dendritic synapses. In G. Stuart, N. Spruston, & M. Häusser (Eds.), *Dendrites* (pp. 310–338). Oxford: Oxford University Press. §5.21.

Mainen, Z. F., & Sejnowski, T. J. (1995). Reliability of spike timing in neocortical neurons. *Science, 268*, 1503–1506. §5.21.

Majewska, A., Tashiro, A., & Yuste, R. (2000). Regulation of spine calcium dynamics by rapid spine motility. *Journal of Neuroscience, 20*(22), 8262–8268. §4.55.

Makovski, T., & Jiang, Y. V. (2007). Distributing versus focusing attention in visual short-term memory. *Psychonomic Bulletin and Review, 14*(6), 1072–1078. §10.13.

Makovski, T., Shim, W. M., & Jiang, Y. H. V. (2006). Interference from filled delays on visual change detection. *Journal of Vision, 6*(12), 1459–1470. §§10.13, 10.15.

Makovski, T., Sussman, R., & Jiang, Y. H. V. (2008). Orienting attention in visual working memory reduces interference from memory probes. *Journal of Experimental Psychology: Learning, Memory, and Cognition, 34*(2), 369–380. §§10.13, 10.15.

Malach, R., Reppas, J. B., Benson, R. R., Kwong, K. K., Jiang, H., Kennedy, W. A., et al. (1995). Object-related activity revealed by functional magnetic resonance imaging in human occipital cortex. *Proceedings of the National Academy of Sciences of the United States of America, 92*(18), 8135–8139. §4.10.

Malcolm, N. (1962). Wittgenstein's *Philosophical Investigations*. In V. C. Chappell (Ed.), *The philosophy of mind*. Englewood Cliffs, NJ: Prentice-Hall. §8n6.

Malenka, R. C., & Bear, M. F. (2004). LTP and LTD: An embarrassment of riches. *Neuron, 44*, 5–21. §§5.6, 5.9.

Maletic-Savatic, M., Malinow, R., & Svoboda, K. (1999). Rapid dendritic morphogenesis in CA1 hippocampal dendrites induced by synaptic activity. *Science, 283*, 1923–1927. §§5.5, 5.9.

Malinow, R. (1991). Transmission between pairs of hippocampal slice neurons: Quantal levels, oscillations, and LTP. *Science, 252*, 722–724. §5.9.

Malinow, R., Schulman, H., & Tsien, R. W. (1989). Inhibition of postsynaptic PKC or CaMKII blocks induction but not expression of LTP. *Science, 245*, 862–866. §5n1.

Malinow, R., & Tsien, R. W. (1990). Identifying and localizing protein kinases necessary for LTP. *Advances in Experimental Medicine and Biology, 268*, 301–305. §5.9.

Mann, E. O., Kohl, M. M., & Paulsen, O. (2009). Distinct roles of GABA(A) and GABA(B) receptors in balancing and terminating persistent cortical activity. *Journal of Neuroscience, 29*(23), 7513–7518. §5.42.

Mann, E. O., Radcliffe, C. A., & Paulsen, O. (2005a). Hippocampal gamma-frequency oscillations: From interneurones to pyramidal cells, and back. *Journal of Physiology, 562*, 55–63. §§4.44, 5.3, 5.40.

Mann, E. O., Suckling, J. M., Hajos, N., Greenfield, S. A., & Paulsen, O. (2005b). Perisomatic feedback inhibition underlies cholinergically induced fast network oscillations in the rat hippocampus in vitro. *Neuron, 45*, 105–117. §§4.44, 5.3.

Mao, B. Q., Hamzei-Sichani, F., Aronov, D., Froemke, R. C., & Yuste, R. (2001). Dynamics of spontaneous activity in neocortical slices. *Neuron, 32*, 883–898. §§4.60, 5.16.

Marco, P., Sola, R. G., Pulido, P., Alijarde, M. T., Sanchez, A., Ramón y Cajal, S., et al. (1996). Inhibitory neurons in the human epileptogenic temporal neocortex: An immunocytochemical study. *Brain, 119*, 1327–1347. §4.33.

Marco, P., & DeFelipe, J. (1997). Altered synaptic activity in the human temporal neocortex removed from epileptic patients. *Experimental Brain Research, 114*, 1–10. §4.33.

Marder, C. P., & Buonomano, D. V. (2003). Differential effects of short- and long-term potentiation on cell firing in the CA1 region of the hippocampus. *Journal of Neuroscience, 23*, 112–121. §4.54.

Marder, E., & Goaillard, J. M. (2006). Variability, compensation, and homeostasis in neuron and network function. *Nature Reviews: Neuroscience, 7*, 563–574. §5.7.

Markram, H., Wang, Y., & Tsodyks, M. (1998). Differential signaling via the same axon of neocortical pyramidal neurons. *Proceedings of the National Academy of Sciences of the United States of America, 95*, 5323–5328. §4.55.

Markram, H., Lubke, J., Frotscher, M., & Sakmann, B. (1997). Regulation of synaptic efficacy by coincidence of postsynaptic APs and EPSPs. *Science, 275*, 213–215. §5.11.

Marr, D. (1982). *Vision.* New York: Freeman. §10.81.

Marshall, L., Helgadottir, H., Molle, M., & Born, J. (2006). Boosting slow oscillations during sleep potentiates memory. *Nature, 444*, 610–613. §5.8.

Martin, K. C., Michael, D., Rose, J. C., Barad, M., Casadio, A., Zhu, H., et al. (1997a). MAP kinase translocates into the nucleus of the presynaptic cell and is required for long-term facilitation in Aplysia. *Neuron, 18*, 899–912. §5.6.

Martin, K. C., Casadio, A., Zhu, H., Yaping, E., Rose, J. C., Chen, M., et al. (1997b). Synapse-specific, long-term facilitation of *Aplysia* sensory to motor synapses: A function for local protein synthesis in memory storage. *Cell, 91*, 927–938. §5.9.

Martin, J., Faure, P., & Ernst, R. (2001). The power law distribution for walking-time intervals correlates with the ellipsoid-body in Drosophila. *Journal of Neurogenetics, 15*, 205–219. §4.70.

Martina, M., Vida, I., & Jonas, P. (2000). Distal initiation and active propagation of action potentials in interneuron dendrites. *Science, 287*, 295–300. §4.33.

Martinez-Conde, S., Macknik, S. L., & Hubel, D. H. (2002). The function of bursts of spikes during visual fixation in the awake primate LGN and primary visual cortex. *Proceedings of the National Academy of Sciences of the United States of America, 99*, 13920–13925. §4.38.

Martinez-Trujillo, J. C., & Treue, S. (2004). Feature-based attention increases the selectivity of population responses in primate visual cortex. *Current Biology, 14*, 744–751. §§4.24, 4.25

Mantini, D., Corbetta, M., Perrucci, M.G., Romani, G.L., & Del Gratta, C. (2009). Large-scale brain networks account for sustained and transient activity during target detection. *NeuroImage, 44*, 265–274. §10.16.

Matsuhashi, M., & Hallett, M. (2008). The timing of the conscious intention to move. *European Journal of Neuroscience, 28*, 2344–2351. §§9.4, 9n1.

Matsukevich, D. N., Maunz, P., Moehring, D. L., Olmschenk, S., & Monroe, C. (2008). Bell inequality violation with two remote atomic qubits. *Physical Review Letters, 100*, 150404. §§A1.6, A1.7.

Matsukura, M., Luck, S. J., & Vecera, S. P. (2007). Attention effects during visual short-term memory maintenance: Protection or prioritization? *Perception & Psychophysics, 69*(8), 1422–1434. §10.15.

Mattingley, J. B., Davis, G., & Driver, J. (1997). Preattentive filling-in of visual surfaces in parietal extinction. *Science, 275*, 671–674. §10.35.

Mattler, U. (2005). Inhibition and decay of motor and nonmotor priming. *Perception & Psychophysics, 67*, 285–300. §10.36.

Matus, A. (2000). Actin-based plasticity in dendritic spines. *Science, 290*, 754–758. §5.2.

Maunsell, J. H., & McAdams, C. J. (2001). Effects of attention on the responsiveness and selectivity of individual neurons in visual cerebral cortex. In J. Braun, C. Koch, & J. L. Davis (Eds.), *Visual attention and cortical circuits* (pp. 103–119). Cambridge, MA: MIT Press. §5.50.

Maunsell, J. H. R., & Treue, S. (2006). Feature-based attention in visual cortex. *Trends in Neurosciences, 29*, 317–322. §§4.24, 4.25.

Maye, A., Hsieh, C.-H., Sugihara, G., & Brembs, B. (2007). Order in spontaneous behavior. *PLoS ONE, 2*, e443. §4.70.

Mayo, J. P. (2009). Intrathalamic mechanisms of visual attention. *Journal of Neurophysiology, 101*, 1123–1125. §4.27.

Mayr, E. (1988). *Toward a new philosophy of biology*. Cambridge, MA: Harvard University Press. §7.17.

McAdams, C. J., & Maunsell, J. H. R. (2000). Attention to both space and feature modulates neuronal responses in macaque area V4. *Journal of Neurophysiology, 83*, 1751–1755. §§4.24, 4.25.

McAlonan, G. M., Wilkinson, L. S., Robbins, T. W., & Everitt, B. J. (1995). The effects of AMPA-induced lesions of the septo-hippocampal cholinergic projection on aversive conditioning to explicit and contextual cues and spatial learning in the water maze. *European Journal of Neuroscience, 7*, 281–292. §5.44.

McAlonan, K., Brown, V. J., & Bowman, E. M. (2000). Thalamic reticular nucleus activation reflects attentional gating during classical conditioning. *Journal of Neuroscience, 20*, 8897–8901. §4.27.

McAlonan, K., Cavanaugh, J., & Wurtz, R. H. (2006). Attentional modulation of thalamic reticular neurons. *Journal of Neuroscience, 26*, 4444–4450. §§4.27, 4.38, 4.39, 4.43, 4.48, 4n11.

McAlonan, K., Cavanaugh, J., & Wurtz, R. H. (2008). Guarding the gateway to cortex: Attention in visual thalamus. *Nature, 456*(7220), 391–394. §4.27, 4.39, 4.43.

McCormick, D. A., Connors, B. W., Lighthall, J. W., & Prince, D. A. (1985). Comparative electrophysiology of pyramidal and sparsely spiny stellate neurons of the neocortex. *Journal of Neurophysiology, 54*, 782–806. §§4.52, 5.3.

McCormick, D., & Prince, D. (1986). Mechanisms of action of acetylcholine in the guinea-pig cerebral cortex in vitro. *Journal of Physiology, 375*, 169–194. §5.39.

McCormick, P. A. (1997). Orienting attention without awareness. *Journal of Experimental Psychology: Human Perception and Performance, 23*, 168–180. §10.28.

McCulloch, W. S., & Pitts, W. H. (1943). A logical calculus of the ideas immanent in nervous activity. *Bulletin of Mathematical Biophysics, 5*, 115–133. §5.14.

McGaughy, J., Decker, M. W., & Sarter, M. (1999). Enhancement of sustained attention performance by the nicotinic acetylcholine receptor agonist ABT-418 in intact but not basal forebrain-lesioned rats. *Psychopharmacology, 144*, 175–182. §5.44.

McGlade-McCulloh, E., Yamamoto, H., Tan, S. E., Brickey, D. A., & Soderling, T. R. (1993). Phosphorylation and regulation of glutamate receptors by calcium/calmodulin-dependent protein kinase II. *Nature, 362*, 640–642. §5n1.

McGlashan, T. H., & Hoffman, R. E. (2000). Schizophrenia as a disorder of developmentally reduced synaptic connectivity. *Archives of General Psychiatry, 57*, 637–648. §5.24.

McLaughlin, J., Skaggs, H., Churchwell, J., & Powell, D. A. (2002). Medial prefrontal cortex and Pavlovian conditioning: Trace versus delay conditioning. *Behavioral Neuroscience, 116*, 37–47. §10n15.

Mehta, M. R. (2004). Cooperative LTP can map memory sequences on dendritic branches. *Trends in Neurosciences, 27*, 69–72. §5.15.

Mele, A. R. (1995). *Autonomous agents: From self-control to autonomy.* New York: Oxford University Press. §7.17.

Mele, A. R. (2006). *Free will and luck.* Oxford: Oxford University Press. §7.17.

Mele, A. R. (2010). *Effective intentions: The power of conscious will.* Oxford: Oxford University Press. §7.17.

Meliza, C. D., & Dan, Y. (2006). Receptive-field modification in rat visual cortex induced by paired visual stimulation and single-cell spiking. *Neuron, 49*, 183–189. §5.11.

Melloni, L., Molina, C., Pena, M., Torres, D., Singer, W., & Rodriguez, E. (2007). Synchronization of neural activity across cortical areas correlates with conscious perception. *Journal of Neuroscience, 27*, 2858–2865. §10.16.

Merikle, P. M., & Joordens, S. (1997). Parallels between perception without attention and perception without awareness. *Consciousness and Cognition, 6*, 219–236. §10.36.

Mesulam, M. M. (1981). A cortical network for directed attention and unilateral neglect. *Annals of Neurology, 10*, 309–325. §4.23.

Meunier, D., Lambiotte, R., Fornito, A., Ersche, K. D., & Bullmore, E. T. (2009). Hierarchical modularity in human brain functional networks. *Frontiers in Neuroinformatics, 3*, 37. §7.15.

Miles, R. (2000). Diversity in inhibition. *Science, 287*, 244–246. §5.3.

Miles, R., Toth, K., Gulyas, A. I., Hajos, N., & Freund, T. F. (1996). Differences between somatic and dendritic inhibition in the hippocampus. *Neuron, 16*, 815–823. §§4.44, 5.3.

Miller, C. A., & Sweatt, J. D. (2007). Covalent modification of DNA regulates memory formation. *Neuron, 53*, 857–869. §5.6.

Miller, E. K., & Desimone, R. (1994). Parallel neuronal mechanisms for short-term memory. *Science, 263*(5146), 520–522. §10.14.

Miller, E. K., Erickson, C. A., & Desimone, R. (1996). Neural mechanisms of visual working memory in prefrontal cortex of the macaque. *Journal of Neuroscience, 16*(16), 5154–5167. §§10.13, 10.14.

Miller, E. K., & Cohen, J. D. (2001). An integrative theory of prefrontal cortex function. *Annual Review of Neuroscience, 24*, 167–202. §5.36.

Millikan, R. (1989). Biosemantics. *Journal of Philosophy, 86*, 281–297. §8.6.

Miraucourt, L. S., Peirs, C., Dallel, R., & Voisin, D. L. (2011). Glycine inhibitory dysfunction turns touch into pain through astrocyte-derived D-serine. *Pain, 152*, 1340–1348. §5n3.

Mishkin, M., & Ungerleider, L. G. (1982). Contribution of striate inputs to the visuospatial functions of parieto-preoccipital cortex in monkeys. *Behavioural Brain Research, 6*(1), 57–77. §4.8.

Mitchell, J. F., Sundberg, K. A., & Reynolds, J. H. (2007). Differential attention-dependent response modulation across cell classes in macaque visual area V4. *Neuron, 55*, 131–141. §§4.48, 4.49, 4.52, 5.50.

Mitchell, J. F., Sundberg, K. A., & Reynolds, J. H. (2009). Spatial attention decorrelates intrinsic activity fluctuations in macaque area V4. *Neuron, 63*, 879–888. §§4.48, 4.49, 5.50.

Mongillo, G., Barak, O., & Tsodyks, M. (2008). Synaptic theory of working memory. *Science, 319*, 1543–1546. §4.55.

Montague, P. R., Hyman, S. E., & Cohen, J. D. (2004). Computational roles for dopamine in behavioural control. *Nature, 431*, 760–767. §3.2.

Montarolo, P. G., Goelet, P., Castellucci, V. F., Morgan, J., Kandel, E. R., & Schacher, S. (1986). A critical period for macromolecular synthesis in long-term heterosynaptic facilitation in *Aplysia*. *Science, 234*, 1249–1254. §5.9.

Moore, J. W., Wegner, D. M., & Haggard, P. (2009a). Modulating the sense of agency with external cues. *Consciousness and Cognition, 18*(4), 1056–1064. §9n2.

Moore, S. J., Cooper, D. C., & Spruston, N. (2009b). Plasticity of burst firing induced by synergistic activation of metabotropic glutamate and acetylcholine receptors. *Neuron, 61*, 287–300. §§5.38, 5.39.

Moore, T., & Armstrong, K. M. (2003). Selective gating of visual signals by microstimulation of frontal cortex. *Nature, 421*, 370–373. §4.24.

Moore, T., Armstrong, K. M., & Fallah, M. (2003). Visuomotor origins of covert spatial attention. *Neuron, 40*, 671–683. §4.24.

Moore, T., & Fallah, M. (2001). Control of eye movements and spatial attention. *Proceedings of the National Academy of Sciences of the United States of America, 98*, 1273–1276. §4.24.

Moran, J., & Desimone, R. (1985). Selective attention gates visual processing in the extrastriate cortex. *Science, 229*, 782–784. §5.50.

Morikawa, H., Khodakhah, K., & Williams, J. T. (2003). Two intracellular pathways mediate metabotropic glutamate receptor-induced Ca^{2+} mobilization in dopamine neurons. *Journal of Neuroscience, 23*, 149–157. §4.40.

Moser, E., Kropff, E., & Moser, M. (2008). Place cells, grid cells, and the brain's spatial representation system. *Annual Review of Neuroscience, 31*, 69–89. §§4.8, 8.22.

Moser, M. B., Trommald, M., & Andersen, P. (1994). An increase in dendritic spine density on hippocampal CA1 pyramidal cells following spatial learning in adult rats suggests the formation of new synapses. *Proceedings of the National Academy of Sciences of the United States of America, 91*, 12673–12675. §5.9.

Moss, H. E., Abdallah, S., Fletcher, P., Bright, P., Pilgrim, L., Acres, K., et al. (2005). Selecting among competing alternatives: Selection and retrieval in the left inferior frontal gyrus. *Cerebral Cortex, 15*(11), 1723–1735. §10.6.

Motter, B. C. (1994). Neural correlates of feature selective memory and pop-out in extrastriate area V4. *Journal of Neuroscience, 14*, 2190–2199. §§4.24, 4.25.

Muir, J. L., Everitt, B. J., & Robbins, T. W. (1994). AMPA-induced excitotoxic lesions of the basal forebrain: A significant role for the cortical cholinergic system in attentional function. *Journal of Neuroscience, 14*, 2313–2326. §5.44.

Mukherjee, P., & Kaplan, E. (1995). Dynamics of neurons in the cat LGN: In vivo electrophysiology and computational modeling. *Journal of Neurophysiology, 74*, 1222–1243. §4.38.

Mulkey, R. M., Herron, C. E., & Malenka, R. C. (1993). An essential role for protein phosphatases in hippocampal long-term depression. *Science, 261*, 1051–1055. §5.9.

Muller, J. R., Philiastides, M. G., & Newsome, W. T. (2005). Microstimulation of the superior colliculus focuses attention without moving the eyes. *Proceedings of the National Academy of Sciences of the United States of America, 102*, 524–529. §4.24.

Müller, W., & Connor, J. A. (1991). Dendritic spines as individual neuronal compartments for synaptic Ca^{2+} responses. *Nature, 354*, 73–76. §5.5.

Muller-Gass, A., Macdonald, M., Schröger, E., Sculthorpe, L., & Campbell, K. (2007). Evidence for the auditory P3a reflecting an automatic process: Elicitation during highly-focused continuous visual attention. *Brain Research, 1170*, 71–78. §§4.22, 10.16.

Murphy, N., Ellis, G. F. R., & O'Connor, T. (2009). *Downward causation and the neurobiology of free will*. Berlin: Springer. §9.14.

Musallam, S., Corneil, B. D., Greger, B., Scherberger, H., & Andersen, R. A. (2004). Cognitive control signals for neural prosthetics. *Science, 305*(5681), 258–262. §10n9.

Nagata, Y., Horiike, K., & Maeda, T. (1994). Distribution of free d-serine in vertebrate brains. *Brain Research, 634*, 291–295. §5n2.

Nagel, E. (1974). What is it like to be a bat? *Philosophical Review, 83*, 435–450. §A2n5.

Naghavi, H. R., & Nyberg, L. (2005). Common fronto-parietal activity in attention, memory, and consciousness: Shared demands on integration? *Consciousness and Cognition, 14*(2), 390–425. §10.65.

Nagode, D. A., Tang, A. H., Karson, M. A., Klugmann, M., & Alger, B. E. (2011). Optogenetic release of ACh induces rhythmic bursts of perisomatic IPSCs in hippocampus. *PLoS ONE, 6*(11), e27691. §5.42.

Nairz, O., Arndt, M., & Zeilinger, A. (2003). Quantum interference experiments with large molecules. *American Journal of Physics, 71*, 319–325. §A1.10.

Nakayama, K., & Mackeben, M. (1989). Sustained and transient components of focal visual attention. *Vision Research, 29*, 1631–1647. §§4.22, 4.48.

Nakayama, K., Kiyosue, K., & Taguchi, T. (2005). Diminished neuronal activity increases neuron-neuron connectivity underlying silent synapse formation and the rapid conversion of silent to functional synapses. *Journal of Neuroscience, 25*, 4040–4051. §5.7.

Neisser, U. (1967). *Cognitive psychology*. New York: Appleton-Century-Crofts. §§10.12, 10.13, 10.56, 10.78.

Neven, H., & Aertsen, A. (1992). Rate coherence and event coherence in the visual cortex: A neuronal model of object recognition. *Biological Cybernetics, 67*, 309–322. §4.45.

Nevian, T., & Sakmann, B. (2006). Spine Ca^{2+} signaling in spike-timing-dependent plasticity. *Journal of Neuroscience, 26*, 11001–11013. §5n5.

Newman, D. (1996). Emergence and strange attractors. *Philosophy of Science, 63*, 245–261. §A2.2.

Newton, J. R., Majewska, A. K., Ellsworth, C., & Sur, M. (2006). Reprogramming cortex: The consequences of cross-modal plasticity during development. In S. Lomber & J. Eggermont (Eds.), *Reprogramming the cerebral cortex* (pp. 349–360). Oxford: Oxford University Press. §§4.63, 5.1.

Nguyen, P. V., Abel, T., & Kandel, E. R. (1994). Requirement of a critical period of transcription for induction of a late phase of LTP. *Science, 265*, 1104–1107. §5.9.

Ni, A. M., Ray, S., & Maunsell, J. H. (2012). Tuned normalization explains the size of attention modulations. *Neuron, 73*(4), 803–813. §5.50.

Niedeggen, M., Wichmann, P., & Stoerig, P. (2001). Change blindness and time to consciousness. *European Journal of Neuroscience, 14*, 1719–1726. §10.16.

Nieuwenhuis, S., Ridderinkhof, K. R., Blom, J., Band, G. P., & Kok, A. (2001). Error-related brain potentials are differentially related to awareness of response errors: Evidence from an antisaccade task. *Psychophysiology, 38*, 752–760. §10.36.

Nir, Y., & Tononi, G. (2010). Dreaming and the brain: From phenomenology to neurophysiology. *Trends in Cognitive Science, 14*(2), 88–100. §§10.77, 10.78.

Nissen, M. J., & Corkin, S. (1985). Effectiveness of attentional cueing in older and younger adults. *Journal of Gerontology, 40*, 185–191. §4.25.

Niswender, C. M., & Conn, P. J. (2010). Metabotropic glutamate receptors: Physiology, pharmacology, and disease. *Annual Reviews of Pharmacology and Toxicology, 50*, 295–322. §5.24.

Nitschke, J. B., & Mackiewicz, K. L. (2005). Prefrontal and anterior cingulate contributions to volition in depression. *International Review of Neurobiology, 67*, 73–94. Figure 7.1.

Norman, D. A., & Bobrow, D. G. (1975). On data-limited and resource-limited processes. *Cognitive Psychology, 7*(1), 44–64. §10.73.

Nowak, L. G., Azouz, R., Sanchez-Vives, M. V., Gray, C. M., & McCormick, D. A. (2003). Electrophysiological classes of cat primary visual cortical neurons in vivo as revealed by quantitative analyses. *Journal of Neurophysiology, 89*, 1541–1566. §§4.52, 5.3.

Nusser, Z. (2000). AMPA and NMDA receptors: Similarities and differences in their synaptic distribution. *Current Opinion in Neurobiology, 10*, 337–341. §4n4.

Oakes, L. M., Ross-Sheehy, S., & Luck, S. J. (2006). Rapid development of feature binding in visual short-term memory. *Psychological Science, 17*(9), 781–787. §4.21.

Oberlander, T. F., Grunau, R. E., Fitzgerald, C., & Whitfield, M. F. (2002). Does parenchymal brain injury affect biobehavioral pain responses in very low birth weight infants at 32 weeks' postconceptional age? *Pediatrics, 110*, 570–576. §10n20.

O'Donnell, P., & Grace, A. A. (1995). Synaptic interactions among excitatory afferents to nucleus accumbens neurons: Hippocampal gating of prefrontal cortical input. *Journal of Neuroscience*, *15*, 3622–3639. §5.36.

Oh, J. S., Kubicki, M., Rosenberger, G., Bouix, S., Levitt, J. J., McCarley, R. W., Westin, C. F., & Shenton, M. E. (2009). Thalamo-frontal white matter alterations in chronic schizophrenia: A quantitative diffusion tractography study. *Human Brain Mapping*, *30*, 3812–3825. §5.24.

Ohno-Shosaku, T., Maejima, T., & Kano, M. (2001). Endogenous cannabinoids mediate retrograde signals from depolarized postsynaptic neurons to presynaptic terminals. *Neuron*, *29*, 729–738. §5.17.

Oppenheim, J., & Wehner, S. (2010). The uncertainty principle determines the nonlocality of quantum mechanics. *Science*, *330*(6007), 1072–1074. §A1.7, §A1n5.

Oppermann, F., Hassler, U., Jescheniak, J. D., & Gruber, T. (2012). The rapid extraction of gist-early neural correlates of high-level visual processing. *Journal of Cognitive Neuroscience*, *24*(2), 521–529. §§4.14, 10.71.

O'Regan, J. K. (1992). Solving the "real" mysteries of visual perception: The world as an outside memory. *Canadian Journal of Psychology*, *46*(3), 461–488. §10.82.

O'Regan, J. K., & Noë, A. (2001). A sensorimotor account of vision and visual consciousness. *Behavioral and Brain Sciences*, *24*, 939–1031. §10.82.

O'Reilly, R. C. (2006). Biologically-based computational models of high-level cognition. *Science*, *314*, 91–94. §8.22.

O'Reilly, R., Noelle, D., Braver, T., & Cohen, J. (2002). Prefrontal cortex and dynamic categorization tasks: Representational organization and neuromodulatory control. *Cerebral Cortex*, *12*, 246–257. §7.11.

Otto, T., Eichenbaum, H., Wible, C. G., & Wiener, S. I. (1991). Learning-related patterns of CA1 spike trains parallel stimulation parameters optimal for inducing hippocampal long-term potentiation. *Hippocampus*, *1*, 181–192. §5.36.

Overton, P. G., & Clark, D. (1997). Burst firing in midbrain dopaminergic neurons. *Brain Research Reviews*, *25*, 312–334. §4.40.

Owen, A. M., Evans, A. C., & Petrides, M. (1996). Evidence for a two-stage model of spatial working memory processing within the lateral frontal cortex: A positron emission tomography study. *Cerebral Cortex*, *6*(1), 31–38. §4.26.

Ozeki, H., Finn, I. M., Schaffer, E. S., Miller, K. D., & Ferster, D. (2009). Inhibitory stabilization of the cortical network underlies visual surround suppression. *Neuron*, *62*(4), 578–592. §4.32.

Palm, G. (1982). *Neural assemblies: An alternative approach to artificial intelligence*. Secaucus, NJ: Springer-Verlag. §4.54.

Palm, G. (1987). Computing with neural networks. *Science, 235*, 1227b–1228b. §4.54.

Pang, K., Williams, M. J., Egeth, H., & Olton, D. S. (1993). Nucleus basalis magnocellularis and attention: Effects of muscimol infusions. *Behavioral Neuroscience, 107*, 1031–1038. §5.44.

Paoletti, P. (2011). Molecular basis of NMDA receptor functional diversity. *European Journal of Neuroscience, 33*, 1351–1365. §4n4.

Pascual-Leone, A., & Walsh, V. (2001). Fast backprojections from the motion to the primary visual area necessary for visual awareness. *Science, 292*, 510–512. §5n11.

Passingham, R. E. (1987). Two cortical systems for directing movement. *Ciba Foundation Symposium, 132*, 151–164. Figure 9.1.

Pasternak, T., & Greenlee, M. W. (2005). Working memory in primate sensory systems. *Nature Reviews: Neuroscience, 6*(2), 97–107. §10.30.

Paterek, T., Fedrizzi, A., Gröblacher, S., Jennewein, T., Zukowski, M., Aspelmeyer, M., et al. (2007). Experimental test of nonlocal realistic theories without the rotational symmetry assumption. *Physical Review Letters, 99*(21), 210406. §A1.6.

Pawelzik, H., Hughes, D. I., & Thomson, A. M. (2002). Physiological and morphological diversity of immunocytochemically defined parvalbumin- and cholecystokinin-positive interneurones in CA1 of the adult rat hippocampus. *Journal of Comparative Neurology, 443*, 346–367. §5.3.

Penrose, R. (1989). *The emperor's new mind: Concerning computers, minds, and the laws of physics.* Oxford: Oxford University Press. §§A1.8, A1.9.

Penrose, R. (1994) *Shadows of the mind.* Oxford: Oxford University Press. §§A1.8, A1.9.

Penrose, R., & Hameroff, S. (1995). What "gaps"? Reply to Grush and Churchland. *Journal of Consciousness Studies, 2*, 99–112. §A1.8.

Penttonen, M., Kamondi, A., Acsady, L., & Buzsáki, G. (1998). Gamma frequency oscillation in the hippocampus of the rat: Intracellular analysis in vivo. *European Journal of Neuroscience, 10*, 718–728. §§4.44, 5.3, 5.43.

Perlmutter, B. A., & Houghton, C. J. (2009). A new hypothesis for sleep: Tuning for criticality. *Neural Computation, 21*(6), 1622–1641. §5.8.

Perrett, D. I., Rolls, E. T., & Caan, W. (1982). Visual neurones responsive to faces in the monkey temporal cortex. *Experimental Brain Research, 47*(3), 329–342. §4.9, 4.10.

Perrett, D. I., Smith, P. A., Potter, D. D., Mistlin, A. J., Head, A. S., Milner, A. D., et al. (1985). Visual cells in the temporal cortex sensitive to face view and gaze direction.

Proceedings of the Royal Society of London, Series B: Biological Sciences, 223(1232), 293–317. §10.21.

Pesaran, B., Nelson, M. J., & Andersen, R. A. (2008). Free choice activates a decision circuit between frontal and parietal cortex. *Nature, 453,* 406–409. §4.23.

Peshkin, M., & Tonomura, A. (1989). *The Aharonov-Bohm effect.* Berlin: Springer. §A1.11.

Petralia, R. S., Yokotani, N., & Wenthold, R. J. (1993). Light and electron microscope distribution of the NMDA receptor subunit NMDARI in the rat nervous system using a selective anti-peptide antibody. *Journal of Neuroscience, 14*(2), 667–696. §5n2.

Phillips, W. A. (1974). Distinction between sensory storage and short-term visual memory. *Perception & Psychophysics, 16*(2), 283–290. §10.13.

Pike, F. G., Meredith, R. M., Olding, A. W., & Paulsen, O. (1999). Rapid report: Post-synaptic bursting is essential for "Hebbian" induction of associative longterm potentiation at excitatory synapses in rat hippocampus. *Journal of Physiology, 518,* 571–576. §5.6.

Pinault, D., & Deschenes, M. (1998). Anatomical evidence for a mechanism of lateral inhibition in the rat thalamus. *European Journal of Neuroscience, 10,* 3462–3469. §4n11.

Pinker, S. (1997). *How the mind works.* New York: Norton. §§1.3, 7.3.

Pins, D., & Ffytche, D. (2003). The neural correlates of conscious vision. *Cerebral Cortex, 13*(5), 461–474. §§10.16, 10.65.

Pinsk, M. A., Arcaro, M., Weiner, K. S., Kalkus, J. F., Inati, S. J., Gross, C. G., et al. (2009). Neural representations of faces and body parts in macaque and human cortex: A comparative FMRI study. *Journal of Neurophysiology, 101*(5), 2581–2600. §4.12.

Pinsk, M. A., DeSimone, K., Moore, T., Gross, C. G., & Kastner, S. (2005). Representations of faces and body parts in macaque temporal cortex: A functional MRI study. *Proceedings of the National Academy of Sciences of the United States of America, 102*(19), 6996–7001. §4.12.

Pinsky, P. F., & Rinzel, J. (1994). Intrinsic and network rhythmogenesis in a reduced Traub model for CA3 neurons. *Journal of Computational Neuroscience, 1,* 39–60. §5.21.

Poirazi, P., & Mel, B. W. (2001). Impact of active dendrites and structural plasticity on the memory capacity of neural tissue. *Neuron, 29,* 779–796. §5.15.

Polger, T. (2004). *Natural minds.* Cambridge, MA: MIT Press. §3.11.

Polich, J. (1986). Attention, probability, and task demands as determinants of P300 latency from auditory stimuli. *Electroencephalography and Clinical Neurophysiology, 63,* 251–259. §4.22.

Pollen, D. A. (1999). On the neural correlates of visual perception. *Cerebral Cortex*, *9*, 4–19. §10.77.

Polsky, A., Mel, B. W., & Schiller, J. (2004). Computational subunits in thin dendrites of pyramidal cells. *Nature Neuroscience*, *7*, 621–627. §5.22.

Polsky, A., Mel, B., & Schiller, J. (2009). Encoding and decoding bursts by NMDA spikes in basal dendrites of layer 5 pyramidal neurons. *Journal of Neuroscience*, *29*(38), 11891–11903. §§4.36, 5.30.

Popper, K. R. (1979). *Objective knowledge: An evolutionary approach*. Oxford: Oxford University Press. §7.17, 10.7.

Popper, K. R., & Eccles, J.C. (1977). *The self and its brain*. New York: Springer. §7.17.

Posner, N. I., & Snyder, C. R. R. (1975). Attention and cognitive control. In R. L. Solso (Ed.), *Information processing and cognition: The Loyola Symposium* (pp. 205–223). Hillsdale, NJ: Lawrence Erlbaum. §10.36.

Posner, M. I., & Petersen, S. E. (1990). The attention system of the human brain. *Annual Review of Neuroscience*, *13*, 25–42. §4.23.

Potts, G. F., Liotti, M., Tucker, D. M., & Posner, M. I. (1996). Frontal and inferior temporal cortical activity in visual target detection: Evidence from high spatially sampled event-related potentials. *Brain Topography*, *9*, 3–14. §4.22.

Poulet, J. F., & Petersen, C. C. (2008). Internal brain state regulates membrane potential synchrony in barrel cortex of behaving mice. *Nature*, *454*, 881–885. §4.42.

Pouille, F., & Scanziani, M. (2001). Enforcement of temporal fidelity in pyramidal cells by somatic feed-forward inhibition. *Science*, *293*, 1159–1163. §§4.43, 4.44, 5.3.

Powell, D. A., & Churchwell, J. (2002). Mediodorsal thalamic lesions impair trace eyeblink conditioning in the rabbit. *Learning & Memory*, *9*, 10–17. §10n15.

Power, A. E., Vazdarjanova, A., & McGaugh, J. L. (2003). Muscarinic cholinergic influences in memory consolidation. *Neurobiology of Learning and Memory*, *80*, 178–193. §5.38.

Pozo, K., & Goda, Y. (2010). Unraveling mechanisms of homeostatic synaptic plasticity. *Neuron*, *66*, 337–351. §5.7.

Priebe, N. J., & Ferster, D. (2008). Inhibition, spike threshold, and stimulus selectivity in primary visual cortex. *Neuron*, *57*, 482–497. §4.32.

Prigogine, I. (1997). *The end of certainty*. New York: Free Press. §4.69, §A1n6.

Prigogine, I., & Stengers, I. (1984). *Order out of chaos*. New York: Bantam. §4.69.

Prince, A., & Smolensky, P. (2004). *Optimality theory: Constraint interaction in generative grammar.* Oxford: Blackwell. §8.22.

Provine, R. R. (1986). Yawning as a stereo-typed action pattern and releasing stimulus. *Ethology, 72,* 109–122. §7n5.

Przybyszewski, A. W., Gaska, J. P., Foote, W., & Pollen, D. A. (2000). Striate cortex increases contrast gain of macaque LGN neurons. *Visual Neuroscience, 17,* 485–494. §5.45.

Puce, A., Allison, T., Asgari, M., Gore, J. C., & McCarthy, G. (1996). Differential sensitivity of human visual cortex to faces, letterstrings, and textures: A functional magnetic resonance imaging study. *Journal of Neuroscience, 16*(16), 5205–5215. §4.12.

Puce, A., Allison, T., Gore, J. C., & McCarthy, G. (1995). Face-sensitive regions in human extrastriate cortex studied by functional MRI. *Journal of Neurophysiology, 74*(3), 1192–1199. §4.12.

Pulvermüller, F. (2010). Brain embodiment of syntax and grammar: Discrete combinatorial mechanisms spelt out in neuronal circuits. *Brain and Language, 112,* 167–179. §4.55.

Putnam, H. (1960). Minds and machines. Reprinted in H. Putnam (1975). *Mind, language, and reality.* Cambridge: Cambridge University Press. §§8.24, 8n9.

Putnam, H. (1967). Psychological predicates. In W. H. Capitan and D. D. Merrill (Eds.), *Art, mind, and religion* (pp. 37–48). (Also published as "The nature of mental states" in H. Putnam [1975]. *Mind, language, and reality.* Cambridge: Cambridge University Press). §§3.11, 8.24, 8n9.

Putnam, H. (1975). *Mind, language, and reality.* Cambridge: Cambridge University Press. §8.24, §8n9.

Putnam, H. (1988). *Representation and reality.* Cambridge, MA: MIT Press. §3.11.

Pylyshyn, Z. W., & Storm, R. W. (1988). Tracking multiple independent targets: Evidence for a parallel tracking mechanism. *Spatial Vision, 3*(3), 179–197. §§4.21, 10.30, 10.32, 10.42.

Qiu, F. T., Sugihara, T., & von der Heydt, R. (2007). Figure-ground mechanisms provide structure for selective attention. *Nature Neuroscience, 10,* 1492–1499. §10.50.

Quine, W. V. (1943). Notes on existence and necessity. *Journal of Philosophy, 60,* 113–127. §8.10.

Quine, W. V. (1960). *Word and object.* Cambridge, MA: MIT Press. §8.10.

Quine, W. V. (1961). Reference and modality. In his *From a logical point of view* (pp. 139–157). Cambridge, MA: Harvard University Press. §8.10.

Quine, W. V. (1966). Three grades of modal involvement. In his *The ways of paradox* (pp. 158–176). Cambridge, MA: Harvard University Press. §8.10.

Quinlan, P. T. (2003). Visual feature integration theory: Past, present, and future. *Psychological Bulletin, 29*(5), 643–673. §10.30.

Quiroga, R. Q., Kreiman, G., Koch, C., & Fried, I. (2008). Sparse but not "grand-mother-cell" coding in the medial temporal lobe. *Trends in Cognitive Sciences, 12*(3), 87–91. §4.11.

Quiroga, R. Q., Reddy, L., Kreiman, G., Koch, C., & Fried, I. (2005). Invariant visual representation by single neurons in the human brain. *Nature, 435*(7045), 1102–1107. §4.11, figure 4.4.

Rabinowitch, I., & Segev, I. (2008). Two opposing plasticity mechanisms pulling a single synapse. *Trends in Neurosciences, 31*, 377–383. §5.7.

Ragozzino, M., Detrick, S., & Kesner, R. (1999). Involvement of the prelimbic—infralimbic areas of the rodent prefrontal cortex in behavioral flexibility for place and response learning. *Journal of Neuroscience, 19*, 4585–4594. §7.11.

Ragozzino, M. E., Jih, J., & Tzavos, A. (2002). Involvement of the dorsomedial striatum in behavioral flexibility: Role of muscarinic cholinergic receptors. *Brain Research, 953*, 205–214. §9.8.

Raichle, M. E., & Snyder, A. Z. (2007). A default mode of brain function: A brief history of an evolving idea. *NeuroImage, 37*(4), 1083–1090.

Railo, H., & Koivisto, M. (2009). The electrophysiological correlates of stimulus visibility and metacontrast masking. *Consciousness & Cognition, 18*, 794–803. §10.16.

Rajimehr, R., Young, J. C., & Tootell, R. B. (2009). An anterior temporal face patch in human cortex, predicted by macaque maps. *Proceedings of the National Academy of Sciences of the United States of America, 106*(6), 1995–2000. §4.12.

Rall, W. (1964). Theoretical significance of dendritic trees for neuronal input-output relations. In R. Reiss (Ed.), *Neural theory and modeling* (pp. 73–97). Stanford, CA: Stanford University Press. §5.15.

Ramachandran, V. S., & Altschuler, E. L. (2009). The use of visual feedback, in particular mirror visual feedback, in restoring brain function. *Brain, 132*(7), 1693–1710. §10.5.

Ramachandran, V. S., & Hirstein, W. (1998). Perception of phantom limbs. *Brain, 121*, 1603–1630. §4n15.

Ramachandran, V. S., Rogers-Ramachandran, D., & Stewart, M. (1992). Perceptual correlates of massive cortical reorganization. *Science, 258*, 1159–1160. §4n15.

Rambhadran, A., Gonzalez, J., & Jayaraman, V. (2010). Subunit arrangement in N-methyl-D-aspartate (NMDA) receptors. *Journal of Biological Chemistry, 285*, 15296–15301. §A1.10.

Ramcharan, E. J., Gnadt, J. W., & Sherman, S. M. (2000). Burst and tonic firing in thalamic cells of unanesthetized, behaving monkeys. *Visual Neuroscience, 17*, 55–62. §4n11.

Ramón y Cajal, S. (1911). *Histologie du Système Nerveux de l'Homme et des Vertébrés.* Paris: Maloine. §5n7.

Rancz, E. A., Ishikawa, T., Duguid, I., Chadderton, P., Mahon, S., & Häusser, M. (2007). High-fidelity transmission of sensory information by single cerebellar mossy fibre boutons. *Nature, 450*, 1245–1248. §5.30.

Rao, R. P., & Sejnowski, T. J. (2001). Spike-timing-dependent Hebbian plasticity as temporal difference learning. *Neural Computation, 13*, 2221–2237. §5.11.

Rao, S. C., Rainer, G., & Miller, E. K. (1997). Integration of what and where in the primate prefrontal cortex. *Science, 276*(5313), 821–824. §4.26.

Rapp, M., Yarom, Y., & Segev, I. (1996). Modeling back propagating action potential in weakly excitable dendrites of neocortical pyramidal cells. *Proceedings of the National Academy of Sciences of the United States of America, 93*, 11985–11990. §§4n2, 5.18, 5.21, 5.23, 5.26, 5n8.

Ravizza, S., & Ciranni, M. (2002). Contributions of the prefrontal cortex and basal ganglia to set shifting. *Journal of Cognitive Neuroscience, 14*, 472–483. §9.8.

Ravizza, S., & Ivry, R. (2001). Comparison of the basal ganglia and cerebellum in shifting attention. *Journal of Cognitive Neuroscience, 13*, 285–297. §9.8.

Ray, S., & Maunsell, J. H. R. (2010). Differences in gamma frequencies across visual cortex restrict their possible use in computation. *Neuron, 67*(5), 885–896. §4.47.

Ray, S. and Maunsell, J. H. R. (2011). Different origins of gamma rhythm and high-gamma activity in macaque visual cortex. *PLoS Biology, 9*(4), e1000610. §§4.35, 4.50, 5.43, figure 5.5, §5n12.

Raymond, J. E., Shapiro, K. L., & Arnell, K. M. (1992). Temporary suppression of visual processing in an RSVP task: An attentional blink? *Journal of Experimental Psychology: Human Perception & Performance, 18*, 849–860. §10.73.

Reavis, E. A., Kohler, P. J., Caplovitz, G. P., Wheatley, T. P., & Tse, P. U. (2012). Additive effects of spatial and feature-based attention on monocular rivalry. Submitted. §10.49.

Reichel, F. D., Todd, J. T., & Yilmaz, E. (1995). Visual discrimination of local surface depth and orientation. *Perception & Psychophysics, 57*(8), 1233–1240. §10.81.

Reinagel, P., Godwin, D., Sherman, S. M., & Koch, C. (1999). Encoding of visual information by LGN bursts. *Journal of Neurophysiology, 81*, 2558–2569. §4.38.

Reitboeck, H. J., Eckhorn, R., & Pabst, M. (1987). A model of figure/ground separation based on correlated neural activity in the visual system. In H. Haken (Ed.), *Synergetics of the brain.* New York: Springer. §4.45.

Remington, R. W., Johnston, J. C., & Yantis, S. (1992). Involuntary attentional capture by abrupt onsets. *Perception & Psychophysics, 51,* 279–290. §4.22.

Remy, S., & Spruston, N. (2007). Dendritic spikes induce single-burst long-term potentiation. *Proceedings of the National Academy of Sciences of the United States of America, 104*(43), 17192–17197. §§5.6, 5.27.

Rensink, R. A., & Enns, J. T. (1995). Preemption effects in visual search: Evidence for low-level grouping. *Psychological Review, 102,* 101–130. §§4.22, 10.35.

Rensink, R. A., & Enns, J. T. (1998). Early completion of occluded objects. *Vision Research, 38*(15–16), 2489–2505. §§4.22, 10.35.

Rensink, R. A., O'Regan, J. K., & Clark, J. J. (1997). To see or not to see: The need for attention to perceive changes in scenes. *Psychological Science, 8*(5), 368–373. §10.13.

Rey, G. (1983). A reason for doubting the existence of consciousness. In R. Davidson, G. Schwartz, & D. Shapiro (Eds.), *Consciousness and self-regulation* (Vol. 3, pp. 1–39). New York: Plenum. §§10.5, A2n1.

Reyes, A., Lujan, R., Rozov, A., Burnashev, N., Somogyi, P., & Sakmann, B. (1998). Target-cell-specific facilitation and depression in neocortical circuits. *Nature Neuroscience, 1,* 279–285. §4.55.

Reynolds, A. M., & Frye, M. A. (2007). Free-flight odor tracking in Drosophila is consistent with an optimal intermittent scale-free search. *PLoS ONE, 2,* e354. §4.70.

Reynolds, J. H., & Chelazzi, L. (2004). Attentional modulation of visual processing. *Annual Review of Neuroscience, 27,* 611–647. §§4.25, 4.48.

Reynolds, J. H., Chelazzi, L., & Desimone, R. (1999). Competitive mechanisms subserve attention in macaque areas V2 and V4. *Journal of Neuroscience, 19,* 1736–1753. §5.50.

Reynolds, J. H., & Desimone, R. (1999). The role of neural mechanisms of attention in solving the binding problem. *Neuron, 24*(1), 19–29, 111–125. §4.21.

Reynolds, J. H., & Heeger, D. J. (2009). The normalization model of attention. *Neuron, 61*(2), 168–185. §§4.21, 4.27, 4.59, 4.60, 5.45, 10.32.

Reynolds, J. H., Pasternak, T., & Desimone, R. (2000). Attention increases sensitivity of V4 neurons. *Neuron, 26,* 703–714. §5.50.

Rhodes, G., Watson, T. L., Jeffery, L., & Clifford, C. W. G. (2010). Perceptual adaptation helps us identify faces. *Vision Research, 50,* 963–968. §§8.18, 8.20.

Rhodes, G., Jaquet, E., Jeffery, L., Evangelista, E., Keane, J., & Calder, A. J. (2011). Sex-specific norms code face identity. *Journal of Vision, 11*(1), 1–11. §§8.18, 8.20.

Ribary, U., Ioannides, A. A., Singh, K. D., Hasson, R., Bolton, J. P., Lado, F., et al. (1991). Magnetic field tomography of coherent thalamocortical 40-Hz oscillations in humans. *Proceedings of the National Academy of Sciences of the United States of America, 88,* 11037–11041. §4.44.

Rich, M. M., & Wenner, P. (2007). Sensing and expressing homeostatic synaptic plasticity. *Trends in Neurosciences, 30,* 119–125. §5.7.

Richmond, B. J., & Wurtz, R. H. (1980). Vision during saccadic eye movements. II. A corollary discharge to monkey superior colliculus. *Journal of Neurophysiology, 43,* 1156–1167. §4.39, figure 4.3.

Riesenhuber, M., & Poggio, T. (1999). Hierarchical models of object recognition in cortex. *Nature Neuroscience, 2*(11), 1019–1025. §4.13, figure 4.3.

Riesenhuber, M., & Poggio, T. (2000). Models of object recognition. *Nature Neuroscience, 3*(Suppl.), 1199–1204. §4.13, figure 4.3.

Riesenhuber, M., & Poggio, T. (2002). Neural mechanisms of object recognition. *Current Opinion in Neurobiology, 12*(2), 162–168. §4.13.

Rizzolatti, G., Riggio, L., & Sheliga, B. M. (1994). Space and selective attention. In C. Umilta & M. Moscovitch (Eds.), *Attention and performance XV* (pp. 231–265). Cambridge, MA: MIT Press. §4.23.

Robbins, T. W. (1997). Arousal systems and attentional processes. *Biological Psychology, 45,* 57–71. §5.38.

Roberts, P. D. (1999). Computational consequences of temporally asymmetric learning rules: I. Differential Hebbian learning. *Journal of Computational Neuroscience, 7,* 235–246. §5n6.

Roberts, S., & Gharib, A. (2006). Variation of bar-press duration: Where do new responses come from? *Behavioural Processes, 72,* 215–223. §4.70.

Robinson, D. L., & Kertzman, C. (1995). Covert orienting of attention in macaques III: Contributions of the superior colliculus. *Journal of Neurophysiology, 74*(2), 713–721. §4.23.

Robitaille, N., & Jolicoeur, P. (2006). Fundamental properties of the N2pc as an index of spatial attention: Effects of masking. *Canadian Journal of Experimental Psychology, 60,* 101–111. §10.28.

Rockland, K. S., & Van Hoesen, G. W. (1994). Direct temporal-occipital feedback connections to striate cortex (V1) in the macaque monkey. *Cerebral Cortex, 4,* 300–313. §4.49.

Rodriguez-Moreno, A., & Paulsen, O. (2008). Spike timing-dependent long-term depression requires presynaptic NMDA receptors. *Nature Neuroscience, 11,* 744–745. §5n5.

Rodríguez-Moreno, A., Banerjee, A., & Paulsen, O. (2010). Presynaptic NMDA receptors and spike timing-dependent long-term depression at cortical synapses. *Frontal Synaptic Neuroscience, 2*(18), 1–6. §5.28.

Roelfsema, P. R., Engel, A. K., König, P., & Singer, W. (1997). Visuomotor integration is associated with zero time-lag synchronization among cortical areas. *Nature, 385*, 157–161. §4.23.

Roelfsema, P. R., Lamme, V. A., & Spekreijse, H. (1998). Object-based attention in the primary visual cortex of the macaque monkey. *Nature, 395*, 376–381. §4.24.

Rogers, J. H. (1992). Immunohistochemical markers in rat cortex: Co-localization of calretinin and calbindin-D28k with neuropeptides and GABA. *Brain Research, 587*(1), 147–157. §5.3.

Roitman, J. D., & Shadlen, M. N. (2002). Response of neurons in the lateral intraparietal area during a combined visual discrimination reaction time task. *Journal of Neuroscience, 22*, 9475–9489. §4.18.

Rokem, A., & Silver, M. A. (2010). Cholinergic enhancement augments magnitude and specificity of visual perceptual learning in healthy humans. *Current Biology, 20*(19), 1723–1728. §4.22.

Rokem, A., Landau, A. N., Garg, D., Prinzmetal, W., & Silver, M. A. (2010). Cholinergic enhancement increases the effects of voluntary attention but does not affect involuntary attention. *Neuropsychopharmacology, 35*(13), 2538–2544. §4.22.

Rolfs, M., Engbert, R., & Kliegl, R. (2004). Microsaccade orientation supports attentional enhancement opposite to a peripheral cue: Commentary on Tse Sheinberg Logothetis. *Psychological Science, 10*, 705–707. §4.23.

Rollman, G. B. (1985). Sensory events with variable central latencies provide inaccurate clocks. *Behavioral and Brain Sciences, 8*, 551–552. §9n1.

Rolls, E. T. (1984). Neurons in the cortex of the temporal lobe and in the amygdala of the monkey with responses selective for faces. *Human Neurobiology, 3*, 209–222. §4.9.

Rolls, E. T. (2007). The representation of information about faces in the temporal and frontal lobes. *Neuropsychologia, 45*, 124–143. §4.12.

Rolls, E. T., Judge, S. J., & Sanghera, M. K. (1977). Activity of neurones in the inferotemporal cortex of the alert monkey. *Brain Research, 130*(2), 229–238. §4.10.

Roopun, A. K., Cunningham, M. O., Racca, C., Alter, K., Traub, R. D., & Whittington, M. A. (2008). Region-specific changes in gamma and beta2 rhythms in NMDA receptor dysfunction models of schizophrenia. *Schizophrenia Bulletin, 34*, 962–973. §5.24.

Rosch, E. H. (1973). Natural categories. *Cognitive Psychology, 4*, 328–350. §8.15.

Rosch, E., & Mervis, C. (1975). Family resemblances: Studies in the internal structure of categories. *Cognitive Psychology, 7,* 573–605. §8.15.

Rosch, E. (1987). Wittgenstein and categorization research in cognitive psychology. In M. Chapman & R. Dixon (Eds.), *Meaning and the growth of understanding: Wittgenstein's significance for developmental psychology.* Hillsdale, NJ: Erlbaum. §8.15.

Roser, M. E., Fugelsang, J. A., Dunbar, K. N., Corballis, P. M., & Gazzaniga, M. S. (2005). Dissociating processes supporting causal perception and causal inference in the brain. *Neuropsychology, 19*(5), 591–602. §5n6.

Roskies, A. L. (2010). How does neuroscience affect our conception of volition? *Annual Review of Neuroscience, 33,* 109–130. §§9.5, 9.14, 9n2, 9n3.

Rosner, R., Egelhaaf, M., Grewe, J., & Warzecha, A. K. (2009). Variability of blowfly head optomotor responses. *Journal of Experimental Biology, 212,* 1170–1184. §4.70.

Rosner, R., Egelhaaf, M., & Warzecha, K. (2010). Behavioural state affects motion-sensitive neurones in the fly visual system. *Journal of Experimental Biology, 213,* 331–338. §4.70.

Rossi, A. F., & Paradiso, M. A. (1995). Feature-specific effects of selective visual attention. *Vision Research, 35,* 621–634. §4.25.

Rothman, S. M., & Olney, J. W. (1995). Excitotoxicity and the NMDA receptor: Still lethal after eight years. *Trends in Neurosciences, 18,* 57–58. §5.5.

Rougier, N. P., Noelle, D. C., Braver, T. S., Cohen, J. D., & O'Reilly, R. C. (2005). Prefrontal cortex and flexible cognitive control: Rules without symbols. *Proceedings of the National Academy of Sciences of the United States of America, 102,* 7338–7343. §7.11.

Rowe, M. A., Kielpinski, D., Meyer, V., Sackett, C. A., Itano, W. M., Monroe, C., et al. (2001). Experimental violation of Bell's inequalities with efficient detection. *Nature, 409,* 791–794. §A1.6.

Royer, S., & Paré, D. (2003). Conservation of total synaptic weight through balanced synaptic depression and potentiation. *Nature, 422,* 518–522. §5.7.

Ryou, J. W., Cho, S. Y., & Kim, H. T. (2001). Lesions of the entorhinal cortex impair acquisition of hippocampal-dependent trace conditioning. *Neurobiology of Learning and Memory, 75,* 121–127. §10n15.

Saalmann, Y. B., Pigarev, I. N., & Vidyasagar, T. R. (2007). Neural mechanisms of visual attention: How top-down feedback highlights relevant locations. *Science, 316,* 1612–1615. §4.24.

Sabatini, B. L., Maravall, M., & Svoboda, K. (2001). Ca(2+) signaling in dendritic spines. *Current Opinion in Neurobiology, 11,* 349–356. §5.22.

Saha, R. N., & Dudek, S. M. (2008). Action potentials: To the nucleus and beyond. *Experimental Biology and Medicine, 233*(4), 385–393. §5.9.

Saint-Cyr, J. A., Taylor, A. E., & Nicholson, K. (1995). Behavior and the basal ganglia. *Advances in Neurology, 65*, 1–28. §9.8.

Salin, P. A., & Bullier, J. (1995). Corticocortical connections in the visual system: Structure and function. *Physiological Reviews, 75*, 107–154. §4.49.

Salinas, E., & Sejnowski, T. J. (2001). Correlated neuronal activity and the flow of neural information. *Nature Reviews: Neuroscience, 2*, 539–550. §5.50.

Salinas, E., & Thier, P. (2000). Gain modulation: A major computational principle of the central nervous system. *Neuron, 27*(1), 15–21. §4.59.

Salisbury, D., Squires, N. K., Ibel, S., & Maloney, T. (1992). Auditory event-related potentials during stage 2 NREM sleep in humans. *Journal of Sleep Research, 1*, 251–257. §§4.22, 10.16.

Salussolia, C. L., Prodromou, M. L., Borker, P., & Wollmuth, L. P. (2011). Arrangement of subunits in functional NMDA receptors. *Journal of Neuroscience, 31*(31), 11295–11304. §A1.10.

Sanchez-Vives, M. V., & McCormick, D. A. (2000). Cellular and network mechanisms of rhythmic recurrent activity in neocortex. *Nature Neuroscience, 3*, 1027–1034. §5.42.

Sarbadhikari, S. N., & Chakrabarty, K. (2001). Chaos in the brain: A short review alluding to epilepsy, depression, exercise, and lateralization. *Medical Engineering & Physics, 23*(7), 445–455. §4.68.

Sarter, M., & Bruno, J. P. (2002). The neglected constituent of the basal forebrain corticopetal projection system: GABAergic projections. *European Journal of Neuroscience, 15*, 1867–1873. §5.45.

Sarter, M., Hasselmo, M., Bruno, J., & Givens, B. (2005). Unraveling the attentional functions of cortical cholinergic inputs: Interactions between signal-driven and cognitive modulation of signal detection. *Brain Research: Reviews, 48*, 98–111. §§5.38, 5.39.

Savain, L. (2010). How to solve the parallel programming crisis. http://www.rebel-science.org/download/cosa002.pdf. §8.1.

Scepkowski, L. A., & Cronin-Golomb, A. (2003). The alien hand: Cases, categorizations, and anatomical correlates. *Behavioral and Cognitive Neuroscience Reviews, 2*(4), 261–277. §10n10.

Schaefer, A. T., Larkum, M. E., Sakmann, B., & Roth, A. (2003). Coincidence detection in pyramidal neurons is tuned by their dendritic branching pattern. *Journal of Neurophysiology, 89*, 3143–3154. §5.21.

Schall, J. D. (1995). Neural basis of saccade target selection. *Reviews in the Neurosciences, 6*(1), 63–85. §4.23.

Schell, M. J. (2004). The N-methyl D-aspartate receptor glycine site and D-serine metabolism: An evolutionary perspective. *Philosophical Transactions of the Royal Society of London, Series B: Biological Sciences, 359*, 943–964. §§2n3, 5.4, 5n2.

Schiller, P. H. (1968). Single unit analysis of backward visual masking and metacontrast in the cat LGN. *Vision Research, 8*, 855–866. §4.39.

Schiller, P. H., & Chorover, S. L. (1966). Metacontrast: Its relation to evoked potentials. *Science, 153*, 1398–1400. §10.16.

Schiller, J., Schiller, Y., & Clapham, D. E. (1998). NMDA receptors amplify calcium influx into dendritic spines during associative pre- and postsynaptic activation. *Nature Neuroscience, 1*, 114–118. §5.6.

Schlegel, A. A., Alexander, S., Roskies, A., Sinnott-Armstrong, W., Tse, P. U., & Wheatley, T. (2012a). Barking up the wrong free: Readiness potentials reflect processes independent of conscious will. Submitted. §9.4, figure 9.2, figure 9.3, §9n5.

Schlegel, A. A., Rudelson, J. R., & Tse, P. U. (2012b). Longitudinal diffusion tensor imaging reveals structural changes in white matter as adults learn a second language. *Journal of Cognitive Neuroscience.* §7.12.

Schmidt, B. K., Vogel, E. K., Woodman, G. F., & Luck, S. J. (2002). Voluntary and automatic attentional control of visual working memory. *Perception & Psychophysics, 64*(5), 754–763. §10.13.

Schneider, W. X. (1999). Visual-spatial working memory, attention, and scene representation: A neuro-cognitive theory. *Psychological Research, 62*(2–3), 220–236. §10.30.

Scholl, B. J., Pylyshyn, Z. W., & Feldman, J. (2001). What is a visual object? Evidence from target merging in multiple object tracking. *Cognition, 80*(1–2), 159–177. §§10.30, 10.32, 10.42.

Schröter, H., & Leuthold, H. (2008). Effects of response sequence length on motor programming: A chronometric analysis. *Acta Psychologica, 128*(1), 186–196. §9n4.

Segal, M., & Andersen, P. (2000). Dendritic spines shaped by synaptic activity. *Current Opinion in Neurobiology, 10*(5), 582–586. §4.55.

Segev, I., & London, M. (2000). Untangling dendrites with quantitative models. *Science, 290*, 744–750. §5.18.

Selfridge, O. (1959). Pandemonium: A paradigm for learning. In *Symposium on the mechanization of thought processes.* London: HM Stationery Office. §4.13, figure 4.3.

Selleri, F. (1988). *Quantum mechanics versus local realism: The Einstein–Podolsky–Rosen paradox.* New York: Plenum Press. §A1.6.

Serences, J. T., Schwarzbach, J., Courtney, S. M., Golay, X., & Yantis, S. (2004). Control of object-based attention in human cortex. *Cerebral Cortex, 14,* 1346–1357. §4.24.

Sergent, C., & Dehaene, S. (2004). Is consciousness a gradual phenomenon? Evidence for an all-or-none bifurcation during the attentional blink. *Psychological Science, 15*(11), 720–728. §§10.65, 10.74.

Sergent, C., Baillet, S., & Dehaene, S. (2005). Timing of the brain events underlying access to consciousness during the attentional blink. *Nature Neuroscience, 8,* 1391–1400. §§10.16, 10.75.

Sergent, J., Ohta, S., & MacDonald, B. (1992). Functional neuroanatomy of face and object processing: A positron emission tomography study. *Brain, 115*(Pt 1), 15–36. §4.12.

Serruya, M. D., Hatsopoulos, N. G., Paninski, L., Fellows, M. R., & Donoghue, J. P. (2002). Instant neural control of a movement signal. *Nature, 416*(6877), 141–142. §10n9.

Shadlen, M. N., Kiani, R., Hanks, T. D., & Churchland, A. K. (2008). Neurobiology of decision making: An intentional framework. In C. Engel & W. Singer (Eds.), *Better than conscious? Decision making, the human mind, and implications for institutions* (pp. 71–102). Cambridge, MA: MIT Press. §4.18.

Shadlen, M. N., & Movshon, J. (1999). Synchrony unbound: A critical evaluation of the temporal binding hypothesis. *Neuron, 24,* 67–77. §4.46.

Shadlen, M. N., & Newsome, W. T. (1994). Noise, neural codes, and cortical organization. *Current Opinion in Neurobiology, 4,* 569–579. §§4.31, 4.62, 5.12, 5.45.

Shadlen, M. N., & Newsome, W. T. (1998). The variable discharge of cortical neurons: Implications for connectivity, computation, and information coding. *Journal of Neuroscience, 18,* 3870–3896. §§4.43, 4.52.

Shadlen, M. N., & Newsome, W. T. (2001). Neural basis of a perceptual decision in the parietal cortex (area LIP) of the rhesus monkey. *Journal of Neurophysiology, 86,* 1916–1936. §4.18.

Shahan, T. A., & Chase, P. N. (2002). Novelty, stimulus control, and operant variability. *Journal of Applied Behavior Analysis, 25,* 175–190. §4.70.

Shallice, T., & Burgess, P. W. (1991). Deficits in strategy application following frontal lobe damage in man. *Brain, 114,* 727–741. §10.61.

Shannon, C.E. (1948). A mathematical theory of communication. *Bell System Technical Journal, 27,* 379–423, 623–656. §8.6.

Shapiro, L. (2000). Multiple realizations. *Journal of Philosophy, 97*, 635–654. §§3.11, 3,12, 4.61.

Sheinberg, D. L., & Logothetis, N. K. (2001). Noticing familiar objects in real world scenes: The role of temporal cortical neurons in natural vision. *Journal of Neuroscience, 21*, 1340–1350. §5.50.

Shelley, C., & Magleby, K. L. (2008). Linking exponential components to kinetic states in Markov models for single-channel gating. *Journal of General Physiology, 132*(2), 295–312. §5.25.

Shen, K., & Meyer, T. (1999). Dynamic control of CaMKII translocation and localization in hippocampal neurons by NMDA receptor stimulation. *Science, 284*, 162–166. §5n1.

Shen, W., Flajolet, M., Greengard, P., & Surmeier, D. J. (2008). Dichotomous dopaminergic control of striatal synaptic plasticity. *Science, 321*, 848–851. §4.40.

Shergill, S. S., Bays, P. M., Frith, C. D., & Wolpert, D. M. (2003). Two eyes for an eye: The neuroscience of force escalation. *Science, 301*(5630), 187. §9n6.

Sherman, S. M. (2001). Tonic and burst firing: Dual modes of thalamocortical relay. *Trends in Neurosciences, 24*, 122–126. §4.38.

Sherman, S. M., & Guillery, R. W. (1996). Functional organization of thalamocortical relays. *Journal of Neurophysiology, 76*, 1367–1395. §§4.38, 4n11.

Sherman, S. M., & Guillery, R. W. (2002). The role of the thalamus in the flow of information to the cortex. *Philosophical Transactions of the Royal Society of London, Series B: Biological Sciences, 357*(1428), 1695–1708. §§4.27, 4.38.

Sherman, S. M., & Koch, C. (1986). The control of retinogeniculate transmission in the mammalian lateral geniculate nucleus. *Experimental Brain Research, 63*, 1–20. §4n11.

Shevell, S. K., St. Clair, R., & Hong, S. W. (2008). Misbinding of color to form in after-images. *Visual Neuroscience, 25*(3), 355–360. §§10.49, 10.50.

Shew, W. L., Yang, H., Petermann, T., Roy, R., & Plenz, D. (2009). Neuronal avalanches imply maximum dynamic range in cortical networks at criticality. *Journal of Neuroscience, 29*, 15595–15600. §4.42.

Shew, W. L., Yang, H., Yu, S., Roy, R., & Plenz, D. (2011). Information capacity and transmission are maximized in balanced cortical networks with neuronal avalanches. *Journal of Neuroscience, 31*, 55–63. §4.42.

Shibasaki, H., & Hallett, M. (2006). What is the Bereitschaftspotential? *Clinical Neurophysiology, 117*, 2341–2356. Figure 9.1.

Shih, S. I., & Sperling, G. (2002). Measuring and modeling the trajectory of visual spatial attention. *Psychological Review, 109*, 260–305. §§10.12, 10.13, 10.70, 10.71.

Shimojo, S., Kamitani, Y., & Nishida, S. (2001). After-image of perceptually filled-in surface. *Science, 293*(5535), 1677–1680. §§10.49, 10.50.

Shipp, S., Adams, D. L., Moutoussis, K., & Zeki, S. (2009). Feature binding in the feedback layers of area V2. *Cerebral Cortex, 19*(10), 2230–2239. §4.21.

Shu, Y., Hasenstaub, A., Badoual, M., Bal, T., & McCormick, D. A. (2003a). Barrages of synaptic activity control the gain and sensitivity of cortical neurons. *Journal of Neuroscience, 23*, 10388–10401. §5.42.

Shu, Y., Hasenstaub, A., & McCormick, D. A. (2003b). Turning on and off recurrent balanced cortical activity. *Nature, 423*, 288–293. §§4.33, 5.42.

Shuai, Y., Hu, Y., Qin, H., Campbell, R. A., & Zhong, Y. (2011). Distinct molecular underpinnings of Drosophila olfactory trace conditioning. *Proceedings of the National Academy of Sciences of the United States of America, 108*(50), 20201–20206. §10.43.

Siegel, M., & König, P. (2003). A functional gamma-band defined by stimulus-dependent synchronization in area 18 of awake behaving cats. *Journal of Neuroscience, 23*, 4251–4260. §4.49.

Siegel, M., Donner, T. H., Oostenveld, R., Fries, P., & Engel, A. K. (2007). High-frequency activity in human visual cortex is modulated by visual motion strength. *Cerebral Cortex, 17*, 732–741. §4.49.

Siegel, M., Donner, T. H., Oostenveld, R., Fries, P., & Engel, A. K. (2008). Neuronal synchronization along the dorsal visual pathway reflects the focus of spatial attention. *Neuron, 60*, 709–719. §4.49.

Siegel, M., Engel, A. K., & Donner, T. H. (2011). Cortical network dynamics of perceptual decision-making in the human brain. *Frontiers in Human Neuroscience, 5*(21). doi: 10.3389/fnhum.2011.00021. §4.23.

Sik, A., Penttonen, M., Ylinen, A., & Buzsáki, G. (1995). Hippocampal CA1 interneurons: An in vivo intracellular labeling study. *Journal of Neuroscience, 15*(10), 6651–6665. §4.44.

Simons, D. J., & Chabris, C. F. (1999). Gorillas in our midst: Sustained inattentional blindness for dynamic events. *Perception, 28*(9), 1059–1074. §10.56.

Simons, D. J., & Levin, D. T. (1998). Failure to detect changes to people during a real-world interaction. *Psychonomic Bulletin & Review, 4*, 644–649. §10.56.

Simons, D. J., & Ambinder, M. S. (2005). Change blindness: Theory and consequences. *American Psychological Society, 14*, 44–48. §10.56.

Singer, W. (1999a). Neuronal synchrony: A versatile code for the definition of relations? *Neuron, 24*, 49–65, 111–125. §§4.43, 4.45, 4.53, 4n3.

Singer, W. (1999b). Time as coding space? *Current Opinion in Neurobiology, 9*, 189–194. §§4.43, 4.45, 4.53, 4n3.

Singer, W. (2004). Synchrony, oscillations, and relational codes. In L. M. Chalupa & J. S. Werner (Eds.), *The visual neurosciences* (pp. 1665–1681). Cambridge, MA: MIT Press. §§4.45, 4.53.

Singer, W., & Gray, C. M. (1995). Visual feature integration and the temporal correlation hypothesis. *Annual Review of Neuroscience, 18*, 555–586. §4.43.

Sinnott-Armstrong, W., & Nadel, L. (2010). *Conscious will and responsibility*. New York: Oxford University Press. §9.2.

Sirigu, A., Daprati, E., Ciancia, S., Giraux, P., Nighoghossian, N., Posada, A., et al. (2004). Altered awareness of voluntary action after damage to the parietal cortex. *Nature Neuroscience, 7*, 80–84. §9.1.

Sirota, A., Csicsvari, J., Buhl, D., & Buzsáki, G. (2003). Communication between neocortex and hippocampus during sleep in rodents. *Proceedings of the National Academy of Sciences of the United States of America, 100*, 2065–2069. §4.60.

Sirota, A., Montgomery, S., Fujisawa, S., Isomura, Y., Zugaro, M., & Buzsáki, G. (2008). Entrainment of neocortical neurons and gamma oscillations by the hippocampal theta rhythm. *Neuron, 60*, 683–697. §4.60.

Sjöström, P. J., Turrigiano, G. G., & Nelson, S. B. (2001). Rate, timing, and cooperativity jointly determine cortical synaptic plasticity. *Neuron, 32*, 1149–1164. §§5.11, 5.12.

Sjöström, P. J., & Nelson, S. B. (2002). Spike timing, calcium signals, and synaptic plasticity. *Current Opinion in Neurobiology, 12*, 305–314. §§5.9, 5.11.

Sjöström, P. J., Turrigiano, G. G., & Nelson, S. B. (2003). Neocortical LTD via coincident activation of presynaptic NMDA and cannabinoid receptors. *Neuron, 39*, 641–654. §§5.28, 5n5.

Sjöström, P. J., & Häusser, M. (2006). A cooperative switch determines the sign of synaptic plasticity in distal dendrites of neocortical pyramidal neurons. *Neuron, 51*, 227–238. §5.27.

Sjöström, P. J., Rancz, E. A., Roth, A., & Häusser, M. (2008). Dendritic excitability and synaptic plasticity. *Physiological Reviews, 88*, 769–840. §§5.9, 5.11.

Slater, R., Cantarella, A., Gallella, S., Worley, A., Boyd, S., Meek, J., et al. (2006). Cortical pain responses in human infants. *Journal of Neuroscience, 26*, 3662–3666. §10n20.

Sligte, I. G., Scholte, H. S., & Lamme, V. A. (2008). Are there multiple visual short-term memory stores? *PLoS ONE, 3*(2), e1699. §10.15.

Sligte, I. G., Scholte, H. S., & Lamme, V. A. (2009). V4 activity predicts the strength of visual short-term memory representations. *Journal of Neuroscience, 29*(23), 7432–7438. §10.15.

Sligte, I. G., Wokke, M. E., Tesselaar, J. P., Scholte, H. S., & Lamme, V. A. F. (2011). Magnetic stimulation of the dorsolateral prefrontal cortex dissociates fragile visual short-term memory from visual working memory. *Neuropsychologia, 49*, 1578–1588. §§10.15, 10.17, 10n22.

Smallwood, J., & Schooler, J. W. (2006). The restless mind. *Psychological Bulletin, 132*, 946–958. §9.4.

Smith, M. A., & Kohn, A. (2008). Spatial and temporal scales of neuronal correlation in primary visual cortex. *Journal of Neuroscience, 28*(48), 12591–12603. §§4.47, 4.48, 5.32.

Snyder, L. H., Batista, A. P., & Andersen, R. A. (2000). Intention-related activity in the posterior parietal cortex: A review. *Vision Research, 40*, 1433–1441. §4.18.

Soames, S. (2007). *Reference and description.* Princeton: Princeton University Press. §8.11.

Sober, E. (1999). The multiple realizability argument against reductionism. *Philosophy of Science, 66*, 542–564. §3.11.

Softky, W. R., & Koch, C. (1993). The highly irregular firing of cortical cells is inconsistent with temporal integration of random EPSPs. *Journal of Neuroscience, 13*, 334–350. §§4.52, 4.62.

Solomon, P. R., Van der Schaaf, E. R., Thompson, R. F., & Weisz, D. J. (1986). Hippocampus and trace conditioning of the rabbit's classically conditioned nictitating membrane response. *Behavioral Neuroscience, 100*(5), 729–744. §10.44.

Solstad, T., Boccara, C. N., Kropff, E., Moser, M. B., & Moser, E. I. (2008). Representation of geometric borders in the entorhinal cortex. *Science, 322*(5909), 1865–1868. §§4.8, 8.22.

Soltesz, I. (2006). *Diversity in the neuronal machine.* Oxford: Oxford University Press. §5.3.

Somogyi, P., Tamas, G., Lujan, R., & Buhl, E. H. (1998). Salient features of synaptic organisation in the cerebral cortex. *Brain Research: Reviews, 26*, 113–135. §5.3.

Somogyi, P., & Klausberger, T. (2005). Defined types of cortical interneurone structure space and spike timing in the hippocampus. *Journal of Physiology, 562*, 9–26. §5.3.

Song, J.-H., & Jiang, Y. (2006). Visual working memory for simple and complex features: An fMRI study. *NeuroImage, 30*(3), 963–972. §10.14.

Song, S., Miller, K. D., & Abbott, L. F. (2000). Competitive Hebbian learning through spike-timing-dependent synaptic plasticity. *Nature Neuroscience, 3*, 919–926. §5.11.

Soon, C. S., Brass, M., Heinze, H.-J., & Haynes, J.-D. (2008). Unconscious determinants of free decisions in the human brain. *Nature Neuroscience, 11*, 543–545. §9.14.

Spencer, K. M., Nestor, P. G., Niznikiewicz, M. A., Salisbury, D. F., Shenton, M. E., & McCarley, R. W. (2003). Abnormal neural synchrony in schizophrenia. *Journal of Neuroscience, 23*, 7407–7411. §4n12.

Spengler, S., Von Cramon, D. Y., & Brass, M. (2009). Control of shared representations relies on key processes involved in mental state attribution. *Human Brain Mapping, 30*(11), 3704. §9.13.

Sperling, G. (1960). The information available in brief visual presentations. *Psychological Monographs, 74*(11), 1–29. §§10.12, 10.13, 10.17, 10.70, 10.71, 10.78.

Sperry, R. (1986). Macro- versus micro-determination. *Philosophy of Science, 53*, 265–275. §A2.2.

Sporns, O., Tononi, G., & Edelman, G. M. (1991). Modeling perceptual grouping and figure ground segregation by means of active reentrant connections. *Proceedings of the National Academy of Sciences of the United States of America, 88*, 129–133. §4.45

Sprengel, R., Suchanek, B., Amico, C., Brusa, R., Burnashev, N., Rozov, A., Hvalby, O., Jensen, V., Paulsen, O. Andersen, P., Kim, J. J., Thompson, R. F., Sun, W., Webster, L. C., Grant, S. G., Eilers, J., Konnerth, A., Li, J., McNamara, J. O., & Seeburg, P. H. (1998). Importance of the intracellular domain of NR2 subunits for NMDA receptor function *in vivo. Cell, 92*, 279–289. §5n1.

Spruston, N., Schiller, Y., Stuart, G., & Sakmann, B. (1995). Activity-dependent action potential invasion and calcium influx into hippocampal CA1 dendrites. *Science, 268*, 297–300. §5.35.

Staff, N. P., Jung, H. Y., Thiagarajan, T., Yao, M., & Spruston, N. (2000). Resting and active properties of pyramidal neurons in subiculum and CA1 of rat hippocampus. *Journal of Neurophysiology, 84*, 2398–2408. §5.35.

Stalnaker, R. (1976). *Propositions: Issues in the philosophy of language.* New Haven: Yale University Press. §8.11.

Stalnaker, R. (2004). Assertion revisited: On the interpretation of two-dimensional modal semantics. *Philosophical Studies, 118*, 299–322. §8.11.

Stapp, H. P. (2004). *Mind, matter, and quantum mechanics* (2nd Ed.). Berlin: Springer. §A1.9.

Stepanyants, A., Hirsch, J. A., Martinez, L. M., Kisvárday, Z. F., Ferecskó, A. S., & Chklovskii, D. B. (2008). Local potential connectivity in cat primary visual cortex. *Cerebral Cortex, 18*(1), 13–28. §4.32.

Stephan, K. E., Friston, K. J., & Frith, C. D. (2009). Dysconnection in schizophrenia: From abnormal synaptic plasticity to failures of self-monitoring. *Schizophrenia Bulletin, 35*, 509–527. §5.24.

Steriade, M. (2001). *The intact and sliced brain.* Cambridge, MA: MIT Press. §4.34.

Steriade, M. (2003). *Neuronal substrates of sleep and epilepsy.* Cambridge: Cambridge University Press. §4n12.

Steriade, M., & McCarley, R. W. (1990). *Brainstem control of wakefulness and sleep.* New York: Plenum Press. §5.38.

Steriade, M., Nunez, A., & Amzica, F. (1993b). A novel slow (< 1 Hz) oscillation of neocortical neurons in vivo: Depolarizing and hyperpolarizing components. *Journal of Neuroscience, 13*, 3252–3265. §5.42.

Steriade, M., Timofeev, I., & Grenier, F. (2001). Natural waking and sleep states: A view from inside neocortical neurons. *Journal of Neurophysiology, 85*, 1969–1985. §5.42.

Stevens, C. F., & Wang, Y. (1995). Facilitation and depression at single central synapses. *Neuron, 14*, 795–802. §5.36, figure 5.5.

Steward, O., & Schuman, E. M. (2003). Compartmentalized synthesis and degradation of proteins in neurons. *Neuron, 40*, 347–359. §5.9.

Stiles, J. R., & Bartol, T. M., Jr. (2001). Monte Carlo methods for simulating realistic synaptic microphysiology. In E. de Schutter (Ed.), *Computational neuroscience: Realistic modeling for experimentalists* (pp. 87–127). Boca Raton, FL: CRC. §4.66.

Stiles, J. R., van Helden, D., Bartol, T. M., Jr., Salpeter, E. E., & Salpeter, M. M. (1996). Miniature endplate current rise times less than 100 microseconds from improved dual recordings can be modeled with passive acetylcholine diffusion from a synaptic vesicle. *Proceedings of the National Academy of Sciences of the United States of America, 93*, 5747–5752. §4.66.

Stocco, A., Lebiere, C., & Anderson, J. R. (2010). Conditional routing of information to the cortex: A model of the basal ganglia's role in cognitive coordination. *Psychological Review, 117*(2), 541–574. §§7.15, 9.8.

Stoet, G., & Snyder, L. H. (2004). Single neurons in posterior parietal cortex of monkeys encode cognitive set. *Neuron, 42*, 1003–1012. §4.19.

Storey, A. E., Walsh, C. J., Quinton, R. L., & Wynne-Edwards, K. E. (2000). Hormonal correlates of paternal responsiveness in new and expectant fathers. *Evolution and Human Behavior, 21*(2), 79–95. §10.5.

Strack, S., & Colbran, R. J. (1998). Autophosphorylation-dependent targeting of calcium/calmodulin-dependent protein kinase II by the NR2B subunit of the N-methyl-D-aspartate receptor. *Journal of Biological Chemistry, 273*, 20689–20692. §5n1.

Strawson, G. (1998/2004). Free will. In E. Craig (Ed.), *Routledge encyclopedia of philosophy* (Vol. 3, pp. 743–753). London: Routledge. §§1.5, 7.4, 7.8, 7.12.

Strawson, G. (2002). The bounds of freedom. In R. Kane (Ed.), *The Oxford handbook of free will*. Oxford: Oxford University Press. §7.12.

Stuart, G., Spruston, N., Sakmann, B., & Häusser, M. (1997). Action potential initiation and backpropagation in central neurons. *Trends in Neurosciences, 20*, 125–131. §§5.18, 5.23, figure 5.4.

Stuart, G., & Sakmann, B. (1995). Amplification of EPSPs by axosomatic sodium channels in neocortical pyramidal neurons. *Neuron, 15*, 1065–1076. §5.18, §5n8.

Sugase, Y., Yamane, S., Ueno, S., & Kawano, K. (1999). Global and fine information coded by single neurons in the temporal visual cortex. *Nature, 400*(6747), 869–873. §4.12.

Sussillo, D., Toyoizumi, T., & Maass, W. (2007). Self-tuning of neural circuits through short-term synaptic plasticity. *Journal of Neurophysiology, 97*, 4079–4095. §§4.42, 4.55.

Sutton, M. A., & Schuman, E. M. (2009). Partitioning the synaptic landscape: Distinct microdomains for spontaneous and spike-triggered neurotransmission. *Science Signaling, 2*, 19. §4n8.

Suzuki, S., & Grabowecky, M. (2003). Attention during adaptation weakens negative after-images. *Journal of Experimental Psychology: Human Perception and Performance, 29*(4), 793–807. §§10.49, 10.50.

Svoboda, K., Tank, D. W., & Denk, W. (1996). Direct measurement of coupling between dendritic spines and shafts. *Science, 272*, 716–719. §5.5.

Swadlow, H. A., & Gusev, A. G. (2001). The impact of "bursting" thalamic impulses at a neocortical synapse. *Nature Neuroscience, 4*, 402–408. §4.38.

Swadlow, H. A., Gusev, A. G., & Bezdudnaya, T. (2002). Activation of a cortical column by a thalamocortical impulse. *Journal of Neuroscience, 22*, 7766–7773. §4.38.

Synofzik, M., Thier, P., & Lindner, A. (2006). Internalizing agency of self-action: Perception of one's own hand movements depends on an adaptable prediction about the sensory action outcome. *Journal of Neurophysiology, 96*(3), 1592–1601. §9n6.

Synofzik, M., Vosgerau, G., & Newen, A. (2008). Beyond the comparator model: A multifactorial two step account of agency. *Consciousness and Cognition, 17*(1), 219–239. §9.13.

Szilard, L. (1929). Über die Entropieverminderung in einem thermodynamischen System bei Eingriffen intelligenter Wesen. *Zeitschrift für Physik, 53*, 840–856. §A1n3.

Takahashi, N., Kitamura, K., Matsuo, N., Mayford, M., Kano, M., Matsuki, N., et al. (2012). Locally synchronized synaptic inputs. *Science, 335,* 353–356. §§4n4, 5.15, 5.22.

Takechi, H., Eilers, J., & Konnerth, A. (1998). A new class of synaptic response involving calcium release in dendritic spines. *Nature, 396,* 757–760. §5.5.

Takehara, K., Kawahara, S., Takatsuki, K., & Kirino, Y. (2002). Time-limited role of the hippocampus in the memory for trace eyeblink conditioning in mice. *Brain Research, 951,* 183–190. §10n15.

Takehara, K., Kawahara, S., & Kirino, Y. (2003). Time-dependent reorganization of the brain components underlying memory retention in trace eyeblink conditioning. *Journal of Neuroscience, 23,* 9897–9905. §10n15.

Takehara-Nishiuchi, K., Kawahara, S., & Kirino, Y. (2005). NMDA receptor-dependent processes in the medial prefrontal cortex are important for acquisition and the early stage of consolidation during trace, but not delay eyeblink conditioning. *Learning & Memory, 12,* 606–614. §10n15.

Tallon-Baudry, C., Bertrand, O., Delpuech, C., & Pernier, J. (1996). Stimulus specificity of phase-locked and non-phase-locked 40 Hz visual responses in human. *Journal of Neuroscience, 16,* 4240–4249. §4.49.

Tamas, G., Buhl, E. H., & Somogyi, P. (1997). Fast IPSPs elicited via multiple synaptic release sites by different types of GABAergic neurone in the cat visual cortex. *Journal of Physiology, 500,* 715–738. §5.3.

Tanaka, K. (1996). Inferotemporal cortex and object vision. *Annual Review of Neuroscience, 19,* 109–139. §4.9.

Tanaka, K., Saito, H., Fukada, Y., & Moriya, M. (1991). Coding visual images of objects in the inferotemporal cortex of the macaque monkey. *Journal of Neurophysiology, 66*(1), 170–189. §4.10.

Tao, H. W., & Poo, M. (2001). Retrograde signaling at central synapses. *Proceedings of the National Academy of Sciences of the United States of America, 98,* 11009–11015. §5.17.

Taylor, D. M., Tillery, S. I., & Schwartz, A. B. (2002). Direct cortical control of 3D neuroprosthetic devices. *Science, 296*(5574), 1829–1832. §10n9.

Taylor, K., Mandon, S., Freiwald, W. A., & Kreiter, A. K. (2005). Coherent oscillatory activity in monkey area v4 predicts successful allocation of attention. *Cerebral Cortex, 15,* 1424–1437. §4.45.

Tegmark, M. (2000). The importance of quantum decoherence in brain processes. *Physical Review E: Statistical Physics, Plasmas, Fluids, and Related Interdisciplinary Topics, 61,* 4194–4206. §A1.8.

Theeuwes, J. (1994). Stimulus-driven capture and attentional set: Selective search for color and visual abrupt onsets. *Journal of Experimental Psychology: Human Perception and Performance, 20*(4), 799–806. §4.22.

Thomson, A. M., Bannister, A. P., Mercer, A., & Morris, O. T. (2002). Target and temporal pattern selection at neocortical synapses. *Philosophical Transactions of the Royal Society of London, Series B: Biological Sciences, 357*, 1781–1791. §4.55.

Tibbetts, P. E. (2001). The anterior cingulate cortex, akinetic mutism, and human volition. *Brain and Mind, 2*(3), 323–341. §10n10.

Tiesinga, P. H. E., & Sejnowski, T. J. (2004). Rapid temporal modulation of synchrony by competition in cortical interneuron networks. *Neural Computation, 16*(2), 251–275. §5.35.

Todd, J. J., & Marois, R. (2004). Capacity limit of visual short-term memory in human posterior parietal cortex. *Nature, 428*(6984), 751–754. §4.26.

Todd, J. J., & Marois, R. (2005). Posterior parietal cortex activity predicts individual differences in visual short-term memory capacity. *Cognitive, Affective & Behavioral Neuroscience, 5*(2), 144–155. §§4.26, 10.14, 10.30.

Todd, J. T., & Norman, J. F. (1995). The visual discrimination of relative surface orientation. *Perception, 24*, 855–866. §10.81.

Tolhurst, D. J., Movshon, J. A., & Dean, A. F. (1983). The statistical reliability of signals in single neurons in cat and monkey visual cortex. *Vision Research, 23*, 775–785. §4.52.

Tong, Z. Y., Overton, P. G., & Clark, D. (1996). Antagonism of NMDA receptors but not AMPA/kainate receptors blocks bursting in dopaminergic neurons induced by electrical stimulation of the prefrontal cortex. *Journal of Neural Transmission, 103*, 889–904. §4.40.

Tononi, G. (2008). Consciousness as integrated information: A provisional manifesto. *Biological Bulletin, 215*(3), 216–242. §8.6.

Tononi, G., & Cirelli, C. (2003). Sleep and synaptic homeostasis: A hypothesis. *Brain Research Bulletin, 62*, 143–150. §5.8.

Tononi, G., & Cirelli, C. (2006). Sleep function and synaptic homeostasis. *Sleep Medicine Reviews, 10*, 49–62. §5.8.

Tononi, G., Sporns, O., & Edelman, G. (1992). Reentry and the problem of integrating multiple cortical areas: Simulation of dynamic visual motion processing in cortical areas MT and MST. *Cerebral Cortex, 2*, 310–335. §4.45.

Toth, L. J., & Assad, J. A. (2002). Dynamic coding of behaviourally relevant stimuli in parietal cortex. *Nature, 415*, 165–168. §4.19.

Traub, R. D., Bibbig, A., LeBeau, F. E., Buhl, E. H., & Whittington, M. A. (2004). Cellular mechanisms of neuronal population oscillations in the hippocampus in vitro. *Annual Review of Neuroscience, 27,* 247–278. §§4.44, 5.3.

Traub, R. D., Bibbig, A., Fisahn, A., LeBeau, F. E., Whittington, M. A., & Buhl, E. H. (2000). A model of gamma-frequency network oscillations induced in the rat CA3 region by carbachol in vitro. *European Journal of Neuroscience, 12,* 4093–4106. §4.44.

Traub, R. D., Kopell, N., Bibbig, A., Buhl, E. H., LeBeau, F. E., & Whittington, M. A. (2001). Gap junctions between interneuron dendrites can enhance synchrony of gamma oscillations in distributed networks. *Journal of Neuroscience, 21,* 9478–9486. §4.44.

Treisman, A. (1992). Perceiving and re-perceiving objects. *American Psychologist, 47*(7), 862–875. §10.30.

Treisman, A. (1996). The binding problem. *Current Opinion in Neurobiology, 6*(2), 171–178. §§4.21, 5.44.

Treisman, A., & Gelade, G. (1980). A feature-integration theory of attention. *Cognitive Psychology, 12,* 97–136. §§5.44, 5.49, 10.30.

Treue, S. (2001). Neural correlates of attention in primate visual cortex. *Trends in Neurosciences, 24,* 295–300. §5.50.

Treue, S. (2003). Visual attention: The where, what, how, and why of saliency. *Current Opinion in Neurobiology, 13,* 428–432. §§4.48, 5.44.

Treue, S., & Martinez Trujillo, J. C. (1999). Feature-based attention influences motion processing gain in macaque visual cortex. *Nature, 399,* 575–579. §§4.24, 4.25.

Trevena, J., & Miller, J. (2010). Brain preparation before a voluntary action: Evidence against unconscious movement initiation. *Consciousness and Cognition, 19*(1), 447–456. §§9n2, 9n4.

Troyer, T. W., & Miller, K. D. (1997). Physiological gain leads to high ISI variability in a simple model of a cortical regular spiking cell. *Neural Computation, 9,* 971–983. §4.32, 5.45.

Tsao, D. Y., Freiwald, W. A., Knutsen, T. A., Mandeville, J. B., & Tootell, R. B. (2003). Faces and objects in macaque cerebral cortex. *Nature Neuroscience, 6*(9), 989–995. §4.12.

Tsao, D. Y., Freiwald, W. A., Tootell, R. B., & Livingstone, M. S. (2006). A cortical region consisting entirely of face-selective cells. *Science, 311*(5761), 670–674. §4.12.

Tsao, D. Y., & Livingstone, M. S. (2008). Mechanisms of face perception. *Annual Review of Neuroscience, 31,* 411–437. §4.12.

Tse, P. U. (1998). Illusory volumes from conformation. *Perception, 27*, 977–994. §10.81.

Tse, P. U. (1999). Volume completion. *Cognitive Psychology, 39*, 37–68. §§4.14, 10.81.

Tse, P. U. (2002). A contour propagation account of surface filling-in and volume formation. *Psychological Review, 109*(1), 91–115. §§4.14, 10.81.

Tse, P. U. (2005). Voluntary attention modulates the brightness of overlapping transparent surfaces. *Vision Research, 45*(9), 1095–1098. §§5n11, 10.48, 10.52, 10.54, 10.64, 10.65, 10.67

Tse, P. U. (2006a). Neural correlates of transformational apparent motion. *NeuroImage, 31*(2), 766–773. §§4.14, 10.18.

Tse, P. U. (2006b). How the evolution of symbolic cognition transformed human morality. In W. Sinnott-Armstrong (Ed.), *Moral psychology* (Vol. 1): *The evolution of morality* (pp. 269–314). Cambridge, MA: MIT Press. §§3.8, 4.21, 7.11, 8.26, 10.30.

Tse, P. U., & Albert, M. (1998). Amodal completion in the absence of image tangent discontinuities. *Perception, 27*, 455–464. §10.81.

Tse, P. U., Baumgartner, F. J., & Greenlee, M. W. (2010). Event-related functional MRI of cortical activity evoked by microsaccades, small visually-guided saccades, and eyeblinks in human visual cortex. *NeuroImage, 49*, 805–816. §4.23.

Tse, P. U., & Caplovitz, G. P. (2006). Contour discontinuities subserve two types of form analysis that underlie motion processing. *Progress in Brain Research, 154*, 271–292. §10.18.

Tse, P. U., & Cavanagh, P. (2000). Chinese and Americans see opposite apparent motions in a Chinese character. *Cognition, 74*, B27–B32. §10.18.

Tse, P. U., & Logothetis, N. K. (2002). The duration of 3D form analysis in transformational apparent motion. *Perception & Psychophysics, 64*(2), 244–265. §10.18.

Tse, P. U., Martinez-Conde, S., Schlegel, A. A., & Macknik, S. L. (2005). Visibility, visual awareness, and visual masking of simple unattended targets are confined to areas in the occipital cortex beyond human V1/V2. *Proceedings of the National Academy of Sciences of the United States of America, 102*(47), 17178–17183. §4.39

Tse, P. U., Reavis, E. A., Kohler, P. K., Caplovitz, G. P. and Wheatley, T. P. (2012). Attention alters perceived features by defining the domain of preconscious operations. Submitted. §10.48.

Tse, P. U., Rivest, J., Intriligator, J., & Cavanagh, P. (2004a). Attention and the subjective expansion of time. *Perception & Psychophysics, 66*(7), 1171–1189. §4.24, §A1n6.

Tse, P. U., Sheinberg, D. L., & Logothetis, N. K. (2002). Fixational eye movements are not affected by abrupt onsets that capture attention. *Vision Research, 42*, 1663–1669. §4.23.

Tse, P. U., Sheinberg, D. S., & Logothetis, N. K. (2003). Attentional enhancement opposite a peripheral flash revealed using change blindness. *Psychological Science, 14*(2), 91–99. §4.48.

Tse, P. U., Sheinberg, D. S., & Logothetis, N. K. (2004b). The distribution of microsaccade directions need not reveal the location of attention. *Psychological Science, 15*(10), 708–710. §4.23.

Tse, P. U., Whitney, D., Anstis, S., & Cavanagh, P. (2011). Voluntary attention modulates motion-induced mislocalization. *Journal of Vision, 11*(3). doi: 10.1167/11.3.12. §10.48.

Tsodyks, M. V., & Markram, H. (1997). The neural code between neocortical pyramidal neurons depends on neurotransmitter release probability. *Proceedings of the National Academy of Sciences of the United States of America, 94*, 719–723. §4.55.

Tsuda, I. (2001). Toward an interpretation of dynamic neural activity in terms of chaotic dynamical systems. *Behavioral and Brain Sciences, 24*(5), 793–810. §4.68.

Turatto, M., Valsecchi, M., Tamè, L., & Betta, E. (2007). Microsaccades distinguish between global and local visual processing. *Neuroreport, 18*(10), 1015–1018. §4.23.

Turrigiano, G. G. (2008). The self-tuning neuron: Synaptic scaling of excitatory synapses. *Cell, 135*, 422–435. §5.7.

Tversky, A., & Kahneman, D. (1974). Judgment under uncertainty: Heuristics and biases. *Science, 185*(4157), 1124–1131. §§8.17, 10.22.

Tversky, A., & Kahneman, D. (1981). The framing of decisions and the psychology of choice. *Science, 211*(4481), 453–458. §8.17.

Uhlhaas, P. J., & Singer, W. (2006). Neural synchrony in brain disorders: Relevance for cognitive dysfunctions and pathophysiology. *Neuron, 52*, 155–168. §4n12.

Uhlhaas, P. J., & Singer, W. (2010). Abnormal neural oscillations and synchrony in schizophrenia. *Nature Reviews. Neuroscience, 11*, 100–113. §4n12.

Uhlhaas, P., Pipa, G., Lima, B., Melloni, L., Neuenschwander, S., Nikolic, D., et al. (2009). Neural synchrony in cortical networks, history, concept, and current status. *Frontiers in Integrative Neurosciences, 3*, 17. §§4.45, 4.53.

Uhlrich, D. J., Manning, K. A., & Xue, J. T. (2002). Effects of activation of the histaminergic tuberomammillary nucleus on visual responses of neurons in the dorsal LGN. *Journal of Neuroscience, 22*, 1098–1107. §4.59.

Ullman, S. (1984). Visual routines. *Cognition, 18*, 97–157. §8.26.

Ungerleider, L. G., & Bell, H. (2011). Uncovering the visual "alphabet": Advances in our understanding of object perception. *Vision Research, 51*, 782–799. §4.8.

Ungerleider, L. G., Courtney, S. M., & Haxby, J. V. (1998). A neural system for human visual working memory. *Proceedings of the National Academy of Sciences of the United States of America, 95*(3), 883–890. §4.26.

Ungerleider, L. G., & Pribram, K. H. (1977). Inferotemporal versus combined pulvinar-prestriate lesions in the rhesus monkey: Effects on color, object, and pattern discrimination. *Neuropsychologia, 15*(4–5), 481–498. §10n12.

Vallar, G. (2001). Extrapersonal visual unilateral spatial neglect and its neuroanatomy. *NeuroImage, 14*, S52–S58. §10.77.

Valsecchi, M., & Turatto, M. (2007). Microsaccadic response to visual events that are invisible to the superior colliculus. *Behavioral Neuroscience, 121*(4), 786–793. §4.23.

Valsecchi, M., & Turatto, M. (2009). Microsaccadic responses in a bimodal oddball task. *Psychological Research, 73*(1), 23–33. §4.23.

van Aalderen-Smeets, S. I., Oostenveld, R., & Schwarzbach, J. (2006). Investigating neurophysiological correlates of metacontrast masking with magnetoencephalography. *Advances in Cognitive Psychology, 2*, 21–35. §§4.22, 10.16.

Van Boxtel, G. J., & Brunia, C. H. (1994). Motor and non-motor components of the contingent negative variation. *International Journal of Psychophysiology, 17*(3), 269–279. §9n4.

Van den Bussche, E., Segers, G., & Reynvoet, B. (2008). Conscious and unconscious proportion effects in masked priming. *Consciousness and Cognition, 17*, 1345–1358. §10.36.

Van Essen, D. C. (2004). Surface-based approaches to spatial localization and registration in primate cerebral cortex. *NeuroImage, 23*(Suppl 1), S97–S107. §4n5.

Van Essen, D. C., & DeYoe, E. A. (1995). Concurrent processing in the primate visual cortex. In M. S. Gazzaniga (Ed.), *The cognitive neurosciences* (pp. 383–400). Cambridge, MA: MIT Press. §4.8.

van Gaal, S., Lamme, V. A., Fahrenfort, J. J., & Ridderinkhof, K. R. (2011). Dissociable brain mechanisms underlying the conscious and unconscious control of behavior. *Journal of Cognitive Neuroscience 23*, 91–105. §10.36.

van Gaal, S., Lamme, V. A., & Ridderinkhof, K. R. (2010). Unconsciously triggered conflict adaptation. *PLoS ONE, 5*, e11508. §10.36.

van Gaal, S., Ridderinkhof, K. R., Fahrenfort, J. J., Scholte, H. S., & Lamme, V. A. (2008). Frontal cortex mediates unconsciously triggered inhibitory control. *Journal of Neuroscience, 28*, 8053–8062. §10.36.

Van Gulick, R. (1995). Who's in charge here? And who's doing all the work? In J. Heil & A. Mele (Eds.), *Mental Causation* (pp. 233–256). Oxford: Clarendon Press. §§1.15, A2.2.

van Lier, R., Vergeer, M., & Anstis, S. (2009). Filling-in after-image colors between the lines. *Current Biology, 19*(8), R323–R324. §§10.49, 10.50.

van Swinderen, B. (2005). The remote roots of consciousness in fruit-fly selective attention? *BioEssays, 27*, 321–330. §10.45

van Swinderen, B. (2007). Attention-like processes in Drosophila require short-term memory genes. *Science, 315*, 1590–1593. §10.45.

van Swinderen, B., & Brembs, B. (2010). Attention-like deficit and hyperactivity in a Drosophila memory mutant. *Journal of Neuroscience, 30*, 1003–1014. §10.45.

van Swinderen, B., & Greenspan, R. J. (2003). Salience modulates 20–30 Hz brain activity in Drosophila. *Nature Neuroscience, 6*, 579–586. §10.45.

van Vreeswijk, C., & Sompolinsky, H. (1998). Chaotic balanced state in a model of cortical circuits. *Neural Computation, 10*(6), 1321–1271. §4.32.

Varela, F., Lachaux, J. P., Rodriguez, E., & Martinerie, J. (2001). The brainweb: Phase synchronization and large-scale integration. *Nature Reviews: Neuroscience, 2*, 229–239. §4.45.

Vecsey, C. G., Hawk, J. D., Lattal, K. M., Stein, J. M., Fabian, S. A., Attner, M. A., et al. (2007). Histone deacetylase inhibitors enhance memory and synaptic plasticity via CREB:CBP-dependent transcriptional activation. *Journal of Neuroscience, 27*, 6128–6140. §5.6.

Velliste, M., Perel, S., Spalding, M. C., Whitford, A. S., & Schwartz, A. B. (2008). Cortical control of a prosthetic arm for self-feeding. *Nature, 453*, 1098–1101. §10n9.

Verkuyl, J. M., & Matus, A. (2006). Time-lapse imaging of dendritic spines in vitro. *Nature Protocols, 1*(5), 2399–2405. §4.55.

Vetter, P., Roth, A., & Häusser, M. (2001). Action potential propagation in dendrites depends on dendritic morphology. *Journal of Neurophysiology, 83*, 3177–3182. §§5.21, 5.22.

Villarroel, A., Burnashev, N., & Sakmann, B. (1995). Dimensions of the narrow portion of a recombinant NMDA receptor channel. *Biophysical Journal, 68*(3), 866–875. §A1.10.

Vogel, E. K., Luck, S. J., & Shapiro, K. L. (1998). Electrophysiological evidence for a postperceptual locus of suppression during the attentional blink. *Journal of Experimental Psychology: Human Perception and Performance, 24*, 1656–1674. §10.16.

Vogel, E. K., Woodman, G. F., & Luck, S. J. (2001). Storage of features, conjunctions, and objects in visual working memory. *Journal of Experimental Psychology: Human Perception and Performance, 27*(1), 92–114. §10.13.

Vogels, T. P., Rajan, K., & Abbott, L. F. (2005). Neural network dynamics. *Annual Review of Neuroscience, 28,* 357–376. §4.68.

von der Heydt, R., Friedman, H., & Zhou, H. (2003). In L. Pessoa & P. DeWeerd (Eds.), *Filling-in* (pp. 106–127). New York: Oxford University Press. §5.37.

von der Heydt, R., Zhou, H., & Friedman, H. S. (1996). The coding of extended colored figures in monkey visual cortex. *Society for Neuroscience Abstracts, 22,* 951. §5.37.

von der Malsburg, C. (1985). Nervous structures with dynamical links. *Berichte der Bunsengesellschaft fur Physikalische Chemie, 89,* 703–710. §4.45.

von der Malsburg, C. (1994). The correlation theory of brain function. In E. Domany, J. L. van Hemmen, & K. Schulten (Eds.), *Models of neural networks II: Temporal aspects of coding and information.* New York: Springer. (Originally published 1981, MPI Biophysical Chemistry, Internal Report 81-2.) §§4.54, 4.55.

von der Malsburg, C. (1995). Binding in models of perception and brain function. *Current Opinion in Neurobiology, 5,* 520–526. §4.45.

von der Malsburg, C., Phillips, W. A., & Singer, W. (Eds.). (2010). *Dynamic coordination in the brain.* Cambridge, MA: MIT Press. §4.45.

von der Malsburg, C., & Schneider, W. (1986). A neural cocktail-party processor. *Biological Cybernetics, 54,* 29–40. §4.45.

von Wright, J. M. (1970). On selection in visual immediate memory. *Acta Psychologica, 33,* 280–292. §4.25.

Voss, M., Ingram, J. N., Haggard, P., & Wolpert, D. M. (2006). Sensorimotor attenuation by central motor command signals in the absence of movement. *Nature Neuroscience, 9*(1), 26–27. §9n6.

Voytko, M. L. (1996). Cognitive functions of the basal forebrain cholinergic system in monkeys: Memory or attention? *Behavioural Brain Research, 75,* 13–25. §5.44.

Voytko, M. L., Olton, D. S., Richardson, R. T., Gorman, L. K., & Price, D. L. (1994). Basal forebrain lesions in monkeys disrupt attention but not learning and memory. *Journal of Neuroscience, 14,* 167–186. §5.44.

Wager, T. D., & Smith, E. E. (2003). Neuroimaging studies of working memory: A meta-analysis. *Cognitive, Affective & Behavioral Neuroscience, 3*(4), 255–274. §4.26.

Walker, E. H. (2001). The natural philosophy and physics of consciousness. In P. van Loocke (Ed.), *The physical nature of consciousness* (pp. 63–82). Amsterdam: John Benjamins. §A1.8.

Wallis, J., Anderson, K., & Miller, E. (2001). Single neurons in prefrontal cortex encode abstract rules. *Nature, 411,* 953–956. §7.11.

Walter, H. (2001). *Neurophilosophy of free will: From libertarian illusions to a concept of natural autonomy.* Cambridge, MA: MIT Press. §10n10.

Walter, W. G., Cooper, R., Aldridge, V. J., McCallum, W. C., & Winter, A. L. (1964). Contingent negative variation: An electric sign of sensorimotor association and expectancy in the human brain. *Nature, 203,* 380–384. §9n4.

Wang, D. L., Buhmann, J., & von der Malsburg, C. (1990). Pattern segmentation in associative memory. *Neural Computation, 2,* 94–106. §4.45.

Wang, H. X., Gerkin, R. C., Nauen, D. W., & Bi, G. Q. (2005). Coactivation and timing-dependent integration of synaptic potentiation and depression. *Nature Neuroscience, 8,* 187–193. §5.12.

Wang, M., Vijayraghavan, S., & Goldman-Rakic, P. S. (2004). Selective D2 receptor actions on the functional circuitry of working memory. *Science, 303,* 853–856. §4.40.

Wang, Q., Cavanagh, P., & Green, M. (1994). Familiarity and pop-out in visual search. *Perception & Psychophysics, 56*(5), 495–500. §10.54.

Wang, Y., Markram, H., Goodman, P. H., Berger, T. K., Ma, J., & Goldman-Rakic, P. S. (2006). Heterogeneity in the pyramidal network of the medial prefrontal cortex. *Nature Neuroscience, 9,* 534–542. §4.55.

Wang, Y. T., & Salter, M. W. (1994). Regulation of NMDA receptors by tyrosine kinases and phosphatases. *Nature, 369,* 233–235. §5n1.

Wang, X. J. (1999). Fast burst firing and short-term synaptic plasticity: A model of neocortical chattering neurons. *Neuroscience, 89*(2), 347–362. §4.35.

Ward, L. M. (2003). Synchronous neural oscillations and cognitive processes. *Trends in Cognitive Sciences, 7,* 553–559. §5.46.

Waters, J., & Helmchen, F. (2006). Background synaptic activity is sparse in neocortex. *Journal of Neuroscience, 26,* 8267–8277. §4.32.

Watson, K. K., Matthews, B. J., & Allman, J. M. (2007). Brain activation during sight gags and language-dependent humor. *Cerebral Cortex, 17,* 314–324.

Wede, J., & Francis, G. (2007). Attentional effects on after-images: Theory and data. *Vision Research, 47,* 2249–2258. §10.50.

Weeks, S. R., Anderson-Barnes, V. C., & Tsao, J. W. (2010). Phantom limb pain: Theories and therapies. *Neurologist, 16*(5), 277–286. §10.5.

Wegner, D. (2002). *The illusion of conscious will.* Cambridge, MA: MIT Press. §§9.1, 9.13, 9.14.

Wegner, D. M., & Wheatley, T. (1999). Apparent mental causation: Sources of the experience of will. *American Psychologist, 54*(7), 480–492. §§9.1, 9.13, 9.14, 9.17.

Wehr, M., & Zador, A. M. (2003). Balanced inhibition underlies tuning and sharpens spike timing in auditory cortex. *Nature, 426*, 442–446. §4.43.

Weible, A. P., McEchron, M. D., & Disterhoft, J. F. (2000). Cortical involvement in acquisition and extinction of trace eyeblink conditioning. *Behavioral Neuroscience, 114*, 1058–1067. §10n15.

Weible, A. P., Weiss, C., & Disterhoft, J. F. (2003). Activity profiles of single neurons in caudal anterior cingulate cortex during trace eyeblink conditioning in the rabbit. *Journal of Neurophysiology, 90*, 599–612. §10n15.

Weiss, C., & Disterhoft, J. F. (1996). Eyeblink conditioning, motor control, and the analysis of limbic-cerebellar interactions. *Behavioral and Brain Sciences, 19*, 479–481. §10n15.

Wenk, G. L. (1997). The nucleus basalis magnocellularis cholinergic system: One hundred years of progress. *Neurobiology of Learning and Memory, 67*, 85–95. §5.45.

Wennekers, T., Sommer, F., & Aertsen, A. (2003). Neuronal assemblies. *Theory in Biosciences, 122*, 1–104. §4.54.

Wessberg, J., Stambaugh, C. R., Kralik, J. D., Beck, P. D., Laubach, M., Chapin, J. K., et al. (2000). Real-time prediction of hand trajectory by ensembles of cortical neurons in primates. *Nature, 408*(6810), 361–365. §10n9.

Westenbroek, R. E., Merrick, D. M., & Catterall, A. (1989). Differential subcellular localization of the RI and RII Na+ channel subtypes in central neurons. *Neuron, 3*, 695–704. §4n2.

Weyand, T. G., Boudreaux, M., & Guido, W. (2001). Burst and tonic response modes in thalamic neurons during sleep and wakefulness. *Journal of Neurophysiology, 85*, 1107–1118. §4.38.

Wheatley, T., & Haidt, J. (2005). Hypnotic disgust makes moral judgments more severe. *Psychological Science, 16*(10), 780–784. §3n3.

Whittington, M. A., Traub, R. D., & Jefferys, J. G. (1995). Synchronized oscillations in interneuron networks driven by metabotropic glutamate receptor activation. *Nature, 373*, 612–615. §§4.44, 5.3, 5.40.

Wickelgren, W. A. (1999). Webs, cell assemblies, and chunking in neural nets: Introduction. *Canadian Journal of Experimental Psychology, 53*, 118–131. §4.54.

Wilent, W. B., & Contreras, D. (2005). Dynamics of excitation and inhibition underlying stimulus selectivity in rat somatosensory cortex. *Nature Neuroscience, 8*(10), 1364–1370. §4.32.

Williams, S. R. (2004). Spatial compartmentalization and functional impact of conductance in pyramidal neurons. *Nature Neuroscience, 7*, 961–967. §5.18.

Williams, S. R., & Stuart, G. J. (1999). Mechanisms and consequences of action potential burst firing in rat neocortical pyramidal neurons. *Journal of Physiology, 521*, 467–482. §5.20.

Williams, S. R., & Stuart, G. J. (2002). Dependence of EPSP efficacy on synapse location in neocortical pyramidal neurons. *Science, 295*, 1907–1910. §5.18.

Williams, S. R., & Stuart, G. J. (2003). Role of dendritic synapse location in the control of action potential output. *Trends in Neurosciences, 26*, 147–154. §5.18.

Wilson, R. I., & Nicoll, R. A. (2001). Endogenous cannabinoids mediate retrograde signalling at hippocampal synapses. *Nature, 410*, 588–592. §5.17.

Wilson, R. I., & Nicoll, R. A. (2002). Endocannabinoid signaling in the brain. *Science, 296*, 678–682. §5.17.

Wilson, T. W., Rojas, D. C., Reite, M. L., Teale, P. D., & Rogers, S. J. (2007). Children and adolescents with autism exhibit reduced MEG steady-state gamma responses. *Biological Psychiatry, 62*, 192–197. §4n12.

Witmer, G. (2003). Multiple realizability and psychological laws: Evaluating Kim's challenge. In S. Walter & H. Heckmann (Eds.), *Physicalism and mental causation* (pp. 59–84). Charlottesville: Academic. §3.11.

Wittenberg, G. M., & Wang, S. S. (2006). Malleability of spike-timing-dependent plasticity at the CA3–CA1 synapse. *Journal of Neuroscience, 26*, 6610–6617. §5.6.

Wittgenstein, L. (1953). *Philosophical investigations*. Oxford: Blackwell. §8.14.

Wittgenstein, L. (1958). *The blue and brown books*. London: Blackwell. §8.14.

Wolf, R., & Heisenberg, M. (1991). Basic organization of operant behavior as revealed in Drosophila flight orientation. *Journal of Comparative Physiology A, 169*, 699–705. §4.70.

Wolfe, J. M. (2003). Moving towards solutions to some enduring controversies in visual search. *Trends in Cognitive Sciences, 7*(2), 70–76. §10.30.

Wollner, D. A. & Catterall, W. A. (1986). Localization of sodium channels in axon hillocks and initial segments of retinal ganglion cells. *Proceedings of the National Academy of Sciences of the United States of America, 83*, 8424–8428. §4n2.

Wolpert, D. H. (2008). Physical limits of inference. *Physica D: Nonlinear Phenomena, 237*, 1257–1281. §A1n3.

Womelsdorf, T., Fries, P., Mitra, P. P., & Desimone, R. (2006). Gamma-band synchronization in visual cortex predicts speed of change detection. *Nature, 439*, 733–736. §4.45.

Womelsdorf, T., & Fries, P. (2007). The role of neuronal synchronization in selective attention. *Current Opinion in Neurobiology, 17*, 154–160. §4.49.

Womelsdorf, T., Schoffelen, J. M., Oostenveld, R., Singer, W., Desimone, R., Engel, A. K., et al. (2007). Modulation of neuronal interactions through neuronal synchronization. *Science, 316*, 1609–1612. §§4.49, 4.60.

Woodman, G. F., & Luck, S. J. (2003). Dissociations among attention, perception & awareness during object-substitution masking. *Psychological Science, 14*, 605–611. §10.28.

Woodruff-Pak, D. S., Lavond, D. G., & Thompson, R. F. (1985). Trace conditioning: Abolished by cerebellar nuclear lesions but not lateral cerebellar cortex aspirations. *Brain Research, 348*, 249–260. §10n15.

Wurtz, R. H., Richmond, B. J., & Judge, S. J. (1980). Vision during saccadic eye movements. III. Visual interactions in monkey superior colliculus. *Journal of Neurophysiology, 43*, 1168–1181. §4.39.

Wyart, V., & Tallon-Baudry, C. (2008). Neural dissociation between visual awareness and spatial attention. *Journal of Neuroscience, 28*, 2667–2679. §§4.49, 10.29.

Wyart, V., & Tallon-Baudry, C. (2009). How ongoing fluctuations in human visual cortex predict perceptual awareness: Baseline shift versus decision bias. *Journal of Neuroscience, 29*, 8715–8725. §§4.49, 10.29.

Xu, Y., & Chun, M. M. (2006). Dissociable neural mechanisms supporting visual short-term memory for objects. *Nature, 440*, 91–95. §§4.26, 10.14.

Yakel, J. L., Shao, X. M., & Jackson, M. B. (1990). The selectivity of the channel coupled to the 5-HT$_3$ receptor. *Brain Research, 533*, 46–52. §A1.10.

Yamane, S., Kaji, S., & Kawano, K. (1988). What facial features activate face neurons in the inferotemporal cortex of the monkey? *Experimental Brain Research, 73*, 209–214. §4.9.

Yamane, Y., Carlson, E. T., Bowman, K. C., Wang, Z., & Connor, C. E. (2008). A neural code for three-dimensional object shape in macaque inferotemporal cortex. *Nature Neuroscience, 11*, 1352–1360. §4.14.

Yang, H., Shew, W. L., Roy, R., & Plenz, D. (2012). Phase synchrony and neuronal avalanches. *Journal of Neuroscience, 32*(3), 1061–1072. §4.42.

Yang, J. (1990). Ion permeation through 5-hydroxytryptamine-gated channels in neuroblastoma N18 cells. *Journal of General Physiology, 96*, 1197–1198. §A1.10.

Yantis, S., & Hillstrom, A. P. (1994). Stimulus-driven attentional capture: Evidence from equiluminant visual objects. *Journal of Experimental Psychology: Human Perception and Performance, 20*(1), 95–107. §4.22.

Yantis, S., & Jonides, J. (1984). Abrupt visual onsets and selective attention: Evidence from visual search. *Journal of Experimental Psychology: Human Perception and Performance, 10*(5), 601–621. §4.22.

Yantis, S., & Jonides, J. (1990). Abrupt visual onsets and selective attention: Voluntary versus automatic allocation. *Journal of Experimental Psychology: Human Perception and Performance, 16*(1), 121–134. §4.22.

Yantis, S., & Serences, J. T. (2003). Cortical mechanisms of space-based and object-based attentional control. *Current Opinion in Neurobiology, 13*, 187–193. §4.25.

Yazawa, S., Ikeda, A., Kunieda, T., Ohara, S., Mima, T., Nagamine, T., et al. (2000). Human presupplementary motor area is active before voluntary movement: Subdural recording of Bereitschaftspotential from medial frontal cortex. *Experimental Brain Research, 131*, 165–177. Figure 9.1.

Yin, H. H., & Knowlton, B. J. (2006). The role of the basal ganglia in habit formation. *Nature Reviews Neuroscience, 7*, 464–476. §4.70.

Yizhar, O., Fenno, L. E., Prigge, M., Schneider, F., Davidson, T. J., O'Shea, D. J., et al. (2011). Neocortical excitation/inhibition balance in information-processing and social dysfunction. *Nature, 477*, 171–178. §4n12.

Ylinen, A., Bragin, A., Nádasdy, Z., Jandó, G., Szabó, I., Sik, A., et al. (1995). Sharp wave-associated high-frequency oscillation (200 Hz) in the intact hippocampus: Network and intracellular mechanisms. *Journal of Neuroscience, 15*, 30–46. §4.35.

Yu, A. J., & Dayan, P. (2005). Uncertainty, neuromodulation, and attention. *Neuron, 46*, 681–692. §4.22.

Yu, L. M., & Goda, Y. (2009). Dendritic signaling and homeostatic adaptation. *Current Opinion in Neurobiology, 19*, 327–335. §5.7.

Yuste, R., & Denk, W. (1995). Dendritic spines as basic functional units of neuronal integration. *Nature, 375*, 682–684. §§5.5, 5.6.

Zeki, S. (2001). Localization and globalization in conscious vision. *Annual Review of Neuroscience, 24*, 57–86. §§5n11, 10.64, 10.65.

Zhang, K., Guo, J. Z., Peng, Y., Xi, W., & Guo, A. (2007). Dopamine-mushroom body circuit regulates saliency-based decision-making in Drosophila. *Science, 316*, 1901–1904. §10.45.

Zhang, L. I., Tao, H. W., Holt, C. E., Harris, W. A., & Poo, M.-M. (1998). A critical window for cooperation and competition among developing retinotectal synapses. *Nature, 395*, 37–44. §5.11.

Zhang, W., & Linden, D. J. (2003). The other side of the engram: Experience driven changes in neuronal intrinsic excitability. *Nature Reviews: Neuroscience, 4*, 885–900. §5.38.

Zhou, H., Friedman, H. S., & von der Heydt, R. (2000). Coding of border ownership in monkey visual cortex. *Journal of Neuroscience, 20*, 6594–6611. §5.37.

Zikopoulos, B., & Barbas, H. (2006). Prefrontal projections to the thalamic reticular nucleus form a unique circuit for attentional mechanisms. *Journal of Neuroscience, 26*, 7348–7361. §4.27.

Zikopoulos, B., & Barbas, H. (2007). Circuits for multisensory integration and attentional modulation through the prefrontal cortex and the thalamic reticular nucleus in primates. *Reviews in the Neurosciences, 18*, 417–438. §4.27.

Zucker, R. S., & Regehr, W. G. (2002). Short-term synaptic plasticity. *Annual Review of Physiology, 64*, 355–405. §4.55.

Zweifel, L. S., Parker, J. G., Lobb, C. J., Rainwater, A., Wall, V. Z., Fadok, J. P., et al. (2009). Disruption of NMDAR-dependent burst firing by dopamine neurons provides selective assessment of phasic dopamine-dependent behavior. *Proceedings of the National Academy of Sciences of the United States of America, 106*, 7281–7288. §4.40.

Author Index

Aaron, G., §§4.60, 5.16

Abbott, L. F., §§3.13, 4.32, 4.34, 4.55, 4.57, 4.68, 5.11, 5.17, 5.36, 5.43, 5.45, 5n4, 5n6

Abdallah, S., §10.6

Abel, T., §5.9

Abeles, M., §§4.42, 4.54, 4n3

Abrams, J., §§4.21, 10.32

Abrams, R. L., §10.36

Acres, K., §10.6

Acsady, L., §§4.44, 5.3, 5.43

Adachi, M., §4n8

Adam, C., §10.16

Adams, D. J., §A1.10

Adams, D. L., §4.21

Aertsen, A., §§4.42, 4.45, 4.54

Afraz, S. R., §4.12

Agassandian, C., §4.33

Aharonov, Y., §A1.11

Ahissar, E., §4.60

Ahissar, M., §4.60

Ahn, K. C., §§5.6, 5n4

Akaoka, H., §4.40

Akbarian, S., §5n2

Akbudak, E., §4.23

Akins, K., §1n1

Akkal, D. fig. 9.1

Albert, M., §10.81

Albright, T. D., §§4.10, 4.23, 10.21

Aldridge, V. J., §9n4

Alexander, S., §§9.4, fig. 9.2, fig. 9.3, §9n5

Alger, B. E., §5.42

Alijarde, M. T., §4.33

Allen, C. B., §5.11

Allen, R. J., §4.21

Allison, T., §4.12

Alseikhan, B. A., §5.9

Alter, K., §5.24

Altschuler, E. L., §10.5

Alvania, R. S., §5.9

Alvarez, B. D., §4.24

Alvarez, G. A., §4.14

Ambinder, M. S., §10.56

Amdahl, G., §8.3

Amico, C., §5n1

Amit, D., §4.32

Amitai, Y., §5.39

Amzica, F., §5.42

Anand, K. J. S., §10n20

Anastassiou, C. A., §4.68

Andersen, P., §§4.55, 5.9, 5n1

Andersen, R. A., §§4.18, 4.23, 10n9

Anderson, E. B., §§4.25, 4.48, 4.52, 4.53, 5.33, 5.38

Anderson, J. R., §§7.15, 9.8

Anderson, J. S., §4.32

Anderson, K., §7.11

Anderson-Barnes, V. C., §10.5

Andrews-Hanna, J. R., §10n23

Angelone, B. L., §10.56

Anstis, S., §§10.48, 10.49, 10.50
Antony, L., §A2.2
Aoki, C., §5.39
Arai, R., §5n2
Arcaro, M., §4.12
Arieli, A., §§4.42, 4.60
Armstrong, D. M., §8n9
Armstrong, K. M., §4.24
Arndt, M., §A1.10
Arnell, K. M., §10.73
Aronov, D., §§4.60, 5.16
Ascher, P., §5.4
Asgari, M., §4.12
Ashby, F. G., §4.21
Aspect, A., §§A1.6, A1.7
Aspelmeyer, M., §§A1.6, A1.7
Assad, J. A., §§4.19, 4.24, 4.25, 4.52
Assal, F. D. R., §10.26
Astafiev, S. V., §4.24
Atasoy, D., §4n8
Atmadia, S., §5.38
Attner, M. A., §5.6
Augustine, G. J., §5.5
Autry, A. E., §4n8
Avery, M. C., §§4.22, 5.39
Avidan, G., §4.10
Awh, E., §10.30
Axelrod, F. B., §10.5
Ay, H., §10n10
Ayala, G. F., §4n12
Azouz, R., §§4.52, 5.3

Baars, B., §10n6
Babiloni, C., §10.16
Bach, J. S., §§7.9, 7.11
Baccala, L. A., §4.38
Bacon, J. P., §10.3
Baddeley, A. D., §§4.21, 10.14
Baddeley, R., §4.34
Bading, H., §§5.5, 5n1
Badoual, M., §5.42
Baerends, E., §7.15
Bailey, C. H., §5.9

Baillet, S., §§10.16, 10.75
Bair, W., §4.52
Bak, P., §4.42
Baker, C. I., §4.26
Bal, T., §5.42
Ballard, D., §4.26
Balleine, B. W., §4.70
Band, G. P., §10.36
Banerjee, A., §5.28
Bangasser, D. A., §10.44
Banke, T. G., §5.4
Bannister, A. P., §4.55
Bapi, R. S., §§7.15, 9.8
Bar, M., §4.14
Barad, M., §5.6
Barak, O., §4.55
Barbaresi, P., §§5.5, 5.28
Barbas, H., §4.27
Barcan Marcus, R. C., §A3
Barcelo, F., §7.11
Bar-Haim, Y., §10.16
Barker, R. A., §9.8
Barlow, H. B., §§4.11, 4.68
Baron-Cohen, S., §A2n5
Barone, P., §4.49
Barry, C., §§4.8, 8.22
Bartalini, S., §10.16
Barth, D. S., §§4.35, 4.44
Barthó, P., §§4.60, 5.16
Bartlett, J. R., §5.37
Bartocci, M., §10n20
Bartol, T. M. Jr., §4.66
Bartos, M., §§4.44, 4.53, 5.40
Bassett, D. S., §§5.24, 7.15
Bastian, J., §5.45
Batardiere, A., §4.49
Batista, A. P., §4.18
Battaglia, F. P., §5.42
Bauer, M., §§4.23, 4.49
Baulac, M., §10.16
Baumgartner, F. J., §4.23
Baxter, M. G., §5.44
Baylis, G., §4.22

Baylis, G. C., §10.21
Baylor, D., §4.68
Bays, P. M., §9n6
Bear, M. F., §§4.7, 4.15, 5.6, 5.9
Beaulieu, C., §4.44
Bechtel, W., §§1n1, 3.11
Beck, J., §10.18
Beck, P. D., §10n9
Beeren, L., §4.70
Beggs, J. M., §4.42
Beierlein, M., §4.44
Beisteiner, R., fig. 9.1
Bekinschtein, T. A., §10.43
Bell, A. H., §§4.12, 10.21
Bell, H., §4.8
Bell, J. S., §A1.6
Ben-Ari, Y., §§4.33, 5n9
Ben-Bashat, D., §4.10
Bender, D. B., §4.10
Bender, K. J., §5.28
Bender, V. A., §5.28
Bennett, C. H., §A1n3
Benson, R. R., §4.10
Berger, R., §5.5
Berger, T. K., §§4.50, 4.55
Bergqvist, L. L., §10n20
Berman, M. G., §4.26
Bernier, B. E., §§5.6, 5n4
Berret, E., §9n6
Berretta, N., §5.28
Berridge, C. W., §5.38
Bertrand, O., §4.49
Betta, E., §4.23
Betz, H., §5.4
Bezdudnaya, T., §4.38
Bi, G. Q., §§5.11, 5.12, 5n5
Bibbig, A., §§4.44, 5.3, 5.40
Bichot, N. P., §4.45
Bickle, J., §§1n1, 3.11, A2n1
Bihan, D. L., §10.16
Binder, P.-M., §A1n3
Binzegger, T., §4.32
Birbaumer, N., §4n15

Bischofberger, J., §§4.44, 5.3
Bisley, J. W., §§4.18, 4.24
Blackstock, W. P., §5n1
Blackwell, J., §4n8
Blagburn, J. M., §10.3
Blair, J. L., §4.33
Blaise, B., §8.1
Blake, R., §§10.49, 10.50
Blakemore, S., §§9.13, 9n6, 10.26
Blanz, V., §§8.18, 8.20
Blaser, E., §4.24
Bliss, T. V., §5.6
Block, N., §§A2n5, A2.1, 10.33
Blom, J., §10.36
Blum, K. I., §5n6
Böbel, E., §10.35
Bobrow, D. G., §10.73
Boccara, C. N., §§4.8, 8.22
Bode, S., §9.14
Boehm, J., §5.9
Boettiger, C. A., §7.11
Bogdahn, U., §7.12
Bohm, D., §§A1.6, A1.11
Bohr, N., §A1.5
Bolton, J. P., §4.44
Boly, M., §10.66
Bondar, I., §§8.18, 8.20
Bonds, A. B., §§4.38, 5.36
Bonhoeffer, T., §§4.55, 5.5, 5.9
Bonnevie, T., §4.44
Booth, D., §10.3
Booth, M. C., §4.34
Boraud, T., §4n12
Börgers, C., §5.50
Borges, K., §4n4
Borker, P., §A1.10
Bormann, J. O., §A1.10
Born, J., §5.8
Boshyan, J., §4.14
Boudreaux, M., §4.38
Bouix, S., §5.24
Bower, J., §5.39
Bowie, D., §4n4

Bowman, E. M., §4.27
Bowman, K. C., §4.14
Boyd, S., §10n20
Bradley, D., §5n2
Bragin, A., §4.35
Braitenberg, V., §4.54
Brasier, D. J., §§5.11, 5.28
Brass, M., §§9.13, 9.14
Braun, J., §10.73
Braver, T. S., §7.11
Bravo, E., §10.65
Brecht, M., §4.21
Breierlein, M., §5.26
Breitmeyer, B. G., §10.50
Brembs, B., §§4.70, 10.3, 10.45
Bremmer, F., §4.60
Brentano, F., §8.5
Brescamp, J. W., §§10.49, 10.50
Bressan, P., §10.28
Bressler, S. L., §4.69
Brickey, D. A., §5n1
Bright, P., §10.6
Brinkhaus, H., §4.55
Britten, K., §4.52
Brooks, D. J. fig. 9.1
Brown, P., §4n12, fig. 9.1
Brown, R. G., fig. 9.1
Brown, V. J., §4.27
Bruce, C., §§4.10, 10.21
Brukner, C., §§A1.6, A1.7
Brunel, N., §4.32
Brunia, C. H., §9n4
Bruno, J., §§5.38, 5.39, 5.45
Bruno, R. M., §§4.22, 4.32
Brusa, R., §5n1
Brush, S. G., §A1.4
Bruss, J., §10.44
Bucci, D. J., §5.44
Buckner, R. L., §10n23
Buda, M., §4.40
Buffalo, E. A., §§4.49, 5.49
Buhl, D., §§4.44, 4.60
Buhl, E. H., §§4.44, 5.3, 5.40

Buhmann, J., §4.45
Bullier, J., §§4.49, 5.45
Bullmore, E. T., §§5.24, 7.15
Bundesen, C., §4.25
Bunjes, F., §9n6
Bunzeck, N., §4.70
Buonanno, A., §5.28
Buonanno, F. S., §10n10
Buonomano, D. V., §4.54
Burge, T., §1.5
Burgess, N., §§4.8, 8.22
Burgess, P. W., §10.61
Burk, J. A., §§5.44, 5.46
Burnashev, N., §§4.55, 5n1, A1.10
Burrone, J., §5.7
Busch, N. A., §9n2
Busch, V., §7.12
Buschman, T. J., §§4.23, 4.24, 4.49
Butterfield, J., §7.18
Buxhoeveden, D., §§4.33, 5.16
Buzsáki, G., §§4.35, 4.42, 4.44, 4.50,
    4.53, 4.55, 4.60, 4n3, 4n7, 5.3, 5.39,
    5.43, 8.7

Caan, W., §4.9, 4.10
Cafaro, J., §4.42
Calder, A. J., §§8.18, 8.20
Cameron, I. G., §9.9
Campbell, D. T., §§1.15, A2.2
Campbell, K., §§4.22, 10.16
Campbell, R. A., §10.43
Cannon, W., §10.5
Cantarella, A., §10n20
Caplovitz, G. P., §§10.18, 10.48, 10.49
Caporale, N., §5.11
Carandini, M., §§4.32, 5.45
Cardin, J. A., §5.42
Carew, T., §1.11
Carey, S., §§9.33, 10.30
Carlén, M., §5.42
Carlson, E. T., §4.14
Carmena, J. M., §10n9
Carrasco, M., §§4.21, 10.32, 10.48

Carretié, L., §4.14
Carruth, M., §5.20
Cartledge, P., §9n2
Casadio, A., §§5.6, 5.9
Casanova, M. F., §§4.33, 5.16
Cashmore, A. R., §§7.12, 9.14
Cassanello, C., §4.19
Cassell, M., §10.44
Castellucci, V. F., §5.9
Cattaneo, A., §5.36
Catterall, A., §4n2
Catterall, W. A., §§4n2, A1.10
Cavanagh, P., §§4.24, 10.17, 10.18,
    10.39, 10.48, 10.54, 10.65, A1n6
Cavanaugh, J., §§4.24, 4.27, 4.38, 4.39,
    4.43, 4.48, 4n11
Celikel, T., §5.11
Chabris, C. F., §10.56
Chadderton, P., §5.30
Chafee, M. V., §4.52
Chakrabarty, K., §4.68
Chakravarthy, V. S., §§7.15, 9.8
Chalmers, D., §§1n1, 8.11, 10.83, A3
Chance, F. S., §5.45
Changeux, J. P., §§2.11, 5.24, 7n7,
    10.16, 10.17, 10.36, 10.54, 10.65,
    10.67, 10.69, 10.77, 10n1, 10n6,
    10n21
Chapin, J. K., §10n9
Chappell, J., §5.44
Charlety, P. J., §4.40
Chase, P. N., §4.70
Chauvel, P., §10.16
Chavkin, C., §5.17
Chelazzi, L., §§4.25, 4.48, 5.50
Chen, G. Q., §2n3
Chen, L., §5n1
Chen, M., §5.9
Chen, M., §5.9
Chen, Z. J., §7.15
Cheng, P., §4n8
Chergui, K., §4.40
Cheyne, D., §4n12, fig. 9.1

Chiba, A., §§4.22, 5.39, 5.44
Childs, J. A., §4.33
Chiron, C., §4.33
Chisholm, R., §8.5
Chiu, J., §§2n3, 4n4
Chklovskii, D. B., §§4.32, 5.15, 5.21
Cho, K. H., §10.88
Cho, S. Y., §10n15
Choi, B., §§4.35, 4.44
Choi, H., §10.18
Chorover, S. L., §10.16
Chou, W.-L., §10.31
Choudhary, J. S., §5n1
Chouvet, G., §4.40
Chow, K. L., §10n12
Chrobak, J. J., §§4.44, 4.50, 4.53, 4n3,
    5.3, 5.39, 5.43
Chun, M. M., §§4.10, 4.12, 4.14, 4.26,
    10.13, 10.14, 10.17, 10.39, 10.65,
    10.73
Chung, C., §4n8
Chung, S., §4.55
Churchland, A. K., §4.18
Churchland, P. M., §§0.3, 1n1, 8.18,
    10.5, A2.1, A2n1
Churchland, P. S., §§0.3, 1n1, 8.18,
    A1.8
Churchwell, J., §10n15
Ciancia, S., §9.1
Ciocchi, S., §9.8
Ciranni, M., §9.8
Cirelli, C., §5.8
Clapham, D. E., §5.6
Clark, D., §4.40
Clark, J. J., §§4.23, 10.13
Clark, L., §9.8
Clark, R. E., §10n15
Clark, V. P., §4.12
Clémenceau, S., §10.16
Cline, H., §5.9
Cobb, S. R., §§4.44, 5.3
Cohen, A. H., §1.11

Cohen, J., §§3.2, 5.36, 7.11, 7.12, 9.14
Cohen, L., §10.16
Cohen, M. A., §§4.14, 10.17, 10.39, 10.65
Cohen, M. R., §§4.25, 4.48, 4.49, 4.53, 5.38, 5.39, 5.45, 5.50, 10.32
Cohen, N. J., §10n12
Colbert, C. M., §4n2
Colbran, R. J., §5n1
Colcombe, A. M., §4.22
Colgin, L. L., §4.44
Collingridge, G. L., §5n9
Colomb, J., §4.70
Colquhoun, D., §§5.23, 5.25, 5.31
Compte, A., §4.52
Compton, A. H., §7.17
Conci, M., §10.35
Conn, P. J., §5.24
Connor, C., §§4.11, 4.14
Connor, J. A., §5.5
Connors, B., §§4.7, 4.15, 5.39
Connors, B. W., §§4.44, 4.52, 5.26, 5.3
Constantinidis, C., §4.52
Constantinople, C. M., §4.22
Conti, F., §§5.5, 5.28
Contractor, A., §5.40
Contreras, D., §§4.32, 4.70
Conturo, T. E., §4.23
Cook, E. P., §4.24
Cools, R., §§7.11, 7.15, 9.8, 9.9
Cooper, D. C., §§5.36, 5.38, 5.39
Cooper, R., §9n4
Corballis, P. M., §5n6
Corbetta, M., §4.23, 4.24, 4.26, 10.16, 10n23
Corkin, S., §§4.25, 10.44
Corlew, R., §5.28
Corneil, B. D., §10n9
Coruzzi, G., §§2n3, 4n4
Cossart, R., §§4.60, 5.16
Costello, P., §§10.28, 10.31, 10.32
Couch, M., §3.11
Coull, J. T., §4.24

Courège, P., §7n7
Courtney, S. M., §§4.24, 4.26, 10.13
Cowan, N., §10.30
Cowan, R. L., §5.42
Crabtree, J. W., §4.27
Craighero, L., §4.24
Craik, K. J. W., §§10.49, 10.50
Craver, C., §1n1
Crick, F., §§0.3, 4.27, 4.39, 4n11, 5.2, 10n10
Crist, R. E., §10n9
Crone, N. E., §4.35
Cronin-Golomb, A., §10n10
Crump, M. J., §10.36
Csicsvari, J., §§4.44, 4.60, 5.3
Cui, C., §2n3
Cull-Candy, S. G., §§5.23, 5.25, 5.31
Cunningham, M. O., §§4.44, 5.24, 5.40
Curtis, C. E., §4.26
Cutrell, E. B., §4.24

Dafydd, M., §9n2
Dale, A. M., §4.14
Dalibard, J., §§A1.6, A1.7
Dallel, R., §5n3
Dan, Y., §§4.34, 5.11, 5.12, 5.21, 5.38, 5.39, 5.42, 5.50, 5n6
Danchin, A., §§5.24, 7n7
Dani, J. A., §5.42
Daoudal, G., §5.38
Daprati, E., §9.1
Davidson, T. J., §4n12
Davis, G., §§5.7, 10.35
Davis, R. L., §4.70
Daw, N. W., §§10.49, 10.50
Dayan, P., §§4.22, 5.39
Deacon, T. W., §§1.15, A2.2
Dean, A. F., §4.52
Deans, M. R., §§4.44, 5.3
Debanne, D., §5.38
DeBruyn, E. J., §4.38
DeBusk, B. C., §4.38
De Capua, A., §10.16

Decker, M. W., §5.44
Deco, G., §5.39
Deecke, L., §9.1, fig. 9.1
DeFelipe, J., §§4.33, 5.2, 5.3, fig. 5.1
de Gardelle, V., §10.36
Dehaene, S., §§2.11, 10.16, 10.17,
    10.29, 10.36, 10.54, 10.65, 10.67,
    10.69, 10.74, 10.75, 10.77, 10n1,
    10n6, 10n21
Deisz, R. A., §4.55
De Koning, T. J., §5.5
deLange, F. P., §10.43
Del Cul, A., §§10.16, 10.65
Del Gratta, C., §10.16
Delicato, L., §5.39
Delpuech, C., §4.49
DeMaria, C. D., §5.9
Demmou, L., §9.8
Denk, W., §§5.5, 5.6, 5.18
Dennett, D. C., §§1.3, 1n1, 7.17, 7.2,
    7n8, 9n1, 10.5, A2n1, A2n5
Denninger, T., §4.44
Denton, D., §10.60
Desai, N. S., §5.7
DeSalle, R., §§2n3, 4n4
Descartes, R., §10.5
Deschenes, M., §4n11
DeSimone, K., §4.12
Desimone, R., §§4.10, 4.21, 4.23, 4.24,
    4.45, 4.47, 4.48, 4.49, 4.53, 4.60,
    5.39, 5.49, 5.50, 10.13, 10.14, 10.21,
    10.32, 10.50
De Souza, W. C., §4.12
D'Esposito, M., §§4.14, 4.26, 7.11, 7.15,
    9.9, 10.14
Destexhe, A., §§4.70, 4n3
Detrick, S., §7.11
Devlin, J. T., §10.13
De Weerd, P., §10.50
DeWitt, B. S., §A2.4
DeYoe, E. A., §§4.8, 5.37
DiCarlo, J. J., §4.14
Dichter, M., §4n12

Dimitrov, D. F., §10n9
Dingledine, R., §4n4,, §5.4
Disney, A., §5.39
Disterhoft, J. F., §10n15,, §5.38
Dodt, H.-U., §5.21
Doeller, C. F., §§4.8, 8.22
Doherty, J. R., §4.24
Doiron, B., §5.21
Domakonda, K., §5.39
Domenici, P., §10.3
Donner, T. H., §§4.23, 4.49
Donoghue, J. P., §10n9
Doty, R. W., §5.37
Douglas, R. J., §4.32
Doyle, B., §7.17
Draganski, B., §7.12
Draine, S. C., §10.36
Dretske, F., §§1n1, 8.6
Drevets, W., §5.39
Drew, P. J., §5n4
Driver, J., §§4.22, 10.35
Drury, H. A., §4.23
Druzgal, T. J., §10.14
Ducati, A., §§5.5, 5.28
Dudek, F. E., §§4.35, 4.44
Dudek, S. M., §§5.6, 5.9
Dugladze, T., §5.43
Duguid, I., §5.30
Dulac, O., §4.33
Dum, R. P. fig. 9.1
Dumas, C., §4.33
Dunbar, K. N., §5n6
Duncan, J., §§4.21, 4.24, 4.25, 5.50,
    10.32
Dupoux, E., §10.36
Duque, A., §§4.32, 4.43, 4.44, 5.3, 5.42
Duran, M., §5.5
Durstewitz, D., §§4.42, 4.68, 5.25, 7.15
Duzel, E., §4.70
Dwyer, T. M., §A1.10

Eagleman, D. M., §10.18
Earley, J.E., §A2.2

Eccles, J.C., §7.17
Eckhorn, R., §4.45
Eddington, A. S., §A1.4
Edelman, G., §§4.45, 5.8, 7n7
Edelman, S., §4.10
Edwards, D. H., §1.11
Egelhaaf, M., §4.70
Egeth, H., §§4.25, 5.44
Ehlers, M. D., §5.7
Ehrenstein, G., §A1.10
Eichenbaum, H., §5.36
Eifuku, S., §4.12
Eilers, J., §§5.5, 5n1
Eimer, M., §§9.1, 9.3, 9.5, fig. 9.2, 9n2
Einstein, A., §A1.5
Elbert, T., §§4.49, 4n15
Ellis, G. F. R., §9.14
Ellis, W. D., §10.50
Ellsworth, C., §§4.63, 5.1
Elsner, A., §10.18
Empson, R. M., §4.55
Emri, Z., §4.44
Engbert, R., §4.23
Engel, A. K, §§4.21, 4.23, 4.45, 4.49,
    4.53, 4.60, 4n3, 5.46
Engert, F., §§5.5, 5.9
Enns, J. T., §§4.22, 10.35
Epstein, R. A., §4.8
Erb, M., §9n6
Erchova, I., §5.11
Erickson, C. A., §§10.13, 10.14
Erisir, A., §5.28
Ermentrout, G. B., §4.23
Ernst, R., §4.70
Ersche, K. D., §7.15
Ertunc, M., §4n8
Esclapez, M., §4.33
Esteban, J., §5.9
Esteky, H., §4.12
Ettlinger, G., §4.8
Euler, T., §5.18
Evangelista, E., §§8.18, 8.20
Evans, A. C., §4.26

Evans, R. H., §5n9
Everett, H., §A2.4
Everitt, B. J., §§5.38, 5.39, 5.44, 5.45
Everling, S., §4.23
Eyherabide, H. G., §§4.38, 5.36
Eysel, U. T., §4.44

Faber, D. S., §§1.11, 4.66
Fabian, S. A., §5.6
Fabre-Thorpe, M., §§4.14, 10.71
Fadiga, L., §4.24
Fadok, J. P., §4.40
Fahrenfort, J. J., §§10.16, 10.36
Fallah, M., §4.24
Fang, F., §§10.28, 10.31, 10.32
Fanselow, E. E., §4.38
Fariñas, I., §§5.2, 5.3, fig. 5.1
Farivar, R., §4.8
Faure, P., §§4.68, 4.70
Faymonville, M. E., §10.66
Fedrizzi, A., §A1.6
Feig, S. L., §4.27
Feigenson, L., §9.33
Feiler, A. M., §4.8
Feinberg, I., §9.13
Feinstein, J., §10.44
Feldman, D. E., §§5.11, 5.28
Feldman, J., §§10.30, 10.32, 10.42
Felleman, D. J., §4.49
Fellous, J., §§5.36, 5.40
Fellows, M. R., §10n9
Fenno, L. E., §4n12
Ferecskó, A. S., §4.32
Fernandez-Duque, D., §10.16
Ferrarelli, F., §§4.27, 5.24
Ferrarini, L., §7.15
Ferrera, V. P., §4.19
Ferster, D., §§4.32, 4.60, 5.16
Feynman, R. P., §A1.11
Ffytche, D., §§10.16, 10.65
Fibiger, H. C., §5.38
Finch, E. A., §5.5
Fine, A., §A1.6

Finke, K., §10.35
Finn, I. M., §4.32
Fisahn, A., §§4.44, 5.40
Fischer, M., §4.55
Fitzgerald, C., §10n20
Fitzgerald, J. K., §4.24
Fitzpatrick, D., §5.3
Fitzsimonds, R. M., §5.17
Fize, D., §§4.14, 10.71
Flajolet, M., §4.40
Fletcher, P., §10.6
Flor, H., §4n15
Floresco, S. B., §4.40
Fodor, J., §§1n1, 3.11, 10.19
Foffani, G., §4.43
Fontanini, A., §5.7
Foote, W., §5.45
Formisano, E., §4.12
Fornito, A., §7.15
Forster, K. I., §10.36
Fougnie, D., §10.13
Fox, M. D., §10n23
Francis, A. A., §5n9
Francis, G., §10.50
Frangou, S., §5.24
Frank, M. G., §5.8
Frank, M. J., §4.40
Frank, R. A. W., §4n4
Frank, S. M., §10.54, figs. 10.3, 10.4
Franks, K. M., §4.66
Freedman, D. J., §§4.19, 4.26, 7.11
Freeman, D. C., §5.36
Freeman, T., §4.34
Freeman, W. J., §4.69
Frege, G., §2.9, 8.8, 8.10
Freiwald, W. A., §§4.11, 4.12, 4.45
Freund, T. F., §§4.44, 5.3, 5.17, 5.43, 5.45
Frey, S., §5.9
Frey, U., §5.9
Frick, A., §5.21
Fricker, D., §§4.44, 5.3
Fried, I., §§4.11, fig. 4.4, §9.14

Friedman, H. S., §5.37
Friedman-Hill, S., §4.52
Fries, P., §§4.21, 4.23, 4.45, 4.47, 4.48, 4.49, 4.53, 4.60, 4n3, 5.39, 5.46, 5.49
Frihauf, J. B., §4.12
Friston, K. J., §5.24
Frith, C. D., §§5.24, 9.13, 9n6, 10.26
Frith, U., §A2n5
Froemke, R. C., §§4.60, 5.12, 5.16, 5.21
Frotscher, M., §5.11
Frye, M. A., §4.70
Fuchs, W., §10.50
Fugelsang, J. A., §5n6
Fujisawa, S., §4.60
Fukada, Y., §4.10
Fukuda, K., §10.30
Furey, M., §5.39
Furlong, P. L., §4.49
Fuster, J. M., §§2n3, 4.26, 10.40, 10.61, 10n10
Futai, K., §5.42
Fyhn, M., §§4.8, 4.44, 8.22

Gaetz, W., §4n12
Gaiarsa, J.-L., §5n9
Gaillard, R., §10.16
Gaissmaier, W., §§8.17, 10.22
Galarreta, M., §4.44
Galili, D. S., §10.43
Galizia, C. G., §10.43
Gallagher, M., §§5.24, 5.44
Gallant, J. L., §§4.24, 4.25, 5.50
Gallella, S., §10n20
Ganguly, K., §5.11
Garcia Dominguez, L., §4n12
Garcia-Larrea, L., §4.22
Garg, D., §4.22
Gaser, C., §7.12
Gaska, J. P., §5.45
Gasquoine, P. G., §10n10
Gazzaniga, M. S., §4.7, §5n6
Gelade, G., §§5.44, 5.49, 10.30
Georgopoulos, A., §§8.1, 8.19

Gerkin, R. C., §5.12
Gervasoni, D., §§4.37, 4.50, 5.45, 5.46
Gharib, A., §4.70
Ghermazien, H., §5.28
Ghose, G. M., §4.24
Ghuman, A. S., §4.14
Gibbs, B. J., §§4.21, 10.30
Gibson, J. R., §§4.44, 5.3
Giese, M. A., §§8.18, 8.20
Gieselmann, M., §5.39
Gigerenzer, G., §§8.17, 10.22
Gil, Z., §5.39
Gilbert, J., §5.7
Gillett, C., §3.11
Gilroy, L. A., §§10.49, 10.50
Giocomo, L., §5.39
Girard, P., §5.45
Girault, J. A., §5n1
Giraux, P., §9.1
Gitelman, D. R., §4.24
Givens, B., §§5.38, 5.39
Glanzman, D. L., §10.43
Gleason, C. A., §§9.1, 9.14
Gloveli, T., §§4.55, 5.43
Gnadt, J. W., §4n11
Goaillard, J. M., §5.7
Goard, M., §§5.38, 5.39, 5.50
Goda, Y., §5.7
Gödel, K., §§7.18, 8.3, A1n3
Godwin, D. W., §§4.38, 4.59
Goebel, R., §§4.12, 4.45, 4.53
Goelet, P., §5.9
Golay, X., §4.24
Gold, J. I., §4.18
Gold, P. E., §5.38
Goldberg, J. A., §4n12
Goldberg, M. E., §§4.18, 4.24
Golding, N. L., §§5.22, 5.27
Goldman-Rakic, P. S., §§4.26, 4.40, 4.52, 4.55
Gold-von Simson, G., §10.5
Gomes, G., §§9n1, 9n4
Gomez, J., §4.33

Gonzalez, J., §A1.10
Goodale, M. A., §4.8
Goodman, P. H., §4.55
Goold, C. P., §5.7
Gordon, R. D., §10.30
Gore, J. C., §4.12
Gorman, L. K., §5.44
Gothard, K. M., §10.21
Goto, Y., §4.40
Gottlieb, J., §§4.18, 4.19
Gotts, S. J., §§4.24, 4.49
Gouaux, E., §2n3
Govindarajan, A., §5.9
Graboi, D., §§4.14, 4.60
Grabowecky, M., §§10.49, 10.50
Grabowski, T., §10.44
Grace, A. A., §§4.40, 5.36
Grafstein, B., §4.68
Graham, N., §A2.4
Grangier, P., §§A1.6, A1.7
Grant, S. G., §5n1
Gray, C. M., §§4.43, 4.44, 4.45, 4.49, 4.52, 4.53, 5.3
Gray, E., §5.2
Graybiel, A. M., §4n12
Green, J. T., §10n15
Green, M., §10.54
Greenberg, M. E., §5n1
Greenberg, P., §10.50
Greene, J., §§7.12, 9.14
Greenfield, S. A., §§4.44, 5.3
Greengard, P., §§.40, 5.9, 5n1
Greenlee, M. W., §§4.23, 10.30, 10.54, figs. 10.3, 10.4
Greenspan, R. J., §10.45
Greenwald, A. G., §10.36
Greger, B., §10n9
Gregoriou, G. G., §§4.24, 4.49
Grenier, F., §5.42
Grewe, J., §4.70
Griffin, I. C., §§10.13, 10.15
Grill-Spector, K., §4.10
Grinvald, A., §4.42

Gritti, I., §5.45
Gröblacher, S., §A1.6
Grodd, W., §9n6
Grol, M. J., §10.43
Gross, C. G., §§4.9, 4.10, 4.12, 4.11, 10.21
Gross, J., §4.23
Grossberg, S., §§4.45, 10.50
Grossi, G., §10.16
Grubb, M. S., §4.38
Gruber, T., §§4.14, 4.49, 10.71
Grunau, R. E., §10n20
Grush, R., §A1.8
Guido, W., §§4.38, 4n11
Guillery, R. W., §§4.27, 4.38, 4n11
Gulyás, A. I., §§4.44, 5.3
Guo, A., §10.45
Guo, J. Z., §10.45
Gupta, A., §§4.33, 4.55, 5.3
Gusev, A. G., §4.38
Gustafsson, L., §4.33
Gutierrez, R., §4.60

Haarmeier, T., §9n6
Hachmeh, K. J., §4.24
Hadj-Bouziane, F., §§4.12, 10.21
Hadjipapas, A., §4.49
Haenny, P. E., §4.24
Hafed, Z. M., §4.23
Hafting, T., §§4.8, 4.44, 8.22
Haggard, P., §§3.1, 3n2, 9.1, 9.3, 9.5, figs. 9.1, 9.2, §§9n2, 9n6
Haglund, M. H., §§4.39, 10.50
Hahn, S., §4.22
Haider, B., §§4.32, 4.43, 4.44, 5.3, 5.42
Haidt, J., §3n3
Hajos, M., §4.27
Hajos, N., §§4.44, 5.3
Hájos, N., §§5.40, 5.43
Haken, H., §4.69
Halasy, K., §§4.44, 5.3
Halgren, E., §10.16
Hall, S. D., §4.49

Hallett, M., §§9.4, 9n1, fig. 9.1
Halpain, S., §5n1
Hama, K., §§4.44, 4.53
Hameroff, S., §A1.8
Hamill, P., §A1.10
Hamzei-Sichani, F., §§4.60, 5.16
Hanes, D. P., §4.23
Hanks, T. D., §4.18
Hanlon, R., §10n16
Hannula, D. E., §10n12
Hansel, D., §4n3
Hardingham, G. E., §5.5
Harel, M., §4.10
Harkany, T., §4.55
Harnett, M. T., §§5.6, 5n4
Harris, K. D., §§4.44, 4.60, 5.16
Harris, W. A., §5.11
Harris-Warrick, R., §§1.11, 4.35
Harting, J. K., §4.27
Hasboun, D., §10.16
Hasenstaub, A., §§4.32, 4.33, 4.43, 4.44, 5.3, 5.42
Hashikawa, T., §5.3
Hasselmo, M., §§5.38, 5.39, 10.21
Hassler, U., §§4.14, 10.71
Hasson, R., §4.44
Hatsopoulos, N. G., §10n9
Hauser, M., §9.33
Häusser, M., §§5.9, 5.11, 5.15, 5.18, 5.21, 5.22, 5.23, 5.27, 5.30, fig. 5.4
Hausser, M., §4.70
Hawk, J. D., §5.6
Hawken, M., §5.39
Hawkes, A. G., §5.25
Haxby, J. V., §§4.12, 4.26, 5.39, 10.13
Hayden, B. Y., §§4.24, 4.25, 5.50
Haynes, J.-D., §9.14
He, A. H., §9.14
He, S., §§10.28, 10.31, 10.32
He, Y., §7.15
He, Z. J., §§4.22, 10.30, 10.35
Head, A. S., §10.21
Hebb, D. O., §§4.54, 5.11

Heckhausen, H., §9n1

Heeger, D. J., §§4.14, 4.21, 4.27, 4.59, 4.60, 5.45, 10.32

Heil, J., §§1.5, A2.2, A2.3

Heinemann, A., §10.36

Heinemann, S. F., §5.40

Heinemann, U., §§4.55, 5.43

Heinze, H.-J., §9.14

Heisenberg, M., §§4.70, 7.17, 10.45

Heisenberg, W., §A1n7

Heitler, W. J., §1.11

Heizmann, C. W., §§4.44, 4.53

Helgadottir, H., §5.8

Helmchen, F., §4.32

Helmholtz, H. L., §§9n6, 10.19, 10n17

Henderson, J. M., §4.14

Hendler, T., §4.10

Hendry, R., §A2.2

Hendry, S. H., §5.3

Henrie, J. A., §4.49

Henriquez, C. S., §10n9

Henson, M. A., §5.28

Hepp, K., §A1.8

Hering, E., §§10.49, 10.50, 10n17

Herrero, J., §5.39

Herrington, T. M., §4.24

Herrmann, C. S., §§5.46, 9n2

Herron, C. E., §5.9

Herry, C., §9.8

Herz, A. V., §§4.38, 5.36

Hestrin, S., §4.44

Hetke, J., §4.35

Hetrick, W. P., §5n2

Higley, M. J., §4.32

Hiley, B. J., §A1.6

Hilkenmeier, F., §4.48

Hille, B., §A1.10

Hillebrand, A., §4.49

Hillstrom, A. P., §4.22

Hillyard, S. A., §§4.21, 10.32

Hinojosa, J. A., §4.14

Hinrichsen, H., §4.42

Hipp, J. F., §§4.23, 4.49

Hirsch, J. A., §4.32

Hirsch, J. C., §4.33

Hirstein, W., §4n15

Hitch, G. J., §4.21

Hobbes, T., §7n1

Hobson, J. A., §§10.77, 10.78

Hochstein, S., §4.60

Hodgkin, A. L., §5.17

Hodgson, D., §A1.9

Hoffman, E. A., §4.12

Hoffman, K. L., §10.21

Hoffman, R. E., §5.24

Hoffmann, K. P., §4.60

Hoffmann, W. E., §4.27

Holcombe, A. O., §4.24

Holland, P. C., §§5.24, 5.44

Holliday, I. E., §4.49

Hollingworth, A., §4.14

Holmgren, C., §4.55

Holt, C. E., §5.11

Holtmaat, A., §5.9

Homayoun, H., §4.36

Hommel, B., §4.23

Hong, S. W., §§10.49, 10.50

Hopfield, J. J., §§4.44, 4.54

Horiike, K., §5n2

Hormuzdi, S. G., §4.44

Horowitz, T. S., §10.58

Horton, J. C., §4n5

Horvath, Z., §4.35

Horwitz, G. D., §4.23

Hou, Q., §5.7

Houghton, C. J., §5.8

Houser, C. R., §5.3

Houtkamp, R., §4.24

Howe, J. R., §§5.23, 5.25, 5.31

Hoyt, W. F., §4n5

Hsieh, C.-H., §4.70

Hsieh, M. H., §2n3

Hsieh, P.-J., §§4.14, 8.18, 10.48, 10.52

Hu, Y., §10.43

Huang, L. Y., §§5n1, A1.10

Huang, M., §§10.28, 10.31, 10.32
Huang, S.-Y., §5.9
Hubel, D. H., §§4.38, 4.9, 5.36
Huganir, R. L., §§5.7, 5.9
Hughes, D. I., §5.3
Huguenard, J., §4.35
Huk, A. C., §4.18
Hume, D., §§5n6, 7n1, 7.2, 7.3
Humphreys, P., §A2.2
Hung, C. P., §4.14
Hupé, J. M., §5.45
Husi, H., §5n1
Huxley, A. F., §5.17
Hvalby, O., §5n1
Hyman, S. E., §3.2

Ibata, K., §5.7
Ibel, S., §§4.22, 10.16
Idiart, M. A., §4.44
Ikeda, A. fig. 9.1
Ikegaya, Y., §§4.60, 5.16
Inati, S. J., §4.12
Ingram, J. N., §9n6
Intraub, H., §4.14
Intriligator, J., §§4.24, A1n6
Ioannides, A. A., §4.44
Irwin, D. E., §§4.22, 10.30
Isaac, J. T., §4.27
Ishai, A., §4.12
Ishida, T., §5n2
Ishikawa, N., §4.52
Ishikawa, T., §5.30
Isomura, Y., §4.60
Israely, I., §5.9
Issa, N. P., §5.8
Itano, W. M., §A1.6
Itzchak, Y., §4.10
Ivry, R., §§4.21, 7.11, 7.15, 9.8, 9.9

Jack, J. J. B., §5.15
Jackson, F., §§10.5, A2n1
Jackson, G. M., §10.35
Jackson, M. B., §A1.10

Jackson, M. E., §4.36
Jacob, V., §5.11
Jagadeesh, B., §4.11
Jahanshahi, M., fig. 9.1
Jahnsen, H., §4n11
Jalali, A., §5.25
Jambaque, I., §4.33
James, A. C., §5.45
James, W., §§7.17, 7n1, 7n6
Jamieson, B., §4.44, 5.3
Jandó, G., §4.35
Jang, H. J., §10.88
Jaquet, E., §§8.18, 8.20
Jarsky, T., §5.22
Jarzylo, L., §5.7
Jastorff, J., §4.14
Jayaraman, V., §A1.10
Jeffery, L., §§8.18, 8.20
Jefferys, J. G., §§4.44, 4.68, 5.3, 5.40
Jen, J., §5n1
Jenkins, I. H., fig. 9.1
Jennewein, T., §A1.6
Jensen, O., §§4.44, 4.49
Jensen, V., §5n1
Jescheniak, J. D., §§4.14, 10.71
Jessell, T., §4.7
Jiang, H., §4.10
Jiang, Y., §§10.13, 10.14, 10.15, 10.28, 10.31, 10.32
Jih, J., §9.8
Jirsa, V. K., §4.68
Jo, Y. H., §10.88
Jobert, A., §10.67
Joelving, F. C., §4.52
Johnson, J. W., §5.4
Johnson, R. C., §5.9
Johnston, D., §§4n2, 5.18, 5n5
Johnston, J. C., §4.22
Jolicoeur, P., §10.28
Jonas, P., §§4.33, 4.44, 4.53, 5.3, 5.40
Jones, B. E., §§5.38, 5.45
Jones, E. G., §§5.2, 5.3
Jones, M. S., §§4.35, 4.44

Jones, R. S., §5.28
Jonides, J., §§4.22, 4.26
Jönsson, C., §A1.10
Joordens, S., §10.36
Joseph, D., §§7.15, 9.8
Joseph, J. S., §10.73
Joubert, O. R., §§4.14, 10.71
Judge, S. J., §§4.10, 4.39
Julesz, B., §10.73
Jung, H. Y., §5.35

Kabara, J. F., §4.38
Kaech, S., §4.55
Kafaligönül, H., §10.50
Kahneman, D., §§4.21, 8.17, 10.22, 10.30
Kainulainen, P., §10.16
Kaiser, J., §4.49
Kaji, S., §4.9
Kalkus, J. F., §4.12
Kaltenbaek, R., §§A1.6, A1.7
Kamitani, Y., §§10.49, 10.50
Kamondi, A., §§4.44, 5.3, 5.43
Kampa, B. M., §§5.21, 5.23
Kampe, K., §5.21
Kanai, R., §§10.32, 10.33, 10n1, 10n18
Kandel, E., §§4.7, 5.9
Kane, R., §7.17
Kang, J., §2n3
Kang, M. G., §5.9
Kang, Y., §4.52
Kano, M., §§4n4, 5.15, 5.17, 5.22
Kant, I., §§7n1, 8.13, 8n5
Kanwisher, N., §§4.10, 4.12
Kaplan, E., §4.38
Kappers, A. L. M., §10.81
Karson, M. A., §5.42
Kass, J. I., §4.35
Kassam, K. S., §4.14
Kastner, S., §4.12
Katai, S., §4.52
Kath, W. L., §5.22
Kato, K., §4.52

Katona, I., §§5.17, 5.40
Katsumaru, H., §§4.44, 4.53
Kavalali, E. T., §4n8
Kawaguchi, Y., §§4.44, 4.53, 5.3
Kawahara, S., §10n15
Kawano, K., §§4.9, 4.12
Kayama, Y., §5.37
Keane, J., §§8.18, 8.20
Keil, A., §4.49
Keller, C., §A1.10
Keller, I., §§9n1, 10.35
Kelso, J. A. S., §4.69
Kelso, S. R., §§4.45, 5n1
Kennedy, H., §4.49
Kennedy, W. A., §4.10
Kepecs, A., §§4.38, 5.30, 5.36, 5.37
Keren, G., §4.25
Kersten, D., §10.22
Kerszberg, M., §10n6
Kertzman, C., §4.23
Kerwin, R., §5.24
Kesner, R., §7.11
Kessler, K., §4.23
Khalsa, S., §10.44
Khayat, P. S., §4.24
Khazipov, R., §5n9
Khodakhah, K., §4.40
Khvotchev, M., §4n8
Kiani, R., §§4.12, 4.18
Kiehl, K. A., §10n10
Kielpinski, D., §A1.6
Kiesel, A., §10.36
Kilgard, M. P., §5.38
Kim, H. G., §5.26
Kim, H. T., §10n15
Kim, J., §§1.5, 3.11, 6.9, A2.1, A2.2, A2.3, fig. A2.1, §A2n1
Kim, J. J., §§5n1, 10n15
Kim, M. S., §10.35
Kim, Y. H., §4.24
Kinoshita, S., §10.36
Kinsbourne, M., §§1.3, 9n1
Kirino, Y., §10n15

Kiss, L., §5.11
Kisvárday, Z. F., §§4.32, 4.44
Kitamura, K., §§4n4, 5.15, 5.22
Kitzbichler, M., §5.24
Kiyosue, K., §5.7
Klaus, A., §4.42
Klausberger, T., §5.3
Kleckner, N. W., §§5.23, 5.31, 5.4
Kliegl, R., §4.23
Kloppenburg, P., §4.35
Klugmann, M., §5.42
Knapen, T. H., §§10.49, 10.50
Knecht, S., §4n15
Knight, R. T., §5.46
Knoblauch, K., §4.49
Knowlton, B. J., §4.70
Knudsen, E. I., §4.48
Knusten, T. A., §§4.12, 10.21
Kobatake, E., §4.10
Koch, C., §§0.3, 3n3, 4.11, 4.38, 4.52, 4.62, 4.68, 4n3, 4n11, fig. 4.4, §§5.15, 5.18, 5.22, 5.45, 7.3, 10.6, 10.28, 10.43, 10.55, 10.71, 10n12, A1.8
Koenderink, J. J., §10.81
Koester, H. J., §5.6
Kohl, M. M., §5.42
Kohler, P. J., §§10.31, 10.49
Kohler, P. K., §10.48
Kohn, A., §§4.47, 4.48, 5.32
Koivisto, M., §10.16
Kok, A., §10.36
Kombian, S. B., §5.17
König, P., §§4.21, 4.23, 4.45, 4.49, 4.53, 4n3, 5.46
Konnerth, A., §§5.5, 5n1
Kopell, N., §§4.23, 4.44, 4.45, 5.50
Korkotian, E., §4.55
Korn, H., §§1.11, 4.66, 4.68
Kornhuber, H. H., §9.1
Koroshetz, W. J., §10n10
Korte, A., §10.18
Korzeniewska, A., §4.35

Kosaka, T., §§4.44, 4.53
Kouider, S., §§10.36, 10.67
Kralik, J. D., §10n9
Kramer, A. F., §4.22
Kramer, M. A., §4.45
Krasne, F. B., §1.11
Krause, M., §4.27
Kraushaar, U., §§4.43, 4.44, 5.3, 5.42
Kravitz, D. J., §4.26
Kreiman, G., §§4.11, 4.14, fig. 4.4, §9.14
Kreiter, A. K., §4.45
Kreitzer, A. C., §5.17
Krekelberg, B., §4.60
Krichmar, J. L., §§4.22, 5.39
Kriegeskorte, N., §4.12
Kripke, S., §2.9, 8.9, 8.10, 8.11, 8.13, A3
Kristeva, R., fig. 9.1
Kronforst-Collins, M., §§5.38, 10n15
Kropff, E., §§4.8, 8.22
Krug, M., §5.9
Kubicki, M., §5.24
Kubischik, M., §4.60
Kubota, Y., §5.3
Kuhl, D., §5.7
Kuhse, J., §5.4
Kunde, W., §10.36
Kuner, T., §5n9
Kunieda, T., fig. 9.1
Kushnir, T., §4.10
Kustov, A. A., §4.23
Kwak, H. W., §4.25
Kwong, K. K., §4.10

LaBar, K. S., §4.24
LaBerge, D., §4.27
Lacey, S. C., §4.26
Lachaux, J. P., §§4.45, 4.49
Lado, F., §4.44
Lagercrantz, H., §10n20
Lähteenmäki, M., §10.16
Laing, C., §5.21

Lakoff, G., §8.15

Lam, H.-M., §§2n3, 4n4

Lamb, T., §4.68

Lambermont, B., §10.66

Lambiotte, R., §7.15

Lamme, V. A., §§4.24, 10.15, 10.16, 10.17, 10.36, 10.65, 10n22

Lampl, I., §§4.60, 5.16

Lamy, D., §§10.16, 10.30

Lamy, M., §10.66

Lancellotti, P., §10.66

Land, B. R., §4.66

Landau, A. N., §4.22

Landauer, R., §A1n3

Landman, R., §§4.49, 5.49, 10.15

Lang, W., fig. 9.1

Langacker, R. W., §8.15

Lape, R., §5.42

Laplace, P.-S., §A1.2

Larkum, M. E., §5.21

Larsen, R. S., §5.28

Latham, P. E., §4.70

Lattal, K. M., §5.6

Lau, B., §5.45

Lau, H. C., §9.1

Laubach, M., §10n9

Laube, B., §5.4

Laureys, S., §§10.65, 10.66

Lauritzen, T. Z., §4.14

Lavond, D. G., §10n15

Le, D. A., §10n10

LeBeau, F. E., §§4.44, 5.3, 5.40

Lebedev, M. A., §10n9

Lebiere, C., §§7.15, 9.8

Le Bihan, D., §10.67

Ledden, P. J., §4.10

Ledent, C., §5.40

Lee, M. C., §5.7

Legendre, P., §4.66

Legenstein, R., §4.42

Lehmann, J., §5.38

Lehtonen, M., §10.16

Leibniz, §7n11

Leitz, J., §4n8

Lem, S., §10n24

Leonard, J. P., §§4.45, 5n1

Leopold, D. A., §§8.18, 8.20

Lepsien, J., §10.13

Lerner, Y., §4.10

LeShan, L., §7.17

Lesica, N. A., §4.38

Leslie, A., §A2n5

Letzkus, J. J., §§5.21, 5.23

Leung, L. S., §4.44

Leuthold, H., §9n4

Levin, D. T., §10.56

Levitt, J. J., §5.24

Levy, R., §4.26

Lewis, D., §8n9

Lewis, R. L., §4.26

Li, C. T., §5.42

Li, F. F., §10.71

Li, J., §5n1

Li, X., §4.55

Liang, H., §§4.49, 5.49

Liang, L., §4.43

Libet, B., §§9.1, 9.14, 9n1

Liddle, P. F., §10n10

Lieberman, D. N., §5n1

Liebovitch, L. S., §5.25

Lighthall, J. W., §§4.52, 5.3

Lima, B., §§4.45, 4.53

Lin, F., §5.25

Lin, S. C., §§4.37, 4.50, 5.45, 5.46, 5.47

Linden, D., §§4.26, 5.9, 5.18, 5.38

Lindinger, G., fig. 9.1

Lindner, A., §9n6

Ling, S., §10.48

Linnaeus, C., §4n14

Liotti, M., §4.22

Lisman, J. E., §§2.5, 4.14, 4.36, 4.38, 4.40, 4.44, 4.50, 4.53, 4.60, 5.9, 5.30, 5.36, 5.37, 5.43, fig. 5.5

Liu, L., §4.70

Liu, Q. S., §5n4

Liu, T., §§4.21, 10.32
Livingstone, M. S., §§4.11, 4.12, 4.39, 5.36
Llinas, R., §4n11
Lobb, C. J., §4.40
Locke, J., §10n5
Lodge, D. J., §4.40
Logan, G. D., §10.36
Logie, R. H., §10.14
Logothetis, N. K., §§4.9, 4.23, 4.48, 5.50, 7.11, 10.18, 10.21
Lomber, S. G., §5.45
Lomo, T., §5.6
London, M., §§4.70, 5.15, 5.18
Longtin, A., §5.21
Los, M. F., §4n8
Lössner, B., §5.9
Lou, L., §10.50
Loukas, C., fig. 9.1
Lowe, G., §5.18
Lozsadi, D. A., §4.27
Lu, S. M., §4.38
Lu, T., §4.43
Lubke, J., §5.11
Luck, S. J., §§4.21, 10.13, 10.15, 10.16, 10.28, 10.32
Luczak, A., §§4.60, 5.16
Lüdke, A., §10.43
Lüthi, A., §9.8
Lujan, R., §§4.55, 5.3
Lukaszewicz, A.-C., §4.22
Lund, J. S., §5.3
Luria, R., §10.30
Lurito, J., §§8.1, 8.19
Lustig, C. A., §4.26
Luu, P., §§5.9, 5n4
Luxen, A., §10.66
Lycan, W., §A2n5
Lynall, M. E., §5.24

Ma, J., §§4.55, 5.18
Maass, W., §§4.42, 4.55
MacDonald, B., §4.12

MacDonald, K. D., §§4.35, 4.44
Macdonald, M., §§4.22, 10.16
Macgregor, R. J., §A1.8
Mack, A., §§10.29, 10.67, 10.71, 10.74, 10n21
Mackeben, M., §§4.22, 4.48
MacKie, K., §5.40
Mackiewicz, K. L. fig. 7.1
Macknik, S. L., §§4.38, 4.39, 10.50
Madden, D. R., §2n3
Maddox, T., §4.21
Maeda, T., §5n2
Maejima, T., §5.17
Maffei, A., §5.7
Maffei, L., §5.36
Magee, J. C., §§5.18, 5.20, 5n5
Magill, P. J, §4n12
Magleby, K. L., §5.25
Magnussen, S., §10.30
Mahon, S., §5.30
Maimon, G., §4.52
Mainen, Z. F., §5.21
Mainville, L., §5.45
Majewska, A., §§4.55, 4.63, 5.1
Makovski, T., §§10.13, 10.15
Malach, R., §4.10
Malcolm, N., §8n6
Maldonado, P. E., §4.52
Malenka, R. C., §§5.6, 5.9, 5n4
Maler, L., §5.21
Malerba, P., §4.45
Maletic-Savatic, M., §§5.5, 5.9
Malinow, R., §§5.5, 5.9, 5n1
Maloney, T., §§4.22, 10.16
Mamassian, P., §10.22
Man, H.-Y., §5.7
Mancia, M., §5.45
Mandeville, J. B., §4.12
Mandon, S., §4.45
Mangin, J. F., §10.16
Mann, E. O., §§4.44, 5.3, 5.40, 5.42, 5.43
Manning, K. A., §4.59

Mantini, D., §10.16

Mao, B. Q., §§4.60, 5.16

Maquet, P., §10.66

Maravall, M., §5.22

Marco, P., §4.33

Marder, C. P., §4.54

Marder, E., §5.7

Mardon, L., §10.50

Margenau, H., §7.17

Marinkovic, K., §10.16

Markram, H., §§4.33, 4.50, 4.55, 4.68, 5.3, 5.11

Marois, R., §§4.26, 10.13, 10.14, 10.30

Marr, D., §10.81

Marrocco, R. T., §4.24

Marsden, C. D., fig. 9.1

Marshall, L., §5.8

Martin, A., §4.12

Martin, J., §4.70

Martin, K. A., §4.32

Martin, K. C., §§5.6, 5.9

Martina, M., §4.33

Martinerie, J., §4.45

Martinez Trujillo, J. C., §§4.24, 4.25

Martinez, L. M., §4.32

Martinez-Conde, S., §§4.38, 4.39

Martinez-Trujillo, J. C., §§4.24, 4.25

Masse, N. Y., §4.24

Massey, J., §§8.1, 8.19

Matsuhashi, M., §§9.4, 9n1

Matsukevich, D. N., §§A1.6, A1.7

Matsuki, N., §§4n4, 5.15, 5.22

Matsukura, M., §10.15

Matsuo, N., §§4n4, 5.15, 5.22

Mattay, V. S., §7.15

Matthias, E., §10.35

Mattingley, J. B., §10.35

Mattler, U., §10.36

Matus, A., §§4.55, 5.2

Mauguiere, F., §4.22

Maunsell, J. H. R., §§4.24, 4.25, 4.35, 4.47, 4.48, 4.49, 4.50, 4.53, 5.38, 5.39, 5.43, 5.45, 5.50, 5n12, fig. 5.5, §10.32

Maunz, P., §§A1.6, A1.7

May, A., §7.12

Maye, A., §4.70

Mayer, M. L., §2n3

Mayford, M., §§4n4, 5.15, 5.22

Mayo, J. P., §4.27

Mayr, E., §7.17

McAdams, C. J., §§4.24, 4.25, 5.50

McAlonan, G. M., §5.44

McAlonan, K., §§4.27, 4.38, 4.39, 4.43, 4.48, 4n11

McBain, C. J., §5.40

McCallum, W. C., §9n4

McCarley, R. W., §4n12, 5.24, 5.38

McCarthy, G., §4.12

McCormick, D., §§4.32, 4.33, 4.35, 4.43, 4.44, 4.52, 5.3, 5.39, 5.42

McCormick, P. A., §10.28

McCulloch, W. S., §5.14

McDermott, J., §§4.10, 4.12

McEchron, M. D., §10n15

McGaugh, J. L., §5.38

McGaughy, J., §5.44

McGlade-McCulloh, E., §5n1

McGlashan, T. H., §5.24

McKenna, P. J., §5.24

McLaughlin, J., §10n15

McMahan, R., §5.44

McNamara, J. O., §5n1

McNaughton, B. L., §5.42

Meek, J., §10n20

Megias, M., §4.44

Mehta, M. R., §5.15

Meisel, L., §§2n3, 4n4

Mel, B., §§4.36, 5.15, 5.22, 5.30

Mele, A., §§1n1, 1.5, 3.1, 3n2, 7.17, A2.2, A2.3

Meletis, K., §5.42

Meliza, C. D., §5.11

Melloni, L., §§4.45, 4.53, 10.16

Melone, M., §§5.5, 5.28

Mercado, F., §4.14
Mercer, A., §4.55
Merchan-Perez, A., §4.33
Meredith, R. M., §5.6
Merikle, P. M., §10.36
Merrick, D. M., §4n2
Mervis, C., §8.15
Merzenich, M. M., §5.38
Meskenaite, V., §5.45
Mesulam, M. M., §§4.23, 4.24
Meunier, D., §7.15
Meyer, J. R., §4.24
Meyer, T., §5n1
Meyer, V., §A1.6
Meyer-Lindenberg, A., §7.15
Michael, D., §5.6
Miles, R., §§4.44, 5.3
Miller, C. A., §5.6
Miller, E. K., §§4.19, 4.23, 4.24, 4.26,
    5.36, 5.50, 7.11, 10.13, 10.14
Miller, J., §§9n2, 9n4
Miller, K. D., §4.32, 5.11, 5.45
Millikan, R., §8.6
Milner, A. D., §§4.8, 10.21
Mima, T., fig. 9.1
Min, B.-K., §9n2
Mingolla, E., §10.50
Mintz, I. M., §4.35
Miraucourt, L. S., §5n3
Mishina, M., §5.28
Mishkin, M., §§4.26, 4.8
Mistlin, A. J., §10.21
Mitchell, J. F., §§4.25, 4.48, 4.49, 4.52,
    4.53, 5.33, 5.38, 5.50
Mitra, P. P., §4.45
Mody, I., §§5.40, 5n1
Moehring, D. L., §§A1.6, A1.7
Moghaddam, B., §4.36
Molden, S., §§4.8, 8.22
Molina, C., §10.16
Molinari, M., §5.3
Molle, M., §5.8
Mongillo, G., §4.55

Monroe, C., §§A1.6, A1.7
Montague, P. R., §3.2
Montarolo, P. G., §5.9
Montgomery, S., §4.60
Monyer, H., §§4.44, 5.43
Moonen, G., §10.66
Moore, J. W., §9n2
Moore, K. S., §4.26
Moore, S. J., §§5.38, 5.39
Moore, T., §§4.12, 4.24
Moran, J., §5.50
Morgan, J., §5.9
Morikawa, H., §§4.40, 5.6, 5n4
Moriya, M., §4.10
Morris, O. T., §4.55
Morris, R. G., §5.9
Morrone, C., §5.36
Moser, E. I., §§4.8, 8.22
Moser, M. B., §§4.8, 5.9, 8.22
Moss, H. E., §10.6
Motter, B. C., §§4.24, 4.25
Mouginot, D., §5.17
Moulder, K. L., §4n8
Moutoussis, K., §4.21
Movshon, J. A., §§4.46, 4.52
Moxon, K. A., §4.43
Mozart, W. A., §§7.7, 7.9–7.11
Mozer, M. C., §10.36
Müller, C., §9.8
Müller, H. J., §10.35
Müller, M. M., §4.49
Müller, W., §5.5
Muir, J. L., §5.44
Mukamel, R., §9.14
Mukherjee, P., §4.38
Mulkey, R. M., §5.9
Muller, J. R., §4.24
Muller, U., §5.24
Muller-Gass, A., §§4.22, 10.16
Mumford, J., §4.33
Mundale, J., §3.11
Munoz, D. P., §§4.23, 9.9
Murphy, N., §9.14

Murray, R. M., §5.24
Murthy, V. N., §5.7
Musallam, S., §10n9

Na, E. S., §4n8
Na, Y., §5.7
Naccache, L., §§10.16, 10.17, 10.29,
    10.54, 10.65, 10.67, 10.69, 10.77
Nádasdy, Z., §4.35
Nadel, L., §9.2
Nagamine, T., fig. 9.1
Nagata, Y., §5n2
Nagel, E., §A2n5
Naghavi, H. R., §10.65
Nagode, D. A., §5.42
Nagy, J. I., §5.38
Nahum, M., §4.60
Naiem, S. S., §5.40
Nairn, A. C., §§5.9, 5n1
Nairz, O., §A1.10
Nakayama, K., §§4.14, 4.22, 4.48, 5.7,
    10.17, 10.30, 10.35, 10.39, 10.65,
    10.73
Nauen, D. W., §5.12
Nee, D. E., §4.26
Neisser, U., §§10.12, 10.13, 10.56,
    10.78
Nelken, I., §4.60
Nelson, M. J., §4.23
Nelson, S. B., §§4.32, 4.55, 5.9, 5.11,
    5.12, 5.28, 5n5
Nelson, T. E., §§4.45, 5n1
Németh, B., §5.43
Nestor, P. G., §4n12
Neuenschwander, S., §§4.45, 4.53
Neven, H., §4.45
Nevian, T., §5n5
Neville, H. J., §10.16
Newen, A., §9.13
Newman, D., §A2.2
Newsome, W. T., §§4.18, 4.24, 4.31,
    4.43, 4.52, 4.62, 5.12, 5.45
Newton, J., §A1.2

Newton, J. R., §§4.63, 5.1
Nguyen, P. V., §5.9
Ni, A. M., §5.50
Nicholson, K., §9.8
Nicolelis, M. A., §§4.37, 4.38, 4.50,
    4.60, 5.45, 5.46, 5.47, 10n9
Nicoll, R. A., §§5.7, 5.17
Niebergall, R., §4.24
Niedeggen, M., §10.16
Nieuwenhuis, S., §10.36
Nighoghossian, N., §9.1
Nikolic, D., §§4.45, 4.53
Nir, Y., §§10.77, 10.78
Nishida, S., §§10.49, 10.50
Nishijo, H., §4.12
Nissen, M. J., §4.25
Niswender, C. M., §5.24
Nitschke, J. B., fig. 7.1
Nitz, D. A., §§4.22, 5.39
Niznikiewicz, M. A., §4n12
Noble, D., §5.15
Nobre, A. C., §§4.24, 10.13, 10.15
Noë, A., §10.82
Noelle, D. C., §7.11
Norman, D. A., §10.73
Norman, J. F., §10.81
Nosyreva, E., §4n8
Nowak, L. G., §§4.52, 5.3
Nunez, A., §5.42
Nusser, Z., §4n4
Nyberg, L., §10.65

Oakes, L. M., §4.21
Oakley, D. A., §9n2
Oberlander, T. F., §10n20
O'Connor, T., §§3.1, 3n2, 9.14
O'Doherty, J. E., §10n9
O'Doherty, J. P., §4.70
O'Donnell, P., §5.36
Öğmen, H., §10.50
Oh, J. S., §5.24
Oh, M. M., §5.38
Ohara, S., fig. 9.1

Ohno-Shosaku, T., §5.17
Ohta, S., §4.12
Ohno, T., §10n24
Olding, A. W., §5.6
Oliveira, I. C., §2n3
Ollinger, J. M., §4.23
Olmschenk, S., §§A1.6, A1.7
Olney, J. W., §5.5
Olton, D. S., §5.44
Ono, T., §4.12
Oostenveld, R., §§4.22, 4.23, 4.45, 4.47, 4.48, 4.49, 4.53, 4.60, 5.39, 10.16
Oppenheim, J., §§A1.7, A1n5
Oppermann, F., §§4.14, 10.71
Orban, G. A., §4.14
O'Regan, J. K., §10.13, 10.82
O'Reilly, R. C., §§7.11, 8.22
O'Shea, D. J., §4n12
O'Toole, A. J., §§8.18, 8.20
Ott, T., §5.9
Otto, T., §5.36
Overgaard, M., §10.16
Overton, P. G., §4.40
Owen, A. M., §4.26
Ozeki, H., §4.32

Pabst, M., §4.45
Pace-Schott, E. F., §§10.77, 10.78
Pais, I., §4.44
Pálhalmi, J., §5.43
Pallotta, B. S., §§5.23, 5.31
Palm, G., §4.54
Pang, K., §5.44
Paninski, L., §10n9
Pantev, C., §4n15
Paoletti, P., §4n4
Paradiso, M., §§4.25, 4.7, 4.15
Paré, D., §§4n3, 5.7
Pari, G., §9.9
Parker, J. G., §4.40
Parker, W. E., §4.8
Parrish, T. B., §4.24
Pascual-Leone, A., §5n11

Passingham, R. E., §§9.1, 10.43, fig. 9.1
Pasternak, T., §§5.50, 10.30, A1.6, A1.7
Paterek, T., §A1.6
Patterson, W. F., §4.23
Pauen, M., §9n2
Paul, D. L., §§4.44, 5.3
Pauls, J., §7.11
Paulsen, O., §§4.44, 5.3, 5.6, 5.28, 5.40, 5.42, 5.43, 5n1, 5n5
Pawelzik, H., §5.3
Payne, B. R., §5.45
Pearl, D. K., §§9.1, 9.14
Perlmutter, B. A., §5.8
Peeters, M., §10.43
Peigneux, P., §10.66
Peirs, C., §5n3
Pena, M., §10.16
Peng, Y., §10.45
Penrose, R., §§A1.8, A1.9
Penttonen, M., §§4.44, 5.3, 5.43
Perel, S., §10n9
Perez Velazquez, J. L., §4n12
Perin, R., §§4.50, 4.68
Pernier, J., §4.49
Perona, P., §10.71
Perrett, D. I., §§4.9, 4.10, 10.21
Perrucci, M.G., §10.16
Pesaran, B., §4.23
Peshkin, M., §A1.11
Petermann, T., §4.42
Petersen, C. C., §4.42
Petersen, S. E., §4.23
Petit, L., §10.13
Petralia, R. S., §5n2
Petrides, M., §§4.26, 8.1, 8.19
Philiastides, M. G., §4.24
Phillips, C., §10.66
Phillips, W. A., §§4.45, 10.13
Philpot, B. D., §5.28
Pietrini, P., §5.39
Pigarev, I. N., §4.24
Pike, F. G., §5.6, 5.40
Pilgrim, L., §10.6

Pinault, D., §4n11

Pinker, S., §§1.3, 7.3

Pins, D., §§10.16, 10.65

Pinsk, M. A., §4.12

Pinsky, P. F., §5.21

Piomelli, D., §5.17

Pipa, G., §§4.45, 4.53

Pittman, Q. J., §5.17

Pitts, W. H., §5.14

Pizzighello, S., §10.28

Plato, §§1.2, 8n2

Plenz, D., §4.42

Podolsky, B., §A1.5

Poggio, T., §§4.13, 4.14, 4.19, 4.26, fig. 4.3, §§5.15, 5.22, 7.11

Poirazi, P., §5.15

Polger, T., §3.11

Polich, J., §4.22

Poline, J. B., §10.16

Pollen, D. A., §§5.45, 10.77

Poll-The, B. T., §5.5

Polsky, A., §§4.36, 5.22, 5.30

Poo, M. M., §§4.34, 5.11, 5.17, 5.21, 5.42, 5n4, 5n5, 5n6

Popper, K. R., §§7.17, 10.7

Posada, A., §9.1

Posner, M. I., §§4.22, 4.23

Posner, N. I., §10.36

Postle, B., §4.26

Potter, D. D., §10.21

Potter, M. C., §10.13

Potts, G. F., §4.22

Pouille, F., §§4.43, 4.44, 5.3

Poulet, J. F., §4.42

Powell, D. A., §10n15

Powell, K. D., §4.18

Power, A. E., §5.38

Power, J. M., §5.38

Pozo, K., §5.7

Preston, A. R., §5.38

Pribram, K. H., §10n12

Price, B. H., §10n10

Price, D. L., §5.44

Priebe, N. J., §4.32

Prigge, M., §4n12

Prigogine, I., §4.69, §A1n6

Prince, A., §8.22

Prince, D., §§4.52, 4.55, 5.3, 5.39

Principe, J. C., §10n9

Prinzmetal, W., §§4.21, 4.22

Prodromou, M. L., §A1.10

Provine, R. R., §7n5

Przybyszewski, A. W., §5.45

Pu, L., §5n4

Puce, A., §4.12

Pulido, P., §4.33

Pulvermüller, F., §4.55

Putnam, H., §§3.11, 8.24, 8n9

Pylyshyn, Z. W., §§4.21, 4.24, 10.30, 10.32, 10.42

Qin, H., §10.43

Qiu, F. T., §10.50

Quine, W. V., §8.10

Quinlan, P. T., §10.30

Quinton, R. L., §10.5

Quiroga, R. Q., §4.11, fig. 4.4

Rabinowitch, I., §5.7

Racca, C., §5.24

Radcliffe, C. A., §§4.44, 5.3, 5.40

Raghavachari, S., §4.52

Ragozzino, M., §§7.11, 9.8

Raichle, M. E., §10n23

Railo, H., §10.16

Rainer, G., §4.26

Raingo, J., §4n8

Rainwater, A., §4.40

Rajan, K., §4.68

Rajimehr, R., §4.12

Rall, W., §5.15

Ramachandran, V. S., §§4n15, 10.5

Rambhadran, A., §A1.10

Ramcharan, E. J., §4n11

Ramón y Cajal, S., §§4.33, 5n7, frontispiece

Rancz, E. A., §§5.9, 5.11, 5.30
Rao, A., §4.24
Rao, R. P., §5.11
Rao, S. C., §4.26
Rapp, M., §§4n2, 4n3, 5.18, 5.21, 5.23, 5.26, 5n8
Ravizza, S., §9.8
Ray, S., §§4.35, 4.47, 4.50, 5.43, 5.50, fig. 5.5, §5n12
Raymond, J. E., §10.73
Read, S., §10.48
Reavis, E. A, §§10.31, 10.48, 10.49, 10.54, figs. 10.3, 10.4
Reddy, L., §4.11, fig. 4.4
Regehr, W. G., §§3.13, 4.32, 4.55, 4.57, 5.17, 5.36, 5.43
Reichel, F. D., §10.81
Reinagel, P., §4.38
Reitboeck, H. J., §4.45
Reite, M. L., §4n12
Remington, R. W., §4.22
Remy, S., §§5.6, 5.27
Renken, R. J., §7.15
Rensink, R. A., §§4.22, 10.13, 10.35
Reppas, J. B., §4.10
Revonsuo, A., §10.16
Rey, G., §§10.5, A2n1
Reyes, A., §§4.55, 5.45
Reyes, P., §10.65
Reynolds, A. M., §4.70
Reynolds, J. H., §§4.21, 4.25, 4.27, 4.45, 4.48, 4.49, 4.52, 4.53, 4.59, 4.60, 5.33, 5.38, 5.45, 5.50, 10.32
Reynvoet, B., §10.36
Rhie, D. J., §10.88
Rhodes, G., §§8.18, 8.20
Ribary, U., §4.44
Rich, M. M., §5.7
Richardson, R. T., §5.44
Richmond, B. J., §4.39, fig. 4.3
Ridderinkhof, K. R., §10.36
Rieger, J. W., §9n2
Rieke, F., §4.42

Riesenhuber, M., §§4.13, 4.19, 4.26, fig. 4.3, §7.11
Riggio, L., §4.23
Rinzel, J., §5.21
Riso, R. R., §5.37
Rivest, J., §§4.24, A1n6
Rivière, D., §10.16
Rizzolatti, G., §§4.23, 4.24
Robbins, T. W., §§5.38, 5.39, 5.44, 5.45, 9.8
Roberts, A. C., §5.28
Roberts, M., §5.39
Roberts, P. D., §5n6
Roberts, S., §4.70
Robertson, L. C., §10.35
Robinson, D. L., §4.23
Robitaille, N., §10.28
Rocca, C., §5.18
Rocha-Miranda, C. E., §4.10
Rock, I., §§10.29, 10.67, 10.71, 10.74, 10n21
Rockland, K. S., §4.49
Rodriguez, E., §§4.45, 10.16
Rodríguez-Moreno, A., §§5.28, 5n5
Roelfsema, P. R., §§4.23, 4.24, 4.45, 4.53
Roger, G., §§A1.6, A1.7
Rogers, J. H., §5.3
Rogers, R. D., §9.1
Rogers, S. J., §4n12
Rogers-Ramachandran, D., §4n15
Roitman, J. D., §4.18
Rojas, D. C., §4n12
Rokem, A., §§4.22, 4.38, 5.36
Rolfs, M., §4.23
Rollman, G. B., §9n1
Rolls, E. T., §§4.9, 4.10, 4.12, 10.21
Roman, G., §4.70
Romani, G.L., §10.16
Roopun, A., §§4.44, 5.40, 5.24
Rorie, A. E., §§4.45, 4.49, 4.53
Rosch, E. H., §8.15
Rose, J. C., §§5.6, 5.9

Rosen, N., §A1.5
Rosenberger, G., §5.24
Roser, M. E., §5n6
Roskies, A., §§1n1, 9.4, 9.5, 9.14, 9n2, 9n3, 9n5, figs. 9.2, 9.3
Rosner, R., §4.70
Rossi, A. F., §§4.25, 4.45
Rossi, S., §10.16
Rossini, P. M., §10.16
Ross-Sheehy, S., §4.21
Roth, A., §§4.70, 5.9, 5.11, 5.21, 5.22
Rothman, S. M., §5.5
Rougier, N. P., §7.11
Rousselet, G. A., §§4.14, 10.71
Rowe, M. A., §A1.6
Roxin, A., §5.22
Roy, E., §4.33
Roy, R., §4.42
Royer, S., §5.7
Rozov, A., §§4.44, 4.55, 5n1
Rudelson, J. R., §7.12
Rudolph, M., §4n3
Rudrauf, D., §10.44
Russell, B., §§2.9, 8.8, 10n5
Rutherford, L. C., §5.7
Ryou, J. W., §10n15

Saalmann, Y. B., §4.24
Sabatini, B. L., §5.22
Sackett, C. A., §A1.6
Sackur, J., §§10.16, 10.17, 10.54, 10.65, 10.67, 10.69, 10.77
Sagi, D., §10.73
Saha, R. N., §5.9
Saha, S., §5.43
Sahakian, B. J., §9.8
Saint-Cyr, J. A., §9.8
Saito, H., §4.10
Sakmann, B., §§4.32, 4.55, 5.6, 5.11, 5.18, 5.21, 5.23, 5.35, 5n5, 5n8, fig. 5.4, §A1.10
Saleem, K. S., §4.26
Salin, P. A., §4.49

Salinas, E., §§4.59, 5.50
Salisbury, D., §§4.22, 4n12, 10.16
Salpeter, E. E., §4.66
Salpeter, M. M., §4.66
Salter, M. W., §5n1
Salti, M., §10.16
Salussolia, C. L., §A1.10
Salzman, C. D., §5.45
Samengo, I., §§4.38, 5.36
Sameshima, K., §4.38
Sanchez, A., §4.33
Sanchez-Vives, M. V., §§4.52, 5.3, 5.42
Sanghera, M. K., §4.10
Santollo, J., §10.44
Santucci, D. M., §10n9
Sarbadhikari, S. N., §4.68
Sarter, M., §§5.38, 5.39, 5.44, 5.45, 5.46
Saruwatari, M., §4.52
Saunier, C. F., §4.40
Savain, L., §8.1
Scanziani, M., §§4.43, 4.44, 5.3
Scepkowski, L. A., §10n10
Schacher, S., §5.9
Schacter, D. L., §10n23
Schaefer, A. T., §5.21
Schaffer, E. S., §4.32
Schall, J. D., §4.23
Scharlau, I., §4.48
Schell, M. J., §§2n3, 5.4, 5n2
Scherberger, H., §10n9
Schiller, J., §§4.36, 5.6, 5.22, 5.30
Schiller, P. H., §§4.24, 4.39, 10.16
Schiller, Y., §§5.6, 5.35
Schlegel, A. A., §§4.39, 7.12, 9.4, figs. 9.2, 9.3, §9n5
Schmechel, D. E., §5.3
Schmid, A. M., §4.14
Schmid, M. C., §10.21
Schmidt, B. K., §10.13
Schmitz, D., §4.55
Schmitz, F., §4.23
Schnakers, C., §10.66
Schneider, F., §4n12

Schneider, W., §§4.45, 10.30
Schnitzler, I., §4.23
Schoepfer, R., §5n9
Schoffelen, J. M., §§4.49, 4.60
Scholl, B. J., §§10.18, 10.30, 10.32, 10.42
Schollmeier, F., §5.9
Scholte, H. S., §§10.15, 10.16, 10.17, 10.36, 10n22
Schooler, J. W., §9.4
Schouten, J. L., §4.12
Schröder, J.-H., §§4.45, 4.53
Schröger, E., §§4.22, 10.16
Schröter, H., §9n4
Schuirer, G., §7.12
Schulman, H., §§5.9, 5n1
Schuman, E. M., §§4n8, 5.9
Schuz, A., §4.54
Schwark, H. D., §5.3
Schwartz, A., §§8.1, 8.19, 10n9
Schwartz, J., §§4.7, 5.9
Schwartz, S., §10.26
Schwarzbach, J., §§4.22, 4.24, 10.16
Sculthorpe, L., §§4.22, 10.16
Searle, J., §8.8
Seeburg, P. H., §5n1
Segal, M., §4.55
Segers, G., §10.36
Segev, I., §§4n2, 4n3, 5.7, 5.18, 5.21, 5.23, 5.26, 5n8
Sejnowski, T. J., §4.66, 5.11, 5.21, 5.35, 5.40, 5.50, 10.18
Selfridge, O., §4.13, fig. 4.3
Selleri, F., §A1.6
Sellitto, C., §§4.44, 5.3
Sen, K., §§4.32, 4.55
Sengpiel, F., §4.34
Senn, V., §9.8
Serences, J. T., §§4.24, 4.25
Sergent, C., §§10.16, 10.17, 10.54, 10.65, 10.67, 10.69, 10.74, 10.75, 10.77
Sergent, J., §4.12

Serruya, M. D., §10n9
Shadlen, M. N., §§4.18, 4.31, 4.43, 4.46, 4.52, 4.62, 5.12, 5.45
Shahan, T. A., §4.70
Shallice, T., §10.61
Shalom, D., §10.43
Shannon, C.E., §§6n1, 8.6
Shao, X. M., §A1.10
Shapiro, K., §4.23
Shapiro, K. L., §§10.16, 10.73
Shapiro, L., §§3.11, 3.12, 4.61
Shapley, R., §4.49
Sheinberg, D. L., §§4.9, 4.23, 4.48, 5.50
Sheliga, B. M., §4.23
Shelley, C., §5.25
Shen, K., §5n1
Shen, W., §4.40
Shenton, M. E., §§4n12, 5.24
Shergill, S. S., §9n6
Sherman, S. M., §§4.27, 4.38, 4.38, 4.59, 4n11
Shevell, S. K., §§10.49, 10.50
Shew, W. L., §4.42
Shibasaki, H., fig. 9.1
Shih, S. I., §§10.12, 10.13, 10.70, 10.71
Shim, W. M., §§10.13, 10.15
Shimojo, S., §§10.49, 10.50
Shin, M., §2n3
Shipp, S., §4.21
Shors, T. J., §10.44
Shu, Y., §§4.33, 4.43, 4.44, 5.3, 5.42
Shuai, Y., §10.43
Shulman, G. L., §§4.24, 4.26
Shulz, D. E., §5.11
Siegel, M., §§4.23, 4.49
Siegle, J. H., §5.42
Sigman, M., §10.43
Sik, A., §§4.35, 4.44
Silberberg, G., §4.50
Silver, M. A., §§4.14, 4.22
Silverstein, C., §10.18
Simon, S. A., §4.60
Simons, D. J., §§10.56, 10n12

Sinai, A., §4.35

Singer, W., §§4.21, 4.23, 4.43, 4.44, 4.45, 4.49, 4.53, 4.60, 4n3, 4n12, 5.46, 10.16, 10.88

Singh, K. D., §§4.44, 4.49

Sinnott-Armstrong, W., §§1n1, 9.2, 9.4, figs. 9.2, 9.3, §9n5

Sirigu, A., §9.1

Sirota, A., §4.60

Sjöström, P. J., §§5.9, 5.11, 5.12, 5.27, 5.28, 5n5

Skaggs, H., §10n15

Slachevsky, A., §10.65

Slater, R., §10n20

Sligte, I. G., §§10.15, 10.17, 10n22

Smallwood, J., §9.4

Smith, A. M., §10n10

Smith, F., §10.50

Smith, E. E., §4.26

Smith, J. E., §4.24

Smith, M. A., §§4.47, 4.48, 5.32

Smith, P. A., §10.21

Smolensky, P., §8.22

Snead, O. C. III, §4n12

Snell, K., §5.5

Snider, R. K., §4.38

Snyder, A. Z., §§4.23, 4.24, 10n23

Snyder, C. R. R., §10.36

Snyder, L. H., §§4.18, 4.19

Soames, S., §8.11

Sober, E., §3.11

Soderling, T. R., §5n1

Softky, W. R., §§4.52, 4.62

Sola, R. G., §4.33

Solomon, P. R., §10.44

Solstad, T., §§4.8, 8.22

Soltesz, I., §5.3

Somers, D., §4.45

Sommer, F., §4.54

Somogyi, P., §§4.44, 4.55, 5.3

Sompolinsky, H., §§4.32, 4n3

Song, J.-H., §10.14

Song, S., §5.11

Soon, C. S., §9.14

Soong, T. W., §5.9

Sørensen, T. A., §10.16

Sorger, B., §4.12

Spalding, M. C., §10n9

Spekreijse, H., §§4.24, 10.15

Spencer, K. M., §4n12

Spengler, S., §9.13

Sperling, G., §§10.12, 10.13, 10.17, 10.70, 10.71, 10.78

Sperry, R., §A2.2

Sporns, O., §4.45

Sprengel, R., §5n1

Spruston, N., §§5.6, 5.18, 5.22, 5.23, 5.27, 5.35, 5.38, 5.39, fig. 5.4

Squires, N. K., §§4.22, 10.16

St. Clair, R., §§10.49, 10.50

Staff, N. P., §§5.27, 5.35

Stalnaker, R., §8.11

Stambaugh, C. R., §10n9

Stanley, C. M., §4.24

Stanley, G. B., §4.38

Stapp, H. P., §A1.9

Stein, J. M., §5.6

Stengers, I., §4.69

Stepanyants, A., §4.32

Stephan, K. E., §5.24

Steriade, M., §§4.34, 4n12, 5.38, 5.42

Sterkin, A., §4.42

Stevens, C. F., §§5.25, 5.36, fig. 5.5, §5n1

Stevens, S. F., §4.66

Steward, O., §5.9

Stewart, M., §4n15

Stiles, J. R., §4.66

Stocco, A., §§7.15, 9.8

Stoerig, P., §10.16

Stoet, G., §4.19

Storey, A. E., §10.5

Storm, R. W., §§4.21, 10.30, 10.32, 10.42

Strack, S., §5n1

Strawson, G., §§1.5, 7.4, 7.8, 7.12

Strick, P. L., fig. 9.1
Stryker, M. P., §5.8
Stuart, G., §§5.18, 5.20, 5.21, 5.23, 5.35, 5n8, fig. 5.4
Su, J., §4n8
Suchanek, B., §5n1
Sucher, N. J., §5n2
Suckling, J. M., §§4.44, 5.3
Sugase, Y., §4.12
Sugihara, G., §4.70
Sugihara, T., §10.50
Sun, Q., §5.7
Sun, W., §5n1
Sundberg, K. A., §§4.48, 4.49, 4.52, 5.50
Sur, M., §§4.63, 5.1
Surmeier, D. J., §4.40
Surtees, R., §5.5
Sussillo, D., §§4.42, 4.55
Sussman, R., §§10.13, 10.15
Sutherland, G. R., §5.42
Sutton, M. A., §4n8
Suzuki, S., §§10.49, 10.50
Svennenfors, B., §4.55
Svoboda, K., §§5.5, 5.9, 5.15, 5.22
Swadlow, H. A., §4.38
Swainson, R., §10.35
Sweatt, J. D., §5.6
Switala, A., §4.33
Synofzik, M., §§9.13, 9n6
Szabó, I., §4.35
Szilard, L., §A1n3
Szyszka, P., §10.43

Tafazzoli, A., §5n2
Taguchi, T., §5.7
Takahashi, N., §§4n4, 5.15, 5.22
Takatsuki, K., §10n15
Takechi, H., §5.5
Takehara, K., §10n15
Takehara-Nishiuchi, K., §10n15
Tallon-Baudry, C., §§4.49, 10.29
Tamás, G., §§5.3, 5.40

Tamè, L., §4.23
Tamura, R., §4.12
Tan, S. E., §5n1
Tanaka, H., §5n2
Tanaka, K., §§4.9, 4.10
Tang, A. H., §5.42
Tang, C., §4.42
Tanimoto, H., §10.43
Tank, D. W., §§4.54, 5.5
Tao, H. W., §§5.11, 5.17
Tapia, M., §4.14
Tashiro, A., §4.55
Taylor, A. E., §9.8
Taylor, D. M., §10n9
Taylor, K., §4.45
Teale, P. D., §4n12
Tegmark, M., §A1.8
Tegner, J., §4.52
Tesselaar, J. P., §§10.15, 10.17, 10n22
Theeuwes, J., §4.22
Thiagarajan, T., §5.35
Thiele, A., §5.39
Thier, P., §§4.59, 9n6
Thompson, I. D., §4.38
Thompson, R. F., §§5n1, 10.44, 10n15
Thomson, A. M., §§4.55, 5.3
Thornton, I. M., §10.16
Tibbetts, P. E., §10n10
Tiesinga, P. H. E., §5.35
Tillery, S. I., §10n9
Timofeev, I., §5.42
Todd, J. J., §§4.26, 10.14, 10.30
Todd, J. T., §10.81
Todd, S., §10.50
Todorov, A. T., §5.25
Tolhurst, D. J., §4.52
Tonegawa, S., §5.9
Tong, Z. Y., §4.40
Toni, I., §10.43
Tonomura, A., §A1.11
Tononi, G., §§4.27, 4.45, 5.8, 5.24, 8.6, 10.77, 10.78
Tootell, R. B., §§4.12, 10.21

Torre, V., §§5.15, 5.22
Torres, D., §10.16
Torrigiano, G. G., §5.7
Toth, K., §§4.44, 5.3
Toth, L. J., §4.19
Towers, S. K., §4.44
Towles, A. C., §5.3
Toyoizumi, T., §§4.42, 4.55
Trampel, R., §9.14
Traub, R. D., §§4.23, 4.44, 5.3, 5.24, 5.40, 5.43
Traynelis, S. F., §§4n4, 5.4
Treisman, A., §§4.21, 5.44, 5.49, 10.30
Treue, S., §§4.24, 4.25, 4.48, 5.44, 5.50
Trevena, J., §§9n2, 9n4
Trinh, D., §5n2
Trommald, M., §5.9
Troyer, T. W., §4.32, 5.45
Tsal, Y., §10.30
Tsao, D. Y., §§4.11, 4.12
Tsao, J. W., §10.5
Tse, P. U., §§3.8, 4.14, 4.21, 4.23, 4.24, 4.39, 4.48, 5n11, 7.11, 7.12, 8.18, 8.26, 9.4, figs. 9.2, 9.3, §§9n5, 10.18, 10.30, 10.31, 10.48, 10.49, 10.52, 10.54, 10.64, 10.65, 10.67, 10.81, fig. 10.3, fig. 10.4, §A1n6
Tseng, C. H., §10n1
Tsien, R. W., §§5.9, 5n1
Tsien, R. Y., §5.15
Tsodyks, M., §4.55
Tsuchiya, N., §§10.28, 10.32, 10.33, 10n18
Tsuda, I., §4.68
Tucker, D. M., §4.22
Turano, F. J., §2n3
Turatto, M., §4.23
Turing, A., §8.1
Turner, R., §9.14
Turrigiano, G. G., §§5.7, 5.11, 5.12, 5.28, 5n5
Tutunculer, B., §4.43
Tversky, A., §§8.17, 10.22

Tye, M., §1n1
Tyzio, R., §5n9
Tzavos, A., §9.8

Ueno, S., §4.12
Uhlhaas, P., §§4.45, 4.53, 4n12
Uhlrich, D. J., §4.59
Ulivelli, M., §10.16
Ullman, S., §§5.45, 8.26
Umilta, C., §4.24
Ungerleider, L. G., §4.8, 4.12, 4.26, 10.13,, §10.21,, §10.50, 10n12
Unno, S., §4.52
Urioste, R., §4.35

Vallar, G., §10.77
Vallortigara, G., §10n16
Valsecchi, M., §4.23
van Aalderen-Smeets, S. I., §§4.22, 10.16
Van Boxtel, G. J., §9n4
van Boxtel, J. J., §§10.49, 10.50
Van den Bussche, E., §10.36
Van der Schaaf, E. R., §10.44
van der Wee, N. J., §7.15
Vanderwolf, C. H., §4.44
van der Zouw, G., §A1.10
van Doorn, A. J., §10.81
Van Essen, D. C., §§4.8, 4.24, 4.49, 4n5
van Gaal, S., §10.36
Vangkilde, S., §10.16
Van Gulick, R., §§1.15, A2.2
van Helden, D., §4.66
Van Hoesen, G. W., §4.49
van Lier, R., §§10.49, 10.50
VanRullen, R., §10.71
van Swinderen, B., §10.45
van Tol, M. J., §7.15
van Vreeswijk, C., §4.32
Varela, F., §4.45
Varela, J. A., §§4.32, 4.55
Vaughan, J. W., §§4.38, 4.59
Vaughn, J. E., §5.3

Vazdarjanova, A., §5.38
Vecchio, F., §10.16
Vecera, S. P., §10.15
Vecsey, C. G., §5.6
Veer, I. M., §7.15
Velliste, M., §10n9
Verchinski, B. A., §7.15
Vergeer, M., §§10.49, 10.50
Verkuyl, J. M., §4.55
Verstraten, F. A., §§10.32, 10.33, 10.43
Vetter, P., §§5.21, 5.22
Vetter, T., §§8.18, 8.20
Vida, I., §§4.33, 4.44, 4.53, 5.40
Vidyasagar, T. R., §4.24
Vierling-Claassen, D., §5.42
Vijayraghavan, S., §4.40
Villarroel, A., §A1.10
Vincent, J. L., §10n23
Vogel, E. K., §§4.21, 10.13, 10.16, 10.30, 10.32
Vogels, T. P., §4.68
Vogt, A., §§4.44, 5.40
Vohs, K., §§3.1, 3n2
Voisin, D. L., §5n3
Von Cramon, D. Y., §9.13
von der Heydt, R., §§5.37, 10.50
von der Malsburg, C., §§4.45, 4.54, 4.55
von Neumann, J., §§6n1, 8n1
von Wright, J. M., §4.25
Vos-Andreae, J., §A1.10
Vosgerau, G., §9.13
Voss, M., §9n6
Voytko, M. L., §5.44
Vuilleumier, P., §10.26

Wager, T. D., §4.26
Wagner, U., §4.55
Wakeman, E. A., §4.34
Walker, E. H., §A1.8
Wall, V. Z., §4.40
Wallis, J., §7.11
Walsh, C. J., §10.5

Walsh, V., §§5n11, 10n1
Walter, H., §10n10
Walter, W. G., §9n4
Wang, D. L., §4.45
Wang, H. X., §5.12
Wang, J., §7.15
Wang, L., §7.15
Wang, M., §4.40
Wang, Q., §10.54
Wang, S. S., §5.6
Wang, X., §§4.43, 5.36
Wang, X. J., §4.35
Wang, Y., §§4.33, 4.55, 5.28, 5.3, 5.36, fig. 5.5
Wang, Y. T., §5n1
Wang, Z., §4.14
Ward, L. M., §5.46
Ward, M. A., §5n1
Warzecha, A. K., §4.70
Warzecha, K., §4.70
Watanabe, M., §§5.28, 9.9
Waterhouse, B. D., §5.38
Waters, J., §4.32
Watkins, J. C., §5n9
Watson, J. B., §10n5
Watson, T. L., §§8.18, 8.20
Waxler, E., §10.44
Webb, W., §4.35
Webster, L. C., §5n1
Wede, J., §10.50
Weeks, S. R., §10.5
Wegner, D. M., §§9.1, 9.13, 9.14, 9.17, 9n2
Wehner, S., §§A1.7, A1n5
Wehr, M., §4.43
Weible, A. P., §10n15
Weinberger, D. R., §7.15
Weiner, K. S., §4.12
Weiss, C., §§5.38, 10n15
Weisz, D. J., §10.44
Wenk, G. L., §5.45
Wennberg, R. A., §4n12
Wennekers, T., §4.54

Wenner, P., §5.7

Wenthold, R. J., §5n2

Wessberg, J., §10n9

Westenbroek, R. E., §4n2

Westin, C. F., §5.24

Weyand, T., §§4.38, 4n11

Wheatley, T., §§3n3, 9.1, 9.4, 9.13,
    9.14, 9.17, figs. 9.2, 9.3, §§9n5,
    10.48, 10.49, 10n13

Whitfield, M. F., §10n20

Whitford, A. S., §10n9

Whitney, D., §10.48

Whittington, M. A., §§4.23, 4.44, 4.45,
    5.3, 5.24, 5.40

Wible, C. G., §5.36

Wichmann, P., §10.16

Wickelgren, W. A., §4.54

Wienbruch, C., §4n15

Wiener, S. I., §5.36

Wiesel, T. N., §4.9

Wiesenfield, K., §4.42

Wilent, W. B., §4.32

Wiley, R. G., §5.44

Wilkinson, L. S., §5.44

Williams, J. T., §4.40

Williams, M. J., §5.44

Williams, S. R., §§5.18, 5.20

Wilson, C. J., §5.42

Wilson, F. D., §5.9

Wilson, R. I., §5.17

Wilson, T. W., §4n12

Winter, A. L., §9n4

Wise, K., §§4.35, 4.44, 5.3

Witmer, G., §3.11

Wittenberg, G. M., §5.6

Witter, M. P., §§4.8, 8.22

Wittgenstein, L., §§2.9, 8.8, 8.14, 8.15,
    8.16, 8n6, 10n5

Wokke, M. E., §§10.15, 10.17, 10n22

Wolf, R., §§4.70, 10.45

Wolfe, J. M., §§10.30, 10.58

Wollmuth, L. P., §A1.10

Wollner, D. A., §4n2

Wolpert, D. H., §A1n3

Wolpert, D. M., §§9.13, 9n6, 10.26

Womelsdorf, T., §§4.23, 4.45, 4.47,
    4.48, 4.49, 4.53, 4.60, 5.39

Woodman, G. F., §§10.13, 10.28

Woodruff-Pak, D. S., §10n15

Worley, A., §10n20

Worley, P. F., §5.7

Wright, E. W., §§9.1, 9.14

Wundt, W., §10n5

Wurtz, R. H., §§4.24, 4.27, 4.38, 4.39,
    4.43, 4.48, 4n11, fig. 4.3

Wyart, V., §§4.49, 10.29

Wynne-Edwards, K. E., §10.5

Xi, W., §10.45

Xu, F., §10.30

Xu, Y., §§4.26, 10.14

Xue, J. T., §4.59

Yakel, J. L., §A1.10

Yamamoto, H., §5n1

Yamane, S., §§4.9, 4.12

Yamane, Y., §4.14

Yan, C., §7.15

Yan, J., §5.3

Yang, H., §§4.42, 7.15

Yang, J., §A1.10

Yanike, M., §4.19

Yantis, S., §§4.22, 4.24, 4.25

Yao, M., §5.35

Yaping, E., §5.9

Yarom, Y., §§4n2, 5.18, 5.21, 5.23, 5.26,
    5n8

Yasuda, R., §5.7

Yau, K.-W., §4.68

Yazawa, S., fig. 9.1

Yeh, S.-L., §10.31

Yilmaz, E., §10.81

Yin, H. H., §4.70

Yizhar, O., §4n12

Ylinen, A., §§4.35, 4.44

Yokotani, N., §5n2

Young, J. C., §4.12
Young, T, §10n17
Young, W. S., §4.66
Yu, A. J., §4.22
Yu, L. M., §5.7
Yu, S., §4.42
Yue, D. T., §5.9
Yuille, A., §10.22
Yuste, R., §§4.55, 4.60, 5.5, 5.6, 5.16

Zacksenhouse, M., §10n9
Zador, A. M., §4.43
Zeilinger, A., §A1.10
Zeki, S., §§4.21, 5n11, 10.64, 10.65
Zhabotinsky, A., §5.9
Zhang, D., §5.7
Zhang, K., §10.45
Zhang, L. I., §5.11
Zhang, W., §5.38
Zhong, Y., §10.43
Zhou, H., §§4.24, 4.49, 5.37
Zhu, H., §§5.6, 5.9
Ziegler, R., §10.50
Zieglgaensberger, W., §5.21
Zikopoulos, B., §4.27
Zilberter, Y., §4.55
Zipfel, W., §4.35
Zucker, R. S., §4.55
Zugaro, M., §4.60
Zukowski, M., §§A1.6, A1.7
Zweifel, L. S., §4.40

Subject Index

Items in boldface are defined in the glossary.

Access consciousness, §10.33

Acetylcholine, §§4.22, 4n4, 5.38, 5.39, 5.40, 5.41, 5.42, 5.44, 5.45, 5.50, 10.87, 10.88, A.10

Achromatopsia, §10n2

Action, §A1n2
 types of, §§3.1, 4.16

Action potential, §§2.4, 5n7

Adaptation, §§10.50, 10.51

Addressing problem. *See* Routing problem

Adequacy, §§7.22, 7n11, 8.4

After-discharge burst, §4.39

Afterimages, §§10.49, 10.50, fig. 10.2, §10n17

AIT. *See* Anterior inferior temporal lobe

Akinetopsia, §10n2

Algorithm, §§7n2, 8.1, 8.2, 8.22, 8.24, 8.26

Alien hand syndrome, §3n3, 10.26

Allocentric coordinates, §4.8

Allodynia, §5n3

Alpha brainwave, §§4.47, 4n6

Amnesia, §10.44

Amodal completion, §1.10

AMPA, §§2n2, 2n3, 4.36, 4n4, 5.6–5.9, 5.19, 5.21, 5.31, 5.38, 5.40, 5n9, 10.87–10.89

Amygdala, §§4.8, 4.14, 9.8, 10.21, 10n12

Anaesthesia, §4.29

Anarchic hand syndrome, §10n10

Annealing, §§4.70, 5.8, 5.51, 5n2

Anterior cingulate, §§3.2, fig. 7.1, §§10.9, 10.40, 10.61, 10n10, 10n23

Anterior inferior temporal lobe, §§4.9, 4.11, 4.12, 4.13, figs. 4.3, 5.6

Anterior insula, §§4.26, 10.61, 10.66, 10n23

Anticipation, §9.5

Antidromic propagation, §5n8

Apical dendrites, §§5.14, 5.21, 5.30, fig. 5.4, §5n8

Aplysia, §10.43

A posteriori knowledge, §§8.10–8.13, A3

Apparent motion, §10.18

Apperceptive agnosia, §10n2

A priori knowledge, §§8.10–8.13

Argument from propositional ambiguity, §§8.10–8.13

"As if" indeterminism, §7.18

Associative learning, §10.43

Astrocytes, §§5.5, 5.28

Attention, §§2.5, 2.10, 2.11, 4.14, 4.21–4.28, 4.38, 4.39, 4.45–4.53, 4.59, 4.60, 4n11, 5.38–5.51, fig. 5.6,

Attention (cont.)
  7.12, 9.8–9.11, 10.6, 10.12, 10.6–
  10.17, 10.23–10.87, figs. 10.1, 10.2,
  10.4, §§10n9, 10n11, 10n12, 10n21
  types of, §10.28
  without consciousness, §§10.28,
  10.31, 10n12
Attentional binding. *See* Binding
Attentional blink, §§10.73, 10.74, 10.76
Attentional modulation of qualia,
  §§10.48, 10.49, 10.88, fig. 10.1
Attentional selection, §§4.27, 5.50, 9.8,
  10.12, 10.23, 10.27, 10.36, 10.41
Attentional shifting, §§7.12, 10.28,
  10.36, 10.37, 10.49, 10.82
Attentional tracking, §§2.10, 10.24,
  10.28–10.47, 10.57, 10.61, 10.81,
  10.84
Attractors, §§4.69, 6.8, 10.11, 10n14
Autism, §§4n12, 10.21
Automatic transmission mode, §§9.8,
  9.9, 10.79
Automaticity, §§10.36, 10.38, 10.46,
  10.86
Automatization, §§10.53, figs. 10.3,
  10.4
Axon hillock, §§4.2, 4.3, 4.6, 4.59,
  4.63, fig. 4.1, 4n2, 5.3, 5.14
Axonal bouton, §5.28

Back-propagating action potentials,
  §§5.14–5.28, 5.31, 5.38, fig. 5.4, §5n8
Backward causation, §§6.16–6.20, A1.11
Balint's syndrome, §§10.35, 10.77
Barcan proof, §A3
Barrel cortex, §4.35
Basal dendrites, §§5.21, 5.22, 5.30
Basal forebrain, §§4.22, 4.37, 5.38,
  5.44, 5.47, 5.48, fig. 5.6
Basal ganglia, §§4.40, 4.49, 4.70, 4n7,
  7.11, 7.15, 9.8, 9.9, fig. 9.1
Baseline firing rate, §§4.29–4.35, 4.42,
  4.46, 4n7, 5.37

Basic argument against free will, §§7.4,
  7.9
Basket cells, §§4.44, 5.3, 5.16, 5.40,
  5.42, 5.43, fig. 5.1
Bayesian inference, §10.19
Behaviorism, §10n5
Beta brainwave, §§4.23, 4n6
Binding, attentional, §§4.26, 4.28, 4.44,
  4.45, 4.47, 4.50, 4.53, 5.48, 5.49,
  10.24, 10.30, 10.33, 10.56, 10.58,
  10.87, 10.88
Binding problem, §§2.5, 2.11,
  4.21–4.28, 4.45–4.53, 5.38–5.51,
  10.17, 10.27, 10.34, 10.35, 10.54,
  10.55–10.57, 10.59, 10.66, 10.69,
  10.77, 10.83, 10.87, 10.88
Biological motion, §4.14
Blindsight, §10.4
Bodycentric coordinates, §4.8
Boolean operations, §§5.15, 5.22
Border cells, §8.22
Bottom-up, §§6.14, 7.6, 7.18, 7n7,
  10.36, 10.48, 10.86, 10.87, 10.88,
  10n8
Boundary conditions, §4.69
Brainstem, §5n3
Brainwaves, §4n6
Broad spiking neurons, §4.52
Brodmann area 10, §§3.2, fig. 7.1,
  10.61, 10n8
Brownian motion, §§4.66, 4.67, 6.23
Buridan's ass, §7.21
Burst coding, §§4.51, 4.53, 5.23, 5.28,
  5.29, 5.32, 5.33, 5.34, 5.35, 5.37,
  5.51, 10.87–10.89
Burst packets, §§4.48, 4.53, 5.34, 5.51,
  10.87–10.89
Burst packet track, §10.89
Burst plasticity, §5.38
Burst refractory period, §5.43
Bursts, §§2.5, 3.13, 4.33, 4.35–4.48,
  4.51–4.53, 4.59, 4.62, fig. 4.5,
  §§4n11, 5.3, 5.6, 5.10, 5.12–5.51,

figs. 5.5, 5.6, §§5n8, 5n10, 5n12, 10.1, 10.87–10.89, A1.10

CA1 synapse, fig. 5.5
Calcium, §§5.4, 5.5, 5.6, 5.9, 5.17, 5.23, 5.35, fig. 5.2, §5n5
Calcium channel, §§5.21, 5.23, 5.30, fig. 5.2
Calmodulin, §5.9
Caricatures, §§2.9, 7.11, 8.20
Categorization, §§4.12, 4.19, 8.15, 8.17, 8n7
Causa sui, §§2.1, 2.4, 2.7, 3.9, 3.10, 3.13, 3.14, 5.51, 6.16, 7.1, 7.4, 7.5, 7.8, 7.10, 7.19, 7.23, 9.15, 10.1, A2.2
Causal closure, §§A2, 6.13
Causal filter, §6.18
Causality, §§A1.2, A1.3, 5n6, 6.10, 6.17, 6.21, 7.2, fig. 9.4, §10.21
Central pattern generator, §1.11
Central processing unit, §8.1
Cerebellum, §§4.70, 4n7, 5n2
Chains of command, §10.25
Chance, §7n6
Chandelier cells, §5.3, fig. 5.1
Change blindness, §10.56
Change detection, §§4.32, 5.37
Chaos, §§4.42, 4.68, 4.69, 5.25, 6.8
Character, §§7.12–7.14
Chattering cells, §4.44
Chemistry, §§6.9, 6n5, A1.3
Choice, §§4.23, 7.2, 7.13, 7.21, 7.22, 10.46
Cholinergic feedback, §§4.22, 5.38, 5.39, 5.40, 5.41, 5.42, 5.44, 10.87, 10.88
Chunking, §§6.15, 10.30, 10.53–10.61, 10.88, figs. 10.3, 10.4
Circular causation, §4.69
Closure, §§A2, 6.13
CNV. *See* Contingent negative variations
Cognitive inference, §10.19

Coherence, §§4.45, 4.48, 4.51
Coincidence detection, §§1.16, 4.4, 4.9, 4.45, 4.51, 4.64, 4n3, 4n4, 5.4, 5.19, 5.22, 5.23, 5.27, 5.28, 5.29, 5.34, 5.39, 5.44, 5.51, fig. 5.2, §§5n1, 6.1, 6.3, 6.5, 6.6, 6.13
Coma, §4.29
Command neuron, §1.11
Common language problem, §§10.24, 10.25, 10n8
Compartmentalization of potential, §§4.1, 4.66, 5.5, 5.15, 5.16, 5.22
Compatibilism, §§2.1, 3.3, 7.2, 7.18, 7n1, 7.18
Complex cell, §§4.9, 6.15
Computational models, §8.3
Computers, §§5.34, 7.15, 7n2, 8.1, 8.2, 8.24, 8n1, 10n7
Condensed matter, §6.8
Conditioning, §§4.40, 4.70, 5n4, 10.43
Cones, §§4.7, 10.50
Configual qualia. *See* Type 2 qualia
Conscious will, §9.1
Consciousness, §§2.10, 2.11, 4.8, 5.24, 7.23, 7n3, chs. 9, 10. *See also* Experience
Conservation laws, §§6.12, 6.13
Constancy operations, §§10.22, 10.23, 10.48, fig. 10.1
Context, §§4.14, 4.15, 9.9, 10.7, 10.9, 10.10, 10.24, 10.25, 10.41
Contingent, §§8.10–8.13
Contingent negative variations, §9n4
Contralateral delay amplitude, §10.37
Corollary discharge. *See* Efference copy
Corticothalamocortical loops, §§4.28, 5.16
Counterfactual definiteness, §A1.6
Couvade syndrome, §10.5
CPU. *See* Central processing unit
Creativity, §§4.70, 5n2, 6.23, 7.7, 7.10, 7.11, 7.13, 7n2, 10.1, 10.85

Criteria, §§3.5–3.7
Criterial causation, §§2.3, 2.6–2.8, ch.
  3, §§4.61, 5.62, 4.69, 4n1, 5.25, 5.51,
  6.1, 6.2, 6.8–6.14, 6.17–6.23,
  7.4–7.11, 7.18, 7.19, 7.22, 7.23, 8.1,
  8.2, 10.1–10.4, A3n3, fig. 3.1
Criterialism, §§2.3, 2.6–2.8, 3.5–3.15,
  fig. 3.1, §§3n5, 4.61, 4.62, 4.69, 4n1,
  5.25, 5.51, 8.8, 8.9, 8.13, 8.14, 8.16
Criticality, §§4.42, 4.70
Critical period, §5.28
Crow brain, §5n2
Cymothoa exigua, §10n9

Daydreaming, §§2.11, 10.60, 10.79,
  10.85, 10n23, 10n24
Death spell, §10.5
Decision-making, §§4.12, 4.15,
  4.17–4.20, 4.23, 7.20, 7.21, 7.22,
  10.36
Decision tree, §9.16
Decoder, §§2.8, 3.10, 3.12, 4.10, 4.9,
  4.11, 4.60, 5.34, 6.2–6.8, 6.11, 6.12,
  6.13, 6.15, 6.18, 6.21, 6.23, 6n1, 6n3,
  7.6, 7.8, 8.6–8.8, 10.58
Decorrelation, §§4.25, 4.48, 4.49, 4.53,
  5.24, 5.38, 5.39, 5.44, 5.45, 5.48,
  5.50, 10.32
Deep cortical layers, §§4.49, fig. 5.4
Default mode network, §10n23
Delay conditioning, §§5n4, 10.43
Delayed match-to-sample experiments,
  §4.19
Deliberative action, §§9.12–9.18, 10.84,
  10.85
Delta brainwave, §§4n6, 5.8
Dendrite, fig. 2.1, §4.45, fig. 4.1,
  §§4n4, 5.2, 5.3, 5.17, 5.18, 5.20,
  5.22
Dendritic branches, §§5.15, 5.16, 5.22,
  5.26
Dendritic spiking, §§5.22, 5.27, 5.31,
  5.38

Dendritic spines, §§5.5, 5.7, 5.9, 5.16,
  5.22, 5.28, 5.51, fig. 5.3, §10.88
Depolarization, §§2n3, 4.1, 4.2, 4.36,
  4.43, 4.51, 4.64, 4n4, 5.2–5.4, 5.6,
  5.11, 5.12, 5.20, 5.23, 5.26–5.36,
  5.42, 5.51, fig. 5.2, §§5n8, 5n9
Depression, §§4n8, 7n9
Depressive synapses, §§3.13, 5.43
Derivative, and synapses, §3.13, and
  bursting, §5.37
Descriptivism, §§2.9, 8.8–8.13, A3
Desert paths, §§10.7, 10.24
Desire, §§7.22, 8.4, 8.5, 8n7, 10.8, 10.9,
  10.10, 10.11, 10.21, 10.25, 10.26,
  10.55, 10.60, 10.86
Determinism, §§A1, 6.10, 6.23, 7.2,
  7.18, 7n9, A2.1, A2.4
Diachronic, §§A2.3, A2n4
Differential equations, §8.3
Digestive system, §§8.2, 8.3
Directionality of time, §6.20
Disinhibition, §§5.45, 5.47
Dissipative structures, §4.69
Distraction, §4.22
DLPFC. See Dorsolateral prefrontal
  cortex
Dopamine, §§2n3, 3.2, 4.40, 5n4
Dorsal attentional network, §10n23
Dorsal stream, §§4.8, 4.26, 10.4,
  10n12
Dorsolateral prefrontal cortex, §§3.2,
  4.26, fig. 7.1, §§7.7, 10.14, 10.40,
  10.57, 10.77, 10.87–10.89, 10n1,
  10n10, 10n22, 10n23
Double bouquet cells, §§5.3, fig. 5.1
Double slit experiment, §§6.13, A1.10,
  A1.11
DOWN states, §5.42
Downward causation, §§1.15, 1.16,
  6.1, 6.2, 6.10, 6.14, fig. 6.2, §§7.18,
  10.1, 10.84, A2.2
Dreaming, §§2.11, 10.22, 10.77, 10.78,
  10.79, 10n4, 10n24

D-serine. *See* Glycine
Dualism, §§A1n1, A2.2

Efference copy, §§9.6, 9.11, 9.13, 9n6, 10.26
Electroencephalogram, §§9.1, 9.17
Eliminative materialism. *See* Epiphenomenalism
Emergent properties, §§1.11, 1.15, 1.16, 6.1, 6.2, 6.10, 6.13
Emotion. *See* Limbic system
Endocannabinoid, §5.17
Endogenous attention, §§2.10, 2.11, 4.22–4.24, 5.51, 9.8–9.10, 10.23, 10.24, 10.27, 10.34, 10.83, 10.84, 10.85, 10.86, 10.87–10.89, 10n23
Endogenous processing, §§9.7–9.9
Endogenous volition, §10.86
Ensemble bursting, §§4.37, 4.51, 5.16, 5.33, 5.46, 5.47
Ensemble coding, §§4.45, 4.46, 4.50, 4.53, 4.65, 5.33, 8.20
Entanglement, §§A1.7, A1.8
Entorhinal cortex, §§4.8, 4.15, 10n15, 10n23
Entropy, §§4.42, 4.68, 6.12, 6n1
Environment, §7.12
Epicircuit. *See* Epiconnectivity
Epiconnectivity, §§3.5, 4.54–4.60, 4.64, fig. 4.5, §8.17
Epigenetics, §4n13
Epilepsy, §§4.31, 4.33, 4.43, 4n12, 5.42
Epiphenomenalism, §§A2.1, A2.3, A2.9, 1.3, 1.5, 1.7, 1.15, 1.16, 1n1, 3.10, 3.11, 4.5, 4.6, 6.2, 6.10, 6.13, 9.15, 10.5, 10n14, fig. A2.1
Episodic memory, §§5.27, 10.24
EPSP. *See* Excitatory postsynaptic potential
Equilibrium, §A1.4
Equivalence class, §§6.4, 6.5, 7n11, 8.5, 8.16, 8.17
Error detection, §§9n6, 10.32

Event-related potential, §§4.22, 9.1
Evolution, §§2n3, 4n14, 5n2, 6.22, 6n7, 7.17, 8.19, 10.7, 10.9, 10.35
Excitation, §§2n3, 4.1, 4.2, 4.36, 4.43, 4.51, 4.64, 4n4, 5.2–5.4, 5.6, 5.11, 5.12, 5.20, 5.23, 5.26–5.36, 5.42, 5.51, fig. 5.2, §§5n8, 5n9
Excitatory postsynaptic potential, §A1.8
Exclusion of over-determination, §A2.1
Executive processes, §§7.7, 7.11, 7.13, 7.14, 7.20, 7.21, 7n3, 9.9, 10.10, 10.14, 10.24, 10.25, 10.27, 10.31, 10.36, 10.37, 10.41, 10.61, 10.62, 10.65, 10.84, 10n9
Exogenous attention, §§4.22, 4.23, 10.9, 10.16, 10.35, 10.36, 10n23
Exogenous processing, §§9.7–9.9, 10.36
Exogenous volition, §10.86
Experience, §§1.7, 1.10, 1.12, 4.8, 2.10, 2.11, 5.24, 5n11, 9.1, 9.6, 9.7, 9.10, 9.11, 9.13, 9.15, 9.17, 10.3, 10.4, 10.5, 10.6, 10.7, 10.10, 10.11, 10.17, 10.19, 10.21, 10.22, 10.23, 10.24, 10.27, 10.32, 10.35, 10.36, 10.40, 10.57, 10.69, 10.83, 10.84, 10n1, 10n4, 10n21
Explicit information, §§4.56, 4.63
Externalism, §§8.7, 8.8, 8.9
Extrasynaptic receptors, §5.38
Extrospective network, §10n23
Eye movements, §§4.14, 4.23, 4.24, 10.28

Face aftereffect, §8.20
Face detector, §§4.9, 4.11, 4.12, fig. 4.4
Face processing, §§4.9, 10.14, 10.21
Face space, §8.16
Facilitating synapses, §§3.13, 5.43
Family resemblances, §§8.14–8.17
Fast-spiking cells, §§4.44, 5.3, 5.42
Fate, §7.22
Feature-averaging, §§10.48, 10.52

Feature-based attention, §10.32
Feature glue, §10.59
Feature soup, §10.66
Features, §§10.30, 10.50, 10.81
Feedback, §§4.14, 4.24, 4.60, fig. 4.1,
    §§4n11, 5.5, 5.6, 5.7, 5.9, 5.17, 5.18,
    5.34, 5.49, 5.50, 7.12
Feeling of agency, §§9.1, 9.6, 9.13,
    9.15, 9.17, 10.26, 10.38, 10.61,
    10.85, 10n9
Feeling of authorship, §§9.11, 9.13,
    9.17, 10.85
Feeling of willing, §§9.1, 9.6, 9.7, 9.10,
    9.13, 9.14, 9.17, 10.38, 10.85
Figure. See Type 3 qualia
Filling-in, §§4.11, 10.48, 10.50, 10.51,
    10.52, fig. 10.1
First law of thermodynamics,
    §§A1n4, 6.9, 6.12
Fixed action pattern, §§1.11, 7n5
Flexible remapping, §§10.31, 10.36,
    10.37, 10.41
Form-motion interactions, §10.18
Fragile visual short-term memory,
    §§10.15, 10.17, 10n22
Free will, §§1.1, 2.3, 2.6, 2.7, 3.1, 3.3,
    3.14, 3n2, 3n3, 4.62, 5.25, 7.1, 7.6,
    7.8, 7.10, 7.11, 7.13, 7.14, 7.16, 7.19,
    7n9, 9.2, 9.14, 10.84, 10.85, 10n10
Free won't, §9.2
Frontal eye fields, §§4.19, 4.23, fig.
    10.4, 10n23
Frontal lobes, §§7.7, 7.14, fig. 7.1,
    §8.22, fig. 9.1, §§10.16, 10.40, 10n10
Frontoparietal network, §§2.11, 4.14,
    4.23, 10.14, 10.17, 10.35, 10.57,
    10.61, 10.65, 10.75, 10.77, 10.78,
    10.87–10.89, fig. 10.4, §§10n1, 10n22
Functionalism, §§1n1, 3.11, 3.12, 8.24,
    8.25, 8n9, 10n9, A2n5
Fungibility, §§6.9, 6n5
Fusiform face area, §§4.9, 4.12, 10.14,
    10.87

GABA, §§4.39, 4.44, 4n4, 4n11, 5.3,
    5.40, 5.42, 5.45, 5.46, A1.10
Gain control, §§3.11, 4.21, 4.28, 4.32,
    4.58, 4.59, 5.7, 5.10, 5.45, 5.47, 5.48,
    5.51, 10.29, 10.48
Gain modulation. See Gain control
Gamma oscillation or brainwave,
    §§4n6, 4.23, 4.35, 4.37, 4.44–4.53,
    4n3, 5.3, 5.16, 5.24, 5.39–5.48
Ganglion cell, §§4.1, 4.7, 4.53, 10.50
Gap junctions, §§4.1, 4.44, 4.66
Garden path, §10.7
Generalization, §8.17
Genetics, §§7.12, 7.15, 7n4, A2.1, A2n3
Gestalt Neuroscience, §§1.10–1.12
Gestalt Psychology, §10n5
Ghost in the machine, §7.15
Gibbs' entropy, §6n1
Gist, §§4.14, 10.71
Glial cells, §§5.5, 5.24
Global workspace model, §10n6
Glutamate, §§2n2, 2n3, 4.36, 4.40,
    4.52, 4n4, 4n8, 5.2, 5.4–5.7, 5.23,
    5.28–5.31, 5.39, 5.41, 5.44, 5.45,
    5.51, 5n1, 5n5, A1.10, figs. 5.2, 5.3
Glycine, §§2n3, 4n4, 5.4, 5.5, fig. 5.2,
    §§5n1, 5n2, A1.10
Grandmother cells, §§4.11, 4n16, fig.
    4.4
Grid cells, §8.22
Grid processing, §8.1
Ground. See Type 1 qualia; Type 2
    qualia
Grouping, §4.22

Habituation, §5.42
Hallucination, §§8.5, 10.22, 10n3, 10n4
Hand detector, §4.9
Heuristics, §10.22
Hidden variables determinisn, §§A1.5,
    A1.6
High-Gamma oscillation or
    brainwave, §§4n6, 4.23, 4.35,

4.49–4.52, 5.6, 5.24, 5.43, 5n12, fig. 5.5

Hippocampus, §§4.8, 4.11, 4.15, 4.35, 4.44, fig. 4.4, 5.3, 5.27, 5.36, 5.40, 5.42, fig. 5.5, 10.16, 10.44, 10n15

HMAX model, §§4.13, fig. 4.3, 5.1, 5.34

Homeostasis, §§4.31, 4.42, 4.62, 4n8, 5.7

Hormones, §10.5

Hunger, §§10.60, 10.61, 10.64

Hypercomplex cell, §4.9

Hyperpolarization, §§2n3, 4n11, 5.31, 5.42

Iconic buffer, §§2.11, 10.12–10.17, 10.72, 10n1, 10n22

Identification, §§10.17, 10.29, 10.67, 10.69, 10.74, 10.75, 10.81, 10.87, 10n21

Identity, §§7n11, 10.29, 10.30

Identity theory, §§2n1, 3.11, 7n11, A3

If-then statement, §8.1

Ignoring, §§4.27, 5.41, 5.48, 5.50, 7.12, 10.9, 10.41, 10.46

Illusions of agency, §§9.13–9.18, fig. 9.4, §§10.84, 10n9, 10n10

Illusion of precise representation, §10.81

Imagination, §10.85

Immune system, §7n7

Implicit information, §§4.56, 4.63

Inaccessible qualia, §10.83

Inattentional blindness, §§10.56, 10.67, 10.71, 10.72, 10.74, 10.76, 10n21

Incompatibilism, §§3.3, 7.17, 7.18

Indeterminism, §§A1, 2.1, 2.6, 3.13, 3.14, 4.6, 6.10, 6.13, 6.20, 6.23, fig. 6.2, §§7.1, 7.2, 7.3, 7.15, 7.16, 7.18–7.22, 7.23, 7n9, A1.4, A1.7, A2.1, A2.4, A2.7

Individuation, §§10.69, 10.81

Inference, §10.19

Information, §§1.2, 1.10, 1.16, 2.3, 2.4–2.8, 3.5, 3.7, 3.9–3.14, fig. 3.1, §§3n5, 4.1–4.15, 4.17, 4.19, 4.29–4.66, 4.69, figs. 4.2, 4.5, §§4n11, 4n16, 5.2, 5.3, 5.5, 5.11, 5.14–5.17, 5.22–5.37, 5.49, 5.51, fig. 5.5, §§6.2–6.16, 6.19–6.23, fig. 6.2, §§6n1, 6n2, 7.6, 7.17, 7n11, 8.5–8.8, 8.19–8.23, 8n4, 10.5, 10.9–10.23, 10.32, 10.81–10.83

Informational entropy, §6n1

Inhibition, §§2n3, 4.39, 4.44, 4n4, 4n11, 5.3, 5.31, 5.40, 5.42, 5.45, 5.46, 8n7, 10.27, A1.10

Inhibitory postsynaptic potential, §§4.2, 4.54, 5.16, A1.8

Insects, §10.3

Insula, §4.26

Intention, §§4.20, 4.27, 7.23, 9.2, 9.4, 9.17, 9n3, 10.2

Intentionality, §8.5

Interneuron, §§4.43, 4.50, 5.3, 5.24, 5.39, 5.42, 5.45, 5.48, fig. 5.1

Interrupts, §10.9

Intraparietal cortex, §§4.18, 10n23

Introspectionism, §10n5

Introspective network, §10n23

Invariance, §§4.10, 4.14, 6.4

Invertebrates, §§10.3, 10.43

Ionotropic receptor, §§2n3, 4.5, 4.36, 4n4, 5.4, 5.6, 5.10, 5.19, A1.10

IPSP. *See* Inhibitory postsynaptic potential

Irreversibility, §6.20

Itching, §§10.60, 10.61, 10.77

Just-in-time processing, §10n24

Kainate receptor, §§4n4, 5.40

Ketamine, §§4n8, 5.24

Kim's argument against mental causation, §A2.3

Kim's challenge, §§A2.2, 6.13, 6.14, 7.4
Knowledge, §10.10

Language, §§4.55, 4.57, 8n4
Lateral geniculate nucleus, §§4.7, 4.9, 4.26, 4.28, 4.32, 4.38, 4.39, 4.43, 4.48, 4.58, fig. 4.2, §§4n11, 5.50, 10.32
Lateral inhibition, §§4.24, 4n11
Lateral intraparietal area, §4.18
Lateral occipital complex, §4.10
Lateralized readiness potential, §§9n2, 9.1, 9.3–9.5, figs. 9.1, 9.2, 9.3
Laughter, §10.60
Learning, §§4.60, 4.70, 5.6, 5.7, 5.8, 5.9, 5.27, 5.38, 5.42, 5.44, 5n2, 5n6, 6.15, 10.53, 10.54, fig. 10.3
LFP. *See* Local field potential
LGN. *See* Lateral geniculate nucleus
Libertarianism, §7.17
Limbic system, §§4.8, 4.15, 9.8, 10.10, 10.11, 10.25, 10.55, 10.61
Linearity, §4.13
LIP. *See* Lateral intraparietal area
LOC. *See* Lateral occipital complex
Local field potential, §§4.44–4.47, fig. 5.5
Locus coeruleus, §4.22
Logical atomism, §10n5
Long-term depression, §§4.31, 4.40, 5.6–5.11, 5.19, 5.20, 5.21, 5.28
Long-term potentiation, §§4.31, 4.40, 5.6–5.11, 5.19, 5.20, 5.21, 5.25–5.28, 5n4
LRP. *See* Lateralized readiness potential
LTD. *See* Long-term depression
LTP. *See* Long-term potentiation
Lurking variable, §§9.3, 9.17
Lust, §10.60
Luxotonic neurons, §5.37

M1, §§3.2, fig. 9.1, §§9n2, 10n8
Magnesium ion, §§4.67, 5.6, 5.10, 5.20, 5.23, 5.25, 5.28, 5.31, fig. 5.2, §§5n1, 5n9
Magnocellular pathway, §4.7
Martinotti cells, §4.51
Maxwell's demon, §A1n3
Medial prefrontal cortex, §10n15
Medial stream, §§4.8, 4.15
Mediodorsal nucleus, §10n15
Medulla, §5n3
Mental calculation, §6.15
Mental content, §§8.4, 8.5, 8.9
Mental imagery, §§6.15, 7.21, 8.5, 9.16, 10.60, 10.78, 10n23, 10n24
Mental rotation, §10.48
Metabotropic receptors, §§2n3, 5.39–5.41, 5n5
Metacognition, §9.4
Metamental states, §A2.8
Metaphors, §8.24
Metasupervenience, §§A2.8, A2n5
Methylation, §§4n13, 7.12
Microconsciousness, §§5n11, 10.23
Microsaccades, §§4.23, 4.38
Microstimulation, §§1.10, 1.12, 4.12, 4.24, 5n11
Midbrain, §5n4
Minicolumn, §§5.15, 5.16
Mirrors, §10.23
Modal logic, §§8.10, 8.13, A3
Models, §§8.3, 8.12, 8.13
Modularity, §§7.15, 10.19, 10.24, 10.36, 10.80, 10n2, 10n9
Monism, §§A1n1, A2.2, 6.9
Morality, §§7.4, 7.12, 7.13, 7.14, 9.2, 10.66
Motion perception, §5n11
Motor execution, §§9.5, 10.53, 10.84, 10n10
Motor plans, §§10.26, 10.27, 10.38, 10.86, 10n8, 10n10

Motor strip see *M1*

MT, §5n11

Multiple criteria decision analysis, §3n4

Multiple realizability, §§1n1, 2.8, 3.11, 3.12, 6.8–6.12, 6.21, 6n6, 8.25, 8n9, A2n5

Multithread processing, §8.1

Muscarinic Ach receptors, §§5.38, 5.40, 5.42

Muscles fig., §§1.11, 9.1, 10.26

Myelination, §7.12

N1 component, §§10.16, 10.75

Narrow spiking neurons, §4.52

Navigation, §4.8

Necessary, §§8.10–8.13, A3

Neglect, §§10.77, 10.81

Neoprimitive, §§10.54, 10.55, 10.58

Neural circuits, §§1.8–1.10, 5.34

Neural code, §§4.57, 5.23, 8.17, 8.24

Neural correlates of consciousness, §10.65

Neuromodulator, §§4n3, 5.24, 5.38, 5.51

Nicotinic Ach receptors, §5.39

NMDA, §§2.5, 2n2, 2n3, 4.36, 4.40, 4.42, 4n4, ch. 5, §§7.6, 7.15, 8.25, 10.1, 10.87–10.89, 10n15, A1.10, A1.11, figs. 5.2, 5.3, §10n15

Noncholinergic feedback, §§5.45–5.50, 10.87

Noncriterial causality, §§A1.1-A1.7, 6.10

Non-deliberative action, §§9.11, 9.14, 9.16

Non-fast-spiking cells, §5.3

Nonlinearity, §§4.13, 4.69

Nonlocality, §§A1n5, A1.6, A1.7, A1.8, A1.11

Nonspiny neurons, §§5.2, 5.3

Nonsynaptic communication, §4.68

Nonsynaptic plasticity, §5.38

Nonteleological qualia, §10.60

Norepinephrine, §4.22

Normalization, §§4.31, 5.7, 5.8, 5.10, 5.45, 5.48–5.50

Norm-based encoding, §§8.18–8.20

Noumenal, §§8.12, 8.13, 8n5, 10.22, A3

Now, §A1n6

Nucleus accumbens, §5.42

Nucleus basalis. *See* Basal forebrain

Object-based attention, §10.32

Object file, §§10.29, 10.30, 10.56, 10.69, 10.87

Obsessive compulsive disorder, §10.9

Occipital lobe, §§10.54, 10.68, 10.75, fig. 10.4

Octopus, §§5n2, 10.45, 10.47

Onset/offset transient, §§4.48, 5.32, 5.36, 5n12, 10.87

Operations, §§8.22, 9.16, 9.18, 10.13, 10.39, 10.48, 10.84

Orienting, §§4.22, 10.29

Orthodromic propagation, §5n8

Oscillation, §§4.29, 4.33, 4.34

Other race effect, §§2.9, 8.20

Outside memory, §§10.82, 10n24

P1 component, §§10.16, 10.75

P3 component, §§10.16, 10.75

Pain, §§5n3, 10.5, 10.9, 10.21, 10.44, 10.55, 10.60, 10.61, 10.86, 10n14, 10n19

Pandemonium model, §§4.13, fig. 4.3, 5.1

Panpsychism, §10n7

Papez circuit, §4.15

Parahippocampal cortex, §§4.8, 10n23

Parallel processing, §8.1

Parietal lobe fig. 10.4, 10n12

Parkinson's disease, §4n12

Parrot brain, §5n2

Parvalbumin, §§5.3, 5.42, 5.43

Parvocellular, §4.7

Pattern causation, §§1.14–1.16, 2.3, 2.6–2.8, ch. 3, §§4.61, 5.62, 4.69, 4n1, 5.25, 5.51, 6.1, 6.2, 6.3, 6.8–6.14, 6.17–6.23, 7.4–7.11, 7.18, 7.19, 7.23, 10.1–10.4, A3n3, fig. 3.1

Perceptual inference, §10.19

Perturbation, §§4.29, 4.32, 4.33, 4.42, 4.62, 4.70, 5.37

Phantom limbs, §4n15, 10.5

Phase, §§1.11, 4.30, 4.33, 4.34, 4.43–4.47, 4.51, 4n3, 4n4, 5.43, 5n12

Phasic firing, §§2.5, 4.33, 4/35–4.41, 4.47, 4.48, 4.51, 4.53, 5.29–5.51, 10.87–10.89

Phenomenal consciousness, §10.33

Phenomenology, §10.17

Phi, §§8.6, 10n7

Philosophy, §§1.6, 1.7, 8.5, 8.7, 8.25

Phosphenes, §5n11

Photon, §4.68

Physicalism, §§1.5, A1.1, A1n1, A2.1, A2.2, 6.9, 6.19, 9.15

Place field, §5.36

Planning, §§4.20, 4.54, 6.15, 7.11, 9.5, 9.9, 9.15, 10.6, 10.10, 10.20, 10.25, 10.61, 10.83

Pleasure, §10.9

Poisson statistics, §§4.35, 4.51, 4.52

Pop-out, §§10.54, 10.58, 10.66, 10.73, 10.76, fig. 10.3

Population coding. *See* Ensemble coding

Possible paths, §§6.14, 6.20, fig. 6.2

Possible worlds, §§8.5, 8.9, 8.11, 8n2, 10.20

Postdiction, §§9.13, 10.18

Posterior cingulate, §10n23

Posterior probability, §§8.17, 8n8

Posthypnotic suggestion, §3n3

Potassium, §5.21, fig. 5.2

Potentiation-action cycle, §4.60

Practice, §§10.53, 10.54, 10.73, figs. 10.3, 10.4

Preattentive processing, §10.30

Precentral gyrus. *See* M1

Precompilation, §§10.20, 10.21, 10.23, 10.58, 10.59, 10.61, 10.83

Preconscious, defined, §10n1

Preconscious perceptual buffer, §§2.11, 4.22, 9.14, 10.18–10.23, 10.28, 10.29, 10.35, 10.48, 10n1, fig. 10.1, §§10.19, 10.28, fig. 10.1

Precuneus, fig. 10.4

Predeterminism. *See* Determinism

Premature babies, §10n20

Premotor cortex, fig. 9.1

Preparation of motor act, §9.5

Prepotentiation, §10.62

PreSMA. *See* Presupplementary motor area

Presupplementary motor area, §3.2, fig. 9.1

Principle of the identity of indiscernibles, §7n11

Principle of the indiscenibility of identicals, §7n11

Prioritization, §10.9

Prior probability, §8n8, 8.17

Property dualism, §A2.2

Proposition, §§8n4, 2.9, 2.10, 3.2, 3.7, 3.8, 3n4, 4.6, 7.20, 7.21, 7n3, 8.4, 8.5, 8.10–8.13, 8.19, 8n4, 9.16, 10.25–10.27, 10.84, 10.n8

Prosopagnosia, §10n2

Prototype theory, §§8.15–8.17

Pseudo-backward causation, §6.18

Psychosis, §5.24

Pulvinar, §§4.8, 10n12

Punishment, §4.40

Pyramidal cell, §§4.43, 4.49, 4.51, 4.52, 4n3, 5.3, 5.6, 5.16, 5.24, 5.33, 5.39, 5.43, 5.48, figs. 5.1, 5.4

Qualia, §§9.18, 10.5, 10.17, 10.24, 10.29, 10.32, 10.34, 10.35, 10.40, 10.53, 10.54, 10.70, 10.84, 10.87–10.89, 10n22, A2n5
and pop-out, §§10.58, 10.76
Qualia soup, §§2.11, 10.34, 10.35, 10.56, 10.57, 10.66, 10.76, 10.77
Qualia without attention, §10.54
Quantum field theory, §6.8
Quantum mechanics, §§6.14, 6.15, 6.17, A1.5, A1.8

Randomness, §§2.6, 3.9, 4.62, 4.66, 4.68, 4.69, 4.70, 5.25, 5.51, 6.23, 7.1, 7.2, 7.3, 7.6, 7.17, 7.21, 10.1, A1.8, A2.11
Rate coding, §§4.51, 5.23, 5.32, 5.33, 5.37, 10.32
Readiness potential, §§9n2, 9.1–9.5, 9.15, figs. 9.1, 9.2, 9.3, §10.84
Read-out neuron, §§4.65, 4n16, 8.6, 8.7
Reafferent kinesthetic feedback, §9.13
Realization thesis, §A2.3, A2.7, A2.12
Realized in. *See* Supervenience
Receptive field, §§1.9, 1.10, 4.7–4.10, 4.18, 4.58, fig. 4.2, §§5.5, 5.50, fig. 5.6, §8.22
Receptor, §§2n2, 2n3, 4.36, 4.61, 4.66, 4n4, 6.9
Recognition, §§4.9, 4.11–4.15, 6.8, 8.17, 8n7, 10.5, 10.53, 10.87–10.89, 10n12
Recurrent input, §§4.32, 5n11
Reductionism, §§A2.1, 6.19, 6.21, 10n5, A1.7
Reference, §§8.4, 8.5, 8.8, 8.9, 8.10, 8n4
Reflex, §§10.6, 10.8, 10.10
Refractory period, §§4.52, 5.43, fig. 5.5
Relativity, §§6.20, A1.7
Religion, §§8.6, 8.7, 10n3

Renormalization, §§4.31, 4.32, 5.7, 5.8, 5.10
Representation, §§8.4, 8.5, 8.8, 8.9, 8.15, 8.17, 8.18
Residual attention, §§10.72, 10.73
Responsibility, §§7.4, 7.12, 7.13, 7.14, 9.2
Resting potential, §§3.6, 5.4, 5.31, Fig. 5.2
Retina, §§4.1, 4.7, 4.68, 10.50, 10n12
Retinotopy, §§4.7–4.10, 4.24, 4.58, 4n5, 5.50, fig. 10.4, §10n17
Retrograde messengers, §5.17
Retrosplenial cortex, §§4.8, 10n23
Reward, §§4.15, 4.40, 10.61
Ribosome, §§6n2, 6n3, 8.6
Rigid designator, §8.9
Rods, §4.7
Routing problem, §4.28
RP. *See* Readiness potential
Rubber hand illusion, §10.22
Rules, §§3.7, 4.19, 6.4, 8.17, 9.9

Saccade, §§4.18, 4.23
Salience, §§5.44, 10.24, 10.28, 10.29, 10.31, 10.38, 10n12
Science, §§1.6–1.12, 3n1
Schizophrenia, §§4n12, 5.24
Scripts, §§9.8, 9.9
Second law of thermodynamics, §§6n1, 6.12, A1.4
Self-causation. *See Causa sui*
Self-report, §9.4
Semantic priming, §§2.9, 8.17
Semantics, §§8.15, 8.16
Serotonin, §§4.61, fig. 4.6, 4n4
Shannon's source coding theorem, §§6n1, 8.6
Shape, §§4.14, 4.22, 4.61
Shunting inhibition, §§5.21, 5.26
Signal detection, §§4.32, 4.60, 4.67, 5.36, 5.39, 5.44, 5.46, 5.50
Similarity, §§8.15, 8.17

Simple cell, §§4.3, 4.53, 4.58, 4.63,
  4.65, fig. 4.2, 6.5, 6.15, 7.11
Simple qualia. *See* Type 1 qualia
Single-shot learning, §5.27
Single-thread processing, §8.1
Size invariance, §4.10
Skepticism, §§6.21, 7.12, 7.13, 7.14,
  7.15, 8.14, 8n6, 10.46, 10.47,
  10.69
Sleep, §§4.38, 5.8
SMA. *See* Supplementary motor area
Social perception, §§10.21, 10.22
Sodium, §§5.21, fig. 5.2
Solipsism, §§8n6, 10.46
Space-based attention, §10.32
Spatial frequency, §4.3
Special sciences, §§A2.1, A2n2
Spike adaptation, §5.39
Spike timing-dependent plasticity,
  §§5.11–5.13, 5.28, 5n4, 5n6
Spiny neurons, §§4.40, 5.2
Split brains, §§10.24, 10n11
Spontaneous firing rate, §§4.34, 4.42
Spontaneous signaling, §4n8
Stack models, §§4.13, 4.14, fig. 4.3,
  5.34
Stage 1 buffer, §§10.15–10.17, 10.30,
  10.48, 10.57, 10.68, 10.75, 10.79,
  10.81, 10.82, 10.87
Stellate cells, §5.2
Stick shift mode, §§9.8, 9.9
Striatum, §4.40, fig. 9.1, 10.4, 10.61
Strong free will, §§7.1, 7.6, 7.8, 7.10,
  7.15, 7.19, 10.1
Stroop task, §§4.27, 9.10, 10.61
Structuralism, §10n5
Subiculum, §4.8
Subjective report, §§10.69, 10.74
Subsidiary working memories, §§10.14,
  10.57, 10.61, 10.87
Substantia nigra, fig. 9.1
Subthreshold potential, §§4.32, 4.62
Superficial cortical layers, §§4.49, 4.50

Superior colliculus, §§4.8, 4.23, 4.49,
  10n12
Superior temporal sulcus, §4.12
Superpositionality of experience,
  §§2.11, 10.23, 10.64, 10.80, 10.81,
  10n2
Supervenience, §§2n1, 7.5, A2.1, A2.2,
  A2.8, A2.10, fig. A2.1
Supplementary eye fields, fig. 10.4
Supplementary motor area, §3.2, fig.
  9.1
Surfaces, §§10.20, 10.30, 10.33, 10.51,
  fig. 10.1
Surface neurons, §5.37
Synaptic addressing problem, §5.15
Synaptic cleft, §§4.66, 4.67, fig. 5.2
Synaptic resetting, §§2.7, 3.9, 3.11,
  3.13, 4.42, 4.54–4.60, fig. 4.5, §§5.6,
  5.9, 5.18, 5.19, 5.23, 5.26, 5.27, 5.51,
  fig. 5.5, §§7.8, 7.17, 10.62
Synaptic tagging, §5.9
Synaptogenesis, §5.8
Synchronic, §§A2.3, A2n4
Synchrony, §§4.37, 4.42, 4.44–4.47,
  4.51, 4.53, 4.60, 4n3, 4n12, 5.3, 5.13,
  5.15, 5.20, 5.22, 5.31, 5.33, 5.35,
  5.39
Syntax, §§8.22, 8.26

Tectopulvinar pathway, §§4.8, 10n12
Teleological qualia, §§10.60
Temporal integration window, §§1.16,
  3.11, 4.3, 4.43, 4.54, 4n3, 5.3, 5.6,
  5.16, 5.20, 5.30, 5.33, 6.2, 6.4, 6.6
Temporal parietal junction, §10n23
Thalamic reticular nucleus, §§4.27,
  4.28, 4.39, 4.43, 4n11, 5.24
Thalamus, §§4.7, 4.9, 4.28, 4.32, 4.38,
  4.39, 4.46, 4.49, 4.58, 4.59, fig. 4.2,
  §§4n11, 5.24, 5.39
Theory of mind, §10.21
Thermodynamic entropy, §§6n1, A1.4
Theta brainwave, §4n6

Thing-in-itself. *See* Noumenal

Thirst, §§10.60, 10.61, 10.86

Thought, §§4.54, 5.6, 5.9, 5.13, 5.24, 5.51, 7.12, 8.4, 8.17, 8.22, 9.9, fig. 9.4, §§10.24, 10.33, 10.38, 10.84

Three-stage model of mental causation, §§3.9, 7.16, 7.23, 10.2, 10.3, 10.84

Time perception, §§5n6, 10.44, A1n6

Time's direction, §§A1.4, A1n6

Tip of the tongue phenomenon, §§10.38, 10n25

Token-level criterial causation, §6.9

Tone probe task, §9.4

Tonic firing mode, §§2.5, 3.13, 4.33, 4.35–4.41, 10.87–10.89

Top-down attention, §§5.47, 5.48, 10.32, 10.36, 10.48, 10.87–10.89

Top-down processing, §§4.14, 4.21–4.28, 4.45, 4.60, 4.69, 5.47, 5.51, 7.6, 7.18, 10.18, 10.86, 10n8

Trace conditioning, §§5.44, 10.43–10.46, 10n15

Tracking. *See* Endogenous attention

Transcranial magnetic stimulation, §10n22

Transcription, §§5.6, 5.9

Transparency, §10.48, 10.49

TRN. *See* Thalamic reticular nucleus

Turing machine, §§8.1, 8.3, 8.24

Two-dimensional semantic analysis, §8.11

Two stage models of free will, §§7.16, 7n8

Type 1 qualia, §§2.11, 10.54, 10.55, 10.68, 10.86, 10.86, 10.87, 10n1, 10n22, 10n24

Type 2 qualia, §§2.11, 10.55, 10.56, 10.78, 10.80, 10n22, 10.87, 10.88

Type 3 qualia, §§2.11, 10.56–10.59, 10.77, 10.86, 10.87, 10.88, 10n22, 10n24

Type identity theory, §3.11

Type-level criterial causality, §§4.61, 4.62, 6.9, 6.10, 6n5

Unconscious inference, §§10.20, 10.21

Unconscious processing, §§7.21, 9.1, 9.7, 9.14, 9.16, 9.17, 10.3, 10.4, 10.19, 10.27, 10.28, 10.29, 10.31, 10.33, 10.36, 10.63

Undulation, §1.11

UP states, §5.42

Urge to move, §§9.4, 9.11

Utilization behavior, §10n10

V1, §§4.8, 4.10, 4.13, 4.28, 4.38, fig. 4.3, 5.39, 5.44, 5.50, fig. 5.5, §§6.15, 10.14, 10.17, 10.78

V2, §§4.8, 4.10, 10.17

V4v, §§4.10, 4.26, 4.47, 4.48, 4.52, 5.33, 5.44, 5.49, 5.50, 10.15, fig. 5.6, §§5n6, 10.44, A1n6, 10.14, 10.17, 10n22

Vectorial processing, §§8.1, 8.18–8.20, 10.58

Vegetative state, §§10.44, 10.66

Ventral lateral prefrontal cortex, §10n10

Ventral stream, §§4.8, 4.10, 4.15, 4.49, 10.87–10.89

Ventral striatum. *See* Striatum

Veridical hallucination, §10n4

Viewpoint invariance, §4.10

Virtual experience, §10.60

Visual background, §10.17

Visual illusion, §§9.14, 10.18, 10.22

Volition. *See* Will

Von Neumann architecture, §8n1

Von Neumann entropy, §6n1

"W." *See* Feeling of willing

Wanderlust, §10.60

Weber's law, §4.32

Will, §§1.1, 3.1–3.4, 4.21, 5.51, 7.5, 7.12, 9.1, fig. 9.4, §§10.37, 10.86

Will, types of, §§3.2, 10.61

Working memory, §§2.11, 4.14, 4.26,
    4.27, 4.53, 5.42, 6.15, 7.7, 7.11, 7.13,
    7.21, 8.19, 8.22, 9.14, 9.16, 10.4,
    10.6, 10.7, 10.8, 10.12–10.15, 10.25,
    10.27, 10.30, 10.31, 10.36–10.41,
    10.57, 10.58, 10.59, 10.79, 10.83,
    10.84, 10.85, 10n1, 10n15,
    10n22–10n24

World-centered coordinates. *See*
    Allocentric coordinates

Zombie, §§7.23, 9.15, 10.2, 10.4, 10.83

Zombie agent, §§3n3, 10.6